I0836601

ENGD BY JOHN SARTAIN PHILA

Yrs. Sincerely
Jas. T. Barclay

THE

CITY OF THE GREAT KING;

OR,

JERUSALEM AS IT WAS,

AS IT IS,

AND AS IT IS TO BE.

BY

J. T. BARCLAY, M.D.,

MISSIONARY TO JERUSALEM.

"Beautiful for situation, the joy of the whole earth is Mount Zion—the City of the Great King."

PHILADELPHIA:
JAMES CHALLEN AND SONS,
BULLETIN BUILDINGS.
J. B. LIPPINCOTT & CO., NO. 20 NORTH FOURTH STREET.
1858.

STEREOTYPED BY MEARS & DUSENBERY. PRINTED BY HENRY B. ASHMEAD.

PUBLISHERS' ANNOUNCEMENT.

THIS work is presented to the public, believing that much will be found in it of great interest and value to all classes of the religious world, and to those who would see the hand of Providence in the history and fortunes of Israel, and the nations with whom they have been associated, for more than three thousand years.

The name of Dr. BARCLAY—a resident missionary in Jerusalem for three years and a half, is now favorably known, both in Europe and in this country, for the valuable discoveries he has made in the Temple Enclosure and other sacred localities, to which he was admitted by special firman, and for the aids he has furnished to many distinguished tourists, in the Holy Land, which have been in all their recent works repeatedly acknowledged.

"The City of the Great King," on every page of it, shows the extent and accuracy of his labors; and his Map of Jerusalem, now before the public, is justly esteemed the only reliable one known. His close observation of facts and conscientious adherence to truth, together with his long and patient labors in the prosecution of his task, cannot fail to commend this book to the confidence of the public.

The Portrait of the Author is a waif, from the hands of the Publishers, given at the request of numerous friends in view of his immediate return to Palestine, probably to be seen no more amongst us. It is from a photograph by McClees, and reflects great credit upon the eminent artist, John Sartain, by whom it was executed.

The Steel Engravings, by Messrs. Buttre, Earle, and Dick, are gems of the first value.

The Chromographs and Lithographs, by L. N. Rosenthal, reflect the highest credit upon his establishment.

The Wood Engravings, by Messrs. Louderback & Hoffmann, from original designs by Moore; and J. H. Byram from transfers, are unequalled.

The Publishers, having spared no pains or expense, to meet the demands of the public, cheerfully commit the work to their hands.

TABLE OF CONTENTS.

Modern Jerusalem.

Millennial Jerusalem.

ILLUSTRATIONS.

Steel Engravings.

Illuminations.

Lithographs.

Wood Engravings.

INTRODUCTION.

On presenting, for the consideration of the public, a new treatise upon a theme so often discussed as the general subject-matter of this volume, a few explanatory observations—demanded alike by the interests of the reader, the writer, and the subject itself—may properly be submitted, by way both of preface and apology.

In this Augustan age of electro-magnetic progression, when time is not only the convertible representative of knowledge, power, and pleasure, but—*manufactured*—is the equivalent of *that* "which answereth all things;" and, indeed, is the very warp and woof of which the web of life is woven—most evident is it that no one has a right to consume his neighbor's time without rendering a valid "*quid pro quo*" in return for the expenditure of a commodity so invaluable. "*Ars longa est—vita brevis.*" And this apothem is especially applicable in this utilitarian age, when the prolific steam press teems with publications on all subjects; and is particularly exuberant in works on Palestine and the Holy City. In announcing a *new work*, therefore, upon a theme so hackneyed, a few prefatory remarks are equally the dictate of propriety and policy—for truly "of making many books" on this subject "there is no end;" and of the remunerative circulation of not a few there is not even a beginning.

Although the author has been much interested and engaged in studies of kindred character for more than a score of years, yet he entertained no idea of publishing a work on the subject, even after two or three years' residence in Palestine, until a propitious Providence placed him in possession of such interesting and important information, that such a publication became loudly demanded by considerations too imperative to be slighted. For, what plea could be urged that would justify him before the tribunal of an enlightened community, in withholding earnestly desired information, on matters so profoundly interesting! Jerusalem! "Name ever dear!" What hallowed memories and entrancing recollections spring at the mere mention of that name! There is music and magic in the very thought! Jerusalem, the joy of the whole earth! The city of the Great King! Zion, the city of solemnities—an eternal excellency! "The hill which God desireth to dwell in: yea, will dwell in it for ever!" The theater of the most memorable and stupendous events that have ever occurred in the annals of the world. Jerusalem! the world-attracting magnet of the devout pilgrim of every age, and the stern warrior of every clime; not the least of whom were the chivalrous Crusaders of our noble ancestry! a spot at once the focus and the radiating point of the strongest emotions of three powerful religions! The land of hallowed associations, endearing reminiscences, and glorious anticipations! The renowned metropolis of the children of miracle, of prophecy, of promise, and of Providence—a people near and dear unto the Lord, and still beloved for their fathers' sakes!

What are the recollections associated with the monuments and antiquities of Memphis, Babylon, Nineveh, Athens, Rome, London, or the cities of the Azteks, compared with those that cluster around the City of the Great King!—whose antiquity is of ancient days—even the days of the great diluvian patriarch Shem!—the city where the "King of Peace and Righteousness" communed with the "Friend of God"—where the son of Jesse tuned his soul-stirring harp, and penned his Psalms for the saints of all ages; where Solomon reared a house for the Lord of Hosts to dwell between the Cherubim; where the Son of God suffered and died, and rose again—whence he ascended on high, and whither he will come again on the clouds of heaven in like manner as he went up—"and his feet shall stand in that day upon the Mount of Olives," and "Jehovah of Hosts shall reign in Mount Zion and in Jerusalem, and before his ancients gloriously," sitting upon his throne in the sublime metropolis (then brought near)—the New Jerusalem above. Then shall the Holy City truly become "the joy of the whole earth!"

> "Glorious things of thee are spoken,
> Zion, city of our God!"

There are matters of momentous concern referable to the late Russo-Turkish war—that most anomalous of all wars—the significant issue and results of which will tell mightily upon earth's destiny, and invest the Jews and their capital and country with unspeakable interest. What mean the various lines of steamers now traversing the length and breadth of the Mediterranean and Red Seas—placing Palestine in such direct, constant, and intimate communication not only with other parts of Asia, but with Europe, Africa, America, and the

Isles of the Gentiles? What the railways now projected between Jaffa and the Persian Gulf, via Neapolis, with which a branch from Egypt is to unite—passing through Jerusalem, a "highway" from Egypt into Assyria? (Is. xix. 23.) And what the electric telegraph at the Holy City—the great central metropolis!—to say nothing of the stupendous scheme of converting the great depressed basin of Arabia Deserta into an inland ocean by letting in the waters of the Red Sea! Above all, what means the astonishing fact that the Sultan has not only made an oblation of the Churches of St. Anne, the Nativity, the Holy Sepulcher, and various other "holy shrines" to the Emperor of the French, but has also given him decidedly the largest and finest square in the Holy City—the site of the Palace of the Knights of St. John—that he may "plant the tabernacle of his palace between the seas, in the glorious holy mountain!" The right of appointing to the high office of "Guardian of the Hill of Zion, and Custodian of the Holy Land," is thus conferred upon Louis Napoleon, the acknowledged patron of the Latin Church, who—laugh as we may at his assumed title of "Son of Destiny"—is nevertheless, beyond all comparison, the most extraordinary personage of the age.

A surprising tide of enterprise is already setting in toward the East, in anticipation of the general breaking up of the Turkish Empire and the enfranchisement of the Jews. The mightiest monarchs on earth are looking with the most profound interest to the Holy Land. Oriental revival is the general order of the day: and that this remarkable tract of country lying between the Euphrates and the Mediterranean, the Arabian Desert and Mount Amanus—"the glory of all lands"—"the delightsome land," as the Lord of Hosts styles it—will receive the first and largest share of this improvement, is most obvious.*

There are truly matters of great interest and grave significancy in connexion with the very liberal firman lately issued by the humbled successor of Mohammed. A very few years ago, no Frank—whether Jew or Christian—was permitted to depose in a Mohammedan court of justice: he was not permitted to build a house of worship, nor could he own a foot of land: and if a Mohammedan abandoned his religion and became either a Jew or Christian, death and

* The highest expectations are justly entertained in relation to the Jewish enterprise recently set on foot at Jaffa, mainly through the efforts of that zealous friend of Israel (himself an Israelite indeed)—the Rev. Ridley Herschel. It is now under the able management of another zealous friend of Israel—Mr. Hershon—from whose devotion and energy much good may be confidently expected. The zeal manifested also in behalf of Israel by H. B. M. consul, and his accomplished lady, is equally creditable to them and to their government; and can but be greatly promotive of their best interests.

The unpretending but efficient colony of Americans, first organized under the zealous advocacy of the late Mrs. Minor, has by no means proved an abortion, as is sometimes asserted, but has accomplished much for agriculture at Jaffa (its present seat of operations), as well as at Bethlehem, where it was first established. And the self-denying and untiring labors of the devoted Miss Williams, in behalf of education and morality, cannot well be too highly estimated.

confiscation were the inevitable consequences. But *now* he can testify on a perfect equality with the *Faithful:* he is permitted to build houses of any kind without let or hindrance: he can not only own land or any other kind of property in fee simple, but sit securely under his own vine and fig-tree—no man daring to molest him: and a Mohammedan may change his religion without forfeiting either his property or his life. And not only are foreigners permitted to own property, but by a late firman they are actually invited to come to Palestine or any other portion of the Ottoman Empire, and occupy as much land as they may desire—paying nothing for twelve years, and subsequently only one-fifth—receiving at the expiration of twenty-one years a complete title. "Lo! what God hath wrought!" The wrath of man hath he caused to praise him, and the remainder hath he restrained.

And what is all this but a Bath-kol of Providence—the voice of "a man" of Palestine—seen in vision, praying us to come over and help them! Now, from all these Providential facts and indications, should we not "assuredly gather that the Lord hath called us for to preach the gospel unto them?" And trusting in the God of Abraham, Isaac, and Israel, are we not "well able to go over and possess the land?" These astonishing concessions on the part of the Turk—though brought about at the solicitation of the Anglo-French alliance—are the Lord's doing, and marvellous in our eyes. Surely the water of the Euphrates, at least so far as it may be regarded as a barrier to the restoration of the Jews, is effectually dried up, and the times of the Gentiles fulfilled! The relaxing grasp of the bigoted Rabbin is another sign of the times scarcely less astonishing and auspicious; and well calculated to arrest the attention of all that would profit by discerning the face of the moral and political sky. The immediately pending future is doubtless big with momentous events concerning Zion and Israel, and well does it behoove us to discern the signs of the times, and turn our eyes toward the devoted, down-trodden, neglected, but still Heaven-remembered city.

The Author, having enjoyed, in every aspect of the matter, opportunities and facilities for research and observation possessed by no one in modern times, ventures to ask the reader's special consideration of the results of his investigations. During a residence of three and a half years in Jerusalem, in the double capacity of physician and missionary, he has enjoyed the most unrestrained intercourse with all classes of Syrian population—from the haughty Basha, down to the humblest Jew, Frank, or Fellah; and has thus become acquainted with the undercurrent of Oriental society, which the mere tourist or pilgrim could never do. But a mere residence under such circumstances—favorable and indispensable as it is to accurate observation and research—constitutes but a small item in the list of advantages enjoyed.

Having succeeded in relieving of a disagreeable affection the Turkish Effendi sent to Jerusalem as architect by the Sultan, for the purpose of repairing the Mosk of Omar and other (so called) sacred edifices, he petitioned the Mejlis or Congress of Jerusalem for permission to associate me with him in designing the necessary repairs, alterations, and decorations—actuated, no doubt, as much by a desire to avail himself of the use of some philosophical instruments I happened to have as through gratitude for the cure, or from appreciation of my technic abilities—exalted as was his professed estimate of them! And his request being finally granted, despite all opposition, I thus enjoyed free access to every part of the ancient Temple area, and other "holy places," that have been seen by no Christian eye since the chivalric but unenlightened era of Frank domination; but on the contrary have been most jealously tabooed, and securely guarded against Christian observation under penalty of death or the far worse alternative of Islamism. By means of such facilities I have been enabled not only satisfactorily to solve many doubts and remove many difficulties that have heretofore obscured the subject, but to make many interesting discoveries.

I had also the good fortune to make some discoveries of the highest interest and importance to Biblical archæology and topography in the environs of the city, during the long period of convalescence from an attack of the Syrian fever, when it became necessary to tabernacle without the walls, and take much exercise.

The publication of the "Biblical Researches" of Drs. Robinson and Smith has indeed constituted a new era in Biblical chorography and archæology, as well as geography; yet important and abundant as their labors confessedly have been, it was impossible for them to remove all the heaps of rubbish, which, in the lapse of centuries of monkish ignorance, superstition, and pious speculation, have so effectually inhumed many hallowed sites of interesting Scripture transactions.

Many others have also done valuable service in elucidating to some extent the greater portion of the vexed questions concerning the topography and archæology of ancient Jerusalem, and in portraying its present condition. But their labors lie scattered here and there, through many volumes—mixed too often with much chaffy speculation and irrelevant matter, from which it is impossible for the general reader to winnow successfully the genuine grains of truth. And even to this day, a complete, reliable manual of Jerusalem as it *was*, or even Jerusalem as it *is*, remains a desideratum. In so saying, however, I mean no disparagement to the many excellent men and polished scholars, who have written upon this much involved question; for they have accomplished as much as could well be expected under the circumstances of the case—their limited sojourn at

Jerusalem, and restricted opportunities of investigation, under the watchful eye of jealous Turkish authority, Jewish bigotry, and Christian superstition. And it is with no view of supplanting, nor in the slightest degree disparaging, such authors that I print; but rather with the hope of rendering the perusal of their works more intelligible, interesting, and satisfactory, by means of accurate maps and other adjuvant illustrations.

With the numerous productions of that large class of tourists and pilgrims, who have blindly taken oral tradition as their guide, these pages will be found in a continual state of antagonism.

The ungracious task, however, of turning out of the way formally to correct every little error, will by no means be attempted; yet there are many mistakes of serious import sanctioned by such high authority, and so long stereotyped, not only by traditionists and plagiarists, but by respectable, independent investigators, that they have at last come to be regarded as topographically orthodox: the correction of such errors as these is deemed matter of prime importance, and will consequently receive due attention—though by so doing, the Author should be regarded as invidiously in the estimation of some, as were the explorers sent out in days of yore to "spy out the land of Canaan, in the sight of the Anakims." While it is entirely true that formal explorations of sacred localities (as is alleged in palliation of these errors) are ordinarily attended with considerable danger; and even mere superficial reconnoissances of many places rather hazardous; yet, making all due allowance on this score, and for the additional consideration that no place on all the earth has been so completely subjected to the process of overturning and levelling as Jerusalem, it is yet not a little singular that so few antiquarian discoveries should have been made in a city, certainly one of the most ancient in all the world, and confessedly the most interesting. And not only is such the case, but unfortunately it is but too true, that in many things relating to the topography and archæology of the Holy City, the greatest names can be quoted in support of the greatest blunders!

"Nether Jerusalem" being a field of research, which, however interesting and important, has been heretofore almost entirely neglected, much attention has been devoted to its exploration. And amongst other interesting matters of research, the much complicated and mystified subject of the water resources of Jerusalem has received due attention. The illustration of numerous obscure topical passages of Scripture being a leading object of this work, the critical student of the Bible will readily excuse the time and space devoted to several matters of topographical character, that have generally been considered rather difficult of solution, if not hopelessly inexplicable. The great importance of correctly understanding the works of Josephus has induced the author to bestow upon the writings of that eminent Jewish historian (whose admirable work is so highly confirmatory and elucidatory of the Sacred Record, and whose testimony it is so important to sustain), very special attention. And the interest naturally attaching to the events of the Crusades will doubtless plead a sufficient apology for the consideration bestowed upon the Mediæval history and condition of the Holy City. No place whatever has been more frequently mapped and planned than Jerusalem and its environs: yet nothing is hazarded in saying that the Author's map is the only correct one in existence. But the Author knows too well the difficulties and dangers inseparable from a survey of Jerusalem and its vicinity, to be censorious on this score. Indeed, but for the ready passport to Moslem favor, afforded by the medical services of a generally known and somewhat naturalized resident, it could have made no pretensions to the minute accuracy now so confidently claimed for it.

The pictorial illustrations are almost entirely original; and not only so, but owing to a fortunate circumstance that placed the Author in possession of excellent French photographic apparatus, are nearly all from photographs taken in special reference to topographical illustration. To his excellent friend Mr. Graham, of the English Mission, he is also deeply indebted for valuable contributions of this character. To insure the greatest possible accuracy, duplicates of many of these originals were also drawn in a large camera (or where lenses were unavailable, by a skilful pencil), and, being satisfactorily verified on comparison with the objects portrayed, they may be regarded as *fac similes* of nature. The greater pains have been taken to insure the utmost accuracy, on account of the miserable caricatures that disgrace so many of our Bibles, and libel the Sacred Localities. The possession of such perfectly reliable maps, plans, diagrams, and pictures, will render superfluous much wearisome verbal description, and yet impart to the reader more accurate and vivid impressions than could possibly be conveyed by the most prolix and detailed explanations. And not only will the subject be far more efficiently, correctly, and indelibly impressed, by thus addressing the mind through the eye, but much valuable time and space be economized. To convey to the mind any adequate idea of complicated or unique structures by the pen, is as difficult as unsatisfactory—yet to do so pictorially is fortunately easy, effective, and satisfactory.

The maps are all entirely original: and being carefully constructed, upon the spot, from actual and minute survey, with every requisite for insuring accuracy, may be regarded as entirely reliable. Great advantage has been derived from the possession of a large and accurate model of Jerusalem and its vicinity—especially in the restoration of ancient Jerusalem.

Owing to their complication with theological questions, deemed matters of paramount importance throughout the Orient, topographical theories differ to an extent that would be absolutely ridiculous were it not so serious a matter. It might well be inferred from the works of Dr. Clark, Mr. Williams, Herr Kraft, Mr. Ferguson, and Mons. de Saulcey, that, on the one hand, no topographical question about the Holy City was susceptible of satisfactory settlement (so diverse and opposite are their conclusions), and on the other, that localities which it is impossible in the very nature of things to identify, have been ascertained with all the certainty of mathematical demonstration.

How many magnificent paper castles of Jerusalem, built of materials hastily gathered during a brief visit, or collected from the conflicting accounts of other travellers, or still worse, from the mere conjectures of an over-confident theorizer, who never even visited the spot, have I seen undermined and subverted by a few metrical appliances, and local matter-of-fact considerations! In the "Chorographical Century of the Land of Israel," (chap. 23,) the learned Dr. Lightfoot thus sensibly discourseth—"Let us have leave not to esteem all things for oracles which they say, who now show those places, since it is plain enough that they mistake in many other things: and let it be without all controversy that they study not so much truth in that affair as their own gain. I wish less credit had been given to them, and more search had been made out of Scripture and other writers, concerning the situation of the places." The astonishing errors into which this great Biblical scholar suffered himself to fall, notwithstanding the foregoing excellent remarks, are well calculated to deter all others from topographical theorizing without actual examination of the premises. The topographic and diagraphic representations of many—indeed nearly all sacred localities, as exhibited in the standard works on Jewish antiquities, are gross perversions, but little better than caricatures—the authors of these works having unfortunately adopted the fanciful scheme of Dr. Lightfoot, whose egregious mislocations of Zion, Siloam, Tophet, and the dividing line between Judah and Benjamin, are the fruitful sources of interminable and ludicrous blunders. But notwithstanding these fundamental errors, his work is one of profound research and rare excellence in nearly every other respect; and is unequalled in all that pertains to the Temple Service.

Few, indeed, can have any proper conception of the laborious investigation involved in bringing out the work attempted in these pages. To delve into the rubbish of Oriental ecclesiastical tradition, and evolve to view many of the Sacred Localities, thus inhumed more effectually than by the mortar, filth, and fragments of twenty centuries—has indeed been "a work of faith and a perseverance of hope," if not "a labor of love." "*Hoc opus, hic labor est!*" but equally true is it that "*Labor ipse voluptas!*"

Many points of the topography of Jerusalem are involved in such perplexing intricacy that they could never be eliminated by adhering to the present traditional terminology of sacred topography, if we would thoroughly lay bare "the foundations of many generations." It is therefore necessary sometimes to disregard the present traditional names, and give them their true designation—a fact that may perhaps at first rather shock the sensibilities of those who entertain an overweening regard for legends of antiquity; but the candid reader is earnestly requested to hold his judgment in abeyance until he shall have read an exposition of all such articles. "Strike—but hear!"

Knowing the value of a well digested chronological synopsis of the leading events of the Crusades, in connexion with the investigation of the antiquities of the Holy City, such a polymicrian time-and-space-saving compilation is given as will obviate the necessity of much tedious reference to historical works, and greatly facilitate the comprehension of the whole subject.

The very full references to the Bible, Josephus, the Talmud, and "Fathers," impart to the work a rather fragmentary appearance, and may perhaps be regarded by some in the light of typographic blemishes; but the critical reader, who feels a special interest in the subject, can but be gratified. All Bible references, not incorporated with the text, might well have been omitted, but for the unaccountable deficiency of all concordances in relation to the names of places, which renders such references indispensable to the full development of the subject. The various matters involved in the consideration of the subject being all classified and treated systematically, great advantage can but accrue to the reader who would fully comprehend the subject.

Being anxious to avoid even the semblance of personal controversy, I shall only refer to writers from whose views I dissent, when compelled to do so. The Author is aware that a larger amount of personal incident, however irrelevant to the main design of the work, would have been more acceptable to many readers, than such formal dissertations.* But in order to place the work within the reach of all that may desire information concerning the Holy City, he feels constrained not only to restrict himself to that subject alone, but to study condensation and facility of reference, by adopting an arrangement—even at the expense of good taste and certain other matters of minor importance—calculated to insure these desiderata.

The same consideration also dictates the propriety of stating quite briefly all that is known of matters about which there is but little misunderstanding, in order that more attention may be bestowed upon the elaboration of topics less understood and more involved in controversy; and especially that the more room may be afforded for the discussion of matters not heretofore brought under consideration at all.

* Many such details being given in the "History of the Jerusalem Mission" compiled by D. S. Burnett, Corresponding Secretary of American Christian Missionary Society—the omission of such incidents in the present work is rendered the more proper.

On the same principle many beautiful photographs are withheld from publication, simply because the public is already furnished with elegant and correct representations of the subjects alluded to, from the portfolios of Bartlett, Tipping, Catherwood, Roberts, and others—supplying them, however, by others perhaps equally as attractive and more subservient to the special end in view. The water supply of ancient Jerusalem, though a matter full of interest, nevertheless has been strangely neglected, and hence the over-proportionate space devoted to that interesting topic.

Mr. Williams well remarks that "it is an obscure and perplexing subject, that well deserves particular attention;" and with Mr. Ferguson, it must be conceded that it is a matter of the deepest interest, and of fundamental importance in the settlement of many points of topographical inquiry.

There is perhaps no stronger aid and incentive to devotion, than the enlightened appreciation and proper improvement of pilgrimages to Sacred Localities; for who is there—having a heart to feel and a mind to conceive—that can seat himself on Mount Olivet and not weep over Jerusalem—can walk about Zion and catch none of the spirit of David—gaze on Calvary and feel no emotion—pass down the Kedron unmoved and unblest! and feel no rapture as he gazes on the Mount of Ascension! Truly, neither the head nor the heart of that person is to be envied that manifests no interest in such a place as the Holy City! that feels for it no yearning of heart, and derives no pleasure from even the inspection of its faithful photographic and topographic portraiture. But though these hallowed spots, in giving a realizing view and impression of the truth of revelation (in no other way so richly to be enjoyed), do greatly enhance our devotional feelings; yet it were enough to make an angel weep to see the misdirected, superstitious, idolatrous devotion paid to sacred localities by the overwhelming majority of pilgrims—for at least nine-tenths of these hyper-devout pilgrims believe that certain sins will immediately be pardoned (and can only be pardoned), by visiting certain localities, to which they have been dispatched as devotees. Is it therefore just matter of regret, as felt by some, that by clearly disproving the identification of some of these traditionary locations, the fallacy of predicating remission of sins upon any such local premises is so plainly indicated? For if it can clearly be demonstrated that tradition is at fault in a few notable instances, doubtless it will greatly tend to prevent that undue reliance upon acts of devotion supposed to be rendered peculiarly efficacious because of the particular locality at which they are performed. The invalidation of a matter so fruitful of evil as this idolatry of locality is observed to be in the latitude of Jerusalem, is by no means to be deprecated, but rather to be desired. And but for this consideration, I should be disposed to leave the poor credulous pilgrim in undisturbed possession of all the enjoyment arising from this blind devotion he pays to sacred shrines, at many a misnamed locality.

The mere entertainment of the reader constitutes no portion of the Author's object in composing these pages: they are the result alone of a conviction of duty—designed for instruction rather than entertainment—and are therefore penned in a style deemed most suitable for the general reader—arranged, however, at the same time for the use of Sunday schools, Bible classes, and ministers of the Gospel. To impart the greatest amount of information in the shortest possible time, consistent with perspicuity, has been almost a necessity—owing to engagements over which he could exercise no control. Much of the work being very hastily written at odd intervals by the wayside, during an extended tour through the United States, and indeed all of it *currente calamo* under most disadvantageous circumstances, can, of course, lay no claim whatever to literary merit—be its pretensions to truthfulness of detail never so confidently asserted. And being put to press without the opportunity of a leisurely revision—no small portion indeed being written while passing through the hands of the compositor for stereotyping—it may well be spared the chastisement of the reviewer's lash for such inelegancies of style and obscurities of expression as would be otherwise justly obnoxious to criticism.

It was with extreme regret that the Author was informed by the Publishers, on reaching the 550th page, that the volume, having already transcended its prescribed limits, must speedily close—for there yet remain about two hundred pages of matter designed for publication, three-fourths of which must now necessarily be excluded, even after greatly abridging the portion inserted. Amongst other matters of interest is a valuable contribution from the pen of his learned friend, Robert Sim, M. D., Surgeon to the Anglican Hospital, on the Lepers of Jerusalem. He cannot but regret that it is necessary also to exclude a whole chapter on a subject profoundly engaging and hitherto entirely uninvestigated, however rich and inviting—the New Jerusalem above, considered in its relations to the earthly City of the Great King. But he more especially regrets that he is thus constrained so materially to abridge the exposition of his views of "Millennial Jerusalem." For this is a subject which, however interesting and important at this ominous crisis of the world's history, is so completely put under ban—owing to the wild extravagancies of reckless theorizers—as scarcely to be esteemed legitimate matter of investigation. Nor is this wariness either very surprising or censurable in view of the many wild vagaries that have been palmed upon the world as the doctrine of Scripture. "Save me from my friends, and I will take care of my enemies," is an expression which even a prophet might be excused for using—for prophecy has far less to fear from its enemies than from some of its professed friends.

Having the sure word of prophecy, whereunto we do well to take heed as unto a light that shineth in a dark place, it is surely not the part of wisdom to be deterred by the carnal doctrines of materialists (spoiled through philosophy and vain deceit), from investigating this important subject and enjoying the blessedness promised to those who heed the words of prophecy.

Happy indeed will the Author be, should the perusal of these pages serve in any degree to render more intelligible, satisfactory, and attractive, any portion of the "Volume of the Book"—"the Living Oracles"—which alone can inform us how to obtain admission into the *Eternal* "City of the Great King"—"the Holy Place of the Tabernacle of the Most High—the Holy Jerusalem descending out of heaven from God."

The Author cannot but express his regret that it was not until the last sheet of his MS. had been sent to the stereotyper, that he met with an excellent English work on Palestine, entitled "The Tent and the Khan, by Robert Walter Stewart, D. D., of Leghorn"—to whose sojourn at Jerusalem reference is made in this volume.

It is with no ordinary satisfaction that the Author finds his discoveries and peculiar views of topography so fully recognised and endorsed by a gentleman, Christian, and scholar so competent to form a correct judgment as Dr. Stewart: and gladly would he have availed himself of this valuable work had it fallen into his hands at an earlier period.

GLOSSARY.

Ain	Fountain.
Amûd	Pillar.
Bab	Gate.
Beit	House.
Bîr	Well.
Birket	Pool.
Dier	Convent.
Haret	Quarter.
Hammam	Bath.
Jammeh	Mosk.
Jebl (*Jebel*)	Mountain.
Kefer	Village.
Khan	Public lodging-place.
Kebla	(Prayer niche) South.
Khûbr or Kûbr	Tomb.
Kubbet	Dome.
Madresseh	School.
Mar	Saint.
Mesjid	Sacred Enclosure.
Mihrab	Oratory—small place of prayer.
Neby	Prophet.
Sûk	Market.
Tarik	Street.
Turbet	Grave-yard.
Wady	Valley.
Wely	Moslem Mausoleum.

References to Josephus are thus expressed: (W. iv. v: 2–6), (Ant. xi. iv: 3–6): Wars, book 4th, chapter 5th, section 2 to 6—Antiquities, book 11, chapter 4, section 3 to 6.

TOWER OF HIPPICUS. CHURCH OF YACOBEIA. ANGLICAN CHURCH & CONSULATE.

CITY OF THE GREAT KING.

CHAPTER I.

"Blest Land of Judea—thrice hallowed of song,
Where the holiest of memories pilgrim-like throng,
In the shade of thy palms, by the shores of thy sea,
On the hills of thy beauty, my heart is with thee."

"THE City of the Great King" is first mentioned on the page of history in the account of the memorable interview between Abraham, the "Father of the faithful," and the "Priest of the Most High God" (Gen. xiv. 18) under the name of Salem. It would appear from that admirable expostulation of Josephus with his infatuated countrymen, recorded in the 4th section of the 9th chapter of his 5th book of the Jewish wars, that the site of Jerusalem was regarded with veneration, not only by their great progenitor but by the Egyptians also, anterior to the heart-rending trial of his faith. "Jehovah-Jireh" ("the Lord will provide") is the cheering appellation by which the eastern portion of the site of Jerusalem is designated by Jehovah, when visited again by the venerable patriarch on another occasion no less memorable—(Gen. xxii. 14). But from the invasion of Palestine by Joshua, to the complete subjugation of the city by David—a period of about five hundred years—it seems to have gone under the name of Jebus or Jebusi (Jos. xviii. 28; Jud.

xix. 10; 2 Sam. v. 6). Thenceforward it was known as Jerusalem,* or more properly Jerushalaim, Holy City, (and that portion of it reëdified and enlarged by David) Zion and the City of David—specific appellations which, though at first appropriated to certain portions only, were afterwards used with such latitude as to indicate the city generally. Josephus remarks (Antiquities, book 7, chap. 3, sec. 2d), that under his forefather Abraham "it was called Salem or Solyma; but after that time some say that Homer mentions it by that name, viz. of Solyma (for he designated the Temple Solyma according to the Hebrew language, which denotes security"). It seems to have borne the name Hierosolyma† even during the reign of Melchisedec. The opinion is entertained by many that Jerusalem is merely a corruption of Jebus-Salem—a name by which it is supposed to have been called when the two cities Jebus and Salem became united—the *b* passing gradually into *r* merely for the sake of euphony; which, however, Aristotle rather discredits, and regards as "very awkward." Others derive the name from Salem or Shalem, *peace*, preceded by the word Jireh slightly altered; and others again from Jeru, *they shall see*, and Salem, *peace*.

The Rabbins reconcile these conflicting theories to their entire satisfaction by the following etymological gloss. "The name of that place is Jehovah-Jireh. Say they, Abraham called the name of the place Jireh; Shem called it Shalem. Saith God, 'if I shall call it Jireh it will displease Shem the just: if I shall call it Shalem it will displease Abraham the just. I will therefore put that name upon it which was put upon it by both—Jireh-Shalem—Jerushalaim—Jerusalem." Herodotus, the Greek historian, styles it Kadytis; but Jerusalem is the name under which it has generally been known since the date of its capture by David down to the

* This name occurs as early as Josh. x. 1, but doubtless proleptically.

† Supposed by some to be compounded of ἱερός and שׁלם, and hence sometimes called "Hierusalem;" but more probably from Salem and Jireh, "*the Lord will provide peace*" by the sacrifice of the sin-atoning Lamb—a suggestion that derives some plausibility from the fact that there are two other places called Salem, from which the sacred locality would thus be significantly contradistinguished.

Name.	Age.

present day. When rebuilt by Hadrian, it passed for a short time under the new name with which he selfishly and impiously dubbed it—Ælia Capitolina; but despite the utmost effort of the mighty heathen emperor, this high-sounding title, however euphonious, was soon exchanged for that far sweeter appellation—Jerusalem: the dwelling of peace; though Zion, the specific name of one of its hills, is perhaps more frequently used in the Bible to designate the city than any other appellation. It is styled at present by the Arabs, Turks, Persians, and other Mussulmans, "El-Khuds," "*the Holy;*" or, Beit-el-Makhuddis, "*the Holy House,*" or "*House of the Sanctuary.*"

But the Holy City is to receive yet another designation. "Thou shalt be called by a new name, which the mouth of the Lord shall name, * * * * thou shalt no more be termed Forsaken; neither shall thy land any more be termed Desolate; but thou shalt be called HEPHZIBAH, and thy land Beulah—for the Lord delighteth in thee, and thy land shall be married * * * * thou shalt be called 'Sought Out,' a city not forsaken.'" (Is. lxii. 2, 4, 12.)

"Jehovah Shammah" ("the Lord is there"), is another appellation sometimes applied to the Holy City by writers: but erroneously; for this is the name of the great political capital of the Holy Land during the millennium. (Ezek. xlviii. 35.)

Under the general name of Jerusalem, the Holy City has now occupied a prominent position on the page of history for nearly thirty-eight long centuries, which shows it to be at least 1168 years older than Rome, the self-yclept "Eternal City," and "Mistress of the world." If any city on earth deserves the appellation of "Eternal," it is Jerusalem. It shall become "an Eternal excellency." God has chosen it as his dwelling-place for ever.

This venerable city, so celebrated in the lays of that Prince of lyric poets—"the sweet singer of Israel,"—as "beautiful for situation, the joy of the whole earth," occupies an irregular site on a kind of cloven tongue of land; being almost surrounded by two valleys and intersected by a third, and is situated on the central chain of limestone mountains, running north and south through Palestine. This sacred site is separated from the hills, or as they are called in one of the "Songs of Degrees," (Ps. cxxv. 2), "*mountains* that are round about Jerusalem," on all sides, except the north-west, where its connexion with the great mountain range of Judea is maintained by a broad ridge or isthmus from the north-west.

The observer, on approaching Jerusalem by way of the Jaffa road, which lies on this ridge, beholds the Kedron valley commencing very gradually on the left of this ridge before he reaches Wely Kamah (more than half a mile from the north-west corner of the city), and then a ridge starting from it on the right separating Wady-el-Werd from the valley of Rephaim; and farther on another ridge or gentle swell also starting on the right (nearly opposite Wely Kamah), dividing the plain of Rephaim from the (so called) Gihon. Just below the Wely this isthmus of Jerusalem gently bifurcates into its two leading ridges or hills—separated by a valley running southwardly, so shallow and broad as scarcely to be perceptible at first, but gradually diminishing in breadth and increasing in depth—the Gihon of the Scriptures, though now nameless. The right-hand bifurcation (the northern part of which is the hill Gareb, and the southern, Zion) is sundered nearly in half by another valley, the Tyropœon, running first to the east and then to the south, having Akra immediately on the north and Zion on the south—Mount Zion being also subdivided by a valley running into the Tyropœon from the south. The left-hand bifurcation of the isthmus is also gradually divided into two ridges—that on the right constituting Bezetha, Moriah, and Ophel—being the larger and more conspicuous—that on the left (unnamed, except Goath, its southern termination) being the smaller and shorter. The valley separating these two ridges is termed in the Scriptures "the valley of the *dead bodies and of the ashes*," and is generally unnoticed by travellers—its termination having been nearly filled up designedly in the construction of the great fossa of Antonia, and that portion of it above

Antonia, which alone was ever very deep, being well stored with the accumulated debris of ages.

Aristeas, who was sent on a mission to the High Priest of the Jews by Ptolemy Philadelphus, thus describes the Holy City as it existed a few centuries before the Christian era:—"It is situated in the midst of the mountains, on a lofty hill, whose crest is crowned by the magnificent temple girt with three walls seventy cubits high, of proportionate thickness, and length corresponding to the extent of the building." The city he supposed to be about five miles in circumference. Towers he represents as arranged like a theatre. The city was built on the declivity of a hill; its streets had raised pavements for passengers, purified at the temple, whilst others walked below—some of the streets ran along the brow of the hill, others lower down, parallel with the course of the valley, connected by cross streets. Brief notices of the Holy City by Tacitus, Herodotus, and other ancient historians, will be found in another part of this work.

No city on earth can boast of a greater celebrity or a higher antiquity than the "City of the Great King;" for there is no just reason to call in question the assertion of the great Jewish historian, that it was founded by "Melchisedec, the righteous king," the second son of Noah—the illustrious ancestor and eminent type of the "Prince of Peace."* Nor is there on all the earth another spot so well entitled to a place in our affections or a page in history, as this venerated place, where Melchisedec was the first "Priest of the Most High God,"—upon one of whose sacred hills Abraham reared an altar to offer up his son—his only son, Isaac, whom he loved—so strikingly typifying the great expiatory sacrifice of the Son of God, and by faith "rejoiced to see His day—and he saw it and was glad."

No slight intimation of the future sacredness and celebrity with which the Holy City was destined to be characterized, is also conveyed to us in the significant names and authority of those mysterious

* That Melchisedec and Shem were the same, scarcely admits of reasonable doubt. According to Jerome, Shem survived Abraham thirty-five years.

personages, one of whom, at the date of its first mention, was king in Jerusalem; the other, when for a time it seemed to bid defiance to the military power of the hosts of Israel, even though commanded by that eminent generalissimo, the terror of whose name was feared and felt even at the remote gates of Gadiz.* For although it would appear from the book of Joshua (i. 8), that a portion of the city at least was captured and burnt by the Israelites, yet it is evident that Joshua never entirely subdued it. (xv. 63.)

No place can boast of a situation more eligible in many respects than that of the City of the Great King; though it unquestionably labors under some disadvantages. This consecrated spot, where the Lord has so graciously recorded his name, may still be regarded as "set in the midst of the nations,"—intermediately and conveniently situated between Asia and Africa, America and Australia, Europe and the "Isles of the Gentiles;" and hither the "tribes," not only of Israel, but of all nations, still go up—for it is the "sacred city," not only of the Jews, but of Moslems and of Christians, "even to the utmost bounds of the everlasting hills." According to accurate observations recently made, it lies in north latitude 31° 46′ 45″ and 35° 13′ east longitude from Greenwich—about thirty-three miles from the Mediterranean, and half that distance from the Jordan and Dead Sea, at an elevation of 2610 feet above the level of the former, and about 3927 above the latter.

At such a towering altitude, the climate of Jerusalem, as may well be supposed, is somewhat different from that of the more depressed regions that surround it: its temperature of course being much less elevated, and, owing to the vicinity of the ever snow-capped peaks of the Lebanon on the north, the burning desert of Arabia on the south, and the mild Mediterranean on the west, it must ever have been as it now is, subject to sudden and considerable vicissitudes of temperature. It will be perceived from the thermometrical

* "We are fleeing from the robber Joshua," said a colony of Canaanites through the monumental column of granite, that even down to the commencement of the present century was plainly legible on the Algerine side of the Straits of Gibraltar.

and barometrical tables, that its highest point—92° F. in the shade, and 143 in the sun—is attained in August; and its lowest—28°—occurs in January. But the extremes of temperature are probably greater now in the general absence of forests and all vegetation, resulting from the suppression of the "latter rain," than in the days of its prosperity. Summer now prevails more than half the year; but, notwithstanding this long prevalence of warm temperature, the heat at Jerusalem is much more endurable than in any portion of the Atlantic coast of the United States, from Maine to Texas. This is due not only to its elevated position, where the evaporation of perspirable matter takes place so readily, and the consequent reduction of temperature is so considerable, but to a north-westerly breeze from the Mediterranean, which uniformly springs up as soon as the ground becomes somewhat heated—about eight or nine o'clock in the morning—and continues till ten at night. This particular current is no doubt attributable, in part, to the rarefaction of the air by the denuded rocky surface of the western slope of the mountain ridge on which the Holy City is situated. A similar breeze would also come in the opposite direction from the eastern declivity, which is equally denuded, arid, and hot, were it not counteracted and neutralized by a similar tendency of the mountains of Moab and Ammon.* The column of atmosphere

* I may mention in this connexion a curious meteorological phenomenon that I observed one night while ensconcing myself beneath a rocky cliff from observation, in the semi-daylight shed by a Syrian full moon. Light fleecy clouds were occasionally passing over our heads, traversing the heavens in an easterly direction. It had for some time appeared to my vision that just as soon as they came directly over the summit of Zion they became entirely dissolved; and on calling attention to the fact, it became evident to all that such was really the case. Now, whether the heat of "the holy hill of Zion" dissolved them when they came so near its summit, or whether a dry, absorbent breeze from Moab and Ammon happened to meet and dissolve them just on this ridge, or whether it was merely an optical illusion owing to the peculiar position of the moon, I shall not undertake to decide; but certain it is that I shall never forget the sensations of that memorable night while memory does her office—for I found myself environed by rather hazardous circumstances—in this effort to reach the temple by a subterranean passage, which no explorer nor "fowler knoweth, and which the vulture's eye hath not seen!" but my ardent hopes were soon foiled by the cupidity and duplicity of my Arab cicerone.

pressing upon the bosom of the Dead Sea and the plain of Jericho, is at least thirteen hundred feet taller than that at Beirût, Tyre, Jaffa, Gaza, or any other seaport of Palestine, and is more than three-fourths of a mile higher than that resting upon Jerusalem and its immediate environs ; hence that teeming tropical luxuriance for which it was so highly extolled by Josephus. It was on account of its production of the celebrated balm and other rare and valuable drugs and fruits, that Cleopatra induced Pompey to take it away from Herod the Great and annex it to the dominions of the Pharaohs. During the palmy days of Judea, when the land was seasonably watered by the latter rains, and subjected to irrigation by means of the "brooks of water, of fountains and depths that spring out of valleys and hills," originally, there was perhaps no spot on all the earth that could compare with that narrow belt of land between "the former and hinder sea" (the Mediterranean and Dead Seas), in point of variety and richness of vegetable productions, and especially that portion of it twelve or fifteen miles east of the Holy City, when it was "well watered, even as the garden of the Lord, like the land of Egypt, as thou comest unto Zoar."

Frost, at the present day, is entirely unknown in the lower portion of the valley of the Jordan, and perhaps as high up as the Sea of Galilee, which is depressed three or four hundred feet below the level of the Mediterranean. Slight frosts, however, are sometimes felt on the sea-coast, and particularly in the vicinity of Mount Lebanon. But at Jerusalem they are quite frequent, and sufficiently severe to blacken the fig leaf prematurely in the fall. And although there may not be a particle of snow or ice for several consecutive years, in general, yet there were several snows—though of short continuance—during the winters of 1853–4 and 1854–5, and pellicles of ice at one time an eighth of an inch thick on thin sheets of water in places protected from the rays of the sun ; and portions of ground similarly situated were slightly frozen for several days.

The hygrometer, perhaps, in no portion of the earth fluctuates more widely than at Jerusalem: no climate perhaps being so humid in winter and arid in summer. Water not only stands in drops on the walls, but sometimes literally flows down freely during a considerable portion of the winter, whenever a cold spell of weather is succeeded by a warm westerly wind. The walls thus saturated with moisture throughout the winter become quite incrusted with a saline deposit left by the water as it exudes and evaporates from the surface after the "winter is over and gone," which, however singular, is easily explained on chemical principles. There being no sand in the vicinity of the city from which to make cement, ashes are substituted for this ingredient of mortar: and hence the chemical reaction that takes place through electrical agencies, in the cement of buildings, results in the formation not only of nitre, but of salts of lime also (the muriate and nitrate), which being dissolved by the winter rain as it percolates through the dome, are deposited in crystalline foliations on the interior, where they alternately deliquesce and effloresce during the hygrometric changes of the summer, and occasionally fall to the floor like fleecy snow, or saline drops from the Dead Sea—so acrid and nauseous are they. But perhaps these extremes of humidity and aridity belong rather to Jerusalem as it now *is* than to Jerusalem as it once *was*, before the curse of heaven was inflicted on the land.

With the exception of the daily mountain breeze of summer, the wind, as to force, frequency, and direction, is very variable—"blowing where it listeth." The sand-storms, though alarming in appearance, are rather grand than terrific: but the fine particles of sand that impart such a peculiar, lurid aspect to the sky, penetrate every crack and crevice, and are exceedingly annoying to housekeepers, reminding one forcibly of the miraculous dust of Egypt. Of all the winds of Palestine, the most disagreeable by far (at least to the unacclimated) is the Sirocco—blowing several successive days from the south, and, like the sand-storms, exerting a sadly depressing influence—mentally, corporeally, and almost spiritually—a feeling of perfect *good-for-nothingness*. Winds are sometimes felt that may well be called Levanters. May not many of the sad and sorrowful expressions in the Psalms of David in some measure be owing to these depressing effects?

The rainy season commences very gradually in the fall, and continues through the spring—undergoing a considerable abatement, however, which the Fellahin anxiously improve with their rude plough and mattock. The climate, however, in relation to rains, has undoubtedly undergone considerable changes since the era of Scripture times—a portion of the rains being still withheld according to prophetic denouncement—though many entertain the opinion that they are gradually being restored.

It is as true now as it ever was, that "when the south wind blows, then we know there will be heat," for "so it cometh to pass" uniformly. But many a cloud now "riseth out of the west," and no one "straightway says there cometh a shower," for "so it is" *not*, in the present altered condition of the country. The chilling north wind, even though saturated with moisture on leaving Lebanon, would become so much warmer before reaching the land of Uz, that it would be extremely absorbent, and highly productive of fair weather at all times; but in speaking of the influence of the north wind upon the weather in Palestine there is an apparent clashing between the text and the margin (Prov. xxv. 23); the meaning of the wise man's expression is no doubt truly rendered in the margin, as well as in the text,—for the influence of such a wind upon the warm, moist atmosphere of the west, south, or south-east, if uncooled and filled with moisture, would certainly be to precipitate their saturated vapor in showers of rain, hail, or snow; yet, if rendered warmer and drier in its passage, it would frequently absorb the clouds; thus verifying the declaration of Job—that "fair weather cometh out of the north." Fine hail mingled with rain is very common throughout the rainy season; and it occasionally falls about the beginning or close of the season as large as peas or beans, and sometimes much larger. Upon the plains of the Jordan and the seacoast, snow rarely ever falls, and perhaps never remains. But those districts appear to enjoy more rain than the mountainous region of Jerusalem. Dews and fogs are much more frequent and copious than would be supposed in such an arid climate, and have furnished the inspired writers with many of their beautiful and expressive figures.

That Palestine was originally a well watered country, is not only to be inferred from its former dense population and its exuberant fertility, as well as from numerous other causes, but is abundantly certified by the declaration of Moses that it was a "land of brooks of water, of fountains and depths that spring out of valleys and hills—that drinketh water of the rain of heaven." How then are we to account for the present sparse supply of fountains and brooks? Not entirely by the diminution of rain—for it rains more copiously in Palestine even at this day than it does in the United States! It is ascribable mainly, no doubt, to the general denudation undergone by the country in the lapse of ages—for, that Palestine was at one time richly clothed with forests and herbage, is not only directly testified in the Scriptures, but the very phrase by which it is so frequently designated—"a land flowing with milk and honey"—significantly implies it. On entering into covenant with Israel, his peculiar people, Jehovah solemnly assures them—"if ye shall hearken diligently to my commandments which I command you this day, to love the Lord your God, and to serve him with all your heart, and with all your soul, then I will give you the rain of your land in his due season, the first rain and the latter rain, that thou mayst gather in thy corn and thy wine and thy oil, and I will send grass in thy fields for thy cattle; the land shall yield her increase, and the trees of the field their fruit; and your threshing shall reach unto the vintage, and the vintage shall reach unto the sowing time; the ploughman shall overtake the reaper, and the treader of grapes him that soweth seed, and the mountain shall drop wine, and all the hills shall melt." And hazardous as it would seem, in human estimation, to suspend the continuance of rain and national prosperity upon the continued faithfulness of human beings, yet it most evidently appears that as long as the Jews continued faithful and obedient as a nation, just so long, and no longer, was their land blessed with prosperity; and whenever they became guilty of defection, the rains of heaven were withheld and their land became desolate. What more conclusive proofs of the Divine origin of the Scriptures could possibly be given than the utterance of such prophecies, so exactly fulfilled in the course of long subsequent ages? Was not the deep interest manifested at the libation of water during the "Feast of Tabernacles," or "Ingathering," occasioned by its association with the punctual recurrence of the rain?

It is generally supposed that the *period* of the rainy season is indicated by the Prophet in the following language (Joel iii. 23): "He hath given you the former rain moderately: and he will cause to come down for you the *latter rain*, in the first month." But the language is rather obscure and indefinite: for even if the italicised term "*month*" (or moonth) be properly supplied, it is still uncertain whether the beginning of the civil or ecclesiastical year be intended by "the first month"—September or March. The autumnal rains are generally regarded as the "former," and the spring showers as the "latter rains" of the Scriptures. "The latter rain of the first month," would thus occur in March (Abib), the commencement of the Ecclesiastic or Sacred year—principally in its first moon; but certainly terminating before harvest—"rain in harvest" being a rare phenomenon. (Prov. xxvi. 1; 1 Sam. xii. 17, and Jer. v. 24.) But the whole subject is very obscure. The present winter rain may be either "the former rain" or the "latter" (and not include both, as is generally supposed): and there may have been another rainy season, now entirely withheld, that occurred after harvest, about midsummer—answering to the latter rain of the Scriptures. And indeed without such a rain, or at least without a shorter continuance of dry weather, how could Palestine ever have been justly characterized as a "land flowing with milk and honey"—"the glory of all lands"—"a delightsome land"—"an exceeding good land"—"a land which the Lord thy God careth for: whose eyes are always upon it from the beginning of the year even unto the end of the year."

It may seem strange to many that Palestine should be so desolate as it is now represented to be, if so much rain indeed falls upon so fertile a soil in so genial a clime; but the difficulty is readily explained when it is remembered that all the rain falls within the space of a few short months, and that during the remaining seven or eight months there is not a single shower or "sprinkle;" and it is hazarding nothing in saying that although so much more rain falls in Palestine than in the United States, yet two years' similar distribution of that rain—falling as it does only during a few winter months—would almost bankrupt the whole country! It is matter of surprise then, not that there should be only a million and a half inhabitants in Syria now so desolate, but that it should sustain even a tithe of that number under existing circumstances.

In such a favored land as this—"a land spied out by the Lord" expressly for his peculiar people—"a land wherein thou shalt lack *nothing*"—with such a rich calcareous soil, under so diversified a climate—what must have been the variety and exuberance of its productions in its palmy era of fructifying showers.* Volney well remarks that "Syria unites different climates under the same sky, and collects within a small compass pleasures and productions which nature has elsewhere dispersed at great distances of time and place. To this advantage, which perpetuates enjoyments by their succession, it adds another, that of multiplying them by the variety of its productions. With its numerous advantages of climate and soil, it is not astonishing that Syria should always have been esteemed a most delicious country, and that the Greeks and Romans ranked it among the most beautiful of their provinces, and even thought it not inferior to Egypt." And to the same effect abundantly testify

* Although the Scriptures afford but little direct testimony upon this subject, yet whoever will attentively read the section on the climate and productions of Palestine, in a subsequent portion of this work, can but be convinced that—even judging from its present cashiered condition—it was well entitled to its distinctive designation—"a delightsome land"—"the glory of all lands."

Aristeas, Tacitus, Ammillianus Marcellinus, Pliny, Josephus, Jerome, &c. &c.

A detailed tabular statement of thermometrical, barometrical, and pluviometrical observations will be found under the head of "Modern Jerusalem," where the subject of climate, as modified by existing circumstances, will be farther considered.

MAP OF ANCIENT JERUSALEM.

A Struthion Pool.
B Birket Israel—Moat of Antonia.
C Royal Cistern.
D Pool west of Temple—Piscina ad latus Templi int.
E Pool of Siloam.
F Intermural Ditch—Lower Pool.

1 Gennath Gate.
2 Valley Gate.
3 Esquiline or Dung Gate.
4 Gate of the Essenes.
5 East (or Sun) Gate.
6 Armory.
7 Palace of High Priest.
8 Governor's Throne.

Fountain Gate, near Siloam.
Gate between two walls, just below Siloam.
Two *outlying* Towers—one over Virgin's Fount, and the other near the Hippodrome.
Tower of Furnaces, near Gennath Gate, in "Sacred Wall."

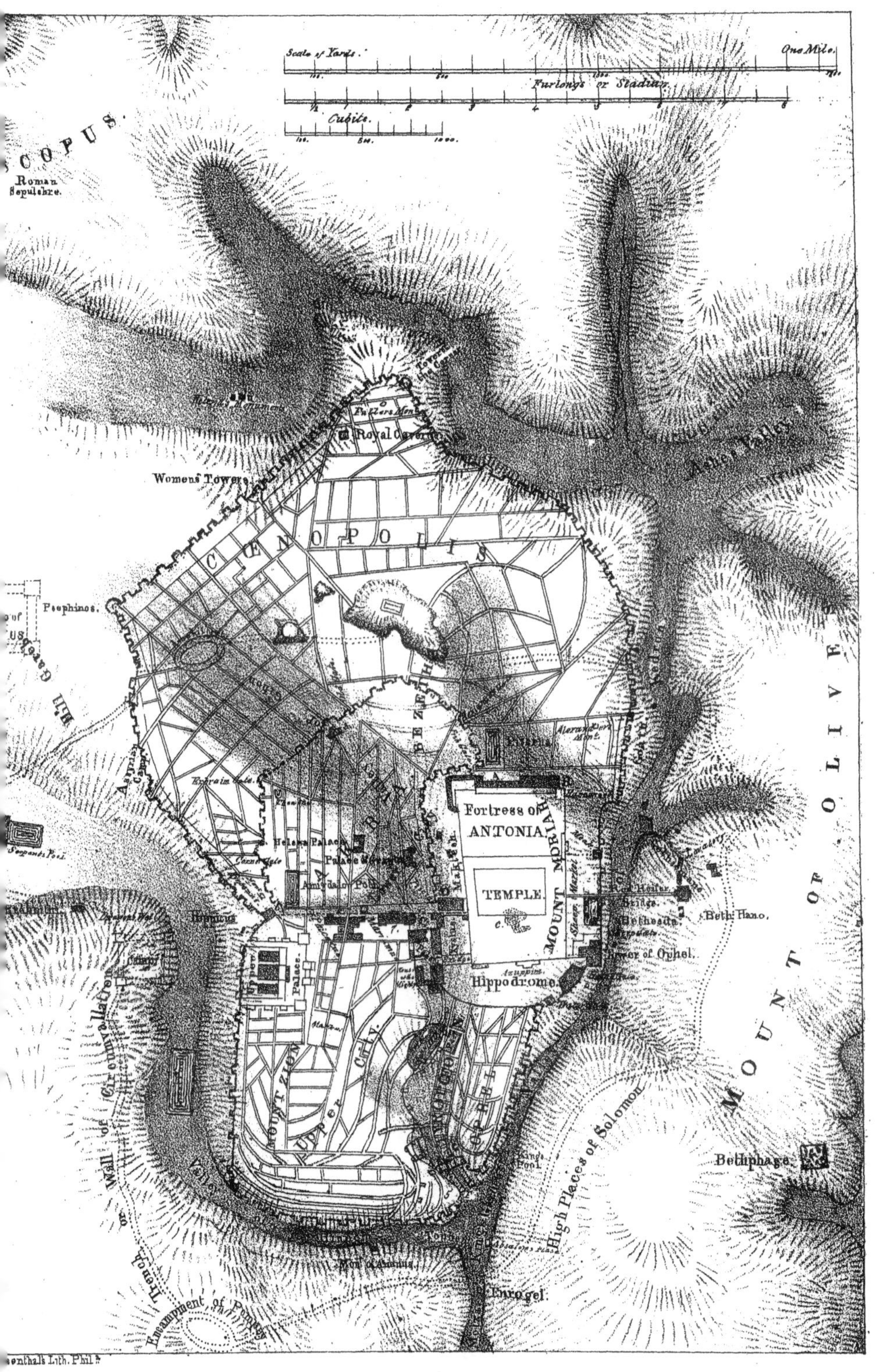

enthal's Lith. Phil.

ANCIENT JERUSALEM.

CHAPTER II.

LOCAL FEATURES OF CITY AND ENVIRONS.

"Walk about Zion—Go round about her."

LAND OF MORIAH—*Vision—Bitterness of the Lord.*

"THE Land of Moriah" seems to have been the name by which the entire site of Jerusalem and its immediate neighborhood was originally designated; and Salem was probably its first capital. But this term, though thus comprehensively used at first, was afterwards restricted to one of the smallest of the several hills upon which Jerusalem is built.

When Abraham's faith was about to be tested, the Lord addressed him in these words: "Take now thy son, thine only son Isaac, whom thou lovest, and get thee into the land of Moriah; and offer him there for a burnt offering upon *one of the mountains* which I will tell thee of." * * * * * "Then on the third day he lifted up his eyes and saw the place afar off." (Gen. xxii. 2, 4.) Now the mountains are still round about Jerusalem, even as in days of yore; and hence there is but one point in all the surrounding country from which this begirded district can be "seen afar off." The traveller from the east is unable to catch the first glimpse of any portion of the city until he reaches the summit of Mount Olivet, half a mile distant; approaching from the north, it is first seen from the heights of Scopus, less than a mile distant; on the west, though a small portion of its loftiest elevations can be seen at Dier Mar Elias, remote about three miles, yet it is not before reaching the crest dividing the valley of Hinnom from the plain of Rephaim, two or three hundred yards off, that any considerable portion can be seen, and even then no part of Mount Moriah is in sight. But from the top of a high promontory, jutting into the deep valley of the Kedron, a few miles south of the city, the hill upon which the temple was built can be plainly seen through the opening made amongst the mountains by the ancient brook; and so narrow is the opening that scarcely any part of the city is visible except this ridge. I had often thought, in looking down that valley, that it was from this very point, or from the summit of a ridge still lower down, that the heart-stricken patriarch "lifted up his eyes on the third day of his journey from Beersheba, and saw the place afar off." And, on making an excursion down the valley, I found the eminence strewed with ruins called "Kirbet Ibrahim," but whether so named in consequence of any such tradition amongst his swarthy descendants, I was unable to ascertain; for so ferocious were the Bedawin then occupying the spot that we were compelled to retreat precipitately, without making any special observations—except, indeed, what we could but note with admiration—that amongst these genuine children of the desert, was a lovely Hagarene, that would suffer only in color by comparison with Venus herself—so perfectly beautiful, graceful, and lovely was she! It is probable, however, that the crusaders had arrived at the same conclusion from the same premises, and had erected on the spot a church and convent, in commemoration of the circumstance. Indeed, so natural and plausible is the conclusion, that it could hardly have escaped the sharp optics of the Empress Helena, in her search for the sacred localities of Palestine.

MOUNT OF OLIVES—MOUNT OLIVET—MOUNT OF UNCTION.

Jebl et-Tûr Jebl es-Zetûn.

So irregular and ill-defined is this far famed mountain, that it is almost impossible to designate its limits, either as to length or breadth. Its principal ridge, however—that which constitutes the distinctive feature of the mountain—lies immediately east of Jerusalem. Its western base may be regarded as coextensive with the Kedron, and is distant from the present Haram wall one or two hundred yards, which was also its average distance from the ancient city. The mean distance of that portion of its summit opposite the city, is about half a mile. But by the nearest pathway it is 918 yards from St. Stephen's gate to the "Church of the Ascension," which is regarded as the principal summit; by the longer foot-path it is 1310 yards, and by the main camel road is perhaps a little farther. Josephus, therefore, in stating the distance of Mount Olivet from the city at five furlongs, or 1010 yards, evidently has reference to the top of the mountain, and not to the foot of it, as is assumed by some writers. A line drawn up the valley lying a short distance south of Bethany, and entering Wady Giddoom, a little below Bethphage, may be regarded as forming, in conjunction with Wady-en-Nair, the southern limit of Mount Olivet. And the road to Anata indicates very nearly its northern boundary. And yet the elevations and expansions north of the spot crossed by the road even as far as Tel el Fûl (the supposed Gibeah of Saul), may well be regarded as a continuation of Olivet. There are more than a dozen spurs that spring from the main body in different directions; and several conspicuous elevations: some might perhaps enumerate a dozen, and others restrict them to two or three. To the spectator on the heights of Zion, or from any other position near the level of Olivet, very little variation of altitude will be apparent; but when viewed from a lower point, the meanderings of the ridge and projection of its spurs produce the impression of many conspicuous eminences; of which that immediately in front, being the nearest, appears the most prominent. And surely there is not in all the world a prospect so delightful to behold, as the panorama to be enjoyed by ascending the minaret alongside the Church of Ascension, that now crowns the elevation nearest the city. Commencing on the south, and looking over the Mount of Corruption, you see in the distance the everywhere visible telegraphic Beth-Haccerem, where Herod had his paradise, and where his execrable bones lie interred; the ocean of hills and mountains to the left is "the hill country of Judea;" and a few miles below Jerusalem you single out an eminence from whose summit you can but conclude that a greater than Herod the Great first "lifted up his eyes and saw the place afar off," where he was commanded to immolate his son—"his only son Isaac, whom he loved." In the distant east, the chatoyant tints of azure-red picture forth the variegated mountains of Moab and Ammon, on one of whose craggy heights a Syrian atmosphere enables you to distinguish the city of Kerak, the site of Kir Moab. You almost fancy you see the very eminence on which proud Balak stood, and "said unto Balaam, Come curse me Jacob—come defy me Israel." Your eyes undoubtedly rest on Pisgah's top, from whose towering height the great lawgiver of Israel was favored with a sight of this "goodly mountain." Chedorlaomer! Amraphel! Tidal! Sodom and Gomorrah! Lot's wife! what overwhelming recollections and sensations oppress us as we gaze down on the pent-up waters of the Dead Sea, and look back through the long vista of thirty-eight centuries! There too, you mark the serpentine course of the turbid Jordan, contrasting so strikingly with the desolate, arid, verdureless desert that occupies three-fourths of the space between Olivet and the Jordan, where John preached and the Messiah was tempted. As you turn your eyes northward to gaze on Mizpah, the great gathering place of Israel—hard by Gibeon and the valley of Ajalon, where, at the command of the son of Nun, the sun and moon were stayed in their courses—your eye is arrested by the white cliffs of Michmash, the height of Ramah, the site of Geba, Anathoth, and many a "scene in fond remembrance set." But a locality far more interesting than all others is just at your feet: and hastily scanning the horizon terminated on the west by the mountains of Bether, celebrated in the "Song of Songs," written by the Preacher that was king in Jerusalem, your eyes are riveted on the City of the Great King and its sacred precincts! What stupendous towers, gorgeous palaces, sumptuous synagogues once adorned the city of Jehovah—and the Temple—how "exceeding magnifical of fame and of glory throughout all countries!" But far more soul-affecting are the emotions that swell up in viewing Golgotha and Gethsemane, on either side of the Kedron below, and the hallowed spot high up on the left, whence the Son of Man ascended up on high, leading captivity captive!

Lunar Station. As this spot (though not the highest point) commands the most extensive prospect, it was probably from a station somewhere near the present Church of Ascension that the appearance of the new moon was announced to the authorities of the Temple, by torchlight signals telegraphed from the land of Moab. This was the great central telegraphic station, which communicated with others on lofty elevations throughout the whole country.

There were also *Proseuchæ*, or houses of prayer, scattered about over the mountain; but of course none of the ruins on Olivet can be recognised at this remote period as the remains of these oratories. If David went the nearest way to Jordan when fleeing from Absalom, as he doubtless did from the stress of the case, and as would also appear from the circumstances connected with the revilings of Shimei; then he no doubt crossed the mountain a short distance north of the present village of Jebl et-Tur, and worshipped at one of these praying places, situated just on the top of the ridge where the last view of the Temple would be taken by one going towards the Jordan, and the first glimpse caught by those coming from Jordan. It was in all probability along the present road from Stephen's Gate across the mountain, which is certainly a very ancient "ascent," that David went up Mount Olivet, and "wept as he went up, and had his head covered, and he went barefoot; and all the people that was with him covered every man his head, and they went up weeping as they went up; and it came to pass that when David was come to the top of the mount where he worshipped God, behold Hushai the Archite came with his coat rent and ashes upon his head." (2 Sam. xv. 30, 32.) Other proseuchæ were of course situated near the "Lavatory;" and no doubt, several also in the Garden of Gethsemane.

Many high places, also, devoted to Ashtaroth, Chemosh, Milcom, Baal, &c., have polluted various parts of this mountain at different times, besides the spur upon which Solomon built idol temples for the heathen portion of his Hareem.

THE LAVATORY was situated on the western slope of Olivet. "That place whereof we are speaking was a pool or collection of waters where people were wont to wash, and it agreeth very well with those things that were spoken before concerning purifications. Here either unclean men or women might wash themselves; and presently, buying in the neighboring shops whatever was needed for purification, they betook themselves to Jerusalem, and were purified in the Temple." Dr. Lightfoot, ii. 305. A bathing establishment so extensive as this Lavatory evidently was, must have required a copious supply of water, and the query may well be raised—"whence did it derive its supply?" Was it from tanks of rain-water, and could they be adequate to such a demand? Was it conducted from the temple by the Red Heifer or the Scapegoat viaduct? or was it dependent upon the Kedron—being brought either by porters or by training the brook along the hillside? In any event it was no doubt situated quite low down the slope: for, if its waters were supplied by the rains, it could only derive a plentiful supply by being located low in one of the principal valleys of the mountain; and, if supplied either by the viaduct or by a diversion of the brook Kedron, it is equally obvious that it must have been situated quite low on the western slope.

Some where near the Lavatory were two very large cedar-trees, and many shops, where pigeons and other articles for purification were sold, called *Beth-hano.*

The place at which the RED HEIFER was burnt to ashes, was situated at the east terminus of the double arched causeway that spanned the Kedron, reaching from Moriah to Olivet, in front of the Gate Shushan. It was vaulted below for fear of pollution, like the south-east corner of the Temple, and the *notable* places in the city for raising "clean persons." "The elders headed the procession, and when the priest came up he bathed himself there." The ceremony is minutely described in the nineteenth of Numbers.

GARDEN OF GETHSEMANE.—*Fat vale—Olive press.* We learn from the Evangelists (Mat. xxvi. 36; Mark xiv. 26; Luke xxii. 39, and John xviii. 1) that this garden was situated over the brook Kedron, on the west slope of Olivet; and its etymology seems to intimate that it was connected with an olive orchard of a fertile valley. It would seem that it was a public place of resort—a kind of pleasure garden perhaps, situated immediately on the side of the foot-path leading to Bethany. The track of an ancient road leading from the Fish Gate to Bethany is still plainly indicated, not only by the physical features of the ground, but by occasional remains of steps cut in the solid rock; and is still in use all the way except where the present path has been made to deviate to the left, for the benefit of the Jebeltûrians and pilgrims to the Cave of Pelagius and the Church of Ascension. The vale of Olivet, through which this path passes, is quite fertile and well stocked with olives, even at the present day, and may well have been the Vale of Gethsemane: the tradition that places the Garden of Gethsemane beside this valley on the right of its lower extremity, cannot easily be disproved, but it is evident that the present enclosure can occupy only in part the site of the ancient garden. For we are informed in the sacred narrative that when the Saviour had entered the garden, he said to the Apostles, "Sit ye here, while I go yonder and pray," and "taking with him the three" that had witnessed his transfiguration, he said to them, "Tarry ye here and watch—and he went forward a little—about a stone's-cast," and there prayed alone—thus plainly implying a considerable extent of area. But the present garden would scarcely be called a stone's-throw in either its breadth or length, being about forty yards in one direction and fifty in the other. The wild rocky space between the eastern wall and the tall watch-tower, about fifty yards distant, could never have been reduced to culture, however valuable land must always have been so near the city; and being so suitable a retreat for prayer, it is a little strange that it was not included in the enclosure by those professing to have identified the ancient locality. But a position in the fat valley above, where there are suitable rocks for oil presses, would be much more in accordance with the etymological import of the name: and if situated near the eastern terminus of the Red Heifer or Scapegoat bridge, there would be more significancy in the expression "he went forth with the disciples *over* the brook Cedron, where was a garden," &c., (John xviii. i.) In this event the Saviour and the Apostles would have crossed the Tyropœon on the Great Solomonic bridge, passed through the Temple (whose gates were kept open at night during the festal seasons), and thus crossed *over* the brook Kedron on the elevated bridge.

THE MOUNT OF CORRUPTION, SCANDAL, OR OFFENCE, where "Solomon (being so strangely "turned aside by his strange wives") did build an high place for Chemosh the abomination of Moab, and for Moloch the abomination of the children of Ammon, was in the hill that is before Jerusalem." (1 Kings xi. 7.) This position is not thus indicated in relation to the Jerusalem that now is, or afterwards was; but as it then existed, confined mainly to Mount Zion. Bearing this in mind, there is no difficulty in correctly locating the scene of these abominable transactions, on the summit immediately east of Siloam and the lower part of Zion; but travellers, unmindful of the local mutations of the Holy City, and locating it on the east, or *before* the present city, have greatly misplaced it. The portion of Mount Olivet thus designated is nearly isolated, being merely conuected to the remainder by the isthmus over which the road to Bethany passes. It rises very precipitously, and to a considerable height above the Kedron, and the valley on the east, which nearly enclose it. The picturesque sepulchral village of Siloam, where, "it is said," Solomon kept his strange wives, occupies a portion of its north-western face, opposite the "Virgin's Fount:" and many other sepulchres are found in its cliffs all around. It is the southernmost or right hand portion of Mount Olivet, as expressed in 2 Kings xxiii. 13: "And the high places that were before Jerusalem, which were on the right hand of the Mount of Corruption, which Solomon, the king of Israel, had builded for Ashtaroth, the abomination of the Zidonians; and for Chemosh, the abomination of the Moabites; and for Milcom, the abomination of the children of Ammon, did the king defile; and he brake in pieces the images and cut down the groves, and filled their places with the bones of men." But if "Mount of Corruption" be the synonym of "Mount of Olives," as many suppose, then not only is the main prominence of this off-shoot of Olivet indicated, but also another considerable prominence on its ridge farther south, opposite En-rogel. The seat of Moloch's worship was afterwards transferred to the Valley of Tophet, below, in a far more detestable and horrible form than that in which it existed on this mountain.

BETHPHAGE—*House of Early Figs—House of the Valleys.* Great diversity of opinion exists in relation to the site of this village; some identifying it with Abu Dis, an Arab village about one mile south-east of Bethany; others assigning it a location on the summit of Olivet, a short distance north of the village of Jebl Tûr; and others, a site not only contiguous to the Holy City, but a portion within the walls; and amongst these latter is the celebrated Dr. Lightfoot. But a simple comparison of the Messiah's triumphal entry into Jerusalem, will show conclusively that in neither of these places could all the requirements of the narrative be met and the conditions fulfilled. Having come nigh unto *Bethphage and Bethany at* the Mount of Olives, the Saviour sent two of his disciples to the village *over against* them, for a colt there tied in a place where *two ways met*, upon which he sat; and when he was come even now at the descent of the Mount of Olives, the multitude shouted hosannas. Now there is not one of those places, nor any other heretofore suggested, to which all the circumstances of the case will apply, except a locality I discovered in making a minute chorographic reconnoisance of the country around Jerusalem. This is a tongue-shaped promontory or spur of Olivet, distant rather more than a mile from the city, situated between two deep valleys, on which there are tanks, foundations, and other indubitable evidences of the former existence of a village. The road from Jerusalem, after passing over the root connecting it with Olivet, sweeps a considerable way up the valley towards the village of Jebl Tûr northward, and then returns down southward on the other side on its way to Bethany, curving around that projection of the mountain, on the farther side of which Bethany is situated. It is fairly to be inferred from the sacred narrative that in making this progression from Bethany to Jerusalem, the Saviour pursued the road ordinarily travelled and best adapted to the circumstances of the multitude that accompanied him, without any unnecessary stoppage or diversion from the route, much less a retrogradation. The point of the road at which he said to two of the disciples, "Go your way unto the village over against you," was perhaps near some tanks and ancient foundations on the top of the intervening ridge, where we would naturally locate the dividing line between the "coasts," or districts of the two villages; and the boundary line would not only be about midway, but the land thus apportioned to each village would be in sight of that village to which it belonged, but out of sight of the other. This position too would at once be near each *village*, and just at the adjunction of the *districts*. The exact application of the expression "over against you," would here fully apply. And whether the two disciples left the main thoroughfare and passed over directly across the valley, or merely quickened their pace a little and turned off to Bethphage by the left-hand pathway, they could easily have the colt in readiness at the point where the Bethphage road entered the main road, by the time Jesus and the multitude that accompanied him had reached that spot. From this point, three or four hundred paces would overcome the ascent to the top and bring them to the "descent of the Mount of Olives," where the whole multitude of the disciples began to rejoice and praise God with a loud voice, for all the mighty works they had seen, saying, "Blessed be the King that cometh in the name of the Lord: peace in heaven and glory in the highest." This view of the position of Bethphage is also fully confirmed by the etymological import of the term, as far as it can be supposed to bear upon the subject. Being so well sheltered from northerly winds, and enjoying so fine a south-eastern and western exposure, it must needs have been well adapted to the production of early fruits; and was, no doubt, well entitled to the appellation "House of Early Figs." And certainly it is justly styled "House of the Valleys,"—if any prefer that etymology.

However much other sacred localities about the Holy City may have altered in the lapse of ages, there is no reason to believe that this hallowed mountain has undergone any material change. True, the palm, the cedar, and the sycamine have long since disappeared from its side; but it is still the home of the *olive*, and its general surface is essentially as it was when King David went up its ascent "weeping and barefooted," and when the Son of man sat upon its brow and wept over the devoted city, or ascended on high from one of its summits. "The Divine Majesty," says Rabbi Janna, "stood three years and a half on Mount Olivet, saying, Seek ye the Lord while he may be found, call on him while he is near." What strong testimony in behalf of the Messiah's divinity, from the pen of a Jew!

It was from this mountain also that "the glory of God"—having left the temple by its eastern gate, ascended on high, after lingering for a time (Ezek. ii., 22, 23), over its hallowed summit.

THE ASCENSION FROM MOUNT OLIVET—
A Sabbath-day's journey from Jerusalem.

Few spots in all the domain of sacred topography are more interesting to the Gentile believer than the one now to be described—the place of the assumption: and although we are entirely dependent upon a few merely allusive paragraphs in the Scriptures for all we know concerning this interesting spot, yet fortunately the language is so specific that its location can be ascertained with great certainty. From this indisputable authority we learn that the spot whence the Saviour ascended on high was on Mount-Olivet;—that it was not only on this mountain but from a portion of it lying a Sabbath-day's journey from Jerusalem; and that it was "as far as to Bethany." (Luke xxiv. 50.) Now the place to which tradition awards the honor of being the last to receive the impress of our Divine Master's feet,* is on Mount Olivet, it is true (and so are many other elevations just as eligible); but is neither "as far as to Bethany," nor is it a Sabbath-day's journey from Jerusalem." The spot now venerated as the place of

* Another impression of His feet is also shown by the votaries of tradition, on the rock in the Kedron just below the bridge opposite "Absalom's pillar."

ascension, over which a portion of the monumental church of the Empress Helena still stands, and which, to the confusion of all cavilling gainsayers, is attested by the veritable foot-print and impress of the staff in the impressible rock, is only about one thousand and thirty-five yards or rather more than half a mile from St. Stephen's Gate, by the path usually travelled, and the same distance from the "Golden Gate" in the Haram wall, now closed; and it is evident from Josephus that the city wall here ran still nearer, eighteen hundred years ago, than it does at present; so that reckoning from the city wall, or even from that of the Temple, by the nearest route, the two places would fall considerably within half a mile of each other. Now this is not half the usual estimate of a Sabbath-day's journey, and considerably less than the smallest computation made upon any data whatever. Authorities decidedly preponderate in favor of the general estimate of rather less than a mile as the length of a Sabbath-day's journey.* We must, therefore, look for some spot on Mount Olivet, thus distant from the wall of Jerusalem: and several such places can be found, both north and south of the present traditionally accredited station. But the sacred narrative requires that it should be not only a Sabbath-day's journey, but "as far as to Bethany"—even unto Bethany—"εως εις Βηθανιαν." Now, it so happens that there is not a more decidedly marked prominence on all Mount Olivet than the hill impending over the ancient "City of Dates," to the top of which is exactly one mile from St. Stephen's Gate, the present place of egress from the city

* It would appear from the Talmudics, that it was no violation of the Sabbath-day, while in the desert, to traverse the whole camp, which is believed to have been twelve miles square; nor was it unlawful to walk through a city on that holy day, no matter how extensive it might be. But after the erection of the Temple, Sabbath locomotion seems to have been greatly circumscribed without the city. No one was permitted to go beyond the limits of the suburbs of the city on that sacred day—a distance of one mile—and this seems to have regulated the Sabbath-day's journey. Some have estimated it as high as two miles, and some, by way of accommodation, as low as seven or seven and a half furlongs; but there is no just reason to question the correctness of the ordinary estimate. The Jewish mile was composed of one thousand paces of five feet, or one thousand six hundred and sixty-six yards, and was therefore nearly one hundred yards shorter than our mile.

to Bethany, and from the Golden Gate also in the ancient Temple wall. But from Shusan or the east gate of the Temple, via the Red Heifer Bridge, it was of course a hundred or two yards less. The present pathway to Bethany, however, is needlessly circuitous (deviating to the left for the benefit of pilgrims), and, if properly located, would be somewhat shortened. The secluded shelter afforded by one of the large projecting rocks that crown the top of this sterile, desolate eminence is just such a retired spot as it might be supposed the great Teacher would select for the delivery of his last charge to the Apostles—sufficiently retired yet easily accessible. This eminence is entirely unprofaned too, by the hands of man—there being no commemorative monument on it, nor (strange to say) any sepulchre within it, nor the mark of the sculptor's tool upon any portion of it; and—as if the Lord would preserve so sacred a spot from idolatrous desecration—the officious hand of tradition has never yet rested upon it, and this with me is a fact of no little significancy, for it does seem that this "*ignis fatuus*" of monastic illumination has rarely ever exhibited its lambent, flickering flame on sacred soil but to mock and bewilder. It may be objected, however, that this spot is not "even unto Bethany"—the town lying about five hundred yards below. But may not the Evangelist have meant the boundary of the "coasts" or *district* of Bethany, instead of the village itself? Such a view of the matter would amply satisfy the demands of the case. But still I incline to the opinion that Luke meant either the village itself or its immediate suburbs. And fragments of columns lying about the remaining foundations of houses in the scarped rock just below the south-east brow of the hill, which is here rather precipitous, indicate that the suburbs of Bethany once extended rather farther towards Jerusalem in this direction than at present, so that the traveller on foot would almost reach it at the end of a mile; while to go around the broad road, he must travel nearly two miles, for the distance is as of old, just fifteen furlongs. In the expression "εως εις Βηθανιαν" Luke therefore would appear to exhibit his usual accuracy of diction, instead of having committed a serious blunder, as some conclude that this heaven-guided historiographer has done. How preposterous is the idea entertained by some of the out-and-out advocates of tradition—that the suburbs of the village of Bethany should extend three-fourths of the way to Jerusalem—thus making the suburbs of the capital only one-fourth as extensive as those of a little village! The summit whence I cannot but believe the Redeemer to have ascended on high, is within a hundred yards of the direct foot-path leading from Jerusalem to Bethany, but yet is quite retired and out of the way. Instead of being conspicuously situated, in full view of all Jerusalem, like the site now reputed the place of ascension, it is entirely out of view of the present city, and could never have been seen from any part of ancient Jerusalem, except perhaps a small portion of Mount Zion. *Here* a meeting with His disciples would have been altogether in consonance with the custom he seems to have observed after his resurrection—of appearing *only* to his disciples, and to *them* only in the recesses of mountains, on the retired sea-shore, or in closed rooms. But such retirement could never be found in such a fertile, prominent, and public spot as that now regarded as the place of ascension. It is not a little singular, that a spot possessing so fully all the requisites indicated by the case, should never before have been regarded as the place of ascension. So satisfactorily demonstrable is the proposition, that I never feel better assured of occupying ground once trodden by the adorable Redeemer, than when I am here; unless it may be, when passing over the narrow neck of land which connects this elevation with the main body of Olivet, for over this thin isthmus, where all the varying paths between Jerusalem and Bethany necessarily become coincident, he must have passed many an evening and morning in journeying between the two places, as his custom was—unless indeed we suppose (contrary to all that either the volume of Revelation or of nature records of him) that he was regardless of the proper adaptation of means to ends; and in going to any given place with his disciples would traverse an extended semicircular path, instead of the nearer and equally available chord—thus travelling twice the requisite distance without any special motive or assignable reason! It is thus perceived that the physical features of the neighborhood singularly concur with the testimony of the inspired eye-witness, to prove that in this instance (as well as in others when tested by reason and Revelation) oral tradition is as groundless and unreliable as the "baseless fabric of a vision;" for if Luke knew anything of the matter, it is utterly impossible that the site pointed out by the finger of tradition can be the true place of the ascension.

Perhaps there is not, on all the wide earth, another Sabbath-day's journey so richly suggestive of the future, or so replete in soul-stirring reminiscences of the past, as the foot-path from the Holy City to the Mount of Ascension. The illustration with which this section is introduced needs no farther explanation than that contained in the following beautifully descriptive, anonymous lines:—

"City of David, for a while farewell;
Thy dazzling shrines, thy narrow squalid streets,
By wearied pilgrims thronged, alike I shun,
And where, with gnarled roots and rugged arms,
Wide straggling o'er the mountain's steep ascent,
Lone ancient Olives linger still, to prove
The name well fitting, breast my upward way.
Its ridge o'erpast, successive sink from view
Thy trench-like valleys, and thy scarped hills,
Thy massive walls, thy towers, thy minarets,
And a new landscape opens to my gaze—
Hill beyond hill, stretching in distant lines
And long succession.
On the horizon's verge,
The last faint tracing on the blue expanse,
Rise Moab's summits, and above the rest,
One pinnacle, where, placed by hand divine,
Israel's great Leader stood, allowed to view,
And but to view that long-expected land,
He may not now enjoy. Below, dim gleams
The sea, untenanted by aught that lives,
And Jordan's waters thread the plain unseen;
Unseen—but marked by "living green."
Nearer approaching, range to range succeeds,
Dark, lava-seeming, dreary solitudes,

View from the summit.

Impervious to the plough, traversed alone
Through gloomy ravines, where of old "a man
Fell among thieves," and where the bandit still
Lurks for his prey, a wilderness of hills.
 But from their base, in gradual ascent,
With yellow grain-fields clothed, and bright relieved
By groves of olives, spreads a sylvan scene.
Beauteous itself, but seeming doubly blest
In nature's bounty, after tracts so wild.
* * * * * And to the hill side,
Here hid among her trees, a village clings,
Roof above roof uprising:
And peopled thick with gayly colored groups,
Housing the golden colored produce of their toil.
Above, one giant patriarch of the woods
Throws the wide shadow of his foliage 'round,
And higher still, the patient laborer
Contends undaunted with the stony waste,
Wresting his hard-won harvest, till the soil
Mocks his vain, fruitless efforts, and alone
Some wandering olive or unsocial fig,
Amid the broken rocks which bound my path,
Snatches scant nurture from the creviced stone.
 And this is Bethany! and here abode
The favored family whom Jesus loved;
To whose warm, humble welcome, 'twas his wont,
Tracking the path that now I passed along,
Oft to retire from foes and wavering friends.
 'Twas here his verdict full acquittal gave,
And high approval of the glowing zeal,
Which, for the "better part," forbore to share
A sister's weak anxieties. 'Twas here
He wept in tender sympathy with woes,
By his command so soon to be absorbed
In grateful joy. Here, by his power divine,
Bade death release its prey, the untrammelled soul
Return to earth and give a living proof
And pledge of future immortality.
And when, his work all ended, he prepared
To reascend his throne, this way he led
His sorrowing followers for a last farewell.
 It seems a humble village, few its homes,
And few and poor its dwellers; cottage roofs,
Except one simple turret, are they all!
Yet save the neighboring city, it were hard

If Palestine were searched, to find a spot
On which the Christian traveller should muse
With fonder interest than Bethany."

If we are to construe the declarations of Luke and Zechariah literally, then this mountain is to undergo a great change when the Son of Man shall so come in like manner as he went up into heaven, "and his feet shall stand in that day upon the Mount of Olives which is before Jerusalem on the east, and the Mount of Olives shall cleave in the midst toward the east and toward the west, and there shall be a great valley, and half of the mountain shall remove toward the north and half toward the south." (Acts i. 11.—Zech. xiv. 4.)

SCOPUS—*Watch-tower—Skopos—Distant View.*—This term is generally but very inappropriately applied to the gentle elevation a short distance north of the city, and immediately south of the great curvature of the Kedron. The hill Scopus is an elevated piece of ground rather more than a mile north of Damascus Gate,—so called on account of the fine view of Jerusalem to be enjoyed from its height. It lies between the two main branches of the valley of the Kedron, and may be regarded as an irregular spur of Mount Olivet. A circular hillock upon this elevation, probably marks the site of the ancient tower. It was here that the Roman general, Cestius, first pitched his camp, and it was also from the heights of this hill that Sennacherib, the vaunting Assyrian monarch, "shook his hand against the mount of the daughter of Zion, the hill of Jerusalem," (Is. x. 32); but all in vain, for like the king of the French, they

"Marched up the hill with twice ten thousand men,
And then—marched back again!"

It was here, likewise, that Titus first pitched his camp, and came well nigh losing his life; but the cup of Israel's iniquity was now full to overflowing, and hence, as Heaven's avenger, he soon destroyed the guilty city. (W. ii. xix : 4–7, and W. v. ii : 4.)

Declivities of Hinnom.—The side of this valley that lies next the city is far less declivitous than the opposite or south-western cliff,

After its gradual commencement at the Upper Pool it becomes quite precipitous throughout its whole extent—being high, perpendicular, and in some places overhanging towards its lower extremity. It forms a distinct but low hill at its commencement—that west of Jaffa Gate—on which Titus made an encampment (now crowned by the convent of St. George). Its termination is also distinctly marked as a hill—that on which the field of Aceldama is pointed out. And much of its middle and upper portion is a low ridge dividing the valley of Ben-Hinnom from the valley or plain of Rephaim. Immediately south of the hill of Aceldama is quite a large promontory or hill, being the termination of that large ridge of which the Hill of Evil Council is the summit. But no special interest attaches to any of these prominences.

HILL OF EVIL COUNCIL—VILLA OF CAIAPHAS—POMPEY'S ENCAMPMENT.—(*Dier Abû Tor, or Dier el Kaddis Modistus.*)—Two or three hundred yards beyond the brow of Gehinnom (commonly called Gihon) is a second elevation of the Hill of Hinnom designated in the traditionary local terminology of Jerusalem "The Hill of Evil Council." It is evidently the hill upon which Pompey pitched his camp; but that its summit was the country seat of Caiaphas, where the Jews took council and devised devices against Christ, is not so easily demonstrated, though its vicinity to the spot he had selected as his final resting-place seems to give some countenance to the tradition. The present remains indicate the former existence of a large and respectable building; and its Arabic name, as well as its peculiar plan, declares it to have been a convent in later ages. The Wely situated in the south-west corner of this ruin is much revered by "*the faithful*" as an oratory or place of prayer. Nearly a hundred yards south-west of it the unsymmetric "tree whereon Judas hung himself" bows its ungraceful head—evidently cultured and trained very carefully in due gibbet form by pio-tradition hands—well meant pious frauds of calculating monks, exhibiting at least the literal truth of the great educational maxim, "just as the twig is bent, the tree's inclined."

"THE HILL GAREB."—The only place in which this hill is mentioned is in Jeremiah (xxxi. 39)—"And the measuring line shall yet go forth over against it upon the Hill Gareb, and shall compass about to Goath"—which plainly defines it to be the ridge running from the north-west corner of the city in the direction of Wely Kamah. It is the isthmus or neck by which Jerusalem is connected with the mountains of Judea—the head of the Kedron valley reposing on its north-east side, and that of the Hinnom on the south-west. This hill gradually coalesces with the low swell that separates the Kedron from the shallow but wide depression north-west of Damascus Gate. Agrippa's Wall, as far as the Tower of Psephinos, was erected nearly upon the middle of this ridge. Some suppose it is so called because Gareb the Ithrite once owned it; others because it contained quarters for the seclusion of lepers.

ASH MOUNDS.—There are several considerable mounds on the elevated ground north-west of the Damascus Gate, of which, that situated about half a mile from the city is the largest. It is contended by many, that these hills are the cinerary products of the Jewish altar of burnt offering: it is evident, however, that their origin is referable alone to the soap manufactories of the city, the leached ashes of which are still deposited there. Quite another disposition of the ashes of the altar was made, as may be seen on reference to the article on the "Ashes Valley."

ROCK MOUND—*near Damascus Gate.*—There is a rock monticule in front of Damascus Gate, two or three hundred yards distant, affording such an eligible site for a large public edifice, that it was perhaps an important place, especially after the Cœnopolis addition of the city. It is an irregular square of sixty or seventy yards on each side; and has several artificial excavations in it; but they do not seem to have been designed for sepulchres, as is generally the case. It is highly probable that it was the site of St. Stephen's Church, reared in the fifth century.

GOATH—*his touching, violent death.*—The only place where this term occurs is in the prophecy of Jeremiah (xxxi. 39,

40), when the prophet, foretelling the reëdification of the Holy City, informs us, in speaking of that portion of it on the north, that "the measuring line shall yet go over against it upon the Hill Gareb, and shall compass about to Goath, and the whole valley of the dead bodies and of the ashes (of burnt idols) and all the fields (or gardens) into the brook of Kedron (even) unto the corner of the Horse Gate toward the east, shall be holy unto the Lord." It was thus evidently on the east of Jerusalem, at the valley of Kedron, in the neighborhood of the Horse Gate, and was embraced within the limits of the great Jewish Cemetery. And that it was not merely a place of sepulture, but also made use of as a place for the execution of malefactors, would also appear from the history of Queen Athaliah, for it was here that this vile usurper was slain, and not by the royal palace on Mount Zion (as is usually contended) on the opposite side of the Temple. This wicked usurper, hearing across the Tyropœon, the rejoicings of the people at the coronation of the young king in the Temple, as she sat in her palace, rushed over the bridge into the Temple, crying "Treason, treason;" but the high priest ordered her immediately to be taken out and put to death, "and they laid hands on her, and she went by the way by the which horses came into the king's house; and there was she slain." (2 Kings xi. 16; comp. 2 Ch. xxiii. 14, 15.) Now, we are not to suppose that horses came into the "king's house" of residence, but into the king's (horses) house or hippodrome, he had built for them just south-east of the Temple, immediately in the vicinity of the Horse Gate. Or as Josephus expresses it (Ant. ix. vii : 3), "Jehoida commanded them to bring Athaliah to the *valley of the Kedron* and slay her there. * * * * Wherefore those that had charge of her slaughter took hold of her and led her to the "*gate of the king's mules* and slew her there" in that part of the Kedron. And that this valley was, at that time, a kind of desecrated place made use of not only as a spot of sepulture, but for the destruction of idols and their appurtenances, is abundantly shown by a passage from the life of good King Josiah (2

Kings xxiii. 2, 6, 12), as well as many other acts of the Kings of Judah. That this quarter was also a general burying ground would appear from the fact stated by Josephus (W. v. vii. 3), that King Alexander was buried in the same general quarter, but farther north.

GOLGOTHA—*a heap of skulls—violent death.*

CALVARY—Κρανιου τοπος—*place of a skull.*

This word is supposed to be compounded of "*gol*" and "*gotha,*" a variation of *goath* or goatha.* And if Hern Kraft is correct in the etymological definition he urges so confidently, "*violent death*"—and those who render the prefix "gol," a *head*, *elevation* or *swell of land*, then we see the propriety of the compound term *golgotha*—a swell or "*hill of violent death.*" Thousands of violent deaths, no doubt, have occurred in that district of the environs of Jerusalem denominated Goath or Gotha, besides the death of Queen Athaliah, or that of the Redeemer of the world—for often has this been the sanguinary battle-ground of the Jews with the Romans under Cestius, Titus, &c.

That the idea of a "skull" is some way or other involved in the Hebrew word *golgotha*, is evident from its version into Greek by John (xix. 17), who says it is "a place called of a skull, which is called in Hebrew Golgotha;" and from Luke (xxiii. 33), who says it is "a place called a *skull,*" (not Calvary,† as is our English version;) but whether because skull-*shaped* or a place bestrewed with skulls, admits of some doubt. Both significations may be true, but the probabilities are rather in favor of the former. The word rendered skull (Jud. ix. 53 and other places), is *golgoleth*, which the Seventy translate as Luke and John render golgotha—skull.

* Persons unacquainted with Oriental languages can hardly conceive Goath and Gotha or Golgotha and Golgoleth to be closely related, much less equivalents; but such variations are very common in the east, at least in the cognate Hebrew and Arabic.

† Calvary is formed by merely anglicising Calvaria, from the Latin Calva, skull. Tradition saith, "it is so called because Adam's skull was found there." His skull is believed by nine-tenths of the pilgrims and Christians of Jerusalem to be interred beneath the altar in the centre of the Greek apartment of the Church of the Holy Sepulchre.

The Arabic term for head (r a s) is as applicable to a head or cape of land as to the head of an animal; and the same may be affirmed of the Hebrew term (golgoleth). Now, there is a kind of head, cape, or promontory of land projecting south-eastwardly into the Kedron valley, a short distance above Gethsemane, to which such a term seems quite applicable, just as the low spur of Lebanon on which Beirût reposes is called Cape or Head of Beirût. May not this similar spur of an unnamed ridge be the site of that awful scene—the crucifixion of the son of God? There is, at this time, no skull-shaped monticule of *rock* to be found in all the region where, according to Jeremiah, Goath or Gotha was located; but this, of course, is no proof that such a prominence did not once exist, for it is evident that neither Jew nor Pagan would have suffered so significant and conspicuous a memorial of the crucified Nazarene long to remain the uncompromising accuser of their faith and morals. It is a little singular that so superficially are the dead buried in the side of that hill to this day, that by merely moving a loose rock or two, skulls are seen in abundance; indeed, the jackal frequently saves the trouble of removing them.

"Now in the place where he was crucified there was a garden, and in the garden a new sepulchre wherein was never man laid." (John xix. 4.) "And the women also which came with him from Galilee followed after, and beheld the sepulchre and how his body was laid." (Luke xxiii. 55.) The language here used is rather indicative of a spot of ground, isolated by an artificial enclosure, if not by natural bounds. The garden and sepulchre were, no doubt, on the lower side of the road—that farthest from the city, and perhaps quite down in the gloomy vale of the Kedron. And where could there be a more appropriate spot for the three days' repose of the "Lamb slain," than the shades of this sequestered vale, hard by the garden of his mental agony? There are still some old sepulchres to be found there, answering quite well the description of the Redeemer's sepulchre. But who could believe that his sepulchre would be spared when the "heathen raged, and the people imagined a vain thing—when the kings of the earth stood up, and the rulers were gathered together against the Lord and against his Christ." Every vestige of the tomb, as well as the cross and the skull-shaped rock on which it may have been placed (if any), was doubtless very early swept off either by Jew or Pagan.* Still there can be but little doubt as to the general locality of these transactions.

It is altogether obvious—from the Old Testament as well as the New—that Golgotha was situated near a garden without the walls. The evangelic narrative also clearly evinces that the scene of the crucifixion was in a conspicuous place, not inhabited (for it was a place of sepulture, as well as execution),—near the wayside, visible from afar as well as from a place just over against—and at the same time nigh unto the city wall—that part of it no doubt forming at once the boundary of the temple and the city: for it is improbable in the highest degree that the Jewish hierarchs, however anxious to gloat on their devoted victim and chuckle at his anguish, would adventure their sanctimonious feet farther than the parapet of the Temple wall on that "high day;" for so immaculate did they wish to appear, that "they themselves went not 'even' into the judgment hall, lest they should be defiled"—much less then would they venture to approach the dying and the dead, whether on the polluted slope of Kedron's sepulchral valley, or any other spot where they would be liable to contract defilement. That these are all requisites of the sacred narrative, is sufficiently obvious from a collocation of the events of the crucifixion as recorded by the four different biographers of the Saviour, all of whom witnessed the mournful scene.

Topographical notice of the route along which the Saviour was taken from the Cœnaculum to the Tomb.—The Cœnaculum, or upper room where our adorable Redeemer ate the last paschal

* It is worthy of remark that it is never alleged by any of the New Testament writers, of our Lord's sepulchre, as it was of David's by Peter on the day of Pentecost, that "his sepulchre is with us unto this day." Had the Jews already swept away all traces of it?

supper, and instituted the commemorative ordinance of his death, is located by tradition in the south-west quarter of Mount Zion. But there is no special authority for the location assigned it on that remote part of the Holy Hill. When our Saviour directed two of the apostles, Peter and John, to go and prepare the passover, they were in Bethany: and in discharging their commission were compelled, unless they would act contrary to all the dictates of convenience, to enter the city either at the Horse Gate, on Ophel, the Fish Gate, on Bezetha, or the intermediate East Gate of the Temple, which, presenting much the shortest and most available route over the Red Heifer Bridge, they would probably select. "And when they were *entered* into the city, there met them a *man* bearing a pitcher of water," which, being a sight so very unusual, indicated him with great certainty, whom they accordingly followed where he entered in. (See xxii. 11.) Now it is not at all probable that a man from that remote western part of the city, where the traditionary Cœnaculum is placed, would come over to the eastern part for water when he was much nearer to the "Lower Gihon" on the west, and Siloam on the south—and even in that event, there would be no propriety in the term "meet"—for let it be noted that *they met a man bearing a pitcher of water*,—a fact quite significant in locating the "upper room"—an *upper room* in more senses than one. Let it now be supposed that the "large upper room furnished and prepared," was situated on the *eastern* brow of Zion; and that the "good man" to whom it belonged had gone to the west part of the city to get a jar of fresh Gihon or Etham water for the feast:—a *man* bearing a pitcher of water, so rare a sight as to be distinctive—must have been poor, and could scarcely afford a guest-chamber that would be adequate to the accommodation of the apostles and the company of the hundred and twenty. The two apostles having passed through the Temple, and crossed the great bridge, would probably not proceed far before they would *meet* him bearing the water, and according to instructions, return with him and then make ready the passover. All the conditions of the case are amply ful-

6

filled in this view of the matter, and the most exact requirements of the narrative satisfied. The supper being ended, the consolatory address concluded, and the hymn sung—they must needs go either through the Temple or the Fish Gate, if they would reach the Garden of Gethsemane by an easy and available route. Being there apprehended, after his agony, and led away to Annas first, he was led down the gloomy vale of Kedron, across Tophet, through Gehenna, and up the steep sides of the "Hill of Evil Council"—if indeed tradition has properly located the country seat of Annas. In order to reach the palace of Caiaphas, the high priest, which was situated on the northernmost part of Mount Zion, hard by the Acro-Zion wall, not far from the Armory, the choice of route would lie between four gates: the Fountain Gate, between the walls at Siloam, through which King Zedekiah fled, the Gate of the Essenes, the Dung Port, and Valley Gate. The route through the Essenes Gate would be the nearest, but steepest way. The remainder of the night after "Annas had sent him bound to Caiaphas, the high priest," his son-in-law, he is detained in the Hall of the High Priest, enduring the insults of the officers and the inquisitorial examination of Caiaphas. The route by which the Saviour was led from Gethsemane to the house of Annas, and thence to the palace of Caiaphas, is mere matter of conjecture; but thenceforth the various points to which he was led are well ascertained; for early in the morning, "the elders of the people and the chief priests and the scribes came together, and led him into their 'Council House,'" to reach which they might either pass through the nearest gate in the Acro-Zion wall, and thus directly across the Tyropoeon, or more probably go around, over the bridge and through the south-west part of the Court of the Gentiles—for the Council House seems to have had an entrance from the Temple as well as from the city. The Sanhedrim and its subalterns, having condemned, mocked, and blasphemously maltreated him, "then led they Jesus from Caiaphas unto the judgment hall of Pilate; and it was early; and they themselves went not into the judgment hall lest they should be defiled; but that they might eat the passover, Pilate then went out to them." "The judgment hall of Pilate" was undoubtedly a large apartment in the Tower of Antonia, situated in the north-west corner of the Temple area, and access to it might be had either by going around the western side of the Temple area, or still more directly by entering the western colonnade of the Temple precincts above. Pilate, without condemning him, sent him to Herod Antipas, Tetrarch of Galilee, who had no doubt come up to the feast, and was occupying the magnificent palace of Herod the Great, near the Tower of Hippicus, where the chief priests and scribes stood and vehemently accused Jesus, and Herod ("that old Fox") with his men of war set him at nought and mocked him, and arrayed him in a gorgeous robe and sent him again to Pilate. The governor having examined him, informed the chief priests and the rulers and the people assembled in the yard of Antonia, that, as neither he nor Herod could find anything worthy of death in the Messiah, he would chastise and release him. But the malicious hierarchs having finally extorted his condemnation, he is taken into the Pretorium by the soldiers, arrayed in mock royalty, buffeted and smitten, treated with the utmost indignity and cruelty, and finally Pilate, occupying his judgment seat out on Gabbatha, or the pavement, brought him out of the Pretorium, and finding his final "*Ecce-homo*" appeal in vain, delivered him to them to be crucified, and that too when he himself, as well as his accuser, and Herod, the *conscientious* murderer of John the Baptist, all pronounced him innocent. And as they came out from the gate in the tower at the north-east corner of the Temple enclosure, they compelled Simon, who passed by "the Temple Gate on his way to Fish Gate, as he was" coming out of the country, "to bear his cross" to Golgotha.

The distance traversed by the Saviour between the upper room and Golgotha was from four and one third to five miles, as follows:—(if the house of Annas be correctly located).

Distance travelled.			Crucifixion witnessed by many.
From Zion to Gethsemane	850	to	900 yards.
" Gethsemane to House of Annas .	2300	"	2400 "
" House of Annas to High Priest's Palace	1400	"	2100 "
" H. P. Palace to Council House .	200	"	400 "
" Council House to Pretorium (in Antonia)	350	"	400 "
" Pretorium to Herod's Palace .	950	"	1000 "
" Herod's Palace back to Pretorium .	950	"	1000 "
" Pretorium to Golgotha	500	"	600 "
	7500	"	8800 "

The extraordinary despatch with which the Saviour was apprehended, tried, condemned, and executed by the Jewish hierarchy, is not alone indicative of their vindictive malice; but clearly shows their fear of a rescue. Equally obvious is the fact that the people within the Temple enclosure were induced to clamor for his blood by the priests, who would probably admit none but such as they could bribe or otherwise influence; and that his condemnation was unwillingly wrung from his judge, is too palpable to be denied. For the popularity of Jesus with the people generally, is not only manifest from the general tenor of the gospel narrative, but is especially evidenced by the fact that "there followed him a great company of people, and of women which also bewailed and lamented him." (Luke xxiii. 27.) The road to Anathoth and Nob, two cities of the priests, was probably the one passing close by (as it now runs through that quarter), and it is quite reasonable to suppose that the passers-by, who wagged their heads and reviled him, were probably of that disaffected region. We are nowhere told that the west side of Jerusalem was a place of sepulture, nor is there any sign that it ever was so used; and even if it had been, the priests would never have hazarded the rescue of their victim by sending him through the city to execution at the place now called Calvary, even had it been (which however it was not) without the city wall. It is true, some of the conditions of the narrative might have met their fulfilment on that side of the city (granting for a moment that the site of the Church of the Holy Sepulchre was at that time beyond the city wall), but there are some that could not possibly be supplied in all that quarter. The crucifixion might certainly have occurred near the city, on that side, close to which a road might have passed. But the well known existence of extensively cultivated and occupied suburbs in that quarter would be fatal to the accommodation of the great crowd, to the prospect from afar, and to the existence of any place "over against" the cross, where the women could note the movements of the soldiers. Nor could the priests be accommodated with a sight, on account of intervening houses and walls; but at the place I venture to designate, not only is there no clashing, but every indication is amply met and minutely fulfilled. Hundreds of thousands could witness it from the western slope of Olivet afar off; and on its lower ledges, just across the Kedron, "over against" Golgotha, the women could sit so near as to observe the disposition made of the Saviour's corpse.

But whether this location be correct or not, most evident is it, that the reputed site was not beyond the city wall, and hence must necessarily be a mislocation. For no engineer having any regard to the security of the wall, the extension of the city, or the general principles of economy or policy, would ever have located the "second wall" of Josephus, so as to exclude the present Church of the Holy Sepulchre, whether the Gennath Gate was located near Jaffa Gate or as low down as the most ardent adherent of tradition would have it. (See Art. Ch. Holy Sepulchre.)

Mount Zion.—Before that portion of the Tyropoeon which divides Zion from Akra became filled up with ruins and the accumulated rubbish of ages, Mount Zion must have been so precipitous on every side, except the narrow neck connecting it to the ridge of Akra—as it is indeed even now almost everywhere—that but slight fortifications were sufficient to render it almost impregnable. Such is the shape of this world-famed mount, that the cleft by which its upper portion was once perhaps deeply divided, imparted to the Holy Hill no slight resemblance to a heart, in the outline of its base.

AKRA.—That portion of the city built upon this hill is by far the most indefensible of all, its wall being located almost entirely upon the slope of the hill. It had, however, within it at one time a rocky eminence very strongly fortified by nature as well as by art; but its advantages in a military point of view, in the hands of its owners, were regarded as more than counterbalanced when possessed by an enemy, owing to the facility it afforded for annoying the Temple worshippers: it was therefore deemed best by the Maccabees to hew down this towering acropolis, and cast it into the neighboring valley, which was accordingly done, as elsewhere related.

BEZETHA, MORIAH, AND OPHEL.—A long and narrow ridge rises gradually a few hundred yards north of Damascus Gate, separating at first the valley in which that gate is situated from that on the east in which Herod's Gate is placed, and lower down the Kedron from the Tyropœon. It runs nearly due south; but inclines somewhat westwardly a few hundred yards before it terminates in a sharp craggy point just below the pool of Siloam. It was originally continuous; but has long since been severed by opening a passage through it about a hundred and fifty yards in width. The portion thus removed was composed of fine building stone divided into regular strata of convenient thickness for quarrying, as is still observable on each side of the cleft, and has no doubt furnished much of the material out of which the city wall, the Temple, and other massive structures were built. The section being perpendicular, it serves an admirable purpose for defence; and hence the wall is nowhere so impregnable as the portion crossing the southern side of this pass. That portion of the ridge thus cut off on the north is now known under the name of Zahara, or Mount of Tombs, in which is the grotto of Jeremiah, and is used only as a Moslem place of interment—*above*, and *below* as a place of quarantine.

That portion of the ridge within the city is called Bezetha, as far down as the Serai—the site of the ancient tower of Antonia—

where it was also divided by a trench cut in defence of that tower. This name was, no doubt, at one time applied to the hill Zahara, as well as to the intermediate portion before its removal.

The title of Moriah, though at one time applied to the site of the whole city and to its environs, is now restricted to that portion of this long ridge within the walls of the Haram esh-Sheriff; and all below the southern wall of the Haram (which is identical, no doubt, with that of the Temple) is called Ophel. Ophel at its upper extremity is perhaps as broad as any other portion of the ridge; but becomes quite narrow a short distance below the Temple, and is very precipitous on the east.

CHAPTER III.

LOCAL FEATURES OF CITY AND ENVIRONS.

—"A land of hills and valleys."

VALLEYS.

REPHAIM—*Giant—Physician—Relaxed—Preserver.*—The Valley of Rephaim seems to have risen in two heads west of Jerusalem, one commencing a few hundred yards west of the Greek Con vent of St. George, and the other near Wely Kamar, and uniting some distance below the Convent of the Cross, forming Wady-el-Werd. And when David "fetched a compass behind them, and came upon the Philistines over against the mulberry-trees, on hearing the sound of a going in the tops of the trees," or "groves of weeping," as Josephus calls them, they may have spread themselves either in its upper or lower branch. In the first instance, David's army would have gone up the Kedron to the neighborhood of Wely Kamah; in the second they would have gone down some distance below En-rogel, and then have ascended a valley terminating just in the rear of the Hill of Evil Council. The latter would appear the more probable, according both to the Bible and Josephus. In the westernmost branch is situated, about one and a quarter miles from Jerusalem, the Convent of the Cross, beneath whose dome, according to tradition, "is the earth that nourished the root, that bore the tree, that yielded the timber, that made the cross"*—a form of ex-

* "Under the high altar you are shown the hole in the ground where the stump of the tree stood; and it meets with not a few visitants, so much more very stocks than itself as to fall down and worship it."—*Maundrell.*

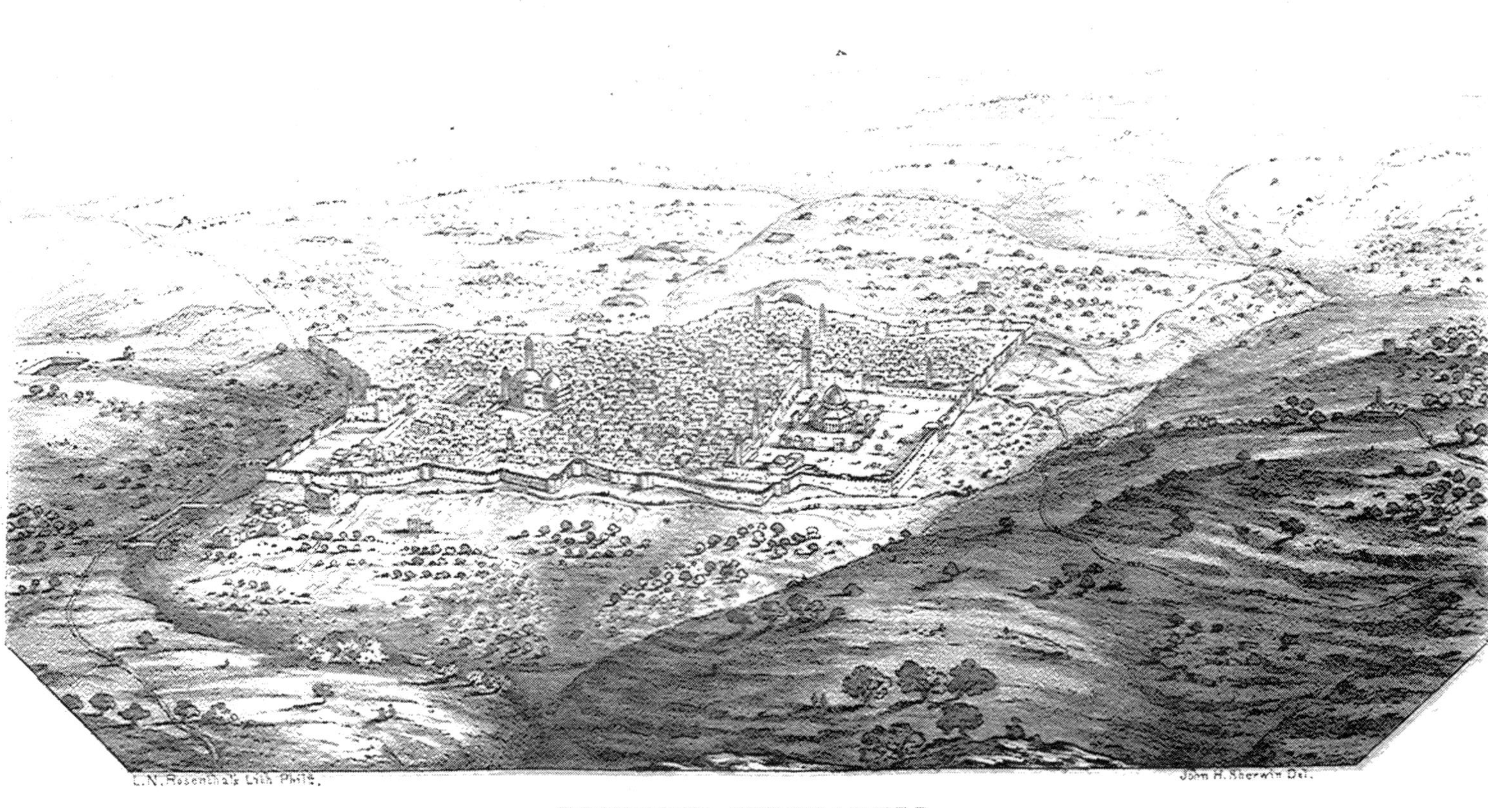

L. N. Rosenthal's Lith Phila. John H. Sherwin Del.

MODERN JERUSALEM,

pression that too often provokes a smile, and gives occasions for jestings that are not convenient, owing to rather an unfortunate resemblance to the phraseology of a well known nursery tale.

TOPHET—*Timbrel—Tabret drum—Betrayed.*—VALLEY OF SLAUGHTER.—This name is applied in Scriptures not only to the lower part of the valley of Hinnom, but to the upper part of the valley formed by the union of Kedron and Hinnom. It was the seat of the idolatrous services rendered to Moloch, who would appear from Jeremiah (xxxii. 35) to be identical with Baal. "Tophet was ordained of old; yea, for the king it is prepared: he hath made it deep and large: the pile thereof is fire and much wood; the breath of the Lord, like a stream of brimstone, doth kindle it." (Is. xxx. 33.) Was not a portion of it also appropriated as the public shambles? The main entrance into it from the city seems to have been by a special gate west of Siloam, called East or Sun Gate (Gate of Baal).

How fearfully was fulfilled the doom denounced against this valley and the city, during the siege of Jerusalem! (Jer. xix. 11.) "Thus saith 'the prophet, speaking the word of the Lord of Hosts,' Even so will I break this people and this city as one breaketh a potter's vessel, that cannot be made whole again; and they shall bury them in Tophet till there be no place to bury." And the historian recording unwittingly its fulfilment, informs us (W. vi., viii. 5) "that the very last struggle between the Jews and Romans occurred on this very spot;" and here, in this secure place where alone they could be interred with impunity, and where the stench would be least annoying, it no doubt was, that "no fewer than 115,880 dead bodies had been carried out for burial through that one gate intrusted to the care of Manneus, who was appointed to pay the public stipend for carrying these dead bodies out"—and after this man ran away to Titus, many of the eminent citizens who told him that no fewer than 600,000 were thrown out at the gates! (v., xiii. 7.)

It was called Tophet, on account of the noise made by *drums* to drown the cries of children when thrown into the lap and arms of the heated brazen idol. But "the days come, saith the Lord, that it shall no more be called Tophet, nor the Valley of the Son of Hinnom, but the Valley of Slaughter: for they shall bury in Tophet till there be no place:" hence its proper appellation at present is "*Valley of Slaughter.*"

VALLEY OF HINNOM—*Riches—Thine they are.*—VALLEY OF BEN-HINNOM—*Valley of the Children of Shrieking—Gehenna*—Γεεννα—*Hades.*—The valley heading very gradually a few hundred yards around Birket Mamilla, running thence toward Yaffa Gate, and thence surrounding Mount Zion on the west, and continuing down below En-rogel, is so called in the Scriptures; but this name is now generally restricted to its lower portion, which is also called Tophet in the Scriptures. In this place—which reaches to the base of the Mount of Corruption—children were, at one time, offered in sacrifice to Moloch ("horrid king") by throwing them into the arms of the heated, hollow, brazen statue of this god—from which they probably fell into the blazing furnace below. With a view of so polluting this place that the idolatrously disposed Jews would loathe and forsake it for ever, good King Josiah utterly polluted it by making it the receptacle perhaps both of filth and dead men's bones. (2 Kings xxiii. 10.) It is generally supposed that fires were continually kept burning here to *consume* the filth; but this is rather inconsistent with the intention of Josiah: though this may have been done after the captivity, when the Jews became so thoroughly weaned from idolatry. Having been the scene of such pollution, wickedness and torment, it became a fit emblem of everlasting punishment. "There are two palm-trees in the valley of Hinnom, between which a smoke arises; and this is that we learn—'the palms of the mountain are fit for iron.' And this is the door of Gehenna."—*Talmud.*

"First, Moloch, horrid king, besmeared with blood
Of human sacrifice, and parents' tears:
Though, for the noise of drums and timbrels loud,
Their children's cries unheard, that passed through fire
To his grim idol. Him, the Ammonite

Worshipped in Rabba and her watery plain,
In Argol and in Basan, to the stream
Of utmost Arnon. Nor content with such
Audacious neighborhood, the wisest heart
Of Solomon he led by fraud to build
His temple right against the temple of God,
On that opprobrious hill; and made his grove,
The pleasant valley of Hinnom thence
And black Gehenna called, the type of Hell."—*Milton.*

VALLEY OF KIDRON, KEDRON OR CEDRON.

(*From Kedar—dark, gloomy, sad, filthy.*)

JEHOSAPHAT—VALLEY OF DECISION.

"There is a spot within this sacred dale,
That felt Thee kneeling, touched thy prostrate brow—
One angel knows it."

The valley commencing on the north-west of Jerusalem, in two gentle depressions on the southern slope of the Scopus, and encompassing the city on the north and east, terminating at its junction with another similar valley on the south and west, is the Kedron of the Bible and of Josephus; but is called Jehosaphat by Jews, Christians, and Mahomedans. Or at least the Arabs call a portion of it Shafat, in contraction it is thought of Jehoshaphat; though they generally call it "Valley of Sitte Myriam"—St. Mary's Valley. Mr. Williams says that they also term it the Valley of Gehinnom, but I have never heard them so denominate it. If restricted, however, to its termination it would be no misnomer—so far at least as Tophet and Hinnom are synonymous. This designation of the valley seems to extend back to the very dawn of inventive, monkish nomenclature of holy places; and is equally gratuitous and absurd, whether due to the mistaken notion that this valley is alluded to by Joel in his prophecy about the "Valley of the Judgment of God" (Yehosaphat), or to the equally mistaken idea that King Jehosaphat was buried in the tomb that now bears his name—for not only is the term a general, instead of a specific one, and the valley far too limited to contain even a ten-thousandth part of the "*all nations*" of Joel, but we are expressly informed that "Jehosaphat was buried in the city of David." The Valley of Jehosaphat, or Decision, is in all probability the great Valley of Megiddo, or Armageddon, the wide plain of Esdraelon, where so many important battles have been fought by Jews, Egyptians, Assyrians, Tartars, Turks, Saracens, Franks, &c.

That this valley was used as a place of sepulture, according to the repeated declarations of Scripture, the tombs that abound throughout its length and breadth, amply testify. Vineyards, figyards, and oliveyards, gardens and patches of green, occupy the entire extent. Valley of Shaveh, or King's Dale, was perhaps the name under which its lower portion was first known. Was it called Kedron, or *Filthy*, on account of receiving the blood and other offal from the Temple? Rabbi Akaba says there was a certain cave (cess-pool) beneath the altar, whereby filth and uncleanness was carried down into the valley of the Kedron; and the gardeners paid so much money as would purchase a trespass offering, for the privilege of fertilizing their gardens with it.

Valley of Shaveh, or King's Dale.—This celebrated dale could be no other than the valley of the Kedron, if the monument now called Tentour Pharoon, just below the south-west corner of the Harem es-Sheriff, be identical, as tradition reports, with the "pillar" "which" Absalom in his lifetime had taken and reared up for himself, which is in the King's Dale: for he said, "I have no son to keep my name in remembrance; and he called the pillar after his own name; and it is called unto this day Absalom's Place." But as tradition is evidently at fault in relation to this pillar, nothing conclusive can be determined by the position of this monument. The King's Gardens undoubtedly occupied the lower portion of the valley of the Kedron at its junction with the valleys of Tyropœon and Hinnom, and it is probable in the highest degree that the entire valley was at that time called the King's Dale.

The King's Gardens.—This royal paradise must evidently have been very extensive—reaching at least from the mouth of the Tyropoœn to the defile in which En-rogel is situated—for we learn from Josephus (Ant. ix. x: 4) that "a great earthquake (doubtless that alluded to by the prophet Zachariah, xiv. 5) occurred before the city at a place called En-rogel, in the reign of Uzziah. Half the mountain broke off from the rest on the west and rolled itself four furlongs, and stood still at the east mountain (Olivet), till the roads as well as the King's Gardens were spoiled by the obstruction." This description is only applicable to the Wady-en-Nair, just below En-rogel: where indeed the hillside still appears as though it may have undergone such a convulsion; though there is room to suspect some exaggeration in relation to the distance the land-slide is said to have slipped; but perhaps his meaning is, not that the avalanche actually travelled or "rolled" that far, but the mass was that length—having separated near the Hill of Evil Council, but only slidden down a few score yards.

The King's Wine Press, for aught that we learn from the Bible, Josephus, or any other authentic source, may have been excavated either in the rocks of the Mount of Corruption, Ophel, Zion, or Aceldama Cliff. There are no observable remains of the vat; but very suitable places all around the King's Gardens for its excavation.

Motsa was probably situated in the lower part of the valley formed by the junction of Kedron and Ben-Hinnom (Wady-en-Nair), a place much better adapted to the growth of willows than any other spot about Jerusalem—a locality which also best accords with the Talmudic account. It seems to have been a grove of willows, reared for the purpose of supplying boughs for celebrating the Feast of Tabernacles. "Below the city," says Dr. Lightfoot, after the Rabbins, "was a place, Motza: hither they came down and cropped off thence long boughs of willow; and going away, placed them near the sides of the altar, bended after that manner that their heads might bow over the top of the altar, &c."

Valley of Gihon—*Valley of Grace or Breast.*—This is the name both of a fountain and a *place* of considerable extent; but it is only the latter that will be here considered.

The first mention of this term occurs in the account of the summary installation of the "King that was preacher in Jerusalem." (1 Kings i. 33.) Few localities have been so much the sport of topographical speculation and tradition as this place, which has been located almost everywhere about Jerusalem, except the right place. The present locality assigned it is the valley south-west of Jerusalem, called in the Scriptures Ben-Hinnom. But the utter incompatibility of that site with the declaration (2 Ch. xxxiii. 14), that "Manasseh built a wall without the City of David, on the *west side* of Gihon in the valley even to the entering in at the Fish Gate," is evidence enough of its mislocation; for a wall built in this valley on its west side, would everywhere be located to great disadvantage, and in many places be no defence whatever, owing to the cliffs of Hinnom overtopping it. But besides this negative proof of its mislocation, the well ascertained position of the Fish Gate clearly shows that the Valley of Gihon could be no other than that heading north-west of Damascus Gate and gently descending southward, uniting with the Tyropœon at the north-east corner of Mount Zion, where the latter turns at right angles and runs towards Siloam. The wall, thus built by Manasseh on the west side of the Valley of Gihon, would extend from the vicinity of the north-east corner of the wall of Zion in a northerly direction, until it crossed over the valley to form a junction with the outer wall at the trench of Antonia—precisely in the quarter where the Temple would be most easily assailed.

Although this location of Gihon may be rather startling to those who are wedded to the school of oral tradition, yet it is unquestionably the only view of the matter by which Manasseh's construction of the wall can be reconciled with the "stubborn facts" of the case: most evident is it that it is perfectly consistent with everything mentioned in connexion with it, either in the Scriptures or Josephus. The correctness of this location is also confirmed by the etymological import of the term. For it is certainly a most graceful and well favored valley.

And if that hemispherical rocky prominence which stands in the centre of the valley, were surrounded by a circular wall of white marble enclosing a rotunda-shaped building, the other etymological term, suggested perhaps by the simile which Israel's great builder of "palaces, temples, and piles stupendous," uses in a closing stanza of his Canticles, would by no means be an inexpressive one. Josephus, in speaking of Herodium, the site of Herod's famous castle—a circular hill like this, but larger—expressly compares it to "a woman's breast."

Fuller's Field and Monument.—Josephus mentions the monument, yet makes no allusion to the Field of the Fuller: and the Bible, which several times speaks of the *field*, makes no mention of the *monument*. But it is sufficiently obvious, from the manner in which such mention is made, that they are in the same general direction; and are, no doubt, reciprocally connected. The field extended perhaps from the monument or its immediate vicinity; and reached within a short distance of the northern curvature of the "Second Wall."

The fountain and pool of Gihon were in this field; and of course a very extended area would be required for the various fulling, bleaching, and cleansing operations practised near the metropolis of such a people as the Jews.

Josephus informs us (W. v. iv: 2), that the "Third Wall," after passing the sepulchral caverns of the Kings, bent again at the Tower of the Corner, at the monument which is called the Monument of the Fuller. At what point this great north-eastern bending of the wall must needs have been, no one acquainted with the physical features of that region can at all doubt. No great error can therefore be committed in assigning the Fuller's Monument a place: though there are now no ruins that can be positively recognised as its remains.

Valley of Dead Bodies and of Ashes—*Intermediate Valley.*—This name might well be regarded as a synonym of the Sepulchral Kedron, but for its specific location elsewhere. It is evident, however, that it is the shallow valley lying between the Kedron and the valley north of Damascus Gate, terminating originally opposite the Garden of Gethsemane, but now drained by the traditionary Bethesda near St. Stephen's Gate. Though nearly reduced to a plain by the accumulations of ages, many of its tombs are still to be seen along its sides north of the city wall. The hill separating it from the Damascus Gate valley (the true Gihon) is still a favorite place of burial—Turbet Zahara, or Mount of Tombs. The only time it is mentioned, is when the prophet is speaking of the enlargement of the city—"The whole valley of the dead bodies, and of the ashes, and all the fields unto the brook Kedron, unto the corner of the Horse Gate, toward the east, shall be holy unto the Lord." (Jer. xxxi. 40.) This valley is known to the Moslem population of Jerusalem under the appellation of Wady-ez-Zahara—a name by which it is also designated in the Koran. Their traditions connect it so unpleasantly with the day of judgment, that, though its upper westernmost portion is much coveted as a place of burial, the living entertain quite a dread of it.

Ashes Valley of Kedron, was probably that beautiful and fertile expansion of this valley north-east of the city, where the ashes of the Temple were deposited. Travellers have generally supposed that the ash-mounds north of the city are the remains of the Temple cinerary deposit; but this is altogether inconsistent with the account of their disposition found in the Talmudic writings, where it is stated that the "ashes from the Temple altar were carried out of the city by the priests, who laid them in a calm place, that the wind might scatter them as little as possible." It is added that "these ashes might not be put to any use;" but it is probably only a profane use that is thus prohibited. For it is highly probable that the first fruits of the harvest were brought from the valley thus richly fertilized. (Lev. xxiii. 10, 11.) Jeremiah declares, in speaking of the enlargement of the city, that "the whole valley of the dead bodies and of the ashes should be holy unto the Lord." (xxxi. 40.) But he there has reference not to this spot, but either to the burial ground on which the ashes and pulverized dust of the idol groves, images, &c., destroyed by Josiah, were strown (2 Kings xxiii. 6, 2 Chr. xxxiv. 4), or to the valley intermedial between the Kedron and the true valley of Gihon, where Damascus Gate is situated, which seems to have been anciently used—indeed its eastern slope is now used in part for a cemetery. The Rabbins depose as follows, according to the citations of Dr. Lightfoot. "The sheaf of first fruits was reaped from the Ashes Valley of Kedron. The first day of the feast of the Passover, certain persons deputed from the Sanhedrim went forth into that valley, a great company attending them, and very many of the neighboring towns flocked together that the thing might be done—a great number being present. They performed the thing with as much show as could be. When it was now even, he, on whom the office of reaping laid, saith:—

"The sun is set."

And they answered,

"Well."

"With this reaping hook."

And they answered,

"Well; with this reaping hook."

"In this basket."

And they answered,

"Well."

"On this Sabbath."

And they answered,

"Well."

"I will reap."

And they answered,

"Well, I will reap."

And they answered,

"Well."

This he said thrice; and they answered thrice,

"Well."

Valley of Cheesemongers—Tyropœon—Τυρος-ποιεω—*Valley of Cheesemakers—Caseariorum.*—This word does not occur in the Scriptures, and all that we definitely know of it from ancient authority is contained in a single paragraph of Josephus—that it issued into the Kedron at the pool of Siloam, and distinguishes the hill of the upper city from that of the lower (W. v. iv: 1). But though only once definitely mentioned, yet the localities in connexion with it are so well identified, that one would suppose no point better established than the location of this valley. Yet, although its position from Siloam as far as Temple street is undisputed, its farther continuation has been the subject of warm and protracted controversy—one party contending that its course continues straight on northward beyond Damascus Gate—the other that it turns to the left, around the north-east corner of Mount Zion in the direction of Temple street, or, as its upper portion is called, David street, to its origin near Jaffa Gate. And that this is its true position there is not the slightest occasion to doubt, though the ravine of which Josephus speaks is now nearly effaced—being concealed by the long-continued accumulation of rubbish. Its situation, however, is still obviously indicated by the overhanging brow of Zion—for the Zion side of the valley being higher than the Akra, is still conspicuous. That it was once very deep is evident; for, without such a ravine as that of which Josephus speaks, Zion could never have been the stronghold that it is represented to have been.

That all that portion of the valley running north and south was once called Gihon is highly probable—see articles Gihon Valley and Gihon Fountain. It is reasonable to suppose that the name Tyropœon was at first restricted to that portion of the valley running eastward, and was only afterward applied to it farther down where the cheesemakers, being crowded out of the central part of the city, were compelled to pursue their avocation lower down in this valley; and of course brought their name with them. There was, no doubt, a broad street extending on the north of the wall along the declivity of Zion dividing this hill from Akra; and the valley very naturally received its name from the cheese bazaars on that street, which, gradually extending downwards, imparted its name to the valley once undoubtedly called Gihon Valley. That there was a valley—perhaps at one time quite deep and extensive, which entered the Tyropœon from the south, after dividing the northern half of Mount Zion nearly equally—is very obvious on inspection, though I have nowhere met with any allusion to it in any author either ancient or modern.

SUBURBS—PARBAR—*Parvar*—Προάστειον.—This term is obviously used by Josephus with considerable latitude, evidently restricted at one time to the vacant space west of the Temple inclusive of the Xystus Yard (Ant. xv. xi. 5), called in the Scriptures Parbar (1 Ch. xxvi. 18), and manifestly at another in its ordinary acceptation to signify unoccupied environs, and yet again to designate the extramural city (W. v. vi: 2). In the former acceptation, the suburbs present the anomaly of being in the very heart of the city, but when first so designated they were probably not walled in—being both *before* and *without* the city. A vacant space seems to have extended all around the sacred enclosure. When we remember, however, that they are the suburbs of the Temple and not of the city, the apparent impropriety of designation vanishes. That portion of the sacred enclosure in which was situated the chamber of Nathan Melek the chamberlain, where the kings of Judah had dedicated horses to the sun (2 Kings xxiii. 11), appears to have been either on the east or south of the Temple, and is distinctly called the suburbs. Josephus, in mentioning that two gates led to the suburbs (*i. e.* on the west), while one led over the bridge to the palace, and the other by many steps over to Akra, seems to intimate that the vacant space (if any) between Akra and Moriah was not expressly called suburbs. Still it is highly probable that there was a vacant space all around the Temple entitled to that appellation—though that on the south being used for exercising with horses and chariots, that on the east as a cattle market, and that on the north for military purposes, may not have been generally so denominated. That the houses of the city were separated some distance from the Temple wall except at one point (probably on the north), is strongly intimated in various portions of the Talmud (see Chagiah, fol. lxxvi. 1). And that the suburbs were not at a distance as contended by some eminent topographers, is abundantly evident from 2 Kings xxiii. 11, where the suburbs obviously reach the gate of the Temple.

MAKTESH.—That portion of the outer or vacant space around the Temple wall, lying between Xystus and the Fish Gate, it would seem from the etymology of the term, as well as from the only place in which it is mentioned in the Scriptures, must be assigned as the Quarter of Maktesh. That this place was quite a mercantile quarter is evident from the fact that the Tabernæ or Temple Bazaars were here situated. The passage just alluded to (Zeph. i. 10, 11) seems to be altogether consonant with this view, and irreconcilable with any other—"There shall be the voice of a cry from the Fish Gate, and an howling from the second, and a great crashing from the hills! howl, ye inhabitants of Maktesh—for all the merchant people are cut down; all they that bear silver are cut off." The mint establishment was doubtless situated in this part of the suburbs, as well as the Council House, Repository of the Archives, &c.

XYSTUS—Συστος—*Gymnasium—Gallery.*—We are mainly indebted for what we know of this place to the casual allusions in Josephus and the Apocrypha. The covered colonnade to which this term primarily applied, was situated in the Tyropœon, immediately at the base of the north-eastern cliff of Mount Zion below the royal palace; and was founded under Antiochus Epiphanes, about 175 B. C.; the term, however, as used by Josephus, applies not only to this colonnade, but to that portion of the Tyropœon between it and the temple, being a part of Parbar or the suburbs—bounded on the south by the great Templo-Zion Bridge, and on the north by the "first wall" of Josephus. The gallery probably extended entirely around this quadrangular area, which, no doubt, was handsomely paved, and adorned perhaps with fountains and reservoirs fed by the aqueduct from Solomon's pools, which skirted the east side of Zion at a considerable height above the Xystus court. The Xystus is no doubt but another name for the memorable gymnasium, built by the infamous high priest Jason (or as he was called by the Jews—Jesus), who gave Antiochus one hundred and fifty talents for the privilege of erecting this structure and an academy for the purpose of liberalizing, or rather gentilizing, the Jews. But though, for a long while, appropriated to athletic exercises after the manner of the heathen, it seems in after ages to have been used merely as the great gathering-place of the Jews. They were here assembled when the great-grandson of Herod the Great, who was afterwards "almost persuaded to become a Christian," addressed them, probably from the top of the colonnade just beneath his palace—which may well have formed the floor of his portico—placing at the same time his beautiful and accomplished, but ill-famed, half-sister, Bernice, at the window or balcony above. Here the Jews were also assembled when Titus addressed them from the lofty cloisters of the Temple. The 3000 Pentecostal converts were also probably congregated here when the Apostle Peter, in discharging the great commission with which he had been invested by the Saviour at Cæsarea Philippi, directed the convinced penitents, in reply to their anxious inquiry what to do to be saved—to "repent and be baptized, every one of them, in the name of Jesus Christ, for the remission of sins."

TYROPŒON BRIDGE—*Templo-Zion Bridge*—"*The Ascent*"—*Causeway or Causey*, 1 Ch. xxvi. 16–18.—This celebrated structure, at which the good Queen of Sheba was so much amazed, afforded a direct passage from Mount Zion to the Temple—obviating the necessity of a toilsome and circuitous walk up and down the declivities on each side of the Tyropœon. Owing to the great accumulation of rubbish at the base of Mount Zion, where its western end evidently abutted, no remains of it are now observable; but on the opposite side, where it united with the Temple wall, there are very considerable remains—and in such a state of preservation as to afford all the elements of calculation requisite for its restoration. The breadth of the Tyropœon at this point, where it approached the nearest to Mount Moriah, is about 118 yards, which, of course, limits the length of the bridge. Its breadth was 51½ feet, and the span of its arches, if uniform, 41 feet (as deduced from the portion now standing). A suitable adjustment of the strength of the piers to the immense masses of stone to be sustained, probably limited the number of arches to five. Some of the rocks now constituting the spring of the broken arch, are about 5¾ feet thick, and vary in length from 21 to 25 feet.

The antiquity of the structure to which these ruins belonged, has been a subject of much discussion from the period when Dr. Robinson first called attention to the subject, and suggested their connexion with the bridge so frequently mentioned by Josephus and generally ascribed to Solomon, down to the present time. This high antiquity, however, is not universally conceded; but questioned, mainly because certain archæologists have denied the discovery—or at least the practical use—of the arch at a period farther back than the sixth century before Christ. But as no one questions that the large reservoirs at El Burak, called Solomon's Pools, are really the work of that monarch, and of course were constructed about 1000 years before the Christian era, the architecture of these works ought to have an important bearing upon the decision of this question. Having, after long awaiting an opportunity, at last succeeded in exploring the room underneath the lowest of these pools, and also that of the "Fountain Sealed," by whose waters they are mainly supplied, I was delighted to find as veritable an arch as ever was made—and with a true keystone, too—and not only arches but vaults! This objection is, therefore, no longer tenable. Arches of a still higher antiquity have also been lately discovered in Egypt and Assyria. Neither their great antiquity nor their Solomonic origin need therefore be any longer called in question.

The Red Heifer Bridge.—That the Kedron valley was spanned by a lofty bridge as well as the Tyropœon, is an unquestionable fact, though not once mentioned by modern writers on the Holy City. It was through the eastern gate of the Temple, according to the Mishna, that the red heifer was conducted forth over the Kedron to be burned on the Mount of Olives; and by the same way, according to some authors, the scape-goat was led forth to the wilderness; but according to others by a mere temporary structure made for the occasion every year. "They built," say the Rabbins, "at no small cost a foot causey, upheld with arches, from the Mount of the Temple to the Mount of Olives, upon which they led away the red heifer to be burned. It was double-arched—arches upon arches—one arch upon two arches, so that the foot of one arch stood upon two arches that were there underneath it."

Comparative Levels.—Having thus noticed all the hills and valleys of Jerusalem and its suburbs, it may be well to record their respective elevations and depressions connectedly, in order that the general topography may be the better understood from this comparison of heights and depths. The best stand-point of observation for general comparison is the plot of ground on which the "Church of Ascension" stands, though this is by no means the most elevated point about Jerusalem, as has been generally supposed. By means of the following table of elevations, beginning at En-rogel (which is 129 feet higher than the valley at the lower edge of the large map, where Wady-Geddoom enters En Nair, and including all the most important points), the reader can readily ascertain the relative elevation of many places not specified.

From	En-rogel	to	Pool of Siloam	117	feet.
"	"	"	Kedron Valley opposite Absalom's Pillar	223	"
"	"	"	Base of the S. E. corner of Haram Wall	348	"
"	"	"	Mugaribeh Quarter	350	"
"	"	"	Mount Ophel immediately south of the Haram	377	"
"	"	"	Mount of Corruption	422	"
"	"	"	Top of wall at S. E. corner of Haram	425	"
"	"	"	Top of Mission House	461	"
"	"	"	North-east corner of city . . .	471	"

From	En-rogel	to	Bethany Mount	484 feet.
"	"	"	Mount Zahara	498 "
"	"	"	Hill of Evil Council	506 "
"	"	"	Zion at S. W. corner of City Wall	511 "
"	"	"	Average height of Zion	521 "
"	"	"	Jaffa Gate	534 "
"	"	"	Bezetha (Summit)	550 "
"	"	"	N. W. corner of city	571 "
"	"	"	The site of Jebel et-Tûr village .	635 "
"	"	"	Wely east of it	653 "
"	"	"	Wely Kamah	655 "
"	"	"	Rock hillock on an elevation of Olivet 1000 feet N. of Jebel et-Tûr village	678 "
"	"	"	Northernmost summit of Olivet .	708 "

The village of Jebl Tûr is 412 feet above the Kedron at "Absalom's Pillar;" it is 104 feet above Zion, and 227 above the Haram area. The south-east angle of the Haram Wall, at its base, is 125 feet above the Kedron valley at "Absalom's Pillar," as Tantour Pharoon is usually called. Mount Zion is 404 feet above Siloam. The north-west corner of the city is 163 feet higher than the Haram area; and the Haram area is 185 above the Kedron.

The greatest difference of level found within the limits of the two miles square embraced by the map is between the loftiest summit of Mount Olivet in the north-east corner, and the depression of Wady en-Nair at its lower edge—837 feet. Within the limits of the present city the greatest difference of altitude—that between the south-east and the north-west corner—is 221 feet. The difference in the ancient city, under its widest extension, was probably about 530 feet.

The Holy City is elevated 2610* feet above the Mediterranean,

* According to Captain Lynch's estimate; but 2749 according to aneroid indication. A few of the foregoing altitudes and depressions were ascertained with the level—some with the aneroid, but most of them by the quadrant.

and 3927 above the Dead Sea. It is 210 feet higher than Damascus, but about 1000 lower than Baalbec. Mount Zion is 148 feet lower than Neby Samwil; and 9 feet below the Frank Mountain—the ancient Beth-Haccerem—a celebrated telegraphic station in former times—but several hundred feet higher than its base.

Boundary Line between Judah and Benjamin.—The division line between Judah and Benjamin is thus indicated in the chorography of the son of Nun:

Lot of Judah.—Their border in the north quarter was from the bay of the sea at the uttermost part of Jordan—thence to Beth-Hogla—along the north of Betharabah to the stone of Bohan—up toward Debir from the Valley of Achor—northward toward Gilgal, before the going up to Adummim on the south side of the river [Kerith], passing towards the waters of En-shemesh—and the goings out thereof were En-rogel; and the border went up by the valley of the Son of Hinnom unto the south side of the Jebusite (the same is Jerusalem). And the border went up to the top of the mountain that lieth before the Valley of Hinnom, westward, which is at the end of the Valley of Giants, northward, and the border was drawn from the top of the hill unto the fount of the waters of Nephtoah, and went out to the cities of Mount Ephraim; and the border went down to Baalah, which is Kirjath-Jearim. (Josh. xv. 5–9.)

Lot of Benjamin.—The south quarter was from the end of Kirjath-Jearim on the west side; and went out to the well of waters of Nephtoah. And the border came down to the end of the mountain that lieth before the Valley of the Son of Hinnom, and which is in the Valley of the Giants, on the north, and descended to the Valley of Hinnom, to the side of Jebusi, on the south, and descended to En-rogel, and was drawn from the north and went forth to En-shemesh ('Apostles fount'), toward Geliloth—over against Adummim, down to Bohan, down to Arabah, along the side of Beth-Hoglah; and the out-goings of the border were at the north bay of the Salt Sea, at the south end of Jordan—this was the south coast. (Josh. xviii. 15–19).

By tracing upon any good map* the boundary line here indicated—for these two courses are the same (merely reversed in order of description),—it will be rendered perfectly obvious that it neither runs through Jerusalem nor by Ain Yalo—as contended by many topographers, but to the south and west of the city, by way of the fountain now called Lifta—which, however, is undoubtedly the *Nephtoah* of the Scriptures. The importance of obviating the serious errors and confusion, consequent upon the mistaken views in relation to the location of this border-line, must plead an apology for this uninteresting little detour.

* In order to understand many portions of the Scriptures, and to harmonize with them the accounts of Josephus and other writers on the Holy Land and the Holy City, a more accurate and detailed map than any heretofore executed, becomes indispensable to the Bible student. Such a work the reader will find in the large sheet lately published by the author, entitled "Map of Jerusalem and Environs, from Actual and Minute Survey," which may here be advantageously consulted.

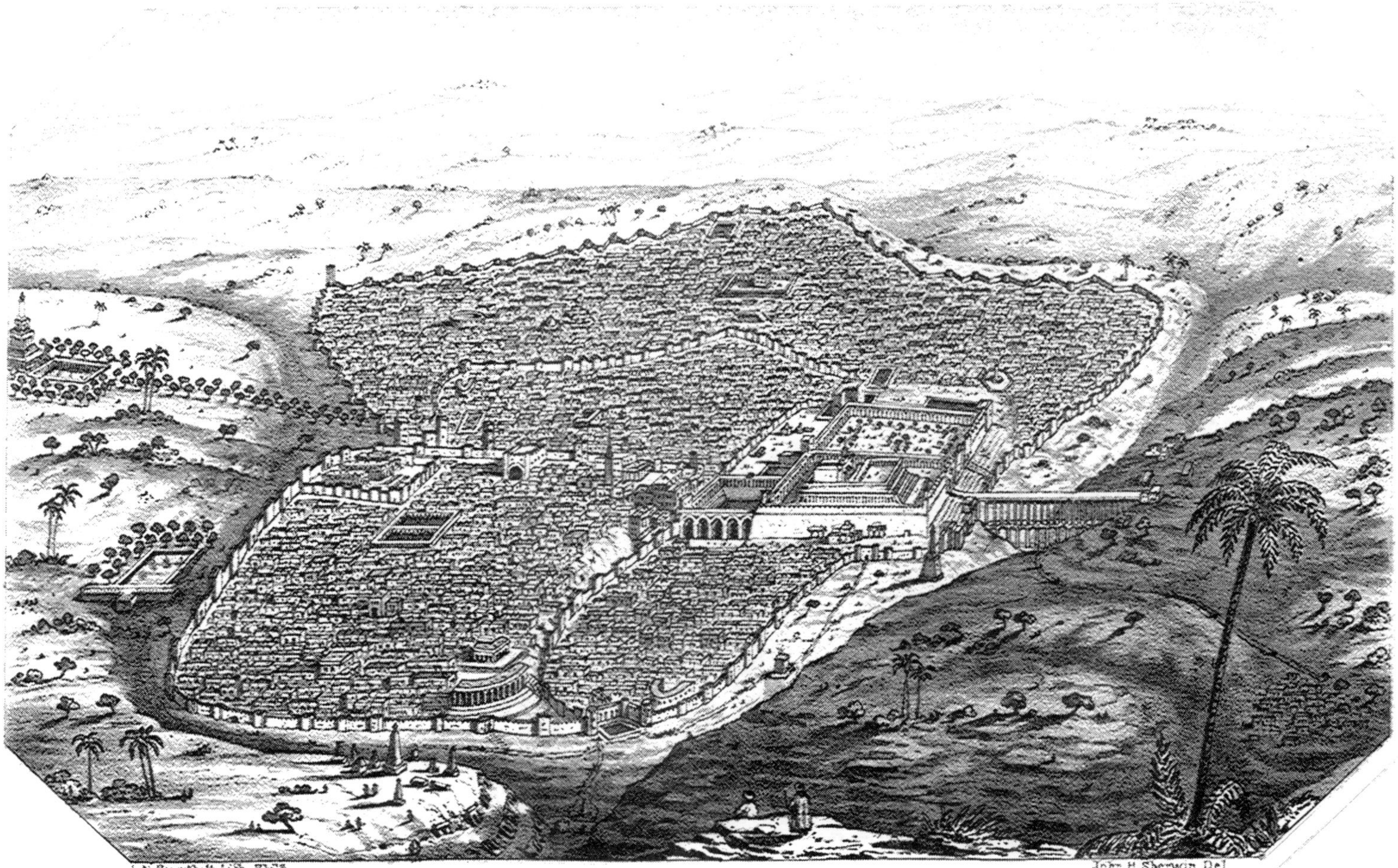

L.N. Rosenthal's Lith. Phila.

John H. Sherwin Del

ANCIENT JERUSALEM

CHAPTER IV.

VARIOUS QUARTERS OF THE CITY.

"Whither goest thou?"
"To measure Jerusalem: to see what is the breadth thereof, and what is the length thereof."
Zech. ii. 2.

SUCCESSIVE DEVELOPMENT.

AFTER the foregoing cursory view of the chorographic position, physical features, and climate of Jerusalem and its vicinity, we are prepared to enter upon the consideration of its various localities in detail. And in order to render the subject as clear as possible, it will be considered in its chronological order of development, commencing with the city of Melchisedec—the first phasis of the Protean capital of the Holy Land.

SALEM—*Perfect—At Peace—Vision of Peace.*—Salem or Shalem was the primeval name borne by that city "whose antiquity is of ancient days"—which finally expanded into "the City of the Great King." (Gen. xiv. 18.) It probably occupied the south-eastern portion of the quarter of the city now generally called Akra—being separated from Mount Zion by the Tyropœon Valley on the south; from Mount Moriah, on the east, by a broad and deep valley—(the true Gihon, afterwards partially filled up by the Asmoneans, but still clearly indicated)—having, however, apparently no good natural defence on the north and west. But it is not to be supposed that the eminent "Priest of the Most High God, and exalted King of Peace and Righteousness," would require a strongly fortified place; but would rather select a site in reference to agricultural advantages, facility of access, supply of water, and general convenience. But although its general surface was lower than any other portion of Jerusalem, yet its lofty *Acropolis*, which was afterwards occupied so long by the Syrians under Antiochus Epiphanes, despite the most strenuous efforts of the Jews to expel them for twenty years, and which required the incessant labor of all Jerusalem three years to level, after the Syrians were finally dispossessed of it, must have been a very commanding site for a palace and fortress. Josephus adds nothing to our topographical knowledge of Salem: neither do the Talmudic authors. It is several times afterward mentioned in Scripture (Heb. vii. 1, 2, and, synonomously with Zion, Ps. lxxvi. 2), but nowhere in such a way as to increase our knowledge of its physical features, except in connexion with the return of Abraham from his Gideon-like expedition, when "the King of Sodom went out to meet him on his return from the slaughter of Chedorlaomer and of the kings that were with him, at the *Valley of Shaveh*, which is *the King's Dale*, and Melchisedec, King of Salem,* brought forth bread and wine." (Gen. xiv. 17, 18.) It is believed to have been founded by Melchisedec (who is no doubt Shem, the second son of Noah), soon after the flood.

The Lower City is an appellation by which Josephus frequently designates this portion of the city, even after it had extended so far up the side of the hill that a small part of it was even more elevated than Zion, which he calls *the Upper City*.

Mount Moriah.—The mount that has absorbed and monopolized the name by which the whole cluster was once denominated is not only the least amongst them, but the term applies only to a small portion of it—that enclosed within the walls of the present Haram-

* The identity of Salem and Jerusalem is still a matter of doubt with many: but the second verse of the seventy-sixth Psalm seems to be decisive on the subject:—"In Salem also is *his Tabernacle;* and his dwelling-place in Zion." The declaration of Josephus to the same effect is very express. "But he who first built it was a potent man among the Canaanites, and is in our tongue called [Melchisedec] the righteous king, for such he really was; on which account he was [there] the first priest of God, and first built a temple [there], and called the city Jerusalem, which was formerly called Salem." (W. vi. 10.)

esh-Sheriff, or the ancient Temple area—the northern portion of the ridge being called Bezetha, and the southern Ophel.

The exact locality of "*Jehovah-Jireh*," the spot selected by Abraham for the sacrifice of Isaac, is generally supposed to be the large elevated rock called emphatically es-Sakhrah, "the Rock" near the centre of the enclosure, directly under the dome of the Mosque of Omar (Kubbet es-Sakhrah). The Copts, however, have located this memorable transaction in their convent, immediately contiguous to the Church of the Holy Sepulchre, hard by the reputed rock of Calvary. Tradition there locates with confidence, amidst heaps of rubbish, the very *tree* (an old olive it is) in which the ram's horns were entangled. But unfortunately for "infallible tradition," a room of masonry has been discovered beneath the tree, and beneath that room a tank of water! But if it be assumed that the altar of Isaac and the cross of the Saviour occupied the same spot, as many contend, then must we look for it not amongst the sacred localities of the Church of St. Sepulchre, nor yet within the Temple enclosure, nor indeed anywhere else within the walls; but on that portion of the ancient Moriah Hill, north-east of the Temple area. That part of Moriah, however, on which David sacrificed at the finale of his perplexing trilemma "that the plague might be stayed from Israel," is undoubtedly situated within the present enclosure, which is identical in position with the ancient Temple area. Within this enclosure then—but certainly not on the elevated rock usually accredited as the spot—was the threshing-floor of Ornan, Arauna or Araniah the Jebusite, where the angel of the Lord commanded Gad to say to David that he should go up and set up an altar to the Lord (1 Sam. xxiv. 15, 25, and 1 Chr. xxi. 18, 28,)—identical with which is the spot where David said, "this is the house of the Lord God; and this is the altar of burnt offering for Israel." (1 Ch. xxii. 1.) The only remaining place where the Scriptures make reference to Mount Moriah by name, is (2 Ch. iii. 1) where Solomon is said subsequently to have built the House of the Lord at Jerusalem, where the Lord appeared to his father David "in the place that David had prepared in the threshing floor of Ornan the Jebusite."

JEBUS—JEBUSI—CITY OF THE JEBUSI.—"The same is Jerusalem." It occupied both the site of Salem and the north-eastern portion of Mount Zion, and was probably captured and enlarged by the Jebusites soon after the death of Melchisedec, 1842 B. C. The city thus enlarged was named by the Jebusites in honor of Jebus the son of Canaan, and well fortified—especially the upper portion of it. (Josh. x. 1, 5, 23; xii. 10; xv. 8, 63, and xviii. 28. Jud. i. 8, 19; x. 12.)

THE CITY OF DAVID.—About five centuries after the first appearance of Jerusalem upon the page of history, it is again mentioned in the Sacred Record when narrating an account of the wars of the Israelites against the Canaanites. The powerful army of the king of Jerusalem and of his five potent allies, was entirely routed by Joshua; and Adoni-Zedec, their "Righteous King,"* (as his name signifies), was slain; and although the city was subsequently smitten, fired, and captured—at least in part—yet it could not have been permanently held by the Israelites, for it is afterwards called "the City of the Jebusites"—"the city of a stranger"—and never was fully possessed by the children of Israel until finally subdued by David. True, we are told that, centuries before that event the children of Judah had fought against Jerusalem and had taken it; and had smitten it with the edge of the sword, and set the city on fire (Jud. i. 8); yet that only part of the city was thus captured, or if entirely subjugated was soon retaken at least in part, is most evident, not only from the name by which the Levite of Ephraim designated it, but from the declaration (contained in the 63d verse of the 15th chapter of Joshua), "as for the Jebusites the inhabitants of Jerusalem, the children of Judah could not drive them out: but the Jebu-

* It may reasonably be inferred from this application that his *Gracious Majesty* Adoni-Zedec exercised a kind of ecclesiastical dominion over the surrounding clans; and that Jerusalem was esteemed a sacred locality, even in the estimation of the heathen. It was probably even at that early period distinctively styled "Holy City."

sites dwell with the children of Judah at Jerusalem unto this day"—(1444 B. C.). The final capture of the city, 1048 years before Christ, is thus recorded (2 Sam. v. 6, 9): "And the king and his men went to Jerusalem unto the Jebusites, the inhabitants of the land: which spake unto David, saying, Except thou take away the blind and the lame, thou shalt not come in hither (thinking David cannot come in hither). Nevertheless David took the stronghold of Zion—the same is the City of David—and David said on that day, Whosoever getteth up to the gutter and smiteth the Jebusites, and the lame and the blind that are hated of David's soul, he shall be chief and captain. Wherefore they say the blind and the lame shall not come into the house. So David dwelt in the fort and called it the City of David; and David built round about from Millo and inward." All at first included under the designation of "City of David" was the stronghold, fort, citadel, castle, or acropolis of the cliffs of Zion above the "ditches, gutters, or trenches;" but is occasionally used in the Scriptures as the synonym of Jerusalem, comprehending the whole city. Josephus, in describing the capture of the city, says: "David began the siege of Jerusalem, and employed his utmost diligence and alacrity therein: * * * so he took the lower city Salem [on Akra] by force; but the citadel held out still: whence it was that the king, knowing that the proposal of dignities and rewards would encourage the soldiers to greater actions, promised that whoever should first go over the ditches that were beneath the citadel, and ascend the citadel itself and take it, should have the command of the entire people conferred upon him.* * * *

"When David had cast the Jebusites out of the citadel, he also rebuilt Jerusalem and named it *the City of David*, and abode there all the time of his reign. * * * Now David made buildings round about the lower city [Salem]; he also joined the citadel to it and made it one body, and when he had encompassed all with walls, he appointed Joab to take care of them. It was David therefore that first cast the Jebusites out of Jerusalem and called it by his own name *the City of David*, for under our forefather Abraham it was called (Salem or) Solyma." (Ant. vii. iii: 62; see also 1 Chr. xi. 4, 8.) The City of David, in its restricted sense, occupied probably about one-fourth of Mount Zion, from which it seems to have been originally somewhat separated by a ravine commencing near its centre, and running northwardly into the Tyropœon.

SION—*Noise.*—ZION—*Monument, Sepulchre, Turret, Dryness, Sunny Place.*—THE UPPER CITY—UPPER MARKET—THE HOLY HILL.—Zion is a term sometimes used synonomously with Salem, Jerusalem and City of David and City of the Great King; but in its literal and restricted topographic meaning, it applies only to the south-western portion of the Holy City—of which the City of David is its north-eastern division. But this term is nowhere to be found in the writings of Josephus—this quarter of the city being called by him the City of David—the Upper City, and the Upper Market Place. In speaking of the hills upon which Jerusalem is built, he says, "that which contains the Upper City is much higher, and in length more direct; accordingly it was called the Citadel by King David; but it is by us called the Upper Market Place." (W. v. iv: 1.) It approximates the shape of a regular parallelogram, and was originally nearly isolated, having apparently been only attached to the south-west corner of Akra by a very short isthmus or neck. The ravine or valley that originally separated it from Akra is now filled up in great measure. Its exact location, however, is quite obvious; for, on passing along from Jaffa Gate towards the Haram, the observer will notice that a few yards to his right Mount Zion rises up quite suddenly, and is many feet higher than Akra. The former depression that originally divided the northern portion of Mount Zion into two parts is also nearly filled up at present, but its position is still plainly indicated along the street of the Jewish Bazaar. The sides of Mount Zion are much higher and steeper than those of any other quarter of Jerusalem, except the eastern declivity of Mount Ophel. The present wall running across Mount Zion excludes about one-half of it from the city—and this excluded half is divided about equally by the pottery aqueduct that now courses around the hill.

UPPER MARKET.—This term is manifestly used to designate the whole of Mount Zion in general; but has also occasionally a more restricted sense—meaning only the large market place on the summit of the Holy Hill.

MILLO—*Fulness.*—Though so often mentioned in the Bible, and so long a matter of discussion, the exact position and nature of this place is still somewhat a matter of doubt. There is every reason to believe, however, that it was that part of Mount Zion where the cleft of Zion declined very rapidly towards the Acro-Zion portion of the Tyropœon Valley. The western wall of Jebus was probably built on the eastern brow of this cliff or ravine, and when David determined to enlarge the city and enclosed the whole of Mount Zion, he concluded to fill up that depression, and render it suitable for building—hence called Millo. It was evidently embraced within the limits of the "City of David," as enlarged by him; and no other place besides this will at all answer the requirements of the case. It was evidently a place of considerable magnitude and importance. Excavations along the Jewish street revealed in several places the foundations of walls six feet in thickness, with arches similar to that, the crown of which may be seen near a dyer's shop on the Zion Gate street, about equally distant from the Anglican Hospital and the bazaars. May not these be the remains of the Millo structures?

Beth Millo—or the house of Millo—was perhaps a strongly fortified edifice at the entrance of the Zion Valley into the Tyropœon. *Silla* seems to have been situated either in the Tyropœon or at the mouth of Zion Valley, and was probably a strong subterranean structure: but we know still less of this place than of Beth Millo. The present Jewish Bazaar indicates the general locality of Millo. Was Silla the name of Zion Valley? "Millo, in the City of David" (2 Ch. xxxii. 5), reads thus in the Septuagint—"to analeema tees poleos David—*the elevation or fortification of the City of David.*"

David seems to have chosen that portion of Zion lying between his palace and Millo as the general site of royal edifices of various characters.

The Jews hold Mamilla or Babilla, the ground about the so called upper pool of Gihon, to be Beth Millo!

OPHEL—OPHAL, OPHLA, OPHLAS, OPEL, APHLA—for by all of these synonyms is it called, either in the Septuagint, the works of Josephus, or our English version of the Scriptures—signifies a swelling, mound, or tower. No mention of this place, either as a quarter of the city, a hill, or a tower, is anywhere made earlier than the reign of Jotham, "who built the high gate of the House of the Lord, and on the wall of Ophel he built much." (2 Chr. xxvii. 3.) In the margin this word is uniformly translated tower. This Tower or Ophel it was that "Manasseh encompassed about, and raised to a very great height." Josephus informs us (W. v. iv: 2), that it was "a certain place which they call Ophlas, where it (the wall) enclosing the city on the south-east, was joined to the eastern cloister of the Temple." But it was not actually united to the Temple enclosure, for we are told that Manahem, when overcome in the Temple, ran away to Ophla. (W. ii. xvii: 9.) The Tower of Ophel was evidently situated near the south-east corner of the Temple enclosure, and consequently near the cattle market; and if at the depressed situation of the south-east corner, a special reason for raising it so high is perfectly obvious. It was no doubt a stupendous and magnificent structure; and is the identical "strong-hold of the Daughter of Zion" so glowingly apostrophized by the prophet Micah (iv. 8).

"And thou, O tower of the flock!
(The strong-hold of the Daughter of Zion)
Unto thee shall it come, even the first dominion,
The kingdom shall come to the Daughter of Jerusalem."

The quarter of Jerusalem called Akra derives its name, confessedly, from the celebrated citadel "Akra," so long occupied by the Syrians. In the same way, it is probable, the ridge of land lying south of the Temple, between the valleys Kedron and Tyropœon, now termed Ophel, may be so called from its great Tower Ophel or Ophla. This ridge is evidently a continuation of Mount Moriah, as Mount Moriah is of Mount Bezetha.

This quarter of the city was the special abode of the Nethinim, Gibeonites, Levites—and probably Stationary Men, as well as Solomon's servants. But there is not now a single tenement upon all Mount Ophel, save a hovel or two of stone and mud, as "a lodge in a garden of cucumbers!"

"Lower City," though very properly applying to the lower part of Akra, under its first phasis as Salem, was yet a very inappropriate term after its extension upward: for while at first all of it was probably below every part of the Zion quarter, then called "Upper City;" yet as it existed in the days of Josephus, a section of it was actually higher than any part of Zion, or the upper city; and a portion of Zion was lower than any part of the lower city; still, however, it occasionally bore its ancient name despite the evident inconsistency.

This quarter of the city has now a general slope to the east of one foot in six or eight; but the lower portion was perhaps much more precipitous originally. The Maccabean princes not only cut away the celebrated rock to which this part of the city no doubt owed its name, but also filled up the valley separating Akra and Moriah—which must not only have altered its own topographic features, but also have had the effect of rendering all the valley above it much wider by the accumulation of the rubbish.

Ophel is adjectively called "*Lower City*" by Josephus in the 6th Book of the Wars, chap. 7, paragraph 2; but Akra is the quarter of the city to which this term is specifically applied.

The Sheep [Market]—*Sheep Quarter.*—According to official returns made by the high priests at the requisition of Cestius Gallus, President of Syria, for the information of the Emperor Nero, no less than 256,500 lambs or kids, but almost exclusively the former, were annually slain at the passover. And a very large number were of course always required to be kept near the Temple in a state of readiness for the altar. A very considerable space was thus required to be set apart for herding these vast flocks of sheep, to say nothing of other victims. It was highly desirable that they should be kept in some large and suitable enclosure, as near the Temple as possible, for convenience of inspection. For this purpose no place could be more convenient and suitable, in every respect, than the extensive yards and courts of Antonia immediately contiguous on the north; but such an appropriation of its premises was utterly incompatible with the purposes for which they were exclusively designed. The Xystus, which was immediately adjacent on the west, though well situated in point of convenience, was not only otherwise appropriated, but much too small. The space immediately adjoining the Temple on the south would be very convenient, but this would be inconsistent with the design of the hippodrome; and moreover, Ophel being the residence of the Nethinim and other attendants upon the Temple services, a sheep quarter there would interfere too much with their facility of access to the Holy House. And besides these insuperable objections it would be very difficult, if not impossible, to supply the requisite amount of water in that part of the city. Nor indeed would it be at all suitable to keep such a vast herd in any part of the city.

Now, on the east of the Temple there was a space between its cloister and the eastern portion of the "first wall" of Josephus, admirably adapted in every respect for this great magazine of sacrifices—which, though within the circuit of the wall, was yet outside the city—in an unappropriated spot, retired yet convenient, both from without and within, easily supplied with water and open to no objection. Here, then, is just the spot for the sheep quarter. And accordingly it is just here we find the *sheep-gate*—which, in entire accordance with the portal nomenclature of the city, is significantly designated. And right at hand we also find the Babel-like Ophel—that "great Tower of the Flock," as the prophet styled it, both of which facts are strongly confirmatory of the correctness of this location. It seems to have been commensurate in length, with the entire breadth of the east side of the Temple, and in order to be sufficiently capacious must have extended in breadth nearly down to the Kedron. It was no doubt divided into numerous compartments for the convenience of the cattle merchants; and supplied with a capacious reservoir, filled perhaps by diverting into it at least a portion of the descending stream of the "swift-gliding Kedron."

How admirably these topographical facts correspond with the Scriptures, and incidentally sustain them! They also show how important to the cause of Christianity it is that the utmost accuracy should be obtained in the location of all sacred places.

Cœnopolis, Bezetha, or the "New City."—Although a small portion of the old city was situated upon the side of Bezetha hill before the erection of the third wall, yet this name only applied to that beyond the old wall; but in process of time it comprehended all the new city, whether built upon this hill or on the adjacent valleys and plain. The general site of Cœnopolis was an irregular shallow, semilunar basin—divided however in its lower portion nearly equally by the hill (Bezetha), which indeed extended nearly across it, though scarcely perceptible at its upper extremity.

The hill, thus gradually and almost imperceptibly rising about midway between Damascus Gate and Kubr es-Sultan, attains a height of more than a hundred feet at its greatest elevation about the point where the wall now crosses it, and gradually becomes lower and lower in absolute but not always in relative height, to its termination at the junction of the Tyropœon and Kedron valleys. But though originally continuous its whole length, it is now entirely severed in one or two places—reduced in height at one point and enlarged in breadth at others, so that it by no means presents the same shape and appearance now that it did originally. Three or four hundred yards below the point crossed by the wall the ridge became quite narrow: and it was here cut down by Herod the Great to a level with the Temple area, at the time that he enlarged its premises and completed the fortification of Antonia. The scarpment thus left by the excision of a portion of the mountain formed the southern face of the Tower. The ridge of Bezetha, however, was not only thus cut away at that point, but a short distance above it was completely severed by a deep trench, and the sides also scarped—thus forming a solid tower of native rock. But the continuity of the mountain was still more completely destroyed beyond the present city wall. The entire ridge has here been cut away nearly to a level with the surrounding ground for the space of about two hundred yards. This great hiatus was perhaps at first a mere narrow trench designed for the security of the wall crossing the summit of the ridge; but being an excellent quarry of building rock, all the rest of the hill occupying this wide gap has been removed for the construction of walls and edifices. In the southern extremity of the northern division of the hill thus severed there is a very large natural cave, where tradition reports that the prophet of Anathoth wrote his doleful "Lamentations" over the desolations of the Holy City; and in the northern extremity of the southern portion I discovered a much larger one, partly natural, but mainly artificial—being evidently a quarry, from which immense quantities of stones have been cut for building purposes. Those extra-cyclopean stones in the south-east and south-west corners of the Temple wall were doubtless taken from this great quarry, and carried to their present position down the gently inclined plane on rollers—a conjecture which at once solves the mystery that has greatly puzzled travellers in relation to the difficulty of transporting and *handling* such immense masses of rock, and enables us to understand why they were called "stones of rolling" by Ezra.

Goath.—Between Bezetha Hill and the Kedron Valley, there is quite a prominent ridge, upon a portion of which the eastern wall of the city now stands. This hill must at one time have been very conspicuous, before the valley separating it from Bezetha became so much filled up. There is no mention of this hill in the works of Josephus or the Talmud, that I am aware of; but the lower portion of it that terminates in the Kedron is unquestionably the *Goath* of the Scriptures. (Jer. xxxi. 39.)

CHAPTER V.

THE CITY WALLS.

"Mark ye well her bulwarks."

WALLS FROM MELCHISEDEC TO ZEDEKIAH.

WALLS OF SALEM.—In treating of the walls of Jerusalem chronologically, which is the plan best adapted to elucidate this intricate and obscure subject, the city of Melchisedec first claims attention. So little, however, is positively known or satisfactorily ascertainable in relation to this ancient city, that its metes and bounds, as laid down on the map, though evidently correct in the main, must yet be received with some grains of allowance, as to exactness of position. Its towering acropolis*—so long and tenaciously held by the Syrians, despite all the efforts of the whole city and nation, was no doubt well nigh impregnable; but its walls on the north and the west being so disadvantageously situated on the slope of Akra, must have been quite assailable, though it is by no means improbable that Akra was divided by a ravine as Zion was; and it must have been either through the northern or western one that the children of Judah effected an entrance and "took the city, and smote it with the edge of the sword and set it on fire." On the south side it was doubtless well secured by the lower portion of the Tyropœon ravine that separated it from Mount Zion, and still more so on the east by the Gihon Valley that divided it from Mount Moriah. It is probable in the highest degree that the east extremity of the north side was

* It was this stronghold (called *Akra* in the Greek tongue) that no doubt gave name to that quarter of Jerusalem.

well defended by a large and deep reservoir, supplied by the waters of Gihon.

WALLS OF JEBUS.—The physical features of the north-east portion of Zion, where the city of the Jebusites was situated, are still so prominent and well defined as to render the location of the walls of this ancient stronghold a matter of much greater certainty than those of Salem. And besides those enduring records of nature, many facts are recorded in the Sacred Scriptures, the Apocrypha, and the works of Josephus, that concur to render their restoration, in great measure, a matter of certainty. It will be seen on reference to the map, that though never heretofore observed, there was an admirable situation for it on quite an isolated protuberance of Mount Zion. The east side was very precipitous, and elevated upwards of a hundred feet above the Tyropœon. This valley was also quite a deep ravine where it bordered Jebusi on the north. Mount Zion declined so rapidly on the south border as to form a good defence in that direction; and on the west there was another valley now nearly filled up; but at the date of David's capture of the city was no doubt a very considerable depression, inasmuch as he found it necessary to fill it up before he could extend the dimensions of the city in that direction. This valley was no other than Millo—(*in loc.*) The present indications of a very steep declivity on its south-western quarter are not very obvious at this remote day, owing to the "heaps" *upon heaps* of rubbish, of which it has been so long the receptacle. But it is to be inferred from the circumstances recorded by the historian in relating the capture of the city by David, that the attack was made on the still deeply precipitous cliffs of the east; which clearly indicates that the city was well fortified by nature as well as art everywhere else. It is probable that the cliffs supporting the citadel were so high and perpendicular, that no additional wall was here deemed necessary, especially as the Jebusites seem have conducted the waters of Gihon into a kind of moat some distance above its base, probably about the elevation at which the waters of Etham now flow in the present aqueduct. Josephus no doubt speaks with his accustomed accuracy when he declares (Ant. v. ii: 2) that "the Upper City (Jebus) was not to be taken without great difficulty through the strength of its walls, and *the nature of the place*," thus situated on the verge of precipices all around.

Walls of Zion.—After capturing Jebus, David immediately selected Jerusalem—or rather the sites of Jebus and Salem, with their immediate environs—as the metropolis of his kingdom; "and built the city round about, even from Millo round about; and Joab repaired the rest of the city." (1 Chr. xi. 8.) This extension of its limits and buildings was most successfully continued under Solomon; who not only "built Millo, and repaired the breaches of the City of David his father" (1 Kings xi. 27), and *built the wall round about* (1 Kings iii. 1), but also surrounded his "magnifical" Temple with massive walls, which he connected with Zion by a stupendous bridge, and by a wall also across the Tyropœon Valley. The "*wall round about*" was, no doubt, the one commencing at the south-east corner of the original Jebus, in continuation of its east side, and coursing around Zion on the most suitable ledges of the impending rocks on the sides of the lower portion of the Tyropœon and Hinnom valleys, as far as the neighborhood of the present Yaffa Gate, whence it was carried in a straight descending course along the side of the upper part of the Tyropœon to Millo, where it became continuous with the northern wall of Jebus. Or, did Solomon commence at the other end (the north-west), and construct the wall around the west and south of Zion, and the south and east of Ophel uniting it to the Temple? If so, it gives new force and interest to the passage informing us that "Manasseh built a wall on the west of Gihon, *even* to the entering of the Fish Gate."

No further mention is made of the walls of Jerusalem until we learn that "Joash, the king of Israel, took Amaziah, king of Judah, the son of Joash, the son of Jehoahaz, at Beth-Shemesh, and brought him to Jerusalem, and brake down the wall of Jerusalem from the Gate of Ephraim to the corner gate, 400 cubits." (2 Chr. xxv. 25; 2 Kings xiv. 13.) This breach was of course soon repaired; and when his more enterprising son, Uzziah, ascended the throne, he "built towers in this neighborhood, at the corner gate, and at the valley gate, and at the turning of the wall, 150 cubits high, and fortified them" (2 Chr. xxvi. 9.) It is said of Jotham, the son of Uzziah, that "he built the High Gate of the House of the Lord, and on the wall of Ophel he built much" (2 Chr. xxvii. 3.) It is evident, however, that in the mean time the limits of the city had been considerably extended on the north and west of the "Lower City"—Salem—its original walls having also been removed. But by whom the wall was made that encompassed the north-west part of the city—commencing near the Jaffa Gate, and terminating at the Temple enclosure on the north, we have no means of ascertaining. The good Hezekiah was very zealous in repairing, fortifying, and beautifying the city of his fathers, and of his fathers' God; but does not appear to have enlarged its borders. "He built up all the wall that was broken down and raised it up to the towers, and *another wall* without (by the side of that destroyed by Joash, probably, called by Nehemiah 'the broad wall,' which was certainly much needed), and repaired Millo in the City of David." (2 Chr. xxxii. 5.)

OPHEL WALL.—Manasseh, also, after his restoration to the throne of Jerusalem, greatly fortified its walls; and considerably enlarged its borders on the south-east, unless indeed his work was mainly a reconstruction of Solomon's or Jotham's—for "he built a wall without the City of David, on the west side of Gihon, in the valley, even to the entering in at the Fish Gate; and compassed about Ophel and raised it up a very great height." (2 Chr. xxxiii. 14.) The Gihon Valley wall here mentioned is undoubtedly that running between Siloam and the Fish Gate, being identical in part with the eastern wall of Jebus (for this valley was no doubt once called Gihon all the way down); but it is doubtful whether he alludes to the *Tower* or to the *Hill* of Ophel as being surrounded with a wall, or to both. But though it does not appear with certainty whether the wall of Ophel was first built by Solomon, Jotham, or Manasseh, certain it is that the wall was at this time about three miles in circuit, which was its utmost limit prior to the captivity; though we have no further topographical particulars of the city till the reign of Hezekiah, when the Lord brought upon Jerusalem Nebuchadnezzar, the king of the Chaldees * * and the city was broken up, and all the men of war fled by night by the way of the gate between two walls which is by the King's Garden * * * and they burnt the House of God, and brake down the wall of Jerusalem, and burnt all the palaces thereof with fire." (2 Kings xxv. 2, 4; 2 Chr. xxxvi. 17–21; Jer. xxxix. 2, 4.)

WALLS FROM NEHEMIAH TO AGRIPPA.

Nehemiah's nocturnal Reconnoissance of the Walls (Neh. ii. 13, 15.)—Biblical expositors having no personal knowledge of the topography of Jerusalem, have all been most signally foiled in their attempts to locate the gates, towers, reservoirs, and other places mentioned by Nehemiah in describing his furtive examination of the walls, their reconstruction and their dedication; and it must be confessed that the pious Tirshatha, designing rather to tell *who* were the builders than *where* they labored and *what* they built, is not as explicit on these points as might be desired for the gratification of our curiosity. But though the subject has heretofore been beset with difficulties deemed insuperable, nothing but an intimate acquaintance with the topography of the site is now necessary to a satisfactory solution of the most formidable of these difficulties, since the satisfactory identification of a few leading points. Nor is any formal disquisition necessary—a very few explanatory remarks merely incorporated with Nehemiah's topographic accounts of the walls (distinguished by Italics) amply sufficing for the complete demonstration of this zigzag problem, which has heretofore so completely baffled the efforts of Biblical topographers. The villages where the restorers resided being generally mentioned, it will be seen that this circumstance affords a general indication of the part of the wall upon which they labored,—such places being on that side of the city nearest their place of abode.

The only apparent exception being perhaps where they repaired more than one piece—having completed their first undertaking (if they worked any more), there being no more work to be done on the side next their residence, or having arrived after the repairs on that part of the city nearest them under operation were completed, they would, of course, go wherever their services would be required. It will be observed that the labor of the priests was confined either to the Temple itself, its immediate vicinity—or some other sacred locality.

(Nehemiah ii. 13, 15.)—"And I went out by night by the gate of the valley, (*near the Tower of Hippicus* (*Jaffa Gate*)) even before the dragon well (*i. e. fountain on the opposite side of the valley*) and to the dung port, and viewed the walls of Jerusalem; which were broken down, and the gates thereof were consumed with fire. Then (*having passed the gate of the Essenes*) I went to the gate of the fountain (*Siloah*) and (*then turning around the point of Ophel came*) to the kings' pool—but there was no place for the beast that was under me to pass (*by the sides of this pool—Solomon's—there being water in the pool and too much rubbbish about it to permit the passage of the beast*). Then went I up in the night by the brook (*Kedron*), and viewed the wall, and turned back, and entered by the gate of the valley, and so returned."

The Reconstruction of the Walls, &c., (Neh. iii.)—"Then Eliashib, the high priest, rose up with his brethren, the priests, and they builded the sheep-gate, they sanctified it and set up the doors of it, even unto the tower of Meah—they sanctified it unto the tower of Hananeel (*this portion having been but little injured*). And next unto him builded the men of Jericho. And next to them builded Zaccur, the son of Imri. But the fish gate did the sons of Hassenaah build, who also laid the beams thereof, and set up the doors thereof, the locks thereof, and the bars thereof. And next unto them repaired Moremoth, the son of Urijah, the son of Koz. And next unto them repaired Meshullam, the son of Berechiah, the son of Meshezabeel. And next unto them repaired Zadok, the son of Baana. And next unto them the Tekoites repaired; but their nobles put not their necks to the work of their Lord. Moreover (*these having repaired the Gate of Benjamin*) the old gate repaired Jehoiada, the son of Paseah, and Meshullam, the son of Besodeiah; they laid the beams thereof, and set up the door thereof, and the locks thereof, and the bars thereof; and next unto them repaired Melatiah, the Gibeonite, and Jadon, the Meronothite, the men of Gibeon, and of Mizpah, unto the throne of the governor on this side of the river. Next unto him repaired Uzziel, the son of Harhaiah of the goldsmiths. Next unto him also repaired Hananiah the son of one of the apothecaries, and they fortified Jerusalem unto the broad wall" (or double wall, "*from the Gate of Ephraim to the Corner Gate, four hundred cubits in length, formerly broken down by Joash, king of Israel*). And next unto them repaired Rephaiah, the son of Hur, the ruler of the half part of Jerusalem. And next unto them repaired Jedaiah, the son of Harumaph, even over against his house. And next unto him repaired Hattush, the son of Hashabniah. Malchijah, the son of Harim, and Hashub, the son of Pahath-Moab repaired the other piece (*beyond the first gate*) and the tower of the furnaces. And next unto him repaired Shallum, the son of Halohesh, the ruler of the half-part of Jerusalem, he and his daughters. The valley gate repaired Hanun and the inhabitants of Zanoah; they built it, and set up the doors thereof, the locks thereof, and the bars thereof, and a thousand cubits on the wall (*passing through a place called Bethzo*), unto the dung gate. But the dung gate repaired Malchiah, the son of Rechab, the ruler of part of Beth-Haccerem; he built it, and set up the doors thereof, and the locks thereof, and the bars thereof. (*Next the Essenes Gate.*) But the gate of the ("Siloam") fountain repaired Shallum, the son of Colhozeh, the ruler of part of Mizpah; he built it, and covered it, and set up the doors thereof, the locks thereof, and the bars thereof, and the wall of the pool of* Siloah (*below the*

* Wall of "shorn skins"—*Septuagint.* Another confirmation of the correctness of these locations.

Fountain of Siloah) by the king's garden, and unto the stairs that go down from the city of David. After him repaired Nehemiah, the son of Azbuk, the ruler of the half part of Beth-zur, with the place over against the sepulchres of David, and to the pool that was made, and unto the house of the mighty (*along the precipitous cliffs of Zion*). After him repaired the Levites, Rehum, the son of Bani. Next unto him repaired Hashabiah, the ruler of the half part of Keilah, in his part. After him repaired their brethren, Bavai, the son of Henadad, the ruler of the half part of Keilah. And next to him repaired Ezer, the son of Jesuah, the ruler of Mizpah, another piece over against the going up to the armory, at the turning of the wall (*i. e. the wall across the Tyropœon—being a continuation of the first wall—connecting Mount Zion with the Temple wall*). After him Baruch, the son of Zabbai, earnestly repaired the other piece, from the turning of the wall (*by the Armory*) unto the door of the house of Eliashib, the high priest. After him repaired Meremoth, the son of Urijah, the son of Koz, another piece, from the door of the house of Eliashib, even to the end of the house of Eliashib. And after him repaired the priests, the men of the plain. After him repaired Benjamin and Hashub, over against their house. After him repaired Azariah, the son of Maasseiah, the son of Ananiah, by his house. After him repaired Binnui, the son of Henadad, another piece, from the house of Azariah, unto the turning of the wall, even unto the corner (*or junction of the "First and Second walls"*).

Palal, the son of Uzai, over against the turning of the wall (*by the Armory*) and the tower which lieth out from the king's high house (*watch-tower by royal palace—in the fortification wall of the palace*) that was by the court of the prison. After him Pedaiah, the son of Parosh. Moreover the Nethinims (*who*) dwelt in (*the portion of Moriah called*) Ophel, (*commencing at Siloam fount*, repaired) unto the place over against the water gate toward the east, and the tower that lieth out. After them the Tekoites repaired another piece, over against the great tower that lieth out even unto the wall of Ophel (*at the place Ophlas*). From above the horse gate repaired the priests, every one over against his house. After them (*going northward around the Temple*) repaired Zadok, the son of Immer, over against his house. After him repaired also Shemaiah, the son of Shechaniah, the keeper of the east gate (*of the Temple, i. e. Shusan*). After him repaired Hananiah, the son of Shelemiah, and Hanun the sixth son of Zalaph, another piece. After him repaired Meshullum, the son of Berechiah, over against his chamber. After him repaired Malchiah, the goldsmith's son, unto the place of the Nethinims (*at the corner by the bridge*) and of the merchants (*in the Tabernæ*), over against the gate Miphkad (*at the other end of the bridge*), and even to the going up of the (*south-west*) corner. And between the going up of the corner (*along the south side of the Temple enclosure*) unto the sheep gate, repaired the goldsmiths and the merchants."

DEDICATION OF THE WALLS—(Neh. xii. 31–40.)—(*The assembly convened near Jaffa Gate where the procession commences.*)—"Then I brought up the princes of Judah upon the wall, (*near the Valley Gate*) and appointed two great companies of them that gave thanks, whereof one went on the right hand upon the wall toward the dung gate (*through Bethzo.*) And after them went Hoshaiah, and half of the princes of Judah. And Azariah, Ezra, and Meshullam. Judah, and Benjamin, and Shemaiah, and Jeremiah. And certain of the priests' sons with trumpets; namely, Zechariah the son of Jonathan, the son of Shemaiah, the son of Mattaniah, the son of Michaiah, the son of Zaccur, the son of Asaph. And his brethren, Shemaiah, and Azarael, Milalai, Gilalai, Maai, Nethaneel, and Judah, Hanani, with the musical instruments of David the man of God, and Ezra the scribe before them. And at the fountain gate, which was over against them, they (*descended through the Tower of Siloam on the interior and then reascending*) went up by the stairs of the city of David, at the going up of the wall, above the house of David, even unto the water gate eastward (*by the staircase of the rampart, having descended to dedicate the fountain structures.*) And the other company of them that gave thanks went over against them, (*both parties having started from the junction of the "First and Second walls,"*) and I after them, and the half of the people upon the wall, from beyond the tower of the furnaces even unto the broad wall. (*beyond the corner gate.*) And from above the gate of Ephraim, and above the old gate (*and the Gate of Benjamin*), and above the fish gate, and the tower of Hananeel, and the tower of Meah, even unto the sheep gate: and they stood still in the prison gate (*or High Gate at the east end of the bridge.*) So stood the two companies of them that gave thanks in the house of God, and I, and the half of the rulers with me"—(*having thus performed the circuit of the investing wall*).

The reader, who will be at the pains critically to read the foregoing delineation of the walls—map in hand—cannot fail to be entirely satisfied of the general correctness of these locations—which tally so completely with the local features and natural condition of the places named. It is highly interesting thus to verify by actual examination those ancient records. Such an investigation cannot fail to afford strong confirmatory evidence of their truthfulness.

WALLS OF JERUSALEM FROM THEIR RESTORATION BY NEHEMIAH TO THE CHRISTIAN ERA.

After lying in ruins more than a century and a quarter while the Jews were in Babylonia, the walls of the Holy City were rebuilt by Nehemiah about four hundred and fifty years before the Christian era—the altar having been set up more than fourscore years previously; and the Temple rebuilt about sixty-five years before their re-edification. And various as were the fortunes of this ill-fated city of the Jews during the period intervening between its restoration under Nehemiah and the Christian era, under its various rulers—Persian, Egyptian, Syrian, Roman, and native, as well priestly as princely—a period of more than five centuries—no material expansion or contraction of its boundaries occurred, though its walls were often demolished, and as often rebuilt. Jonathan Maccabeus "built a wall in the midst of the city in order to exclude the market place from the garrison (of Syrians) which was in the citadel (Akra). But we are not told *where* it was: a circumstance, however, but little to be regretted, inasmuch as it was doubtless removed as soon as Simon wrested this celebrated fortress from the Syrians and determined to destroy it.

The walls demolished by Nebuchadnezzar and reëdified by Nehemiah, were no doubt identical in capacity as well as position with those of the city at the period of the Messiah's sojourn upon earth, with the exception of a slight alteration by Herod the Great in the neighborhood of Antonia; and this perhaps was a mere enlargement of the area of the Temple at the expense of the city in that quarter. But about ten years after the ascension of the Saviour, King Agrippa the Elder projected and partially completed an immense wall on the north of the city, which, though the truckling king felt constrained to relinquish lest he should incur the displeasure of the Emperor Claudius, the Jews yet found means of completing, independently of royal favor.

As there is some advantage in following the course pursued by Nehemiah and Josephus (our chief authorities), in starting at the point where the three grand divisions of Jerusalem come in juxtaposition, this point of departure will be adopted in treating of the walls of the city, as they existed in the days of their investment by Titus.

"THE FIRST OR OLD WALL"*—(*enclosing Zion and Ophel*).—Starting at the Tower of Hippicus, in the north-west corner of Zion, the wall ran eastward † along the northern brow of Zion just on the

* There is no reason to believe that this ordinal classification of the walls was any other than an arbitrary one, merely adopted for convenience in describing the siege; for Josephus afterwards reverses the order—making the first third, and the third first—the second retaining its name alone from the force of circumstances.

† Dr. Robinson well observes (Bib. Res. i. 411), that "the phrases *pros dusin, pros noton, pros anatoleen*, in this passage as applied to the wall, can only mean *towards*, or *on the west, south*, east, &c., equivalent to the *western, southern, eastern* wall. This is shown both by the nature of the case, and by the similar phrase *te pros anatoleen, stoa tou hierou*, in the same sentence, which no one ever thought of rendering

south brink of the Tyropœon Valley, thirty cubits above the bottom of the ravine, and was united to the west colonnade of the Temple; having crossed over the cleft of Zion (Millo), passed the Xystus, and united with the Council House or Sanhedrim at its junction with the Temple wall. Returning to the same point to locate the remainder of the wall, we trace it thence through a place called Bethzo, along the verge of the Hinnom, occupying perhaps the site of the present wall as far as its south-west corner; thence it doubtless ran a straight course to the English cemetery, though probably lower down than at present indicated, and thence—did we locate it to the best advantage—its course would be contracted considerably within the line indicated on the map: but the immense population of the city imperatively requires us to give the wall the utmost extension compatible with the physical features of the ground, and the requirements of the descriptive narratives—having special regard to strength of position—for on this western and southern border of Zion the wall was deemed so impregnable that no enemy ever ventured to attack it. There are no reliable indications of the ancient foundations now visible, unless we may regard as such the scarped rock forming the north-eastern boundary of the English cemetery; which, however, would restrict the limits of the city entirely too much, and render too acute the corner of the wall at Siloam to be justified either upon principles of civil economy or military policy. The wall could have been located advantageously almost anywhere upon the craggy precipices of this rocky hillside, due regard being had to the towering cliffs on the opposite side of Hinnom. The southern side—as also the western—was quite straight until Siloam was approached, when, instead of continuing directly forward to Solomon's Pool in the course naturally indicated by the locality at the mouth of the Tyropœon, it underwent a great deflection around the Pool of Siloam. This was accomplished by running northward

otherwise than *the eastern portico of the Temple.* Had this form of expression been always so understood, it would have saved great confusion among commentators both as to the course of the wall and the position of Siloam."

seventy or eighty yards, then eastward about half that distance, and back again southward seventy or eighty, to the point of Ophel—thus forming the two walls between which Zedekiah escaped (Jer. xxxix. 5). Around this point it underwent another deflection, and was carried along the brow and side of Ophel in a direction mainly facing the east, but evidently having somewhat of a southern aspect below the south-eastern angle of the Temple wall, in order to be conformed to the curvature of Ophel; and was joined to the Temple wall on the east—no doubt at its farther extremity, in order not only to protect the Temple from profanation on that side, but for the purpose also of forming the cattle market. In order to complete the enclosure, so much of the Temple wall as lies between this point and the Council House—either including or excluding the Temple area—must also be regarded as a portion of the "First Wall."

Josephus has rather strangely omitted all direct mention of a wall built by Manasseh, which was evidently in existence in his day, running from Siloam to the Xystus, and dividing Zion from Ophel; but, as it was an inner wall that was never attacked by the Romans, there was no especial occasion for describing it in an account of the city designed mainly to illustrate its capture. This omission, however, is amply supplied by Nehemiah, who sufficiently describes it (iii. 15–19).

"Second Wall" (*enclosing Akra, in conjunction with part of the first wall and the Gihon Valley wall*).—Of this wall Josephus merely informs us that it took its beginning from that gate which they call "Gennath, which belonged to the First Wall: it only encompassed the northern quarter of the old city, and reached as far as the Tower of Antonia."

The present traditionary Pool of Hezekiah being recognised as the Amygdalon of Josephus, the position of Gennath Gate, though so long and angrily controverted, is very easily and satisfactorily established. We learn from the great Jewish historian that the celebrated tenth legion of the Roman army, together with the fifteenth, raised mounds at that portion of the Second Wall opposite Amygdalon, thirty cubits distant. This wall, therefore, ran within about fifteen yards of this pool; and of course the Gate of Gennath was situated about that distance above the point of the old First Wall that would be cut by an extension of the west wall of the Amygdalon Pool.

REMAINS AT DAMASCUS GATE—ANCIENT TOWER ROOM.

REMAINS AT DAMASCUS GATE.—The very ancient, massive, and characteristically Jewish remains found in the two towers on each side of Damascus Gate, indisputably indicate that spot as a portion of the "Second Wall." The resemblance between the architecture of the outer Temple wall (which was undoubtedly built either by Solomon or his immediate successors) and the lower portions of the Damascus Gate towers (and also of the wall for some distance on each side), is so very striking, that it cannot fail to arrest the attention of the most superficial observer, and produce the conviction that they are the works of the same age and of one common system. The Gate of Damascus, without doubt, is identical with the "Old Gate" of Nehemiah; and, in the accompanying representation of the lower room on the east of the gate, the reader has before him the best specimen of ancient Jewish mural structure that the battering-ram and tooth of time have spared to us.

The upper portion of the masonry, it is obvious, is of modern and inferior workmanship. The slab in the foreground of the picture belongs to the winding stairway commencing on the left, leading to the top of the tower and wall, the step-rocks of which are about seven feet in length and three feet in breadth. This stairway is not contained in a circular tube, as in modern buildings; but is square-shaped, as represented in the annexed ground plan of the tower-room, in which the three lowermost steps are represented. It was also, in all probability, this kind of ascent by which "they went up with winding stairs into the middle chamber, and out of the middle into the third"—situated in the southern wing of the Porch of the Temple. (1 Kings vi. 8.)

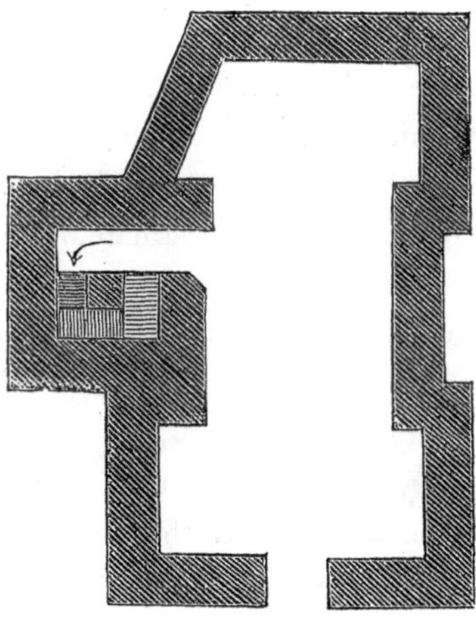

GROUND PLAN OF ROOM AND WINDING STAIRWAY IN TOWER AT DAMASCUS GATE.

So disadvantageous would be a line drawn directly from these towers to Antonia for a defensive wall, and so very advantageous a location the top of that portion of Bezetha Hill extending between the Seraglio and the section through the hill, that the wall must either have rested on this crest or on the slope just beyond it eastwardly, and upon the site now occupied by the wall thence to Damascus Gate. Such considerable remains of an ancient wall are still to be seen where the present northern wall near its western termination makes the greatest southern declination, that they can but be regarded as a portion of the old second wall. But for these remains, however, the wall would have been located, on the plan, with a more graceful curve at that point, in accordance with the intimations of the word used by Josephus in describing this wall.

"THIRD WALL"—(*enclosing Cœnopolis, Bezetha, or the New City.*)—This wall began at the Hippic Tower and ran to Psephinos: thence extending over against Helena's Monuments, it reached a great length; passing through the royal sepulchral caverns, and bending at the corner tower and Fuller's Monument, joined the old wall at the Cedron—which is summarily expressed by Jeremiah (xxxi. 39) in these words: "The measuring line shall yet go forth over against it (the city) upon the hill Gareb, and shall compass about to Goath." This wall (as seen on the map) was laid down from repeated examinations of its site, just as it is believed King Agrippa's engineer would have located it, had he been instructed to select the best site for the erection of a wall designed to include a large area within a wall most eligibly situated. And it is found to quadrate as well with recorded facts, circumstances, and indications, as with the configuration of the ground. A slight examination of the map will obviate the necessity of a long verbal account; and perhaps subserve a better purpose. A wall of much smaller circuit than this must not only have been located to great disadvantage, but the city thus restricted would have been totally inadequate to the accommodation of its teeming population. The northern wall was three stadia south of Helena's Monument. If then, this tomb was identical with "The Tombs of the Kings," which is only 520 yards from Damascus Gate (on the line of the old "Second Wall"), the "Third Wall" must have been within 214 yards, or only a little more than one stadium from the "Second" !!! The rocks supposed by Dr. Robinson to belong to the foundation of the "Third" wall are only 2 stadia from the "Second" wall, and most disadvantageously situated for a wall. The stones of the Third Wall were 20 cubits long and 10 broad; whereas these are not one-fourth that size. But the entire absence of all sepulchres between Kubr Moluk and the city is *decisive* upon this point; and has an important bearing in relation to the position of Helena's tomb. Except by implication, in describing the capture of the Temple, Josephus makes no allusion to the Gihon Valley wall, which is described (2 Chr. xxxiii. 14) as running along the west side of the valley, even to the Fish Gate.

If success has attended the attempt thus to locate the walls according to the nature of the ground and the various requirements of all the circumstances of the case, the location of the gates and towers will be easily accomplished without any clashing between Josephus, Nehemiah, and others. Josephus states that "the whole compass of the city was thirty-three furlongs," which exactly corresponds with my restoration—provided measurement be made between the main outer leading points, without taking the recesses into account, which undoubtedly was the plan pursued in making his estimate. In proof of which it need only be remarked, that were all the towers located (according to the data he furnishes) in a regular line, instead of the zigzag projections and indentations described by Tacitus, the circumference of the city would be considerably more than double the extent assigned it by Josephus. In speaking of Jerusalem, Tacitus remarks—"Walls constructed with skill. In some places projecting forward: in others retiring inwardly, with the angles so formed that the besiegers were always liable to be annoyed in flank. The extremities of the rock were sharp, abrupt, and craggy. In convenient places near the top, towers were raised sixty feet high, and others on the declivity of the sides, one hundred and twenty feet."* That the subject may be the better understood, the towers and gates will come under consideration in the regular order of their position—whether mentioned by Josephus, Nehemiah, or other writers. A few words of explanation, however, in relation to the number and arrangements of the towers, are demanded first. The hundred and ninety towers assigned to the walls by Josephus, would *seem* to be exclusive of those around that portion of the Temple called Antonia, as well as those on the Gihon Valley wall, and the wall between Ophel and Zion, which in the aggregate form a greater length of fortification than the whole second wall. The *supposition*, however, that these one hundred and ninety towers are to be distributed amongst *all* the walls, greatly relieves the difficulty which has heretofore so distressingly puzzled the "restorers of Jerusalem's paths." For it will be observed that the data given by Josephus, involve quite a serious dilemma. Deducting the forty towers of the second wall (for it is obvious that this wall formed no portion of the circumference of Jerusalem at that time), there remain one hundred and fifty in the outer wall: multiplying this number therefore by two hundred, the number of cubits they were separated (*i. e.* from centre to centre), we have thirty thousand cubits, or about seventy-four stadia—more than twice the alleged compass of the city!! And the difficulty is still increased if we allow a clear interval of two hundred cubits between each tower, instead of reckoning from the centre of one to the centre of the other! Such is the dilemma in relation to the wall, allowing the intervals of the towers to be correctly stated: nor is the dilemma into which the towers are thrown—allowing the extent of the wall to be correctly stated—less harassing. For, dividing thirty-three stadia, its alleged extent, by two hundred cubits, we have only sixty-six towers; not half the requisite number. But serious as the difficulty appears, it is susceptible of satisfactory explanation, when we

* Muri per artem obliqui, aut introrsus sinuati, ut latera oppugnantium ad ictus patescerent. Extrema rupis, abrupta et turres, ubi mons juvisset, in sexaginta pedes: inter deveca, in centenos vincenosque attollebantur.

take into consideration the serrated nature of the walls as described by Tacitus, and extend the second wall, as may be fairly done by the addition of the Gihon Valley wall, which indeed is necessary to effect its completion and junction with the first wall; and regard as a continuation of the third wall so much of the Antonia wall as intervenes between the tower of Antonia and the point of junction between it and the first wall on the eastern declivity of Moriah. The wall dividing Zion and Ophel cannot with propriety be considered as a portion of either the first, second, or third wall of Josephus; though it is undoubtedly a part of the first wall described by Nehemiah. But there is no occasion so to regard it, in order to reconcile the above discrepancy—the considerations already adduced being amply sufficient. And besides all this, it is not at all improbable that instead of "cubits," the word in the original was *feet;* as he sometimes makes use of both measures in his descriptions of places: a suggestion that derives some plausibility from the consideration that towers two hundred *feet* apart would not only be much more conducive to security, but also more in consonance with the practice of that age of the world—many walls having towers only one hundred and fifty feet apart. Before attempting the hypothetical restoration of the walls of Jerusalem, it will be well also to bestow some attention on his account of the site of the city—which is accordingly here inserted for the benefit of the general reader.

"The city of Jerusalem was fortified with three walls, on such parts as were not encompassed with impassable valleys; for in such places it had but one wall. The city was built upon two hills which are opposite to one another, and have a valley to divide them asunder; at which valley the corresponding rows of houses on both hills end. Of these hills, that which contains the upper city is much higher and in length more direct. Accordingly, it was called the "Citadel" by King David; he was the father of that Solomon who built this Temple at the first; but it is by us called the 'Upper Market Place.' But the other hill, which was called

Akra, and sustains the lower city, is of the shape of the moon when she is gibbous; over against this was a third hill, but naturally lower than Akra, and parted formerly from the other by a broad valley. However, in those times when the Asmoneans reigned they filled up that valley with earth, and had a mind to join the city to the Temple. They then took off part of the height of Akra, and reduced it to be of less elevation than it was before, that the Temple might be superior to it. Now, the Valley of the Cheesemongers, as it was called, and was that which we told you distinguished the hill of the upper city from that of the lower, extended as far as Siloam; for that is the name of a fountain which hath sweet water in it, and this in great plenty also. But on the outsides these hills are surrounded by deep valleys, and, by reason of the precipices to them belonging on both sides, they are everywhere impassable.

"Now, of these three walls, the old one was hard to be taken, both by reason of the valleys, and of that hill on which it was built and which was above them. But besides that great advantage as to the place where they were situated, it was also built very strong; because David and Solomon and the following kings were very zealous about this work. Now that wall began on the north at the tower called 'Hippicus,' and extended as far as the 'Xystus,' a place so called, and there joining to the Council House, ended at the west cloister of the Temple. But if we go the other way westward, it began at the same place, and extended through a place called 'Bethso' to the Gate of the Essenes, and after that it went southward, having its bending above the fountain Siloam, where it also bends again towards the east at Solomon's Pool, and reaches as far as a certain place which they called 'Ophlas,' where it was joined to the eastern cloister of the Temple."

"The second wall took its beginning from that gate which they called 'Gennath,' which belonged to the first wall; it only encompassed the northern quarter of the city and reached as far as the Tower Antonia. The beginning of the third wall was as far as the Tower Hippicus, whence it reached as far as the north quarter of the city and the Tower Psephinos, and then was extended till it came over against the monuments of Helena, which Helena was queen of Adiabene, the daughter of Izates: it then extended further to a great length and passed by the sepulchral caverns of the kings, and bent again at the tower of the corner, at the monument which is called 'the Monument of the Fuller,' and joined to the old wall at the valley called the 'Valley Cedron.' It was Agrippa who encompassed the parts added to the old city with this wall, which had been all naked before; for as the city grew more populous it gradually crept beyond its old limits, and those parts of it which stood northward of the Temple and joined that hill to the city, made it considerably larger, and occasioned that hill which is in number the fourth, and is called 'Bezetha,' to be inhabited also. It is over against the Tower Antonia, but is divided from it by a deep valley which was dug on purpose, and that in order to hinder the foundations of the Tower of Antonia from joining to this hill, and thereby affording an opportunity for getting to it with ease, and hindering the security that arose from its superior elevation; for which reason also that depth of the ditch made the elevation of the towers more remarkable. This new built part of the city was called 'Bezetha' in our language, which, if interpreted in the Grecian language, may be called the 'New City.' Since, therefore, its inhabitants stood in need of a covering, the father of the present king, and of the same name with him, Agrippa, began that wall we spoke of; but he left off building it when he had only laid the foundation, out of the fear he was in of Claudius Cæsar lest he should suspect that so strong a wall was built in order to make some innovation in public affairs; for the city could no way have been taken if that wall had been finished in the manner it was begun; as its parts were connected together by stones twenty cubits long and ten cubits broad, which could never have been either easily undermined by any iron tools or shaken by any engines. The wall was, however, ten cubits wide, and it would probably have had a height greater than that, had not his zeal who began it been hindered from exerting itself. After this it was erected with great diligence by the Jews as high as twenty cubits, above which it had battlements of two cubits, and turrets of three cubits altitude, insomuch that the entire altitude extended as far as twenty-five cubits." (W. v. iv: 1, 2).

Having thus briefly described the various quarters of the city, he speaks of the walls and fortifications as follows:—"Now the towers that were upon it were twenty cubits in breadth and twenty cubits in height; they were square and solid, as was the wall itself, wherein the niceness of the joints and the beauty of the stones were no way inferior to those of the Holy House itself. Above this solid altitude of the towers, which was twenty cubits, there were rooms of great magnificence; and over them upper rooms and cisterns to receive rain-water. They were many in number, and the steps by which you ascended up to them were every one broad; of these towers, then, the third wall had ninety, and the spaces between them were each two hundred cubits; but in the middle wall were forty* towers, and the old wall was parted into sixty, while the whole compass of the city was thirty-three furlongs."

THE TRENCH, OR WALL OF CIRCUMVALLATION.—Titus, provoked by the stubborn resistance of the Jews, who not only pertinaciously rejected all his overtures of mercy, but studiously defied and insulted him, decided at last, in a council of war, to encircle the whole city with an intrenchment, not only to prevent their escape, but cut off all supplies, and enhance his renown by a speedy capture of the city. This infatuated people had now filled up the measure of their sins; and the time had at length arrived when they were fearfully to realize the literal fulfilment of the awful doom denounced against them by the Son of Man thirty years before, as, weeping, he gazed upon the devoted city from the heights of Olivet; "Saying, If thou hadst known, even thou, at least in this thy day, the things that

* In the only copy I have had an opportunity of consulting in the original—that according to Havercamp and Hudson—the number of towers in the second wall is set down at *fourteen*—*τεσσαρεσκαιδεκα*—instead of forty—and in the Latin version it is XIV also.

belong unto thy peace! but now they are hid from thine eyes. For the days shall come upon thee, that thine enemies shall cast a trench about thee, and compass thee round, and keep thee in on every side, and shall lay thee even with the ground, and thy children within thee; and they shall not leave in thee one stone upon another; because thou knewest not the time of thy visitation." (Luke xix. 42–44.)

All we know about the location and structure of this extensive rampart, we learn from the account given us by Josephus in the 1st and 2d sections of the 12th chapter of his 5th book of the Wars of the Jews—the descriptive portion of which is here inserted:—"Titus began the wall from the "camp of the Assyrians," where his own camp was pitched, and drew it down to the lower parts of Cœnopolis; thence it went along the Valley of Cedron to the Mount of Olives: it then bent towards the south, and encompassed the mountain as far as the rock called Peristereon, and that other hill which lies next it, and is over the valley which reaches to Siloam: whence it bended again to the west, and went down to the Valley of the Fountain, beyond which it went up again at the Monument of Ananus the high priest, and, encompassing that mountain where Pompey had formerly pitched his camp, it returned back to the north side of the city, and was carried on as far as a certain village called 'The House of the Erebinthi;' after which it encompassed Herod's Monument, and there on the east was joined to Titus's own camp where it began. Now the length of this wall was forty furlongs, one only abated. Now on this wall without were erected thirteen places to keep garrisons in, the circumference of which put together amounted to ten furlongs: the whole was completed in three days; so that what would naturally have required some months, was done in so short an interval as is incredible. When Titus had therefore encompassed the city with this wall, and put garrisons in proper places, he went round the wall at the first watch of the night, and observed how the guard was kept; the second watch he allotted to Alexander; the commanders of legions took the third watch. They also cast lots among themselves who should be upon the watch in the night-time, and who should go all night long round the spaces that were interposed between the garrisons."

Topographers have differed widely in their location of this trench—as well they might, without an intimate acquaintance with the environs of Jerusalem. To mark out on paper a line of intrenchment thirty-nine stadia in length, is indeed such a very easy matter that it may be effected in the study, to the entire satisfaction of the designer and the general reader; but to adapt it to the actual state of the localities and all the requirements and conditions of the case, is quite a different thing, and can only be accomplished by oft-repeated personal examination of the ground. Such a critical inspection alone can solve the problem—which must puzzle every careful reader of Josephus—how it was possible, even with all the disposable force of the Roman army, to construct such a fortification in the brief space of three days, by exposing to view the great extent of ground along the general direction indicated that was already sufficiently fortified by nature. So extensive indeed are the cliffs and projecting ledges of rock on the naturally terraced slopes of the "mountains round about Jerusalem," along that line, that to connect them by raising a wall and digging a trench in the intermediate space, not thus fortified by the hand of nature, was a work that could easily be accomplished in three days. The circumvallation through Cœnopolis could very speedily be effected by reserving certain rows of houses and filling them with the stones of the neighboring houses, blocking up the openings left by cross streets, and thus constructing a continuous wall. The position occupied by the Assyrian camp—whence the wall of circumvallation started—is a subject that has been much controverted; but if pitched upon the most eligible location, according to the principles of ancient castrametation, it would undoubtedly be placed upon the broad ridge or expansion north-west of the city, whence, too, it would not only entirely quadrate with the other points, but also best derive a supply of water—a very material consideration, certainly. In its course hence down to "the *lower parts of Cœnopolis,*" on the western side of Kedron, it would no doubt embrace in its track that rocky knoll, about three hundred yards north-west of Damascus Gate, as a natural fortress for a garrison; and also take advantage of the precipitous southern face of Turbet es-Zahara as a portion of its line of defence, whose summit would also form an excellent site for another garrison. Thence to Mount Olivet, the map exhibits it located to the best advantage, according to the configuration of the ground and rocks. The summit of Olivet, where the tenth legion had first encamped just in front of the ruins of Viri Galilæi, would doubtless be too distant to fall within the line of operations; and, besides, the ledges of rock far below it are so much more easily fortified than the smooth rockless surface above, that the rampart would no doubt be constructed there. It next passed by the Peristereon, which the Rabbins affirm was a building for the sale of doves, but it is generally supposed to have been a place fancifully so called from a remote resemblance to a dove-cote. The present village of Silwan is beyond doubt the true representative of *Peristereon*, and not the tombs of the prophets, as contended by some. The rock cliff thus styled may not improbably have been so called on account of its fancied resemblance to a dove-cote (the literal meaning of the term), the numerous doorways to the sepulchres with which it was pierced giving it that appearance. The term "*rock*" is here used by the historian as the equivalent of "*another hill,*" and therefore implies far too large a mass to be mistaken for the small projecting rock at the tombs of the prophets, or any others whatever on Mount Olivet except this.

"*The Other Hill*" alluded to is, of course, the contiguous one just south of Peristereon, overhanging the Kedron Valley at Siloam. Both of these hills were, no doubt, well garrisoned. In looking down into the bottom of the reputed Aceldama, we see all that now remains of the *Monument of Ananus or Ananias*—according to the very plausible conjecture of Dr. Schultz. *The mountain where Pompey had formerly pitched his camp* can well be no other than the Hill of Evil Council, on whose mount a garrison was certainly placed. THE HOUSE OF EREBINTHUS, or Chick-pea village, is located somewhat conjecturally at a very fitting place; but if not occupying the precise spot, it certainly cannot be much misplaced. The wall of circumvallation, if located to best advantage, must needs pass by the camp occupied by Titus opposite Hippicus (the present Greek convent of St. George), and, of course, this valuable station would be well garrisoned.

HEROD'S MONUMENT may either have been situated immediately beside the pool on its western extremity, or upon a slight eminence (Charnel House of the Lion), west of the so called Upper Pool of Gihon, whence, in all probability, the wall of circumvallation ran directly east to the camp of Titus, where it commenced. The entire circuit of intrenchment thus indicated on the map is just about thirty-nine stadia in extent, and seems to fulfil all the conditions of the case.

POPULATION OF THE CITY AT THE TIME OF ITS SUBVERSION.—It would seem from the statements of Josephus, that about 2,000,000 Jews either perished or were captured during the siege of Jerusalem; and on account of this supposed exaggerated estimate of the population of the city, the great historian has been attacked most virulently. But it seems to be forgotten that he by no means assigns this as the *regular* population of the city; but expressly includes in this number the multitudes that came up to the Feast of Unleavened Bread, and were enclosed within its walls, when the threatened day of national retribution came upon them unawares—for as a snare the Roman army spread its meshes, and came upon them that dwelt upon all the face of the land. (Luke xxi. 34, 35.) The number in attendance at the passover, as officially reported on a former occasion, was more than 2,500,000, and at another time 3,000,000. The regular and constant population of the city, about three centuries before Christ, was computed at only 120,000 by Hecateus, according to Eusebius. But after its enlargement by Agrippa, Tacitus computes it at 600,000. Now, if it be borne in mind that every householder was expected to entertain many guests at least three times a year, and that their tenements were probably built in special reference to such accommodation of those that came up to the festivals, there will be no great difficulty in believing that this immense crowd could be *temporarily* lodged, if not comfortably and permanently accommodated. It is true that the area of the city, even according to the extended limits that I assign it, would by no means be adequate to their comfortable accommodation, if we suppose them all to be stowed away on the ground floor; but why need we restrict their lodgment to one or two, or even three stories? The area of the city under its greatest extension did not contain more than 2,500,000 square yards of surface; which, deducting the space occupied by walls, would allow but little more than nine square feet for each person—rather close packing, it is true; but if distributed through several stories, would be very tolerable during a festival week, when so much of the time would be spent on foot. There are many houses on Mount Zion at this time as much crowded as Josephus has represented them during the siege; and any one who has spent a night in the Church of the Holy Sepulchre during the Easter festivities, has seen them packed away at the rate of eight or nine feet to the individual, or less, for twenty-four hours successively—eating, sleeping, worshipping, carousing, &c.

The polished Occidental, with his refined views and feelings, can form no adequate idea of the unceremonious way in which the Orientals live, in consequence of their disregard of the refinements, conventional arrangements, and comforts of civilized society in other more enlightened parts of the world. It is alleged by some very credible writers, that the great inequality of surface in the city would sufficiently account for this teeming population. It is contended on the other hand, however, that the accommodations would not thereby be increased, inasmuch as no more houses can be built in a city intersected with hills and valleys than if it were a plain surface. But, while it is literally true that no more houses could be constructed in the one case than in the other, yet it must be admitted, that a city on hillsides can be made to contain more inhabitants than if its site were a plain; for in the former case, regular ground streets may be dispensed with almost entirely—the tops of each range of lower houses serving as a street in front of the houses above, as in the case of Safet, and many other towns in Palestine, at the present day. The increased ventilation and light thus enjoyed would also render it much more agreeable and healthy.

It will be remembered by the Bible reader that the Passover—the feast upon which the Jews were attending when shut up by Titus—was one of the great assemblies of the nation, at which every male in Israel was enjoined to be in attendance, and for the entertainment of these hosts of Israel, the house-tops, courts, and all other available spaces, were tented, and put in requisition. Nor must it be forgotten that "Jerusalem was builded as a city that is compacted together." All things being fairly considered, there would appear, therefore, no just grounds for the charge of exaggeration brought against Josephus, in reference to his statement of the numbers besieged in Jerusalem.

CHAPTER VI.

TOWERS, GATES, ETC.

"Tell the towers thereof"—"Go through—go through the gates."

Most of these structures having been already satisfactorily located in considering the account given by Nehemiah, the task of locating the remainder mentioned by Josephus and others is greatly facilitated. Some have been already sufficiently described, while a full account of others will be reserved for a more appropriate place.

Hippicus.—In walking about Zion and going round about her, to "mark her bulwarks, tell her towers, and consider her palaces," we commence, like Josephus and Nehemiah, at the Tower of Hippicus; which is not only in a better state of preservation than any of the rest, but is at once the most celebrated in history and the most important in topography. And, though the position of this renowned tower has been much disputed, there can be no reasonable doubt but that the largest of the towers in the present City Castle, near the Jaffa Gate, generally styled the "Tower of David," is (in part at least) the far-famed Hippic Tower. Time and the elements—and the still greater destroyer, man—have shorn it of half its height—the ancient portion now remaining being only about forty feet high—which being entirely solid, without the least vacuity, has bid defiance alike to battering-ram, cannon-balls, prying curiosity, and the elements, for nineteen long centuries. But though it answers so well in many respects to the description given by Josephus, yet its dimensions (fifty-six by seventy feet) are considerably greater than those of Josephus—twenty-five cubits square—which, reduced to feet by the ordinary metrical standard, would be about thirty-eight by thirty-eight; but it must be remembered that absolute accuracy is scarcely to be expected under the circumstances amidst which Josephus wrote his work—for it is very probable that in many unimportant matters he depended entirely upon his recollection. The stones composing it are scarcely half as large as those of the Temple wall; and though they are rebated in the characteristic style of Jewish architecture, yet their faces are not reduced to a plain smooth surface, like those in the Temple and city wall, but are very protuberant and rough. The additional height of fifteen or twenty feet is constructed of much smaller stones, and is no doubt the work of the Crusaders. Josephus, in giving an account of the structures of King Herod, after describing the Psephine Tower, thus speaks of this structure:—"Over against it was the Tower Hippicus; and hard by, two others were erected by King Herod in the old wall. These were, for largeness, beauty, and strength, beyond all that were in the habitable earth; for, besides the magnanimity of his nature, and his magnificence towards the city on other occasions, he built these after such an extraordinary manner, to gratify his own private affections, and dedicated these towers to the memory of those three persons who had been dearest to him, and from whom he named them. They were his brother, his friend, and his wife. The wife he had slain out of his love (and jealousy), as we have already related; the other two he lost in war as they were courageously fighting. Hippicus—so named from his friend—was square; its length and breadth were each twenty-five cubits, and its height thirty, and it had no vacuity in it. Over this solid building, which was composed of great stones united together, there was a reservoir twenty cubits deep, over which there was a house of two stories, whose height was twenty-five cubits, and divided into several parts; over which were battlements of two cubits, and turrets all around of three cubits high, insomuch that the entire height added together amounted to fourscore cubits." (W. v. iv: 3.) This fortress is sometimes, but without the least propriety, called the "Tower of David"—for that structure, mention of which is made in that inimitable Song of Songs (Canticles iv. 4), is undoubtedly the Armory on the opposite side of Zion.

THE VALLEY GATE—where Nehemiah commenced his nocturnal exploration. There is scarcely a valley about the Holy City in which this gate has not been located by different topographers, and made to quadrate with their peculiar theories; yet most evident is it that it occupied a position between the Tower of Furnaces and the Esquiline Gate, a thousand cubits north of the latter—somewhere quite near the present Jaffa Gate; but may have been subsequently absorbed in the fortifications of the Tower of Hippicus. (2 Chr. xxvi. 9; Neh. ii. 13, 15, and iii. 13.)

THE DRAGON'S WELL OR FOUNTAIN was probably situated on the opposite side of the Hinnom. (See article on *Waters of Jerusalem.*) (Neh. ii. 13, and iii. 13.)

DUNG GATE.—At the distance of one thousand cubits south of Hippicus, was the Dung Port of Nehemiah, overhanging Hinnom; and between Herod's Palace and this gate was BETHZO, a place of which we know nothing further than its mere name, which seems to be indicative of its esquiline character. (W. v. iv: 2.)

GATE OF THE ESSENES.—Next in order came the gate of this ancient sect, which I locate at a slight depression in the Hill of Zion, where the present road from Neby Daoûd enters Hinnom. The Esquiline Gate must have been very inaccessible, as well as otherwise inappropriately situated just over the large Pool es-Sultan, unless approached by a mere foot-path; but Zion was very accessible from this gate. There is no other portal mentioned between this and the "Gate of the Fountain," unless the East or Sun Gate may have been situated there; nor is there any special occasion for any—there being no spot where Zion could be ascended in all this quarter—except near the fountain. (W. v. iv: 2.)

THE TOWER OF SILOAM, of which mention is made in Luke xiii. 4, was probably situated near the south-west corner of the lower Pool of Siloam, at the south-east point of Zion, just at the "Tree of Isaiah;" and if the Jews were in the habit of lounging about that delightful spot as the Arabs now are, no surprise is to be felt at the number crushed to death—"those eighteen on whom the tower fell and slew them."

THE EAST GATE OR SUN GATE was either the GATE OF THE FOUNTAIN leading from Zion directly to the lower Pool of Siloam (Skin Pool, now a garden and figyard), facing the east; or it gave exit directly from Zion to Hinnom or Tophet, where the brazen idol of Moloch or Baal was worshipped—from which fact, perhaps, it was called Sun Gate after Baal, as the Temple of Baal at Balbec is also called Heliopolis or Temple of the Sun. (Jer. xix. 2.) The East Gate, mentioned Neh. iii. 29, and 1 Chr. xxvi. 14, is the Shusan Gate of the Temple wall—with which this structure must not be confounded.

THE STAIRS OF DAVID were in the immediate vicinity of the Fountain Gate, occupying probably the same site now descended by a flight cut in the native rock. (Neh. iii. 15, and xii. 37.)

INTERMEDIATE GATE, or gate betwixt the two walls by the King's Gardens. The point at which the Tyropœon enters the Kedron was much the lowest in all the course of the wall, and hence it was deemed necessary to fortify it, both by stone and water, in the manner represented on the map. This gate seems to have been in the short wall connecting Ophel with Zion, built probably upon the broad foundation of the lower side of the pool. "Here it was that Zedekiah the king of Judah and all the men of war fled and went forth out of the city by night, by the way of the King's Garden, by the gate betwixt the two walls," "when they saw Nergal-Sharezer, Shamgar-Nebo, Sarsechim, Rabsaris, Rabmag, with all the residue of the princes of the king of Babylon, come in and sit in the middle gate of the city." (2 Kings xxv. 4; Jer. xxxix. 3, 4, and lii. 7.)

THE HOUSE OF DAVID doubtless spanned the Tyropœon at this

point, and was probably a stoa surrounding, or at least connected with, the pool. (Neh. xii. 37.)

KING'S POOL, as Nehemiah (or SOLOMON'S POOL, as Josephus,) calls it, is generally supposed to be the Fount of the Virgin, which lies three or four hundred yards above Siloam; but this small intermitting subterranean fountain conveys so poor an idea of a *royal pool*, that I have no hesitation in discarding such a view, and locating this pool about midway between Siloam and the Virgin's Fount, in a very suitable spot for the construction of a large reservoir—at the lower end of Siloam village, and just at the head of the King's Gardens—supplied by the Kedron mainly, but doubtless by the Virgin's Fount also, before the subterranean channel was cut, which now conducts its water to Siloam. (Neh. ii. 14; W. v. iv: 2.)

POOL OF SILOAM (see article on *Waters of Jerusalem*) and KING'S GARDENS (see page 92.)

THE TOWER THAT LIETH OUT was probably built over the Virgin's Fount, to render it available to the Jews when besieged by their enemies. A hole in the rocky roof above, through which the water may have been drawn up into the tower, gives some countenance to this idea. Why any out-lying tower here, where the wall perched on so steep a hillside, was so very inaccessible, except for the object indicated? (Neh. iii. 26.)

THE WATER GATE would naturally be situated in the most accessible and available spot, as indicated on the map where there is a curve and concavity in Mount Ophel. The nature of the ground would here require the wall to decline somewhat to the right before passing around to be united to the Temple. There was also another water gate situated within the Temple, on Chel, or the rampart south. (Neh. iii. 26; and viii. 1; and xii. 37.) And also a gate of the same name, through or by which an aqueduct entered the Hippic premises.

THE GREAT TOWER THAT LIETH OUT may well have occupied the large rock eighty or ninety yards south of the south-east corner of the Temple, that still juts out prominently. (Neh. iii. 27.) Or was it the *Tower* of Ophel?

THE HORSE GATE was situated in the vicinity of the Hippodrome, which evidently occupied a spot near the south-east corner of the Temple wall. In accordance with the indications contained in the 4th verse of the 31st chapter of Jeremiah, Nehemiah locates this gate in the Valley of the Kedron, in the corner of the wall on the east. Some have located it in the Xystus, and others on Mount Zion—than which, more inappropriate places could scarcely be found; while here, at this corner, it is at once naturally and conveniently situated at an unfrequented place, close to the Hippodrome, convenient to fresh water, and near the cattle quarter—a most appropriate locality, certainly. It was through this gate that the wicked, usurping Queen Athaliah was led forth to be executed. (2 Kings xi. 16–19; 2 Chr. xxiii. 15; Neh. iii. 28; Jer. xxxi. 40.) Next in order

OPHLAS, or the Tower of Ophel, which was unquestionably situated in the quarter immediately east of the Temple, was probably a very large and strong fortress, built apparently in protection of the immense sacrificial sheep-cote in connexion with it. (Jos. W. v. iv: 2—vi. vi: 3; 2 Chr. xxxiii. 14; Neh. iii. 27.) Micah evidently apostrophizes it under the name of "TOWER OF THE FLOCK." (iv. 8.)

THE SHEEP GATE, as we would naturally conclude, was situated near the Temple, and as is implied in its name, was designed rather for the admission of sheep into their particular quarter, than that of persons into the city. (See *Sheep Quarter*.) (Neh. iii. 1, 6, 12; xii. 39; John v. 2.)

THE TOWER OF MEAH seems to have been erected on the slope of Moriah, where the wall turned at right angles to join the Temple, and was probably built, like the Tower of Ophel, in defence of the cattle market. (Neh. iii. 1, and xii. 39.) Was Meah a lofty watch-tower—a hundred cubits high—as its name may be supposed to import?

THE TOWER OF HANANEEL was a famous land-mark, and evidently located at one extreme of the city, prior to its enlargement by

Agrippa. The position assigned it not only fulfils this condition, but the defensive demands of the ground in this quarter also: for it was more assailable at this point than anywhere else between Meah and the Fish Gate. Does not the massive structure now forming the north-east corner of the Haram enclosure, stand as the representative of this far-famed tower? (Jer. xxxi. 38; Zech. xiv. 10; Neh. iii. 1, and xii. 39.)

THE FISH GATE is next mentioned; and although it has been so variously and strangely located by different topographers, no doubt can well be entertained as to the correctness of the position assigned to it on the map—near the great "Piscina," or Fish Pool; and hence its name. (2 Chr. xxxiii. 14; Neh. iii. 3; Zeph. i. 10.)

THE GATE OF BENJAMIN is placed next on the list (as it needs must be, if significantly located), and was planted just where the situation of the wall relative to the bulk of the district of Benjamin required its location. A gate of this name is mentioned in the 37th chapter of Jeremiah, 13th verse; but must not be confounded with the Benjamin Gate mentioned Jeremiah xxxviii. 7; that gate being evidently identical with the High Gate of Benjamin, at the Zion extremity of the great bridge. It was out of this gate that Jeremiah was passing, directly on his way to Anathoth, when Irijah, the son of Shelemiah, took Jeremiah the prophet, saying, "Thou fallest away to the Chaldeans."

THE OLD GATE undoubtedly occupied the site of the Damascus Gate, very considerable and interesting remains of which are still to be seen in the towers on either side of it. An inspection of the plan and perspective view of the ancient remains on the east side of the Damascus Gate (page 132), though somewhat patched up by modern additions, will give the reader the best idea anywhere to be had of ancient Jewish tower and stairway. Between this gate and the Gate of Ephraim is the judgment hall of the Persian Satrapy of Judea, called

THE THRONE OF THE GOVERNOR—Neh. iii. 6, 7, and xii. 39—no remains or special indications of which, however, now exist.

THE GATE OF EPHRAIM, like that of Benjamin, is most appropriately indicated by the narrative of dedication, just at that portion of the wall that faces the canton of the tribe. (2 Kings xiv. 13; Neh. xii. 39.)

THE BROAD WALL is no doubt the doubly built four hundred cubits which Joash broke down from the Gate of Ephraim to the Corner Gate—at the northern extremity of which was the Gate of Ephraim, and at the southern the CORNER GATE. (Neh. iii. 8, and xii. 38.)

THE CORNER GATE OR "GATE THAT LOOKETH" (in the margin).—We would naturally look for this structure at the north-west corner of the city; but it would rather seem to be situated about midway between that corner and the general cornering point near Hippicus, at the most indefensible part of the wall—just the position indicated by the two only references made to it, and required by the nature of the ground. The term, however, is sometimes used in a general sense to indicate *any* gate at or near a corner.

THE TOWER OF FURNACES.—From the Corner Gate the wall ran nearly south until it united with that coming from the Temple (the "First Wall" of Josephus), when it bent at right angles and ran west to the point whence we started. This latter wall is "the other piece" in which the Tower of Furnaces was situated—being at the west end of it. (Neh. iii. 11, and xii. 38.)

THE FIRST GATE.—It would appear from analogy that this gate was situated in the "First Wall" somewhere near the present Jaffa Gate—the general topographical starting-point—but was afterwards closed; and hence the expression "*place* of the first gate." It was undoubtedly near "a turning of the wall," if not close to *the* Corner Gate. No definite conclusion is warranted by its mention, Zechariah xiv. 10—the only place where it occurs; and although the Old Gate may be thought as well entitled to the appellation as any other, from its undoubted claim to the highest antiquity, yet it is called *first* in respect to importance rather than *first* in order of erection or numerical enumeration; and the sense of the passage evidently requires that it should exist in a portion of the city wall opposite the well ascertained site of Benjamin's Gate. It would seem from the 47th verse of the 5th chapter of 1st Esdras that there was also a "first gate" of the Temple; but whether it was the outer gate, afterwards called Shusan, or the inner one, subsequently known as "the Beautiful Gate," does not distinctly appear. It must be borne in mind that Jerusalem was in ruins at the time Zechariah made mention of this gate.

THE SEPULCHRES OF DAVID.—There is an admirable situation for rock sepulchres about midway the eastern semilunar, sloping curve of Mount Zion, between Siloam and the great bridge; and it is apparently just here that Nehemiah assigns the royal sepulchres a place. (Neh. iii. 16.) That tradition has egregiously misplaced the "Tomb of David," is too obvious to need demonstration. (See article "*Neby Daûd.*")

"THE POOL THAT WAS MADE" may well have occupied any part of the Tyropœon Valley: but it is probable that the one here alluded to was situated rather nearer the Temple than the royal sepulchres were. This is probably the "old pool" (Is. xxii. 11), whose waters serving a much better purpose as a defence in the ditch between the two walls were sent there, and the pool that was made was suffered to fill up.

THE HOUSE OF THE MIGHTY was no doubt situated on the brow on Zion, at the west end of the bridge; and separated from the palace only by a broad street or open space. It is the same building elsewhere called the *guard chamber*, because perhaps the head-quarters of the Cherethites, Pelethites, and others composing the royal body guard were here lodged. (Neh. iii. 16; 2 Chr. xii. 10, 11; 2 Kings xi. 19.)

THE ARMORY, OR HOUSE OF THE FOREST OF LEBANON, called so doubtless from the immense number of spears, bows and arrows, balista, battering rams, &c., stored away in this great military magazine, was situated in the north-east corner of Mount Zion, at the turning of the wall, immediately above the north-west corner of the Xystus—having the palace of the king on the south, and the palace of the high priest on the west. (1 Kings x. 17; Neh. iii. 19; Is. xxii. 8.)

THE HOUSE OF ELIASHIB THE HIGH PRIEST was undoubtedly between the Armory and Millo; and identical with the *palace of the high priest* mentioned by Josephus and the Evangelists on the northern slope of Zion, (see page 82.) (Neh. iii. 20.)

THE KING'S HIGH HOUSE, by the court of the prison, was a very lofty watch-tower west of his palace, near to which was an isolated tower—not in connexion with the wall. (Neh. iii. 25.)

THE PRISON seems to have been on the royal premises west of the palace. (Neh. iii. 25; Jer. xxxii. 2, 12; xxxvii. 21.) But the *Scribes' House* was also used as a prison. (Jer. xxxvii. 15.)

THE COMMON PRISON, if on the royal premises, was, probably, not so well furnished as that designed for state prisoners, and differed from it merely in this respect: but nothing is certainly known in relation to its position. (Acts v. 18, 19; xii. 4, 5, 7, 17.)

PRISON GATE.—Besides the ordinary gate of the prison, there was also a gate of that name in the Temple (Neh. xii. 39, 40), and was identical, no doubt, with the gate *Shallecheth*, which seems to have been provided with stocks for the security, if not for the punishment, of prisoners.

MIPH-KAD GATE—*judgment—correction;* identical with the High Gate of Benjamin, where there were stocks, either for the correction or detention of prisoners—hence the name. (Neh. iii. 6; Jer. xx. 2.) It was situated at the west end of the Tyropœon Bridge—the great "Causey."

THE SCRIBES' CHAMBER was in the King's House. (Jer. xxxvi. 12.) This office pertained only to the royal household; and must not be confounded with the "Repository of Archives," in or near Parbar—the outer place of the Temple.

SECOND GATE.—A gate in the upper part of Gihon Valley wall seems to be indicated by the prophet: * * * "The noise of a cry from the Fish Gate, and an howling from the 'second,' * * * howl, ye inhabitants of Maktesh, for all the merchant people are cut down, and all that bear silver are cut off." (Zeph. i. 10.) If this language indicate the existence of a gate called "second," it was probably that near the Fish Gate, giving entrance into the second part of the city. *Maktesh,* if its etymology be significant, would point to the Tyropœon, in the neighborhood of the Temple, occupied by the merchants, goldsmiths, moneyers, &c., where the Mint was also probably situated. The Talmud also mentions a second or "*Bird Gate,*" but does not locate it. Was it so called because the birds required under the Jewish ritual were there kept for sale?

We have thus completed the tour of all the outer walls of the city, as they stood prior to the addition of the third wall by Agrippa, A. D. 40. But before considering the structures in this latter wall, it will be well to notice the towers and gates of the wall along the Gihon Valley and lower Tyropœon, as well as those that Josephus describes on the line of the "First Wall." Those of the Gihon Valley and lower Tyropœon wall being elsewhere described, need here only be enumerated in their associated position. Commencing below, they are as follows:—The Tower of Siloam, Gate of the Fountain, Stairs of the City of David, House of the Mighty, Gate of the Bridge, Palace and Xystus, Armory and Gate in the upper part of the Gihon Valley wall. There were doubtless several gates and towers in the Gihon Valley wall between the Armory and the gate near Antonia.

TOWERS ON THE "FIRST WALL," OR "OLD WALL."

Hard by the *Tower of Hippicus* (which was not in actual contact with the wall, as might be inferred from one or two passages, but some distance south of it), Josephus informs us that two others were erected—"The second tower which he named from his brother, *Phasaelus,* had its breadth and its height, equal each of them forty cubits; over which was its solid height of forty cubits, over which a cloister went round about, whose height was ten cubits, and it was covered from enemies by breastworks and bulwarks. There was also built over that cloister another tower, parted into magnificent rooms, and a place for bathing; so that this tower wanted nothing that might make it appear to be a royal palace. It was also adorned with turrets and battlements, more than was the foregoing, and the entire altitude was about ninety cubits; the appearance of it resembled the tower of Pharos, which exhibited a fire to such as sailed to Alexandria, but was much larger than it in compass. This was now converted into a house wherein Simon executed his tyrannical authority. The third tower was MARIAMNE, for that was his queen's name. It was solid as high as twenty cubits; its breadth and its length were twenty cubits, and were equal to each other; its upper buildings were more magnificent, and had greater variety than the other towers had; for the king thought it most proper for him to adorn that which was denominated from his wife better than those denominated from men, as those were built stronger than this last that bore his wife's name. The entire length of this tower was fifty cubits. Now, as these towers were so very tall, they appeared much taller by the place on which they stood: for that very old wall wherein they were, was built on a high hill, and was itself a kind of elevation that was still thirty cubits taller; over which were the towers situated, and thereby were made much higher to appearance. The largeness also of the stones was wonderful, for they were not made of common small stones, nor of such large ones as men could carry, but they were made of white marble, cut out of the rock; each stone was twenty cubits in length, and ten in breadth, and five in depth. They were so exactly united to one another, that each tower looked like one entire rock of stone, so growing naturally, and afterwards cut by the hand of artificers into their present shape and corners; so little or not at all did their joints or connexion appear." (W. v. iv: 3.)

THE TOWER OF MARIAMNE was probably situated a short distance west of the depression in Mount Zion, which is still visible, though greatly filled up at or near Millo; and PHASAELUS was probably at or near the junction of the first and second walls, near the Gate

Gennath, where the Tyropœon must have been quite shallow, and the wall must have required very strong fortifications.

GENNATH GATE.—Only one gate of the first or old wall is specially mentioned—the Gate of Gardens, as the name imports. It is generally supposed to be so called because it led to gardens close at hand; but, inasmuch as Jerusalem was surrounded with gardens, this designation is not sufficiently distinctive; and, besides, the immediate environs in this quarter were occupied by houses, as we learn from Josephus. Was it not rather so called because it opened into the public pleasure garden attached to Herod's Palace? All we know of it is from the following words of Josephus:—"The second wall took its beginning from that gate which they call Gennath, which belonged to the first wall." The nature of the ground and the circumstances of the case equally require its location just at the spot assigned it on the map. There was, of course, another gate in the "old wall" where it crossed the Tyropœon opening to the Xystus, and one at Millo where Mount Zion was accessible through the Valley of Zion; but so very inaccessible must the wall have been along the intervening spaces, that the erection of other gates would have been useless—and hence the necessity for the great Templo-Zion Bridge. The gate mentioned by Josephus as that through which water was brought into the Hippic Tower is evidently the Gennath. (W. v. iv: 2.)

TOWERS, GATES, ETC., IN THE THIRD WALL.

The buildings of the "Second Wall" having been already considered, (pp. 131–134) those of the "Third Wall" will now come under review.

In the 5th book, 4th chapter, and 3d section of the Wars of the Jews, Josephus thus describes the

TOWER OF PSEPHINOS.—"Now, the third wall was all of it wonderful; yet was the Tower Psephinos elevated above it at the northwest corner, and there Titus pitched his own tent; for, being seventy cubits high, it both afforded a prospect of Arabia at sun-rising, as it did of the utmost limits of the Hebrew possessions at the sea westward. Moreover, it was an octagon." (W. v. iv: 3.) The spot upon which Psephinos stood was only a few feet higher than the site of the Church of Ascension, from the rear of which the Dead Sea is visible; and as the Mediterranean can be seen from the hills around Neby Samuel, which is only forty or fifty feet higher than the site of Psephinos, it is not at all improbable that this is the sea alluded to, and not the Dead Sea, as supposed by some authors; for Mount Olivet would entirely exclude the view of that depressed sheet of water. There are strong indications of the ancient wall nearly all the way to the site of the Psephinos Tower.

THE TOWER OF THE CORNER.—Although there are no reliable remains to indicate the spot, yet, with Josephus in hand and the localities before the eye, no great error can well be committed in locating this tower, as is done on the map, at the spot where the nature of the ground requires that the wall should bend almost at right angles. "The Monument of the Fuller" would, of course, fall a short distance within this angle of the wall. This view receives some confirmation by the vicinity of the royal sepulchres—"sepulchral caverns of the kings"—(Tombs of the Kings) to the wall, seventy or eighty yards to the north of which, the wall passes on upon an eligible site. (W. v. iv: 2.)

THE WOMEN'S TOWERS would, of course, fall somewhere between Psephinos and the Fuller's Monument. If Titus approached the city by the road now generally travelled from Gabaath Saul (Gibeah of Saul), supposing the present Tel el-Ful to be the capital of Saul's dominions, then they were situated somewhere near the Tombs of the Kings. But if the road leading at that time from Gabaath (as it probably did) approached the wall where the road from Beit Hannina now enters, (*i. e.* through the ash-mound Tel el-Massabin)—for Titus seems to have approached the wall somewhat at right angles, as that road now does, and not obliquely like the other—then the Women's Towers were situated much further south-west, probably on the scarped rock covered by the ashes—certainly near this spot. Excavations made in this ash-mound would, no doubt, reveal two rock eminences through which the road now passes—on which towers could be so securely built and easily defended as to justify the appellation of *Women's* Towers. *Helena's Tomb* was opposite the Women's Towers; and if the latter is correctly located, they would, probably, be some distance off, as is strongly implied. (W. v. iii: 3).

Of the ninety towers and numerous gates of this extensive wall, these are all that are designated by name. But it may be well, in this connexion, to bring under consideration such gates, towers, and other mural structures not elsewhere described, as are incidentally mentioned in the Sacred Scriptures or the writings of Josephus and the Talmudists.

GATES IN OTHER WALLS.

THE GATE OF THE FOUNDATION was unquestionably the same as the High Gate of Benjamin at the western end of the bridge (2 Chr. xxiii. 5), and was so called because it was built upon the massive foundations constituting the abutments of the west end of the Tyropœon Bridge.

THE GATE OF SUR (*withdrawing*) would appear to be the gate entering the court of the palace. (2 Kings xi. 6.)

GATE OF THE GUARD—seems to be used synonymously with the Gate of the Foundation; but was most probably a gate leading into the court of the Guard Chamber, or House of the Mighty. It was certainly somewhere near, or directly at the west end of the bridge. (2 Kings xi. 6, 19, and 2 Chr. xxiii. 5.)

GATE OF BENJAMIN, by the palace, or more distinctively—

HIGH GATE OF BENJAMIN—is different from Benjamin Gate mentioned Zech., xiv. 10, Jer. xxxvii. 13, and xxxviii. 7—the latter being a gate in the outer wall of the city, and the former at the west end of the Temple Bridge, "by the House of the Lord." There were stocks in this gate; and it was therefore a kind of prison, and called Miph-kad, or Judgment Gate. (2 Chr. xxiii. 20, and xxvii. 3; Jer. xx. 2.) It was situated at the Zion end of the great bridge. King Zedekiah was sitting here in judgment when the kind-hearted Ebed-Melech, the Ethiopian, interceded in behalf of Jeremiah, who had been cast into a dungeon beneath the royal treasury of the palace. (Jer. xxxviii. 7–13.)

THE GATE SHALLECHETH was at the east end of the Tyropœon Bridge, being the entrance to the great Stoa Basilica of the Temple; whilst Miph-kad, at the other extremity, gave admittance to the royal premises on Zion.

THE HIGH GATE seems to be used as a mere abbreviation for the High Gate of Benjamin, at the Zion end of the great bridge.

THE HIGH GATE OF THE HOUSE OF THE LORD would appear to be the gate at the east end of the bridge, opposite the High Gate of Benjamin—and was no doubt placed in a tower at the west end of the Stoa Basilica. (2 Chr. xxiii. 20, 27.) It would seem to be identical with the Gate Shallecheth, by the causeway of the going up. (1 Chr. xxvi. 16.) Many of the gates about the Temple seem to have been known under various synonyms.

THE HIGHER GATE OF THE HOUSE OF THE LORD was probably the Gate Nicanor. (2 Kings xv. 35.) The position of this gate—upon the upper terrace—well entitles it to such an appellation.

THE NEW GATE—"The New Gate in the higher court of the Lord's House," is the Gate Nicanor, synonymous, no doubt, with the last mentioned—giving entrance into the Court of Israel from the Court of the Women, or the New Court.

THE GATE OF JOSHUA is only once mentioned (2 Kings xxiii. 8), and then in such a way—though with apparent exactness—that it is impossible to locate it with any certainty whatever.

THE KING'S ENTRY, OR GATE EASTWARD—may either have been the Gate Shushan or that at the west end of the bridge, otherwise called the High Gate of Benjamin. The name was probably applied to both. (1 Chr. ix. 18.)

THE MIDDLE GATE is mentioned Jeremiah xxxix. 3, but not in such a way as to indicate its position. We may suppose, with some degree of certainty, that it was situated in the interior of the city; a fit place would be in the wall running from the "First Wall" to the "Second," dividing Akra from the immediate environs of the Temple. It is evident at least that the defence of the city was considered hopeless after the capture of the wall in which this gate was situated.

CHAPTER VII.

CASTLES, CITADELS, FORTRESSES, PALACES, ETC.

"Consider her palaces."

Fort of Zion.—Besides the large towers already described, there were still more capacious and strongly fortified military structures, styled citadels, forts, palaces, strongholds, &c. All that portion of Mount Zion, wrested from the Jebusites by David, seems at one time to have passed under the name of Fort or Stronghold of Zion (2 Sam. v. 7, 9); but it was no doubt specially applied to the cliffs above the Xystus. This term would seem also to be applied to the rock and fort of Akra, the great Acropolis, afterward so famous in the Syrian wars. (2 Sam. v. 17.) The Cave of Macpelah is also called a stronghold.

The Castle of Zion is also a term used to designate all that portion of the Holy Hill mentioned above and in the parallel passage of Chronicles. (1 Chr. xi. 4, 7.)

"The Tower of David" is but another name for the *Armory*. That it was a tall round structure, is certainly intimated by the following lines from the pen of the "Sweet Singer's" gifted son. "Thy neck is like the tower of David, builded for an armory, whereon they hung a thousand bucklers, all shields of mighty men." (Cant. iv. 4.)

The Citadel is also what Josephus calls this portion of Zion (Ant. vii. iii: 1), but he afterwards appropriates it to Baris in the Lower City, so long held by the Syrians, "which was high and overlooked the city." (Ant. xii. v: 4; and vii. 6; also xiii. v: 11.) And the appellation was not only applied to the fortifications on that celebrated rock, but to all that part of the city—which retained the name long after the castle had been removed, and the very rock upon which it was founded razed to its base by the Jews, "that it might not be any more a place of refuge to their enemies when they took it * * * that so the Temple might be higher than it." (Ant. xiii. vi: 7; and Wars i. i: 4.)

MILLO appears also to have been a military fortification (see article) at the junction of the Tyropœon and Zion valleys.

THE CASTLE, so frequently mentioned or alluded to in the New Testament, is no doubt the Tower of Antonia; the term would, therefore, seem to have been applied at first to a portion of Mount Zion, then to a portion of Akra, and finally was monopolized by the fortress of Moriah. (See ANTONIA, article *Temple.*)

It was in an apartment in this castle, or rather in the palace pertaining to it, called the JUDGMENT HALL, that our adorable Redeemer was so cruelly mocked, scourged, and condemned to death by Pontius Pilate. (John xviii. 28, 33; xix. 3.) And it was from the stairway leading up to this castle from the grand colonnade of Antonia, that Paul delivered that admirable address recorded in the 22d of Acts, when rescued from the infuriated Jews by the chief captain of the Temple. (Acts xxi. 34, 37; xxii. 24; xxiii. 10, 16.) The Pretorium does not appear to be the Judgment Hall, but the Common Hall, another room in the palace whither the Roman soldiers led the Saviour to mock and maltreat him. (Compare Mat. xxvii. 27; and Mark xv. 16.)

Baris was a term applied to the acropolis of Akra. When Simon, the celebrated high priest and general of the Jews, had finally rescued this citadel from the Syrians, he persuaded the citizens of Jerusalem to destroy the citadel together with the rock upon which it was built. Some idea of the extent of this acropolis may be inferred from the fact that its demolition occupied the multitude three whole years, both day and night. The slight elevation in that quarter of Akra where the house of Rabbi Schwartz is situated, not far from the west end of the Cotton Bazaar, may possibly indicate its position.

Baris is also the name of a tower in Ecbatana: it seems to have been a generic term for fortified places; and as such is sometimes employed to designate the Tower of Antonia.

Strato's Tower.—This appellation is best known in history as the original name of Cæsarea Palestina; but it is also the name of a famous tower of the Temple area somewhere between the Holy House and the Tower of Antonia. It was while passing through the dark subterraneous passages of this tower, on his way to pay his respects to King Aristobulus his brother (lying sick in the Tower of Antonia), that Antigonus was unfortunately slain by a cunning and mean device of the queen. (W. i. iii: 1–6; and Ant. xiii. xi: 1–3).

The King's House, or the Royal Palace.—In all Jerusalem there is not a more eligible spot for a palace than the high north-east cliff of Zion nearest the Temple—the site of the American Christian Mission premises—and accordingly it is precisely at this spot that Josephus locates with so much precision the royal residence of the Asmonean and Herodian sovereigns; nor is there the slightest reason to doubt that it was the royal abode of the Davidian dynasty also: indeed, no other locality is at all consistent with the frequent allusions to the "King's House" in the Old Testament. Herod the Great—it is true—that great fortress and palace builder—had *another* palace erected in the west of the city, as he also had at Herodium and various other places. But this seems at all times to have been the fixed official abode of the chief Executive of Israel. We have a brief account of Solomon's palace (which, by way of intimating its magnificence we are told was "thirteen years in building,") in the 7th chapter of the 1st book of the Kings; but Josephus gives a much more detailed account in the following words. "It is necessary that I describe the entire structure and disposition of the parts, that so those that light upon this book may thereby make a conjecture, and, as it were, have a prospect of its magnitude.

"This house was a large and curious building, and was supported by many pillars, which Solomon built to contain a multitude, for hearing causes and taking cognisance of suits. It was sufficiently capacious to contain a great body of men, who could come together to have their causes determined. It was a hundred cubits long, and fifty broad, and thirty high: supported by quadrangular pillars, which were all of cedar; but its roof was according to the Corinthian order, with folding doors, and their adjoining pillars of equal magnitude, each fluted with three cavities: which building was at once firm and very ornamented. There was also another house so ordered, that its entire breadth was placed in the middle; it was quadrangular, and its breadth was thirty cubits, having a temple over against it, raised upon massy pillars; in which temple there was a large and very glorious room, wherein the king sat in judgment. To this was joined another house, that was built for his queen. There were other smaller edifices for diet and for sleep, after public matters were over; and these were all floored with boards of cedar. Some of these Solomon built with stones of ten cubits, and wainscoated the walls with other stones that were sawed, and were of great value, such as are dug out of the earth for the ornaments of temples, and to make fine prospects in royal palaces, and which make the mines whence they are dug famous. Now the contexture of the curious workmanship of these stones was in three rows, but the fourth row would make one admire its sculptures, whereby were represented trees, and all sorts of plants, with the shades that arose from their branches, and leaves that hung down from them. These trees and plants covered the stone that was beneath them, and their leaves were wrought so prodigious thin and subtile, that you would think they were in motion; but the other part, up to the roof, was plastered over, and, as it were, embroidered with colors and pictures. He moreover built other edifices for pleasure; as also very long cloisters, and those situated in an agreeable place of the palace; and among them a most glorious dining-room, for feastings and compotations, and full of gold and such other furniture as so fine a room ought to have for the conveniency of the guests, and when all the vessels were made of gold. Now it is very hard to reckon up the magnitude and the variety of the royal apartments; how many rooms there were of the largest sort, how many of a bigness inferior to those, and how many that were subterraneous and invisible; the curiosity of those that enjoyed the fresh air; and the groves for the most delightful prospect, for the avoiding the heat and covering of their bodies. And to say all in brief, Solomon made the whole building entirely of white stone and cedar wood, and gold and silver." (Ant. viii. v: 2.)

Such was the sumptuous residence of that illustrious king of Israel; and very similar, no doubt, was the palace of the no less splendor-loving Herodian family, situated on the same spot, and thus described by the same author: "King Agrippa built himself a very large dining-room in the royal palace at Jerusalem, near to the portico. Now this palace had been erected of old by the children of Asmoneans, and situate upon an elevation, and afforded a most delightful prospect to those that had a mind to take a view of the city, which prospect was desired by the king; and then he could lie down, and eat, and thence observe what was done in the Temple: which thing, when the chief men of Jerusalem saw, they were very much displeased at it; for it was not agreeable to the institutions of our country or law that what was done in the Temple should be viewed by others, especially what belonged to the sacrifices. They therefore erected a wall upon the uppermost building which belonged to the inner court of the Temple towards the west; which wall, when it was built, did not only intercept the prospect of the dining-room in the palace, but also of the western cloisters that belong to the outer court of the Temple also, where it was that the Romans kept guards for the Temple at the festivals. At these doings, both King Agrippa, and principally Festus, the Procurator, were much displeased." (Ant. xx. viii: 11.)

But, through the influence of Nero's wife—the Jew-befriending Poppea, "who was a religious woman"—the wall was permitted to remain. And this same wall, by-the-bye, completely refutes the traditionary location of this palace on Bezetha. This splendid Palace extended from the western extremity of the Great Bridge along the brow of the cliff; and the distance separating it from the Armory could have been but small, if built, as it probably was, upon the foundation of Solomon's. Its position is well defined in the following extract from Josephus: "concerning the effort made by Agrippa to quell the insurrectionary movements of the Jews. He therefore called the multitude together into a large gallery [the Xystus], and placed his sister Berenice in the house of the Asmoneans, that she might be seen by them (which house was over the gallery, at the passage to the Upper City, where the bridge joined the Temple to the gallery). (W. ii. xvi: 3.)

The Palace of Berenice appears to have been situated just in the rear of Agrippa's, not far from that of the high priest—probably on the foundation of that built by Solomon for his wife—and was destroyed at the same time that Agrippa's and the high priest's were. (W. ii. xvii: 6.)

The Upper Palace of Herod the Great.—This seems to have been one of the most splendid of all the magnificent palaces of the Magnificent Herod; and hence the great topographer of Jerusalem and historiographer of Israel thus minutely describes it:—"He also built himself a place in the Upper City, containing two very large and most beautiful apartments, to which the Holy House itself could not be compared [in largeness]. The one apartment he named Cæsareum, and the other Agrippium, from his [two great] friends." (W. i. xxi: 1.) But he enters more fully into detail in the following account of it when speaking of the position of the Mariamne and Phasaelus Towers, on the north side of the First or Old Wall:—

"Now as these towers were themselves on the north side of the wall, the king had a palace inwardly thereto adjoined, which exceeds all my ability to describe it; for it was so very curious as to want no cost or skill in its construction, but was entirely walled about to the height of thirty cubits, and was adorned with towers at equal distances, and with large bedchambers, that would contain beds for a hundred guests apiece, in which the variety of the stones is not to be expressed; for a large quantity of those that were rare of their kind was collected together. These roofs were also wonderful, both for the length of the beams and the splendor of their ornaments. The number of the rooms was also very great, and the variety of the figures that were about them was prodigious; their furniture was complete, and the greatest part of the vessels that were put in them was of silver and gold. There were besides many porticoes, one beyond another, round about, and in each of these porticoes curious pillars; yet were all the courts that were exposed to the air everywhere green. There were moreover several groves of trees and long walks through them, with deep canals, and cisterns that in several parts were filled with brazen statues through which the water ran out. There were withal many dove courts of tame pigeons about the canals; but, indeed, it is not possible to give a complete description of these palaces; and the very remembrance of them is a torment to one, as putting one in mind what vastly rich buildings that fire which was kindled by the robbers hath consumed; for these were not burnt by the Romans, but by those internal plotters, as we have already related, in the beginning of their rebellion. That fire began at the Tower of Antonia, and went on to the palaces, and consumed the upper parts of the three towers themselves." (W. v. iv: 4.)

"THE PALACE THAT APPERTAINED TO THE HOUSE."—It is uncertain whether, by this appellation, the royal palace on Zion was intended, or a palatial castle at that time existing on the acropolis of Akra. (Neh. ii. 8.)

THE MACCABEAN PALACE, we learn from Josephus (Ant. xx. ix: 11), "was erected of old by the children of Asmoneus, and was situate" upon the exact site of the Herodian palace, then occupied by King Agrippa—the Davidian, Asmonean, and Herodian Palaces having all been built upon the cliff of Zion nearest the Temple.

PALACE OF PONTIUS PILATE. (See *Tower of Antonia*, Chapter IX.)

THE PALACE OF THE HIGH PRIEST—Where the council of scribes, elders, and priests was convened by Caiaphas for the trial of the Saviour—was situated between Millo and the Armory, on the north-eastern slope of Mount Zion. As thus situated on a declivity, a story below the chief suite of rooms was very natural, and indeed almost unavoidable: and this circumstance enables us the better to understand the expression (Mark xiv. 66)—"Peter was *beneath* in the palace." We are likewise informed—a fact which might also be inferred from its peculiar situation—that there was a porch in front of this lower story where Peter was. (Neh. iii. 20, 21; Matt. xxvi. 58, 69, 71; Mark xiv. 54, 66, 68, 69; Luke xxii. 54, 55; John xviii. 16; Jos. Wars ii. xviii: 6.)

PALACE OF QUEEN HELENA.—All that we know of the palace of this royal convert to Judaism and munificent benefactress of the Jews, is the mere assertion of Josephus that it "was in the middle of Akra." (W. vi. vi: 3.)

PALACE OF MONOBASUS.—We know nothing farther of the palace of this eminent proselyte of the Jews, than what Josephus records in the 1st section of the 6th chapter of his Wars of the Jews:—"Simon held the Upper City and the Great Wall as far as Kedron, and as much of the Old Wall as bent from Siloam to the east [facing the east],* and which went down to the Palace of Monobasus, who was king of the Adiabini beyond the Euphrates." It is thus found located in the extreme south-eastern portion of Mount Zion. As neither King Monobasus the elder or younger ever resided at Jerusalem, this palace was probably the residence of the five sons whom Izates sent to Jerusalem out of his family of forty-eight children; and was named in honor of his father. Being called by Jo-

* See note, page 129.

sephus, the "Palace of Monobasses who was king of the Adiabene," it cannot have been the property of the Monobasus a relative, who was killed at Jerusalem by the Romans.

THE ROYAL PALACE OF GRAPTE—Another relation of Izates the king of Adiabene, is only mentioned once, and then in such a way as to give no certain clue to its location; but it was probably near the Temple—and on Akra. (W. iv. ix: 11.)

COUNCIL HOUSE, OR CHAMBER OF THE SANHEDRIM—Was situated near the spot where the "First Wall" of Josephus abutted against the western wall of the Temple, with which it was, no doubt, connected, either by an intervening portico or by actual junction. We learn from the Talmud that it was built upon piers and arches—in order, no doubt, to elevate it to the level of the Temple area. The present Mekhemeh or Council Chamber of the Turkish Divan, where the Mejlis or Congress of Jerusalem holds its deliberations, having one entrance directly into the Haram and another into the elevated causeway street, probably occupies its identical site; and the Sanhedrim, like the Mekhemeh, may have been built over the pool. (W. v. iv: 2; and vi. vi: 3.)

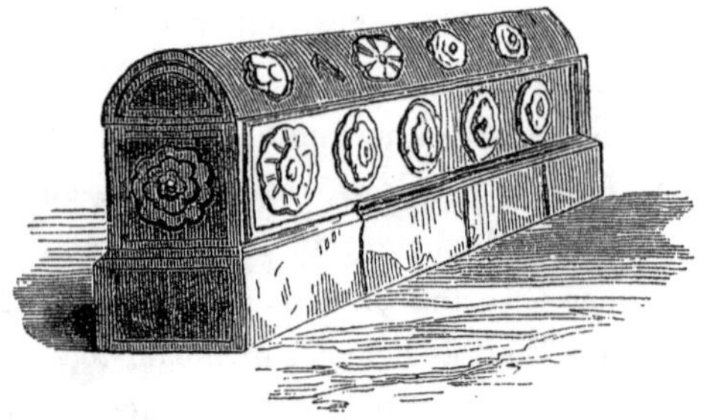

SARCOPHAGUS FROM KUBR EL MOLUK.

REPOSITORY OF THE ARCHIVES, where the civil documents of the Jews were kept, was situated on Akra Hill, or in the valley apparently not far from the Council Chamber—and, probably, in the "outer place" that seems to have surrounded the Temple. (W. ii. xvii: 6; and vi. vi: 3.)

Mint.—We have no definite information in relation to the Mint of Israel, either in the Scriptures, Josephus, or any other work with which I am acquainted; but we may reasonably conclude that it was situated in the neighborhood of the Council Chamber, Hall of Archives, and other public buildings in the "outer place." It was just here (along the western wall of the Temple) that the merchants seem to have been especially congregated, as well as the goldsmiths and moneyers. And a passage in the prophecy of Zephaniah seems to render it probable, in the highest degree, that the Jewish coinage was minted in this quarter, which would seem, with very little doubt, to be the place denominated Maktesh. "Howl, ye inhabitants of Maktesh, for all the merchant people are cut down: all they that bear silver are cut off." (i. 10–12.)

In more modern times (about the era of the Crusades) minting operations have been conducted in the Tower of Hippicus.

The House of Azuppim, or Gathering, seems to have adjoined the Temple on the south—and may have been the magazine for storing away the tithes contributed for the Levites. (1 Chr. xxvi. 16, 17.)

Chamber of Nathan Melek the Chamberlain.—This edifice was in the suburbs as we learn from 2d Kings xxiii. 11, either on the south side between the Hippodrome and the nearest of the two southern gates of the Temple, or by the gate Shushan in the Sheep Quarter, most probably the latter.

The King's House by the Horse Gate (*the King's Horse's House*).—This is by no means the king's palace, as is generally supposed, but is evidently the royal stables, quite distant from the palace. Queen Athaliah, the wicked usurper, was put to death at the Horse Gate near this edifice by order of Jehoiada the high priest. It would have been strange, indeed, after all the pains taken by Jehoiada to exclude her army from the Temple, at the coronation of the young king, had they incurred the hazard of her rescue by sending her back over the bridge to her army, instead of taking her for execution in the opposite direction—to the desecrated

Valley of Kedron. But that this view of the matter is correct we have the positive testimony of Josephus, who informs us that "Jehoida called for the captains of hundreds, and commanded them to bring Athaliah to the valley of Kedron and slay her there * * * * * wherefore, those that had the charge of her slaughter took hold of her and led her to the Gate of the King's Mules and slew her there." (Ant. ix. vii: 2.) The Gate of the King's Mules is, no doubt, the Horse Gate of the Scriptures—and the Hippodrome is, probably, the King's (Horse's) House: though this term, in its largest sense, would include the race-ground attached, as well as the royal stable. (2 Kings xi. 16; and 2 Chr. xxiii. 15.)

The Hippodrome.—Although the kings of Israel were forbidden to "multiply horses to themselves," yet, if they did not entirely disregard the prohibition themselves, they so far disobeyed it as to give them to the Sun (Baal probably), and built them a fine palace near the Horse Gate. (Ant. vii. x: 2, 8; Wars ii. iii: 1.)

The College *or School, or Second Part*, where Huldah the prophetess dwelt, was perhaps situated in the suburbs of Antonia, amongst the other public buildings. Was it the School of the Prophets—and were the vestments of the high priest reposited there previous to their removal to the Tower of Antonia? (2 Kings xxii. 14; 2 Chr. xxxiv. 22.)

Synagogues.—There were from four hundred and sixty to four hundred and eighty synagogues in the city, for giving instruction in the Bible and in the traditions of the elders.

Amphitheatre.—Herod the Great built a very large amphitheatre in the plain near Jerusalem—probably some distance north-west of Damascus Gate. (Ant. xv. viii: 1.) But no remains of it are now to be seen; and in the absence of all definite information, we are left entirely to conjecture as to its exact location.

Theatre.—The location of Herod's Theatre is nowhere indicated, but it was no doubt a considerable distance from the Temple and other venerated places—it may have been somewhere in the north-western corner of the old city—on Akra, near the "Street of the Strangers," who would be its principal patrons. (Ant. xv. viii: 1.)

THE OPEN MARKET PLACE, in which Pontius Pilate insidiously attacked the Jews on account of their persevering opposition to his "images," is by some called a *Circus;* but we have no intimation of its locality. (Ant. xviii. iii: 1, and Wars ii. ix: 3.)

UPPER MARKET.—Although this term was generally used to designate the whole "Upper City" or Mount Zion, yet it would also seem to be used in a more restricted sense, to indicate a market place also on the Holy Hill. There were also market places of a general as well as special character in other parts of the city.

The Timber Market, we learn from Josephus, was situated in Cœnopolis, or the "New City."

Wool Market.—The "Street of Wool Dealers" was probably situated at the lower extremity of the city, near the "Skin Pool," or lower Pool of Siloam. And in the same quarter also, we should locate the "Street of Butchers." There were *Garment Bazaars* in Cœnopolis; but doubtless in the older part of the city also.

The Bakers' Street is mentioned (Jer. xxxvii. 21), but not located; neither is the *Braziers' Bazaar*, of which Josephus speaks; nor the "*Strangers' Street*," mentioned by the Talmud—farther than its relative position—that it was an upper street. It may readily be inferred, however, that all such resident Gentiles would be required to take up their abode as far from the Temple as possible—probably in the upper corner of Akra—the highest part of the city prior to the annexation of the suburbs.

Mention is made by the Talmud of a great court walled in with stone, called *Beth-Jazzek*, where a grand assembly of those deputed to testify in relation to the moon were handsomely entertained every month. But we are not informed in what part of the city it was situated.

The Street of the House of God (plateia), is evidently the easternmost portion of the Court of the Gentiles, equal in breadth to the distance between the eastern portico called Solomon's Porch, and the Sacred Fence. (Ezra x. 9.) (See section on the *Temple.*)

The East Street mentioned in the 4th verse of the 29th chapter of 2 Chronicles, is but another name for the same "broad space."

The Street of the Water Gate mentioned by Nehemiah (viii. 1, 3, 16), was doubtless the vacant space in the Hippodrome area, just in front of the Water Gate of the city wall, though it is also applicable to that portion of the Court of the Gentiles lying between the Sacred Fence and the southern portico—the royal Basilica immediately in front of the Water Gate of the Temple.

The streets of the Holy City seem to have differed from those of all other cities in the provision made to prevent "clean" passengers from coming into contact with the "unclean"—one side being elevated for the benefit of the former, and the latter being compelled to walk in a depressed portion. They are represented by Josephus as being very narrow; but, being paved with white marble, must have presented a neat and elegant appearance, and certainly convey no mean intimation of the magnificence of the City of the Great King.

Herod's Monuments.—Which of the Herods this structure was monumental of, we are not informed; but it was no doubt Herod the Great—the great palace, fortress, and monument builder. It adjoined the reservoir called the Serpent's Pool (which seems to have been identical with that now called the Upper Gihon), and was not, therefore, a sepulchral structure. I have elsewhere ventured the conjecture that these monuments were reared by Herod the Great in commemoration of his great achievement in bringing water from Etham at so high an elevation. (See article, Ch. x.) (Wars v. iii: 2, and v. xii: 2.)

The Monument of King Alexander was evidently situated northward from the Temple—on the Hill Goath—not far from the present Birket Hammam, where it would be very conspicuous. This was no doubt the mausoleum of Alexander Janneus—erected to his memory by his truckling *herodian* queen (Alexandra), and his *dear friends*, the Pharisees, in consequence of the ruse devised by the dying king. (Ant xiii. xv: 5; Wars, v. vii: 3.)

Monument of the High Priest John Hyrcanus.—This monumental structure is very definitely located by Josephus, in the south-western corner of Cœnopolis, between the Second and Third Wall, and not far from the First or Old Wall, in the immediate vicinity of Hippicus and the Almond Pool. Being so far from the sepulchral grounds of the city, it was no doubt a mere cenotaph of the admiration-loving hierarch, designed to emblazon his *good deeds*—for we cannot for a moment conceive that the Jews would tolerate a sepulchre anywhere near this great thoroughfare. (Wars v. vi: 2; and v. vii: 3, &c.)

A Hospital, it would seem, was also built by this prince-hierarch.

MONUMENTAL PILLARS AND TABLETS OF SIMON MACCABEUS, H. P.—There were triplicates of these brazen tablets: one set of which was deposited in the public treasury; another was conspicuously placed in the Temple; and the third attached to pillars erected on Mount Zion, doubtless in a public and conspicuous place—probably near his palace. There is nothing definitely stated as to the size, shape, and architecture of these pillars; but our conjectures may possibly assume a more definite and reliable character by referring to the account of the monumental structures he erected over the graves of his father, mother, and four brothers at Modin (1 Mac. xiii. 27–29)—"Simon also built a monument upon the sepulchre of his father and his brethren, and raised it aloft to the sight with hewn stone, before and behind; moreover, he set up seven pyramids, one against another, for his father, his mother, and his four brethren, and in these he made cunning devices, about the which he set great pillars, and upon the pillars he made all their armor for a perpetual memory, and by the armor, ships, carved that they might be seen of all that sail on the sea." (Mac. xiv. 25–49.)

MONUMENT OF THE FULLER.—Whether this monument was erected by the fullers of Jerusalem in honor of their craft, or whether it perpetuates the name of an individual, we are not informed; but as it is evidently located in the neighborhood of the Fullers' Field, where fulling operations were probably performed, in the vicinity of the Upper Gihon waters, it was no doubt connected with the full

12

ing profession. (For *Fullers' Field and Monument*, see article.) (Wars v. iv: 2.)

Absalom's Pillar, Place, or Hand.—We learn that "Absalom in his lifetime had taken and reared up for himself a pillar, which is in the king's dale: for he said, 'I have no son to keep my name in remembrance:' and he called the pillar after his own name: and it is called unto this day Absalom's Place." (2 Sam. xviii. 18.) We are informed by Josephus that this marble pillar was two stadia from the city; and from a Talmudic note we learn that the part of the royal dale in which it was erected was its lower portion, called Motsa.

A comparison of these facts with those stated under the article *Tantour Pharoun*, which tradition confidently points out as Absalom's Pillar, will clearly evince their non-identity. Nor is there any other monument in all the King's Dale, nor anywhere else, answering the description of this pillar.

Monument of Ananus, or Annas, or Annanias, the high priest.—The late lamented Schultz has quite satisfactorily identified the sepulchre of that notorious high priest with the traditionary Aceldama. It is fully described in the account of the *Sepulchres of Hinnom*. (Wars v. xii: 2.)

There remains not a single ascertainable vestige of the monuments of Absalom, Herod, Alexander, Hyrcanus, Simon Maccabeus, or the Fullers: and though the underground work of those of Helena and Ananus may be reliably indicated, yet there is certainly not a single stone of their cippi, stela, or other superstructure remaining. Of course we are entirely ignorant of their architecture, execution, and general design. Their types, however, may be found amongst some of the well-preserved existing sepulchral monuments of Kedron; which, though they may not claim coëval origin with all of those just mentioned, were nevertheless their contemporaries in part, and may at least serve to give a sufficiently correct idea of their general character, design, and appearance.

CHAPTER VIII.

TOMBS AND SEPULCHRAL MONUMENTS.

"Strong vaulted cells where martyr'd seers of old
Far in the rocky walls of Zion sleep;
Green terraces, and arched fountains cold,
Where lies the cypress shade so still and deep.
Th' unearthly thoughts have passed from earth away,
As fast as evening sunbeams from the sea.
Thy footsteps all, in Zion's deep decay,
Were blotted from the holy ground. Yet dear
Is every stone of hers. For Thou wert surely here."

WELL did the expatriated cup-bearer of Artaxerxes Longimanus, when soliciting the office of Tirshatha of Jerusalem, style the capital of his father-land "the place of his father's sepulchres"—for no expression could more forcibly characterize the Holy City than the term necropolis—its rocks being everywhere perforated with tombs, and its soil covered with grave-stones. Most ardently does every Jew still desire a final resting-place in the Holy City, and especially in the Valley of Jehosaphat, not only because he dreads the under-ground passage (should he die abroad), but because he believes that the Lord will there finally plead for "his people" and judge the nations. It is a much cherished belief amongst the Jews that beneath the adjacent mountain all their dead are inhumed, and shall there be raised. "When the dead shall live again," say they, "Mount Olivet is to be rent in two, and all the dead of Israel shall come out thence: yea, those righteous persons, who died in captivity, shall be rolled under the earth, and shall come forth under the Mount of Olivet"—so declare the Rabbins.

These myriads of sepulchres, though originally designed, almost without exception, for the interment of the dead of Israel or their proselytes, have, in turn, served also for the sepulture of various other races subsequently occupying the devoted city—Pagan, Moslem, and Christian; and not only have these rock-hewn sepulchres been tenanted by the Gentile dead, but by the living also. Thousands of Cenobites have had no other dwelling at Jerusalem than these cold, damp, dark habitations of the dead. And even down to the present day the Arabs of Siloam occupy, either wholly or in part, the catacombs of the Hill of Offence—though generally having a small anteroom in front of the tomb. And in the Turkish burial field, on the hill to the right of Damascus Gate, called Turbet es-Zahara, or Mount of Tombs, the order of nature is exactly reversed by these Troglodytes—the dead being above the living.

This was, until recently, the quarantine station; and many a Frank traveller has been compelled to share this revolting species of temporary inhumation with the Turks and Arabs.

The process of quarrying and blasting is so much facilitated in cliffs perforated and intersected with tombs, that the sepulchres immediately around the city are rapidly disappearing before the hands of the mason, the dark habitation of the dead being thus converted into lighted residences for the living.

On the east side of Olivet and the southern slope of Scopus, I discovered a few sepulchres precisely resembling some that I saw at Rome; instead of large loculi for sarcophagi, mummies or corpses like the Jewish tombs, they have a great many small recesses in the sides of the room, barely large enough to contain a small cinerary urn or lachrymary vessel. But with this exception, nearly all the excavated rock tombs of Jerusalem are undoubtedly of Jewish origin. The Jewish sepulchres, although regulated by one general principle, yet differ very much in point of capacity, finish, and internal arrangement. Lazarus seems to have been interred in a mere natural cave with a small mouth—such as still abound in the vicinity of Jerusalem and Bethany. And the cave of Macpelah was unquestionably in its natural condition when first used for the burial of Sarah.* In the sides of some of these natural grots, loculi or roughly executed receptacles for the dead, are still to be found; but it is probable that in the earlier periods of the Jewish age the corpses were often merely laid on the floor swaddled in the winding-sheet. Indeed there is abundant proof that such a burial has been practised in quite modern times. Usually, however, the Jewish sepulchre is a small room excavated in the solid rock and provided with several receptacles for the dead. They are occasionally provided with an anteroom, and susceptible of unlimited enlargement, which is effected by adding room to room, literally, in the rear, on the sides, or below. A perpendicular surface is generally sought through which a small door is cut; but the position of this door in reference to the room is very irregular—the workmen having evidently paid more regard to the grain and flaws of the rock than to the symmetry of the room.

The rock being much more homogeneous and seamless far down than it is near the surface, the sepulchre is occasionally excavated very deep; and hence the entrance to such tombs is cut far below the general surface, and is reached by a narrow passage cut through the solid rock, either with or without steps, according to the degree of declination. The removal of the occluding rock from the door at the extremity of a steep passage of this kind would, of course, be no easy matter. And hence we can well sympathize with the women who were early at the sepulchre of the Lord on the morning of the resurrection—so anxiously inquiring "who shall roll us away the stone from the door of the sepulchre"—for it was very

* It is well remarked by Jahn (the great archæologist) that "the sepulchres of the common people were, without doubt, mere excavations in the earth, such as are common at the present day. Persons of a higher rank owned large subterranean recesses or caverns, either the work of nature or merely artificial excavations of the earth cut out from rocks."

great. It is generally assumed—in order to account for the fact that the Apostles stooped down to see the "linen clothes and napkin"—that the tomb of Joseph had an anteroom; and that, the door of this intermediate wall being low, they were compelled to stoop in order to see into the tomb proper. But this, and all the other circumstances of the narrative, are perfectly explicable upon the supposition that the tomb was entered by an inclined passage. Such doors as were situated in the perpendicular cliff far above ground could not, of course, be closed by rolling a stone against them—neither could very large doorways resting upon the level of the ground—they, however, may have been closed by one or more stone *plugs*, by movable masonry, or even by a wooden door; though no such fixtures are now to be seen.

But though usually situated very near, if not below, the general surface of the ground, yet they were sometimes disposed to exalt them very high, as we frequently observe on the sides of high cliffs, as well as learn from the rebuke administered by Isaiah to Shebna the treasurer. (Is. xxii. 16.) Several tombs at Wady Farar are more than a hundred feet above the valley; and in the "Mount of Temptation" they are several hundred above the base of the mountain: it is not certainly known, however, that these were ever used as tombs. It is supposed by some that they are mere cells for eremite monks, excavated during the reign of the Franks in Palestine.

The outer door is generally without the least ornament; but in tombs of superior order is provided with jambs, lintels, and handsomely sculptured pediments, and still more rarely with a portico and façade. A receptacle for water was also excavated within a few feet or yards of the door. Considerable diversity prevailed within, in relation to the arrangement of the loculi or various kinds of receptacles for the individual corpses. They are generally simple rectangular cavities, but sometimes arched—seven or eight feet in length, and two or three in breadth and height, penetrating into the rock their entire length endwise; in other cases, however, they are excavated laterally, and occasionally a shallow arch or narrow vault is excavated over them, the corpse or sarcophagus in the former case being laid perpendicular to the side of the room, and in the latter parallel to it; and this undoubtedly was the arrangement of the tomb of Joseph of Arimathea. Several tiers are sometimes found; but generally there is only one series. Small niches, scarcely large enough to hold a cranium, are also occasionally to be found executed in various parts of the sepulchres. Have these been, in after ages, made by the Romans to receive the urn containing their ashes? Or would the proud Roman condescend to store away his ashes in a sepulchre once defiled by the remains of the despised Jew? It is conjectured by some that their only object was to contain a lamp; by others, incense, water, or treasure.

These various arrangements will be better understood by reference to the illustrative plans, elevations, and sections. That nearly all these sepulchres are Jewish is conclusively shown by the general resemblance borne to a tomb I discovered about two miles north of Jerusalem, most unequivocally Jewish, which it will be well to figure and describe as the true type of Jewish sepulchral architecture.

JEWISH TOMB AT EL-MESSAHNEY.

Though hewn out of the solid rock, the characteristic Jewish rebatement, like that of the ancient temple wall, was so boldly executed that much of it is as sharp and perfect as though chiselled but yesterday. Much of the portion of rock containing the entablature has long since fallen and disappeared; but several feet of it remain in such a fine state of preservation that its minutest details are still observable. Though undoubtedly of the highest antiquity, there is no piece of ancient architecture about Jerusalem in a better state of preservation than this. It has been suggested by my friend Dr. Stuart of Scotland, now missionary at Leghorn, that it was the place of sepulture used by the high priests prior to the destruction of the sacerdotal city of Nob by King Saul. And if the style of architecture can be referred to so remote a period, it would be difficult to withhold concurrence from such an opinion. Certain it is that this city was situated in this immediate vicinity—for the first glimpse of Jerusalem is caught from the road on the hill just above, leading from Geba, Gibeah, &c., just where we may naturally suppose the haughty Assyrian monarch would first "shake his hand against the mount of the Daughter of Zion, the hill of Jerusalem, as he remained at Nob that day." (Is. x. 32.) The internal construction and general style of execution seem also to favor the idea that it was designed for the highest dignitaries either of church or state; and Mount Zion being the appointed site of the Tombs of the Kings, this may have been selected as a final resting-place for the sacerdotal line prior to the period of the monarchy. It is observed that the second loculus on the right occupies more than twice as much space as any other; a circumstance that may well have constituted it the place of honor for the repose of the last deceased high priest. The door is not only much larger than usual, but is arched—still so low, however, that it is necessary to stoop considerably either to enter or see far into it—as is generally, but by no means universally the case. It differs also from other tombs in having a window—(not seen in the cut—being buried beneath the rubbish). Was this opening designed for ventilation, or the admission of sufficient light to display the corpse laid out in state in the large loculus? This tomb is now used during the winter as a lodgment for a goat-herd and his flock, and there are numerous others all around frequently put in requisition by the Arabs for the same purpose; and on seeing the Fellahin coming out of them, one is forcibly reminded of the "man coming out of the tombs with an unclean spirit, having his dwelling among the tombs." And on coming in contact with one of these Fellahin he will be found possessed of a spirit about as unclean, and with almost literally a legion of evil-spirited fleas, of which he may soon be in great measure exorcised at your expense, and you set a capering down these steep places like the swine of Gadara.

PLAN OF EL-MESSAHNEY TOMB.

The seventeen loculi of this sepulchre all enter the walls endwise, and not laterally as in many others. The dimensions will be understood at once on inspection of the annexed plan. The order of architecture is, undoubtedly, Roman Doric; and is rather unfavorable to its very high antiquity, except upon the supposition of subsequent remodelling. This tomb is situated at the upper end of extensive foundations and ruins called El-Messahney, where Jewish rocks are to be found three and a quarter feet long, and portions of columns three and a half in diameter, evidencing the former existence of a very considerable city.

TOMBS OF THE JUDGES.

TOMBS OF THE JUDGES.—The accompanying vertical section and elevation of the north side of the Tombs of the Judges (arbitrarily so called), will still farther illustrate the architecture of Jewish sepulchral structures. Over the outer door A is a richly sculptured Grecian pediment mounted on handsome mouldings. A very richly executed doorway, B, leads from the vestibule or ante-room C into the main room, on the north side of which are seen thirteen loculi contained in two tiers. In front of three pairs of the upper row are three arches, broad enough to contain a sarcophagus or swarthed corpse, at right angles to the others and parallel to the wall. Another door, D, gives entrance into another room on the same story, exhibiting nine repositories, somewhat different from the others. In the north-east corner of the main room is a stairway leading down to a room beneath the last-mentioned loculi, containing ten or twelve receptacles still somewhat different from the foregoing. And in the south-west corner of the large room is a stairway leading down into an unfinished apartment. There are only sixty places for the repose of the dead in this catacomb, although it wears its present appellation in honor of the Jewish Sanhedrim, that was composed of *seventy-two* senators, elders or judges: but this tradition is comparatively modern, and entitled to no credence whatever. It was at one time called "Tombs of the Prophets," a title now generally applied to an extensive catacomb on Mount Olivet.

THE TOMB OF HELENA is an object so interesting in itself and of such importance in a topographical point of view, that the ascertainment of its position is worthy of special consideration. Queen Helena, the widow and sister of Monobasus, king of the Adiabenians, influenced by religious considerations on becoming a convert to the Jewish faith (which her son Izates, who succeeded to the throne, had also embraced), removed to Jerusalem just before the occurrence of that great dearth foretold by Agabus (Acts xi. 28), which came to pass in the days of Claudius Cæsar, about A. D. 44. It would appear from the 20th book of the "Antiquities" that during her residence in the Holy City she built for herself a sepulchre, in accordance with the custom of the age; but on being informed of the death of Izates she returned to Adiabene, and there died soon after her arrival. Monobasus (the 2d), however, who had now ascended the throne, "sent her bones as well as those of Izates his brother to Jerusalem, and gave orders that they should be buried at the pyramids which his mother had erected: they were three in number, and distant no more than three furlongs from the City of Jerusalem." We learn from the "Wars" (v. iv: 2) that these monuments were on the north of the city, somewhere in the region between Psephinos and the "Sepulchral Caverns of the Kings." And from the 2d section of the 2d chapter, that they were also opposite the "Womens' Towers," somewhere near the road by which Titus approached the city; and furthermore (chap. iii. section 3), that they were between these towers and Titus's camp on Scopus. Jerome informs us that this mausoleum of Helena lay on the left (east) of Paula as she approached the city, apparently from the north. Very little can be inferred from this—for should it be incidentally mentioned that the custom house of Jerusalem was on the left of a traveller who entered the city on a certain occasion, it would be concluded that the traveller approached the city either by the Jaffa or Bethlehem road—whereas travellers even from Damascus and the Jordan, if they have baggage, are compelled to enter Jaffa Gate, and thus leave it on the left on entering that gate. And Pausanias relates that "the door of this sepulchre (of wonderful work) was manufactured of marble, as also the other parts of the sepulchre; which, on a certain hour of a certain day of the year, is opened by the concealed operation of certain machinery, &c., closing again after a short time, and had one tried to open it at another time, he must first have broken it with violence." These are all the data, as yet furnished by the ransacked folios of antiquity, for making out the site of this interesting locality. The opinions of Pococke, Chateaubriand, Clarke, Robinson, and other weighty authorities, are cited in favor of the supposition that these monuments and the Tombs of the Kings are identical. But the very term by which Josephus expresses their construction, seems flatly to contradict such a conclusion: and indicates at least that, unlike Kúbr el-Moluk, the principal structure of her monuments was above ground, for no expression could be more inappropriate than to say that these "royal caverns" were "*erected*"—the term used in relation to Helena's sepulchre. The "door" of her sepulchre is also said to have been made of the same material composing the remainder of the structure—which is by no means the case with the Tombs of the Kings. Moreover this material is said (in the Latin version of the account) to be *marble**—by which of course cannot be meant the coarse limestone composing the Tombs of the Kings—but evidently in contradistinction from this native rock. Instead of being deeply sunken in the earth like the Tombs of the Kings, these monuments would appear to have been mainly if not entirely constructed above ground; and besides, Pausanias does not speak of them as a series of tombs but as a single tomb.† The Adiabenian style of sepulchral architecture

* "Ostium fabricatum est e marmore, uti cæteræ sepulchri partes."

† Ταφος.

was probably as diverse from that of the Jewish as were their respective religions; and hence the notoriety of this exotic sepulchre. In pyramids thus constructed of marble, high and dry, we may conceive of machinery that would remain in good order a considerable length of time; but, deeply immured in the "misty vapors" of this damp subterranean dungeon of the dead, what species of mechanism could preserve its integrity a single moon? And to recognise in the plain pannelled doors of the interior of the Tombs of the Kings, or the circular door without, the door of wonderful work described by the Greek writer—even making the most liberal allowance for Oriental hyperbole—is truly more wonderful than the wonderful door itself!

If it could be established (as assumed) that the present Tel el-Fûl is the "Gabaa" of St. Jerome, and was the place from which Lady Paula came last and *directly*, previously to entering Jerusalem, and that "the great northern road at present is unquestionably the same that it formerly was," then the probability of identity between Helena's Monuments and the Tombs of the Kings "would be greatly increased." But to make these assertions under the actual state of the case savors somewhat of begging the question: for a much better road could have been made higher up, where the Kedron Valley, instead of being narrow and rapidly declivitous, expands into a plain: and if the present Jeba is "Gabaa," or if St. Paula had turned aside to visit some other very interesting localities north of Jerusalem, then the Tomb of Helena would have occupied a site far different from that assigned it by these authors. There is no evidence whatever that the present road was in existence at that day; and, unquestionably, if a good northern road had been desired from that part of the city, it would have been located much higher up, and most eligibly, just where the present road to Mizpah and Gibeon crosses the valley. After oft-repeated examination and protracted consideration of the subject, I can come to no other conclusion than that these monuments were situated, as marked in the map of Ancient Jerusalem, a short distance to the right of the present Mizpah road, by way of the Tombs of the Judges. There is quite a picturesque situation for a mausolean structure on a rocky hill in the Valley of Kedron, or Jehosaphat, as it is generally called, five or six hundred yards from Ashmound, or Tel el-Massabin; in which is a tomb containing two or three rooms of small dimensions. But the tomb having the strongest claim to be regarded as Helena's, is one situated a short distance east of the valley, about one hundred yards north of the present Nablous road—of which the following is a plan. There are loose rocks and rubbish above it, clearly indicating the existence of a former building; and a pair of steps in the north-west corner of the vestibule, proving the existence of a communication between the sepulchre and the building by which it was crowned. True, it is situated to the right or west of the present road leading from Tel el-Fûl—the road by which it is supposed St. Paula approached the city; but were the road located to the best advantage, it would fall about one hundred yards to the left or east of such road. Its distance from Ashmound—through which there are some indications that the northern wall formerly ran—is a little upwards of six hundred yards—just about three furlongs. There are six or eight loculi in this sepulchre, three of which are much superior to the others: were these for Helena, Izates, and Grapte? The main outer entrance from the court was probably closed and secured on the interior; and the tomb could then only be opened by descending through the stairway from above. May not this passage have terminated in one of the pyramids, or the substruction on which all three were sustained? Be this as it may, all the indications of the case are met in this location. But, besides all this, was the construction

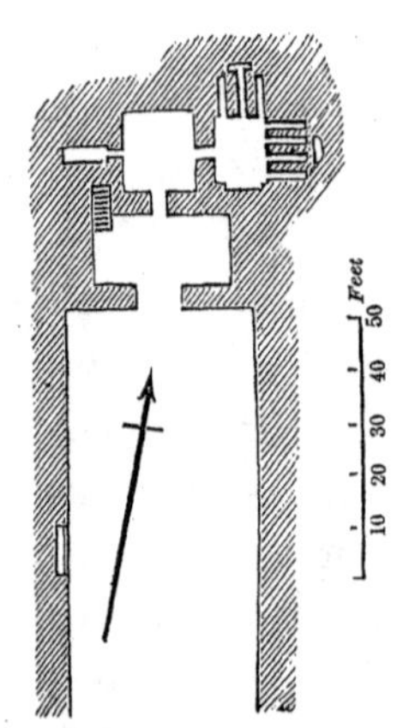

PLAN OF TOMB—SUPPOSED TO BE QUEEN HELENA'S.

of such an extensive series of elegant rooms as those of Kubr Moluk within the compass of possibility during the space of time necessarily so limited by the circumstances of the case?

TOMBS OF THE KINGS—KUBR EL-MOLUK—KUBR ES-SULTAN.—A more costly and imposing structure than either of those just noticed, and indeed more magnificent than any others about the Holy City, is that which, in consequence of this superiority, has secured for itself the title of "Tombs of the Kings," according to ecclesiastic tradition—and its equivalent in the legends of the Moslem "Kubr es-Sultan." It is situated just half a mile north of Damascus Gate, on the west side of a sunken court, about 90 feet square and upwards of 20 feet deep. These finely-constructed catacombs are entered through a splendid, but now much decayed and defaced, portico or portal and hall, on its western side, 13½ feet high and 28½ wide. Near its south-western corner is a door beneath the level of the floor, 2½ feet broad, and less than 3 feet high, opening into an anteroom, about 19 feet square. In the western side of this room is a door leading into another room 13½ feet square, having in it about a dozen receptacles for the dead, and a passage leading by a stairway into a room 10 × 12, situated a story lower. There are two rooms entered from the south side of the anteroom or hall, each having half a dozen loculi; and from the north side of the westernmost one is a flight of steps conducting to another room in the lower story 10 feet square. The loculi in each of these lower rooms and in some other parts of these tombs are parallel to the wall, or in other words present their side, being accessible throughout, but most of them are perpendicular to the wall, and of course accessible only at one extremity. This is the only tomb certainly known to have contained sarcophagi, many richly carved fragments of which are strewn about the rooms and court. But the only one known to be in existence is that in the Mekhemeh or Council House of Jerusalem, which supplies the Divan of Jerusalem Effendis with drinking water! *Sic transit gloria mundi!* Alas! poor Yorick!! To some of these loculi are attached, either at their extremities or sides, other small receptacles. Many large pieces of richly pannelled stone doors lie scattered about the rooms. The jambs of the interior doorways have such an inclination that the ponderous doors even with all the friction of mortice and tenon hinge, would always close from the force of gravity, but the outer door was closed by a contrivance so unique as to deserve a detailed account. Imme-

KUBR MOLUK—TOMBS OF THE KINGS.

diately in front of the doorway (the top of which is more than a foot below the floor of the porch), is a deep trench, commencing a foot or two west of the door, and extending three or four yards along the wall eastward. The bottom of this trench is a short distance below the sill of the door, and is probably an inclined plane. Along this channel a large thick stone disk traverses, fitting very accurately against its western end, which is made concave, so as to be exactly conformed to the convexity of this large millstone-like

disk, when rolled to that end—thus closing the doorway most effectually. In order to introduce this circular door *in situ*, it was necessary originally to make an opening into this channel, which was done at its east end, and afterwards sealed (hermetically, no doubt) by a slab, four and three-fourths feet long, two and a half broad, and more than half a foot in thickness. Two or three feet in advance of this channel was a subterranean (or rather subrupean) passage to its west extremity. These arrangements were all formerly excluded from view by the floor of the porch (now broken away), and the smaller inner doorway (closed by the stone disk) was approached by a passage eight or ten feet long, whose mouth was entered from a circular excavation eight feet in diameter, and five or six in depth. This basin was probably kept well supplied with water, for which perhaps the large tank just without the court (at the foot of the inclined plane) was provided, except when the sepulchre was opened; and the object of the L shaped passage to the west end of the doorway track was to scotch the door. The whole of this narrow passage may also have been blocked up with masonry, with a view of rendering access the more tedious and difficult. These various contrivances seem undoubtedly to have been designed specially for the security of the sepulchre, by rendering access as difficult, uncertain, and tardy as possible. Few would even suspect the true and only way of access into the interior, and fewer still attempt an entrance! This contrivance may assist us in understanding the query in relation to the entrance of the Holy Sepulchre, "Who shall roll us away the stone from the door of the sepulchre?" Though it would be equally applicable to several other arrangements of the door. The way into this house of Death—strangely enough—thus becomes an apt emblem of the way to Life Eternal—"for straight is the gate and narrow is the way which leadeth unto life, and few there be that find it."

The portal was once sustained, or rather ornamented, by two pillars and two pilasters—mere vestiges of which, however, now remain; and the perpendicular surface of rock over the portal was so highly adorned with classic mouldings, clusters of grapes and wreaths of flowers, as to leave its age and style of architecture altogether a matter of fanciful speculation. In the absence of a more appropriate epithet, its style of architecture may well be termed "Romanized Hebro-Grecian."

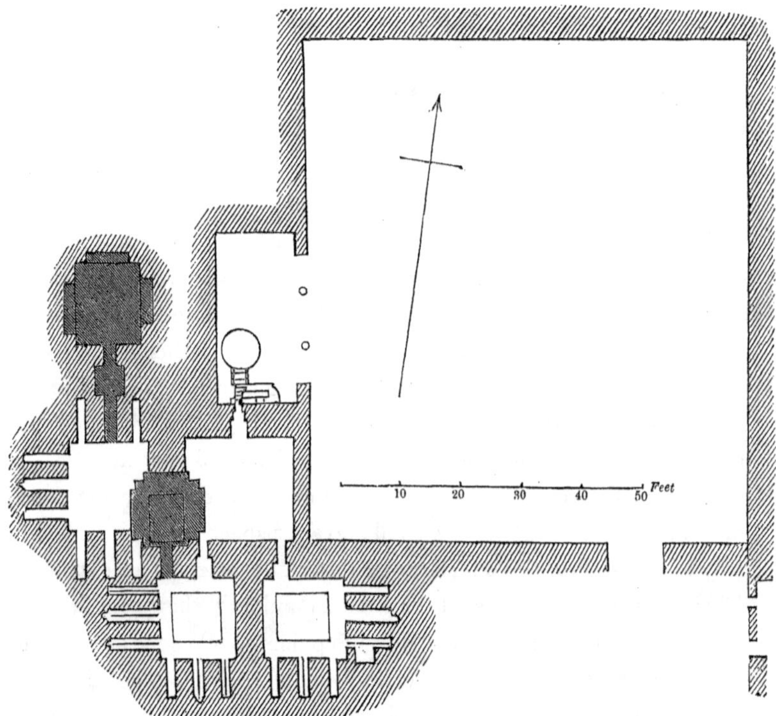

PLAN OF TOMBS OF KINGS.

Few subjects connected with the archæology of Jerusalem have excited more discussion than these elegant catacombs; but that the appellation by which they are now generally known (Tomb of the Kings of Judah) is an egregious misnomer, is most evident to every Bible reader that knows the relative locality of this place and Mount

Zion. For we are repeatedly informed that "the sepulchre of the kings of Judah," where the kings of Judah were all buried (except five*), was in the city of David (about one mile distant from the so called "Tombs of the Kings). And yet—notwithstanding the express authority of Nehemiah (iii. 16) for locating them in that part of the city of David containing the royal sepulchres between the Pool of Siloam and the House of the Mighty, near "unto the stairs that go down from the city of David,"—a learned and elegant French writer is confident that he has succeeded in establishing the identity of the sepulchres of the kings of Judah with the present so called Tombs of the Kings!!! They are regarded by one of the most distinguished Biblical antiquarians and Oriental scholars living, as the celebrated sepulchre of Helena, queen of Adiabene; but this is undoubtedly a mistake, for he relies mainly upon what Pausanias says about the door of Helena's tomb—that it "was of the same rock, and was so contrived that it could only be opened when the returning year brought around a particular day and hour;" but this conjecture is abundantly disproved by what has been said in relation to its doors, as well interior as outer, and especially when it is remembered that the doors are made of a rock quite differing from that of the catacombs, and have no appearance of any attachment of mechanism. And besides, what would this widowed old lady want with a sepulchre containing about thirty loculi, even if her son, niece, and five grandsons, sent to Jerusalem by Izates to be educated, were also interred with her? Did we not know that some of the Maccabean family were buried at Modin, and were constrained thence to infer that all of this royal line were buried in that city, we might assign this tomb to them. But though it cannot well be ascribed to them, may it not belong to the next succeeding dynasty?

* Jehoram was "buried in the City of David, but not in the sepulchres of the kings." (2 Ch. xxi. 20.) Uzziah the leper was "buried with his fathers in the *field* of the burial which belongeth to the kings." (2 Ch. xxvi 23.) 2 Ch. xxviii. 27, Manasseh "was buried in the garden of his own house, in the garden of Uzziah; and Ammon his son was buried in the same place." (2 Kings xxi. 18, 26.)

Herod the Great, we are informed, was buried at Herodium; but it is quite questionable whether any of his family would like to lie beside him, even in death! May not these tombs, then, have been the place of interment for the remainder of the Herodian family? The "Monuments of Herod"—as elsewhere suggested—were not sepulchral structures, but most probably monumental erections, commemorative of some special act of his magnificent reign. There are several other tombs east of this, of somewhat similar character, but of far inferior workmanship and extent. Are these, together with "Kubr el-Moluk," what Josephus styles the "Sepulchral Caverns of the Kings"? Or does that appellation belong alone to Kubr el-Moluk?

"The Sepulchral Caverns of the Kings."—These royal excavations, which Josephus incidentally mentions in describing the location of the northern portion of the Agrippan Wall (W. v. iv: 2), were situated on the north of the city; but whether they were included or excluded by the wall is not asserted. But if the wall was located in reference to the best position for defensive purposes, and the Royal Caverns be indeed identical with Kubrel-Moluk, then would they necessarily fall within the enclosure. There are one or two other large sepulchral excavations a short distance east of this, but none of them materially near the city; we are, therefore, constrained to look for them in this immediate neighborhood. And as Kubr el-Moluk amply fulfils all the indications of the case, and there are no other structures in all that neighborhood to which the conditions are at all applicable, we are shut up to the conclusion that in this elegant series of excavated chambers we have "the Sepulchral Caverns of the Kings"—the final resting-place of all the Herodian dynasty, except the "great" monster himself, as above intimated—a supposition considerably strengthened by their comparative freshness and fine state of preservation. (See article *Kubr el-Moluk.*)

"The Sepulchres of the Kings of Judah" were situated within the city of Jerusalem, according to Josephus, and in the southern portion of it, called Mount Zion or the City of David, according to the sacred Scriptures. These sepulchres were no doubt hewed in the rock beneath the "field of the burial which belonged to the kings." (2 Chr. xxi. 20; xxvi. 23; xxviii. 27.) There were also various other sepulchres upon Mount Zion in which the kings of Israel were interred—but only in dishonor. There are several sepulchres on the southern and eastern slopes of Zion in very good preservation, evidently far within the circuit of the ancient wall. May not these be the tombs of those kings who were denied interment within the royal sepulchres of Zion, but were yet suffered to be buried on Mount Zion in their own gardens—Jehoram, Ahaz, Manasseh, and Ammon? It is evident from the whole tenor of Jewish history and polity, that only such privileged persons as kings, and probably high priests exercising royal functions, enjoyed the distinction of city burial. May not the traditional tomb of David be one of the most splendid amongst the tombs of these ostracised kings or princely hierarchs? For, although Jewish, Christian, and Moslem tradition all most confidently depose in behalf of the present site, yet most evident is it from Nehemiah's account of the reëdification of the wall (iii.), that David's sepulchre, instead of being on the very summit of Zion, was on its eastern declivity, not far from the middle wall. Its locality seems to have been well known at the introduction of the Christian era (Acts ii. 29); but it is highly probable that even if the great veneration they entertained for their revered prophet-king would not lead them to conceal the royal sepulchres with immense masses of rubbish before the capture of the city by Titus, the process would soon be accomplished by the elements of nature in such a situation. The "Sepulchres of the Kings" were, no doubt, a series of excavations entered by one door only—like that of the Judges, Kubr el-Moluk, &c.—and could, therefore, be easily and effectually concealed by a bank of earth.

"*The Sepulchre of David*" was merely one room, with possibly a suite of treasury vaults, in the foregoing royal sepulchres. (See article above; and for traditional tomb of David, see article *Neby Daûd.*)

SEPULCHRE OF SIMON THE JUST, THE SON OF ONIAS.—This traditionary tomb is on the eastern side of the valley of the Kedron. north-east of the Tombs of the Kings, and is much visited by pilgrims—abundant evidence of which is seen in the Hebrew inscriptions written on the walls. It is quite an extensive tomb, but in no way remarkable (except for its large door); and, like all other tombs with accessible doorways, is used most of the year as a sheep-cote.

Sepulchres of various kinds are very numerous on both sides of the valley all the way down to Hinnom. But perhaps there are none worthy of special notice nearer than the labyrinthian one, on the slope of Olivet, named both of the Prophets and Apostles; though there are several on each side, and especially around the cove of the Kedron, I venture to identify with the "Ashes Valley," that are very extensive.

TOMBS OF THE PROPHETS.

TOMBS OF THE PROPHETS.—A sufficiently correct idea of this structure, called Tombs of the Prophets or Apostles (for they are known under both designations, and are doubtless entitled as well to the one as the other), may be had by inspecting the small plan on the map, in connexion with the accompanying view of the interior. The excavations extend about twenty-eight yards from north to south, and thirty or forty from east to west; but upwards of fifty yards measured on the circuit of the outer semicircular range. About thirty loculi are now accessible; but several diverging passages being too much choked by rubbish to be explored, there may be many more according to the assertion of several ancient authors. Some regard these catacombs as the tombs of the Prophets, others as those of the Apostles—though certainly rather more capacious and stylish than either necessity or consistency would require for the Galilean fisherman and the Tarsan tentmaker—while others connect them with the idolatrous services of Baal, owing to the fancied resemblance of the large dome-shaped anteroom to a supposed furnace where the "offering of the dead" may have been eaten. But surely a far more plausible solution of the enigma of their hsitory would be their assignment to the Jewish hierarchy—being so conspicuously situated opposite the Temple. Lord Nugent suggests that they may have belonged to the School of the Prophets in Jerusalem.

The ground plans of the Church and *Sepulchre of the Virgin Mary*, and the tombs of James the Less, of the Prophets and of Jehosaphat are delineated with sufficient precision on the large map of Modern Jerusalem to give a correct idea of their extent, form, and general arrangement. St. Mary is said by tradition to have been buried in the cruciform portion of the tomb called the "Church of the Virgin Mary;" higher up the long flight of sixty-five steps by which access is had to this deep sepulchral church, the traveller is shown the *crypts of St. Anna, Joseph, and Joachim.* But *quis credat?—Judeus Apella? Non ille!*

The Monumental Structures dedicated to Jehosaphat, James, and Zechariah, are situated in the narrow part of the Kedron, rather less than two hundred yards from the east wall of the Temple, nearly opposite its south-eastern corner, and just at the base of Mount Olivet. The lower one, called, in the current traditionary nomenclature of Jerusalem, "Zechariah's Tomb"—is about twelve or thirteen yards south of the "Tomb of St. James," and the upper one, called "Absalom's Pillar," is about forty steps north of that sepulchre.

Tomb of Zecharias (so called) is a true monolith; and is isolated from the rock that surrounds it on three sides by a passage, several yards wide. Its general appearance at present is that of a four-sided pyramid, of equal base and height, mounted on a cube of about twenty feet each way; but at least one-fourth of its lower portion is concealed from sight by accumulated earth, containing Hebrew graves; and thousands of names are engraved upon its sides in Hebrew characters. No entrance being perceptible in any direction, it is *supposed* to be solid. Beautiful Ionic capitals crown the pillars and pilasters. The two middle pillars on each side are half round; two pilasters meeting at the corners give the appearance of massive square pillars; and on each side of the pilasters are quarter-round pillars. The effect is pleasing; and although the architecture is by no means imposing, the monument is impressive in the highest degree.

Tantour Pharoun—Absalom's Pillar.—This monumental pillar is monolithic as high as the cornice, and is detached from the surrounding ledge of Olivet just as Zechariah's. Its entire height does not appear—a fourth of it probably being concealed by accumulated stones and rubbish. Its present ascertainable height is about fifty feet, and its breadth about twenty-three or twenty-four. It exactly resembles Zechariah's in the character and disposition of the pillars and pilasters with which it is ornamented, and is therefore referable to the same age. The triglyphs, guttæ, and other ornaments of the entablature are clearly Doric, while the capitals are Ionic. There is a concavity both in the living rock and the superstructure of masonry: that below is about eight feet square, with arched recesses on the south and west, and handsomely ornamented ceiling; but that extending upward in the masonry about twenty feet, is very irregularly shaped, and apparently unfinished. This vacuity was only entered originally on the east side, through a very low and narrow doorway above the cornice, opening to a short flight of steps; but in the lapse of ages another has been effected on the west by the pious indignation of Moslems, Jews, and Christians, who never pass this monument without testifying their detestation of Absalom's wicked conduct, by casting a stone at his supposed resting-place. For tradition unhesitatingly points out this as the "pillar" mentioned in the 18th verse of the 18th chapter of 2 Samuel—that Absalom had taken and reared up for himself, which is in the King's Dale; and it is called unto this day Absalom's Place. But we learn from Josephus that the monument called Absalom's Place or Hand was constructed of marble, and that this "marble pillar" stood two furlongs from the city. Now the monument just described could not have been more than half that distance from the city when there was a wall in that quarter; for it is rather less than two stadia from the Temple Wall. But even were it situated at the required distance from the city, it could not still be recognised as Absalom's Pillar; for, instead of being constructed of marble, it consists of the common limestone of the country. Nor has the rapacity of Jerusalem's ferocious despoilers spared a single *marble* structure in all the city or its borders! We learn, moreover, from Jewish writers, that this monument was situated in Motsa, lower down. Absalom's Pillar is therefore now nowhere to be found. And although there is sufficient space within for a corpse, yet there is no special sepulchral arrangement, nor could a sarcophagus ever have been introduced through the only opening that appears to have been left in it. It is therefore probable that this structure, as well as that of Zecharias, was merely designed as a cenotaph. They have been arbitrarily named at various times in honor of Hezekiah, Uzziah, Isaiah, Jehosaphat, Simon the Just, &c. But it is very evident,—whether a judgment be formed from the order and embellishments of their architecture, or their fine state of preservation,—that this structure can scarcely date back so far as the age of David. For, with the exception of injuries inflicted by the ruthless hand of man, their finest embellishments are in a very good state of preservation, and present no such marks of antiquity as would justify their reference to so remote an era. If erected by Absalom, this monument has resisted the decomposing influences of the cold, heat, and damp of nearly three thousand years! There is a strange and puzzling admixture of the Greek and the Egyptian styles about both these monuments, and also one or two lower down, by Silwan village, that defies alike the analytic powers of the architect and the antiquary; but most observers would probably be brought by a critical examination of the subject to the conclusion that they cannot long antedate the Christian era, and probably belong to the Herodian age of Jewish history.

Few perhaps would widely dissent from the opinion expressed in the following extract from the Biblical Researches—than the authors of which none are better qualified to form a correct judgment. "The intermingling of the Greek orders, and a spice of the massive Egyptian taste, which are visible in these monuments, serve also to show that they belong to a late period of the Greek and Roman art; and especially to that style of mingled Greek and Egyptian which prevailed in the Oriental provinces of the Roman Empire. The chief seat of this style was perhaps at Petra; where it still appears in much of its pristine character in the very remarkable excavations of Wady Musa. When we visited that place, some weeks afterwards, we were much struck at finding there several isolated monuments, the counterparts of the monolithic tombs in the Valley of Jehosaphat. The architectural remains of Petra are not held, I believe, to be in general older than the Christian era; nor is there any reason to suppose that the Jewish monuments in question are of an earlier date. Indeed, if they existed prior to the destruction of Jerusalem, they are probably to be referred to the times of the Herods; who themselves were of Idumean descent, and maintained an intercourse between Petra and Jerusalem. In that age too, as we know, other foreigners of rank repaired to Jerusalem and erected for themselves mansions and sepulchres. It would not, therefore, be difficult to account in this way for the resemblance between these monuments and those of Petra." (i. 521.)

THE TOMB OF JEHOSAPHAT is entered through a door in the north-east corner of the passage that isolates the pillar of Absalom, over which is a beautiful and elaborately carved pediment. Availing of a favorable opportunity, I succeeded in exploring this secluded mansion of the dead throughout, but, instead of finding ancient manuscripts (as I had been led to entertain the hope of doing), my pains were only rewarded by a room full of rotten leather parings, and a hecatomb of skeletons—Jewish, no doubt, as the Jews lay special claim to this sepulchre, and very jealously guard it. Tradition and the Bible are directly at variance in relation to the sepulchre of good King Jehosaphat; the one contending that this is his identical tomb, and the other that "he was buried with his fathers in the City of David." (2 Chr. xxi. 1.) And yet there are some that halt between the two opinions! And stranger still, others who insist upon it that we are bound to believe "infallible tradition!" Surely, "full well do such reject the word of the Lord, that they may keep their own tradition."

The main entrance to the Tomb of St. James is from the court of Zechariah's obeliscal monument; but there is also a stairway from above by which it may be entered. It is contended by some of the advocates of tradition that it is not really his sepulchre, but merely the place of his temporary retreat after the Messiah's crucifixion, where "he swore he would no more eat bread till he should see his Lord risen;" and it is added—"on the third day our Lord, returning from his triumph over hell, showed himself to James, saying, Arise, James, and eat, for I have now risen from the dead." The "looker on" in Zion, will delight to linger in this picturesque portico, if not too much annoyed by the herds of goats and sheep sheltered here—or, still worse, by the legions of parasites of the flocks, with which the sepulchre teems.

Under certain circumstances it may be worth while climbing the mountain to take a hasty peep at a large stone sarcophagus in the "*Cave of St. Pelagius*," beneath the dome crowning the Mosque of Jebl Tûr, in a basement story at the south-west corner. It is believed by Oriental Christians to have contained the remains of

Margarita the famous courtesan of Antioch, who, on conversion to Christianity, came and ended her days here as a monk—or as others assert—as a nun, under the assumed name of Pelagia. The Jews, however, claim it as the *Tomb of Huldah the prophetess;* and the Muhammedans also venerate it as the "narrow house" of one of their Santons or Saints. An almost effaced inscription written in very old and ill-shaped Greek letters on a tablet upon the rock bids Aletial (which is probably a veiled name for the Magdalen) to "take courage!" The Muhammedans set a very high estimate upon a piece of precious stone serving as lintel of the entrance door, and although it appears to be nothing more than a highly polished block of a jaspery kind of agate, may once have been entitled (as it is now esteemed by its possessors) a "precious stone." One very similar to it may be seen, without difficulty or danger, over the door of Wely Kamah, north-west of the city. But the adventurous explorer would be wise to tarry here as short a time as possible, lest, before he is aware of it, he find himself in the midst of the peltings of a pitiless storm of stones showered upon him by all the boys and girls of Jebl Tûr, as well as the "children of an older growth"—for they never omit exercising this precious privilege of pelting Franks, graciously vouchsafed them by special firman from the Sublime Porte, unless the blows are warded off by the adroit management of the potent piastre—in the shape of a shield yclept "*buckshish!*"

"The Valley of the Dead Bodies" is, undoubtedly, an appellation appropriately applied to the Valley of the Kedron, which, it would appear, has always been the great burying ground of Jerusalem; but as a specific designation, it is applied to the depression north of the Temple area. Multitudes were, no doubt, buried in earth-graves which have in many places been swept away, while in other spots they have been deeply inhumed by successive accumulations of rubbish, forming stratum after stratum for sepulture. But most of the rock tombs still remain in a tolerably good state of preservation, and particularly those in the towering cliffs of the *Mount of Offence,* now appropriated to domestic use by the Silwanite Arabs; and, as the monks will have it, once the abode of Solomon's strange wives. In the north-western *cliff of Ben Hinnom*, and indeed in all the lower north-eastern portion of the slope of the Hill of Evil Council, there are great numbers yet remaining notwithstanding the destructive agency of gunpowder brought to bear upon them so effectually by the vandal Greeks of late years. The doorways of these tombs are not elaborately carved; but some of them are surmounted by chaste Doric pediments.

Toward the lower extremity of this region of Gehenna may be observed, at a considerable distance, a conspicuously situated and well finished sepulchre, sometimes called the "whited sepulchre;" and near it is the "*Latibulum Apostolorum*"—"Apostles' Retreat"—where it is said the Apostles (ten of them at least) concealed themselves during the period of the Saviour's inhumation! Over the entrance may still be deciphered the celebrated inscription ΤΗΣ ΑΓΙΑΣ ΣΙΩΝ, which suggested to a learned traveller the strangely preposterous conceit of the identity of this hill with Mount Zion! But the suggestion of the lamented Shultz that this inscription merely indicates this tomb as the cemetery of "The Holy Church of Mount Zion" (Agia), is no doubt correct and sufficiently explanatory of the inscription. During the occupancy of these mansions of the dead (the larger by Cenobite communities, and the smaller by anchorites and half-dead half-alive hermits of every hue and dye), the walls of many of them were pictorially sanctified, and others inscribed with epitaphs, proprietors' names, &c.—a few in Hebrew but generally in ancient Greek characters, &c.; but they are now so much effaced that though many attempts have been made to decipher and translate them by archæologists—learned and unlearned—nothing has yet been evolved but contradiction and absurdity—

"Optics keen have they, I ween,
Who read what is not to be seen."

Amongst these tombs is one with a single loculus and anteroom, which was regarded by the above thaumaturgic mountain-moving traveller as the tomb of Joseph of Arimathea—"the true Holy Sepulchre!" as if there were not hundreds of others like it all around Jerusalem! and strangely enough forgetting that the Saviour must needs suffer without the walls (for, if it was on Mount Zion, as he conjectured, it was of course within the walls). Some of these charnel-houses have an arrangement of the receptacles within, not elsewhere to be observed: they are neither sarcophagi nor loculi—technically speaking—but undetached thin stone troughs or coffins, arranged somewhat after the manner of berths in a vessel, containing perhaps a dozen skeletons in each depository, in most revolting pell-mell disorder. In exploring the lower story of one of these cells of death, which we accidentally stumbled upon, we found some consecrated wafers, water in a Jordan-can, saint-seeming pictures, and images of the Madonna and Infant Saviour sculptured in Jerusalem marble; the monumental offering, apparently, of a Greek devotee. The room in which this offertory was found, is entered by a door in the floor above, and seems altogether to have escaped observation in modern times; though the condition in which the pictures and bread, the oil and the lamp, were found, forbids the idea that they could have lain there more than a few score years. The extent of the tomb is equal to that of Jehoshaphat, immediately behind the Pillar of Absalom, and like that is literally strewn with dead bodies, and but seldom explored by travellers. The outer doorway is a mere hole in the earth, rudely faced with rocks; but the door of the tomb itself is considerably below the general surface of the ground, and is reached by a rapid descent through a rudely-lined passage of five or six yards in length. The accompanying representation of this entrance will also give a general idea of many other entrances to these sepulchral excavations.

ACELDAMA.—Just above the Retreat is shown a place called *The Field of Blood* to this day—"The Potters' Field," bought with the reward of iniquity—called in the Jews' own proper tongue "Aceldama"—that was appropriated by the *benevolent* and conscientious chief priests and elders as a place to bury strangers in. The vault or cemetery itself is about sixty feet square, twenty or thirty in depth, and is only subterranean in part. The rock being very friable, has long since crumbled to pieces on the lower side, where the former entrance was, and been replaced by an artificial wall of rather inferior construction. The vault thrown over it is even with the ground on the upper side, but is probably twenty feet above the ground on the side next to Hinnom. There are two doors above, and a third opening from an adjoining cave; but no means of descending it. The remains of large square pillars of the Jewish order render it highly probable that the superstructure was always artificial to a great extent. The interior has undergone so much disintegration in the lapse of ages that the loculi are scarcely discernible in some places. This disintegrated dirt being supposed very favorable to speedy decomposition, much of it has been sent to foreign cemeteries; and it has been the custom for ages past, until quite a recent period, to cast into this pit the corpses of the poor penniless pilgrim dying at Jerusalem, many of whose skulls are seen lying about the floor.* There is a bed of whitish earth not far from this famous receptacle of the dead, generally supposed to be clay, but evidently calcareous in its nature. It is, however, triumphantly pointed at by the advocates of tradition, in proof of the correct identification of Aceldama. And although this alleged identity cannot be disproved, yet it is much more probable that it is the tomb of the high priest Annas or Ananias, or Ananus as Josephus calls him (W. v. xii: 2), whose monument was certainly in this immediate vicinity—just where we would be inclined

* Sir J. Maundeville says, that "in that felde ben manye tombs of Christine men: for there ben manye pilgrymes graven."

to look for it—conspicuously situated in full view of the Temple. In conformity with the general belief that the earth of Potters' Field possessed the peculiar property of expediting the putrefactive process, we are told by Monroe, that, "By order of the Empress Helena, two hundred and seventy ship-loads of it were translated to Rome and deposited in the Campo Santo, near the Vatican; where it was wont to reject the bodies of the Romans, and only consume those of strangers!" The interior of the Campo Santo at Pisa is also filled with this soil, when I saw it two years ago producing a rank crop of alopecurus and other grasses.

"The *Tree whereon Judas hung himself*," and from which, "falling headlong, he burst asunder in the midst, and all his bowels gushed out," is now shown beyond the limits of the field, about one hundred yards south-east of the summit of the Hill of Evil Council. During the Frank kingdom, it was located in Gehenna, at the foot of the cliff opposite the traditional Aceldama—a much more likely site, certainly, for here the cliff is thirty or forty feet in height; and should he have fallen into the rocky gorge below, from an overhanging limb at this place, such a doom of the traitor would have been as natural as well merited.

Neby Daud—The Traditional Tomb of David.—This most sacred of all the sacred localities of the Turks in El-Khuds (the Holy) is situated beneath the Cœnaculum, or "large upper room," in the hamlet called Neby Däûd, near Zion Gate; and is in the cherished custody of the very élite of Turkish society. Hence a suite of apartments was assigned Ibrahim Pasha in this revered place as his abode during his sojourn at the Holy City.

No spot about the Holy City is half so jealously guarded as this sanctum sanctorum of the Moslems, so confidently believed by Jew and Christian as well as Mussulman to contain the dust of the "Sweet Singer of Israel." Hence the superstitious awe with which it is venerated by Mussulmans, is only equalled by the itching curiosity of Jews and Christians to explore the hidden arcana of its mysterious recesses. Many have been the attempts by foul means and by fair, by lavish buckshishes as well as by furtive efforts, to gain admittance; but all efforts have proved entirely abortive, until quite recently, when my daughter had the good fortune to be admitted, without money, without price, and without intrigue—simply through the strong attachment of a Moslem lady. Many have succeeded to their heart's content in bribing the body guard of the royal prophet; indeed a few hundred dollars will readily compass such a feat. But then the good old sheikh has rather a curious way of fulfilling the terms and conditions of his covenant, by palming off a tumulus of richly canopied stone and mortar on the floor of an *upper room*, which, however, he is willing to swear by the beard of Mohammed is the veritable tomb of King David, Solomon, Hezekiah, Uzziah, &c., &c., &c. Indeed, I was myself victimized "on that wise." Having succeeded in relieving a favorite slave of the old effendi—and, what was far more highly appreciated, successfully treated a favorite wife of one of his sons, who was laboring under that most vexatious of all Oriental female complaints, sterility—he evidenced his profound gratitude by perpetrating the same fraud upon me.

My daughter, however, was far more fortunate than any of us, as will be perceived on reading the following extract from her journal. It was just at that critical juncture of Ottoman affairs attendant upon the breaking out of the war between Russia and Turkey when the Sultan had sent an imperative firman to the Holy City, enjoining all the faithful, under penalty of "five hundred sticks," to repair to the Haram every Friday at twelve o'clock, to pray for the success of the war against the infidels; of course, all the "faithful" were conscienciously bound to be there at the specified time! It fortunately so happened, too, that my daughter's hands being well tattooed with henna at the time, she was in possession of a most desirable—indeed, indispensable passport. Circumstances seemed to be so propitious in every respect, and the contingency of danger so remote and improbable, that, after holding a brief family council, we could but agree that she should accept the pressing invitation of the generous lady, who, by-the-bye, being a relative of the old

Neby Däûd effendi, and intimately acquainted with all the premises as well as the keepers and domestics, was the best possible cicerone—considerations certainly of no small moment in such an adventure, especially in the event of any exigency.

Extract.—"Early one morning, during the great Mohammedan feast of Rhamadan, I was called to the 'parley' room, to see my friend Moosa. This little fellow having become rather a frequent visiter, I was at first inclined to excuse myself; but remembering he had lately hinted at the possibility of my gaining an entrance into the Tomb of David, and in consideration, too, of the fact, that being their fasting season, the everlasting finjan of coffee and douceur of sweetmeats—those otherwise indispensable marks of Turkish civility—might now be dispensed with, I concluded to make my appearance. On entering the room my pleasing suspicions were confirmed, by seeing him close the door and mysteriously place his forefinger on his lips, in token of profound secrecy. He laid his ponderous turban on the divan beside him, doffed his slippers, crossed his legs, and then disclosed the nature of his errand. In short, I was informed that his sister was ready for an adventure; and, as I was too, we were not long in reaching 'Turfendah,' (his sister), who immediately commenced operations. My hair was taken down and braided in scores of little plaits. A red cloth cap, with a blue silk tassel, was placed on my head, and around it a gauze turban, with gold tassels and embroidery. My robe and trowsers were of the finest Damascus silk, my girdle of cashmere, and tunic of light blue stuff, embroidered in silver flowers. My hands were already dyed with 'henna,' having undergone this process on the occasion of a former adventure in the Mosque of Omar, and still retained the deep yellow hue; my skin was pretty deeply tanned, too, from a residence of several years under a burning Syrian sun, which was quite an addition to my Turkish appearance. The sheet, veil, and slippers came in due order; and having secreted my pencil and sketch-book in the folds of my girdle, we sallied forth, accompanied by Turfendah's favorite slave.

"The reputed Tomb of David is just outside of Zion Gate, hard by the Cœnaculum and American cemetery. It is surrounded by an irregular pile of buildings, and surmounted by a dome and minaret. In the interior are some of the most grotesque architectural embellishments imaginable, on the capitals of some remains of the Crusaders' architecture. Just think of the frightful owl occupying the place of the classic acanthus and the mythic lotus! We passed the several halls and corridors, evidently of the style of the Quixotic era of the Crusaders' domination, before reaching the consecrated apartment, whose entrance is guarded by double iron doors. We found here an old derwish prostrate in prayer, on the cold stone floor. Not being privileged, as we, to enter the sacred precincts, he was content with gazing at the Tomb through the iron bars; for it is a rare thing for even a Mussulman ecclesiastic to gain admittance—my companion and her family only enjoying this privilege, because they are very near relatives of the curator of the tomb. Our slave was despatched for the key, which she had no difficulty in obtaining, on the plea that her mistress wished to pray on the holy spot. But what was my consternation on seeing another slave return with her! I confess that I trembled, and was thinking I had best leave my awkward slippers behind, in case of retreat, as they would greatly impede my progress, and might thereby cause me to lose my head! She peered under my veil, asked who I was, and seemed satisfied with the careless reply of Turfendah, that I was merely a friend of hers from Stamboul! She invited us up stairs to see the old keeper's hareem; and Dahudeah (Moosa's little wife) who is always glad to exchange the purgatory of a residence with her lord and master, for a visit of a few days here; for I can testify from personal observation, that the young effendi lords it over her in true Oriental conjugal style! Turfendah regretted she could not accept her kind invitation, and, as she was so much exhausted from fasting, she would prefer deferring it to another time! The slave then left, to our mutual relief, and, having dismissed the old derwish, the doors were closed and doubly locked. The room is insignificant in its dimensions, but is furnished very gorgeously. The tomb is apparently an immense sarcophagus of rough stone, and is covered by green satin tapestry, richly embroidered with gold. To this a piece of black velvet is attached, with a few inscriptions from the Koran, embroidered also in gold. A satin canopy of red, blue, green, and yellow stripes, hangs over the tomb; and another piece of black velvet tapestry, embroidered in silver, covers a door in one end of the room, which they said, leads to a cave underneath. Two tall silver candlesticks stand before this door, and a little lamp hangs in a window near it, which is kept constantly burning, and whose wick, though saturated with oil—and, I dare say, a most nauseous dose—my devotional companion eagerly swallowed, muttering to herself a prayer with many a genuflexion. She then, in addition to their usual forms of prayer, prostrated herself before the tomb, raised the covering, pressed her forehead to the stone, and then kissed it many times. The ceiling of the room is vaulted, and the walls covered with blue porcelain, in floral figures. Having remained here an hour or more, and completed my sketch, we left; and great was my rejoicing when I found myself once more at home, out of danger, and still better, out of my awkward costume." * * *

The result of her pencilling is before the reader, and sufficiently speaks for itself.

No small portion of the interest attaching to the Tomb of David is due to the treasure supposed to be still buried somewhere below. Josephus informs us (Ant. vii. xv: 3), that "David was buried by his son Solomon in Jerusalem, with great magnificence and with all the other funeral pomp with which kings used to be buried with; moreover, he had great and immense wealth buried with him, the vastness of which may be easily conjectured at by what I shall now say: for, a thousand and three years afterwards, Hyrcanus the high priest, when he was besieged by Antiochus that was called the Pious, son of Demetrius, and was desirous of giving him money to get him to raise the siege and draw off his army; and having no other method of compassing the money, opened one room of David's sepulchre, and took out three thousand talents, and gave part of that sum to Antiochus, and by this means caused the siege to be raised. Nay, after him and that many years, Herod the king opened another room, and took away a great deal of money; and yet neither of them came at the coffins of the kings themselves, for their bodies were buried under the earth so artfully, that they did not appear to those that entered into their monuments."

Of this last robbery (by the high priest) the Jewish historian gives us farther particulars in another place (Ant. xvi. vii: 1): "As for Herod, he had spent vast sums about the cities, both without and within his own kingdom; and as he had before heard that Hyrcanus, who had been king before him, had opened David's sepulchre and taken out of it three thousand talents of silver, and that there was a much greater number left behind, and indeed enough to suffice all his wants; he had a great while an intention to make the attempt; and at this time he opened that sepulchre at night, and went to it, and endeavored that it should not be at all known in the city, but took only his most faithful friends with him. As for any money, he found none, as Hyrcanus had done, but that furniture of gold, and those precious goods that were laid up there; all these he took away. However, he had a great desire to make a more diligent search, and to go farther in, even as far as the very bodies of David and Solomon; where two of his guards were slain by a flame that burst out upon those that went in, as the report was. So he was terribly affrighted, and went out, and built a propitiatory monument of that fright he had been in; and this of white stone, at the mouth of the sepulchre, and that at a great expense also. And even Nicholaus, his historiographer, makes mention of this monument built by Herod, though he does not mention his going down into the sepulchre, as knowing that action to be of ill repute."

Benjamin of Tudela, who is generally regarded as a trustworthy chronicler, visited Jerusalem about A. D. 1860–1870, and tells the following rather hard story about this mysterious place. "On Mount Zion are the sepulchres of the house of David and those of the kings who reigned after him. In consequence of the following circumstance, however, this place is hardly to be recognised at present. Fifteen years ago, one of the walls of the place of worship on Mount Zion fell down, which the patriarch ordered the priest to repair. He commanded to take stones from the original wall of Zion, and to employ them for that purpose; which command was obeyed. Two laborers who were engaged in digging stones from the very foundation of the walls of Zion, happened to meet with one which formed the mouth of a cavern. They agreed to enter the cave and search for treasure; and in pursuit of this object they penetrated to a large hall, supported by pillars of marble incrusted with gold and silver, before which stood a table with a golden sceptre and crown. This was the sepulchre of David, king of Israel; to the left of which they saw that of Solomon, and of all the kings of Judah, who were buried there. They further saw locked chests, and desired to enter the hall to examine them, but a blast of wind like a storm issued from the cavern, and prostrated them almost lifeless upon the ground. They lay in this state till the evening, when they heard a voice commanding to rise up and go forth from the place. They proceeded, terror-stricken, to the patriarch, and informed him of what had occurred. He summoned Rabbi Abraham el Constantini, a pious ascetic, one of the mourners of the downfall of Jerusalem, and caused the two laborers to repeat the occurrence in his presence. Rabbi Abraham hereupon informed the patriarch that they had discovered the sepulchres of the house of David and of the kings of Judah. The patriarch ordered the place to be walled up, so as to hide it effectually from every one to the present day. The above-mentioned Rabbi Abraham told me all this."

If these accounts be credible, the royal sepulchres must have been successfully concealed from the Egyptians, the Chaldeans, the Romans, the Persians, and all other captors of the Holy City—which is rather a large draft upon one's faith to credit, especially as the site was evidently known in the days of Nehemiah and of the

Apostles It would appear that in the 16th century there were two travellers, Furer and Radzivil, who succeeded in bribing their way into an apartment in the hamlet of Neby Däûd something like the one represented by the chromograph: and it is a well-known fact that Sir Moses and Lady Montefiore were permitted—but at an immense cost, as I learn—"to behold through the lattice of a trellissed door" what they regarded as "the sacred and royal deposit of the best and noblest of kings."

That David and all his successors were buried far under ground is a well-established fact. The oblong tumulus must therefore be regarded as the representative of the "propitiatory monument" that Herod built over the mouth of the cave—if indeed it be not palmed off as the identical monument itself—though it is the common belief that the royal seer lies within this very tumulus just behind the tablet of black velvet.

A candid review of all the facts of the case constrains me to abandon the view I once entertained as to the genuineness of the site, and brings me confidently to the conclusion that the Tomb of David is several hundred yards east of the traditional locality. It is not even positively known that there are such extensive and well-executed excavations at the traditional site as would at all justify the tradition—even were all other matters more strictly in accordance with the demands of the case.

There are several other small but quite well-executed sepulchres, as also several natural caverns, a short distance below Neby Däûd; and it is not at all improbable that the tomb now claimed to be David's, is indeed a royal sepulchre, but the property of one of the leprous or dishonored kings instead of that of the great prophet-king of Israel.

Charnel-House of the Lion.—Amongst the numerous church edifices reared by the Franks during the period of their domination in Palestine was the Church of St. Mamilla or Babilla, over extensive sepulchral excavations three or four hundred feet west of the traditional Pool of Gihon. It is called Charnel-House of the Lion, because the Christians slain at the sack of Jerusalem by the Persians under Chosroes II. are said to have been dragged and thrown into the cavern by a tender-hearted lion; and the especial design of the church was daily to chant prayers over their remains. These catacombs appear to have been merely a natural cave at first, but were subsequently enlarged and strengthened by excavation and masonry. It is a soft, easily disintegrated rock, however, and much of it, like the bones of the poor Christians, has mouldered into dust. The catacombs are in the midst of the Turkish burying-ground, where there are several welies containing the remains of distinguished Moslem *saints*, and several natural caverns and artificial excavations in which are great numbers of skeletons. And in the Muhammedan cemetery along the east side of the Haram and on the Hill of Goath, portions of partially decayed corpses may frequently be seen protruding from the ground. Still more loathsome is the sight occasionally witnessed in the Jewish burying-ground, where for want of room they are frequently buried in tiers—the topmost one, of course, being very superficially covered. The Jews have a small cemetery on Mount Ophel, and quite a large one on Mount Zion; but by far the largest occupies the valley of the Kedron and the western slope of Olivet, stretching from the village of Silwan nearly to the Garden of Gethsemane, about two hundred yards in breadth.

The Christian cemeteries occupy but little space, and are all on Mount Zion. A parcel of ground near the "Birket Mamilla" was first secured for the Anglican Cemetery; but the "faithful" became so scandalized and horrified by this vicinage of "Christian dogs," that, after enduring much vexatious litigation, the English missionaries were very willing to exchange it for a site on the brow of Zion just above the "Birket es-Sultan," quite a picturesque and eligible situation. The other Christian cemeteries are near Zion Gate, as indicated on the large map—Armenian, Latin, Greek, and American. The traveller can but look with melancholy interest on the slab that covers the remains of Costigan, the unfortunate explorer of the Dead Sea, as he strolls through the Latin graveyard. Dr. Robinson gives the following affecting account of the last end of a young American *Protestant*, of whom I have heard much also from others.

"In the Latin quarter one inscription struck my eye particularly; it contained the name of my own country, and marked the grave of a young American. Ten years ago I had known him in Paris in the flower of his youth, a favorite in the family of La Fayette, and moving in the gay circles of that gay metropolis. He had soon after wandered off to Egypt and the east; and, in 1830, died here alone and friendless in the Latin convent. The epitaph with which the monks have honored him declares, that 'of his own accord he abjured the errors of Luther and Calvin, and professed the Catholic religion.' Poor youth! he knew too little of the doctrines of the Reformers, and still less of those of the Romish Church. No friend was near to watch over his last moments; and the strongest inference that can be drawn from the above language is, that in order to be left in quiet he gave assent to all their questions. Or, not improbably, the assertion may rest merely on the fact, that in his dying hour, when consciousness perhaps was gone, they administered to him extreme unction. The stone purports to have been placed by 'weeping friends'—rejoicing Catholics of course; for no others could have put an inscription like the following over his grave.

D. O. M.
HIC JACET
C. B. Ex Americanæ Regionibus
Lugduni Galliæ Consul, Hierosolymis tactus intrinsecus sponte
Erroribus Lutheri et Calvini abjectis
Catholicam Religionem professus, Synanche correptus
E vita decessit IV nonas Augusti MDCCCXXX
Ætatis suæ
XXV
Amici mœrentes posuere
Orate pro eo."

To Professor Robinson I am also indebted for the following

AMERICAN CEMETERY—NEAR NEBY DAUD.

account of the American Cemetery, liberally provided for their Jerusalem Mission by the American Board of Commissioners for Foreign Missions, several years prior to their abandonment of that station. It is still owned by the Mission, however; and any Protestant dying at Jerusalem is allowed to repose within its walls on payment of a small sum—and if poor, without money and without price. "A little to the southward of the Latin Cemetery, and adjacent to the north-west enclosures connected with the Mosque and Tomb of David, is a small plat of ground which has been purchased by the American missionaries as a place of burial for their dead. To this measure they were driven almost by necessity. Two of their members, Mrs. Thomson and Dr. Dodge, had already died in Jerusalem. For the former a grave was sought and obtained without difficulty in the Cemetery of the Greeks. In the case of the latter, the same permission was granted, and a grave dug; but as they were about to proceed to the burial, word was brought that the permission had been recalled and the grave filled up. On a strong representation of the case to the heads of the Greek convent, the burial was allowed to take place, with the express understanding that a like permission would never more be given. In consequence, the missionaries purchased this little spot upon Mount Zion, and enclosed it with a common wall of stone. The plat contains two or three olive-trees, and looked green and peaceful; but it was yet untenanted. After the purchase had been made, and possession delivered, the authorities of the city hesitated to give it the last legal sanction. They did not object to the transaction itself; but, as they wanted a bribe of some fifty dollars in their own pockets, they professed to entertain scruples, whether it was fitting that Christian corpses should be buried so near the sacred Tomb of David. The matter had not at that time been brought to a close, and, until this was done, the missionaries did not choose to transfer thither the relics of their friends. I have since learned, that during the last year (1840) the Mission caused a permanent wall to be erected around the plat, with a door under lock and key; and shortly afterwards, on the death of a child of Mr. Nicolayson, the body was interred with all due formalities within the precincts. All this was done without opposition on the part of the authorities; and as such matters are here usually settled by full possession and prescription, no further difficulty is apprehended." The remains of Dr. Fisk, and several other Americans have since been interred in this unpretending graveyard.

This brief notice must suffice for the sepulchres and sepulchral buildings without the city; but, within the walls, there is an edifice to which so profound an interest attaches that it justly demands a more detailed notice. I allude to the entire group of buildings known under the general appellation of "The Church of the Holy Sepulchre."

According to Eusebius, the Emperor Constantine (being divinely moved thereto soon after his memorable "*in-hoc-signo-vinces*" vision) caused the dirt and other obstructions with which Hadrian is said to have covered a certain rock cavern, as well as the sanctuary of Venus which had been erected upon this immense pile of earth, to be removed, and a magnificent temple to be built about it—under the *impression* that this cavern was no other than the identical sepulchre in which the Saviour was buried. It was accordingly accomplished in the finest style; and the various edifices, called collectively the Temple, dedicated A. D. 335. The monticule containing the alleged sepulchre of the Lord was cut away until it became only a foot or two in thickness around the cavern, which seems at the same time to have been converted into a double-roomed sepulchre, and was covered with marble within and without—this Ædicula being the true Church of the Anastasis, around which a very large circular building was erected, and, on the east, various other magnificent structures—the Martyrium, Basilica, &c.

It is gravely affirmed (not by Eusebius, however, but by all immediately-succeeding writers) that the true cross on which Emmanuel had suffered was brought to light and verified under the following circumstances. The Empress Helena, on making a pilgrimage to the Holy City, having by divine direction and guidance at last discovered the sepulchre, was much perplexed by three crosses, a tablet, and some large nails close by. The tablet, however, not being in connexion with either of the crosses, it was still uncertain which was the "true cross." But Bishop Macarius happily suggested an expedient by which their harassing doubts were immediately relieved, and the perplexing question at once and for ever settled infallibly. The three crosses were successively presented before a noble lady of the Holy City that lay hopelessly sick. The first one exhibited produced no effect whatever; neither did the second; but no sooner was the third one placed near her than she sprang up, perfectly restored!

This magnificent pile, thus erected by order of Constantine, remained about three hundred years; when it was studiously destroyed by the Persian and Jewish army under Chosroes II., who doomed it to the ordeal of fire, A. D. 614. Another series of buildings was, however, soon erected on the site of the former, but, as would seem, considerably varied in form, dimensions, and style.

from a Photograph. J. C. Buttre.

Church of the Holy Sepulchre

The Church of the Holy Sepulchre, as well as all other Christian edifices, seems to have escaped the hand of spoilation from this time onward, till the city fell under the dominion of the Fatimites; for be it said, to the honor of Omar and in justice to Arab character, that he sacredly observed the stipulations of his covenant in behalf of the Christian buildings. In 969, however, the Khalif Muez gave orders to destroy the buildings, as far at least as destruction could be compassed, by fire. And during the Khalifate of el-Hakim, in 1010, the Church of the Holy Sepulchre was entirely demolished by the Governor of Ramley, under his orders—the building being not only razed to its foundations, but special efforts made to deface and destroy the sepulchre itself.* Glaber, a contemporary chronicler, relates that they endeavored to break in pieces even the hollow tomb of the sepulchre with iron hammers, but without success: and Ademar, another chronicler and palmer, states that, when they found it impossible to break in pieces the stone of the monument, they tried to destroy it by the help of fire; but that it remained firm and solid as adamant!!!

Its reconstruction was commenced under the successor of Hakim, and completed in 1048, but evidently in a much less imposing style; and in this state the buildings were found by the Crusaders in 1099, when they captured the city; but were soon afterwards enlarged and beautified.

In 1808 this entire pile of buildings was again doomed to destruction by fire; but, phœnix-like, rose from its ashes in 1810. The following account of this conflagration is given by one who not only believes most firmly that the alleged site of Calvary and the Tomb is the genuine one, but that, notwithstanding all the fires and spoilations to which the place has been subjected, the original shell of rock still remains:—"I need not enter into the details of that fire. It will be sufficient for my purpose to state that the heat was so excessive that the marble columns which surrounded the circular

* Professor Willis.

building, in the centre of which stood the sacred grotto, were completely pulverized. The lamps and chandeliers, with the other vessels of the church—brass, and silver, and gold—were melted like wax: the molten lead from the immense dome which crowned the Holy Sepulchre poured down in torrents; the chapel erected by the Crusaders on the top of the monolith was entirely consumed; half the ornamental hangings in the ante-chapel of the Angel were scorched; but the cave itself, though deluged with a shower of lead and buried in a mountain of fire, received not the slightest injury internally; the silk hangings and the painting of the Resurrection remaining, in the midst of the volcanic eruption, unscathed by the flame, the smell of fire not having passed upon them." But, whether or not this thin wall of native limestone around the sepulchre can have escaped the destroying agency of a heat that converted the more refractory marble into lime—even if it had not been previously demolished by the destroying hand of man—the reader must needs judge for himself; for, though it would be so easy to settle the question by giving ocular proof of its continued existence if still there, the "Guardians of the Sepulchre" take special care not to permit examination to be made by any heretical "outsider." But the traditionist that has credulity enough to believe in the "invention" of the cross, as its discovery is called—that shallowest of all the shallow *inventions* of the "mystery of iniquity"—will find but little difficulty in believing the alleged asbestine character of the sepulchre, or the salamandrine properties of its tapestry and paintings: still less will he find in believing that the mighty heathen emperor of the world, instead of utterly destroying the little rocky prominence containing the sepulchre (or *cave*, as Eusebius calls it—antron), was content in his spiteful hate merely to cover it up with earth: and none whatever, that the imperial architect was silly enough to erect the temple of the Goddess of Love upon this *pile of earth!!!*

But, indeed, whether this locality can *possibly* be the site of the crucifixion and burial of the Redeemer, in view of the historical evidence of the evangelic narrative, with which it is so irreconcilable, the archæological reasons so entirely inconsistent with it, and the topographical argument with which it is still more at variance—the reader must also judge for himself. It must also be borne in mind that although such a strenuous effort is made to press into the service of this locality, tradition of the highest antiquity, yet on investigation it is all resolved at last into a mere *presumption* that inasmuch as a temple was reared to Venus on that spot, *ergo* it may have been Calvary and the Garden of Sepulture! For, even admitting the genuineness of the *inventive* miracle by which the true cross is alleged to have been certified, the question as to the identification of the true sepulchre is by no means determined. But, supposing for argument's sake that the alleged site had been maintained by an unvarying tradition a hundred years older than that claimed by the warmest advocates of the legendary school, may not that tradition have been founded in error, as that in relation to the Church of Ascension most clearly is, and at least two also of those fixing the martyrdom of St. Stephen indubitably are—traditionists themselves being judges?

The historical and archæological aspect of the matter being sufficiently presented in considering the question of Golgotha, as well as incidentally here and elsewhere, the topographical bearing of the subject will now be briefly considered, referring the reader for a thorough consideration of the whole matter to the masterly argument of Professor Robinson, in his "Biblical Researches," and the "Bibliotheca Sacra," No. XI., 1846.

The crucifixion and burial of the Saviour having occurred without the walls, it must be conceded by the most devoted advocate of oral tradition that if it can be shown that the traditional Calvary and Sepulchre (or the site of the Church of the Holy Sepulchre) was within the city walls at the period of the crucifixion, then it must be admitted that a grand mistake has been made in fixing upon that spot; and hence the obvious corollary, that churches and kingdoms have long been fighting for that which neither is nor could be what tradition alleges. This whole question, though supposed to involve such momentous interests, being altogether topographical in its character, is susceptible of a settlement possessing nearly all the conclusiveness of an ocular demonstration. The decision of the matter wholly depends upon the location of the "Second Wall," which is thus described by Josephus (Wars v. iv: 2): "The Second Wall took its beginning from that gate which they call 'Gennath' which belonged to the First Wall; it only encompassed the northern quarter of the city, and reached as far as the Tower of Antonia." The position of Gennath—the starting point of the Second Wall—is therefore the pivot upon which the whole controversy turns. Now there is no doubt as to the *termination* of this wall,—the Tower of Antonia being a well ascertained point. But the precise part of the First Wall in which the Gennath Gate was placed, is a matter that has been keenly controverted on account of its bearing upon this question—"*topographers*" contending that its position must necessarily have been quite high up near the Hippic Tower, and "*traditionists*" that it was situated much lower down—some locating it as far east as the Turkish Bazaar.

In support of the assertion that Gennath Gate was situated as low down as the bazaars, it is alleged by those who contend that the Church of the Holy Sepulchre occupies the true site of the crucifixion and resurrection:—

1st. That the old columns still to be seen at the "Porta Judiciaria" and further southward parallel to the bazaars, are portions of the "internal decorations" of a gateway in the ancient outer wall.

2d. That a broken arch on the eastern side of the large open area fronting the Church of the Holy Sepulchre, was a gateway in the same wall.

3d. That the house at the intersection of the westernmost bazaar with David street, in which are found a few courses of stones resembling those in the Hippic Tower, but much smaller, is one of the towers of the ancient Second Wall—Mariamne perhaps.

4th. That Zion being more easily accessible at this point than it is below or above (for a considerable distance), was a very suitable place for a gate; and

5th. That the crown of an old arch on the street leading hence to Zion Gate, thirty or forty yards south of David street, near a dyer's shop, is Gennath Gate itself.

It is most obvious that if the wall was indeed so far east, it would necessarily leave the Church of the Holy Sepulchre about one hundred yards outside on the west, and therefore the traditional sites *may possibly* be the true ones. But there are very serious objections and obstacles in the way of such a location of the wall.

A wall pursuing this course (going thence to Antonia via Damascus Gate, as is contended) could with no sort of propriety be said to *encompass* the northern quarter of the city within its narrow scope—the space thus included being a long irregular parallelogram. The remains still found in the tower rooms at Damascus Gate so unmistakeably proclaim these structures to have been a part of the ancient "Second Wall," that traditionists are compelled to assign them a place in their location of the wall, however unnatural the parallelogram thus made. It would thus leave nearly one-half of the northern wall of Zion unprotected at its weakest point, contrary to the declaration of Josephus. A wall thus situated on the steep slope of Akra would also be entirely unavailing as a defensive structure. Nor could there have been any object in locating a wall so disadvantageously in respect to security and the quantity of ground enclosed, when there was a site so much better but a short distance above, where nearly twice as much area would be included by the same extent of wall—or one certainly not exceeding it more than fifty or one hundred yards in length. The exclusion of the Birket el-Batrack, or the traditional Pool of Hezekiah, so that it would be unavailable to the citizens but available for the enemy in time of siege, is also *another* most serious objection to this location of the wall. Not only, however, do these strong objections obtain, but the arguments urged in behalf of such a location are altogether inapplicable. The "pillars" along the bazaar, instead of forming a portion of an imaginary gateway, extended formerly (as is clearly proved by the remains still existing between the covered bazaar and the "Judgment Gate") about one hundred and fifty yards, and evidently belong to the propyleum or colonnade of the Basilica of the Church of the Holy Sepulchre, as satisfactorily appears from accounts of the Chronicles.* Equally evident is it from the same authorities, that the broken portal or "smaller half of an arch" is the remains of one of the entrances to the palace of the "Knight's Hospitalers." The alleged Tower of Mariamne is considerably too far north to belong to the First Wall, which Josephus says was elevated on the brow of Zion thirty cubits above the valley in which this house stands, even if its rocks were not too diminutive to be the remains of the tower described by Josephus. This depression is certainly more suitable for a gate than the adjoining ground, either above or below; but even if it could be shown that there ever was a gate there, it would yet remain to be proved that it was the *Gennath*—and besides, if this depression be not the site of Millo and Silla, where are we to look for these places? The gateway which is sought to be identified with Gennath, unfortunately ranges north and south (!!) instead of east and west as required; and moreover belongs to a wall (I observed at intervals, while excavations were being made in that part of Zion), running in quite another direction within fifteen or twenty feet of the Zion Minaret (nearly two hundred yards further north), and containing several well preserved arches. The curious traveller may see a portion of this wall beneath the Askenazim Synagogue, some of whose arches are six feet thick and twelve in span, with stones generally $3 \times 2 \times 2$; though some of them are six feet in length. The arch near David street may be a portion of the Millo works; and the wall farther on southward may well be the representative of the ancient boundary of Jebus "when

* Those near the middle are gray granite, and may have belonged to the propyleum, but those now remaining at the northern and southern extremity are of native reddish marble, and probably belonged to the colonnade or portico.

David captured it and built round about from Millo and inward." But it is not only obvious that none of the evidence adduced by traditionists in support of this location of the Second Wall and Gennath Gate can be relied upon; but it is evident from various considerations that this gate was much higher up—quite near the Tower of Hippicus. We know that Herod the Great had a magnificent garden on Mount Zion, in this immediate vicinity; and giving entrance, as it probably did, either directly into the garden or into a street leading by it, it is appropriately called "*Garden*" or "*Gennath*" Gate on that account.* It is probable also that it did not exist until the erection of the Third Wall, but was then rendered necessary to form a direct communication between Zion and Cœnopolis; though it may always have been used to give exit directly from Zion into the country.

Not only would a gate, situated in the westernmost part of the northern wall of Zion, be more convenient and serviceable than at any point lower down, but such is the nature of the ground that it must almost necessarily have been situated just there, near to Hippicus. We nowhere learn that Zion was ever attacked on the north until Akra had been previously captured; and this is in exact accordance with the declaration of Josephus, that this wall was protected by the "Second." Hence, Gennath Gate, where the "Second Wall" started from the "First," must, of necessity, have been situated near the western extremity of the northern boundary of Zion—and of course near Hippicus. It is evident that the monument of the high priest John was situated between the Second and Third Walls, opposite the Amygdalon Pool which was east of it, and that this pool is identical with that now called Hezekiah's Pool. From the immediate neighborhood of this pool, on its west, there ran a

* A late and elegant writer wonders that "no one has appeared to observe the interesting fact, however slight may seem its importance in this argument, that this gate opened toward that garden in which we suppose the Saviour found a tomb." But how could any sober-minded person make such a far-fetched conjecture, when he could but know that all that district was already built up, and was soon afterward enclosed by Agrippa!

wall to the Tower of Hippicus, which was repaired by Simon—"quite to the gate by which water is brought into Hippicus." There was, therefore, a gate in the First Wall, near this tower, through which water was conducted into it. Now, the Second Wall having started from a gate near Hippicus, the conclusion is almost irresistible that this gate through which water was brought into Hippicus was the Gennath.

The four tombs ascribed to Joseph of Arimathea, Nicodemus, Melchisedec, and Adam, are alleged by traditionists in proof that this site was beyond the walls; but there is no tradition relating to them earlier than the sixteenth century, and it is certain that the one built in the wall cannot be much older than eight hundred years—Hakim having entirely destroyed the church in the year 1010. But it were really trifling with the subject to seriously undertake a refutation of the puerile argument attempted to be drawn from the present existence of these tombs. For, what does it signify, if they have indeed all been excavated long before the erection of the Second Wall, when that district was clearly beyond the limits of the city, or what if made after the demolition of that wall and before its reconstruction, when it was again outside the city; or what—"*the end justifying the means*"—if they were all—as *one* certainly was—foisted there by the hand of well-meaning Pia Fraus!

But, though the pilgrim may turn away with disgust from these bald impositions upon his confidence, yet he will not fail to visit with interest the tombs of Godfrey of Bouillon and his brother Baldwin—the almost illegible inscriptions on which, when correctly deciphered, read thus:—

> "Hic jacet inclytus dux Godefridus de
> Bulion, qui totam istam terram ac-
> Quisivit cultui Christiano, cujus anima
> Regnit cum Christo. Amen."

> "Rex Balduinus, Judas alter Machabeus,
> Spes Patriæ, Vigor Ecclesiæ, Virtus utriusquæ,
> Quem formidabant, cui dona tributa ferebant
> Cædar et Egyptus, Dan ac homicid Damascus,
> Pro Dolor! In modico clauditer hoc tumulo."

One of the latest and most captivating writers upon the Holy City, albeit his style is rather poetic, jocose, and *airy* for so grave a subject, has so succinctly stated his creed on this mooted point that I may as well transcribe it—appending a concise remark or two, *en passant*, for the benefit of whom it may concern.*

"These points then," he avers, in announcing the four articles of his easy topographic faith, "appear to me sufficient evidence on which to rest my faith in the authenticity of the Holy Sepulchre:

"1. It is not credible that this locality was forgotten by Christians within three hundred years after the great events of the crucifixion, burial, and resurrection." [*And yet tradition itself does not even assert any such knowledge of its locality, or even existence; but simply that Constantine built the Church of the Holy Sepulchre upon a spot where it was thought Hadrian had erected a temple to Venus; and what if the valley-filling, mountain-levelling, Christian-hating Jews had levelled the monticule and scattered it, cave and all, to the four winds! What would the memory of the "oldest inhabitant" avail, if nothing were left to remember?*]

"2. Critical scholars and learned men employed in investigating the topography of the Holy Land, had no doubt of its authenticity in the fourth century." [*These critical scholars and learned men (in the fourth century—no short time that!!) were not a whit more competent than scores of moderns, who have come to a very different conclusion: and besides, the works of these fathers furnish abundant evidence that they were quite as gullible by "pious fraud" as some*

* An instance of this author's unpardonable looseness is found in the assertion made when speaking of this very subject—that "the springs of the upper Pool of Gihon formerly found their way across to the Valley of Jehosaphat;" across Mount Zion and Mount Moriah!!! Another evidence of his great inaccuracy also occurs in treating of the same theme, when speaking of the *size* of the stones in the traditionary Gate of Gennath. Equally mistaken is he in his *perhaps*, that "this gateway is the most massive perfect arch, ancient or modern, in Jerusalem." Had he pursued his investigations a little farther south, he would not only have found several "more perfect arches," but convincing proof also that this poor tortured gateway is far from being any part of the Second Wall.

other people in the world. Was not their faith founded alone in that incredible miracle ? ! !]

"3. No one, so far as we know, thought in that age of disputing the fact, but all men acknowledged its truth." [*That all men acknowledged its truth, I trow, would be rather difficult to prove at this late Anno Domini; and several persons may have thought of doubting it, and yet the fact be unknown to us after the lapse of more than fifteen hundred years !*]

"4. It is not doubted by any one that this is the locality in which those learned men placed their confidence, it having been well preserved from that time to this." [*Granted: but what of that? If it was an error then—as stubborn facts positively declare it was—just as great is the error now.*]

The gifted author thus continues:—"This is, I say, sufficient, without those additional considerations which I shall hereafter present. But of course, these grounds of faith may be undermined. It is not pretended that they sustain a certainty. He who would overcome the argument may do it in two ways:—"

"1. By proving that this is not the locality, from some evidence therewith connected." [*Which is clearly done by irrefragable evidence, drawn from historical, topographical, and archæological facts and considerations.*]

"2. By proving that some other place is the locality, and thereby establishing a sort of alibi. The second proposition it will not be necessary to consider, since no one can maintain it." [*Why can no one maintain it? The kind of alibi required, it will be found, may at least be plausibly inferred, from the considerations adduced in the article Golgotha. But to show that the events could not have transpired at the spot assigned them by tradition will amply suffice, and virtually amounts to an alibi. The physical features of the everlasting hills are rather more permanent and reliable than the oracles of Protean tradition; and it must needs be confessed by the most devoted traditionist, that that which is topographically impossible can-*

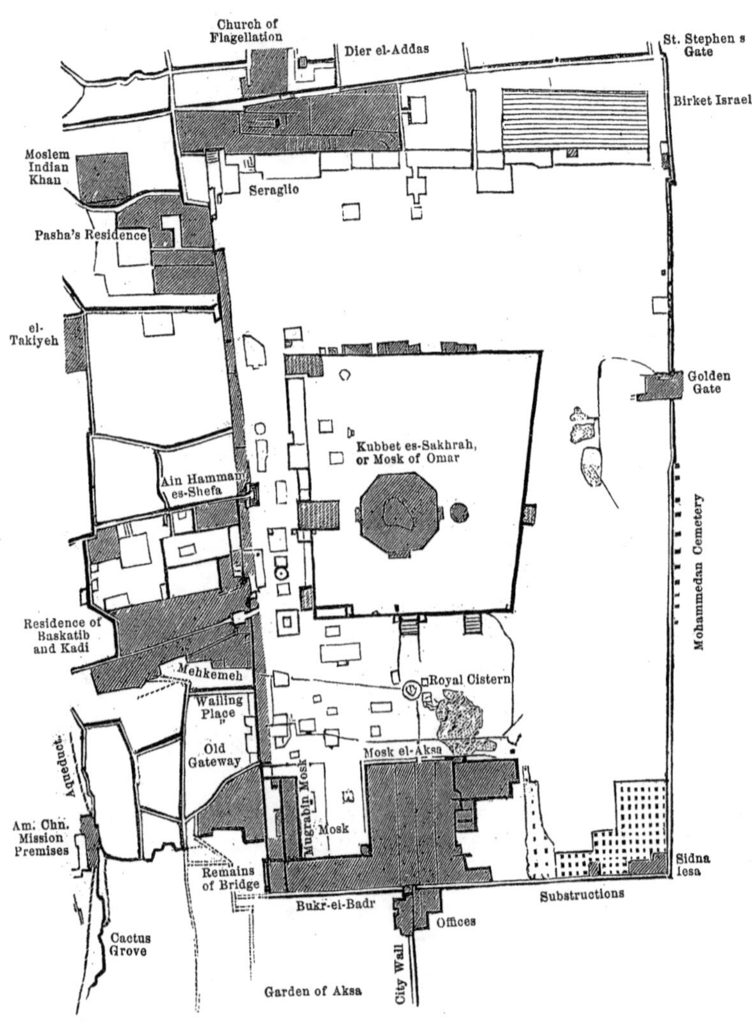

EL-HARAM ESH-SHERIF, OR MESJID EL-AKSA—THE AREA OF THE TEMPLE—AND ADJACENT PORTION OF THE CITY.

not be traditionally true—be the assumption never so confidently made and plausibly maintained.]

The admirable steel engraving cannot fail to impart to the reader a very impressive idea of the exterior appearance of the buildings: and, of the many sketch plans and diagrams of the interior of the premises that I have seen, the accompanying one is the best. And being not only approved by writers of the traditionary school, but quite in accordance with the large official plan given me by the architect effendi, it will serve the purpose of giving a sufficiently correct idea of the internal arrangements of this extensive group of buildings, without encumbering the subject with the details of the large Turkish plan.

Passing through the motley groups of pilgrims of every hue and dye that throng the "Mart of Holy Wares" in the court of the church, the visiter enters the vestibulum through the only door, (1), now permitted to remain open; and is equally surprised and mortified to find the whole premises under the surveillance of a haughty Turkish guard, mounted upon a rude kind of divan on the left, well armed with guns, swords, and cowhides—the latter of which, at least, they put in requisition on the most trivial occasions, and have no special objections to using the former.

The large marble slab, (3), around which the pilgrim sees so many devoutly kneeling, he is gravely told, is the "stone of unction," on which our Lord was washed and anointed for burial!

Leaving the vestibule, and turning to the left, the pilgrim is shown a small circular enclosure, (11), where Mary is said to have stood while the body of our Lord was being anointed.

We next enter a large rotunda, the main body of the building, about thirty-three yards in diameter, surrounded by an imposing colonnade, supporting the galleries and a lofty dome. It is on a slightly-elevated platform, directly beneath the skylight of this dome, that we find the beautiful marble Ædicula, or little church, containing the alleged tomb in which the Lord of Life lay. It is only about ten feet in breadth, and twice as much in length and height.

The accompanying representation conveys a correct idea of its outer appearance under ordinary circumstances; but, during festal occasions, it is very highly decorated.

ROTUNDA AND MAUSOLEUM OF CHURCH OF HOLY SEPULCHRE.

Pilgrims, travellers, and visiters of every hue and dye of the Frank order, are expected if not required to make bare both head and foot, on entering any of the sacred localities of the Holy City—whether Jewish, Moslem, or Christian; and at this point of his pilgrimage through these premises, the visiter is expected to doff his shoes as well as his hat; and if he would escape the scoffs and scowls of cowled monks, he must be very careful not to be guilty of crossing his hands behind his back—such a posture of ease being regarded as very disrespectful by the jealous custodians of the Sepulchre—some of whose watchful eyes follow you wherever you go, unless you are seen bowing before some of the shrines and pictures, or otherwise indicating, by crossing, kissing, and other bodily exercise, that you are a devotee of tradition. I once saw an English pilgrim of quite respectable exterior, leave the ranks of the procession in which he was marching around the corridor, and deliberately knock off the hat of a gentleman who was tacitly looking on from a short distance. And a gentleman standing by, was next morning challenged by the fiery bigot to *fight a duel*, merely because he had ventured a spirited remonstrance.

Leaving his hat and shoes at the door, the pilgrim enters the *anteroom* of the sepulchre—for although tradition declares that the little "*sanctuary*," as it is called, was originally a cave of one room, it is now found divided into two apartments. In the centre of this anteroom is a large block of stone, elevated on a pedestal, which the poor beguiled pilgrim is made to believe is the identical stone with which the mouth of the sepulchre was once stopped; though the Armenians allege with equal confidence that the stone they exhibit at the house of Caiaphas is the veritable one that the "angel rolled back from the door and sat upon." The pilgrim, having paid his devotions at this shrine, enters the inner room through a low narrow door. Here, at the right-hand on entering, is a marble sarcophagus partially imbedded in masonry, which tradition declares is the identical tomb of the rich man of Arimathea, in which the Son of God was buried! And though you may give no credit whatever to the tradition, and may be heartily disgusted with the mummery all around,

yet little is hazarded in saying that when you place your hands on that cold marble (as you find yourself doing by involuntary and irresistible impulse), you will feel an indescribable emotion felt never before or since.

The officiating priest liberally besprinkles you with sanctified rose water, and politely offers to consecrate any article you may desire; but still you feel anxious to breathe the open air once more, though the sanctuary is well ventilated, and sufficiently lighted by a number of lamps of gold, silver, and brass. The accompanying wood cut is a very accurate representation of the interior.

In the rear of the sanctuary is the joint shrine of the Copts, Abyssinians, and Syrians, (15), the most devout apparently of all the sects at Jerusalem. And yet the rites and ceremonies performed by these poor superstitious creatures are absurd and ridiculous in the extreme. The *religious antics* played off before high Heaven by these semi-nude jugglers, when it becomes their turn to march in procession around the sepulchre, were enough to make an angel weep!

It is part and parcel of the pilgrim's duty to render devotion at the tombs of Melchisedec, Joseph of Arimathea, and the honorable senator of Israel, situated beyond the colonnade, opposite the coptic shrine, (16, 17).

Entering the hall north of rotunda, you are shown the spot where Christ stood when he was taken for a gardener by Mary Magdalen, indicated by mosaics in the paved floor, (27), and the spot where Mary stood also, (28); and near these places, on the right, is the altar of the Franks, (29). You are now on Roman territory, and may hear some delightful music at matin and vespers, from the choir and organ in the gallery on the left.

Proceeding farther on, you enter another room by a low flight of steps—the Latin church—in the corner of which (at 30), you are permitted to thrust a cane through a small opening and touch something which you are told is the "Pillar of Flagellation" to which they say Christ was bound when scourged. The "Chapel of the Apparition," (32), or place where Christ first appeared to his mother after his resurrection, is also specially pointed out in this room, and with equal particularity and assurance, the place of the "recognition of the cross," (33).

Returning through the great rotunda and entering the Greek apartment beneath the lofty arched doorway, you observe near the middle of this fine large room a small pillar railed in, which infallible tradition declares is planted in the centre of the earth, in the very spot whence was taken the earth out of which Adam was made! It is called the "navel of the world," and though his tomb is in quite another part of the premises, yet they say his skull is buried beside this monumental pillar. Passing by the various shrines, thrones, and stalls in the Greek apartment, which abounds in puerile ornamentation with gold leaf, lamps, and ostrich eggshells, we enter the surrounding corridor, where we find "the Chapel of Mocking," (39), the "Chapel of the Parting of the Garments," (38), the "Chapel of Longinus the Centurion," (37), the "Chapel of Bonds"—where Christ was bound, (35), the "Chapel of the Virgin," (36), the "Chapel of the Crown of Thorns," &c.

Descending from this corridor by a long flight of steps, we reach an apartment in which are the chapels of "St. Helena" and the "Penitent Thief," (41, 42). And descending another flight in the south-east corner we reach the small grotto in the lowest spot about the premises—the "Chapel of the Cross," (44).

The chapel or "Mount of Crucifixion," on the "rock Calvary," is situated about midway between the sepulchre and the "Chapel of the Invention," i. e. about forty yards from each. It is reached by ascending a flight of steps *said* to be cut in the solid rock, but the entire surface being covered with marble or other stone, it is impossible to see the native limestone except where openings are left to exhibit the alleged holes in which the crosses were set, and the rent made in the rock. The Mount of Crucifixion is said to be a solid oval-shaped rock, about eight or ten yards in length, and half that breadth, but there is no proof whatever that there is any *live-rock* within the masonry—and in the present state of the case, it is impossible to say whether the holes and the "rent" are really in an elevation of native rock, or in a few isolated stones, duly prepared by pious hammer and chisel operation, to testify for the crosses and the earthquake.

The identification and aggregation of so many sites of important events within so small a compass is an absurdity at which credulity itself must stagger, and the most ardent devotee of tradition stand abashed.

CHAPTER IX.

THE TEMPLE.

"See what manner of stones and what buildings are here!"

"Palaces, temples, and piles stupendous,
Whose very ruins are tremendous."

THE splendid Temple of Solomon, which was reared by that great monarch according to the divinely ordered model * delivered to him by his father, and dedicated A. M. 3001, was entirely destroyed by Nebuchadnezzar four hundred and twenty-four years afterwards. Its reëdification was commenced sixty-nine years subsequently by Zerubbabel; but, owing to the numerous hindrances of those "troublous times," it was not completed till 511 B. C., when it was dedicated, seventy-three years after its destruction by Nebuchadnezzar. It was "*this house*,"† as reëdified and beautified by Herod the Great, that was filled with glory by the "Desire of all nations," and finally destroyed by the Romans A. D. 70. "Forty and six years was this temple in building" (John ii. 20), up to the first year of the Saviour's ministry, and was not even then completed, notwithstanding Herod had spent two whole years in the collection of materials, and constantly

* See 1 Chr. xxviii. 11, 12, 19.

† But, although the sacred fane has existed under several different phases, and it is common to designate them as first, second, and third Temples, yet it may be properly spoken of as only *one* Temple: and the prophet Haggai appears not only to identify the Zerubbabel Temple with that of Solomon, but it would seem that the future Millennial Temple may also be regarded as identical—as would appear from a comparison of 2 Chr. ii. 3-9, with Heb. xii. 26.

kept employed ten thousand artificers under the supervision of one thousand priests. Tacitus well characterized this superb structure as a "temple of immense wealth"—"*immensæ opulentiæ templum.*"

The temple of Zerubbabel is usually said to have been double the size of that of Solomon; but if the dimensions given in the 6th chapter of Ezra (3d verse) relate to the main building, as they most obviously do, then it was even less in length, no greater in breadth, and only half its height. Certain it is that it was not "magnifical" like that of the magnificent king, neither in material nor fabric. Herod's temple was ten cubits longer than Solomon's, and thirty longer than Zerubbabel's. It exceeded them likewise in breadth. And while it was forty cubits higher than Zerubbabel's, it was twenty less than Solomon's, except during the short period that the twenty extra cubits of wooden structure remained on its summit. It is probable, however, that the Temple proper, or the Holy House itself (*i. e.* the Holy Place and the Holy of Holies), was identical in each of these temples—the variations in size occurring only in the circumjacent chambers, and the pronaos, vestibule or porch. But it was only Solomon's Temple that could boast of the Ark, the Mercy Seat, the Shechinah, the Holy Fire, and the Urim and Thummim.

The Temple of Herod, immediately previous to its destruction by Titus, is that referred to in the following pages, unless otherwise expressly specified; and, as Josephus and the Talmud are almost the only authorities besides the brief descriptions contained in "Kings and Chronicles," I shall make large extracts from their detailed statements, in elucidation of the Bible account. Indeed, with the aid of the carefully and minutely executed plans, elevations, and sections, but little verbal description will be necessary to the fullest elucidation of the subject. It must be remembered, however, that the term "Temple" is used by Josephus and indeed by all authors, not excepting the sacred writers, with considerable latitude of meaning. In its most restricted sense it is used only to designate the Holy House, but very generally also not only the

Courts of the Priests, Israel, and the Women, but also that of the Gentiles. In a still wider sense the term is likewise used by Josephus so indefinitely as to include the Tower of Antonia as well as its yard, courts, &c., &c. The term sanctuary is used with less latitude of application, and is generally applicable no farther than the Court of Israel. But yet Ezekiel designates the entire enclosure of one mile square by this term in describing the Millennial Temple.*

That the Temple was situated *somewhere* within the oblong enclosure on Mount Moriah, all topographers are agreed, although there is not the slightest vestige of the sacred fane now remaining; and the greatest diversity of sentiment prevails as to its exact position within that large area. Some would restrict it to a square of six hundred feet in its south-west corner; others would place it exactly in the centre of the area; others again would make the large rock under the Kubbet es-Sakhrah the very rock on which Abraham offered up Isaac, and David sacrificed to stay the hand of the destroying angel,† and hence assign it a conspicuous place in the Temple, as the site of the Altar of Burnt Offerings, the Altar of Incense, or the Ark of the Testimony. But these are all, most evidently, mislocations—the limits of the first location being too contracted, those of the second entirely too extensive, and any allotment of the es-Sakhrah within the area of the Holy House or contiguous courts being entirely irreconcilable, not only with its relative position and elevation, but its actual size.

The Holy Place was forty cubits long, and twenty wide, and the Holy of Holies only twenty cubits square; of course, then, this huge rock, which is sixty feet in length (north and south), and fifty-

* *'Ιερὸν* is the the term generally rendered Temple in the instances above referred to; which generally means the Temple or fane, with its courts and appurtenances; while *Ναος* is restricted to the Holy House; and *Προναον* applies alone to the porch or vestibule.

† The narrative of this transaction is recorded 2 Sam. xxiv., and 1 Chr. xxi., and xxii. 1; in the former, David is said to have "bought the *threshing-floor and the oxen* for fifty shekels of silver;" and, in the latter, to have given "to Ornan, for the *place*, six hundred shekels of gold;"—purchasing no more at first than the rock itself, but afterward a large portion of Mount Moriah.

five in breadth (east and west), could not be accommodated in either of those apartments, upon any known computation of the cubit whatever. It is also far too large to have been included beneath the altar of Solomon, which was only twenty cubits square. But even were it small enough, it is not sufficiently elevated: for whereas, this rock is only about fifteen feet above the surrounding surface of the ground, the floor of the Court of the Priests, on which the Altar of Burnt Offerings was reared, was about forty feet above the general level. We also learn from the Talmud that the Holy House was reared upon a substructure of *masonry* forty feet in thickness, which of course entirely precludes the idea of the Sakhrah being its floor.

The belief that this rock is the identical threshing-floor of Araunah, the Jebusite, is almost universally entertained; and could it be identified as such, would be decisive as to the general location of the "House of the Lord God;" but that it is that memorable spot, is improbable in the highest degree. For it is by no means level enough for such a purpose—being considerably higher in the middle than elsewhere, and sloping irregularly in different directions. Rising too, as it does, nearly perpendicularly to a height of eight or ten feet, it could never have been sufficiently accessible for a threshing-floor. The narrative seems to require a surface much more even than this, and depressed, rather than elevated. The altar of David is several times said (both in Chronicles and Kings, as well as Josephus) to have been reared "*in*" the threshing-floor of Araunah—"*therein*" a circumstance in no way applicable to the present or any other prominently projecting rock; but sufficiently applicable to a low flat surface, especially if surrounded by other rocks or shrubbery.

The declaration of David that "this is the House of the Lord, and this is the altar of burnt offering for Israel" (1 Chr. xxii. 1), though evidently seeming to indicate the locality of either the house or the altar, yet, when it is remembered that Jacob used language concerning a certain spot at Bethel, almost identical with this, it may be understood in a more general sense. But still, as we learn (2 Chr. iii. 1) that "Solomon built the House of the Lord at Jerusalem, in the Mount Moriah, where the Lord appeared to David his father, in the place that David had prepared in the threshing-floor of Araunah the Jebusite," we could but locate it there, provided such a rock could now be found. It is not very likely, however, that the polytheistic, Jew-hating Hadrian would allow such a memorial of the one living and true God to remain, as the foundation marks of the Temple would be. In erecting his celebrated temple to Jupiter Capitolinus (when this idol-loving monarch even changed the name of the City of the Great King to Ælia, after his own name), he would doubtless remove all the landmarks of the place selected by Jehovah to record his name; and had the present es-Sakhrah in any way appertained to the Temple, not a vestige of it would have been permitted to remain—religious and political considerations equally concurring to forbid such a piece of impolicy.

But, allowing the present southern boundary of the Haram es-Sheriff to be coincident with that of the ancient Temple—of which scarcely a doubt can be entertained—the area assigned to the Temple, both by Josephus and the Talmud, presents an insuperable argument against the supposition that the es-Sakhra could have fallen within the Holy House or anywhere in its immediate vicinity. But in order to understand the subject the better, we must first bring Antonia under consideration.

Antonia, though devoted alone to military purposes, was considered an integral portion of the Temple, being indeed the fortress of the Temple, as the Temple was of the city: it is expedient, therefore, to bring them under consideration thus connected. We are entirely indebted to the learned Jewish historian so often quoted, for all we know concerning this fortress; but so complete is his description that we have but little occasion to regret the silence of the Talmud and other ancient writings about it. (See Wars v. v: 2, 8. Ant. xv. 4, 7.)

The Maccabees, finding the citadel on Akra better calculated to overawe the temple, when in the hands of an enemy, than to defend it, when possessed by themselves, doomed it to destruction in the reign of Simon, about 140 B. C., and in lieu of it erected this fortress, probably in the reign of John Hyrcanus. "It was of old called Baris or the Citadel; but afterwards got the name of Antonia, when Anthony was lord of the East, about which time Herod the Great re-fortified it and named it in honor of his great benefactor;" but it was not until his thorough reparation of the Temple and its appurtenances that it was finally completed—being then made no less a palace than a fortress.

The Acropolis, or fort itself, was situated at the north-west corner of the great quadrangular enclosure of Mount Moriah; but its extensive colonnades, courts, and appendages, extended as far as the sacred edifices, and covered an area about equal to that included within the outer cloisters of the Temple. The native rock upon which the citadel stood, was at the junction of the northern and western cloisters—being fifty cubits high and covered with polished stones, within which (on its top) was a wall three cubits high, and within this enclosure the main citadel was erected to the height of forty additional cubits. As to the interior space between this acropolis and the northern wall of the Temple enclosure (properly speaking), it "had the largeness and form of a palace, being parted into all kinds of rooms and other conveniences, such as courts and places for bathing, and broad spaces for camps; insomuch, that having all conveniences that cities wanted, it might seem to be composed of several cities, but by its magnificence it seemed to be a palace." The elevation on which the citadel stood was made by cutting through the Hill Bezetha. The mound thus isolated was trimmed down perpendicularly on the south and indeed all round. All the rocky surface in the north-west corner of the great area of the Temple was reduced, while the south-east corner was elevated on piers and arches in order to produce a uniform surface. The height of the Antonia rock at present is only twenty or thirty feet.

Besides this great tower on the rock at the north-west corner, it had also others at or near the three other corners, two of which were fifty cubits in height, but that at the south-east corner was no less than seventy cubits high, and commanded a fine interior view of the temple and its entire premises. The Acropolis was entirely separated from the Hill Bezetha, of which it was formerly a continuation, by a very deep trench cut through the solid rock. This huge L-shaped tower communicated with the massive cloisters that entirely surrounded the remainder of the fortress, at its inner angle. The exact extent of Antonia is nowhere specified; but we learn from Josephus (Wars iii. v: 2), that inclusive of the Temple it was six stadia: and as we are told (Ant. xi. xv: 3), that the Temple was a stadium on each side, it follows, of course, that these were also the general dimensions of Antonia. And that the entire enclosure of the Temple mount was a kind of oblong figure, capable of being reduced nearer to the form of a true square, we may also safely infer, from a remark made by Josephus on the capture of Antonia by the Roman army, that "the Jews by demolishing the Tower of Antonia had made their Temple four-square, while at the same time they had it written in their sacred oracles—that then should their city be taken, as well as their Holy House, when once their Temple should become four-square." An "occult passage" was constructed by Herod between the fortress Antonia and the Nicanor or Corinthian Gate, on the eastern side of the inner court of the Temple, where he erected a tower "that he might the more easily be enabled to quell any sudden insurrection of the people." But, to return to the consideration of the Temple area, properly so called.

A line running east and west across the area, along the upper side of the Sakhrah, makes the following apportionment of its upper and lower divisions:—for the lower or Temple portion, south wall 916, east 820, north 975, west 870: for the upper or Antonia enclosure, south 975, east 710, north 1030, west 730. The lower portion or Temple area is thus found to be nearly square, though only one or at most *two* of its corners is an exact right angle. The upper portion thus assigned to Antonia, though differing considerably from an exact square (as must necessarily always have been the case), yet is very nearly the same in capacity—being only one hundred and thirty-six feet less than the lower division, and inclusive of the tower around its north-west corner, exceeds it about two hundred feet—the one being 3581 feet, and the other 3445, exclusive of the tower. The area of Mount Moriah is thus divided into two distinct and nearly equal precincts, as the statements of Josephus require. But, though thus divided in accordance with the requirements of Josephus and the indications of the ground, yet, according to the ordinary estimate of Hebrew measures, the dimensions of these precincts considerably exceed those assigned them, not only by Josephus, but by the still larger estimates of the Talmud:—the former rating each side at 400 cubits (or a stadium), and the latter at 500 cubits. But the greatest diversity of opinion exists amongst archæologists in relation to the value of the cubit, stadium, &c., and it therefore becomes necessary to ascertain the length of these measures before we can proceed intelligently in our investigations.

The Jews, as well as other ancient nations, not only made use of different cubits and stadia or furlongs at different times, but also at the same time; and this too without the slightest specification: hence the necessity of research and discrimination on our part, if we would avoid erroneous conclusions. We may reasonably conclude that the Hebrew cubit was identical with the Egyptian Derah, (or drah, as the pîk* or cubit is pronounced at Jerusalem), which being used for gauging the waters of the Nile, has, no doubt, been preserved unaltered—a conclusion that receives some corroboration from the fact that it exactly measures certain rooms found in the Great Pyramids without excess or deficiency. Possessing no metrical standards of their own, and yet having constant occasion for measures, it is not at all improbable that the oppressed Israelites brought with them from Egypt the measures to which they had there become accustomed.

* From Πῆχυς, a cubit.

The Egyptian cubit or drah, as found on existing nilometers, is as 1824 compared with the English foot as 1000; or 21.8888 inches long. A cubit found at Memphis was 6 palms or 24 fingers on one side; and the other was 4 fingers greater.

The "cubit after a man" is the distance between the elbow and the tip of the middle finger, one-fourth the height of a well proportioned man, and is divided into 6 minor palms of four fingers each (24 fingers in all), and hence its division into 24 parts or finger-breadths. The average length of this cubit may fairly be set down at the usual estimate, 18 inches.

The "common cubit" is also estimated at 18 inches.

Some of the Rabbins rate the cubit at only 15 inches or 5 hand-breadths, and hence allow 18 inches only to the measure styled "a cubit and a hand-breadth."

Another Rabbinical estimate is 24 inches. But the Talmudists rate it at 22½ inches, adding a fourth to the Roman cubit.

The "sacred cubit" is by some supposed to have been 36 inches.

The Constantinople cubit, pîk or drah, is 30 inches; and the "builder's drah" of Jerusalem in common use, varies in length from 25 to 26½ inches.

The Arab cubit is rated at 18 inches, and the Greek and Roman cubits are just about the same—the former probably a fraction more, the latter a little less.

But although the Jewish cubit, in the earlier periods of their history, may have been identical with the Egyptian, it is by no means improbable that, when they came under the dominion of the Romans, they made much use of their metrical system, even though they may not have adopted it altogether. And this conjecture certainly derives some support from a circumstance mentioned by Josephus, in which he incidentally gives us a clue to the comparative value of the cubit and stadium. In describing the Temple he makes use of the stadium, cubit, and foot; and several times makes the stadium or furlong the equivalent of 400 cubits. If, then, the value of the stadium can be satisfactorily ascertained, we are at once furnished with a key to the estimates of Josephus and those of the Talmud too—for although different dimensions are assigned by these authorities for the walls of the Temple area, yet there is such a general agreement in their admeasurements within, that the same cubit, is, no doubt, used by both—the above estimate being merely conjectural.

A stadium, it would appear from the best authorities, contains 600 feet, Greek measure; and the Greek foot bearing the ratio of 25 to 24 compared with the Roman, 625 Roman feet constitute a stadium. Now, the Greek foot is rather longer, and the Roman rather shorter than the English—the former being as 12.135 inches to 12 of English measure, and the latter about 11.650. About 606¾ feet English measure, therefore, make a stadium or furlong, and are the equivalent of 600 Greek feet, and 625 Roman. On this computation—400 cubits being equal to the stadium of 606¾ feet (Eng.)—the cubit used by Josephus must be 1.517 feet; but for facility of calculation the small fraction of seventeen-thousandths may ordinarily be disregarded, and 18 inches be adopted as the value of the cubit under consideration. A larger estimate, it is true, would serve much better to reconcile some of the statements of Josephus to the stern requirements of existing localities; but on the other hand, were it smaller, it would be better adapted to the adjustment of certain other difficulties. A fact mentioned by Chrysostom, in relation to the low stature of the Apostle Paul, may not be without relevancy and significancy in the settlement of this question. Had the cubit been more than 18 inches it would scarcely have been deemed a fact sufficiently notable to justify the record, that he was "only 3 cubits high"—4½ feet; and, on the contrary, had it been less, Lucian, the satirizing Christian-hater, would not have failed to harp upon the *Lilliputian* stature of the "high-nosed, bald-pated Galilean," as he derisively terms him.

We are now prepared to understand and appreciate the following account of the sacred fane and its appurtenances, collated from the works of Aristeas, Tacitus, Josephus,* and the Talmud.

Aristeas gives the following brief account of the Temple and its services† in writing to his brother Philocrates. "The city is situated in the midst of mountains on a lofty hill, whose crest is crowned by the magnificent Temple, girt with three walls, seventy cubits high, of proportionate thickness and length, corresponding to the extent of the building. Its costly portals, with its jambs and lintels, were very worthy of admiration; and the vail, resembling gates in appearance, was a pleasing object to contemplate, as it waved perpetually to the passing breeze throughout its whole length. The altar, suitable to the place, and to the burnt sacrifices that were offered thereon, had an ascent well arranged for the services of the priests, who ministered in garments of fine linen reaching to their ankles. The Temple had an eastern aspect; its spacious court, paved throughout with marble, covered immense reservoirs containing large supplies of water, which gushed out by artificial contrivance to wash off the blood of the numerous sacrifices offered there on the festivals. The order and reverence of the ministering priests, and the undivided attention with which they waited on their respective duties, many of which were very arduous, was truly admirable. To some was assigned the charge of the wood, to others the oil, or the fine flour, or sweet spices; others exhibited great strength and dexterity in heaving and burning the holocausts of bullocks and sheep. Yet such deep silence prevailed that you would imagine the place to be devoid of men, although there were seven hundred ministering, and a vast multitude more bringing up the sacrifices. With such awe and reverence, worthy of a great Deity, were the proceedings conducted. Nor did the high priest Eleazar inspire less veneration while performing the sacred service, setting

* Whiston's Josephus, London, 1852, is the edition referred to. It will be borne in mind that no words included in brackets are any part of the original text: those bracketed in the ordinary type of the work being chargeable to the Editor, and those italicised to myself.

† I adopt the version of Mr. Williams.

off to the best advantage his vestments of glory and beauty, adorned with precious stones, and surrounded at the skirts with golden bells, alternated with pomegranates, girt about with a richly variegated girdle; bearing on his breast the oracle set with twelve different stones, according to the names of the tribes of Israel; and on his head the mitre, worn over the linen bonnet and exhibiting the name of God engraven on a golden plate over the forehead."

Tacitus remarks that "the Temple itself was a strong fortress, in the nature of a citadel. The fortifications were built with consummate skill, surpassing in art as well as labor all the rest of the works. The very porticoes that surrounded it were a strong defence."

And Josephus, in writing "against Apion" (ii. 22), thus extracts from Hecateus' description:—"There is about the middle of the city a wall of stone (his allusion is evidently to the Holy House and its immediate court), the length of which is five hundred feet, and the breadth a hundred cubits, with double cloisters, wherein there is a square altar, not made of hewn stone, but composed of white stones gathered together: having each side twenty cubits. Hard by it is a large edifice, wherein there is an altar, and a candlestick, both of gold, and in weight two talents; upon these there is a light that is never extinguished, neither by night nor by day. There is no image, nor anything, nor any donations therein; nothing at all is there planted, neither grove nor anything of that sort. The priests abide therein, both nights and days, performing certain purifications, and drinking not the least drop of wine while they are in the Temple."

"1. Now this Temple, as I have already said, was built upon a strong hill." (Ant. viii. iii: 2.) "The king laid the foundations of the temple very deep in the ground, and the materials were strong stones, and such as would resist the force of time; these were to unite themselves with the earth, and become a basis and a sure foundation for that superstructure which was to be erected over it: they were to be so strong in order to sustain with ease those vast superstructures and precious ornaments, whose own weight was to be not less than the weight of those other high and heavy buildings which the king designed to be very ornamental and magnificent."

"At first the plain at the top was hardly sufficient for the holy house and the altar; for the ground about it was very uneven, and like a precipice; but when King Solomon, who was the person that built the Temple, had built a wall to it on its east side, there was then added one cloister founded on a bank cast up for it, and on the other parts the holy house stood naked; but in future ages the people added new banks, and the hill became a larger plain. They then broke down the wall on the north side, and took in as much as sufficed afterward for the compass of the entire temple; and when they had built walls on three sides of the Temple round about, from the bottom of the hill, and had performed a work that was greater than could be hoped for (in which work long ages were spent by them, as well as all their sacred treasures were exhausted, which were still replenished by those tributes which were sent to God from the whole habitable earth), they then encompassed their upper courts with cloisters, as well as they [afterward] did the lowest [court of the] Temple.

"The lowest part of this [*wall occupying the depths of the ravines*] was erected to the height of three hundred cubits, and in some places more;* yet did not the entire depth of the foundations appear, for they brought earth and filled up the valleys, [*that intersected the east side of Moriah*], as being desirous to make them on a level with the narrow streets of the city, wherein they made use of stones of forty cubits in magnitude; for the great plenty of money they then had, and the liberality of the people, made this attempt of theirs to succeed to an incredible degree; and what could not be so much as hoped for as ever to be accomplished, was, by perseverance and length of time, brought to perfection.

Ant. xv. xi: 3. "The hill was a rocky ascent that declined by degrees towards the east parts of the city till it came to an elevated level. This hill it was which Solomon, who was the first of our kings, by Divine revelation encompassed with a wall; it was of excellent workmanship upwards, and round the top of it. He also built a wall below, beginning at the

* This, of course, is greatly exaggerated; for the entire difference of level between the Kedron Valley opposite the Temple and the top of the royal cloister could only have been two hundred and eighty-seven *feet!* the valley at Absalom's Pillar being only one hundred and twenty-five feet below the base of the south-east corner of the Temple; and the Tyropœon could not certainly have been much more depressed than the Kedron.

bottom, which was encompassed by a deep valley; and at the south side he laid rocks together, and bound them one to another with lead, and included some of the inner parts, till it proceeded to a great height, and till both the largeness of the square edifice and its altitude were immense, and till the vastness of the stones in the front were plainly visible on the outside, yet so that the inward parts were fastened together with iron, and preserved the joints immovable for all future times. When the work [for the foundation] was done in this manner, and joined together as part of the hill itself to the very top of it, he wrought it all into one outward surface, and filled up the hollow places* which were about the wall, and made it a level on the external upper surface, and a smooth level also. This hill was walled all around, and in compass four furlongs [*exclusive of Antonia*] [the distance of] each angle containing in length a furlong: but within this wall, and on the very top of all, there ran another wall of stone also, having on the east quarter a double cloister of the same length with the wall; in the midst of which was the temple itself. This cloister looked to the gates of the temple; and it had been adorned by many kings in former times; and round about the entire temple were fixed the spoils taken from barbarous nations; all these had been dedicated to the temple by Herod, with the addition of those he had taken from the Arabians."

"2. Now, for the works that were above these foundations, these were not unworthy of such foundations; for all the cloisters were double, and the pillars to them belonging were twenty-five cubits in height, and supported the cloisters. These pillars were of one entire stone each of them, and that stone was white marble; and the roofs were adorned with cedar, curiously graven. The natural magnificence and excellent polish, and the harmony of the joints in these cloisters, afforded a prospect that was very remarkable; nor was it on the outside adorned with any work of the painter or engraver. The cloisters [of the outmost court] were in breadth thirty cubits, while the entire compass of it was, by measure, six furlongs including the Tower of Antonia; those entire courts that were exposed to the air were laid with stones of all sorts."

Ant. xv. xi: 5. "Now, in the western quarter of the enclosures of the temple there were four gates; the first led to the king's palace, and went to a passage over the intermediate valley; two more led [*underneath*] to the suburbs of the city [*Parbar west of the Temple;*] and the last led to the other city, [Akra,] where the road descended down into the valley by a great number of steps, and thence up again by the ascent; for the city lay over against the temple in the manner of a theatre, and was encompassed with a deep valley along the entire south quarter; but the fourth front of the temple, which was southward,

* This, of course, is merely a general expression; for it is evident that various reservoirs, the substructures of the south-east corner and the subterranean avenues, are to be excepted.

had, indeed, itself gates in its middle, as also it had the royal cloisters, with three walks, which reached in length from the east valley unto that on the west, for it was impossible it should reach any farther: and this cloister deserves to be mentioned better than any other under the sun; for while the valley was very deep, and its bottom could not be seen, if you looked from above into the depth, this farther vastly high elevation of the cloister stood upon that height, insomuch that if any one looked down from the top of the battlements, or down both those altitudes, he would be giddy, while his sight could not reach to such an immense depth. The cloister had pillars that stood in four rows one over against the other all along; for the fourth row was interwoven into the wall, which [also was built of stone;] and the thickness of each pillar was such that three men might, with their arms extended, fathom it round, and join their hands again; while its length was twenty-seven feet, with a double spiral at its basis; and the number of all the pillars [in that court] was an hundred and sixty-two. Their chapiters were made with sculptures after the Corinthian order, and caused an amazement [to the spectators] by reason of the grandeur of the whole.

"These four rows of pillars included three intervals for walking in the middle of this cloister; two of which walks were made parallel to each other, and were contrived after the same manner; the breadth of each of them was thirty feet, the length was a furlong, and the height fifty feet: but the breadth of the middle part of the cloister was one and a half of the other, and the height was double, for it was much higher than those on each side; but the roofs* were adorned with deep sculptures in wood, representing many sorts of figures; the middle was much higher than the rest, and the wall of the front was adorned with beams, resting upon pillars, that were interwoven into it, and that front was all polished stone, insomuch that its fineness, to such as had not seen it, was incredible, and to such as had seen it was greatly amusing."

Ant. viii. iii: 9. "But he made that temple which was beyond this, a wonderful one indeed, and such as exceeds all description in words; nay, if I may so say, is hardly believed upon sight; for when he had filled up great valleys with earth, which, on account of their immense depth, could not be looked on when you bended down to see them, without pain, and had elevated the ground [*for the space of*] four hundred cubits, he made it to be on a level† with the top of the mountain on which the temple was built, and by this means the outmost temple, which was exposed to the air, was even† with the temple itself. He encompassed this also with a building of a double row of cloisters, which stood on high upon pillars of native stone, while the roofs were of cedar, and were polished in a manner proper for such high roofs; but he made all the doors of this temple of silver."

"When you go through these [first] cloisters, unto the second [court of the] temple, there was a partition made of stone all round, whose height was three cubits, [*the Thrigcos, Gison or Sacred Fence*]:‡

* Roofs: this word seems generally to be used by Josephus in this descriptive essay as the equivalent of *ceiling*.

† In this allusion to the even surface of the Temple area, he is speaking only in general terms; for he elsewhere specifies their relative elevations.

‡ The Talmud says it was wood, and ten hand-breadths high. It was probably a wooden balustrade of that height, supported by stone pillars, and a foundation of stone about a cubit and a half in height.

its construction was very elegant; upon it stood pillars, at equal distances from one another, declaring the law of purity, some in Greek, and some in Roman letters, that "no foreigner should go within that Sanctuary;" for that second [court of the] temple was called "the Sanctuary," and was ascended to by fourteen steps from the first court. This court was four-square, and had a wall about it peculiar to itself; the height of its buildings, although it was on the outside forty cubits, was hidden by the steps, and on the inside that height was but twenty-five cubits; for it being built over against a higher part of the hill with steps, it was no farther to be entirely discerned within, being covered by the hill itself."

Ant. xv. xi: 5. "Thus was the first enclosure. In the midst of which, and not far from it, was the second, to be gone up to by a few steps: this was encompassed by a stone* wall for a partition, with an inscription, which forbade any foreigner to go in, under pain of death.

"Beyond these fourteen steps there was the distance of ten cubits, [Chell or Rampart]: this was all plain, whence there were other steps, each of five cubits apiece, that led to the gate, which gates on the north and south sides were eight, on each of these sides four, and of necessity two on the east; for since there was a partition built for the women on that side, as the proper place wherein they were to worship, there was a necessity of a second gate for them: this gate was cut out of its wall, over against the first gate."

Ant. xv. xi: 5. "Now this inner enclosure had on its southern and northern quarters three† gates [equally] distant from one another; but on the east quarter, towards the sun-rising, there was one large gate [*the 'Beautiful'*] through which such as were pure came in, together with their wives; but the temple farther inward in that gate was not allowed to the women—[*unless they brought a sacrifice.*]

"7. There was also an occult passage built for the king; it led from Antonia to the inner temple, at its eastern gate [*the Nicanor*], over which he also erected for himself a tower, that he might have the opportunity of a subterraneous ascent to the temple, in order to guard against any sedition which might be made by the people against their kings.‡

* See note ‡ on preceding page.

† He here omits the fourth, giving admittance into the women's court; but elsewhere supplies the omission.

‡ It does not distinctly appear whether this subterranean passage terminated at Nicanor or the Beautiful Gate; but it was probably Nicanor.

"There was also on the other sides one southern and one northern gate, through which was a passage into the court of the women; for as to the other gate, the women were not allowed to pass through them; nor when they went through their own gate could they go beyond their own wall, except to lay hands on their sacrifice. This place was allotted to the women of our own country, and of other countries, provided they were of the same nation, and that equally; the western part of this court had no gate at all, but the wall was built entire on that side; but then the cloisters which were betwixt the gates, extended from the wall inward, before the chambers; for they were supported by very fine and large pillars. These cloisters were single, and, excepting their magnitude, were no way inferior to those of the lower court."

Ant. viii. iii: 9. "He also built beyond this court [*court of the Gentiles*] a temple [or inner court], the figure of which was that of a quadrangle, and erected for it great and broad cloisters; this was entered into by very high gates, each of which had its front exposed to one of the [four] winds, and were shut by golden doors. Into this [*court of the*] temple all the people entered that were distinguished from the rest by being pure and observant of the laws."

"3. Now nine of these gates were on every side covered over with gold and silver, as were the jambs of their doors and their lintels; but there was one gate that was without [the inward court of] the Holy House, which was of Corinthian brass, and greatly excelled those that were only covered over with silver and gold. Each gate had two doors, whose height was severally thirty cubits, and their breadth fifteen. However, they had large spaces within of thirty cubits, and had on each side rooms, and those both in breadth and in length, built like towers, and their height was above forty cubits. Two pillars did also support these rooms, and were in circumference twelve cubits. Now the magnitude of the other gates were equal one to another; but that over the Corinthian Gate, which opened on the east over against the gate of the Holy House itself, was much larger; for its height was fifty cubits; and its doors were forty cubits; and it was adorned after a most costly manner, as having much richer and thicker plates of silver and gold upon them than the other. These nine gates had that silver and gold poured upon them by Alexander, the father of Tiberius. Now there were fifteen steps, which led away from the wall of the court of the women to this greater gate; whereas those that led thither from the other gates were five steps shorter."

Ant. xv. xi: 5. "But still more inward there was a third [court of the] temple, *beyond the court of Israel*, (*called the court of the priests*), whereinto it was not lawful for any but the priests to enter. The temple itself was within this: and before that temple was the altar upon which we offer our sacrifices and burnt offerings to God.

"4. As to the holy house itself, which was placed in the midst [of the inmost court] that most sacred part of the temple, it was ascended to by twelve steps; and in front its height and its breadth were equal, and each a hundred cubits [*i. e. the pronaon*], though it was behind forty cubits narrower;* for on its front it had what may be styled shoulders on each side, that passed twenty cubits farther."

Ant. viii. iii: 2. "They erected its entire body, quite up to the roof, of white stone; its height was sixty cubits, and its length was the same and its breadth twenty. There was another building erected over it [*i. e. over the pronaon or porch*], equal to it in its measures; so that the entire altitude of the temple was a hundred and twenty cubits. Its front was to the east. As to the porch, they built it before the temple: its length was twenty cubits, and it was so ordered that it might agree with the breadth of the houses; and it had twelve cubits in latitude, and its height was raised as high as a hundred and twenty cubits."

Ant. xv. xi: 3. "So Herod took away the old foundations, and laid others, and erected the temple upon them, [*the pronaon*] being in length a hundred cubits, and in height twenty additional cubits, which [twenty] upon the sinking of their foundations, fell down: and this part it was that we resolved to raise again in the days of Nero. Now the temple was built of stones that were white and strong, and each of their lengths was twenty-five cubits, their height was eight, and their breadth about twelve; and the whole structure, as also the structure of the royal cloister, was on each side much lower, but the middle was much higher, till they were visible to those that dwelt in the country for a great many furlongs, but chiefly to such as lived over against them, and those that approached to them. The temple had doors also at the entrance, and lintels over them, of the same height with the [interior] temple itself. They were adorned with embroidered vails, with their flowers of purple, and pillars interwoven; and over these, but under the crown work, was spread out a golden vine, with its branches hanging down from a great height, the largeness and fine workmanship of which was a surprising sight to the spectators, to see what sort of material these were and with what great skill the workmanship was done."

* From which remote resemblance to a lion, the Temple was sometimes called Ariel.

"Its first gate was seventy cubits high, and twenty-five cubits broad; but this gate had no doors; for it represented the universal visibility of heaven, and that it cannot be excluded from any place. Its front was covered with gold all over, and through it the first part of the house, that was more inward, did all of it appear; which as it was very large, so did all the parts about the more inward gate appear to shine to those that saw them; but then, as the entire house was divided into two parts within, it was only the first part of it that was open to our view.

"Its height extended all along to ninety cubits in height, and its length was sixty cubits, and its breadth twenty; but that gate which was at this end of the first part of the house was, as we have already observed, all over covered with gold, as was its whole wall about it: it had also golden vines about it, from which clusters of grapes hung as tall as a man's height; but then this house, as it was divided into two parts, the inner part was lower than the appearance of the outer, and had golden doors of fifty-five cubits altitude, and sixteen in breadth; but before these doors there was a vail of equal largeness with the doors. It was a Babylonian curtain, embroidered with blue, and fine linen, and scarlet, and purple, and of a contexture that was truly wonderful. Nor was this mixture of colors without its mystical interpretation, but was a kind of image of the universe; for by the scarlet there seemed to be enigmatically signified fire; by the fine flax the earth, by the blue the air, and by the purple the sea; two of them having their colors the foundation of this resemblance; but the fine flax and the purple have their own origin for that foundation, the earth producing the one, and the sea the other. This curtain had also embroidered upon it all that was mystical in the heavens, excepting that of the [twelve] signs representing living creatures.

"5. When any persons entered into the Temple, its floor received them. This part of the Temple, therefore, was in height sixty cubits, and its length the same; whereas its breadth was but twenty cubits: but still that sixty cubits in length was divided again, and the first part of it cut off at forty cubits, and had in it three things that were very wonderful and famous among all mankind; the candlestick, the table [of show bread,] and the altar of incense. Now, the seven lamps signified the seven planets; for so many there were springing out of the candlestick. Now, the twelve loaves that were upon the table signified the circle of the zodiac and the year; but the altar of incense, by its thirteen kinds of sweet-smelling spices with which the sea replenished it, signifies that God is the possessor of all things that are both in the uninhabitable and habitable parts of the earth, and that they are all to be dedicated to his use. But the inmost part of the temple of all was of twenty cubits. This was also separated from the outer part by a veil. In this there was nothing at all. It was inaccessible and inviolable, and not to be seen by any, [*except the High Priest on the day of atonement*] and was called the Holy of Holies.

Ant. viii. 3. "Now when the king had divided the temple into two parts, he made the inner house of twenty cubits [every way], to be the most secret chamber, but he appointed that of forty cubits to be the sanctuary; and when he had cut a door place out of the wall, he put therein doors of cedar, and overlaid them with a great deal of gold, that had sculptures upon it. He also had veils of blue, and purple, and scarlet, and the brightest and softest of linen, with the most curious flowers wrought upon them, which were to be drawn before those doors. He also dedicated for the most secret place, whose breadth was twenty cubits and the length the same, two cherubims of solid gold; the height of each of them was five* cubits; they had each of them two wings stretched out as far as five cubits; wherefore Solomon set them up not far from each other, that with one wing they might touch the southern wall of the secret place, and with another the northern; their other wings which joined to each other were a covering to the ark, which was set between them; but nobody can tell, or even conjecture, what was the shape of these cherubims. He also laid the floor of the temple with plates of gold; and he added doors to the gate of the temple agreeable to the measure of the height of the wall, but in breadth twenty cubits, and on them he glued gold plates; and to say all in one word, he left no part of the temple, neither internal nor external, but what was covered with gold. He also had curtains drawn over these doors, in like manner as they were drawn over the inner doors of the most holy place; but the porch of the temple had nothing of that sort."

"Now, about the sides of the lower part of the temple there were

* In this account of the Cherubim, Josephus, though apparently describing those of Solomon's Temple, is undoubtedly guided by their restoration for the Herodian Temple—so very different is it from the account given in the 6th chapter of 1 Kings.

little houses with passages out of one into another; there were a great many of them, and they were of three stories high; there were also entrances on each side into them from the gate [*or porch*] of the temple. But the superior part of the temple had no such little houses any farther, because the temple was there narrower, and forty cubits higher, and of a smaller body than the lower parts of it.*

Ant. viii. iii: 2. "He also built round about the temple, thirty small rooms, which might include the whole temple, by their closeness one to another, and by their number, and outward position round it. He also made passages through them, that they might come into one through another. Every one of these rooms [*in the lower range*] had five cubits in breadth, and the same in length, but in height twenty. Above these were other rooms, and others above them, equal, both in their measures and number [*in their respective tiers*], so that these reached to a height equal to the lower part of the house; for the upper part had no buildings about it."*

Thus we collect that the whole height, including the sixty cubits from the floor, amounted to a hundred cubits.†

Ant. viii. iii: 2. "The king also had a fine contrivance‡ for an ascent to the upper room over the temple, and that was by steps in the thickness of its wall; for it had no large door ou the east end, as the lower house had, but the entrances were by the sides, through very small doors. He also overlaid the temple, both within and without, with boards of cedar, that were kept close together by thick chains, so that this contrivance was in the nature of a support and a strength to the building."

"6. Now, the outward face of the temple in its front wanted nothing that was likely to surprise either men's minds or their eyes:

* The wall of the Holy House was three cubits thicker below than above, and suffered a decrement in thickness of one cubit at heights of twenty, forty, and sixty cubits; as explained in the 6th verse of the 6th chapter of 1 Kings:—"The nethermost chamber (or row of chambers) was five cubits broad, and the middle was six cubits broad, and the third was seven cubits broad: for without, in the wall of the house, he made narrowed rests round about, that the beams should not be fastened in the walls of the house."

† By some blunder, the height of the naos, which is ninety cubits, is confounded with that of the pronaon, one hundred. Or, was its original height raised ten cubits when the height of the pronaos was increased to one hundred and twenty?

‡ This is more particularly described in 1 Kings vi. 8:—"And they went up with winding stairs into the middle chamber, and out of the middle into the third." A specimen of this "winding" or spiral stairway is still to be seen in the old tower east of Damascus Gate ("Old Gate"). It is not in a cylindric case, as in modern spiral stairways, but in a hollow shaft left in the thickness of the wall.

for it was covered all over with plates of gold of great weight, and, at the first rising of the sun, reflected back a very fiery splendor, and made those who forced themselves to look upon it to turn their eyes away, just as they would have done at the sun's own rays. But this temple appeared to strangers, when they were at a distance, like a mountain covered with snow; for, as to those parts of it that were not gilt, they were exceeding white. On its top it had spikes with sharp points, to prevent any pollution of it by birds sitting upon it. Of its stones, some of them were forty-five cubits in length, five in height, and six in breadth. Before this temple stood the altar, fifteen cubits high, and equal both in length and breadth; each of which dimensions was fifty cubits.* The figure it was built in was a square, and it had corners like horns, and the passage up to it was by an insensible acclivity. It was formed without any iron tool, nor did any such iron tool so much as touch it at any time.*

"There was a wall of partition, about a cubit in height, made of fine stones, and so as to be grateful to the sight; this encompassed the holy house and the altar, and kept the people that were on the outside off from the priests."

Ant. viii. iii; 9. "He also placed a partition round about the temple, which in our tongue we call Gison, but it is called Thrigcos by the Greeks, and he raised it up to the height of three cubits, and it was for the exclusion of the multitude from coming into the temple, and showing that it was a place that was free and open only for the priests."

The Phastophoria—Covert of the Sabbath.—This lofty watch-tower—"where," according to Josephus (W. iv. ix: 12), "one of the priests stood of course, and gave a signal beforehand with a trumpet at the beginning of every seventh day in the evening twilight, as also at the evening when the day was finished, as giving notice to

* The altar of Solomon's Temple, as Josephus elsewhere mentions, was only twenty square and ten high. That described in the Talmud was thirty-two square and nine high. Is not this discrepancy between Josephus and the Talmud susceptible of reconciliation upon the supposition that Rabbi Yehuda describes it as restored by Zerubbabel—Josephus, as enlarged by Herod? It would require a great deal of room for the accommodation of the colossal altar described by Josephus; unless its base (which is highly probable) was merely a slightly-elevated platform.

the people when they were to leave off work, and when they were to go to work again"—was situated either at the eastward or Shusan Gate; or in the south-west corner of the Court of the Gentiles, at the entrance to the Tyropœon Bridge.

It would appear from the following note of Mr. Whiston upon this passage, that this building—not a little resembling the present minarets of Jerusalem, both in architecture and object—was identical with the *Covert for the Sabbath* that they had built in the house and the king's entry without. "This beginning and ending the observation of the Jewish seventh day or Sabbath with a priest's blowing of a trumpet, is remarkable, and nowhere else mentioned that I know of. Nor is Reland's conjecture here improbable, that this was the very place that has puzzled our commentators so long, called 'Musach Sabbati,' the covert of the Sabbath, if that be the true reading, 2 Kings xvi. 18; because here the proper priest stood dry, under a *covering*, to proclaim the beginning and ending of every Jewish sabbath." The portion of this watch-tower called the covert or covering, was probably a kind of cupola of gold, very curiously wrought, inasmuch as it was deemed worthy the acceptance of the king of Assyria by King Ahaz.

"*Street of the House of God.*"—This is clearly a mistranslation—there being no streets in the Temple. It is called "broad court" in the 9th chapter of Esdras (vi. 38, 41); and the original Hebrew term is entirely susceptible of this translation, as is also the corresponding term in the Septuagint—p l a t e i a. The circumstances of the case also plainly indicate that this street was no other than the Court of the Gentiles—that being the only place where the "*great multitude*" could be accommodated. It must be borne in mind that the Court of the Gentiles is frequently called the *great Outer* or *Lower Court;* that of the Women, the *New Court;* and that of the Priests, the *Inner* or *Innermost Court.* The Higher Court includes both the Court of the Priests and that of Israel. "The porters lodged round about the House of God, because the charge was upon them. In four quarters were the porters—toward the east, the west, the north, and the south."—*Talmud.*

Josephus minutely describes the pillars of Jachin and Boaz in his account of Solomon's Temple: but fails to mention them, as he also does the Court of Israel, in his description of Herod's Temple. It cannot be supposed, however, that the jealous, formal, mint-tithing Jews of that generation would have tolerated the omission of these famous pillars, nor the "narrow lights," nor indeed anything else, authorized by the original "pattern" of Solomon's Temple. An account of the Temple furniture and service, however cursory, would be quite interesting; but nothing less than a monograph on the Temple would justify such details. But although the prescribed limits of this work necessarily preclude the propriety of entering into minutiæ, yet it may be well to admit additional memoranda from original works on Jewish antiquities, in order that we may be enabled the better to understand the brief accounts contained in the Scriptures: and at the same time to supply *temple-builders* with ample materials for the restoration of the Sacred Edifice.

The Talmud not being available to the general reader, the following carefully culled extracts from this rare work are presented, in the hope that they will prove as acceptable, as they are valuable, in elucidating the Temple service arrangements.*

"The hill of the temple was 500 cubits by 500, and surrounded by a wall 25 cubits high on the interior. The southern outer wall was farther from the temple wall than any of the others—was supplied with two gates, Chuldah by name, equidistant from the corners and from each other.†

"The eastern wall was nearer to that of the temple; had only one gate, called Shushan on account of the picture or sculpture of Shushan they had been commanded by the kings of Persia, at the time

* They are derived both from the Mishna and Gamara—text and commentary; but are mainly extracted from that division of the Talmud called Middoth or Measures.

† These were doubtless the Double and Triple Gates—though their respective distances are not stated with rigid accuracy.

when they were liberated from their captivity, to make on the eastern gate in order to remind them of their captivity. The battlement over the east gate was lower than elsewhere—being only 6 cubits high: so that the priest, when sprinkling the blood of the red heifer on Mount Olivet, could, by looking over this and through the inner gates, see the altar.

"The northern wall, which was still nearer to that of the temple, had but one gate called Tetdi or Tudy—and was for no special purpose.

"The western wall, which was the nearest to that of the temple, had but one gate, and was called Coponius or Kephinus. Most service was done in the south part of the temple area, because most of the rooms were there. There was, therefore, most space on the south side—and where there was most space there was most use.

"The partition, a sort of lattice work of *wood*, between the outer wall and the exterior space *surrounding* the temple wall, was 10 hand-breadths high, and had thirteen openings afterwards used as bowing places. The space between the said lattice work and the temple wall, was ten cubits, and was called the Rampart, which also surrounded the Temple. There were twelve steps on the eastern side leading to the court of the women.

"The court of the women was 135 square, and divided by a wall from the court of priests.

"At the inner corners of the women's court there were four apartments, each being 40 square, or 40 × 30. That of south-east was for polling the hair of the Nazarites, and cooking their peace-offerings.

"The north-eastern apartment for wood—where the blemished priests picked the sound wood, from the worm-eaten and unsound pieces, for the altar.

"The north-western apartment for the lepers—where, after having discharged such duties as devolved upon them in the country, they bathed themselves.

"The south-western apartment was the place for oil and wine, used in meat and drink offerings, &c. Both men and women worshipped in this court—the men on the floor and the women in the galleries.

"The gate called Nicanor, was at the eastern side of the court of Israel. A stairway of 15 steps led from the women's court to this gate.

"An apartment was to the right of the gate for the vestry-man of the priests.

"An apartment to the left of the gate for the culinary utensils.

"Under the court of Israel there was an apartment where the Levites kept their musical instruments, having an opening to the women's court.

"The court of Israel was 135 cubits long and 11 broad: and was cloistered like the women's court; the cloisters extending all the way round on every side, except the east, where there was only a wall and roof.

"A step or platform 1 cubit high extended through the whole length of the temple, beneath the roof of the courts of Israel and the priests, separating the one from the other, upon which there was a pulpit $1\frac{1}{2}$ cubits from the surface, upon which it stood; where the Levites stood to sing and to bless the people; and was ascended by means of these steps.

"The court of the priests was 135 cubits long and 11 broad. The railing of the pulpit served for a partition between the two courts.

"*Near* Solomon's altar (which was 20 × 20) and close to the *outside* of south-west corner, were two drainholes; but Herod's altar being larger, they fell within the base of this altar. The blood and offal of the victims mixed with water, was conducted subterraneously to the Kedron.

"The altar was 10 cubits high—32 by 32 at its base, but diminished to 24 × 24 at top by three abatements of dimensions. It was in its first abatement—or "foundation"—that these holes were pierced to be continuous with the old openings.

"A red band of scarlet thread surrounded the altar at a height of 5 cubits. An inclined plane of undressed stone 32 by 16, was laid to the south of the altar for the priest to ascend and descend. There was a room underneath where surplus food was sometimes placed. The "circuit" of the altar, on which the priests walked, was 6 cubits from the floor—even with the sill of the temple door.

"Two tables stood at the western side of the inclined plane, one of gold and the other of marble.

"A place 1 × 1 with marble cover and ring, for cleansing the conduit.

"The space from the inclined plane to the temple was 12½ cubits.

"From the altar to the rings, 8 cubits.

"Six rows of rings each containing 4; to the north of the altar.

"From the tables to the hooks (driven in a beam of wood resting on stone pillars for suspending the victims, 8 cubits.

"The slaughtering *department* had 8 hooks to hang the meat upon.

"From the hooks to the *enclosure* of the temple 8 cubits The Temple had 6 departments on the southern side: the easternmost of which was the magazine for salt.

"The apartment of a man whose name was Parvah the magician. Tradition says that this apartment was built magically. But some say that the name Parvah was owing to the skinning of the sheep which was done in this room, the name of a skin being Parvah.

"An apartment, for washing the sacrifices, from which there was a stairway leading to the terrace of the apartment called Parvah upon which there is a baptistery for the high priest to dip himself five times on the day of atonement.

"At the northern side near the east there was an apartment for the shearing of the sheep, half of it belonging to the temple and the other half to the common. Had two openings; one to the temple, and one to common.

"An apartment called (Golah) owing to a well it had—the water being drawn by means of a wheel.

"An apartment for wood.

"A very large house, built on arches, and was supplied with several fireplaces for the priests to warm themselves as they were ministering barefooted; had two gates, one opening to the temple and one to common; had four small rooms, two projecting into the temple, and two to the common.

"An apartment for selected sheep, without blemish or spot, for daily offerings.

"An apartment for making show-bread.

"The apartment in which the Asmoneans laid away the stones of the desecrated altar.

"This apartment was also called the house of fire, as it was supplied by a fireplace for the priests to warm themselves after coming out from the bath, by means of steps leading down from the same room.

"A place of 1 cubit square, where a ring with a chain was fastened, upon which the keys were suspended.

"The gate through which offerings were brought in.

"The gate called Nitsouts, had two walls projecting at the sides of the gate upon which upper room was built on arches for watch, and had an opening to the rampart.

"The gate through which wood was brought in, and was called burning or kindling.

"The gate through which all the first-born of such animals as were fit for offering were brought in, and was called first-born or firstlings.

"The water to be poured out on feast days was brought in through this gate.

"An apartment close to the water gate. All the gates were covered with gold except Nicanor, which was Corinthian brass or aurichalchum. Two small doors in Nicanor: right and left watch rooms, by sides of gates—twenty-four in all.

"The brazen sea stood between the porch and the altar towards the south.

"Between the porch and the altar there was a space of 22 cubits: there were also twelve steps occupying 19 in extent, and a pavement 3 = 22.

"The wall of the porch was 5 cubits thick, and the height of the opening was 40 cubits, width 20 cubits. House and porch braced by connecting beams.

"The porch was 11 cubits broad from east to west, and 70 cubits long from north to south (inside), exclusive of the shoulder-rooms for slaughter knives (15×2=30+70=100). There were five beams of timber curiously wrought over the gate of the portico.

"The apartment for the slaughter knives 15 cubits from north and 15 from south.

"Two tables in the porch, close to the door, one of gold and the other of marble. Gold chains suspended from projecting pieces of stone, by which the priest ascended to golden offerings.

"From north-west corner was a spiral stairway to roof of chambers. Around the top of the temple was a battlement 3 cubits high: and a scare-crow 1 cubit high, to deter ravens and other birds from lighting on the house.

"The wall of the temple was of veined marble: and it seemed like the waving of the sea—one row of stones did so curiously go in, and another come out—one border or edge going in and another out.

"Besides a deep foundation in the earth there was another above surface of 6 cubits, upon which the house was built, and it was broader than the superstructure.

"The interior of the temple was 40 cubits from east to west, and 20 cubits from north to south.

"There was a place at the right of entrance, and a marble cover which had a ring in it in order to lift it up to take ashes from under it, to put it into the proof water of jealousy.

"Two golden vessels in which the high priest put the blood of the goat on the day of atonement.

"The candlestick at the left of the entrance, and a table to the right, and the altar of gold projecting a little from between.

"A space of one cubit thick between the walls of the temple and the holy of holies.

"The holy of holies, 20 cubits square. In its door were two

smaller ones. The room over the holy and most holy places was entered on the south by a door over the chambers. In its floor were holes through which priests were let down once a year to whitewash. The ceiling of the holy place was 55 cubits, but in the most holy, only 20; though it had another 40 cubits high. The ceiling of the porch was 90 cubits high.

"The wall of the temple, 6 cubits to the north and 6 to south.

"Side chambers 6 cubits broad, 15 on north, 15 south, and 8 west, equal 38—in three stories—the lowest entered from below, the upper ranges, from spiral stairways in the north end of the portico—and by the same contrivance from the lower story, 10 cubits above the roof of the chambers was a row of lights, narrow without and broad within.

"On roof of chambers there were holes; and projecting pieces of cedar mark the line between holy and holy of holies.

"The wall of that department 6 to the north and 6 to south.

"The third surrounding space 3 to the north and 3 to south was called the department where the waters fall—(the Impluvium).

"The wall 5 to the north and 5 to south.

"The wall of the temple 6 to the west.

"Haanoth, Tabernæ or *Bazaars for the sale of salt, wine, oil,* &c., were situated near the gates."

The close resemblance between the Talmudic account of the Temple of Herod, and that so minutely described by Ezekiel (Chs. 40–44), readily suggests the conclusion that the Rabbins have drawn very freely upon the prophet for the minutiæ of their description.

The following condensed items of measurement, carefully extracted from the works of Josephus and the Talmud, though occasionally somewhat variant* and apparently contradictory, will nevertheless aid materially in a correct apprehension of the Temple

* In stating the size of the doors, the Talmud seems to give the dimensions of the *leaf,* and Josephus that of the opening in the wall, containing the side posts, lintel, and space above; the one describing interior dimensions and the other outer.

structures. Unless otherwise expressed, the measurements are in cubits.

Holy house; height, 90 without and 60 within.

Porch or pronaos; height without, 100 (at one time 120), breadth, 100.

Apportionment of Holy House and Porch from East to West.

Wall of porch	5
Inner space of porch (or vestibule)	11
Wall of holy place, east	6
Holy place (length)	40
Wall between holy and holiest	1
Holy of holies (length)	20
Wall of holy house, west	6
Breadth of rear chambers	6
Thickness of chamber wall	5
Width of impluvium in the rear of the chambers	5
Rear wall	6
	111

Apportionment of Holy House, Chambers, &c., North and South.

Outer surrounding wall	5
Interval for impluvium (gallery)	3
Lateral chamber wall	5
Breadth of chambers	6
Wall of holy house	6
Breadth of holy house	20
Wall of holy house	6
Breadth of chambers	6
Breadth of chamber wall	5
Impluvium (or place of coming down of waters)	3
Outer investing wall	5
	70

The thickness of *one* of these walls, according to Josephus, was 8 cubits.

Arrangements for Sacrificing (extending across the Court of the Priests 22 in front of the Porch).

Space from north wall to pillars	8
Pillars to marble tables	4
From tables to rings	4
Ring apartment	24
From rings to altar	8
Altar and plane united	62
Plane to south wall of court	25
	135

Measurements from Josephus and the Talmud.

Dimensions across the Sanctuary, East to West.

Court of Israel (breadth)	11
Court of priests "	11
Altar "	32
Between altar and temple	22
Temple (length)	100
Between west end of temple and the wall west	11
	187

Altar, 32 square, diminishing to 24 at top, and 9 high. (Talmud.) (Josephus says 50 square, and 15 high.) Pavement from altar to steps, 3 wide.

Thrigcos or Gison, 1 (Josephus); 3 (Talmud).

Court of priests, 135 long, 11 wide. Platform, 1 high. Pulpit, 1½ high (or).

Court of Israel, 135 long, 11 wide.

Sanctuary, inside measure, 135 × 187.

Women's court, 135 square. Apartments in each corner, 40 × 30.

Buildings around inner court; height outside, steps excepted, 40; inside, 25; cloisters single, but pillars fine and large.

Gates to inner courts: 4 on north, 4 south, 1 east; height 20 × 10. (Jos. 30 × 15, and double.) Beautiful gate, 30 × 15. Corinthian or Nicanor; height 50, doors 40 × ?

10 steps in each gate, but 15 semicircular ones from women's court to Israel's.

Chel or rampart surrounding sanctuary, 10.

Steps to chel, 12, (Josephus 14,) and ½ high.

Hil, Soreg, or sacred partition fence, stone and 3 high. (Talmud, 1½ and wood.) An opening before each gate.

Steps to Hil.

Cloisters or porticoes: on south, triple and 70 broad (30 + 45 + 30 *feet*); height 100 in the middle, and 50 north and south. Height of pillars, 27 *feet.* 162 in number.

On east, west, and north, double, and 25 (cubits) high. Breadth, 30.

Length, 400 cubits, or 1 stadium or furlong.

Exterior wall, 400 cubits in length. (Talmud, 500.) Including Antonia, 6 furlongs around.

Gates in outer wall; on west 4, south 2 (?), on east 1 (Talmud), on north 1 (Talmud).

Opening to vestibule, 40 × 20. (Josephus, 70 × 25.)

Door to holy place, 55 × 16; to holy of holies, 20 × 10.

Five bars across doorway, 22, 24, 26, 28, 30; and one in it 20 long.

Steps to porch, width 19; generally 1 broad, but 4th and 8th 3 broad, and 12th 4 broad—tesselated. Height of each step, ½.

All the gates in the outer wall, 20 high × 10 broad.

Elevations westward from Court of Gentiles to floor of Holy House.

From court of Gentiles to partition fence	2½
" area within sacred fence to chel	7½
" chel to inner gates	5
" women's court to court of Israel	7½
" court of Israel to court of priests	2½
" court of priests to floor of holy house	6
	31
Difference between floor of outer court and floor of holy house (elsewhere stated)	22

With these copious materials and authentic data, there is but little difficulty in the mere restoration of the Temple ; but its exact location and accommodation within the enclosed area of Mount Moriah is a subject which, though so long and keenly discussed, has never yet been satisfactorily determined. Existing remains do not allow us to entertain the idea that the Temple-mount area was ever exactly square, as we would infer from Josephus and the Talmud ; and hence we are constrained to come to the conclusion that Josephus and the Rabbins merely intended to speak approximatively in so expressing themselves. But this is not the greatest difficulty ; for the actual deviation in dimension is still more serious than that in form—the *shortest* side of the present Temple enclosure being 166 feet longer than a side of the square assigned it by the Talmud, and 316 longer than the estimate of Josephus—the cubit being rated at 18 inches.

But "facts are stubborn things;" and although Josephus is so prone to exaggerate in magnitudes and distances when the glory of his nation or the military fame of his great patron can be thereby enhanced, yet in this instance he has undoubtedly understated dimensions—for according to the stern requirements of the ground and the remains upon it, the outer Temple wall must have been at least a stadium and a half in length, instead of a stadium, at which he so frequently rates it. But it must not be forgotten that in writing his account of it, the author is doing so at considerable disadvantage—being far away at Rome ; and there is every reason to believe that in many such matters he was more dependent upon memory than upon any special materials that he had personally collected before leaving the Holy City. The probability is that the Talmudic is the more correct estimate—for Rabbi Yehudah, the compiler of the Talmud, residing as he did at Tiberias, had the opportunity of speaking with sufficiently minute correctness on this point ; for though in general he merely reflects the tradition of the Rabbins, and of course cannot speak from personal observation as to much of his description, yet, though living a century and a half after the destruction of the Temple, there were doubtless sufficient remains to indicate its main apportionment. But still, notwithstanding such discrepancies between these authors individually, and the still more serious want of agreement between them and the facts of the case in relation to this item; yet the outer enclosure of the Temple never having been regarded as holy ground, we are not to expect the same accuracy that these authors observe in describing the sacred structures and courts of the interior. And hence the general estimate of the outer enclosure which each of them has made, may fairly be considered as sufficiently accurate for all general purposes. It is perfectly obvious that the buildings of the Temple could never have been compressed within the area of a stadium square—the mere sanctuary, independent of the Court of the Gentiles, being more than 400 cubits in length; nor could they have well been included within the 500 cubits square assigned for their accommodation by the Middoth, without inconvenient crowding. The larger limits of the area of the Haram seem indispensable to their proper display and arrangement. The satisfactory disposition of es-Sakhrah is a problem that has puzzled Biblical topographers not a little. But it is altogether obvious that no accommodation heretofore proposed meets the requirements of the case; and just as evident is it, that unless in some way excluded from view, it would be an entirely useless and very unsightly object in the Court of the Gentiles, or somewhere else still more inconveniently situated. I have therefore, in accordance with certain indications on its surface, located it within the north cloister of the Temple, where it would not only be out of the way, but serve a useful purpose as a foundation for a tower, or a safe depository for treasure. Its northern end is scarped, and has every appearance of having at once sustained and formed part of a wall. But for this scarpment it might be plausibly objected that a broader cloister would be required to conceal it, than that assigned this wall by Josephus; its upper surface, however, is so much reduced in length by this scarpment that the space jointly occupied by the cloister and wall would exactly cover it—supposing the wall to be a foot or two thicker on this vulnerable side of the Temple than on its other sides where it was almost impregnable.

Having thus disposed of this difficulty, it becomes very easy to locate the Sanctuary according to the requirements of the Middoth, so that most room would be on its south, and less and less opposite its eastern, northern, and western faces. Such a position, too, will at once explain why one of the southern gates of the Sanctuary was called "Water Gate"—for it thus became located immediately over the great subterranean reservoir of the Temple. This division of the Temple area by a wall running as low down as the Sakhrah is also more in conformity with the requirements of Josephus, as well as with the indications of nature.

The outer foundation walls of the Temple were not perpendicular; but inclined inwardly probably as much as three feet in a height of seventy or eighty, which would reduce the length of the south wall to 910 feet at the top. Nor was the exterior wall of the cloisters a continuation of this wall, but was an independent structure, built partly on the substructions, and in part only upon this wall, its surface not being *flush* or even with that of the foundation wall, but a short distance within its outer edge, so as to leave a shoulder of two or three feet all around. Now allowing eight feet for the cloister wall, three for this shoulder, and three for the *talus* or inward inclination, the east and west walls would be 888 feet apart at their junction with the south wall; and the east and west cloisters being each 45 feet in width, the cloisters would thus be 798 feet distant from each other at that point. Making similar allowance on the other sides, the distance between cloister and cloister will be found on the west 680, on the north 857, and east only 630. Now this last measure so nearly approximates a stadium, that a person forming an estimate of the Temple area by pacing this colonnade might well be excused for setting it down at a stadium, and concluding that the others were the same length, and all the corners right angled—for the most practised eye could not detect the deviation of such an area from the form of an exact square. The average of these distances, it is seen on calculation, is 741 feet, which is 141 or one-fifth more than the number assigned by Josephus, but nine feet less than the Rabbinic specification; measured, however, from wall to wall, the average distance is 869, or 119 feet longer than the measure apparently assigned it in the Middoth. But as there were towers, apparently, at the junction of the cloisters, in each corner, it is probable that the mensuration applies not to the actual length of the walls, but to the space between these corner structures.

As a dernier resort, the strict constructionist might easily take advantage of the fact mentioned by Josephus in speaking of the outer or foundation wall, that "*within* this wall and on the very top of all, there ran another wall, &c.," and construct an exact square either of 400 or 500 cubits a side, but for the inconsistency of such an appropriation of the Temple area with his account of the siege, and the inconvenient crowding of the buildings thus rendered unavoidable, without any apparent reason.

Under all the circumstances of the case, we can arrive at no other conclusion than that the present wall of the Haram is identical in position with that of the ancient Temple, and that the square stadium assigned the Temple area by Josephus, and the 500 cubits by the author of Middoth, or the compiler of the Talmud, are only general estimates, and must be made to yield to the uncompromising facts of the case.

After these extended introductory remarks, we are now prepared to understand the more succinct accounts of the Temple contained in the Scriptures—here carefully collated for easier comparison and comprehension. Several apparent incongruities, difficulties, and discrepancies in the two accounts will be observed—of immaterial import and easily explicable.

1 Chron. xxviii. 11, 21. Then David gave to Solomon his son the pattern of the porch, and of the houses thereof, and of the treasuries thereof, and of the upper chambers thereof, and of the inner parlors thereof, and the place of the mercy seat, and the pattern of all that he had by the Spirit, of the courts of the House of the Lord, and of all the chambers round

about, of the treasuries of the house of God, and of the treasuries of the dedicated things. And also for the courses of the priests and Levites, and for all the works of the service of the house of the Lord, and for all the vessels of service in the house of the Lord. * * * * "All this," said David, "the Lord made me understand in writing by his hand upon me, even all the works of this pattern."

1 Kings VI.

1. And it came to pass after the four hundred and eightieth year after the children of Israel were come out of the land of Egypt, in the fourth year of Solomon's reign over Israel, in the month Zif, which is the second month, that he began to build the house of the Lord.

2 Chr. III.

1. Then Solomon began to build the house of the Lord, at Jerusalem, in Mount Moriah, where the Lord appeared unto David his father, in the place that David had prepared in the threshing-floor of Ornan the Jebusite.

1 Kings v. 17. And the king commanded, and they brought great stones, costly stones, and hewed stones, to lay the foundation of the house.

Ezra vi. 3, 4. In the first year of Cyrus the king, the same Cyrus the king made a decree concerning the house of God at Jerusalem—"Let the house be builded, the place where they offered sacrifices, and let the foundations thereof be strongly laid; the height thereof threescore cubits, and the breadth thereof threescore cubits; with three rows of great stones, and a row of new timber."* "Whose height shall be sixty cubits, and the breadth sixty cubits, with three rows of hewn stones; and one row of new wood of that country."

1st Esdras vi. 25.

2. And he began to build in the second day of the second month, in the fourth year of his reign.

2. And the house which king Solomon built for the Lord, the length thereof was threescore cubits, and the breadth thereof twenty cubits, and the height thereof thirty cubits.

3. Now these are the things wherein king Solomon was instructed for the building of the house of God. The length by cubits after the first measure was threescore cubits: and the breadth twenty cubits.

8. And he made the most holy house, the length whereof was according to the breadth of the house, twenty cubits, and the breadth thereof twenty cubits: and he overlaid it with fine gold, amounting to six hundred talents.

3. And the porch before the temple of the house, twenty cubits was the length thereof, according to the breadth of the house; and ten cubits was the breadth thereof, before the house.

4. And the porch that was in the front of the house, the length of it was according to the breadth of the house, twenty cubits; and the height was a hundred and twenty: and he overlaid it within with pure gold.

* This reduction in height was probably intended by Cyrus to prevent the conversion of the porch into a citadel. The sixty cubits in breadth was, no doubt, inclusive of the chambers on each side. But his restrictions seem to have been set at nought by the builders.

Harmony of Kings, Chronicles, &c., descriptive of the Temple.

1 Kings VI.	2 Chr. III.

4. And for the house he made windows of narrow lights.
5. And against the wall of the house he built chambers round about, against the walls
of the house round about, both of the temple and of the oracle; and he made chambers
6. round about. The nethermost chamber was five cubits broad; and the middle was six
cubits broad, and the third was seven cubits broad; for without in the wall of the house
he made narrowed rests round about, that the beams should not be fastened in the walls
of the house.
7. The house, when it was in building, was built of stone made ready before it was
brought thither; so that there was neither hammer, nor axe, nor any tool of iron heard
8. in the house while it was in building. The door of the middle chamber was in the
right side of the house; and they went up with winding stairs into the middle chamber,
and out of the middle into the third.

9. So he built the house and finished it; and covered the house with beams and boards of cedar.	5. And the greater house he ceiled with fir-tree which he overlaid with fine gold, and set thereon palm-trees and chains.

10. And then he built chambers against all the house five cubits high; and they rested
on the house with timber of cedar.
15. And he built the walls of the house within with boards of cedar, both the floor of
the house and the walls of the ceiling; and he covered them on the inside with wood,
16. and covered the floor of the house with planks of fir. And he built twenty cubits on
the sides of the house, both the floor and the walls with boards of cedar; he even built
17. them for it within, even for the oracle, even for the most holy place. And the house,
18. that is, the temple before it, was forty cubits long. And the cedar of the house within
was carved with knops and open flowers: all was cedar; there was no stone seen.
19. And the oracle he prepared in the house within, to set there the ark of the covenant
20. of the Lord. And the oracle in the fore-part was twenty cubits in length, and twenty
cubits in breadth, and twenty cubits in the height thereof; and he overlaid it with pure
gold; and so covered the altar which was of cedar.

21. So Solomon overlaid the house within with pure gold: and he made a partition by the chains of gold before the oracle, 22. and he overlaid it with gold. And the whole house he overlaid with gold, until he had finished all the house; also the whole altar that was by the oracle, he	7. He overlaid also the house, the beams, the posts, and the walls thereof, and the doors thereof, with gold; and graved cherubims on the walls. 9. And the weight of the nails was fifty shekels of gold. And he overlaid the upper chambers with gold.

30. overlaid with gold. And the floor of the house he overlaid with gold within and
without.

6. And he garnished the house with precious stones for beauty; and the gold was gold of Parvaim.

23. And within the oracle he made two cherubims of olive-tree, each ten cubits 24. high. And five cubits was the one wing of the cherub, and five cubits the other wing of the cherub: from the utter-	10. And in the most holy house he made two cherubims of image-work, and over- 11. laid them with gold. And the wings of the cherubims were twenty cubits long: one wing of the one cherubim was five

Harmony of Kings, Chronicles, &c., descriptive of the Temple.

1 Kings VI.

most part of the one wing to the uttermost part of the other wing were ten
25. cubits. And the other cherub was ten
cubits; both the cherubims were of one
26. measure and of one size. The height of
the one cherub was ten cubits, and so
27. was it of the other cherub. And he set
the cherubims within the inner house:
and they stretched forth the wings of the
cherubims, so that the wing of the one
touched the one wall, and the wing of

2 Chr. III.

cubits, reaching to the wall of the house;
and the other wing was likewise five
cubits, reaching to the wing of the other
12. cherub. And one wing of the other
cherub was five cubits, reaching to the
wall of the house; and the other wing
was five cubits also, joining to the wing
13. of the other cherub. The wings of these
cherubims spread themselves forth twenty
cubits; and they stood on their feet, and
their faces were inward.

the other cherubim touched the other wall: and their wings touched one another in
28. the midst of the house. And he overlaid the cherubims with gold.
29. And he carved all the walls of the house round about with carved figures of cherubims and palm-trees, and open flowers, within and without.

14. And he made the veil of blue, and purple, and crimson, and fine linen, and wrought cherubims thereon.

31. And for the entering of the oracle he made doors of olive-tree; the lintel and side
32. posts were a fifth part of the wall. The two doors also were of olive-tree; and he
carved upon them carvings of cherubims, and palm-trees, and open flowers, and overlaid them with gold, and spread gold upon the cherubims, and upon the palm-trees.
33. So also made he for the door of the temple posts of olive-tree, a fourth part of the
34. wall. And the two doors were of fir-tree; the two leaves of the one door were folding,
35. and the two leaves of the other door were folding. And he carved thereon cherubims,
and palm-trees, and open flowers; and covered them with gold fitted upon the carved
work.

IV. 22. And the entry of the house, the inner doors thereof for the most holy place, and the doors of the house of the temple were of gold.

36. And he built the inner court with three
rows of hewed stone, and a row of cedar
beams.

9. Furthermore, he made the court of the
priests, and the great court, and doors
for the court, and overlaid the doors of
them with brass.

VII.

15. He cast two pillars of brass of eighteen*
cubits high apiece; and a line of twelve
cubits did compass either of them about.

III.

15. Also he made before the house two
pillars of thirty and five* cubits high,
and the chapiter that was on the top of

* This discrepancy is reconcileable by supposing either that about eighteen cubits was the height of each pillar (and about thirty-six their joint height), or that each pillar was about thirty-five or thirty-six cubits in height, but *cast* in two pieces eighteen cubits in length. The latter is by far the more probable explanation—whether the symmetry of the pillar be considered, or the height of the temple door before which they were placed. The chapiters seem to have consisted of several pieces, and being sometimes spoken of collectively, and at others in detached pieces, some confusion seems to have arisen in consequence.

Harmony of the Scriptures descriptive of the Temple.

1 Kings VII.

16. And he made two chapiters of molten
brass to set upon the tops of the pillars;
the height of the one chapiter was five
cubits, and the height of the other cha-
17. piter was five cubits. And nets of
checker work, and wreaths of chain
work, for the chapiters which were upon
the tops of the pillars; seven for the one
chapiter, and seven for the other chapi-
18. ter. And he made the pillars, and two
rows round about upon the one net-work,
to cover the chapiters that were upon
the top with pomegranates; and so did
19. he for the other chapiter. And the chapiters that were upon the top of the pillars, were of lily-work in the porch, four
20. cubits. And the chapiters upon the two
pillars had pomegranates also above,
over against the belly which was by the
net-work; and the pomegranates were
21. two hundred, in rows round about upon the other chapiter. And he set up the pillars
in the porch of the temple: and he set up the right pillar, and called the name thereof
22. Jachin; and he set up the left pillar, and called the name thereof Boaz. And upon the
41. top of the pillars was lily-work; so was the work of the pillars finished. The two pillars
and the two bowls of the chapiters that were on the top of the two pillars; and the two
net-works, to cover the two bowls of the chapiters which were upon the top of the pil-
42. lars. And four hundred pomegranates for the two net-works, even two rows of pomegranates for one net-work, to cover the two bowls of the chapiters that were upon the
pillars.

2 Chr. III.

16. each of them was five cubits. And he
made chains as in the oracle, and put
them on the heads of the pillars; and
made an hundred pomegranates, and put
17. them on the chains. And he reared up
the pillars before the temple—the one on
the right hand, and the other on the left;
and called the name of that on the right
hand Jachim, and the name of that on
the left Boaz.
IV. 12. The two pillars, and the pommels, and
the chapiters which were on the top of the
two pillars, and the two wreaths to cover
the two pommels of the two chapiters
which were upon the top of the pillars.
13. And four hundred pomegranates on
the two wreaths; two rows of pomegranates on each wreath, to cover the two
pommels of the chapiters which were
upon the pillars.

Jer. lii. 21. And concerning the pillars, the height of one pillar was eighteen cubits; and a fillet of twelve cubits did compass it; and the thickness thereof was four fingers: it was hollow. (22). And a chapiter of brass was upon it; and the height of one chapiter was five cubits, with net-work and pomegranates upon the chapiters round about, all of brass. The second pillar also and the pomegranates were like unto these. (23). And there were ninety and six pomegranates on a side; and all the pomegranates upon the net-work were an hundred round about.

1 Kings VII.

23. And he made a molten sea, ten cubits,
from the one brim to the other: it was
round all about, and his height was five
cubits: and a line of thirty cubits did
compass it round about.
24. And under the brim of it round about
there were knops compassing it, ten in a

2 Chr. IV.

2. And he made a molten sea of ten cubits
from brim to brim, round in compass, and
five cubits the height thereof: and a line
of thirty cubits did compass it round
about.
3. And under it was the similitude of oxen,
which did compass it round about; ten

Harmony of the Scriptures descriptive of the Temple.

1 Kings VII.	2 Chr. IV.
cubit, compassing the sea round: the knops were cast in two rows when it was cast.	in a cubit compassing it round about. Two rows of oxen were cast when it was cast.
25. It stood upon twelve oxen, three look- ing toward the north, and three toward the west; and three looking toward the south, and three looking toward the east; and the sea was set above upon them; and all their hinder parts were inward. 26. And it was an hand-breadth thick, and the brim thereof was wrought like the brim of a cup, with flowers of lilies; it contained two thousand baths.*	4. It stood upon twelve oxen, three look- ing toward the north, and three looking toward the west, and three looking toward the south, and three looking toward the east; and the sea was set above upon them; and all their hinder parts were in- 5. ward. And the thickness of it was an hand-breadth, and the brim of it lilies; and it received and held three thousand 10. baths.* And he set the sea on the right side of the east end, over against the south.

27. And he made ten bases of brass; four cubits was the length of one base, and four
28. cubits the breadth thereof, and three cubits the height of it. And the work of the bases
29. was on this manner; they had borders, and the borders were between the ledges. And
on the borders that were between the ledges, were lions, oxen, and cherubims: and upon
the ledges there was a base above; and beneath the lions and oxen were certain addi-
30. tions made of thin work. And every base had four brazen wheels, and plates of brass;
and the four corners thereof had undersetters; under the laver were undersetters molten
31. at the side of every addition. And the mouth of it within the chapiter and above was
a cubit: but the mouth thereof was round, after the work of the base, a cubit and a
half; and also upon the mouth of it were gravings with their borders, four-square, not
32. round. And under the borders were four wheels, and the axle-trees of the wheels were
33. joined to the base, and the height of a wheel was a cubit and a half cubit. And the
work of the wheels was like the work of a chariot wheel; their axle-trees and their
34. naves, and their felloes and their spokes were all molten. And there were four undersetters to the four corners of one base; and the undersetters were of the very base
35. itself. And in the top of the base was there a round compass of half a cubit high; and
36. on the top of the base the ledges thereof and the borders thereof were of the same. For
on the plates of the ledges thereof, and on the borders thereof he graved cherubims,
lions, and palm-trees, according to the proportion of every one, and additions round
37. about. After this manner he made the ten bases; all of them had one casting, one
measure, and one size.

38. Then made he ten lavers of brass; one laver containing forty baths; and every laver was four cubits; and upon every one of the ten bases one laver.	6. He made also ten lavers; and put five on the right hand and five on the left, to wash in them; such things as they offered for the burnt offering they washed in

* Two thousand probably being the capacity of the upper basin or sea proper; and the *foot*, pedestal, or receptacle on and *in* which it is believed to have stood, containing one thousand.

Harmony of Kings, Chronicles, &c., descriptive of the Temple.

1 Kings VII. — 2 Chr. IV.

39. And he put five bases on the right side
of the house; and five on the left side

them; but the sea was for the priests to
wash in.

of the house; and he set the sea on the right side of the house, eastward, over against
the south. And Hiram made the lavers and the shovels and the basins.

8. He made also ten tables, and placed
them in the temple, five on the right side, and five on the left: and he made an hundred
basins of gold. (11). And Hiram made the pots and the shovels and the basins.

45. And the pots and the shovels and the
basins; and all the vessels which Hiram
made to king Solomon for the house of
the Lord were of bright brass.

16. The pots also and the shovels and the
flesh-hooks, and all their instruments, did
Huram his father make to king Solomon
for the house of the Lord, of bright brass.

48. And Solomon made all the vessels that
pertained to the house of the Lord; the
altar of gold and the table of gold whereupon the show-bread was.

19. And Solomon made all the vessels that
were for the house of God, the golden
altar also, and the tables whereon the
show-bread was set.

1. Moreover he made an altar of brass,
twenty cubits the length thereof, and twenty cubits the breadth thereof, and ten cubits
the height thereof.

49. And the candlesticks of pure gold, five
on the right side and five on the left, before the oracle, with the flowers, and the
50. lamps and the tongs of gold; And the
bowls and the snuffers, and the basins
and the spoons, and the censers, of pure
gold; and the hinges of gold; both for
the doors of the inner house, the most
holy place, and for the doors of the house,
to wit, of the temple.

7. And he made ten candlesticks of gold,
according to their form, and set them in
the temple, five on the right hand and
19. five on the left. And Solomon made all
the vessels that were in the house of God,
the golden altar also, and the tables,
20. whereon the show-bread was set. Moreover the candlesticks with their lamps,
that they should burn after the manner
before the oracle, of pure gold.

21. And the flowers and the lamps, and the
tongs made he of gold—and that perfect gold. (22). And the snuffers and the basins,
and the spoons and the censers, of pure gold.

VI. 37. In the fourth year was the foundation of the house of the Lord laid, in the month
38. of Zif: and in the eleventh year, in the month Bul (which is the eighth month), was
the house finished throughout all the parts thereof; and according to all the fashion of
it. So was he seven years in building it.

1st Chr. xxvi. 12—18—(*Gates of the outer enclosure of the Temple*). On the north was one gate under Zechariah the porter (a wise counsellor), and four Levites: On the east, one, under Shelemiah the porter, and six Levites: on the south, two, under Obed-edom and Sons porters, and four Levites: and on the west, three (Shallecheth above, and two in Parbar), under Shuppim and Hosah porters, and four Levites.

Of the four gates of the western wall of the Temple, mentioned by Josephus, the one that led "by the causeway of the going up" to the king's palace across the Tyropœon, was undoubtedly situated immediately over the remains of the bridge now visible, thirty-nine feet from its southern extremity—termed Shallecheth, 1 Chr. xxvi. 16, and High Gate, 2 Chr. xxiii. 20. The passage over the bridge seems to have corresponded exactly with the middle walk of the royal portico. Of the two that led to Parbar or the suburbs (1 Chr. xxvi. 16, 18), the portal I discovered underneath the present Mograbin Gate is undoubtedly one; the other probably occupied the site of the present gate, near the Mekhemeh; and the Cotton Bazaar Gate is no doubt the representative of that which "led to the other city." The Talmud makes mention of only one gate in this wall—Coponius, or Kephinus; but this is evidently a mere omission--not being visible from within, inasmuch as they were situated in the bottom of the wall in Parbar, and gave entrance to the Temple through subterranean passages. That it had more than one, is sufficiently evident from the 16th and 18th verses of the 26th chapter of 1 Chronicles; and that it had four, we have the explicit testimony of Josephus. The gate Coponius may have been named after the Roman general, as Antonia was in honor of Mark Antony—and may have been the gate leading from Antonia into the Lower City, and if so was doubtless very stately and magnificent; but the probability is that it is but another name for the gate leading over to Zion—and if allusion is made only to the Temple gates, strictly speaking, this must necessarily be the case. The expressions used both by Josephus and Rabbi Yehudah in relation to the gates on the south—though somewhat equivocal in some respects—are sufficiently descriptive of the triple and double gateways now found there. Some of the Talmudists are very explicit—not only assigning two gates, but making them equidistant from the corners, and from each other. That there were more than one, seems also to be intimated 1 Chr. xxvi. 15. They are situated just as might be inferred from what Josephus says of them—the one for general purposes, and the other probably for the priests, Levites, Nethenim, Stationary-men, &c., "*about* its middle." The western one, is the

Huldah Gate of tradition. May not the other be what the Talmud calls the Priests' Gate? Josephus, in his description of the Temple, is entirely silent in relation to the gates of the north and east enclosures; but in giving an account of the siege (W. vi. iv: 2) he incidentally speaks of "gates" in the northern wall: there were, therefore, at least two on that side. The Talmud only makes mention of one (Tidi), of which nothing special is said. That there was one on the east side, we learn directly from the Talmud, and incidentally from the Bible (1 Chr. xxvi. 14); and even if there were no written intimation of it, we would be bound to infer its existence from a necessity for a short and direct communication between the altar and Sheep Quarter. It is called Shusan; and besides giving entrance immediately to the Court of the Gentiles, had, no doubt, also a subterraneous passage for victims, terminating in or near the slaughtering department, close to the altar. It was lower by five cubits than any other gate, in order that the priests, when sprinkling the blood of the red heifer (about to be burnt on Mount Olivet) toward the altar, might be enabled to look over this gate (along the lofty bridge), and through the Beautiful and Nicanor Gates, and get a view of the altar.

The Rabbins say, that "such a foot causey also (as the Red Heifer Bridge) they made, upon which they led away the scape-goat; both were built at the charges of the public treasure, which was in the Temple."

In order to make assurance doubly sure in guarding the "clean person" that was to sprinkle the "clean water" upon the unclean, the more effectually against defilement from contact with the dead, or a near vicinity to a grave, the Jews resorted to the following expedient, as detailed by Dr. Lightfoot out of the Rabbinical writings. "Therefore that such persons might be had, there were arches wrought in a rock in Jerusalem, after the manner forementioned, and houses built over those arches. Some courts were built upon a rock, under which there was made a hollow, that by no means any sepulchre might be there. Hither they brought some teeming women, that they might be delivered there, and might there also bring forth their children, and the reason of that curiosity was, that those children, there born and brought up, where they were so secure from being touched by a sepulchre, might be clean without doubt, and fit to sprinkle with purifying water, such as were polluted with a dead carcase. (L. ii. 34.) This was one of the 'memorable places' of the city, and thither, as to a place secure from graves, certain women with child were brought, when they were near to the time of their delivery, and there they were brought to bed; and their children were there brought up continually, for this very employment, that they might be ready as they were capable, and as there was occasion to sprinkle these other, which, when any of them went to do, he rode on a seat on oxen's back, first to the Pool of Siloam, where he lighted in the water, for there he might presume there was no grave to defile him, filled his pitcher, and got up again, rode to Mount Olivet, besprinkled the party that was to be cleansed, and rode in like manner to his cell again." (i. 982.) The place where the cow was burnt was also arched over for fear of pollution. The elders headed the procession, and when the priests came up, he bathed himself there. Nine cows had been burnt from from Moses to the Messiah, and another performance of the ceremony was in contemplation about the time of his death.

What rapturous emotions of wonder, awe, and delight must have filled the mind and heart of the devout worshipper going "up to the House of the Lord!" Crossing the cyclopean Tyropœon Bridge, and entering the Temple area by the High Gate of the House of the Lord—the royal entrance—what a magnificent spectacle was presented to his admiring gaze by the triple cloister, called the Stoa Basilica—the royal portico, just in front of him, with its triple colonnades of its one hundred and sixty-two magnificent columns! On his left, and extending all around on the west, north, and east sides, were superb cloisters and colonnades, but not so broad, lofty, elegant, and imposing as the southern or royal cloister immediately in front. To these colonnades and cloisters (most of which were occupied by the Levites), the Doctors of the Law were accustomed to resort in order to expound the law, and be interrogated by the people. It was no doubt in one of these places that the sorrowing mother of the young child Jesus found him "sitting in the midst of the doctors, both hearing them and asking them questions." It was here too that the Messiah so often refuted the scribes, Pharisees, and doctors of the law. It was also in the eastern cloister, called "Solomon's Porch," that Peter preached his second recorded discourse. (Acts iii.) And probably also, it was in this same place that the first converts "continued daily with one accord, praising and blessing God." The pinnacle of the Temple, upon which our Lord was tempted of the devil, was perhaps the loftiest part of the southern portico, and not the summit of the house itself, as generally supposed. It is at least certain that from this point to the ground, on the exterior, was by far the greatest elevation about the premises; and Josephus declares that "if any one looked down from the top of the battlements into the Valley of the Kedron, which here bends around the Temple, he would be giddy, while his sight could not reach to such an amazing depth." Passing through this enclosing cloister, the worshipper found himself in a very large and magnificent court, paved with the finest variegated marble, surrounded on all sides by the magnificent piazza or covered walk in front of the cloisters. This is the great Court of the Gentiles, containing fifteen or twenty acres, and was entered by several subterranean gateways, as well as those on its own level. It was in this outer court that Jesus found in the Temple those that sold oxen, and sheep, and doves, and the changers of money sitting. And when he had made a scourge of small cords, he drove them out of the Temple, and the sheep and the oxen, and poured out the changers' money, and overturned the tables, and said unto them that sold doves, Take these things hence; make not my Father's house an house of merchandise. (John ii. 14–16.)

The north-western quarter of this area was occupied by that splendid pile of buildings consisting of the Holy House, and its immediate courts and appendages. This more sacred enclosure was separated from the remainder of the great outer court by the sacred balustrade or wall of partition, called Hil, or Soreg, beyond which it was death for any Gentile or even an unclean Jew to go. It was for the supposed offence of "polluting the Holy Places beyond, by bringing some Gentiles within this place, that such a clamor was raised against the Apostle Paul. (Acts xxi: 28.)

The purified worshipper, on proceeding beyond this wall through any of its numerous openings, ascended a flight of steps, and found himself on a broad platform, extending all around the cloisters and courts within, called the rampart or Chel. Passing through the large gate on the east, or either of the easternmost gates on the north or south sides, he finds himself in the new court—generally styled Women's Court, where the treasury chests were kept—the large court, in which worship was generally offered, and beyond which the women were not permitted to go, except when they brought a sacrifice. It was to this court, no doubt, that the "two men went up to pray," as related by the beloved Physician (Luke xviii: 10—14), "the one a Pharisee, the other a publican," and here too, our Saviour delivered the discourse recorded by the Apostle John, (viii: 1—20.)

The magnificent Corinthian-brass gate on the east of this court, was the Beautiful Gate, where the cripple was healed by the Apostle. (Acts iii. 2–11.) Ascending a flight of semicircular steps, and passing through another magnificent gate called Nicanor, on the western side of the court, whose ponderous leaves required the strength of twenty men to open or close them, the worshipper found himself in the small Court of Israel, just beyond which was the Court of the Priests, in which stood the Holy Fane itself—whose splendor and magnificence surpassed all description.

It was upon these steps that the Levites are supposed to have stood when they chanted the "Psalms of Degrees," (120–134,) at the Feast of Tabernacles. It was here that the wife suspected of infidelity underwent the trial of bitter water; and here too that the mother appeared for purification; and the leper stood to be cleansed from his loathsome disease.

The upper half of the Temple area appertained to the Castle or Acropolis of Antonia, and was adorned with magnificent palatial as well as military structures, courts, bathing-places, &c., &c.

The *Judgment Hall*, where the "King of the Jews" was so wickedly and cruelly mocked and maltreated, was doubtless a large room in this magnificent palatial fort. *Gabbatha*, or the *Pavement*, a place evidently contiguous to the Hall, is generally supposed to have been the mere paved floor of the area of Antonia. But as the etymology of the term would seem to require elevation, it is rather to be inferred that if it was not a regularly elevated platform, surmounted with a seat of judgment, it was at least a portion of the upper cloister used as a tribunal or judgment seat. The Castle being built upon the lofty solid rock, it could have no low story; the Hall must therefore necessarily have been located as high, probably, as the top of the cloisters. (John xviii. 28, and xix. 13.)

There appears to have been a stairway, leading from the Antonia yard at this corner, to the Castle, or at least to the cloisters above, in connexion with it. It was here that Paul was led up into the Castle and made his defence from the stairs. (Acts xxi. 35–40.)

"Concerning the high veneration which the Jews cherished for their Temple, Dr. Harwood has collected some interesting particulars from Philo, Josephus, and the writings of Luke. Their reverence for the sacred edifice was such, that rather than witness its defilement, they would cheerfully submit to death. They could not bear the least disrespectful or dishonorable thing to be said of it. The least injurious slight of it, real or apprehended, instantly awakened all the choler of a Jew, and was an affront never to be forgiven. Our Saviour, in the course of his public instructions, happening to say, 'Destroy this Temple, and in three days I will raise it up again,' (John ii. 19)—it was construed into a contemptuous disrespect, designedly thrown out against the Temple—his words instantly descended into the heart of a Jew, and kept rankling there for several years; for upon his trial, this declaration, which it was impossible for a Jew ever to forget or to forgive, was alleged against him, as big with the most atrocious guilt and impiety. (Matt. xxvi. 61.) Nor was the rancor and virulence, which this expression had occasioned, at all softened by all the affecting circumstances of that excruciating and wretched death they saw him die—even as he hung upon the cross, with infinite triumph, scorn and exultation, they upbraided him with it, contemptuously shaking their heads, and saying, 'O thou who couldest *demolish* our Temple and rear it up again, in all its splendor, in the space of *three* days, do now *save thyself*, and descend from the cross!' (Matt. xxvii. 40.) Their superstitious veneration for the Temple further appears from the account of Stephen. When his adversaries were baffled and confounded by that superior wisdom and those distinguished gifts he possessed, they were so exasperated at the victory he had gained over them, that they went and suborned persons to swear that they had heard him speak blasphemy against Moses and against God. Thus inflaming the populace, the magistrates, and the Jewish clergy, he was seized, dragged away, and brought before the Sanhedrim. Here the false witnesses, whom they had procured, stood up and said—'This person before you is continually uttering the most reproachful expressions against this sacred place,' (Acts vi. 13), meaning the Temple. This was *blasphemy* not to be pardoned. A judicature composed of high priests and scribes would never forgive *such* impiety. We witness the same thing in the case of Paul, when they imagined that he had taken Trophimus, an Ephesian, with him into the Temple, and for which insult they had determined to imbrue their hands in his blood. (Acts xxi. 28, &c.)

"We have only to add that, from several passages of Scripture, it appears that the Jews had a body of soldiers who guarded the Temple, to prevent any disturbance during the ministration of such an immense number of priests and Levites. To this body of men, whose office it was to guard the Temple, Pilate probably referred when he said to the chief priests and Pharisees, who waited on him to desire he would make the sepulchre secure, "You have a watch: go your way, and make it secure as you can." (Matt. xxvii. 65.) Over these guards *one* person had the supreme command, who, in several places, is called Captain of the Temple, or Officer of the Temple Guards. (Acts iv. 1; v. 25, 26; xviii. 12.) Josephus mentions such an officer. (Ant. 20, 2; Wars, c. 17, 2.)

The holiness of the place, and the injunction (of Lev. xix. 3), "Ye shall reverence my sanctuary," laid the people under an obligation to maintain a solemn and holy behavior when they came to worship in the Temple. We have already seen that such as were ceremonially unclean were forbidden to enter the sacred court on pain of death; but, in the course of time, there were several prohibitions enforced by the Sanhedrim, which the law had not named.

The following have been collected by Lightfoot, out of the Rabbinical writings. (1.) "No man might enter the mountain of the house with his staff." (2.) "None might enter in thither with his shoes on his feet"—though he might with his sandals. (3.) "Nor might any man enter the mountain of the house with his scrip on." (4.) "Nor might he come in with the dust on his feet," but he must wash or wipe them, "and look to his feet when he entered into the house of God," to remind him, perhaps, that he should then shake off all worldly thoughts and affections. (5.) "Nor with money in his purse." He might bring it in his *hand*, however; and in this way it was brought in for various purposes. If this had not been the case, it would seem strange that the cripple should have been placed at the gate of the Temple to ask *alms* of those who entered therein. (See Acts iii. 2.) (6.) "None might spit in the Temple. If he were necessitated to spit, it must be done in some corner of his garment." (7.) "He might not use any irreverent gesture, especially before the gate of Nicanor," that being exactly in front of the Temple. (8.) "He might not make the mountain of the house a thoroughfare," for the purpose of reaching the place by a nearer way: for it was devoted to the purposes of religion." (9.) "He that went into the court must go leisurely and gravely into his place; and there he must demean himself as in the presence of the Lord God, in all reverence and fear." (10.) "He must worship standing, with his feet close to each other, his eyes directed to the ground, his hands upon his breast, with the right one above the left." (See Luke xviii. 13.) (11.) "No one, however weary, might sit down in the court." The only exception was in favor of the kings of the House of David. (12.) "None might pray with his head uncovered. And the wise men and their scholars never prayed without a veil." This custom is alluded to in 1 Cor. xi. 4, where the Apostle directs all men to reverse the practice adopted in the Jewish Temple. (13.) Their bodily gesture, in bowing before the Lord, was either "bending on the knees," "bowing the head," or "falling prostrate on the ground." (14.) Having performed the service, and being about to retire, "They might not turn their backs upon the altar." They therefore went backward, till they were out of the court.

The Sacred Furniture of the Temple.—The ultimate fate of the holy vessels and sacred apparatus of the Temple is a subject that has excited much inquiry, and well merits a passing notice. It is a very general belief that amongst the spoils of the Temple carried to Rome by Titus were the identical candlestick, golden altar and table, the silver trumpets, &c., that had been provided by Solomon; but this is a great mistake. Such of this furniture as was brought back from Babylon by the Jews on returning from captivity was carried to Antioch by Antiochus Epiphanes, when he despoiled Jerusalem, "and emptied the Temple of its secret treasures and left nothing at all remaining." The sacred trophies carried away by Titus were those with which the Holy House was furnished by Judas Maccabeus on purifying the Temple after its profanation and desertion. On reaching Rome, the golden vessels and other sacred implements were deposited in the temple of Concord; and although some of them may have fallen a prey to the devouring element when that temple was destroyed, A. D. 191, yet history distinctly informs us that they fell into the hands of Alaric, when he sacked the city, A. D. 410. And about half a century afterwards most or all of them seem to have been carried to Carthage by Genseric, king of the Vandals, when the city fell into his ruthless hands, but seem to have been returned to Rome, or at least recovered by the Romans, after the victory of Belisarius. There appear to be reliable notices of them both at Ravenna and at Constantinople afterwards; and tradition, at least, reports that they were finally restored to Jerusalem by the Emperor Justinian, and it is supposed by many that they still lie concealed in some of the secret subterranean recesses of the Temple Mount.

A finely executed piece of sculpture representing the articles of Temple furniture exhibited in the triumphal procession of Titus, is still to be seen, in a tolerable state of preservation, within the Arch of Titus at Rome.

REFERENCES TO PLAN OF TEMPLE.

SECTIONS AND ELEVATIONS.

GROUND PLAN OF THE TEMPLE.

1, 1, 1, 1, 1 Piazza or Colonnade and Cloister—enclosing the whole area of Antonia and the Temple, and also dividing the former from the latter. That on the south is the Royal Colonnade or Stoa Basilica; and that east of the Sanctuary, Solomon's Porch.
2 The traditional Gate of Huldah.
3 Triple Gate—probably the "Priest's Gate"—to the east of which is a small doorway, giving entrance to the substructures.
4 Shusan or East Gate.
5 The present Golden Gate—formerly giving entrance apparently to a tower, probably the Tower of Meah.
6 The gate which led to Akra by steps.
7 and 8 The two Parbar Gates.
9 Shallecheth, High Gate or Prison Gate (Coponius also). Titdi Gate seems to have been in the wall dividing the Temple from Antonia.
10, 10, 10 Court of the Gentiles.
12 Court of Women.
13 Court of Priests.
14 Court of Israel.
15 Hil, Soreg or Sacred Partition Fence.
16 Steps leading to Chell or Rampart surrounding the Cloisters.
- a Gate of Kindling.
- b Gate of Firstlings.
- c Water Gate.
- d Women's Gate, south.
- e Beautiful Gate.
- f Women's Gate, north.
- g Gate of Offerings or Corban.
- h Gate Nitzouts.
- i Gate of Song?
- j Nicanor.
- k Thrigcos.
- l Altar.
- m Inclined Plane or Steps to Altar.
- n Brazen Sea.
- o, o Places for Slaughtering Knives.
- p Slaughtering Apartment, rings, tables, beams, hooks, &c.
- q Porch.
- r Holy Place—containing Altar of Incense, Candlestick, and Table of Showbread.
- s Most Holy Place, containing Ark, &c. Around the Holy and Holiest, or the Holy House, are
- t The Chambers—and beyond and around these
- u The Impluvium.

17 Room for Lepers.
18 Room for Wood.
19 Room for Nazarites.
20 Room for Oil.
21 Treasury Chests.
22 Royal Cistern.

In the cloisters on the north and south sides of the Court of the Priests, are various apartments, for different purposes:—Golah, sheep-shearing, selected sheep, bath and house of kindling, washing sacrifices, Paroch, sheep-skins, bath, salt magazine, wood, warming apartments, showbread room, room of the Asmoneans (where the desecrated stones of the Altar were kept), and Gazith, where the Sanhedrim sometimes sat. Beneath the Court of Israel, and opening into the Court of Women, were the wardrobe rooms, and apartments for musical instruments, culinary utensils, &c.

TEMPLE AND PRECINCTS.

END VIEW FROM SOUTH—A.

- a Royal Buildings on Zion.
- b Tyropœon Bridge.
- c Gate Miphkad.
- d High Gate of Benjamin, Shallecheth, &c.
- e Holy House (side view).
- f Royal Portico.
- g Southern Wall of Temple Area.
- h Double Gate, leading subterraneously to the Upper Area. (Huldah's.)
- i Triple Gateway, leading subterraneously to the Area above.
- j Small door, leading to the substructures of the south-east corner. (Apparently modern.)
- k Pastophoria, or "Covert of the Sabbath."
- l Tower of Ophel.

SECTION THROUGH THE TEMPLE AND COURTS, THE XYSTUS AND THE RED HEIFER BRIDGE—B.

- a Armory and other public buildings on Mt. Zion.
- b Xystus (northern end).
- c Western Cloister.
- d Hil or Sacred Fence.
- e High wall in the rear of the Temple.
- f Holy House.
- g Altar.
- h Covered Colonnade—the Court of the Priests.
- i Gate Nicanor, in front of Court of Israel.
- j Beautiful Gate.
- k Eastern Cloister—Solomon's Porch.
- l Pool of Bethesda.
- m City Wall.
- n Red Heifer Bridge.

SIDE VIEW FROM THE EAST—C.

- a Pastophoria.
- b Upper-Central Colonnade in the Royal Basilica.
- c, c Tops of the northern and southern ranges of the Inner Cloisters.
- d Shusan or East Gate.
- e Front view of the Temple.
- f Towers of the range of Cloisters north of the Temple.
- g Tower.
- h Tower at north-east corner of Temple.

VIEW FROM THE NORTH—E.

- a Eastern Cloister of the Temple Area.
- b Tower of the eastern range of the Cloisters of the Court of the Women.
- c Top of the Cloisters on the east of the Inner Temple.
- d Side view of the Temple.
- e Tower of Antonia.

VIEW FROM THE WEST—D.

- a Tower of Antonia.
- b Towers of the range of Cloisters north of the Temple.
- c, c Towers at the north-west and south-west corners of the north and south ranges of the inner Cloisters.
- d Rear view of the Temple.
- e Prison Gate at east end of Royal Basilica.
- f Upper and central range of Colonnades in Royal Basilica.
- g Northern Parbar Gate.
- h Southern Parbar Gate.
- i "Gate that led to the other city."
- j Abutment of Tyropœon Bridge.

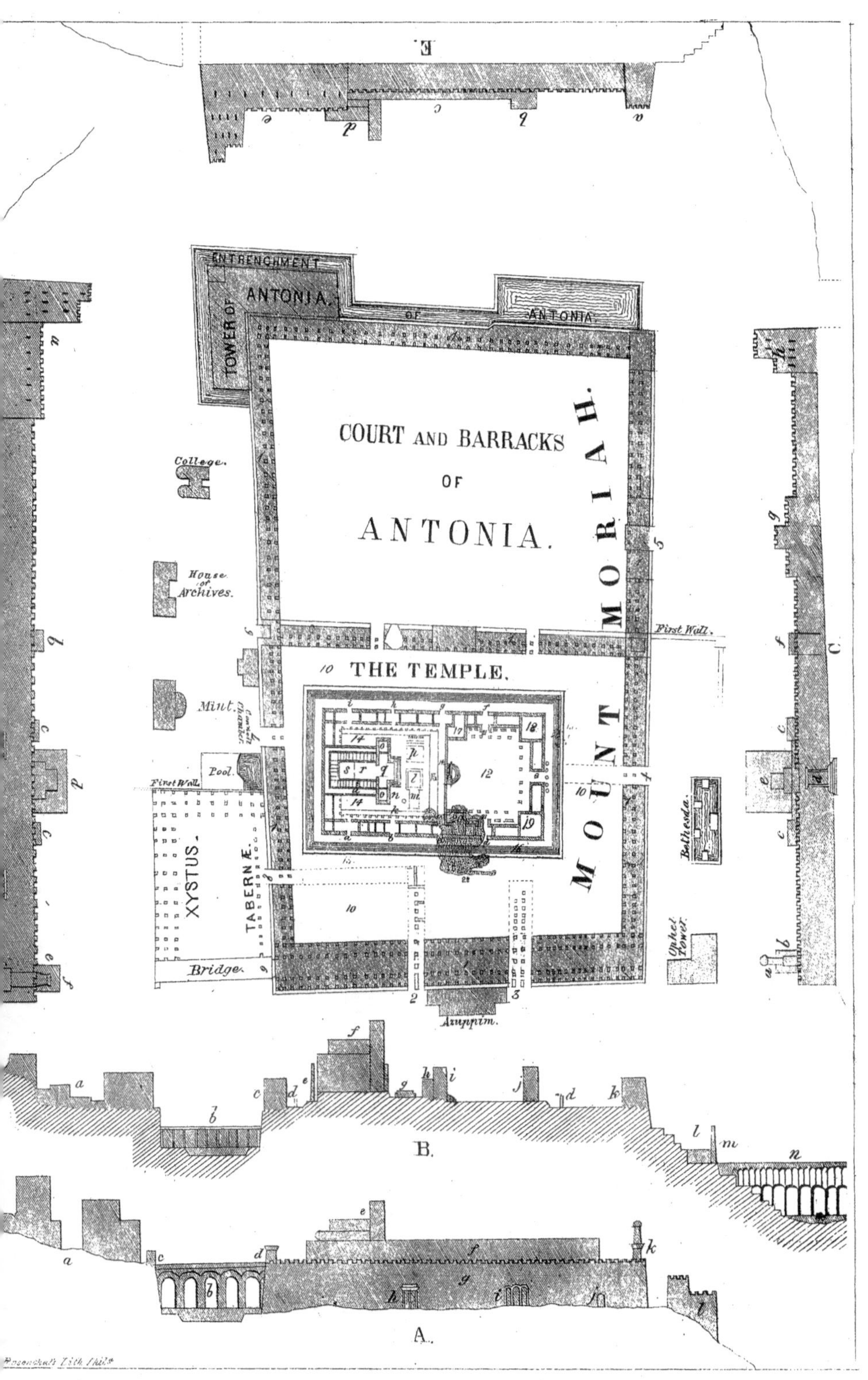

PLAN, ELEVATION AND SECTION OF THE TEMPLE AND ITS PRECINCTS.

CHAPTER X.

WATER SUPPLY OF JERUSALEM.

"A good land—a land of brooks of water, of fountains and depths that spring out of valleys and hills."

THAT the proud capital of Israel was originally well supplied with water is not only fairly inferable from the peculiar customs of the Jews, and palpably evident from the numerous and magnificent waterwork remains of antiquity; but is abundantly proved by the inimpeachable testimony of ancient writers—both sacred and profane. The entire absence of rain during so large a portion of the year, and the surprising fertility of the soil when irrigated under a Syrian sun, could but induce the Jews to bestow much attention upon the construction of cisterns not only for storing away the rain falling on housetops for table use and other domestic purposes, but such of that falling in the fields as could be conducted by channels into large artificial basins or caverns, for agricultural as well as horticultural purposes. The winter rain was to them what the Nile was to the Egyptians. And accordingly the vestiges of such channels and reservoirs are to be seen everywhere throughout the country. We can arrive at no other conclusion than that the reservoirs and baths must have abounded in the Holy City, when it is remembered the divers washings of the law were so greatly multiplied by the traditions of the elders, that "the Pharisees, and all the Jews, except they wash their hands oft, eat not; and when they come from the market, except they wash they eat not; and many other things * *

* * as the washing of cups and pots and brazen vessels, and of tables." (Mark vii. 3, 4.)

Upon this much controverted subject Dr. Trail expresses himself very appositely as follows:—(Trail's Jos. pp. 58–61.)

Perhaps upon no city of the ancient world had greater cost been bestowed, or more skill shown, in securing for it an unfailing supply of water; and such was the repute of Jerusalem in this particular, that its strength as a fortification is frequently alluded to by profane writers, as including this grand and indispensable means of sustaining a lengthened siege. Thus, Strabo having mentioned the fact generally that Jerusalem, situated in the midst of a district destitute of water, was itself abundantly supplied therewith, presently afterwards; and, while referring to the capture of the city by Pompey, states that he took it, notwithstanding its substantial munitions, and its being abundant in water, while all around was dry:—εντος μεν ευυδρον, εκτος δε παντελως διψηρον (p. 762), 1106.* To the same purport is the often-cited passage in Tacitus (Hist. v. 12), who describes the Temple with its porticoes, as a fortress; and such, in fact, it was, well fitted to sustain the frequent sieges to which it was liable. 'Fons perennis aquæ, cavati sub terra montes: et piscinæ cisternæque servandis imbribus.'†

In truth, the provision made—and it appears to have been from the earliest times of the monarchy—for securing a supply of water to the city generally, and to the Temple especially, was of the most elaborate kind; and so well contrived were these works, that they continued to be effective for their purposes through the course of many centuries; and indeed are so, in great measure, to the present time. Almost every house of the better class, in the modern Jerusalem, has its capacious tank, occupying the basement, and which, collecting the water of the rainy season from its courts and roofs, furnishes an ample supply during the months of drought. Yet, these

* "Within, truly well watered; but without, altogether dry."

† "A fountain of perennial water, mountains hollowed out, underneath: also fish pools and cisterns—rain-water being preserved."

private reservoirs are not alone relied upon—or were not so in the age of national prosperity.

Whether there be indeed any natural spring of water deep-seated within the Temple enclosure, and the waste of which runs off at Siloam, cannot perhaps at present be certainly determined: it is a question which, with many others of the same kind, must await the time when the Holy City comes under the sway of some civilized government.

Whatever may be the source of the waters which supply the Haram so copiously, it is certain that these resources were not relied upon as sufficient to secure an unfailing abundance of this necessary element. We find, therefore, and at so great a distance from the city as seven miles, extensive and well constructed reservoirs, undoubtedly of the highest antiquity, the intention of which was to collect water to be conveyed thither by ducts, carried upon or beneath the surface, and on a due level around the slopes of the country, a distance, in its windings, of not less than twelve miles. But even this was not enough, for nearer at hand, and more under command, the entire surface water of the country, west of the city, found its way into two reservoirs—the upper and the lower Gihon Pools, as already mentioned. From these tanks—covered no doubt originally—two aqueducts conveyed the water; the one directly to the city near the Jaffa Gate, the other in a circuit round Zion, on its southern side, and toward the Temple.* The waters of the Upper Pool, when redundant, flowing on to the more spacious reservoir, called the Lower Pool, and upon the brink of which means were taken for readily watering the cattle of the surrounding country. * * * * * * * * * *

* The learned commentator is probably mistaken in this assertion—at least there are no vestiges of such an aqueduct at the present day; and, moreover, the pool being deeper than any portion of Zion that was ever included within the city walls, there could have been no special occasion for such an aqueduct. The aqueduct now conveying water around the slopes of Zion, is from neither the Upper nor Lower Pool, but from "Solomon's Pools." at Etham.

There are frequent allusions in Josephus and other writers to deep-seated aqueducts within and without the city.

In the many sieges which the Holy City has sustained during the lapse of ages, the same course of events nearly is presented—the sufferings of the besieged from hunger, and of the besiegers from thirst. A scarcity of water does not seem ever to have aggravated the miseries that were endured within the walls;* while the want of it without has, in each instance, tormented the assailants.

Wealth, intelligence, and constructive skill, to an extent which has not been well understood by modern writers, were undoubtedly at the command of the early Jewish monarchs; and while the storms of war, ravaging their land from age to age, have swept from the surface almost every monument of its early greatness, so much of the national resources as were providently expended beneath the surface, in works of primary importance, has been—in its wrecks at least—conserved, these to the present time, to claim, what they so well deserve, the enlightened attention of Biblical archæologists. The Temple of Solomon and of Herod has been rased, yet its substructures still, and not obscurely, shadow forth its greatness. The cedar roofs of a hundred palaces, blazing with gold, are no more; but the ample and well-contrived reservoirs which those palaces bestrode, still exist; and still subserve their purpose. The terraced gardens, the "paradises" of the kings and nobles of Jerusalem, have long been desolated; but even now around the slopes of the hills may be traced, mile after mile, the aqueducts whence those gardens drew perpetual verdure, and which then poured their superfluous streams into the deep bosom of Moriah!

It may be appropriate, in passing, to call the reader's attention to that occult connexion of causes which, no doubt, had much influ-

* This is not literally true, though asserted by so many authors; for, in the 161st or 162d Olympiad, when Antiochus laid siege to Jerusalem, the Jews "were once in want of water," as Josephus informs us, Ant. xiii. ix: 2. It is also more than intimated by Ezekiel that there was a very great scarcity of water in the final siege by the Chaldeans. (Ezek. iv. 17.)

ence in securing to the ancient, and so to the modern Jerusalem, an unfailing supply of water. The Jewish public worship was, if we might so term it, a ceremonial of ablution; and Judaism, considered as a personal and domestic scheme of life, was a routine of endless washings. Now, one would have thought, on grounds of ordinary calculation, that the founder of such an institute—of this public ritual, and of this individual ceremonial—the promulgator of this religion of "divers baptisms," of this scheme of life for a nation, demanding that their persons and utensils should often be washed, and should daily be plunged in water, was looking forward, from the scorched wilderness of Sinai, to some region of many streams, and of gushing fountains, as the destined home of his people. One would have thought that Moses was intending to make—not Jerusalem, but Damascus the metropolis of the Israelitish worship. Jerusalem, reared among limestone mountains, and scarcely blessed, within a circuit of many miles, with so many as two or three natural springs,* and yet this very city, this central point as it is of drought, has, from age to age, known no thirst within its walls! The series of writers from Strabo down to William of Tyre, use almost the same phrases, at once in describing the aridity of the region, and in attesting the fact that within the city there was always water enough and to spare!

Now it is obvious to remark that this abundance, so important to the health and comfort of a densely crowded city, has been the consequence of this very peculiarity of the religious system of the people. This system, demanding so large a supply of water, has, from the earliest age, secured to the population as ample a supply as is enjoyed by the inhabitants of cities that are the most favored in this respect by their nearness to rivers, and by the copiousness of natural springs. In Jerusalem the collection and conservation of the rains of the winter months, became, at the impulse of a reli-

* The Doctor is again at fault in this assertion. Within a circuit swept by a radius of seven miles, there are no less than thirty or forty natural springs.

gious necessity, the first law of the municipal economy of the state."

But besides the above-cited testimony of Strabo and Tacitus, who depose as to the water resources of Jerusalem, in the first century of the Christian era, just at the period of its subversion by the Romans, it may be well, by way of attestation, at least to adduce the testimony of other historians and travellers of a date anterior to that event, as well as long subsequent to it—even down to our own days.

That Jerusalem was well supplied with water during the high-priesthood of Simon the Just, three hundred years before the Christian era, we may well infer from the 50th chapter and 3d verse of Ecclesiasticus, where, amongst other matters concerning the reparation of the Temple, it is specially recorded that "in his days the cistern to receive water, being in compass as the sea, was covered or lined with plates of brass."* What is here called a "*sea*" is no doubt the great subterranean cistern I discovered beneath the Temple area, reference to which is also made by a highly favored explorer of Jerusalem, a few years after the high-priesthood of Simon—the celebrated Aristeas, who was sent by Ptolemy Philadelphus on a special mission to Eliezur, high priest of the Jews, rather more than two and a half centuries before Christ, for the purpose of securing an authentic and authorized version of the Hebrew Scriptures into Greek—the Septuagint. (Ant. xii. ii: 1, 15.) Aristeas, in writing his brother an account of his visit to the Holy City, speaks thus of its water resources and appliances:—"A powerful natural spring is received into subterranean reservoirs, the extent of which is surprising and beyond description, to the circumference of five stadia about the Temple. They are connected by numberless pipes, through which the waters flow from one to another. There are above, frequent hidden apertures to these depths, known only to those employed at the sacrifices, through which the water, gushing out with force, washes off all the blood of the numerous victims. The reservoirs have their floors and sides cased with lead,*

* Brass—lead—a pointed, yet immaterial discrepancy.

and are covered over with a quantity of earth." According to Dr. Lightfoot, vol. i. p. 2010, "Aristeas, who was an eye-witness and spectator of it, giveth testimony of this conveyance of water in these words:—'There was a continual supply of water, as if there had sprung an abundant fountain underneath: and there were wonderful and unexpressible receptacles underground, as appeared five furlongs' space about the Temple, each one of which had divers pipes, by which waters came in on every side: all these were of lead, under ground, and much earth laid upon them. And there were many vents on the pavements, not to be seen at all but to those that served; so that in a trice and easily all the blood of the sacrifices could be washed away, though it were never so much. And I will tell you how I came to know of these underground receptacles: they brought me out more than four furlongs' space out of the city, and one bad me stoop down and listen what a noise the meeting of the waters made.'"

The Talmud, in speaking of the "draw-well room," says, "that fountain was twenty-three cubits deep." "It was at the west end of the famous room Gazith," says the same authority, "where a well was sunk with a wheel over it, and from thence they fetched up water to serve all the court. It was not a little water that was used; and yet the temple never wanted. In some places there were baths on the very tops of the gates: on the roof of the water gate and the incense room there were baths for the high priest; for although the bathing-place on the top of Happorah was the place where he washed oftenest on the day of expiation, yet here he washed first. On the top of the adjoining room there was also another bath. Five times he bathed his body and ten times he washed his hands, on the day of expiation."

Aristeas, however, though so well sustained by the Talmud, is universally charged with the grossest exaggeration in this account; and by many is discredited in toto. But my explorations of the sacred enclosure go so far to exculpate and sustain his statement, that—bating the allowable hyperbole of an Oriental and especially a native of the land of hieroglyphics, where there were no "fountains and depths springing out of valleys and hills"—it may certainly be regarded as highly reliable in the main. That there was an actual independent, though perhaps small, fountain* in the Temple enclosure at one time, is probable in the highest degree; and that it was supplied with fresh water by an aqueduct, as well as with rain-water, is certain. The present aqueduct can be traced within a few yards of it, and running directly towards it; and it is evident from the Middoth that there was a large subterranean reservoir in the south quarter of the Temple, supplied by an aqueduct from Etham—the discharge of which into the reservoir is supposed by some to have been "the coming down of the waters." If there really never was a native fountain there, then we must in charity allow that the Egyptian chronicler failed to discriminate between the gushing of a natural fountain and the effusion of this artificial waterspout.

But it is not until we have taken into consideration the immense capacities of the "Brazen or Molten Sea" and ten lavers, the great number of personal ablutions performed by such a vast company of priests, the many sacrificial washings, and the innumerable purifications to be performed over running water, that we are prepared to form any proper estimate of the immense amount of water constantly flowing through the Temple.

THE MOLTEN SEA that stood in the Court of the Priests, mounted upon twelve brazen oxen, was an immense receptacle, about fifteen feet broad and seven and a half in depth: its contents were at least two hundred barrels, and its capacity is even rated by some authors as high as three hundred hogsheads. And the basin in which this great receptacle stood is supposed to have contained half this amount. The ten lavers probably contained about seven barrels each.

THE IMPLUVIUM was a narrow receptacle of water, extending around three sides of the Holy House more than three hundred feet

* I have since received a communication from the effendi, stating that he has discovered a very weak fountain in the immediate vicinity of the es-Sakhrah, but some distance below the surface.

in length, four and a half in breadth on the sides of the Temple, and seven and a half in its rear.

Eusebius, who was a native of Palestine, and died there about the year 340, in making extracts from authors that lived between the Apostolic age and the age in which he flourished—incidentally gives us some information on that subject. He quotes Timochares as saying, "the whole city flowed with water, so that even the gardens were irrigated of those flowing waters out of the city. But round about for forty stadia to be without [water], but from these forty stadia water again to exist." The surveyor of Syria speaks of a fountain existing in that place, pouring forth water plentifully: and Philo mentions the peculiarities of "the fountain and the pipes of the high priests' fountain spouting water." The Bourdeaux Pilgrim remarks in the Jerusalem Itinerary, A. D. 333—"There are, in Jerusalem, two large fish pools by the side of the Temple, *i. e.*, one at the right-hand, the other at the left, which Solomon made." * * * * * "There are there great receptacles of subterranean water and fish pools, built with great labor; and in the house itself, where the Temple was which Solomon built." (Itin. Hierosol. p. 152.) And again: "But farther in the city are twin fish pools having five porches which are called Bethsaida." (Itin. Hierosol. p. 589.) He also mentions that the Basilica of Constantine, surrounding the Church of the Holy Sepulchre, had receptacles of water at its side whence water was raised, and a bath in the rear where infants were washed. It is stated as a fact, that while Julian was attempting the reëdification of the Temple, about A. D. 362, on removing a certain foundation stone, the entrance to a rock-hewn cavern was discovered, in which, on lowering a laborer by a cord, water was found half way up his thigh. Jerome informs us that even in his day—about the beginning of the fifth century—"Tophet was a fine and pleasant place, well watered with fountains, and adorned with gardens." And Omar is said to have performed his ablutions at two fountains in Hinnom. The "Placentine Pilgrim," who wrote about A. D. 600, says "that an apple, thrown into a certain crypt on the side of

Golgotha rock, where noise of running water is heard (*flumina aquarum*), it would afterward be found at Silwan." On the hypothesis suggested in relation to the course of Hezekiah's subterranean conduit, it would pass just by the rock alluded to.

When Omar took the city (A. D. 637), water was found copiously flowing down a pair of steps connected with the Temple. Two fountains were also in the "Valley of Hinnom" at that time. The beautiful Saracenic fontal structures in the lower part of the city, of which four now remain around the Haram enclosure, between St. Stephen's Gate and Temple street, in quite good state of preservation, abundantly attest the fact that the city was well supplied with running water during its occupancy by the Saracens. Mr. Williams, in the first volume of his "Holy City," gives a very interesting account of Omar's reception by the Patriarch, which he has gleaned from various sources, as follows:—(p. 316) "Water was running down the steps, and through the street which led to the city gate, so that great part of the stairs was under water. Then said the Patriarch to him: 'Thou canst go no farther except by crawling on hands and knees.' The Khalif, nothing daunted, proceeded thus through the water channel, until he came to a level space at the top of a hill, where there were ruins. Here he looked about him and contemplated for awhile; then he said: '*Ullah Acbar!* By Him, in whose hands is my life, this is that which the Apostle of God (on whom be the peace and blessing of God!) described to me.'" The steps down which the water was flowing into the street, were those leading to the double gate in the southern wall of the Temple, from the area above or the gate I discovered in the west wall beneath the present Mugrabin Gate similarly arranged—more probably the former; as the water from the great Temple reservoir, in front of Akra (supplied by aqueduct from Etham), would most readily find egress through that channel from the overflowing or bursting subterranean lake. William of Tyre speaks of the fountains that were brought from "outer parts by aqueducts into fish pools of great quantity (*Maximæ quantitatis*) outside the Temple, but beneath the city, beyond the exuberant impluvium, (A. D. 1182.) And, about the same time, mention is made by Albert of Aix (50, 6), of a royal cistern before the doors of the palace, in an excavation, after the manner of a lake in amplitude and magnitude. And, in the Gesta Francorum, abundant mention is made of the fact that there was a superfluity of water within the city, and especially in reservoirs near or within the sacred enclosure. Brocardus mentions, in 1283, a large reservoir near St. Ann's Church, called "Piscina Interior," just opposite Birket Israil, which he calls very great ("*grandis valde*") even compared with the latter! May they not always have been filled, and well stocked with fish? for William of Tyre informs us that they were filled with living water brought from a distance by aqueducts. And hence the name of the gate. It was filled with water as late as 1509, according to Anselm. Mentioned also by Felix Fabri,* and many other authors. Piscinæ gemilares. And into the lower one (Birket Israil) George Sandys reported so late as his visit in 1610, that "a barren spring doth drill from between the stones of the northern wall, and stealeth away almost undiscerned."

Having taken this general view of the subject, we are the better enabled to understand what may be contained in the Scriptures in relation to the waters of Jerusalem and environs.

THE BROOK KIDRON.—This is the first water mentioned by name in the annals of Jerusalem and its environs. The term Kidron occurs eleven times in the Scriptures, and always with the prefix "brook" except once; and yet it is strenuously contended by some that it was a mere *valley*, and had no stream of water in it—because, forsooth, it has none now, in the present day of scanty rain and still scantier herbage! But that there was a stream of water in the Valley of the Kidron during the Bible period of its history is evi-

* "Nutritur (Jerusalem) aquis de cælo vel a longinquo inductis. Credo quod hodie major cura sit, quo modo civitas provideatur de aquis quam prius unquam fuerit, qui Saraceni continuis et cottedianis baptismatus utuntur, magis quam Judeis igitur lavatoria multa habent, et mirabili industria inducunt aquas in Jerusalem."

dent from the Hebrew term with which it is ten times found connected, which emphatically means a stream of water. Hence we read (1 Kings xv. 13) that "Asa destroyed the idol, and burnt it by the brook Kedron"—and (2 Kings xxiii. 6) "And he brought out the grove from the house of the Lord, without Jerusalem, *unto* the brook Kedron, and burned it *at* the brook Kedron"—expressions which would be entirely unnatural and unmeaning upon the supposition that Kedron was an unwatered valley. Equally inappropriate would be the expression of Nehemiah (ii. 15), as he went up this same valley in his nocturnal reconnoissance of the city walls—"then went I up in the night by the brook," &c.*

The fountain that bursts forth during the winter, in a valley entering the Kedron from the north, and flowing several hundred yards before it sinks, may perhaps be the representative of the true Kedron. It is not at all impossible that the Kedron may yet be gliding along far below the present rubbish surface of the earth—indeed it is quite probable—for the murmuring of a stream may be distinctly heard in the valley about two miles below the city apparently quite deep. A similar noise was also heard by a shepherd during the period of my sojourn in Jerusalem, about two miles south-east of the city, at a spot where the natural cleavage of the rock was easily effected even by Arab implements; and, on removing the rocks to the depth of

---

* Dr. Robinson observes that the Septuagint, as well as the New Testament and Josephus, has *Keimarrous;* which would seem to imply a *winter* torrent. But it must not be forgotten that, in Nehemiah's account of his nocturnal exploration, the term valley twice occurs, and that neither time is it a word having any relation to water; but when he comes to the *brook*, then this word is put in requisition.

He also remarks that the Hebrew term here always used with Kedron—*Nakhál*—"may be taken as nearly equivalent to the Arabic Wady;" thus intimating that it may be a dry valley. It is the same term, however, that is used in 2 Chr. xxxii. 4: "brook that ran through the land." Still more decisive is the passage in 1 Sam. (xxx. 9, 10): where the Hebrew term used to designate the "brook" over which two hundred men were so faint that they could not pass, is *Nahal*—the identical word by which the Kedron is indicated. But the application of this term to the perennial stream that is to go forth from the Millennial Jerusalem ("in summer and winter shall it be"), is yet more unambiguous. (Ezek. xlvii. 5, 6, 7, &c. Zech. xiv. 8.)

about ten or twelve feet, water was found—though in small quantity, in midsummer, when I visited it. Streams that run beneath the earth for some miles when their source is not very abundant, but also upon the surface when the supply is too great to be vented by the channel below, are not at all unfrequent in Palestine. And this fact may serve to illustrate the present condition of the Kedron. Dr. Robinson, it would seem, had never heard of this occasional stream; and, in commenting on the fact that the Kedron is at present "the dry bed of a wintry torrent," concludes thus: "nor is there any evidence that there was anciently more water in it than at present." (Bib. Res. i. 402.) But, surely, the Doctor does not make sufficient allowance for the diminished amount of rain in the present denuded state of the country, nor give credence enough to the testimony of travellers of former times. For Benjamin of Tudela, who visited Jerusalem in 1163, in speaking of what he saw in the Valley of Kedron on leaving the Gate of Jehosaphat, makes special mention of the great spring of Shiloah that enters the *brook* Kedron. Dr. Lightfoot, in giving the Rabbinical account of Jerusalem, makes special mention of the "Valley of Kedron, in which is a brook whence the valley takes its name." And Sir John Maundeville, in speaking also of the Valley of Jehosaphat, so lately as 1322, says: "in the middle of the valley is a *little river*, which is called the *brook Cedron.*" William of Tyre and Brocardus testify that its subterranean waters were to be heard in their day. The traveller who observes two immense pools in a valley on one side of Jerusalem, and none in a valley several times as expansive on the other side, may well express his surprise. But that there was at least one there in ancient times, and that a very large one, too, we are assured by the highest possible authority. Nehemiah, during his furtive examination of the prostrate wall of Jerusalem, having passed around the west and south sides, comes next to the eastern side; and, leaving "the gate of the fountain" (Siloam), comes to "the king's pool"—but could *ride* no further, there being "no room for the beast that was under him," on account of this pool (no doubt), which, under such circumstances, would scarcely afford room for the Tirshatha to pass through the ruins on the side-walk of the pool. This pool may well be located anywhere in the lower part of the valley, which is here quite a defile, every part of which is admirably adapted to the construction of such reservoirs. If situated higher up, in the neighborhood of the Virgin's Fount, it would account for his silence in relation to that fountain, and might extend a great way up; but if situated quite low down, where I have restored it in consequence of existing indications, where the cliffs of Olivet become less precipitous, it would serve the additional purpose of a military defence to that portion of Mount Ophel and also be more convenient to the King's Gardens. It is just here, too, where the wall makes a more decided curve in facing the east, that Josephus locates "Solomon's Pool," (Wars, v. iv: 2,) which is perhaps identical with this "King's Pool" of Nehemiah. Unless these are different pools, then no more than one reservoir is *mentioned* by any author in all the Valley of Kedron; but one is still to be found (in a very dilapidated and patched-up condition*) four or five hundred yards north of the Tombs of the Kings; and about midway between that and the shallow wady down which the winter stream flows, are some slight vestiges of two or three others. It is highly probable, also, that a portion of the waters of Kedron was conducted along the western slope of the valley, high enough to be received into the Sheep Market, where cattle were temporarily kept in preparation for the altar.

WATERS OF GIHON—"*The brook that flowed through the land.*"—The next mention of the waters of Jerusalem occurs in the narrative of Solomon's sudden accession to the throne. (1 Kings i. 33, 38, 45.) It would appear (from 2 Chr. xxxiii. 30) that there were two fountains or other water localities in Gihon—the upper and the

* And although this may appear to be a modern structure, yet it is doubtless very ancient; for Dr. Robinson well observes that "these reservoirs" he learned to consider as one of the least doubtful vestiges of antiquity in all Palestine; for among the present race of inhabitants such works are utterly unknown. (Bib. Res. i. 483.)

lower. The lower and nearer one was undoubtedly that at which Solomon was anointed king; and was situated somewhere between Akra and Bezetha (or Moriah), serving, perhaps, as a trench to Salem on the north, east, or west. An additional reason for assigning it such a position is found in the fact, that the acclamations of the people and the sound of the trumpets, which so alarmed Adonijah and his fellow-rebels, could be so much better heard from this place than from the spot usually assigned as the scene of the royal unction. The objection that so seriously militates against the site generally selected as the scene of coronation, as to its relative height compared with that of the palace, is altogether without application on this hypothesis: on the contrary, its depressed situation is highly confirmatory of its position—so much lower than the palace on Zion, being in exact accordance with the sacred narrative. The ground at the traditionary "Upper Gihon," where this transaction is generally supposed to have occurred, being as elevated as the highest part of Zion, they could not with any propriety be said to "*go down*" from the citadel where the palace was situated. But such a theory could never have originated except upon the erroneous presumption that the royal palace was at this time situated on the summit of Zion, by the present Jaffa Gate. Josephus mentions (Ant. vii. xiv: 5) that the inauguration occurred at the *fountain;* while the sacred narrative and the circumstances of the case seem to locate it at the lower pool. But this apparent contradiction is at once reconciled on recollecting that he also calls the Pool of Siloam, which he says "hath sweet water in it, and that in great plenty also," by the same appellation. There may have been two fountains (for aught contained in the Scriptures)—an upper and a lower—but the probability is that there was only one, strictly speaking, situated high up in the valley, whose waters were brought by a causeway (in which was the "conduit"), and emptied into a pool near the city wall; and being, as a matter of course, a place of general resort, it was here that the inaugurating ceremonies were performed. As a general rule, there is no fountain in Palestine without a large receptacle for its waters; and where these reservoirs are, there is the gathering of the people. And that this was equally the case in those remote ages of the world is perfectly obvious from such remains of antiquity now visible, and from incidental allusions of the Scriptures—one of which will properly introduce the next reference to the water resources of Jerusalem; *i. e.* Isaiah vii. 3; where the prophet goes out to meet King Ahaz "at the *end* of the conduit of the *upper* pool in the highway (or causeway) of the Fullers' field." As the upper pool here indicated seems to be mentioned in contradistinction from a lower one, there were perhaps two pools in the Fullers' Field. The prophet is sent to "the end of the conduit of the upper pool;" but the idea conveyed by "the end of the conduit" is not very definite. The end thus designated was evidently not inside the city, but some distance off, inasmuch as Isaiah went forth to it. Perhaps it was a building to which water was subterraneously conveyed from the upper pool *at* the fountain, and there distributed by hydrants into baths and other small receptacles—the surplus and waste water merely running off to the lower pool, which was probably situated immediately by the side of the wall as a defensive measure. This aqueduct probably ran along upon or beside the highway or causeway, which was permitted to remain after the concealment of the water. At all events, there must have been some kind of landmark by which the former site of the aqueduct could be known to those acquainted with the spot, even after the water had been concealed far beneath the surface of the earth. For when Rabshakeh held that memorable parley with the Jews, "he stood by the conduit of the upper pool which is in the highway of the Fullers' field." (2 Kings xviii. 17; Isaiah xxxvi. 2.) It is evident that while these circumstances are all entirely applicable on the north of the city, some of them are totally inapplicable on the west side. But, conceding the proper location of the Fullers' Field, their occurrence within the limits of this field necessarily locates them in the broad shallow valley on the north of the city.

The next allusion that the Scriptures make to the waters of Jerusalem is a very comprehensive one. (2 Chr. xxxii. 2–4.) We here learn that, "when Hezekiah saw that Sennacherib was come (to Lachish), and that he was purposed to fight against Jerusalem, he took counsel with his princes and his mighty men to stop the waters of the fountains which were without the city; and they did help him. So there were gathered much people together, who stopped all the fountains, and the brook that ran through the midst of the land, saying, Why should the king of Assyria come, and find much water?" Where these various fountains were, we have now no positive means of ascertaining; though En-rogel and the spring now called the Virgin's Fount may well be numbered amongst them. Josephus mentions the existence of various fountains without the city, but does not locate or even name any of them in this connexion but Siloam. (W. v. ix: 4.) "The brook," however, is located with sufficient precision to enable us to trace it very definitely. We are told that it "ran through the midst of the land." Now a stream running through either the Kedron or Hinnom Valley could in no proper sense be said to run through *the midst of the land;* but one flowing through the true Gihon Valley, and separating Akra and Zion from Bezetha, Moriah, and Ophel, as a stream once doubtless did, could with peculiar propriety be said to "run through the midst of the (holy) land" on which the (Holy) City was built. And that this is the correct meaning of the phrase is not only apparent from the force of circumstances, but is positively so declared in the Septuagint, where, moreover, it is also called a river;* which at least implies a much larger stream than the Kedron, and comports well with the marginal reading, where it is said to "*overflow* through the midst of the land." Previous to the interference of man, there was, no doubt, a very copious stream that gushed forth somewhere in the upper portion of that shallow, basin-like concavity north of Damascus Gate—which is unquestionably the upper extremity of the Gihon Valley—and pursuing its meandering course through this

* Greek, *Potamos;* literally, *river flowing* through the *city*.

valley, entered the Tyropœon at its great southern curve, down which it flowed into the Valley of Kedron.

If we are to understand that the flow of these fountains was entirely arrested, they were doubtless reopened on the retreat of the invading army. But we learn from the 30th verse that one of these fountains never visibly flowed again on the exterior of the city, having been permanently conducted into the city through a secret subterranean channel; for, "This same Hezekiah also stopped the upper watercourse of Gihon, and brought it straight down to the west side of the city of David."

Now, had the so-called "Upper Pool of Gihon" been the "upper watercourse or out-flow of Gihon" (of Scripture), as is generally alleged (though there is not the slightest intimation of such a thing, either in the Bible, the works of Josephus, or any other reliable authority), there would be no propriety in mentioning that its waters were brought down "to the west side of the city of David;" for they were already on that side. But if the fountain thus sealed was situated on the north side, then it would have been a fact sufficiently notable to deserve a special notice. But that the waters stored up in that pool were designed for quite another purpose is most obvious; for to this day they are conducted—not through a deep rock-cut channel, as Hezekiah's no doubt was—but most of the way by a trifling foot-wide ditch *on* the surface of the ground, to a reservoir on Akra near the Jaffa Gate, traditionally called Hezekiah's Pool, but which most certainly is the Amygdalon Pool of Josephus. If by "the city of David" is here meant the whole city of Jerusalem, and the water was conducted literally to the west side of Jerusalem, the enterprise was very difficult of execution, and by no means as useful as it would have been if located more centrally. It is observable, too, that in this immediate connexion this term is restricted to the lower portion of Zion.*

But besides this fact, and the equally significant one that such an

* 5th verse. . . . . The preposition "in" is not in the original.

enterprise would possess greater availableness as well as facility of execution—no small considerations under such circumstances—there is another fact materially favoring the idea that, instead of the whole city being intended, only the lower portion of Zion or the original "City of David" is meant. In exploring the subterranean channel conveying the water from Virgin's Fount to Siloam, I discovered a similar channel entering from the north, a few yards from its commencement; and, on tracing it up near the Mugrabin Gate, where it became so choked with rubbish that it could be traversed no further, I there found it to turn to the west, in the direction of the south end of the cleft or saddle of Zion: and, if this channel was not constructed for the purpose of conveying to Siloam the surplus waters of Hezekiah's aqueduct, then I am unable to suggest any purpose to which it could have been applied. But why it was not brought down on the Zion side, who can divine? Was it because Zion was already well watered in its lower portion by the "Great Pool"—the Lower Pool of Gihon, according to the terminology of tradition? Perhaps so. Williams renders it thus:—"He stopped the upper outflow of the waters of Gihon, and led them down westward to the city of David." An accomplished Hebrew scholar, a resident of Jerusalem, himself a Jew—the son of a Rabbi*—thus translates this passage:—"This same Hezekiah stopped the mouths of the waters of the upper Gihon, and levelled them down westward to the city of David;" or, in other words, he turned the stream into a more westward direction. In referring to this transaction, the writer of the book of Maccabees thus describes it (xlviii. 17):—"Hezekiah strengthened his city, and brought in water into the midst of it; he dug with iron into the rock, and built fountains for the waters."

But, although the above suggestions have been submitted, yet, supposing the true Fountain of Gihon situated in the present basin across the intervening Hill of Gareb, just opposite the traditionary

* M. J. Diness; now a Christian, and the dragoman of the American Christian Mission.

one, there is not the slightest difficulty in the exact fulfilment of every indication of the passage most literally construed. If we regard as parallel to this the 20th verse of the 20th chapter of 2 Kings, then it would appear that he not only brought the water into the city, but also made a pool for it:—"He made a pool and a conduit, and brought water into the city." But whether the pool was inside or without, we are not positively informed.

In reproving the Jews for confiding more in human means than Divine aid, Isaiah comments upon the defensive measures adopted by Hezekiah and his princes, when threatened by Sennacherib, in the following terms:—"Ye have seen also the breaches of the city of David, that they are many; and ye gathered together the waters of the lower pool. And ye have numbered the houses of Jerusalem; and the houses ye have broken down to fortify the wall. Ye made also a ditch between the two walls for the water of the old pool, but ye have not looked," &c., &c. (Isaiah xxii. 9–11.) The "ditch" and the "lower pool" here alluded to are, therefore, evidently trenches for military defence; and, of course, the pool commonly ascribed to Hezekiah—being obviously designed for no such purpose—cannot be either of them. In exploring the Temple area and its immediate vicinity, I discovered a large pool beneath the Mechemeh and Temple street, extending eighty-four feet alongside the Temple wall, which is here constructed of large Jewish rocks like those at the Wailing-Place, is ten feet deep, and still partially coated with cement. But its entire extent from east to west could not be ascertained—a wall having been built across it at a distance of forty-two feet from the Temple wall, for the purpose of supporting the buildings above. Can this be the "*ditch* between the two walls for the water of the old pool"—or the trench built by Hezekiah between "the First" and "Second Walls" of Josephus, as a defence to the *First* Wall passing from Zion to the Temple, and which was supplied with water by a branch of Hezekiah's aqueduct? Or are we to recognise the empty pool below Siloam as "the ditch?" It is not so easy a matter to locate the "lower pool" satisfactorily;

unless, indeed, the *Lower Pool* of Siloam (the depressed figyard in the mouth of the Tyropœon), be intended by it—the waters from various sources being here "gathered together," in the mouth of the Tyropœon, just where the nature of the locality would require such a defence. But in this event, the lower pool and the ditch between the two walls would be regarded synonymously.

The foregoing are all the references to the waters of Jerusalem previous to its destruction by the Chaldees, with the exception of the allusion to Siloam, contained in Isaiah's reproof of the Jews (viii. 6), which will now come under review in considering the water resources of Jerusalem subsequent to its restoration.

SILOAM, SILOAH—*Sent—the Pool and Fountain.*—The Fountain of Siloam is alluded to in the 8th of Isaiah, the 14th verse of the 2d chapter of Nehemiah, and the 15th of the 3d. The *fountain*, though a real one to all appearance (as it was called), was evidently the mere outflow of the water brought from the Virgin's Fount by the rock-cut canal through Mount Ophel, and is by no means an independent fountain. The *present* Pool of Siloam is undoubtedly the representative of the ancient *fountain*, so called both by Nehemiah and Josephus, but probably much reduced in size. It is frequently referred to, and is located with great precision by Josephus. And the etymology of the term conclusively identifies it—Sent. The water poured out at the Feast of Tabernacles was drawn from the Fountain of Siloam, as the Rabbins declare:—"Thence, also, they draw the water that was to be mingled with the ashes of the red heifer." This water of separation then was very far from being *clean water*, in the sense sometimes understood. "The priests, eating more liberally of the holy things, drank the waters of Siloam for digestion sake." This, beyond all question, is the pool in which the "blind man washed and received sight" at the command of the Messiah; who, having anointed his eyes with "clay and spittle," "said unto him, Go, wash in the pool of Siloam (which is, by interpretation, Sent)." (John ix. 7, 11.)

No reader of the Bible can gaze upon this placid sheet without being reminded of Isaiah's remark about "the waters of Shiloah, that go *softly*." Their *present* taste, however, is anything but pleasant, and is rather indescribable. But they were probably nearly tasteless—or, as Josephus pronounces them, sweet—in former ages when they flowed copiously.

SHILOAH—SHELACH—*Shear-skin Pool.*—It is generally supposed, but erroneously it would seem, that the Pool of Shiloah mentioned Nehemiah iii. 15 is identical with this. In the Septuagint, it is rendered "*pool of skins by the king's wool*," instead of "pool of Shiloah by the king's garden." But it is quite probable that, in correcting one error, the Greek translators have fallen into another; as suggested by Dr. Lightfoot in the following remarks (Chorographic Inquiry, &c., vol. 2, sec. 2):—"We have the mention of it also Nehemiah iii. 15—the pool of Siloam by the king's garden—where we may observe that it is here written Shelah; different from Shiloah (Isaiah viii. 6) by a difference hardly visible in Bibles not pointed—indeed sometimes overlookt by myself, and so, as is evident, by others. For Shelah is rendered in the same sound with Shiloah. * * * The Greek interpreters did, indeed, observe the difference, and thus render the words:—'the pool of skins by the king's wool.' Nor doth the Italian overlook it, for that renders it thus:—la piscina di Selac presse al orto del Re—the fish pond of Selac, hard by the garden of the kings.' * * * It is observable in the Greek version, that, whereas they render the word by 'the king's wool or hair,' they may seem to have read *a fleece of wool*, for *a garden*." The uppermost pool would appear to be the true Siloah or Siloam Pool (though called a fountain); and the lowermost one, adjoining the king's gardens, Shelach, or *the pool of skins*.

DITCH BETWEEN THE TWO WALLS—*Trench—Mikvah—Reservoir.*—The depressed garden occupying all the gorge between the promontories of Zion and Ophel, except spaces barely broad enough for a road on each side, is obviously the site of an ancient pool, probably that of the "lower pool" of Isaiah—where the expression "gathered together" would be more significant than elsewhere. It was about one hundred and thirty feet long and about the same in breadth, but evidently somewhat curved at the northern end, leaving an interval of only a few paces between it and the Pool of Siloam. That a large pool existed here till a comparatively late period, is evident from the accounts of pilgrim tourists; but this will be considered when treating of the waters of Jerusalem after its restoration by Hadrian. It would seem not improbably to be identical with the Lower Pool. (Isaiah xxii. 11.) The precise meaning of Mikvah is "a place where waters flow together"—a term exactly indicative of the character of this lowest of all the pools of Jerusalem, where all the waters of the city literally flowed together.

Lower Pool (Isaiah xxii. 9).—Was there any such pool actually made by Hezekiah? or did he merely destroy the Pools of Gihon, and collect their waters (the water formerly in the "old pool") into the Ditch (or Reservoir) below Siloam—the Pool of Skins? "Ye have seen the breaches of the city of David, that they are many: and ye gathered together the waters of the lower pool." This is the only reference made to this reservoir in the Scriptures; and Josephus makes no mention of it whatever. It would seem to have been a kind of defensive moat or trench; and, if so, the "Lower Pool of Gihon," which has generally been regarded as identical with it, can by no means be so considered. This being the lowest and most defenceless place about the city, there is no spot where we could more reasonably expect to find the "Lower Pool" than just here.

The Pool that was made.—This pool was situated somewhere between the House of the Mighty and the Stairs of the City of David—probably opposite the Tombs of the Kings of Judah, and not far from them, on the eastern slope of Zion; or else in the Tyropœon Valley: but there are no appreciable remains of it at the present day, neither could any be expected in such a place; for, if left in a perfect state of preservation, a single age might suffice not only to fill it up with debris, but inhume it far below the surface of the earth.

THE OLD POOL (Isaiah xxii. 11).—The pool here mentioned may either be "the pool that was made," or the old Pool of Gihon north of the city; for the "ditch or trench between the two walls" must necessarily have been the ultimate receptacle for the contents of both of these pools.

EN-ROGEL—*Fullers' Eye.*—The earliest mention of En-rogel occurs in the book of Joshua, where it is twice mentioned (xv. 7, and xviii. 16) as a landmark of division between Judah and Benjamin. In the Septuagint it is called *fountain* in each of these places, as it is also by Josephus; and in 2 Sam. xvii. 17, where it is next mentioned as the lurking-place of Zadoc and Abiathar, until they could receive tidings of the state of matters in Jerusalem, in order to bear them to David while fleeing from Absalom. The next and only other mention of En-rogel is in connexion with the rebellion of King David's other rebel son. For it was doubtless just here, upon some one or other of the large rocks still remaining between the Mount of Offence and Hill of Evil Council, that the evil-counselled "Adonijah slew sheep and oxen and fat cattle, by the stone of Zaheleth, which is by En-rogel," and called his accomplices to eat. But alas! when the state of matters in the city became known, "all the guests of Adonijah were afraid, and made an end of eating, and rose up and went every man his own way; and Adonijah feared because of Solomon, and arose and went and caught hold of—the horns of the altar—instead of the sceptre! It is, without doubt, the present Bir Ayûb—situated at the junction of the three valleys, Hinnom, Kedron, and En-Nair. Some writers however entertain the opinion that, instead of being an independent well of water, this shaft merely affords us a peep at the subterranean Kedron passing through it. But that the present Bir Ayûb or Yûab is this same ancient fountain, no reasonable doubt need be entertained. It probably continued to flow perennially (when unsealed) until the utter desolation of Judea, and the consequent cessation of the latter rain; after which time it became necessary to deepen it from time to time.

Motza—*Springhead.*—The Rabbins inform us that the place where "willows of the watercourses" were grown for keeping the Feast of Tabernacles, was called Motza: and it no doubt owed its name to one or more springs for watering the willows of the brook. This term is applied to the immense "fountain and depth" near Jericho, whose waters were healed by Elisha—translated very properly, "spring of waters." As applied to Gihon, it is rendered "watercourse." (2 Chr. xxxii. 30.) Can the present ephemeral fountain a few hundred yards below En-rogel, called "Ain ed-Durrage," be the representative of Motza?

The Dragon's Well—*Ain Tannim—The Spring of Fountains* (Neh. ii. 8)—Was evidently situated somewhere in the neighborhood of the Valley Gate, below the present Jaffa Gate. The appellation of Dragon may have been given it on account of some fanciful figure sculptured on the trough, or because it was thought to be a fitting abode for that fabulous creature; or because lizards, which here exist in such variety of sizes and shapes, resorted in great numbers to its recesses and crévices. The Septuagint version calls it "Fountain of Figs," and leads us to infer that it made its way out from a large mouth or fissure in the rocky cliff of the hill, just across the Valley of Hinnom, and was shaded by a clump of fig-trees. It is not at all improbable that in the lapse of two centuries between Nehemiah and the days of Ptolemy Philadelphus, its name may have been thus changed; and, if so, the Seventy would of course feel justified in substituting the new name instead of the old, in order that their description might be intelligible. And this is by no means a solitary instance of such alterations in that invaluable translation. There is every reason to believe that it was a fountain; and not a mere well, in our acceptation of the term. In confirmation of this view, Jerome declares that, so late as his day, this valley was well supplied with fountains and waters.

Aqueduct of Pontius Pilate.—Josephus informs us, in "The

Wars of the Jews" (ii. ix: 4), that Pontius Pilate "expended that sacred treasure called *corban* upon aqueducts, whereby he brought water from a distance of four hundred furlongs"—a distance of fifty miles; but, in the "Antiquities," he tells us (xviii. iii: 1) that, in bringing "this current of water to Jerusalem," he derived the *origin* of the stream from the distance of *two hundred* furlongs," or about twenty-five miles. In the last instance, he doubtless specifies the distance of the *source;* and in the former the length of the *aqueduct*, occasioned by the meandering unavoidable in such a hilly country. But that it must have been a work of considerable magnitude, and at least as long as he represents it, is evident from the necessity of expending the funds of the sacred treasury for its construction. Solomon's Pools being less than one-third of the shortest distance mentioned by Josephus, the idea generally entertained—that Pilate's Aqueduct was supplied by these reservoirs—which would otherwise be reasonable enough, is entirely precluded. There are more than half a dozen springs at Neby Samwil, which, though sufficiently elevated and copious and still nearer, are of course excluded by the same consideration. Neither would the copious fountains at Hebron be distant enough, even if sufficiently elevated: nor is there any place whatever, south, east, or west of Jerusalem, of the requisite distance, from which the supply could be brought. It results therefore, as a matter of necessity, that it was situated somewhere on the mountain ridge running north from Jerusalem—of which, however, no vestige is now known to exist.

Stone Aqueduct.—The waters immediately round about the sacred precincts must be embraced in the account of Aristeas, as well as those within the sacred precincts;—for the entire area of the Temple at that time was only about four stadia. Nor must it necessarily be understood that the extent of water "to the circumference of five stadia about the Temple" was *continuous*—for the reverse is plainly implied by the mention of "connecting pipes"—and, thus interpreted, the account is perhaps chargeable with no exaggeration whatever. "The frequent hidden apertures above," if not the open-

"WATERING-PLACE" IN THE LINE OF STONE AQUEDUCT BETWEEN SOLOMON'S POOLS AND JERUSALEM—THE TRADITIONAL MOUTH OF THE CAVE OF ST. MARY.

ings now remaining, are at least represented by them: and through similar openings water was probably drawn up to a higher level and stored away (as we know from the Bible and Talmud it was in the brazen laver and other places); from which of course it would gush forth with great violence on opening the communication "to wash off the blood of the numerous victims." And if Jerusalem and the Temple were thus well supplied with water prior to the reign of Herod the Great, how much more copiously after the accession of that great fountain-builder, aqueduct-maker, and rebuilder of the Temple, to the throne of Israel!

The Talmud cites Jewish authority for relating that "between Hebron and Jerusalem is the Fountain of Etham, from whence the waters are conveyed by pipes into the great pool at Jerusalem."

And it is certainly probable in the highest degree that Solomon himself is the author of these water-works between Jerusalem and Etham which Josephus informs us (Ant. viii. vii: 3), was "a certain place, about fifty furlongs distant from Jerusalem, which is called Etham; very pleasant it is in fine gardens, and abounding in rivulets of water." The king that was preacher in Jerusalem thus writes of them (Ecc. ii. 6): "I made me pools of water, to water therewith the wood that bringeth forth trees." Certainly these immense reservoirs could never have been constructed merely for irrigating the gardens and plantations at Etham: the surplus water was doubtless brought then, as it is now to the Holy City, by pipes. The allusion most probably was to the King's Pools, or as Josephus expressly calls it, "Solomon's Pools" in the Kedron, which being built first, and the name thus appropriated, would naturally retain the distinctive appellation. Josephus relates (Ant. xv. ix: 4), that Herodion, sixty stadia from Jerusalem, was "well worth seeing both on other accounts, and also on account of the water which is brought thither from a great way off, and at vast expenses; for the place itself is destitute of water." Now although it has been positively denied that this water could be brought from Solomon's Pools (Etham), inasmuch as the pools are lower than the city (as they allege); yet having proved by the theodolite that the reverse is the case, I commenced search for the remains of an aqueduct between the two places, and at last found numerous remains of a very substantial aqueduct between the large pool at the base of the citadel hill, and a copious fountain at Artos considerably lower than the "pools," but in the same valley. It is, therefore, by no means a far-fetched suggestion, that even had the rivulets of Etham not previously been conducted to Jerusalem, Herod would have brought them there, else why not conduct them as well as the lower fountain to Herodion?

The examination and reflection I have bestowed upon the subject lead me irresistibly to the conclusion that he found an inferior kind of pottery conduit there that poured its surplus waters into the "Great Pool" of the Jewish writers, which is no other than the traditional "Lower Pool of Gihon," the largest at Jerusalem, the "Lacus Germanicus" of the Crusaders, around which the present aqueduct courses, still giving off a branch to it; but instead of repairing it, he had a new and greatly superior one constructed by Roman engineers, who of course were better skilled in the principles of hydrodynamics than the Israelites were a thousand years previously—in the days of Solomon—by which he was enabled to bring the water by a much more direct route, and to a higher level than that formerly attained—to the so called *Upper Pool of Gihon!* And it was probably to commemorate this very event that he had a monument reared at this very spot, which is no other than the "Serpent's" Pool of Josephus. Travellers have long noticed a short piece of this admirable work, a few hundred yards east of Rachel's Tomb; but no other portions of it were known to be in existence until I accidentally stumbled upon it in riding over a field near Mar Elias. Having thus found it in a spot favorable for observation, the theodolite soon revealed other portions of it by indicating the exact level and best locality for its construction. I thus discovered portions of it on the plain of Rephaim, not far from the "Hill of Evil Council;" and, on applying the theodolite, found that it could be very easily carried even above the "Upper Pool of Gihon"—the Serpent's Pool of Josephus. The bottom of this pool being only about four feet below the sill of Jaffa Gate, its water could easily be conducted into the city, so as not only to fill entirely the moat of the Hippic Tower, but could be reservoired on the very summit of Zion as well as in the "deep canals and cisterns" in the palace grounds of King Herod: but, inasmuch as there were in them "brazen statues through which the water ran out," they must either have been situated lower on the sides of Zion, or—what is more probable—the aqueduct coursed around the pool at a higher level (like that at the lower pool), sending off to it its surplus waters at Herod's Monument, and entering the city on the surface of the ground "at the gate where water was brought into the Tower of Hippicus"—as the language of Josephus seems to import. (W. v. vii: 3.)

The rock-cut conduit discovered by my friend Professor Johns, in preparing for the erection of the Anglican Church on Mount Zion, is not a "venerable sewer," as it has been stigmatized, but doubtless conveyed water to the Temple: it would seem, at all events, that it ran from one of these pools due north for a short distance, and then turned due east along the brink of the Tyropœon towards the Temple. It was probably from this aqueduct, or in one of the occasional subterranean reservoirs along its course, that Ananias the high priest was dragged from his hiding-place, and slain. (W. ii. xvii: 9.) The city is indebted to Sultan Muhamed, it seems, for its present supply of fresh water—such as it is: The inscription on the fountain at the "Lower Gihon Pool" ascribes its entire construction to his munificence. But it is very probable that, having no mechanics equal to the task of erecting one out and out, or even repairing the large aqueduct that I ascribe to Herod the Great, he was content merely to repair an old one—that of Solomon.

Maundrel well remarks, in speaking of certain fragments of this stone aqueduct which he saw in 1697, that "the whole work seems to be endued with such absolute firmness, as if it had been designed for eternity; but the Turks have demonstrated, in this instance, that nothing can be so well wrought but that they are able to destroy it; for of this strong aqueduct, which was carried formerly five or six leagues with so vast expense and labor, you see now only here and there a fragment remaining."

AMYGDALON POOL—POOL OF HEZEKIAH—*Birket el-batrak.*—If Herod the Great was the author of the waterworks just ascribed to him, then may he also have built the pool situated midway between the Tower of Hippicus and the Church of the Holy Sepulchre, usually ascribed to King Hezekiah. That Herod built the Hippic Tower, now generally called the Castle of David, is almost universally conceded: and that whoever built that tower also made the pool, few perhaps would doubt on comparing them—so very similar is their architecture. There is none of this massive rough Jewish architecture, however, to be seen about the Serpent's Pool; but this may perhaps be satisfactorily accounted for, either on the supposition that such large stones would naturally be used up in some of the various rebuildings of the walls in later ages, and their place supplied by the present smaller ones, or that Herod found the pool there already—having been built by some less architecture-loving monarch, in plain style, merely as a receptacle for the rain-water draining from the wide basin near the head of which it is situated. The pool built by Hezekiah must have been very hastily constructed, while the one that bears his name was evidently executed deliberately and in the very best style of Jewish architecture. And, besides this—if neither of the pools alluded to by Isaiah (xxii. 9, 11) be this, as is highly probable—indeed almost absolutely certain, the one being in a low place and the other the result of certain waters being "gathered together"—neither of which attributes can be predicated of the present pool. It is clear however that, by whomsoever it was made, this pool is evidently the Amygdalon of Josephus: and that it was constructed by Herod the Great is probable in the highest degree.

Moat of Antonia—Pool of Bethesda—*Probatica Piscina—Sheep Pool—Piscina Gemilares* (*twin pools*)—*Gemini Lacus*.—The northern enclosure of the Temple was formerly between two and three hundred yards farther south than it is at present: but we are informed by Josephus that when Herod rebuilt the Temple, he extended it to twice its former dimensions; and of course, from the very nature of the case, all the enlargement must have occurred on the north side. The Temple was far more vulnerable on that side than anywhere else; and hence the necessity for such an extensive entrenchment as that which we now find on the north, upon whose southern edge the northern cloisters of the Haram are in part built. Its depth is upwards of fifty feet, even at the present day, although it has been the general receptacle of trash and rubbish in this part of the city for centuries past. Between its eastern border and the wall of the city there is room for a wide street leading from St. Stephen's Gate to a gate of the Haram. The main pool is about one hundred and thirty-one feet broad and three hundred and sixty-five in length: its length, however, is continued one hundred and forty-two feet farther, though the breadth of this extension is only forty-five feet. That they were both originally designed to hold water is evident from the cement with which they were lined—much of which still remains; and where it has fallen off a singular contrivance for securing its adhesion is observable.

We readily recognise in this piece of water the "Piscina Gemillares of the "Jerusalem Itinerary." But that it could be the Pool of Bethesda or Sheep Pool (Piscina Probatica), is not only highly improbable, but is elsewhere abundantly disproved. Was this vast pool dependent upon the rains for its supply of water, or was it furnished by a subterranean aqueduct from the Amygdalon Pool? Or may it not have been supplied by the aqueduct of Pontius Pilate? Such a supposition would satisfactorily account for his appropriation of the "sacred treasure" to its construction.

THE POOL STRUTHION—*Sparrow Pool.*—Though Josephus so frequently alludes to the great entrenchment on the north of the Temple, he only calls it an "abyss," in general, without specifically designating it: but the narrow portion is most probably what he calls Struthion—where Titus built one of his towers. This pool doubtless extended all around the exterior of the tower. Amongst "other conveniences" of the "inward parts," were "places for bathing."

PISCINA INTERIOR—*Piscina Grandis Valde.*—Besides the large double pool entrenching Antonia on the north, there was evidently another still larger pool in the same quarter, a little farther north, which, though apparently neither mentioned in the Bible, the works of Josephus, or any other very ancient authority, was evidently there at the date of Jerusalem's destruction. The earliest known mention of it is by Brocardus in 1283, (unless this is one of the pools mentioned by Eusebius and his translator in the fourth century;) then by Marinus Sanutus in 1321; next in the "Gesta Dei" (p. 573) in 1611, after which it is frequently mentioned; but it has long since disappeared entirely—its rocks having probably been used for other purposes, and its cavity filled up by accumulation of rubbish. The term *interior*, it is true, could with no propriety have been distinctively applied to it during the existence of ancient Jerusalem; but was appropriate enough after the demolition of the ancient "Second Wall" and the erection of the present walls—during which period alone it is described. It is highly probable that it was designed to prevent the application of the battering-ram at that point, and located immediately east of the "Second Wall," where it joined Antonia, and was more assailable than it was farther north. It must have been in the immediate vicinity of the Fish Gate; and, if stocked with fish, as its name would seem to imply, would account more satisfactorily than the suggestion generally received for such a designation of that gate, and especially so if the neighboring "twin-lake" was also a piscinary. It is rendered highly probable, from what Sandys says (p. 149), that it was supplied, in part at least, by a fountain; and certain it is that the great water-loving warrior, Herod the Great, would never have constructed so important a pool as the Trench of Antonia, without providing it with an abundant supply of living water. And indeed William of Tyre expressly mentions that they were filled with water brought from a distance by aqueducts.

"Lacus Quidam."—This piece of water is mentioned by several authors; but not in such a way as to locate it more definitely than to produce the impression that it was a short distance above the entrenchments of Antonia. Can it be merely an allusion to the Piscina Grandis Valde? or was it a reservoir situated higher up in the valley? Most probably the latter.

"Piscina a Francis Inventa."—This pool, it would seem, was situated somewhere about St. Anne's Church. Is it a mere synonym for "Lacus Quidam?" or yet another pool?

Pool of Bethesda—*House of Mercy—Effusion—Washing—Piscina Magna.*—"Now there is at Jerusalem, by the sheep market, a pool, which is called in the Hebrew tongue Bethesda, having five porches. In these lay a great multitude of impotent folk, of blind, halt, withered, waiting for the moving of the water. For an angel went down at a certain season into the pool, and troubled the water: whosoever then first, after the troubling of the water, stepped in, was made whole of whatsoever disease he had. And a certain man was there, which had an infirmity thirty and eight years. When Jesus saw him lie, and knew that he had been now a long time in that case, he saith unto him, Wilt thou be made whole? The impotent man answered him, Sir, I have no man, when the water is troubled, to put me into the pool: but while I am coming, another steppeth down before me. Jesus saith unto him, Rise, take up thy bed, and walk. And immediately the man was made whole, and took up his bed, and walked: and on the same day was the Sabbath." (John v. 2–9.)

The location of this celebrated pool is a subject of no little controversy among biblical topographers and antiquaries, on account of the deep interest naturally attaching to the scene of an event so mysterious, in relation to this interesting locality. Pilgrims and tourists, in general, concur with the monks in the opinion that the present Birket Israel is the "*Sheep Pool*" or Bethesda of the Scriptures, and triumphantly cite, in confirmation, the two long subterraneous vaulted passages proceeding from its south-west corner, as two of the "five porches" or stoas. But that this immense trench, which, we learn from Josephus, and see from its design, was constructed as a defence to Antonia, can be Bethesda, is an idea too absurd and improbable to need formal refutation. Its depth alone is sufficient to refute such a notion—being upward of fifty feet at the present time, and was originally an "abyss," as we are informed by Josephus. A learned friend, after minute personal examination of all the premises, regards Siloam as the true Bethesda, and advocates its claims upon the strength of six old pillars still remaining on its east side. But to lay "a great multitude of impotent folk" in *porches* so small as must needs have been built between these pillars, would be as great a miracle as "the troubling of the water" or the healing of the "impotent man." Another learned friend also—than whom, too, there is no higher authority in biblical topography, archæology, or chorography—after critically examining all the localities and bearings of the matter, has arrived at the conclusion that the traditionary "Fount of the Virgin" is no other than the Pool of Bethesda! But in the process of reasoning, by which he arrived at this conclusion, he seems, by no means, to have observed that caution and accuracy that generally characterize his work and render his labors so reliable and valuable. The term by which the Pool of Bethesda is designated in the original* is enough of itself to refute the idea that the Virgin's Fount could ever fulfil the indications involved. Nothing less than a pool of sufficient dimensions to permit the free exercise of swimming, *will at all answer its requirements: and surely no claim of the sort* will be urged in behalf of the Virgin's Fount. The capacity of the grotto, too, is entirely inadequate to the accommodation of a *multitude.* But not to dwell upon these incapacitating circumstances, and to say nothing of the impracticability of arranging "five stoas" in such a locality, and the inaccessibility of the deep subterranean water by invalids, this fountain is not *by* the sheep-gate (or market)—*a sine qua non*, in its location. And more unsatisfactory than all, is the miracle-nullifying suggestion invoked in the substitution of the natural operation of a syphon for the supernatural agency of an angel, or, indeed, *messenger* of any kind: for though the water *below* this receptacle may figuratively be called an *angel*, yet surely that above it is no better entitled to such an appellation than any other stream—be the same intermitting, remitting, or constant.

But although there is such a diversity of opinion about the situation of this noted pool, its position, I think, may be ascertained with considerable accuracy, if the locality assigned the sheep as their quarter be reliable—the space immediately east of the Temple. *Gate* is perhaps the word that should supply the omission or ellipse in the 2d verse, according to the marginal correction, instead of *market.* And the position of this gate being accurately made out, we cannot possibly far mislocate Bethesda. It would, of course, be *near* the gate and probably within the limits of the sheep quarter: and if the text of several old manuscripts can be relied on, the ellipsis should be supplied with *pool*, instead of gate or market, which amendment would almost necessitate such a location alongside this sheep pool whence water was supplied for watering and washing the sheep. And if, at the same time, the sheep would find shelter

* Κολυμβῆθρα, a pond—swim-pool.

beneath its cloisters from the scorching sun, the bleak wind, and pelting storm, it would pre-eminently be a "house of mercy" as well as a pool of "effusion" and "washing" to these victims, at the same time that it was a merciful place of resort for invalids. It is a fact, highly confirmatory of this view of its situation, that a large pool was known to exist just at this spot about three centuries afterwards.

The Bordeaux Pilgrim, who visited Jerusalem in the year 333, makes mention of two great pools ("piscinæ magnæ"), the one on the right hand of the Temple, the other on the left. In exact accordance with his assertion, I have found one of them where it had heretofore entirely escaped observation, and could suitable excavations be made, the other would no doubt be brought to light in a position corresponding to this, just where I have reasoned out its location from the data afforded by the Bible and Josephus, applied in accommodation to the physical requirements of that quarter of the city. There are no special vestiges of the pool to be seen at this time; but could the immense banks of rubbish be removed from the place indicated, I doubt not that the veracity of the Pilgrim would be as fully sustained in relation to this pool as to the other. In order that it might the more easily have been supplied with water, we would naturally conclude that this pool was situated on the lower side of the sheep quarter, *within* it, if the omission be supplied by *gate*, but *without*, if supplied by *market* or *quarter*—and in either event, one of its porches, stoas, or cloisters would be built (in part at least) upon the massive wall of the lower side: and it is probable that King Jotham was engaged in the erection of these very works, when it is said of him (2 Chr. xxvii. 3) that "on the wall of Ophel he built much."

Does not the name by which the large pool within the walls, just north of the Antonia entrenchments, is called—*Piscina Interior*—plainly intimate the existence of another in that neighborhood without the walls, called *Piscina Exterior*—and if so, could it well be any other than Bethesda, as here indicated?

THE GREAT POOL—(*Lower Pool of Gihon—Lacus Germani*)—*Birket es-Sultan.*—The Upper Pool of Gihon, so called in the nomenclature of tradition, is the spot where it is generally supposed Solomon was anointed king of Israel, although this "Lower Pool" would certainly quadrate rather better with the circumstances of the case: but it is evident, as elsewhere demonstrated, that neither place answers the requirements of the narrative; and the truth is—abundant as pools of water seem to have been about Jerusalem from the earliest period of its history—neither of them was then in existence. Besides those already existing when Solomon ascended the throne, he soon constructed others:—"I builded me pools of water to water therewith the wood that bringeth forth trees" says "the King that was Preacher in Jerusalem." Nehemiah and Josephus very definitely locate one of these pools just above the King's Gardens, evidently supplied by the brook that flowed in the valley of the Kedron, and perhaps by the Virgin's Fount also. Others we recognise at Etham. Had he merely been in quest of an eligible site for pleasure gardens, Neby Samwil would have possessed far superior advantages, being two or three miles nearer, a better site for gardens, possessing sufficient water, and so elevated that it commanded a lovely prospect even as far as the shores of the Mediterranean. But most evident is it that horticultural irrigation is not the only purpose for which these grand reservoirs were made: to furnish the Temple with water was evidently a leading object in their construction—a purpose that must have been fondly cherished by a monarch who lavished such vast sums in the erection and adornment of an edifice requiring so large a supply of water in fulfilment of the great design for which it was built. "There is a river, the streams whereof shall make glad the city of God, the holy place of the Tabernacle of the Most High!" Nor can it be objected with any propriety that "had these pools really been built by Solomon for the purpose of furnishing the Temple with water, he would scarcely have failed to inform us so" in the passage cited, for such a mention of them would have been entirely *outré* and inapposite in the enumeration of sensual pleasures that he terms "*vanities*." Now the position of the "lower pool of Gihon" is precisely where it ought to be upon the presumption that it was built to reservoir the surplus waters of Etham—a few feet lower than the level of the Etham aqueduct coursing around it. The conjecture, therefore, affords a plausible solution of the anomaly of its position, for it would certainly have been situated either higher up or lower down but for this consideration. But fortunately we are not left to mere conjecture, however plausible, in designating the uses and character of this great work. Dr. Lightfoot informs us in his great work on the chorography and topography of Jerusalem, that the Jewish writers frequently allude to the fact, that "in the way betwixt Hebron and Jerusalem is the Fountain of Etham, from whence the waters are conveyed by pipes into the *Great Pool* at Jerusalem." Now this pool is not only situated just where it ought to be, to subserve the purposes indicated, but it is emphatically the *great* pool of Jerusalem, having about three times the capacity of any other about the city. To this conclusion also, the name by which alone it is designated by the natives, significantly points—Birket es-Sultan, or King's Pool. And that this is a very ancient pool, and indeed one of Solomon's construction, is still further evident from a comparison of its general design, structure, and appearance with those of Etham, acknowledged to be his on all sides—being made unlike all others, but identically like them, by clearing away the soil, erecting two cross-walls (the lower very massive, the upper rather slight), connecting them by side-walls, scarping the shelving ledges of rock on its sides, and plastering the whole over with water cement.

During the existence of the Frank kingdom it seems to have gone under the appellation of "Lacus Germanicus," but why thus styled is not known: and by some it is believed—absurdly enough surely—to be the "Pool of Bathsheba." But that it can be no other than what is here indicated is certainly obvious enough to satisfy the most sceptical.

When full, this pool presented an area of nearly four acres of water—being by far the largest about the city. Dimensions 260 feet by 600.

WATERS OF ETHAM.—The above Rabbinical account of the waters of Etham is abundantly confirmed by Josephus, who testifies that "there was a certain place about fifty furlongs distant from Jerusalem, which is called Etham; very pleasant it is in fine gardens, and abounding in rivulets of water; thither did Solomon use to go out in the morning sitting on high."

"SERPENT'S POOL"—"UPPER POOL OF GIHON"—*Birket Mamilla or Babilla*—"*Lacus Patriarchi.*"—The observant traveller, in passing between Jerusalem and Bethlehem, can scarcely fail to notice, close by the celebrated Pea-Patch,* and immediately on the side of the gullied road, opposite Rachel's Tomb, and within a hundred yards of the present pottery aqueduct at that point, a few large, well squared, and nicely perforated stones, protruding out of the low ridge of earth. They belong to a well executed aqueduct that, in some places, penetrates deeply beneath the ground, in others lies on its surface, and occasionally ascends perpendicularly several yards above the ground, terminating in an open gutter on the top of a thick wall, thus surmounting a gentle slope, then continuing in a solid rock-cut channel, at the end of which it is again received into the regular aqueduct formed by the adjunction of the large cubical blocks. These joints are perforated with a bore six or eight inches in diameter, and are quite exact cubes with the exception of the conical projection from one side through which the bore extends, that fits into the conical opening of the next succeeding block, similarly fashioned: and so tenacious is the cement by which they are united, that it is almost impossible to disunite them without fracture.

* "In which are picked up a little sort of small round stones, exactly resembling peas; concerning which they have a tradition here, that they were once truly what they now seem to be; but that the Blessed Virgin petrified them by a miracle, in punishment to a surly rustic, who denied her the charity of a handful of them to relieve her hunger."—*Maundrel.*

Starting at the above place, where the aqueduct is covered by a low ridge of rock-covered earth, running parallel to the road for some distance, I succeeded in discovering various portions by means of the theodolite—enough to show conclusively that it was designed to convey water from Solomon's Pools to Jerusalem, on a higher level than that of the present far inferior conduit of pottery. At a point nearly midway between Mar Elias, and Jebel Tantûr or Elkhamis, close beside the Beit Jala road, is a large half-buried piece of cylindric-shaped reddish marble immediately adjoining this aqueduct, situated just on the great watershed of Palestine between the Mediterranean and Dead Seas. The Arabs venerate it very much as the door occluding the entrance of the "Cave of Sitte Myriam," and rarely pass it without devoutly piling up a small pyramid of stones near it. But it is evidently nothing more than a watering-place of this aqueduct—a large marble basin, dislocated and broken. Its present dimensions are 7 feet in length, 5⅓ in height, and 6¼ broad: internal depth 2½ feet.* Application of the level to the northernmost portion of the aqueduct now to be seen on the plain of Rephaim, shows that the water could be very easily conducted to the summit of Mount Zion, and in so doing would pass just around the "Upper Pool of Gihon," as the pottery aqueduct does around the lower one. Now, if the wall of circumvallation has been properly located—of which there can be no reasonable doubt—it here *encompassed* Herod's Monument, just at a point from which the camp of the Assyrians was situated a short distance east. (W. v. xiii: 2.) And this monument we are told (W. v. iii: 2), "adjoined to the Serpents' Pool." Now it so happens that at this identical spot we find the so called "Upper Pool of Gihon"—a large reservoir of water, which if it be not the Serpents' Pool of Josephus, then where are we to look for that pool? The result of my investigations is the irresistible conviction that this piece of water is no other than the Serpents' Pool. And if we could even bring ourselves to the conclusion that Herod the Great in his reëdi-

* See cut, page 317.

fication, enlargement, and adornment of the Temple, would fail to furnish what it most of all needed—a good supply of fresh water—it is yet certain that he introduced an ample supply upon the premises of his own magnificent palace and pleasure grounds on Mount Zion. This supply he could derive from no other place so well as from Etham: it is therefore a most reasonable supposition that he did thus introduce those waters; and as it was a very considerable enterprise for that age, we may easily account for the erection of the monumental structure in actual conjunction with the pool—evincing thus vauntingly the same boastful spirit that animated the emperor—when, on the completion of the Church of St. Sophia, he exclaimed, "O Solomon, I have surpassed thee!" For account of the waters of Herod's pleasure grounds, see Jos. W. v. iv: 4.

> "The city, lakes and living springs contains,
> And cisterns to receive the falling rains;
> But bare of herbage is the country round,
> Nor springs nor streams refresh the barren ground.
> No tender flower exalts its cheerful head:
> No stately trees at noon their shelter spread."—*Tasso.*

"THE LAVATORY" *on Mount Olivet.*—It would appear from the Rabbins that this was a bathing establishment on the western slope of Olivet; but we have no definite specifications as to its size or even location, except that it was somewhere opposite the Temple. It was probably located not far from the eastern extremity of the Red Heifer Bridge, in order that the bather, being "made every whit clean" by his ablution in the Lavatory, might be the more effectually secured against any possible defilement before reaching the Temple.

THE DEEP CANALS AND CISTERNS—pertaining to the palace grounds of Herod the Great, were upon the very summit of the Holy Hill—the north-west corner. The language in which Josephus describes them in giving an account of that royal palace induces the belief that they were very extensive. These—unlike most of the water in the city—were evidently not stagnant, but living waters, supplied by aqueducts, in all probability, brought from Etham. It is evident at least that the "brazen statues," through which the water poured into these canals and cisterns, could not be fed by any source now supplying water to the city. The aqueduct brought to light by Professor Johns would seem to have conducted a portion of the surplus water to the Temple or lower palace, after it had irrigated and adorned those royal pleasure grounds; and the remainder, after operating in a jet-d'eau in the western part of the palace grounds, which probably reached a considerable way down the hill, was distributed through that part of the city; and the surplus sent to the Virgin's Fount *via* the subterranean passage I explored in part.

The foregoing account of the palaces, towers, fortresses, walls, waterworks, and other structures and resources of Jerusalem, proclaims it to have been one of the most magnificent cities on earth: and especially when it is remembered that they are only such as have been incidentally mentioned—constituting a portion only, and perhaps but a small portion, of its buildings and resources. And to this effect also abundantly testify her silent but not inexpressive tombs.

Such, then, was the City of the Great King—the perfection of beauty—the joy of the whole earth! But, as Josephus well remarks (Wars, vi. x: 6), "Yet hath not its great antiquity, nor its vast riches, nor the diffusion of its nation over all the habitable earth, nor the greatness of the veneration paid to it on a religious account, been sufficient to preserve it from being destroyed." And alas, how great has been her fall! "How doth the city sit solitary that was full of people! how is she become as a widow! She that was great among the nations and princess amongst the provinces, how is she become tributary!" But, notwithstanding her low estate and deep degradation—trodden under foot of the Gentiles—"the Lord shall yet comfort Zion, and shall yet choose Jerusalem"—yea, God will establish her for ever, and make her an *eternal excellency*.

CHAPTER XI.

JERUSALEM FROM ITS SUBVERSION BY TITUS, TO ITS CAPTURE BY THE SARACENS.

ÆLIA CAPITOLINA.

"* * The city is full of violence: wherefore I will bring the worst of the heathen, and they shall possess their houses: I will also make the pomp of the strong to cease, and their holy places shall be defiled." (Ezek. vii. 24.)

"Reft of thy sons, amid thy foes forlorn,
Mourn, widowed Queen! forgotton Zion, mourn!
Is this thy place, sad city, this thy throne,
Where the wild desert rears its craggy stone;
Where suns, unblest, their angry lustre fling,
And wayworn pilgrims seek the scanty spring?
Where now thy pomp which kings with envy viewed?
Where now thy might, which all those kings subdued?
No martial myriads muster in thy gate;
No suppliant nations in thy temple wait
No prophet-bards, thy glittering courts among,
Wake the full lyre and swell the tide of song:
But lawless Force and meagre Want are there,
And the quick-darting eye of restless Fear;
While cold Oblivion, 'mid thy ruins laid,
Folds his dark wing beneath the ivy shade."

HAVING thus brought under notice the condition of the ancient Jewish metropolis in all its various phases from its inception under Melchisedec down to the reign of Agrippa; when, having attained the zenith of its glory and depth of its iniquity, it was subverted by the Romans; we will now consider such brief notices of its condition in early Christian and Medieval times, as will enable us the better to appreciate its present condition, and also serve the purpose of greatly illustrating the works of the chroniclers, Crusaders, and modern travellers. The reader will at the same time have ample opportunity of forming a proper estimate of the religion of the Holy City for the last fifteen hundred years. It will also abundantly appear how cautious we ought to be in receiving the various traditionary identifications of sacred localities.

Jerusalem was subverted by Titus in the year of our Lord 70; and although it may not be literally true, as is sometimes asserted, that the Romans at this time actually ran a plough over the city and sowed it with salt, yet was every part of it most completely destroyed, except a portion of the wall and a few of the towers on the west. Josephus remarks in the 1st chapter and section of the 7th book of the Wars, that "Cæsar gave orders that they should demolish the entire city and temple, but should leave as many of the towers standing as were of the greatest eminency; that is, Phasaelus and Hippicus and Mariamne, and so much of the wall as enclosed the city on the west side * * * * but as for all the rest of the wall, it was so thoroughly laid even with the ground by those that dug it up to the foundation, that there was nothing left to make those that came thither believe it had ever been inhabited."* And in this utter state of desolation it seems to have lain until Adrian ordered it to be rebuilt, A. D. 136, in honor of Jupiter and himself, under the name of Ælia Capitolina, excluding nearly all the quarter of Cœnopolis, and about one-half of Mount Zion. The wall on the north no doubt occupied very nearly the site of the old Second Wall from the north-west corner to Bezetha Hill; but instead of then running to the north-west corner of the Temple, it was continued east a few hundred yards, and then turned at right angles due south to join the north-east corner. The present wall, perhaps, occupies very nearly the site of that then erected by the Emperor.

* It is supposed by many that a portion of the city (that near the western wall, perhaps) was also spared; but, if so, where is the propriety of the above language?

A temple in honor of Jupiter Capitolinus we are told was built upon the site of the Holy House, and another to Venus over the Sepulchre of the Saviour. The erections of this period, both military and religious, seem to have been really magnificent.

But little is known of Jerusalem from Adrian to Constantine. The Jews, who had been forbidden by Adrian to come within sight of the Holy City under pain of death, were permitted to visit it on payment of a certain tax under Constantine; and about this time also, the Christians of Jerusalem, who on the investment of the city by Titus had fled to Pella, now returned, as is supposed, and re-established themselves in the Holy City.

Very little is known of Jerusalem, until, upon the conversion of Constantine, A. D. 326, it ceased to be a heathen city; and losing the name by which Adrian had endeavored to consign the Holy City to oblivion, it resumed its ancient designation. The idol temples immediately gave place to Christian church edifices. Constantine—or rather his mother, the Empress Helena—greatly adorned the city and designated the sacred localities.

Amongst the buildings erected by the pious Emperor and his zealous mother (who made a pilgrimage to Palestine when fourscore years of age), may be enumerated the Basilica of Constantine, the Churches of Calvary and the Resurrection, Gethsemane and the Ascension.

Julian the Apostate, in order to disprove certain prophecies, permitted and even assisted the Jews to rebuild the Temple; but globes of fire, as it is related by the historians of that day, issuing from the foundations compelled the workmen to desist.

Justinian erected a splendid hospital or Zenodochium, and the magnificent Church of St. Mary, about the year 530 according to Procopius.

But all Christian edifices were destroyed by the Persians and Jews under Chosroes II., on his capture of the city A. D. 614; though on the recovery of the city by Heraclius, and indeed before that event, many of these churches were rebuilt. The city was now freed from the tyranny of the disciples of Zoroaster, but was soon brought under a far more galling and permanent yoke—that of Mohammedanism.

> "Jerusalem! Jerusalem! thy *cross* thou wearest now!
> An iron yoke is on thy neck, and blood is on thy brow;
> The golden crown—the crown of Truth—thou didst reject as dross;
> And now thy cross is on thee laid—the crescent is thy cross."

The city was captured by Omar in 634; and the covenant into which he entered, not to destroy the property of Christians, whether public or private, was faithfully observed. He found the venerated rock es-Sakhrah (which is still to be seen beneath the so-called Mosk of Omar) covered with filth, placed there by the Christians in contempt of the Jews; and piously assisting with his own hands in the removal of this immense heap, he erected a wooden house of prayer over it. The present splendid edifice, however, that bears his name, was erected by Abd el-Melek Ibn Marwan, at an immense cost, in 688. The mosk built by Omar was far more in keeping with his primitive simplicity of character—a plain quadrangular, large but mean wooden structure, which in the course of half a century gave place to the present elegant octagonal edifice.

The large fabric now generally called Mosk el-Aksa, is not an original Saracenic structure, but is unquestionably the Church of Mary built by Justinian, merely a little Saracenized before its consecration to Islamism.

Amongst Turks and Arabs, Jerusalem still retains the name given it by Omar—Beit el-Makudis or in its abbreviated form el-Kudis or el-Kuds—*the Holy House.*

CHAPTER XII.

"Her gold is dim; and mute her music voice;
The heathen o'er her perished pomp rejoice."

Notices of Jerusalem—From the Travels of Bishop Arculf, who visited the City near the close of the Sixth Century—Edited by the Venerable Bede. Ven. Bede de Sanctis Locis.

"ARCULF, the holy bishop, a native of Gaul, resided nine months at Jerusalem. He counted in the circuit of the walls of the Holy City, eighty-four towers and six gates:—the Gate of David on the west of Mount Zion, the Gate of the Valley of the Fuller, St. Steven's Gate, Benjamin Gate, the Little Gate, leading by a flight of steps to the Valley of Jehosaphat, and the gate called Tecuitis. On the spot where the Temple once stood, near the eastern wall, the Saracens (under Omar) erected a square house of prayer in a rough manner, by raising beams and planks upon some remains of old ruins; this is their place of worship; and it will hold about three thousand men. There were many large and handsome houses of stone in all parts of the city.

"The Church of the Holy Sepulchre is very large and round, encompassed with three walls, with a broad space between each, and containing three altars of wonderful workmanship, in the middle wall at three different points: on the south, the north, and the west. It is supported by twelve stone columns of extraordinary magnitude; and it has eight doors or entrances through the three opposite walls, four fronting the north-east, and four to the south-east. In the middle space of the inner circle is a round grotto, cut in the solid rock, the interior of which is large enough to allow nine men to pray, standing, and the roof of which is about a foot and a half higher than a man of ordinary stature. The entrance is from the east side, and the whole of the exterior is covered with choice marble, to the very top of the roof, which is adorned with gold, and supports a large golden cross. Within, on the north side, is the tomb of our Lord, hewn out of the same rock, seven feet in length, and rising three palms above the floor. These measurements were taken by Arculf with his own hand. This tomb is broad enough to hold one man lying on his back, and has a raised division in the stone to separate his legs. The entrance is on the south side, and there are twelve lamps burning day and night, according to the number of the twelve apostles; four within at the foot, and the other eight above, on the right hand side. Internally the stone of the rock remains in its original state, and still exhibits the marks of the workman's tools; its color is not uniform, but appears to be a mixture of white and red. The stone that was laid at the entrance to the monument is now broken in two; the lesser portion standing as a square altar before the entrance, while the greater forms another square altar in the east part of the same church, covered with linen cloths.

"To the right of this round church (which is called the Anastasis, or Resurrection), adjoins the square church of the Virgin Mary, and to the east of this another large church is built, on the spot called in Hebrew Golgotha, from the ceiling of which hangs a brazen wheel with lamps, beneath which a large silver cross is fixed in the very place where stood the wooden cross on which the Saviour of the human race suffered. Under the place of our Lord's cross, a cave is hewn in the rock, in which sacrifice is offered on an altar for the souls of certain honored persons deceased, their bodies remaining meanwhile in the way or street between this church and the round church. Adjoining the Church of Golgotha, to the east, is the basilica or church erected with so much magnificence by the

Emperor Constantine, and called the Martyrdom, built, it is said, in the place where the cross of our Lord, with the other two crosses, were found by divine revelation, two hundred and thirty-three years after they had been buried. Between these two last-mentioned churches is the place where Abraham raised the altar* for the sacrifice of his son Isaac, where there is now a small wooden table, on which the alms for the poor are offered. Between the Anastasis, or round church, and the basilica of Constantine, a certain open space extends to the Church of Golgotha, in which are lamps burning day and night. In the same space between the Martyrdom and the Golgotha, is a seat, in which is the cup of our Lord, concealed in a little shrine, which Arculf touched and kissed through a hole in the covering. It is made of silver, of the capacity of about a French quart, and has two handles, one on each side. In it also is the sponge which was held up to our Lord's mouth. The soldier's lance, with which he pierced our Lord's side, which has been broken into two pieces, is also kept in the portico of the Martyrdom, inserted in a wooden cross. Arculf saw some other relics, and he observed a lofty column in the holy places to the north, in the middle of the city, which, at mid-day at the summer solstice, casts no shadow, which shows that this is the centre of the earth. Arculf next visited the holy places in the immediate neighborhood of Jerusalem. In the Valley of Jehosaphat he saw the round church of St. Mary, divided into two stories by slabs of stone; in the upper part are four altars; on the eastern side below there is another, and to the right of it an empty tomb of stone, in which the Virgin Mary is said to have been buried; but who moved her body, or when this took place, no one can say. On entering this chamber, you see on the right hand side a stone inserted in the wall, on which Christ knelt when he prayed on the night in which he was betrayed; and the marks of his knees are still seen in the stone, as if it had been

* But, unfortunately for its antiquity, beneath this place, recent excavations have revealed a room! and beneath that room a tank of water!!!—*Author.*

as soft as wax. In the same valley, not far from the Church of St. Mary, is shown the tower of Jehosaphat, in which his tomb is seen; adjoining to which little tower, on the right, is a separate chamber cut out of the rock of Mount Olivet, containing two hollow sepulchres, one, that of the aged Simeon the Just, who held the child Jesus in the Temple, and prophesied of him; the other of Joseph, the husband of Mary. On the side of Mount Olivet there is a cave, not far from the Church of St. Mary, on an eminence looking towards the Valley of Jehosaphat, in which are two very deep pits. One of these extends under the mountain to a vast depth; the other is sunk straight down from the pavement of the cavern, and is said to be of great extent. These pits are always closed above. In this cavern are four stone tables; one near the entrance is that of our Lord Jesus, whose seat is attached to it, and who, doubtless, rested himself here while his twelve apostles sat at the other tables. There is a wooden door to the cave, which was often visited by Arculf.* After passing through the Gate of David, which is adjacent to Mount Zion, we come to a stone bridge, raised on arches, and pointing straight across the valley to the south; half-way along which, a little to the west of it, is the spot where Judas Iscariot hanged himself; and there is still shown a large fig-tree, from the top of which he is said to have suspended himself, according to the word of the poet Juvencus.

"Informem rapuit ficus de vertice mortem."

"On Mount Zion, Arculf saw a square church, which included the site of our Lord's Supper, the place where the Holy Ghost descended upon the apostles, the marble column to which our Lord was bound when he was scourged, and the spot where the Virgin Mary died. Here also is shown the site of the martyrdom of St. Stephen.† He saw, on the south of Mount Zion, a small field

* They appear to be nothing more than tanks of a large size.—*Author.*

† It is now shown nearly midway between Gethsemane and Stephen's Gate; and at another time was confidently located near Damascus Gate!!!—*Author.*

(Aceldama) covered with a heap of stones, where the bodies of many pilgrims are carefully buried, while others are left to rot on the surface.

"Arculf states that few trees are found on Mount Olivet, except vines and olive-trees, but wheat and barley flourish exceedingly; the nature of the soil, which is not adapted to trees, is favorable to grass and flowers. The height of this hill appears to be equal to that of Mount Zion, although it is much more extensive in length and breadth: the two mountains are separated by the Valley of Jehoshaphat. On the highest point of Mount Olivet, where our Lord ascended into heaven, is a large round church, having around it three vaulted porticoes.

"The inner apartment is not vaulted and covered, because of the passage of our Lord's body; but it has an altar on the east side, covered with a narrow roof. On the ground, in the midst of it, are to be seen the last prints in the dust, of our Lord's feet, and the roof appears open above where he ascended; and although the earth is daily carried away by believers, yet still it remains as before, and retains the same impression of the feet. Near this is a brazen wheel, as high as a man's neck, having an entrance towards the west, with a great lamp hanging above it on a pulley, and burning night and day. In the western part of the same church are eight windows; and eight lamps, hanging by cords opposite them, cast their light through the glass as far as Jerusalem; which light, Arculf said, strikes the hearts of the beholders with a mixture of joy and divine fear. Every year, on the day of the Ascension, when mass is ended, a strong blast of wind comes down, and casts to the ground all who are in the church. All that night, lanterns are kept burning there, so that the mountain appears not only lighted up, but actually on fire, and all on that side of the city is illuminated by it. There is also a much frequented church to the north of Bethany, on that part of Mount Olivet where our Lord is said to have preached to his disciples."

Memoranda from the Travels of Bishop Willibard. By a Nun of Heidenhum. A. D. 721–727.

"Our bishop arrived here [in Jerusalem] on the Feast of St. Martin, and was suddenly seized with sickness, and lay sick until the week before the nativity of our Lord. And being a little recovered he rose, and went to the church called St. Zion, which is in the middle of Jerusalem, and, after performing his devotions, he went to the Porch of Solomon, where is the pool where the infirm wait for the motion of the water, when the angel comes to move it, and then he who first enters it is healed. Here our Lord said to the paralytic, 'Rise, take up thy bed and walk.' St. Mary expired in the middle of Jerusalem, in the place called St. Zion; and as the twelve apostles were carrying her body, the angels came and took her from their hands, and carried her to Paradise. Bishop Willibard next descended to the Valley of Jehoshaphat, which is close to the city of Jerusalem, on the east side. And in that valley is the church of St. Mary, which contains her sepulchre, not because her body rests there, but in memory of it. And having prayed there, he ascended Mount Olivet which is on the east side of the valley, and where there is now a church, where our Lord prayed before his passion, and said to his disciples, 'Watch and pray that ye enter not into temptation.' And thence he came to the church on the mountain itself, where our Lord ascended to heaven. In the middle of the church is a square receptacle, beautifully sculptured in brass, on the spot of the Ascension. And there is on it a small lamp in a glass case, closed on every side, that the lamp may burn always, in rain or in fair weather; for the church is open above, without a roof. And two columns stand within the church, against the north wall and the south wall, in memory of the two men who said, 'Ye men of Galilee, why stand ye gazing up into heaven?' and the man who can creep between the wall and the columns, will have remission of his sins."

It was in the beginning of the ninth century that Haroun er-

Raschid bestowed upon Charlemagne the jurisdiction of the church of the Holy Sepulchre and its appurtenances.

Notes, &c., from Bernard the Wise, who visited Jerusalem, A. D. 867.

On arriving at Jerusalem he was in the Hostel founded by the glorious Charles (Charlemagne), in which are received all the pilgrims who speak the Roman tongue, to which adjoins a church in honor of St. Mary, with a most noble library, founded by the same emperor, with twelve mansions, fields, vineyards, and a garden in the Valley of Jehoshaphat. In front of the hospital is a market, for which every one who trades there pays yearly to him who provides it, two aurei. Within the city, besides others, there are four principal churches, connected with each other by walls—one to the east, which contains the Mount of Calvary, and the place in which the cross of our Lord was found, and is called the Basilica of Constantine; another to the south; a third to the west, in the middle of which is the Sepulchre of our Lord, having nine columns in its circuit, between which are walls made of the most excellent stones, of which nine columns, four are in front of the monument itself, which, with their walls, include the stone placed before the sepulchre, which the angel rolled away, and on which he sat after our Lord's resurrection. I must not omit to state that on Holy Saturday, which is the eve of Easter, the office is begun in the morning in this church, and after it is ended the "Kyrie Elyson" is chanted until an angel comes and lights the lamps* which hang over the aforesaid sepulchre; of which light the patriarch gives their shares to the bishops and to the rest of the people, that each may illuminate his own house. * * * There is, moreover, in the city another church on Mount Zion, which is called the Church of St. Simeon, where our Lord washed the feet of his disciples, and in which is suspended our Lord's crown of thorns. St. Mary is said to have

* The celebrated Greek fire. The angel is what the late Robert Hall so characteristically calls "liquid hell-fire and distilled damnation"—alcohol!—*Author.*

died in this church. Near it, towards the east, is a church in honor of St. Steven, on the spot where he is believed to have been stoned. And indirectly to the east is a church in honor of St. Peter, in the place where he denied our Lord. To the north is the Temple of Solomon, having a synagogue of Saracens. To the south of it are the iron gates through which the angel of the Lord led Peter out of prison, and which were never opened afterwards. Leaving Jerusalem, we descend into the Valley of Jehoshaphat, which is a mile from the city(!), containing the village of Gethsemane, with the place of the nativity of St. Mary. In it is a round church of St. Mary, containing her sepulchre, on which the rain never falls, although there is no roof above it. There is also a church on the spot where our Lord was betrayed, containing the four round tables of his supper. In the Valley of Jehoshaphat there is also a church of St. Leon, in which it is said that our Lord will come at the Last Judgment. Thence we went to Mount Olivet, on the declivity of which is shown the place of our Lord's prayer to the Father. On the side of the same mountain is shown the place where the Pharisees brought to our Lord the woman taken in adultery, where there is a church in honor of St. John, in which is preserved the writing in marble which our Lord wrote on the ground. At the summit of the mountain, a mile(!) from the Valley of Jehoshaphat, is the place of our Lord's ascension, in the middle of which, on the spot from which he ascended, is an altar, open to the sky, on which mass is celebrated. * * * On Mount Olivet, near Bethany, is a pool in which, by our Lord's command, Lazarus washed himself after he had been raised from the dead. On the western declivity of Mount Olivet is shown the marble from which the Lord descended on the foal of an ass. Amongst many other monasteries, one mile to the south of Jerusalem is the Church of St. Mamilla, in which are many bodies of martyrs slain by the Saracens, and diligently buried there by her. * * * I will add, in conclusion, that we saw, in the village of Gethsemane, squared marble stones of that fineness that a man might see anything he liked in them, as in a looking-glass.

The following compendious "Chronology of the Crusades," (taken from Procter's excellent work) may here advantageously find a place.

"The predisposing causes of those famous enterprises are generally attributed to the impulsive influence of religion upon the barbaric mind, the institution of chivalry, the union of martial and superstitious feelings, and the influence of fanatical enthusiasm. But the proximate causes are seen in the persecuting frenzy of Hakem, the third Fatimite khalif, and in the fanatical cruelties of Seljukian Turks. The reports of returned pilgrims respecting the insulting and savage cruelty of the latter, as well as the destruction of the Church of the Resurrection by the former, excited general indignation; but it was not till the return of Peter Gautier, an officer of Amiens, who had renounced his profession in order to undertake a pilgrimage, that any proposal was made for attempting the expulsion of the infidels from the Holy Land. Peter (the Hermit) laid before Pope Urban II. a project he had formed for expelling the infidels from Palestine; which, being backed by the complaints of the Greek Emperor, Alexis, and the urgent appeals of Peter, the Pope was induced to espouse the projected enterprise; accordingly he recommended to all Christian princes, first at the Council of Placentia, and afterward at that of Clermont, the duty of zealously engaging in this holy war. At the latter council the Pope obtained from the ambassadors present a commission for Peter Gautier to proceed forthwith in the prosecution of his chivalric design. The ensuing spring (1096) was appointed for the departure of the first army."

A. D.

The Crusades—Abortive Expeditions.

1096 Peter the Hermit, issues from the western frontiers of France, leading an immense concourse of the lowest orders.

The rabble multitude is divided:—

The first division, of 20,000, is led by Walter the Pennyless through Hungary.

In Bulgaria they are all destroyed, except Walter and a few who escape to Constantinople.

The second division, of 40,000, under Peter the Hermit, advance into Hungary.

They destroy Malleville (Zemlin) and slaughter its inhabitants.

Carloman, King of Hungary, marches against them.

The Bulgarians cut them off by thousands.

At Nissa they are routed with great slaughter; their camp is despoiled, and their baggage plundered, &c.

The remnant arrive at Constantinople in great distress; they pass into Asia Minor.

They are nearly all cut off by the Turks in the plain of Nice; only 3000 escape.

Fall of Walter the Pennyless.

Third division, of 15,000, from Germany, under Gondenschal, a German monk.

Their atrocious wickedness in Hungary ends in their ruthless massacre at Belgrade.

A. D

1096 *Fourth division*, of 200,000, composed of one huge mass of the vile refuse of France, Flanders, the Rhenish Provinces, and England.

They are guided by two 'divinely inspired' animals—a goat and a goose.

Massacre of Jews at Mayence and Spires, and other places in Germany.

The Crusaders overthrown in Hungary.

["So dreadful the carnage that the course of the Danube was choked with the bodies, and its waters dyed with the blood of the slain." "Before twelve months had expired since the spirit of crusading was roused into action by the Council of Clermont, and before a single advantage had been gained over the infidels, the fanatical enthusiasm of Europe had already cost the lives, at the lowest computation, of 250,000 of its people. But while the first disasters of the Crusade were sweeping this mass of corruption from the surface of society, the genuine spirit of religious and martial enthusiam was more slowly and powerfully evolved. With maturer preparation, and with steadier resolve, than the half-armed and irregular rabble, the mailed and organized chivalry of Europe was arraying itself for the mighty contest; and a far different, a splendid and interesting spectacle opens to our view."—*Procter.*]

THE FIRST CRUSADE.

1096 Though not undertaken by any of the crowned heads of Europe, was eagerly embraced by the most distinguished feudal princes of the second order, viz.:—

Godfrey of Bouillon, with his two brothers, Eustace and Baldwin, and a kinsman also named Baldwin; Hugh, Count of Vermandois, and Robert of Normandy, brothers of the French and English Kings; Robert of Flanders, Stephen of Chartres, and Raymond of Thoulouse—the first temporal prince who assumed the crown; Boemond, son of Robert Guiscard, Prince of Tarento, and his cousin Tancred.

Order of Departure.

The *first division*, under Godfrey, consisted of the nobility of the Rhenish provinces and the north of Germany.

Godfrey receives assistance from Carloman of Hungary and the Emperor Alexius: he peaceably arrives with his army on the fertile plains of Thrace.

The *second division*, under the Counts of Vermandois and Chartres, embraced the chivalry of Central and Northern France, the British Isles, Normandy, and Flanders.

Their passage from Italy is opposed by the Emperor Alexius, and Hugh is made prisoner at Durazzo.

Thrace ravaged by the Crusaders, under Godfrey, in retaliation for the opposition offered Hugh of Vermandois by the Emperor Alexius.

The *third division*, under Boemond and Tancred, composed of Southern Italians—10,000 horse, and 20,000 foot.

The *fourth division*, under the Count of Thoulouse, includes his own vassals and native confederates, comprehended under the general appellation of Provençals.

1097 Godfrey at open war with Alexius: seizure of the bridge of Blachernæ; attack upon Constantinople.

Hugh of Vermandois mediates.

A. D.

1097 Messages from Boemond and the Count of Thoulouse, requesting Godfrey to defer negotiations till they should arrive.

Godfrey submits; hence an

Accommodation between the wily Alexius and the crusading princes; the latter swears fealty, the former delivers his son as hostage.

Approach of the third division to the Byzantine capital.

Boemond at first refuses to do homage to Alexius, but afterward submits.

The fourth division next approaches—its leader, Raymond, sternly refuses homage to Alexius whom he menaces.

Alexius craftily gains the ascendancy over the mind of the aged, though stern, Raymond.

Muster of the several divisions in the plain of Asia Minor; numbers estimated—including 100,000 mailed cavalry, and a prodigious number of priests, women, and children—at about 700,000.

Siege of Nice, June 20; it falls into the hands of the Greeks by stratagem.

Battle of Dorylæum in July; ultimate victory of the Crusaders.

Evacuation of Asia Minor by the Sultan of Roum.

Triumphant entry of the crusading hosts into Syria.

Battle between Tancred and Baldwin.

Baldwin separates from the main body and proceeds eastward, victoriously overrunning the whole country as far as the Euphrates.

The Crusaders lay siege to Antioch.

Famine and pestilence in the Christian camp; desertion of great numbers to Baldwin in Mesopotamia, &c.; cowardice of the Duke of Normandy, Count of Chartres, the Viscount of Melun, and Peter the Hermit.

1098 *The Latin principality of Edessa founded* by Baldwin.

Siege of Antioch renewed; the Turks defeated through the treachery of Phirouz; city surprised and captured; the Turkish garrison escape within the citadel.

The Sultan of Persia unites the Turks against the Christian invaders; twenty-eight emirs lead a force of from 3000 to 4000 cavalry to relieve the garrison in the Citadel of Antioch.

Blockade of the Crusaders in the city.

Second famine; horrible distress, attended by cannibalism, and vice of every kind.

Alexius abandons their relief.

The despairing Crusaders are called into action by superstition and the imposture of a priest.

Great battle of Antioch; the Turks routed with terrible slaughter.

Foundation of the Latin principality of Antioch; Boemond its ruler.

Disunion among the crusading princes.

Third famine and pestilence in Antioch, which sweep off 100,000 persons—cannibalism again resorted to.

1099 The Crusaders, now numbering only 1500 cavalry and 20,000 infantry, and an equal number of unarmed camp followers, &c., proceeded from Antioch to Jaffa by sea.

Jerusalem invested by the Crusaders, June.

Chronology of the Crusades.

A. D.

1099 Sufferings of the besieged from thirst.

Arrival of Genoese galleys in Jaffa; the mariners are brought to the camp to construct three movable towers.

Jerusalem taken by the Crusaders, July 15; frightful massacre of the Mussulmans and Jews.

Extirpation of the Mussulman inhabitants; the law of conquest supplies to Jerusalem a new and Christian population.

Foundation of the Latin kingdom of Jerusalem; its first king is

Godfrey of Bouillon, elected by the army.

He modestly declines the title of king, accepting only that of "Defender of the Tomb of Christ."

[Thus the great design of the *first Crusade* had been accomplished, in the triumphant recovery of the Holy Sepulchre.]

Foundation of the *Knights of St. John of Jerusalem*—the origin of which was an hospice founded in Jerusalem, in 1048, by a few merchants of Memphis, for the accommodation of pilgrims from Europe. An hospital for the sick was afterward added, hence the term—knights hospitallers; the members of which are also known as the knights of Rhodes. When the Crusaders entered Jerusalem, many of the chevaliers determined on joining the order—Godfrey granted a donation, which example was followed by other princes. To the usual vows of chastity, poverty, and obedience, was added a vow to be always ready to fight against Mohammedans, and all who forsook the true religion. Thus was the chivalric institution—the offspring of feudalism—made subservient to the interests of the church. See 1118.

Flourishing period of chivalry.

[On the continent, the lowest tenant, by military service, was fully included in the pretensions and privileges of nobility, except in the case of imperial feuds, which were not accounted noble beyond the third degree of subinfeudation. Hence the land which bristled with fortresses afforded as many titles of nobility; and every country was filled with a numerous order of minor counts, barons, and vavassors—the vassals of the greater feudatories, and themselves each the chieftain of a train of knightly dependants. The least of these last, who was bound or entitled to serve his lord as a horseman or chevalier—*from whence are derived the original distinction, and the very name of* CHIVALRY—was a member of the same aristocracy as the duke or count, the privileges of which order, according to feudal customs, formed an impassable line between it and the commonalty. The exact epoch at which Chivalry acquired a religious character, it is not easy to determine. In the age of Charlemagne, the form of knightly investiture was certainly unattended by any vows or ecclesiastical ceremonies: but in the eleventh century, it had become common to invoke the aid of religion in the inauguration of the knight. There is abundant proof, however, of the success of the church, before the Crusades, in infusing some religious principle into the martial spirit of Chivalry. The original obligations of this institution included loyalty and honor, courtesy and benevolence, generosity to enemies, protection to the feeble and the oppressed, and respectful tenderness to woman.]

Chronology of the Crusades.

A. D.

1099 Approach of a great Fatimite army, swelled by Turks and Saracens.

Battle of Ascalon; the Crusaders victorious; they acquire much booty.

The princes depart for Europe, except Tancred, who remains with Godfrey.

Daimbert, patriarch of Jerusalem.

1100 Capture of Boemond, prince of Antioch, by an Armenian chieftain.

Death of Godfrey, aged 40, five days preceding the first anniversary of his reign.

Baldwin I., prince of Edessa, elected king of Jerusalem: he resigns to Baldwin du Bourg, the brother of Godfrey, the principality of Edessa.

1101 First Crusade by land; or

Supplementary Crusade under Counts Vermandois and Chartres.

1102 Vermandois is wounded in a battle with the Mussulmans of Cilicia; dies at Tarsus;

Rash assault by a vanguard upon the Egyptian invaders; Chartres taken and murdered; Baldwin rescued from death by a grateful emir.

1103 Azotus reduced by Baldwin; the siege of Acre formed.

1104 Arrival of seventy Genoese ships with Crusaders, which results in the conquest of Acre by Baldwin I.

1106 The Count of Thoulouse is joined by several French princes, who had arrived in the Supplemental Crusade, (1101.)

Tortosa taken by Raymond.

1108 Bertrand, son of Raymond, effects the conquest of Tripoli.

1109 Tripoli and its vicinity erected into a county, by Baldwin, for the house of Thoulouse. Hence "County of Tripoli."

1111 The Crusaders take Berytus.

Sidon captured by the Crusaders.

[With an interval of four years, two fleets of Scandinavian cruisers, who had performed the long voyage from the Baltic, through the Straits of Gibraltar, to the Syrian shores, co-operated with the Christian forces of Palestine, in the siege of Sidon. Although the first attempt was repulsed, the second proved successful.]

1112 Critical position of the State of Edessa, surrounded by Armenians and Turks.

Heroic exploits of its prince, Baldwin du Bourg, and his relative, Joscelyn de Courtenay.

Arrival of large numbers of pilgrims and Crusaders from Europe.

1113 The order of Knights Hospitallers of St. John confirmed by Papal Bull.

The Suljuk Turks of Aleppo, Damascus, and Iconium, aided by Mohammedans of Arabia, Egypt, and Persia, harass and often defeat the Crusaders.

1117 Birth of Noureddin, the younger son of Zenghi, second of the Attabek princes.

1118 Expedition against Egypt conducted by Baldwin.

Death of Baldwin I. (in March) on his march toward Egypt; his cousin.

Baldwin II. (Prince of Edessa), King of Jerusalem.

The order of *Knights Hospitallers* of the order of St. John (called also Knights of Malta) becomes a military order. Hence

Knights Templars: institution of the order of the Temple of Solomon.

[The object of the institution of this order was to act in a military capacity to protect pilgrims. See 1099.

A. D.

1118 [The military orders were, in the first instance, subjected to the rule of St. Augustin; modified, of course, in some degree, by the peculiar object of their institution. The most ancient of these was the order of the Knights Hospitallers of St. John of Jerusalem, established in the first instance (1048) for the reception and care of pilgrims visiting the Holy City. This order became monastic in 1092, and in 1118 added the military qualification.]

1120 Zenghi, governor of Mosul, (1145, 1146.)

1124 Tyre reduced by Baldwin II., aided by the Doge of Venice, who obtains the sovereignty of one-third of the city.

[All the maritime republics of Italy, with their characteristic mercantile cupidity, extorted great commercial advantages, as the price of their services to the Crusaders. And throughout the Christian possessions in Palestine and Syria generally, the three republics of Genoa, Pisa, and Venice contended, often with bloodshed, for the right of establishing places of exchange, and enjoying the common or exclusive privileges of trade.]

Archbishopric of Tyre established.

Extension of the Latin kingdom of Jerusalem, from the sea-coast to the deserts of Arabia, and from the city of Beritus, on the north, to the frontiers of Egypt, on the south, forming a territory about 60 leagues in length, and 30 in breadth; and exclusive of the county of Tripoli, which stretched northward from Beritus to the borders of the Antiochian principality.

1131 Abdication of Baldwin, with the consent of his nobles and prelates, in favor of his son-in-law.

Foulques (of Anjou) King of Jerusalem.

Baldwin retires to a convent.

1144 *Baldwin* III., King of Jerusalem, (13 years old,) in conjunction with his mother, Melesinda.

[Soon after the martial sceptre of the house of Bouillon had devolved upon a woman and a minor, the Christian power in the East began to decline.]

1145 Fall of Edessa; Zenghi, the Turkish emir of Aleppo, takes it by storm.

Indignation excited in Europe by the event.

St. Bernard preaches a Second Crusade, which is promoted by Louis of France.

[At the soul-stirring exhortations of St. Bernard, the great feudatory princes of Bavaria, Bohemia, Carinthia, Piedmont, and Styria, with a crowd of inferior chieftains, assumed the cross; and the conversion of the emperor Conrad III., after some struggle between the sense of political interest and religious duty, completed the triumph of the pious orator.]

Decline of the power of the Crusaders.

1146 Zenghi murdered by his own troops at the siege of Jabbar; his son, *Noureddin*, the third of the dynasty of the Attabeks of Syria, becomes King of Aleppo and Damascus.

He maintains war against the Crusaders.

1147 *The Second Crusade;* led by the Emperor Conrad III., and by Louis VI., King of France.

A. D.

1147 [The number of the Crusaders has been estimated as approaching near to a million; of which 70,000 were mailed cavalry, and 250,000 were trained infantry; the rest were clergy, pilgrims, women, and camp followers.]

Treacherous policy of Comnenus, the Greek emperor; he harasses the Crusaders in their march through Bulgaria.

Conrad, on arriving at Constantinople, indignantly refuses to have an interview with Comnenus.

Louis arrives at Constantinople after the departure of Conrad; he accepts the apologies, and is induced to delay his march by the treacherous emperor.

Almost total destruction of the imperial army in the passes of Lycaonia by the Sultan of Iconium.

Louis encamps at Nice; here he is joined by Conrad and the remnant of the imperial army.

The united forces come to Ephesus; here they separate—the Germans proceed by sea to Palestine; the French by land.

Sanguinary defeat of the Turks by Louis, on the banks of the Meander.

1148 Surprise and defeat of Louis in the mountains between Pisidia and Phrygia; narrow escape of the king.

Retreat upon the port of Attalia.

Louis transports his nobles and knights by sea to Palestine.

The infantry and pilgrims left behind perish, either by the cimetars of the Turks, or the unnatural cruelty of the Greeks.

The sovereigns of Jerusalem, Germany, and France, resolve on reducing Damascus.

1149 Great victory of Saladin over the Christians at Antioch; Raymond is killed, Joscelyn de Courtenay made prisoner.

Unsuccessful siege of Damascus.

Return of Louis; he lands at St. Gilles on the Rhone, in October.

[Louis left Metz in 1147, at the head of 70,000 knights, mounted and armed, and a band of infantry and camp followers, amounting to about 200,000. He returned a fugitive, with about 300 followers, in barks furnished by Sicily.]

1150 Return of Conrad with the miserable remnant of his army.

[Thus ended abortively the Second Crusade, leaving the Christian cause in Palestine again deserted, save by the scanty bands, but enduring courage of its habitual defenders.]

1151 Increasiug danger of the Latin kingdom of Palestine from the arms of Noureddin, the Attabek of Aleppo.

Victory of Baldwin III. over the Turks at Jericho.

1153 Ascalon falls by the chivalry of Baldwin.

1162 Death of Baldwin III.; his brother *Almeric* succeeds as King of Jerusalem.

[Though Baldwin was destitute of any high degree of ability, his character was graced by many noble and chivalric qualities. As he left no children, he was succeeded by his brother Almeric, whose equal mediocrity of talent was unrelieved by the same virtues.]

Chronology of the Crusades.

A. D.

1162 Almeric neglects immediate dangers, and wastes his energies in projects for the conquest of Egypt;

Victory of Almeric over Shiracouch.

Pelusium besieged and taken.

1163 Surprise and sanguinary defeat of Almeric, near Artesia, by Noureddin.

1167 Second signal defeat of Shiracouch on the Egyptian frontiers; the Turks capitulate and engage to evacuate Egypt.

1168 Project of Almeric for the permanent subjugation of Egypt.

Pelusium taken, and cruelly sacked by Almeric.

He advances before the wall of Cairo.

Death of Noureddin.

1169 Failure of the project of Almeric, owing to the faithlessness of the Greek Emperor and the craft of the vizier Shaweer.

Retreat of Almeric into Palestine.

Rise of Sallah-u-deen, or Saladin—the scourge of the Christian fortunes in Palestine.

1171 Saladin deposes the sons of Noureddin, and unites under his sway all the Mussulman states from the Nile to the Tigris.

Dissensions and weakness of the Latin kingdom of Palestine.

1173 Death of Almeric; his son

Baldwin IV. (a leper) King of Jerusalem.

Regency of the king's sister, Sybilla, and her husband, Guy de Lusignan.

Disaffection of the barons of Palestine.

1176 Siege of Alexandria.

1177 Defeat of Saladin before Jerusalem.

1183 Abdication of Baldwin IV.; his nephew

Baldwin V. (an infant) under the protection of Joscelyn de Courtenay.

Raymond, regent of the kingdom.

Subjugation of Aleppo by Saladin.

Death of the ex-king, Baldwin IV.

Suspicious death of Baldwin V.

1186 *Guy de Lusignan*, King of Jerusalem.

Civil war; Raymond of Tripoli allies himself with Saladin against Lusignan.

1187 Saladin demands redress for an outrage perpetrated by Reginald de Chatillon.

Lusignan refuses justice, whereupon

Saladin invades Palestine with an army of 80,000 horse and foot.

Battle of Tibérias; sanguinary defeat of the Crusaders; Guy de Lusignan made prisoner; Chatillon decapitated by Saladin himself, and 230 of the Knights of St. John taken prisoners and inhumanly murdered by his orders.

[The Christians were betrayed by the Count of Tripoli. See 1086.]

Fall of Cæsarea, Acre, Jaffa, and Beritus.

Tyre besieged; Saladin abandons the siege and marches against Jerusalem.

Saladin takes Jerusalem, October 2.

[Thus after a possession, by the Christians, of 88 years, Jerusalem was again defiled by the religion and empire of the votaries of Mohammed.]

A. D.

1187 Fall of Bethlehem, Nazareth, Ascalon, and Sidon.

Tyre, defended by Conrad of Montferrat, holds out against Saladin.

[The news of the fall of Jerusalem, &c., filled all Western Christendom with horror and grief.]

A "Saladine" tithe is exacted in Europe for fitting out armaments for Palestine.

1188 Popular expeditions preceding

THE THIRD CRUSADE—by sea.

["All the principal sovereigns of Europe, except those of Spain, vowed to lead their national forces to the recovery of Jerusalem; but even their earnest preparations were too tardy for popular impatience."]

Myriads arrive in Palestine from the ports of Italy, the Baltic, the North Sea, England, and the Mediterranean, at their own expense.

1189 Siege of Acre commenced; 100,000 Crusaders, led by many noblemen and prelates under Lusignan, appear before the city.

["On both sides the frightful consumption of human life was fed by new arrivals; and during nearly two years the strength of Christendom and Islam was concentrated and exhausted in an indecisive conflict before the single city of Acre."]

Departure of King Richard from England, Dec. 11.

1190 Richard I. of England, and Philip-Auguste of France, assemble their forces (amounting to 100,000 men) on the plain of Vezelay, July 1.

Louis departs from Genoa for Sicily.

Richard's army sails from Marseilles.

Violent proceedings of King Richard toward Tancred, &c., in Sicily.

Dissensions between Louis and Richard.

Frederic (Barbarossa) defeats the Sultan of Iconium, who sues for peace.

Death of Frederic—drowned while attempting to swim across the river Calycadnus in Cilicia, June 10.

The Duke of Suabia takes the command.

Antioch taken by the imperial army.

Fearful destruction of life in the army of the German Crusaders.

Institution of *Teutonic Order* of knights.

[About 60 years before this time, a German crusader and his lady founded hospitals in Jerusalem for poor pilgrims of both sexes, of their nation; and when subsequent endowments had enriched these houses, the male brethren devoted themselves to military as well as charitable services. But their efforts had obtained little distinction; and their fraternity was dissolved by the expulsion of the Christians from Jerusalem. Its purposes were now recalled to the national attention by the private charity of some individuals among the German army, who opened their tents for the reception of their sick and wounded countrymen. A number of knights having joined this benevolent association, the Duke of Suabia seized the occasion to incorporate them into a regular order of religious chivalry. Note to 1099.]

Arrival of Philip of France before Acre from Sicily.

Conquest of Cyprus by King Richard.

Chronology of the Crusades.

A. D.

1190 Richard's fleet dispersed by a storm.

1191 A Mussulman troop-ship, manned by 1500 hands, destroyed by Richard.

Arrival of the English before Acre, June 10.

King Richard insults Leopold of Austria before Acre.

Acre capitulates, July 12; 5000 hostages left by Saladin, till the ransom money of 200,000 pieces of gold should be paid.

[The conquest was dearly acquired by the loss of 100,000 Christians.]

Cold-blooded massacre of the Mussulman hostages; followed by the retaliating slaughter of the captive Christians by Saladin.

Open rupture between Richard and Philip.

Philip of France retires from the crusade, leaving 10,000 of his troops under the Duke of Burgundy.

Conrad, Prince of Tyre, King of Jerusalem.

Assassination of Conrad; followed by

Marriage of Henry, Count of Champagne, with Conrad's widow; hence

Henry, of Champagne, King of Jerusalem.

The kingdom of Cyprus founded.

King Richard departs from Acre at the head of the combined army, 30,000 strong.

The Crusaders winter on the coast.

1192 Arrival of the Christian host in the valley of Hebron; terror of the infidels.

The Austrians desert the Crusade; also the Duke of Burgundy and the French.

Unexpected retreat of the Crusaders from before Jerusalem.

Jaffa seized by Saladin.

Gallant exploits of Richard at Askelon, &c.

Battle of Askelon (called by some the battle of Ashdod or Azotus); defeat of Saladin; 20 emirs and 40,000 Turks and Saracens (including 7000 cavalry) killed, September 7.

Ascalon, Jaffa, Cæsarea, and other places fall into the hands of the Crusaders.

Truce for three years between Saladin and Richard; the latter dismantles Ascalon, and the former engages not to molest Tyre, Acre, Jaffa, Antioch, and Tripoli, and to grant free access to all Christians visiting Jerusalem.

Departure of Richard's fleet, having on board his queen, sister, and the daughter of the captive king of Cyprus.

Richard sails from Acre, October 9.

End of the third Crusade.

Richard lands at Corfu in November, and leaves it about the middle of the same month.

1193 Death of Saladin, March 4.

[He is, perhaps, the brightest examplar in history of an Asiatic hero; and his virtues, like the dark traits which obscured them, exhibit the genuine lineaments of his clime and race.]

Division of Saladin's empire; his brother

Saphadin reigns in Syria, while his three sons erect distinct thrones at Cairo, Damascus, and Aleppo.

A. D.

1194 A new Crusade preached in Germany.

1195 Crusade of German chivalry; three great armaments under the guidance of nobles and prelates successively arrive at Acre.

Union of the Mussulman powers of Egypt and Syria against the Crusaders.

1196 Indecisive results of this campaign.

Jerusalem still in the hands of the infidels.

1197 Death of Henry, nominal king of Jerusalem.

Almeric of Lusignan marries the widow of Henry, and is recognised King of Jerusalem and Cyprus.

A fourth Crusade promoted by Innocent III.

1198 Folques of Neuilly atones for a life of sin by preaching a new Crusade.

["Without the rude originality of Peter the Hermit, or the learning of St. Bernard, he, nevertheless, kindled the flame of religious enthusiasm throughout Flanders and France."]

1200 Many French barons, &c., take the Cross; the chief promoter is Thibaud, Count of Champagne.

The barons of France implore, upon their knees, the maritime aid of Venice.

The Venetians agree to convey the armaments to Palestine for 85,000 silver marks.

1201 The Crusade delayed—1st, by the death of Thibaud; 2d, by dissensions among the leaders; 3d, by the deficiency of 30,000 marks to pay for transhipment.

THE FOURTH CRUSADE.

1202 Departure of the Crusaders under the Marquis of Montserrat; Zara captured; denunciations of the Pope; return of De Mountfort; new destination of the armament, owing to the successful negotiations of the friends of young Alexius with the Latin barons, &c., to replace his father on the throne of the East, which his uncle had usurped.

1203 The Crusaders sail for Constantinople.

Negotiations with Alexius; siege.

Flight of Alexius; Isaac restored.

Disunion between the Latins and Greeks.

Young Alexius induces the Crusaders to defer their expedition till the next year.

Third part of Constantinople burned in a feud.

The Crusaders demand the fulfilment of Alexius's pecuniary agreement; they defy the two emperors, which leads to

Open hostilities; the Crusaders and the Greeks at war.

1204 Revolution in Constantinople; the two emperors deposed by Mourzoufle; Alexius is murdered.

Death of Isaac in prison.

Second siege of Constantinople.

Treaty of partition by the Crusaders.

Capture of Constantinople, April 12.

A second conflagration; destruction of the remains of ancient letters and art, &c.

Pillage; public distribution of the spoils.

Chronology of the Crusades.

A. D.

1204 *Baldwin*, of Flanders, the first Latin Emperor of the East.

The Eastern kingdom divided between the Latin barons and the Venetians.

Capture of Mourzoufle; he is thrown from the summit of the Theodosian pillar.

Theodore Lascaris devotes himself to the rescue of his country from the Latin domination.

1204 *End of the Fourth Crusade.*

[In the division and enjoyment of a conquered empire, the confederated barons seemed to have forgotten the original object of their expedition; and the vain trophies of a victory, not over Paynim, but Christian enemies—the gates and chain of the harbor of Constantinople—sent by the new Emperor of the East to Palestine, were the only fruits of the fourth Crusade, which ever reached the Syrian shores.]

1204 Truce with Saphidin for six years.

["The cupidity of the leaders of the fourth Crusade occasioned the loss of the fairest opportunity of re-establishing the Christian fortunes in Palestine. The dissensions of the Mussulman princes, and the ravages of a dreadful famine, and consequent pestilence in Egypt, would have effectually paralyzed all opposition from that dangerous quarter to the success of the crusading arms. But the hopes excited for the Christian cause were completely lost in the diversion of the fourth Crusade against the Eastern Empire."]

1210 *John de Brienne*, King of Jerusalem.

Saphidin applies for a prolongation of the truce, which the Latins refuse.

1211 The Mussulman arms are successful against the Latins, who are in great straits.

1213 Appeal of John de Brienne to the Pope for succor against the infidels.

1214 The Pope decrees another Crusade.

1215 The 4th Lateran council zealously adopt

THE FIFTH CRUSADE—by sea.

1217 First expedition, the Hungarian Crusaders under their King Andrew.

Second expedition; Germans, Italians, French, English, under Duke of Austria.

1217 Abortive campaign of King Andrew.

The Turks expel the Saracens from Jerusalem.

1218 Return of Andrew of Hungary.

Numerous accessions from Germany.

The Crusaders invade Egypt.

Siege and capture of Damietta.

1219 Two of the sons of Saphidin, Coradinus and Camel, offer the cession of Jerusalem, on condition that the Crusaders evacuate Egypt.

This most acceptable offer rejected, through the cupidity of the papal legate.

1220 Disastrous condition of the Crusaders near Cairo; the legate sues for peace.

Peace purchased by the surrender of Damietta to the Sultan of Cairo.

1221 Disgraceful return of the Crusaders from Egypt to Acre.

1224 Embassy of Herman de Saltza, Grand-Master of the Teutonic knights, to the Emperor Frederic, offering him the hand of Iolanta, daughter and heiress of John de Brienne, King of Jerusalem.

A. D.

1225 Marriage of the Emperor Frederic and Iolanta; her dower consisting of the transfer of the sovereign rights of her father to Frederic.

Frederic promises to lead an army into Palestine, for its reconquest, within two years.

1228 Frederic (emperor) arrives in Palestine with a reinforcement in 28 galleys.

Difficulties of Frederic, arising from the iniquitous persecution of the Pope.

Negotiations with the Sultan Coradinus; peace concluded for ten years; free access to Jerusalem granted to the Christians; with possession of Bethlehem, Nazareth, &c.

1229 Frederic crowns himself in Jerusalem; the patriarch having refused to perform the ceremony.

Return of Frederic to Germany; and

End of the Fifth Crusade.

Death of the Empress Iolanta in giving birth to a son.

1230 Civil war; struggle for the Crown between the partisans of Frederic, and those of Alice, widow of Hugh de Lusignan.

Reconciliation effected by the mediation of Pope Gregory IX.

Renewal of hostilities between the Emirs of Syria and the Latins.

Several thousand pilgrims slaughtered.

Sanguinary defeat of the Knights Templars, by the Emir of Aleppo.

1232 Another Crusade projected by the Council of Spoletto: the Dominicans and Franciscans are authorized to preach it.

Appropriation of the moneys collected for the Crusade, by the Pope and his agents.

1235 Armenia seized by the Mogols.

1236 The Christians expelled from Jerusalem by the Sultan of Egypt.

1237 Martial and religious enthusiasm excited throughout Europe.

The nobles of France and England take the Cross.

THE SIXTH CRUSADE—two expeditions.

1238 I. Expedition of the French Crusaders under Thibaud, Count of Champagne, Duke of Burgundy, &c.

Defeat of the Crusaders at Gaza; Count de Bar slain, Armory de Montfort, and many nobles and knights taken captive.

Retreat of the King of Navarre upon Acre.

The French leaders, &c., return home.

II. Expedition of Richard, Earl of Cornwall, who lands at Acre, accompanied by the flower of the English chivalry.

His arrival strikes the Mussulmans with terror, and inspires the Christians with confidence.

Richard demands the restoration of the prisoners taken at the battle of Gaza.

He marches upon Jaffa; but

The Sultans of Egypt and Damascus hasten to negotiate for peace.

1240 Jerusalem restored to the Christians.

Restoration of 600 Christian prisoners.

Return of Richard, Earl of Cornwall.

End of the Sixth Crusade.

A. D.

1241 The fortifications of Jerusalem rebuilt by the Knights Templars.

The ravages of the Moguls in Asia Minor drive several tribes into Syria for settlements. One of these tribes—

The Kharizmian horde (20,000 cavalry), under Barbacan, enter Palestine, being guided by an Egyptian emir.

1242 Jerusalem captured by Barbacan, and finally lost to the Christians.

Indiscriminate massacre of the inhabitants; pillage of the city; general ruin.

The Knights Templars unite with the Moslems of Damascus, Aleppo, Ems, against the Egyptians and Kharizmians.

1243 Terrible defeat of the Christian chivalry and their Moslem allies.

Fall of Tiberias, Ascalon, &c.

Palestine overrun by the Kharizmians.

1244 The Christian chivalry confined to Acre.

Disunion between the Kharizmians and Egyptians; the former expelled from Palestine.

Holy Sepulchre in the hands of infidels.

THE SEVENTH CRUSADE.

1245 The new Crusade was resolved upon at the Council of Lyons; temporal wars to be suspended for four years.

Crusade embraced in England and France.

1247 Cyprus the rendezvous of the French Crusaders; here they spend eight months.

1248 Louis sails for Egypt with 1800 vessels, and 50,000 men.

[In imitation of the plan of the fifth Crusade, Egypt, as the principal seat of the Moslem power, was again selected for the theatre of operations.]

A storm disperses the fleet; only 700 knights, under the king, make the port.

Panic of the Mussulmans; they evacuate Damietta to the French.

Arrival of those dispersed by the storm, with a body of English nobles under William Longsword.

March of the French toward Cairo.

1249 Rashness of the Count d'Artois at Mansora; himself, William Longsword, and a host of knights slain.

Death of Nedjmeddin, Sultan of Egypt.

Louis defeats the Moslems at Mansora.

Crusaders in distress; famine and pestilence make frightful ravages among them.

1250 Total rout of the Crusaders at Mansora, and capture of Louis; destruction of at least 30,000 Christians.

Revolution in Egypt; Louis in danger.

Surrender of Damietta to the Turks, April 5, in exchange for the king and nobles.

The king proceeds to Acre; but most of his nobles return home.

[During four years, the treasures which Louis was enabled to raise were lavishly expended in refortifying Jaffa, Cæsarea, Sidon, and Acre.]

1253 Dissensions among the Moslem emirs of Syria and Egypt; hence the hopes of the Christians revive.

1254 Renewal of hostilities; the Moslem hordes approach Acre, but soon retire.

A. D.

1254 The news of the death of the queen-mother of France hastens the Departure of Louis for Europe.

End of the Seventh Crusade.

1255 Commercial and political rivalry of the Venetian States the cause of troubles in Palestine.

Disunion between the several orders.

1257 Sanguinary battles between the Templars and Knights Hospitallers; complete and merciless destruction of the former.

Preparations of the Templars in Europe for inflicting a desperate vengeance upon the Hospitallers.

1260 Approach of the Mamelukes; occupation of Damascus and Aleppo.

1263 Mameluke invasions, under Bondocdar.

Desperate and unequal battles between the now united orders and the Mamelukes.

1265 Loss of Azotus; Latins put to the sword.

1266 Surrender of Saphoury; Bondocdar (or Bibars) treacherously violates his treaty, and murders all his prisoners.

1267 Loss of Cæsarea, Laodicea, and Jaffa.

1268 Fall of Antioch before Bibars of Egypt; massacre of 40,000(?) Christians; 100,000 are sold as slaves.

Antioch abandoned to desolation and ruin.

Acre is alone in the hands of the Christians.

1269 Another crusade is proposed and eagerly adopted in Europe.

THE EIGHTH AND LAST CRUSADE.

1270 Undertaken by Louis IX., but diverted to Africa.

Prince Edward of England separates from the French before Tunis, and proceeds to Sicily.

1271 From Sicily he departs for Palestine at the head of about 1000 Englishmen.

Edward arrives in Palestine in May.

The report of his arrival strikes Bondocdar with terror: he retires from before Acre.

Edward, with only 9000 men, marches against the infidels, and routs them with slaughter.

Assault on Nazareth; capture of the city, and dreadful slaughter of the Moslems.

Edward's army fall victims to disease.

Edward is himself taken ill.

Narrow escape from assassination; Edward kills the assassin (a Mussulman).

[None of the writers contemporary with this event knew anything of that beautiful fiction—the creation of a much later age—which ascribes the recovery of Edward to the affectionate devotion of his consort, Eleanor, in sucking the venom from his wounds.]

Truce for ten years offered by the Sultan of Egypt; accepted by Edward.

1272 Edward and his wife Eleanor return home.

End of the Eighth Crusade.

1274 Pope Gregory X. endeavors to revive the crusading spirit in Europe.

A. D.

1276 The Latins twice plunder the peaceable Moslem traders; satisfaction for which Keladun, Sultan of Egypt, vainly demands.

1280 Invasion of Palestine by the Mamelukes, who renew their ravages every year.

1289 Dismemberment of the county of Tripoll from the Latin kingdom, by the Mamelukes.

Tyre and Sidon destroyed by the Turks, so that they might not afford protection any longer to the Christians.

1290 Further outrages on Mussulman merchants by the inhabitants of Acre.

Sultan Khatil demands reparation : denied.

1291 Khatil, having vowed to exterminate the faithless Franks, leads an army of 200,000 men against Acre.

Fall of Acre, the last Christian possession in Palestine.

End of the War of the Crusades.

["The cessation of the Crusades was not produced by any abatement of the love of arms, or of the thirst of glory, in the chivalry of Europe. But the union with these martial qualities of that fanatical enthusiasm which inspired the Christian warriors of the eleventh century, had been slowly, and almost thoroughly dissolved."]

CHAPTER XIII.

JERUSALEM UNDER CHRISTIAN DOMINATION.

FROM THE JOURNAL OF SAEWULF—A. D. 1102, 1103.

(*Immediately after the foundation of the Latin Kingdom in Palestine.*)

"BELOW Mount Calvary, where the patriarch Abraham raised an altar, is the place called Golgotha, where Adam is said to have been raised to life by the blood of our Lord which fell upon him, as is said in the passion, 'and many bodies of the saints which slept arose.' * * * At the head of the Church of the Sepulchre is the place called Compass, which our Lord Jesus Christ himself signified and measured with his own hand as the middle of the world. * * * On the other side of the Church of St. John, is a very fair monastery of the Church of the Holy Trinity, in which is the place of the Baptistery. * * * Without the gate of the Holy Sepulchre, to the south, is the Church of St. Mary, called the Latin. Adjoining to this church is another, called St. Mary the Little, occupied by nuns who serve devoutly the Virgin and her Son. Near which is the Hospital, where is a celebrated hospital, founded in honor of St. John the Baptist. * * * * There still are seen in the rock, in the Temple of our Lord, the footsteps of our Lord when he concealed himself and went out. * * * There is the gate of the city on the eastern side of the Temple which is called the Golden, where the Emperor Heraclius entered Jerusalem victorious when he returned from Persia with the cross of our Lord; but the stones first fell down and closed up the passage so that the gate became one mass, until, humbling himself at the admonition of an angel, he descended from his horse, and so the entrance was opened to him. In the court of the Temple of the Lord to the south is the Temple of Solomon,* of wonderful magnitude; on the east side of which is an oratory, containing the cradle of Christ and his bath, and the bed of the Virgin Mary. From the Temple of the Lord you go to the Church of St. Anne, the mother of the blessed Mary, towards the north. Near it is the pool, which in Hebrew is called Bethsaida, having five porticos,† of which the Gospel speaks. A little above is the place where the woman was healed by our Lord, by touching the hem of his garment. * * * About a stone's throw from the Church of the Ascension is the spot where, according to the Assyrians, our Lord wrote the Lord's prayer in Hebrew with his fingers, on marble; and there a very beautiful church was built, but it has since been entirely destroyed by the pagans, as are all the churches outside the walls, except the Church of the Holy Ghost, about an arrowshot from the wall to the north. In that church is a chapel, where the blessed Mary died. On the other side of the church is the chapel where our Lord Jesus Christ first appeared to the apostles after his resurrection. * * * The stoning of St. Stephen took place about two or three arbalist (or cross-bow) shots without the wall to the north, where a very handsome church was built, which has been entirely destroyed by the pagans. The Church of the Holy Cross, about a mile to the west of Jerusalem, in the place where the Holy Cross was cut out, and which was also a very handsome one, has been similarly laid waste. Under the wall of the city, outside, on the declivity of Zion, is the Church of St. Peter, which is called the Gallican, where, after having denied

* The present el-Aksa.

† This must either have been the Trench of Antonia, the Pool of Struthion, or the Piscina Grandis Valde—one of the Geminalles; and that the five porticos were really there need not be doubted. The *pious* hands that could sculpture the impress of the Redeemer's feet in so many hard rocks, would surely not scruple to build these porticos!

his Lord, he hid himself in a very large crypt, as may still be seen there."

Adventures of Sigard, the Norse King Crusader, 1107, 1111. (*About the time that Tripoly, Beirût, and Sidon fell into the hands of the Crusaders under Baldwin* 1*st.*)

"A young king just and kind,
People of loyal mind,
Such brave men soon agree—
To distant lands they sail with glee.
To the distant Holy Land,
A brave and pious band,
Magnificent and gay,
In sixty long ships glide away.
Our king, whose land so wide
No kingdom stands beside,
In Jacob's Land next winter spent,
On holy things intent."

It is related in the Saga that amongst other splendid exploits he took a castle and killed every man in it because they refused to be baptized—

"The men he treated as God's foes
Who dared the true faith to oppose—
No man he spared who would not take
The Christian faith for Jesus' sake."

King Baldwin made a sumptuous feast for King Sigard and many of his people; and gave him numerous holy relics. By the orders of King Baldwin and the patriarch, there was taken a splinter off the Holy Cross, and on this holy relic both made oath that this wood was of the Holy Cross upon which God himself had been tortured.

An Account of Jerusalem during the Frank occupation of Palestine, written about 1150: *by a Mussulman.*

"Beit el-Mocaddas (Jerusalem) is an illustrious city, ancient and full of old monuments. It bears the name of Ilia (Ælia Capitolina), so designated by Hadrian, its reformer. Situated on a mountain of easy access on all sides, it extends from west to east. On the west is the gate called el-Mihrab; beneath is the Dome of David (from which is announced the hours of prayer); on the east is the gate called Mercy, which is generally shut, and not to be opened except during the feast of doves; on the south the Gate of Zion; on the north the gate called Amoud el-Ghorab. In going from the western gate to el-Mihrab, one diverges towards the east by a large street, and reaches the great church called the Resurrection, and which the Mohammedans call Comamè. This church is the object of the pilgrimage of Christians from all the countries of the east and the west. One enters it through the west door, and arrives under the dome which covers all within, and which is one of the most remarkable things in the world. The church is below this gate, and it is impossible to descend into the inferior portion of the edifice by this side. One descends from the north side through a door opening on a staircase, which has thirty steps, which door is called Bab Santa Maria. At his entrance into the church, the spectator finds the Holy Sepulchre, a considerable edifice, having two doors and surmounted by a dome of very solid construction, very strong and built with admirable taste; of these two doors, the one is made to face from the northern side to the door of Santa Maria, the other to face the south, and its name Bab el-Salsubié (door of the Crucifixion); the piazza of the church is on this side, being opposite the east; towards the east is another considerable church, immense, where the Christians celebrate their holy services, and offer their prayers and oblations.

"At the east of this church, in descending by a gentle declivity, one arrives at the prison where the Lord Messiah was detained, and the spot where he was crucified. The great dome is circular, piercing the open heavens, and one sees all around the interior, pictures representing the Lord Messiah, St. Mary his mother, and St. John Baptist. Amongst the lamps which are suspended above the Holy Sepulchre, one distinguishes three which are of gold, and are hung in a particular place. If you seek for the principal church, you diverge towards the east, and reach the holy dwelling-house which was built by Solomon, son of David, and which was a place of pilgrimage from the time of the power of the Jews. This their temple was afterwards forcibly taken and they were banished, from the epoch of the arrival of the Mohammedans. Under the Mohammedan dominion it was aggrandized, and this is (at present) the great mosque known to the Mohammedans by the name of Misdjed el-Aksa. There is nothing that exists in the world that equals it in grandeur, with the exception of the great Mosque of Cordoue in Andulasia; for according to accounts, the roof of this mosque is grander than that of Mesjid el-Aksa. Furthermore the area of this last forms a parallelogram, of which the extent is two hundred fathoms, and the base one hundred and twenty-four. The half of this space—that which is near the Mihrab, is covered by a roof (or rather by a dome) of stones, sustained by many rows of columns; the other is open to the sky. In the centre of the edifice is a great dome known by the name of the Dome of the Rock. Through the care of divers Mohammedan caliphs it was ornamented with arabesques in gold, and other beautiful works. Beneath is the rock tomb; this rock is of quadrangular form, like a buckler; one of its extremities is elevated above the ground to the height of nearly a half fathom; the other adheres to the soil; it is nearly cubical, and its width nearly equals its length: that is to say, nearly ten cubits (Ziraa). Beneath is a cavern or a dark retreat, of ten cubits in length and five in width, and whose height is more than a fathom. One cannot penetrate its darkness but by the light of torches; the dome is pierced by four doors; facing that which is on the west one sees the altar on which the children of Israel offered their sacrifices; near the eastern door is the church called the Holy of Holies, of an elegant construction; on the south is a chapel which was used by the Mohammedans; but the Christians have seized upon it, and it has remained in their power until the epoch of the stipulation of the present work. They have converted this chapel into a convent, where the monks of the order of the Templars reside—that is to say, the officers of the House of God. Finally, the northern door is situated opposite a garden, well planted with divers species of trees, and surrounded by columns of marble, sculptured with much taste; at the end of the garden is a refectory for the priests and for those who are destined to enter the orders.

"In seeking for the place of worship, and directing your steps towards the east, you arrive at the door of Mercy, closed as we have said, but near to which is another door, through which one can come in and go out, and which is called Bab el-Asbat (or the Tribes of Israel). At the distance of a bow-shot from the latter is a very large and beautiful church, dedicated to St. Mary and known by the name of Gethsemane; here is the tomb of the Virgin in sight of the Mount of Olives, distant from Bab el-Asbat about a mile. On the road by which one ascends this mountain, one sees another church, large and solidly built, which is called the Church of Pater Noster; on the summit of the mountain is a large church, where men and women live confined, thus awaiting the divine reward; at the south-east of the mountain is the tomb of Lazarus, who was raised to life by the Lord Messiah; and at two miles from the Mount of Olives is the village from whence the ass was taken which served to bear our Lord on his entrance into Jerusalem; this village is actually deserted and ruined.

"In seeking for the gate of Zion, you find at the distance of a stone's throw, the Church of Zion, a beautiful and strong church, where one finds the room in which our Lord ate with his disciples—thus that table still subsisting, and one can visit it on a Thursday. From the Gate of Zion one descends into a ditch known under the name of the Valley of Gehennah, near to which is the Church of St. Peter. From this valley is the source of Silwan (Siloam), where the Lord Messiah gave sight to the blind man who could never otherwise have enjoyed the light of day. At the south of this source is the field which was assigned by the Messiah for the burial of strangers. Not far from there are great numbers of houses cut in the rock, and inhabited by some pious cenobites."

NOTICES BY RABBI BENJAMIN OF TUDELA, 1160–1173.

(*About the period of King Baldwin's death.*)

"Jerusalem has four gates, called the gates of Abraham,* David, Sion, and Jehosaphat. The latter stands opposite the place of the Holy Temple, which is occupied at present by a building called Templo Domino. At Jerusalem you also see the stables erected by Solomon,† and which formed part of his house. Immense stones have been employed in this fabric, the like of which are nowhere else to be met with. If you leave the city by the Gate of Jehosaphat, you may see the pillar erected on Absalom's place, and the sepulchre of King Uzziah, and the great spring of Shiloah, which runs into the brook Kedron. Over this spring is a large building, erected in the times of our forefathers. Very little water is found at Jerusalem: the inhabitants generally drink rain-water, but the country about Bethlehem abounds with rivulets, wells, and springs of water, which they collect in their houses. The dyeing house is rented by the year, and the exclusive privilege of dyeing is purchased from the king by the Jews of Jerusalem, two hundred of whom dwell in one corner of the city, under the Tower of David. There are two hospitals that support four hundred knights, and afford shelter to the sick: these are provided with everything they may want, both during life and in death: the second is called the Hospital of Solomon—being the place originally built by King Solomon. This hospital also harbors and furnishes four hundred knights. On Mount Sion are the sepulchres of the house of David, and those of the kings who reigned after him."

For the marvelous story related by the Rabbi, concerning the Tomb of David, see *Neby Daûd*.

* Damascus Gate must thus be called by the Rabbins; the Golden Gate or St. Stephen's being doubtless the Jehosaphat.

† The substructions of the south-east corner of the Temple area.

An Account of Jerusalem during its occupancy by the Franks; about the period of their expulsion by Saladin, at the close of the 11th century.

DESCRIPTION OF JERUSALEM BY A NORMAN CHRONICLER.

"I. *In what condition Jerusalem and its holy places remain at this day.*—Because most of good Christians spoke, and were honored in speaking voluntarily of the holy city of Jerusalem, and its holy places, where Jesus Christ lived and died; we will speak as it was in the day when Saladin and the Saracens conquered it from the Christians. Any can, who wish to hear; those whom it displeases will trespass here.

"There were in the city of Jerusalem four main gates of the cross, the one at the right of the other, between the posterns. Now you will name them as they will be. The Gate of David was towards the setting sun and was at the right of the (Obres) gates, which were towards the eastern sun from behind the Temple of the Lord. This gate was near or contiguous to the Gate of David. When one was before this gate one turned to the right hand in a street before the Tower of David. One could go to Mount Zion through a postern which was there in this street at the left hand. Thus as one went out from the postern was a Monastery of St. James (de Galica), whose brother was St. John the Evangelist. The reason the monastery was built, was because it was said that St. James had the true copy. The great street went straight from the Tower of David to the (Obres) gates. It was called the David street until it turned to the left hand. By the Tower of David was a large place where wheat was sold. And when one had gone down this street a little which was called the street of David, one found a street at the left hand which was called the street of the Patriarch, because the Patriarch lived at the head of this street. The Patriarch had a gate there where one entered in the house of the hospital. Next was a gate through which one entered the Monastery of the Sepulchre, but was not (mie la mistre) the main one. When one came to the bank, where the street of David ended, one found a street which was named the street of Mount Zion. And at the end of the bank one found a street covered by vaults, which was called the street of Herbs; there were sold all the herbs and all the fruits and spices of the city. At the head of this street was a place where fish was sold. And there was a large place at the left hand where cheese, poultry, and eggs were sold. At the right hand of this market were the goldsmiths (lié as suries) Roman weight. And there the palms were sold, that the palm bearer brought from beyond the sea. At the right hand of this market were the shops of the Latin goldsmiths. At the head of the shops was a convent of nuns, which was called St. Mary the Great. Next to this convent of nuns one found a convent of black monks which was called St. Mary the Latin. Next, at the right hand, one found the House of the Hospital.

"II. *Of the same.*—At the right of the hospital was the main door of the Sepulchre. Before this door of the Sepulchre was a very pretty place paved with marble. At the right hand of this Sepulchre was a monastery which was called St. James of the Jacobins. At the right hand, before this door of the Sepulchre, was a flight of steps by which one went up to Mount Calvary. There underneath the mount was a very pretty chapel, and there was one other door in this chapel by which one entered the monastery of the Sepulchre, and there descended by other stairs which were there. Thus one entered the monastery beneath Mount Calvary which was Golgotha; at the right hand were the cloisters of the Sepulchre and a chapel which was called Holy Trinity. This chapel was most grand, for there all the ladies of the city were married, and there was the fount where all the children of the city were baptized. This chapel was contiguous to the Sepulchre, and had a door through which one entered the monastery: at the right of this door was the tomb. At the right of the tomb were the monasteries, circular and open above and without covering. And within this tomb was the stone of the Sepulchre, and the tomb has a vaulted roof (au chavech): this tomb, thus at the head of the altar from without, which was called (Chavec). There they daily chanted at dawn. There was a beautiful place all around the tomb, all paved, and they went in procession all around the tomb. Next, toward the east was the choir of the Sepulchre, there where the chanters chanted; it was long. Between the choir, there where the chanters chanted, and the tomb, was an altar where the Greeks chanted. There was one other enclosure, between two; there was one through which one went from the one to the other. And in the middle of the choir of the chanters was a letter of marble which was called the Compass (lassus list) in the epistle . . . At the right hand of the main altar of this choir was Mount Calvary. If which when they chanted the mass of the Resurrection, the deacons when they chanted the gospel, turned towards Mount Calvary when they said Crucifixion. Afterwards they turned towards the tomb when they said (resurrexit, non est hic), if rightly shown: 'Ecce locus ubi posuerunt eum:' and then they returned to the book which declared the glad tidings. At the head of the choir was a door through which the chanters entered into their offices at the right hand. Between this door and Mount Calvary was a very deep ditch to which one descended by steps. There was a place which was called St. Helena. There St. Helena found the cross, the nails, the hammer, and the crown. In this ditch, in the time that Jesus Christ was on earth, the bodies of the thieves were buried when they were hung and were crucified. And when one clenched hands on oath, and did justice, it was done on Mount Calvary. When one did justice and taught the law, and there dwelt the members that they judged to speak to the malefactors. All thus that the chanters were of the sepulchre; at the left hand were their dormitories, at the left their refectories, and contiguous to Mount Calvary. Between these two offices were their cloisters and their open spaces. In a place of the (peel) was a large opening, through which one saw into the chamber of Helena, for otherwise one saw not to eat (on goute).

"III. *Of the same.*—The banks were contiguous to the street of

Herbs, which was called (Malquismat). In this street meat for the pilgrims was cooked, which was sold; and here (*chier*) was washed. And one went from the street to the sepulchre. All before this street (of Malquismat) was a street which was called the covered street, there where clothes were sold; and was all covered above. And through this street one went to the Sepulchre. This street, which went from the bank to the (Oires) door, was named the street of the Temple; for this one called it the door of the Temple, which came thus to the Temple—that to the Oires. At the left hand, as one descended this street to go to the Temple, there was the butchery, where was sold the (*char*) of the butchery to those of the city. At the right hand was another street through which one went to the hospital. This street was called the German street. At the left hand on the bridge was the Monastery of St. Gile. At the head of this street was found a door, which was called the precious door: Jesus Christ through this gate entered into the city when he was on earth. This gate was in a wall which was between the city and the Oires gates.

"IV. *Of the same.*—Between the wall of the city and the wall of the gates (Oires) was the Temple. And there was there a large place which was most of a tract of land, and a 'stone's throw' from there, thus as it comes to the Temple. This place, it was paved which, one called this place the pavement. At the right hand, as one issued from this gate, was Solomon's Temple, there where the brothers of the Temple lived. At the right of the precious gates, and of the gates Oires, were the Monasteries of the Temple of the Lord. And it was above as one ascended by high steps. And when one ascended these steps, one found a large ditch; and this pavement went all around the Monastery of the Temple. The Monasteries of the Temple were all round. And at the left hand of the raised platform of the Temple were the offices of the Abbey and of the chanters. And from this portion were steps by which one ascended to the Temple from the bass pavement to the upper. Towards the eastern sun, contiguous to the Monastery of the Temple, was a chapel of Monseigneur St. James the Apostle, the Less; because it was when in this chapel that he was there martyred, when the Jews lived there on the Temple securely. Within this chapel was the place where Jesus Christ delivered the offendress, who was taken to be martyred because she was taken in adultery. At the head of this pavement, towards the eastern sun, one descended by some steps to go to the gates (Oires). When one had descended, one found there a large place, thus as one came to the gates: there was the other which Solomon built. Through these gates one could not pass, being walled; and one could not pass but twice during the year when they were unwalled: and they went in procession the day of Palm Sunday, because that Jesus Christ passed there on this day, and was protected by a procession; and the day of the feast of the holy cross in Steuben, for through these gates was carried the cross into Jerusalem, when the Roman Emperor Heraclius conquered it from Persia, and through this door recovered it into the city, and these in procession against it. Because that one went from out the city through these gates, there was a postern (par encoste), which was called the Gate of Jehosaphat. Through this postern, those of the city went out from this part. And this postern was at the left hand of the gates Oires, towards the west. There one descended from the upper pavement to the lower Temple, from which one went to the Temple of Solomon. At the left hand, as one went from the upper pavement to the lower, there was a monastery which was called La Biets. There was the cradle in which God was rocked in his infancy, as has been said. Where was the Monastery of the Temple were four gates of the cross; the first was towards the setting sun: through this, those of the city entered into the Temple, and through that towards the eastern sun one entered into the chapel and (enrissat on ileaque) to the gates (Oires). Through the gate towards the west, one entered into the Temple of Solomon, and through the gate toward the north one entered into the Abbey.

"V. *Of the same.*—Now you have been told of the Temple and of the Sepulchre as they are, and of the hospital, and of the streets which were from the Gate of David, from this to the gates (oires), the one at the right of the other. That towards the north was called the Gate of St. Estiene (St. Steven). Through this gate all the pilgrims entered, and all those who from towards Acre came to Jerusalem, and from all the land from the river until the Sea of Ascalon. From without this gate, thus as one entered it, at the right hand, was a monastery of Monseigneur St. Estiene, who was stoned to death. Before this monastery, at the left hand, was a large house, which was called the stable; there slept the asses, and there were kept the saddles of the hospital, which was the cause of its being named the stable. This Monastery of St. Estiene the Christians of Jerusalem built before they were besieged, for this that the monastery was near the wall. The stable was not built thus, was then grand master of the pilgrims, who by (truce ?) came to Jerusalem when the Saracens had it, and when the Saracens left not a gatherer of herbs within the city, because that the house of the stable was grand master. At the right hand of the gate of Jerusalem, contiguous to the wall, before the lazaretto, was a postern which was called the Postern of St. Ladre. When the Saracens had conquered the city from the Christians, through there they put the Christians for to go secretly to the Sepulchre. For the Saracens wished not that the Christians (veissent la convine) of the city; for this they put them through the door of the Patriarch, which was in the street of the monastery of the Sepulchre, one did not put them through the main door. But know well to see that the Christian pilgrims who wish to go to the Sepulchre, and to other holy places, that the Saracens had great (*treis*), and great (*leviers*), and great services. The Saracen took them (well chascun arc XX[m] besans). But in escomenia after all the Christians who lodged gave them, by which they came down much. When one entered into the city through the Gate of St. Estiene, one found two streets, the one to the right and the other to the left, which went to the Gate of Mount Zion, which was right west. And the Gate of the Mount, it was at the right, went to a postern which was called the tannery, and went right beneath the bridge. This street, which went to the Gate of Mount Zion, was called the street of St. Estiene. From this which came to the banks of the Syrians was at the right hand, which was called the street of the Sepulchre; there was the gate of the house of the Sepulchre; through these those of the Sepulchre entered to their houses and to their families. When one came before this bank, there turned to the right a street covered with vaults, through which one went to the Monastery of the Sepulchre. In this street the Syrians sold their clothes and made their wax candles. Before this bank, fish was sold. Contiguous to this bank were the three streets which were contiguous to the other banks of the Latins. Of which the one of these three streets was named the Covered Street. There the Latins sold their clothes; and the other street of the herbs and the third Malquismat. Through the street of herbs one went to the street of Mount Zion, from which one went to the Gate of Mount Zion and very (*cupoit*) is the street of David. Through the covered street one went in a street by the bank of the Latins; this street was called the Street of the Arch of Judas, because it was said that Judas hung himself there; there was there an arch of stone. At the left hand of this street was a Monastery of St. Martin. And near this gate was a Monastery of St. Peter. There it was said that Jesus Christ made the mixture which he put in the eyes of those who had bad sight. Out of the Gate of Mount Zion one found three ways: one way to the right hand, which went to the Abbey and to the Monastery of Mount Zion. And between the Abbey and the wall of the city was a great gathering place, and a monastery in the middle of the way; at the left hand it went along the wall of the city right to the gates (oires), and from there descended to the Valley of Jehosaphat and if one went to the fountain of Siloam. And by this gate, at the right hand, on this road, was a Monastery of St. Peter in (Galiciente). In such a monastery was a ditch there where one said that St. Peter lamented himself when he denied Jesus Christ, and he heard the cock crow and then he wept. The way at the right of this door towards the west, if one went over the mount on which one could pass if one descended the mount and went through this door to Bethlehem.

"VI. *Of the same.*—When one had descended the mount, one found a lake in the valley which was called the Lake of the Germans, that the Germans made to collect the water which descended from the mountain when it rained, and there watered the horses from the city. From another part of the valley at the left hand, near from below was a charnel-house, which was called Aceldamah. There they buried the pilgrims who died at the Hospital of Jerusalem. This valley where were some charnel-houses where was bought some silver with which Judas sold his dear Lord, as the Evangelist testifies. Outside the gate was a lake towards the setting sun, which was called the Lake of the Patriarch, there where they collected the water of (iluec) all around to water the horses. Near this lake was a charnel-house which was called the Charnel-House of the Lion. It became already, as was said, had one day which was passed, that it had between the Christians and the Saracens a battle, between this charnel-house and Jerusalem, where most of the Christians were killed, and that the Saracens of the battle became all to make next day (ordoir pour la puror). Such as it came that a lion came by night and carried them all in this ditch if it is as reported: for this they called it the Charnel-House of the Lion, and above this charnel-house was a monastery, where they chanted every day at (ileques). At one place was a convent of nuns, there where they said was collected one of the pieces of the true cross.

"VII. *Of the same.*—Now returning to the door of St. Estiene, to the street which went to the left hand which went to the Gate of the Tannery. When one had gone a great piece of this street, to the left hand which was called the street of Jehosaphat; quant (en avoit pou alé avant), one found a square oven of a way of which the way which came towards the left to the Temple and went to the Sepulchre. At the head of this way was a door towards the Temple, which was called the Doleful Door. At the right hand, on the (carfor) of this way, was the (*ruisians*), of which the Evangelist testifies, by which he says that our Lord should pass, when he was taken to be crucified. At the right was a Monastery of St. John the Evangelist, and there was there a great house. This house and monastery were of nuns of Bethany; there they lived when there was war with the Saracens. Now to return to the street of Jehosaphat. Between the street of Jehosaphat and the wall of the city, at the left hand, was a street thus, as (*á a vile*). There lived the most of those from Jerusalem, and this street was called (La Merie). In such a (Merie) was a Monastery of St. Mary Magdalen, and near to the monastery was a gate. One could not issue from out to the (chans), but between the wall one went. At the right hand of this street of Jehosaphat was a monastery which was called the (Repons). There it is said that Jesus rested himself when they took him to crucify him, and there was the prison where he was placed the night he was taken in Gethsemane. A little before in this street, was east, the Pilate house. At the left hand, before this house was a door through which one went to the Temple.

"Near the door of Jehosaphat, at the left hand, was a convent of nuns which was called St. Anne. Opposite this convent was a fountain which was called the fountain below the pool. This fountain (*ne quent point, ains estoit desure!*)

"In this fountain, in the time of Jesus, the angels descended and moved the waters, and the first sick persons who descended in it were healed of their diseases. This fountain had porches where the sick ate, as is said. From the door of Jehosaphat one descended into the Valley of Jehosaphat. There was a convent of black monks. In this convent was a monastery of St. Mary. In this monastery was the grave where she was buried. The Saracens, when they had taken the city, pulled down this convent and carried the stones of it to the shut city, but the monastery they did not pull down. Opposite this monastery, at the foot of Mount Olivet, was a monastery in a rock which was called Gethsemane. There was Jesus Christ taken. At the other part of the way as one ascends

Mount Olivet, as much as one would throw a stone, was a monastery which was called St. Saviour. There Jesus went at twilight, the night he was taken, and there the sweat of his body was as blood. In the valley of Jehosaphat were recluses and (velaes), and was all fortified, and I know not to name it but by Siloam. And on the Mount of Olives was a convent of white monks. Near this convent, at the right hand, was a road which went to Bethany, all the side of the mountain. On the turn of this road was a monastery which was called St. Paternoster. There it was said Jesus Christ made the Paternoster and taught it to his Apostles. Near there was the fig-tree which the Deity reprobated when he went to Jerusalem between the monastery which was called Belfage. There came Jesus the day of Palm Sunday and the (joi) sent him the ass. Now you have been told the convents and monasteries of Jerusalem, without Jerusalem and within, and the streets of the Latins. But I have not named the convents and monasteries of the Syrians, nor of the Greeks, nor of the Jacobins, nor of the Boanins, nor of the Nestorians, nor of the Hermits, nor of the other manners of the people who were subservient to Rome of which there were monasteries and convents in the city; for this you have not (*veil mie*) to speak of all these people that I name here who were (*mie*) subservient to Rome as one has said."

Jerusalem again under Moslem Domination.

SIR JOHN MAUNDEVILLE, A. D. 1322, 1356.

"Before the Church of the Sepulchre the city is weaker than in any other part, for the great plain that is between the church and the city. And towards the east side, without the walls of the city, is the vale of Jehosaphat which adjoins to the walls as though it were a large ditch. And over against the vale of Jehosaphat, out of the city, is the Church of St. Stephen, where he was stoned to death. And then beside is the golden gate which may not be opened, by which gate our Lord entered on Palm Sunday, upon an ass; and the gate opened to him when he would go unto the Temple; and the marks of the ass's feet are still seen in three places on the steps which are of very hard stone. Before the Church of St. Sepulchre, two hundred paces to the south, is the great Hospital of St. John, of which the Hospitallers had their foundation. And within the palace of the sick men of that hospital are one hundred and twenty-four pillars of stone; and in the walls of the house, besides the number aforesaid, there are fifty-four pillars that support the house. From that hospital, going towards the east, is a very fair church which is called Our Lady the Great, and after it there is another church very near, called Our Lady the Latin; and there stood Mary Cleophas and Mary Magdalene, and tore their hair when our Lord was executed on the cross."

Description of Jerusalem. (About the time that it passed from the sway of the Sultan of Egypt into the hands of the Ottomans.) Extracted from "The Sublime Companion to the History of Jerusalem and Hebron. By Kadi Mejr-ed-din, Ebin-yemen, Abd-er-Rahman, El-Alemi." A. D. 1495. *Translated by Von Hammer; with corrections from an original Arabic MS. in the British Museum. By Geo. Williams, B. D. (With a few immaterial omissions.)*

CHAP. XX. DESCRIPTION OF THE MESJID EL-AKSA.

§ i. Mesjid el-Aksa is the name given to the body of the Mosk, which extends from south to north, with a lofty dome adorned with mosaics, under which is the Mihrab and the Minbar. It is divided into seven compartments (Akwar), supported by columns and piers, of which are forty-five columns, thirty-three of marble, twelve of stone. The thirteenth column is towards the eastern gate, near the Mihrab of Zachariah. There are in all forty piers of stone. The roof, which is of great elevation, is of wood. In the middle of its southern part is the dome, on the sides of which are two compartments. The four others are arranged two on the east and two on the west side. The other half of the roof is of stone and mortar.

That which is of wood is leaded without. One part of the Mosk on the south and east is lined with marbles of different colors.

The great Mihrab on the east side of the Minbar is said to be the Mihrab of David. Others say that his is the Mihrab outside the Jamia on the south wall, to the east, near the place called the Cradle of Jesus. I have spoken before of the Mihrab of David at the Castle. For his residence was there, as was his oratory.

When Omar came to Jerusalem he followed his (David's) example, praying in the same place, which was also called the Mihrab of Omar, because there he first prayed on the day of the conquest of Jerusalem. But it was originally the Mihrab of David. In confirmation of this is the tradition of Omar demanding of Kaab, "Where shall we establish our oratory?" The small Mihrab on the west side of the Minbar, surrounded with an iron fence, is called the Mihrab of Moaviah.

§ ii. *Dimensions.*—The length from the great Mihrab to the opposite gate is 100 common Ziraas,* exclusive both of the apse of the Mihrab and of the portico without the northern gate. The width from the eastern gate, leading towards the Cradle of Jesus, to the western gate, is 77 common Ziraas.

On the east is a Mosk, built wholly of stone, called the Mosk of Omar, because this building is one of the remaining buildings of Omar; and the Mihrab in this place is called the Mihrab of Omar, viz. that which is near the Minbar opposite to the great north door, as lately described.

On the north of the Mosk of Omar is a porch, called the Porch of 'Ozair (*i. e.* Ezra), from which a door leads into the Mosk of Omar, and near this porch is another where is the Mihrab of Zachariah, near the eastern gate. Within the Mosk on the west is a large building divided into two compartments, running east and west, called the Mosk of the Women. It has ten arches supported by nine piers, very well built, erected, it is said, by the Fatimites.

* This measure is probably the Constantinople Drah or Pik = thirty inches. The Jerusalem Drah is four or five inches shorter.

Within the Mosk (Jamia) behind the Kibla, is the Corner of the Circumcision. This oratory is surrounded with an iron fence, and adjoins the Minbar. Near the Circumcision Corner, on the west side, is the Dar-el-khotabut [the place where the Khòtba, or prayer for the reigning sovereign, is offered]. The Minbar is of wood, inlaid with ivory and ebony, constructed by the Sultan Melik el-Aadel Nureddin es-Shahid, at Aleppo, in the year 564 (A. D. 1186), and thence conveyed to Jerusalem by Saladin after his conquest, according to the intentions of Nureddin, which were thus accomplished after his death. The date of its construction is inscribed upon it. Opposite the Minbar is the gallery (dikkah) of the Muezzins, formed of beautiful marble.

This Mosk has ten gates of entrance. Seven on the north, one opening into each of its seven compartments. Outside these gates are seven porches raised on seven arches opposite these gates. They have fourteen marble columns built into the piers. The eastern gate leads to the Cradle of Jesus; another is opposite to this, on the west side, and the tenth is that which leads to the Women's Mosk.

§ iii. *The Well of the Leaf.*—This is within the Mosk at the side of the great gate. There are various traditions concerning this Well, one of which is reported by Abu-Bekr, Ibn-Miryam, and by Attye, Ibn-Kaisi. According to him, the Prophet said, "One of my people shall enter into Paradise walking, while yet alive." It happened in the time of Omar that some persons came to Jerusalem to pray. A man of the tribe of the Beni-Temim, named Sherik Ibn-Habasha, went to bring water for his companions, and his bucket fell into the well. He went down to recover it, and found a door in the well which led to gardens. He entered the door to the gardens, and walked in the gardens, and took a leaf from their trees, which he placed behind his ear. He returned by the well, came to the governor, and reported what he had found in the gardens, and about his entering them. He sent some men with him to the well, who descended with him, but they did not find any door, nor arrive at the gardens. And he wrote to Omar, who answered, that the tradition of the Prophet concerning the man that should enter Paradise alive, was true; but it should be ascertained whether the leaf was fresh or dry; for if it had changed color it could not be from Paradise, where nothing changes. The tradition adds, that it had not changed. It is said, that the well is that which is in the Mesjid el-Aksa, on the left as you enter the Jamia. On the south-east is a great magazine called the Magazine of the Joiners, in which are kept the utensils for the Mosk. It was probably constructed by the Fatimites. There is a second mouth to the Well of the Leaf.

The second Mihrab of David is without the Jamia, but within the Mesjid, on the southern wall, on the east side—a great Mihrab celebrated among the people as the Mihrab of David, near the Cradle of Jesus.

§ iv. *The Mart of Science.*—At the eastern end of the Mosk, towards the second Mihrab of David, is a place with a Mihrab, called the Mart of Science. I know not the reason of this name, which probably owes its origin to the inventive spirit of the servants of the Mosk, to excite the curiosity of the pilgrims. Some historians write that the Gate of Repentance was on this side. When an Israelite transgressed, his sin was found in the morning written on the door of his house, then he went to this place to repent and beseech God. The sign of his pardon was the disappearance of the writing; and so long as it was not obliterated he dared not approach any one. This place was assigned as an Oratory to the Hanbelites, by the Sultan Isa, son of Abu-Bekr, of the family of Eyûb, Lord of Damascus.

§ v. *The Cradle of Jesus.*—This is a subterranean Oratory near the Mart of Science. It is said that Miryam, the mother of Jesus, prayed here. To pray here with success one must recite the Surat Miryam, and pray like Omar, who recited the Surat Sad at the Mihrab of David. They recite also here the prayer of Jesus, when he was received into heaven from the Mount of Olives.

§ vi. *The Mosk of the Moghrebins.*—Outside the Jamia, to the west, in the front of the Mesjid, is the building called the Mosk of the Moghrebins, where the Malekites pray. This building was apparently first erected by Omar Ibn-Khatab, on whom be the peace of God! For, according to the tradition of Shedad, when Omar had entered the Mesjid el-Aksa he went to its west front, bearing in his dress the filth that he had taken from the Sakhrah. We carried it, says Shedad, like him, and came to the Valley Jehennom. Thence he returned, and we with him, until we stopped to pray with him in a place where the people prayed. The same Shedad reports that Omar, on the day of the conquest, went towards a place on the west side, saying, Let us here establish a Mosk: and this Jamia is in the west face of the Mesjid. Possibly the building was constructed by Omar, or the Ommiades left it behind them. It extends from east to west in the Mesjid.

§ vii. *The Rock Es-Sakhrah.*—This rock is in the middle of the Mesjid, on a raised platform, covered with a beautiful building. It is a Dome rising 50 common architectural Ziraas above the platform, which is itself elevated 7 Ziraas from the ground; so that the total elevation of the Dome above the ground is 58 Ziraas. The Dome is supported by columns of marble, and piers very well built. It has twelve columns of marble and four piers. The rock itself is surrounded with a wooden rail, and the columns and piers which carry the Dome are surrounded with an iron fence. The Dome is covered with a roof of gilded wood, supported by sixteen columns and eight piers. The pavement and walls below the Dome are of marble within and without. It is ornamented above, both within and without, with variegated stones, and the building which surrounds the Dome is octangular. The interior circumference is 224 Ziraas, the exterior 240, by the ordinary Ziraa.

§ viii. *The Sacred Footprint.*—It is on a stone detached from the rock on the south-west, and is on marble pillars.

§ ix. *The Cave.*—Beneath the rock is a Cave on the south, to which is a descent by stone steps. The steps are interrupted in the middle by a small bench excavated in the rock on the east side, where the pilgrims rest. Here is a marble column, the base of which stands on this bench, joined on the south to the side of the Cave; the capital supports the side of the Sakhrah, as if to prevent it from leaning towards the south side, or in any other way.

This cave is one of the most sacred places on earth. The author of Messir-el-ghoram says that he found, in the Commentary on the work Muta (a collection of traditions of the Imam Malek), on that verse in the Koran, "We sent water from heaven"—that all the water on earth comes from under the Sakhrah; which is a marvel, because being itself without support on any side, it is supported only by Him who supports the heavens, which can only fall upon the earth by his permission.

On the south side is the footprint of the prophet, which was there impressed when he mounted the celestial beast Borak, for the nocturnal journey: which occasioned the rock to incline on this side out of respect. On the other side you see the prints of the fingers of the angels who supported the rock while it bowed. Beneath the rock is a cave in which prayers are heard at all events. When I would enter there (continues the author of Messir-el-ghoram), I feared that it would sink down under the burden of my sins; but having seen that sinners covered with all kinds of iniquity entered and came out safe and sound, I took courage to enter; I still hesitated, however; at last I entered, and was astounded to see the rock detached on all sides, and not joined to the earth. So writes the author of Messir-el-ghoram; but, adds our author, it is a well-known fact among men, that this rock is suspended between heaven and earth. It is said that it remained so suspended until a pregnant woman, when she had entered under the rock, being terrified with this appearance, miscarried there. Then it was surrounded with the present building, to conceal the terrific marvels of the place. Ibn el-Arabi relates in his work that he came to the East, A. H. 485 (A. D. 1107),—which is the time of his arrival at Jerusalem, and that then the rock was already surrounded with a rotunda. God best knows how this is! The Dome and the rotunda which encircle it have a double roof, of which the lower is of gilded timber, and the upper covered with lead, and there is a considerable space between the two. The building has four gates towards the Cardinal points. That on the south leads straight to the Jamia, properly called Aksa. On the right side within the Dome is a Mihrab, opposite the gallery of the Muezzins, on a column of marble of very elegant workmanship. The eastern gate leads towards the steps of Borak, opposite the Dome of the Chain. This eastern gate is called the Gate of Israfil (the angel of death). The northern gate is called the Gate of Paradise. There is seen the black pavement, of which I have spoken elsewhere. The western gate is opposite to that which is called the Cotton Merchants'.

§ x. *The Dome of the Chain.*—This dome is very beautiful: I have spoken of it among the buildings of Abd-el-Melik Ibn-Merwan. It served as a model for that of the Sakhrah, and stands between the eastern gate and the steps of Borak; supported by seventeen marble columns, exclusive of those of the Mihrab. Tradition says, that the prophet on his nocturnal journey saw the Houris in this place. The platform round the Dome of the rock is square; so, however, that it is somewhat longer from south to north than from east to west, as will appear when we speak of its dimensions, please God.

Before each of the gates of the Sakhrah are columns supporting the prominent part of the roof (porches); the platform is paved with white marble. From whatever quarter you approach there are stone stairs, the heads of which are surmounted by arches raised on columns. Two of these stairs are on the south side; one of which is opposite to the great gate of the Mosk, commonly called el-Aksa. At the top of these stairs is a marble Minbar and near it a Mihrab, where prayer is made on festivals and in times of drought. This Minbar it is said was erected by the Judge of the judges, Burhan-ed-din Ibn Jema. . . At first it was built hastily only in wood. The second of these stairs leads towards the Dome of the Roll, which is towards the Mount of Olives. It faces the wall of the Mosk el-

Aksa. The stairs on the east are called the steps of Borak, and lead to the olives planted from the east side of the Mosk to the Gate of Mercy. Two other stairs are on the north, one opposite to the Gate Hitta, the other opposite to the Gate of the Dewatar. On the west side there are three stairs, one opposite to the Gate of the Inspector (Bab-en-Nazir), the second opposite the Gate of the Cotton Merchants (Katanin), the third opposite the Gate of the Chain (Bab-es-Salsala). This last was made in our times, in the year 877 (A. D. 1499). Near these stairs is the Dome called the Grammarians', constructed by the great Melik Isa.

§ xi. *The Dome of the Prophet's Ascension.*—On the right of the Rock, on the west of the platform, rises the Dome of the Ascension, much visited by pilgrims, built by the Amir Isfehsalan Az-ed-din, son of Amru Osman, Governor of Jerusalem, A. H. 596 (A. D. 1218). It existed before, but was then repaired.

§ xii. *The Place of the Prophet.*—This is said to have been once a beautiful little Dome, standing on the platform on the side of the Dome of the Ascension; but when the platform was paved this cupola disappeared, and its place was marked by a Mihrab, described in red marble, in the pavement on the side of the Sakhrah, which still exists. It is said that this is the place where the prophet prayed with the angels and cherubim, on the night of his nocturnal journey, and from which he afterwards ascended to heaven. Two prints of his feet are to be seen there, one in gold the other in silver, marking the spot of the Ascension, which took place on the right side of the Sakhrah. [Directions and formula for praying there.]

§ xiii. *The Place of the Prophet El-Khudr* (*S. George.*)—Below the platform on the west, towards the Dome of the Prophet, is a place called Bakh-bakh [wonderful and beautiful!] which is the place of El-Khudr, who prayed there; it is now abandoned. There is beneath the platform, towards the Gate of Iron (Hadîd), adjoining the stairs which lead to the platform, [a chamber] called the Cave of Spirits, which is rarely visited by pilgrims. On the west side of the Mesjid are rocks said to be of the time of David. It is evident that they are natural rocks, rooted in the ground, and never removed.

§ xiv. *The Dome of Solomon.*—On this side, near the gate of the Dewatar, is a Dome solidly built on the natural rock, called the Dome of Solomon; and the rock must be that where he stood to pray after having finished the Temple. . . This dome dates from the time of the Ommiades.

§ xv. *The Dome of Moses.*—The Dome which stands near the Gate of the Chain (es-Salsala) is called the Dome of Moses; but this is not Moses the prophet. The true origin of this name is unknown. It was built by Melik Saleh Nejem-ed-din Eyûb, son of Melik el-Kaamel, in the year of his death, *i. e.* A. H. 647 (A. D. 1269). It was formerly called Kubbet-es-Sijret (Dome of the Tree). On the west side of the Mesjid are cloisters solidly built, running from south to north. The first is near the Gate of the Moghrebins (*i. e.* the Gate of the Prophet), and the last at the Gate of the Inspector (Nazir), and beyond [to] near the Gate El-Ghuanimi.—All these cloisters were built under the direction of Melik Naser Motammed, Ibn Kelaûn. Those from the Gate of the Moghrebins to that of the Chain (es-Salsala) were built in A. H. 713 (A. D. 1335), those from the Gate of Nazir to that of Ghuanimi in the year 707 (A. D. 1329). On the area of the Mesjid, between these cloisters and the platform of the Court of the Sakhrah, there are a number of small elevations for prayer and a great quantity of trees—as sycamores, figs, and others. The cloisters on the north of the area run east and west from the Gate of the Tribes (es-Sabat) to the School el-Jawlié, now called the House of Prefecture.

As to the cloisters which extend from the Gate of the Tribes to the School of Ghader, I cannot speak positively. Most probably they were erected at the same time as the neighboring Minaret built by Sultan Eshref Ibn Hosein, A. H. 769 (A. D. 1391). The cloisters below the School of Ghader were built at the same time as were those of the School of Kerim. The cloisters near the Gate of Hitta to that of the Dewatar were built by Melik Efhad, at the same time with his sepulchre, which is near the former of these two gates; for they are mentioned in the deed of foundation. As for the cloisters commencing at the Gate of the Dewatar, and extending to the western wall of the Mesjid, and the five schools outside them—the School of Emin and the Persan are ancient. They were repaired during the reign of Melik Isa, in the year 610 (A. D. 1232). The cloisters beneath the other three schools, viz. that of Esaad and Sabib, were built at the same time with these Schools, whose dates will be given in the chapter on the Schools. The lower cloisters beneath the Prefecture [Es-Seraiyah] were built at the same time with the minaret of the Gate El-Ghuanimi; for the date is preserved in the chronography written above: but the writing has become illegible from age, and its height from the ground. The two cloisters were built a year after the minaret....... On the east side are many olives, planted in the time of the Greeks, and the remains of the ruined cloisters on the side of the Cradle of Jesus date from the times of the Ommiades.

§ xvi. *The Dome of the Roll.*—This is on the platform of the Sakhrah on the south-west. I have been told that it is so called because one of the ancient kings, on a visit to Jerusalem, having ascended the Mount of Olives, threw a roll which fell here; which gave occasion to the building of this Dome and to its name. Men have invented diverse accounts of this matter: God only knows the truth!

§ xvii. *Retreat of Kashan.*—This is a place near the Dome of the Roll, on the side of the platform of the Sakhrah towards the south. Sheikh Abd-el-Melik of Mosul here lived as a hermit. Its walls are cased with tiles of Kashan, whence it derives its name.

§ xviii. *The Cell of Bostam.*—Under the platform of the Sakhrah, on the east, near the olives, where the poor of Bostam met for prayer. The door is now closed.

§ xix. *The Cell of Samed.*—Near the Cell of Samed on the north, adjoining the Stairs of Borak. The door is now closed, as that of the former building. There are in the Mesjid thirty-four wells for collecting the rain-water. One of these is that of the Leaf, already mentioned (§ 3), in the Jamia. There are seven others on the platform of the Sakhrah, the remainder in the ground of the area around the four sides of the platform. Some have no opening, others have as many as three, so that there are more than forty mouths to these wells. Some are in ruins, and some stopped.

§ xx. *Dimensions of the Area of the Mesjid.*—I took these dimensions myself with cords, and found the length—commencing from the south wall near the Mihrab of David, to the end of the cloisters on the north of the Gate of the Tribes—669 common Ziraas, without reckoning the thickness of the two walls. Should any one else find it 2 or 3 Ziraas more or less, it must be ascribed to the difficulty of surveying; for I surveyed it twice myself before I obtained the true measure. The width from east to west, commencing from the eastern wall adjoining the tombs at the Gate of Mercy to the end of the western cloisters beneath the School of Tunjûz, is 406 common architectural Ziraas, without reckoning the thickness of the two walls.

§ xxi. *Observation.*—I have at the commencement called attention to the fact that the place now called by the name Aksa (*i. e.* the most distant), is the Mosk [Jamia] properly so called, at the southern extremity of the area, where is the Minbar and the great Mihrab. But in fact Aksa is the name of the whole area enclosed within the walls, the dimensions of which I have just given, for the Mosk proper [Jamia], the Dome of the Rock, the Cloisters, and other buildings, are all of late construction, and Mesjid el-Aksa is the correct name of the whole area.

§ xxii. *Dimensions of the Platform of the Sakhrah.*—The length from the southern wall between the two southern stairs, passing with the measure between the eastern door of the Sakhrah and the Dome of the Chain, to the northern wall opposite the Gate Hitta, is 253 Ziraas; the width from east to west, commencing at the eastern wall adjoining the olives, to the western wall opposite to the School of

Eshrif, is 189 common architectural Ziraas. The dimensions of the Mosk proper (Jamia), the elevation of the Dome of the Sakhrah, and its circumference, have been before indicated (sup. §§ ii. vii). If there be an error in the measures it must be very slight. The dimensions here given differ from those which I have given in the account of its construction under the reign of Abd-el-Melik Ibn Merwan. The reason is, that the measures vary according to the usage of the time, though their names remain the same: some who have given these measures employ the Ziraa of iron; others, the hand-Ziraa (the length of the arm)—God knows best! There are besides in the area a number of small oratories, &c., the description of which would be too long, for he only who has seen this sanctuary can form a just idea of it, and all that I have said concerning it is only by way of approximation.

§ xxiii. *The Ancient Aksa.*—Beneath the Mesjid on the south side is a great building, in which are piers supporting the roof, and it is under the place of the Minbar and Mihrab. This place is called the ancient Aksa, and these are perhaps the remains of Solomon's building, as may be judged from their solidity.

§ xxiv. *The Stable of Solomon.*—At the side of that, also beneath the Mesjid, under where the olives grow, there is a walled place called the Stable of Solomon. It runs in under the greatest part of the Mesjid, and occupies the subterranean space of most of the above-noticed southern localities of the Mesjid. It is probably Solomon's building.

§ xxv. *The Minarets.*—In describing the Mosk as it was built in the time of Abd-el-melik Ibn-Merwan, we have already spoken of the four Minarets, of which three are on the west side of the Mosk, the fourth at the Gate of the Tribes. They still exist, but it is plain that they have been repaired and rebuilt in more modern times, on the old foundations. The first Minaret, and most beautiful, is at the south-west near the School of Fakhr, against the back of which it rests. It was perhaps built by the founder of that school; but God knows best! The second is at the Gate of the Chain, served by the most eminent Muezzins: it gives the direction to the other Minarets, which follow it in announcing prayer. I have been informed that it was erected by Tûnjuz, prefect of Syria, when he built the celebrated school at the side of the Gate of the Chain. The third Minaret is at the north-west extremity of the Mesjid. It is the largest and most solid of the four; it was built by Kadi Sheref-ed-din Abd-er-Rahman, son of the Wisîr Fakhr-ed-din el-Khalili, inspector of the religious foundations of the Harams of Mecca, Medina, and Jerusalem. I have seen the patents for this office [or the expenses of this work], drawn up by Sultan Hossam-ed-din Lajin, in the year 697 (A. D. 1319), at which time probably this Minaret was erected. Others think it was of the time of Kelaûn, which is possible. The fourth Minaret near the Gate of the Tribes is the most elegant. It was built in the reign of the Sultan Eshref, in the month of Shaaban, A. H. 769 [A. D. 1391].

§ xxvi. *Gates of the Mesjid.*—There are first the two gates pierced in the east wall, of which God speaks in the Koran, saying, "He raised a wall, whose gate on the inside is the Gate of Mercy, and on the outside the Gate of Torture." The valley behind this last is called Wady Jehennom. They are now stopped. Remains of the work of Solomon may still be seen on the inside of the enclosure, the only remains that are found within the Mesjid. This place is much reverenced and visited by pilgrims. I heard from a sage that these two gates were closed by Omar Ibn Khatab, and will only open at the end of the world, when Jesus the Son of Mary shall descend upon the earth. It seems they were closed for fear, and to secure the Haram and the city, because they face the desert, and there could be no advantage in having them open (to facilitate the entrance of the Bedawin). The place above the Gate of Mercy is called the Convent of Nasr, from Sheikh Nasr, who delivered scientific lectures there for a long time. He was replaced by the Imam Abu Hamid el-Ghazali, and this place was called the cell of Ghazali. Being afterwards repaired by Melik Isa, it soon fell again to ruin, so that only some remains of its walls now appear. There is on the east side near the two gates above mentioned a third closed gate, opposite the stairs of the Sakhrah, called the Steps of Borak. It is called the Gate of Borak, because by this gate the Prophet entered on his nocturnal journey; and the gate of funerals, because they went out by it. The Gate of the Tribes, so called from the Tribes of the Children of Israel, Joseph, Reuben, Simeon, and Judah, at the extreme north-east side, not far from the Gates of Mercy and Repentance. It is said that between the Gate of Mercy and that of the Tribes is the place of Elias and El-Khudr.

The Gate Hitta is on the north side. This gate has its name from the command given by God to the Israelites, to say Hitta (*i. e.* Pardon!), as they entered it.

The Gate of the Nobility of the Prophets is on the north. It is apparently this by which Omar entered on the day of the conquest. But God best knows all things! It is now called the Gate of the Dewatar, from the school of the same name at its side. There are then three gates on the north; that of the Dewatar, that of the Tribes, and that named Hitta. The Gate El-Ghuanimi is at the extremity of the west wall, where it turns north, so called after the minaret of that name. It leads to the quarter of the Children of Ghuanimi, and was formerly called the Gate of Abraham.

The Gate of the Nazir (Inspector) is an ancient gate repaired in the time of Melik Isa, about A. H. 600 (A. D. 1222). It was formerly called the Gate of Michael. This is the gate to which Gabriel tied the celestial beast Borak on the night of Mohammed's journey. The Gate of Iron is solid and beautiful, made by Argun el-Kameli. The Gate Katanin (of the Cotton Merchants), so called from its leading to the cotton bazaar. An inscription under it states that the Sultan Melik en-Nasr Mohammed, Ibn Kelaun, repaired it in 737 (A. D. 1359). It is an extremely solid gate, and in its neighborhood is the Gate of the Bath, by which you can come to the Bath of the Mesjid. It is ancient, and was in ruins when Alla-ed-din el-bassir renewed its building, when he built the Mutta-weddy.

The Gate of the Chain and the Gate Sekiné both lead over the great street, called the Street of David. These are the principal gates and most frequented, because they lead towards the bazaar and the principal streets of the city. The Gate of the Chain was formerly called the Gate of David.

The Gate of the Moghrebins, so called from its vicinity to the door of the Jamia of the Moghrebins (Western Africans)... and because by that, one goes to the quarter of the Moghrebins. This gate is at the south-west extremity of the enclosure, and is also called the Gate of the Prophet....

There are then eight gates on the west side commencing with that of Ghuanimi, to that of the Moghrebins, and three to the north, *i. e.* eleven in all, exclusive of the two Gates of Mercy and Repentance, and the closed door in the east wall—with which there are fourteen. ... On the east and south sides, the Mesjid looks towards the desert: on the south, to the Fountain of Siloam, &c.; on the east is also the Mount of Olives and the Valley of Jehennom; on the north and west only the enclosure is bounded by houses. I have already said that the Mesjid was once in the middle of the city, surrounded on all sides by buildings, but after the old constructions were destroyed no one undertook to rebuild them, and the affairs of the world became exhausted.—So things remained as we see them in these days.

Schools and Sepulchral Monuments within and around Jerusalem.—These charitable foundations comprehend Schools (Medressé), Convents (Khankeh), Cells (Zaweh), and Caravanserais (Robat), founded and endowed by religious sultans, princes, and local governors, or officers, civil and ecclesiastical, or by private individuals, chiefly in the 7th, 8th, and 9th centuries of the Hejira; for from the time of its recovery from the Franks the Musulmin vied with each other in their endeavors to repair the temporary desecration of their Holy House by special reverence and acts of extraordinary devotion.

The Convent of Fakhr, near the Mosk of the Moghrebins, within the Mesjid, near the gate which leads to the Quarter of the Moghrebins founded by Kadi Fakhr-ed-din Abu-Abdullah Mohammed, inspector of the troops, a Coptic convert to Islam, who died A. H. 732 (A. D. 1354), upwards of 70 years of age. [This is doubtless the present house of Abu Se'ud Effendi.]

The School of Tunjûz, founded by Emir Tunjûz, prefect of Syria, opposite the Gate of the Chain (Bab-es-Salsala). The founder left many monuments of his piety, as *e. g.* the marbles near the Mihrab of the Great Mosk, on the west side. This building was commenced in A. H. 720 (A. D. 1342). He also caused to be made the marble basin between the Sakhrah and the old Mosk, and the Bath at the Gate of the Cotton Merchants (Bab-el-Katanin). [Hammam es-Shefa.] . . .

The School of Saleh, near the Gate of the Tribes (Bab-es-Sabat), founded by Melik Saleh-ed-din. It is the ancient Church of St. John, where the Virgin Mary was buried. It was founded A. H. 588 (A. D. 1210). The revenues of the Sheikhs are the best that have been founded in the countries of Islam.

The Cell of Yona, near the Gate of the Inspector (Bab-en Nazir). The School of Jehark, on the north of the Cell of Yona. These two places were formerly a Christian Church divided in two, so that one-half became the Cell of Yona, the other the School of Jehark, founded in A. H. 791 (A. D. 1413), by the emir of that name, grand-master of the Squires of Melik Barkuk, killed at Damascus. The School of Efdhal, formerly called the Dome of the Moghrebins, founded by Melik Efdhal Nur-ed-din Abulhasan Ali, son of Saleh-ed-din, for the use of the Moghrebins. He founded also the Mosk by the side of the Church of the Holy Sepulchre, A. H. 589 (A. D. 1205), where his father died. The minaret only was built before the year 870 (A. D. 1492).

The Cell Derkah, near the Hospital of Saleh. This building was in the time of the Franks the establishment of the Hospitallers, and had been built by Helena, mother of Constantine, who built the Church of the Holy Sepulchre. The minaret is in ruins. Here the Governors of Jerusalem formerly dismounted. This Cell was endowed A. H. 613 (A. D. 1235), by Melik Mozaffer-Shehab-ed-din Gazi, son of Sultan Melik-el-Aadel Abu Bekr, son of Eyûb, Lord of Miafarakein.

The Serpents' Mosk, near the Church of the Holy Sepulchre, where is the talisman against serpents. It was built by the Khalif Omar.

The Convent of Saleh, under the Church of the Holy Sepulchre, founded in 585 (A. D. 1207) by Melik Saleh-ed-din. [This is el-Khankey.]

The Red Convent, near the last named, destined for the poor.

The School of Maimûn, at the City Gate, ez-Zahari. It was formerly a Greek Church, endowed in A. H. 593 (A D. 1215), by Emir Faris-ed-din Abu-Said Maimun, son of Abdullah el-Karsi, treasurer of Melik Saleh-ed-din.

§ xxviii. *The Minarets of Jerusalem.*—Besides the four Minarets of the Mesjid el-Aksa, there is without a small Minaret at the School of Moazzem (opposite the Gate of the Dewatar), and another at the Convent of Saleh-ed-din, built by Sheikh Borhan-ed-din, Ibn Ghanem, before the year 820 (A. D. 1442). I have been informed by Sheikh Shems-ed-din Mohammed, son of Sheikh Abdullah of Bagdad, that Borhan-ed-din's design to build this Minaret greatly distressed the Christians, because it would out-top the Church of the Holy Sepulchre. They offered a large sum of money to the Sheikh to abandon his design, but he continued to build, to their great annoyance. Then the Prophet appeared in a dream to a man whom he ordered to salute Ibn-Ghanem in his name, and to assure him of his intercession in the Day of Judgment, in recompense for his having raised this Minaret above the head of the Infidels. We have said above that the Minaret, which is on the south of the Church of the Holy Sepulchre, was built before the year 870 (A. D. 1492), on the ancient foundations. The Minaret at the side of the Cell Derkah was partly ruined by the earthquake of the year 863 (A. D. 1485), and the Minaret of the Mosk near the Jews' Synagogue was built since the year 800 (A. D. 1422). The City of Jerusalem, as it now stands, is a large city built partly on the mountain and partly in the valley. Everywhere are found vestiges of ancient buildings on which the modern are reared. It has a large number of reservoirs for collecting the rain-water. Among the most solid buildings of Jerusalem is the Cotton Bazaar, on the west side of the great Mosk, of such height and strength as is found in few other cities: then the three Bazaars near the Gate of the Mihrab, commonly called the Gate of Hebron (Bab el-Khalil), which are also the work of the Greeks, and extend in the direction of Damascus. The first, on the west side, is the Bazaar of the Grocers, assigned by Saleh-ed-din as endowment to the School which he built. The middle one which joins this is the Herb Bazaar, and the third on the east is the Bazaar of Stuffs. The rents of these last belong to the Mosk of Aksa. Travellers say that they know no Bazaar which can be compared with these. They are one of the ornaments of Jerusalem.

Selami Ibn Kossair relates, that when Omar had taken Jerusalem he stopped at the upper part of the Bazaar, and inquired "Whose row is this?" *i. e.* the row of Shops of the Cloth Bazaar. The answer was "The Christians'." "And whose," he asked, "is this western row, where the bath is?" He was answered—"The Christians'." Then he made a sign with his hand, saying, "This for them, and that for us." This, *i. e.* the middle Bazaar, which runs between the two rows, and is to be understood of the great Bazaar where is the Dome covered with lead. It is clear, he describes the place where are now the three Bazaars before mentioned, for the old rows have disappeared, and the present buildings have taken their place.

There are at Jerusalem nearly twenty Churches and Convents of the times of the Greeks. The principal and most solid of all is that of the Holy Sepulchre, annually visited by a great number of pilgrims from all lands, who arrive there for the day of the Resurrection. The Church of Sion which belongs to the Franks, at the southern extremity of Jerusalem. The Church of S. James, or the

Convent of the Armenians, near the former. The Church of the Cross (Masulabi), which belongs to the Georgians without Jerusalem, on the west. These four Churches are the pillars of the Christians. . . The last was taken away from them during the reign of Nasr Mohammed, son of Kelaun, and converted into a Mosk. But in the year 705 (A. D. 1327) an ambassador arrived from the King of the Georgians and the Emperor of Constantinople to demand the restitution of this Church, which was accordingly restored to them.

§ xxviii. *Celebrated Quarters of Jerusalem.*—Quarter of the Moghrebins, near the walls of the Mesjid, on the west, where the Moghrebins (Western Africans) sojourn, from whom it is named. The Quarter of Sheraf in its neighborhood, also on the west, and its name is derived from a man who was of the nobles of the city, called Sheraf, and he has descendants known by the name of Beni Sheraf. It was formerly called the Kurds' Quarter. The Quarter of Alem, named after Alem-ed-din Suliman, son of Mohezeb, deceased in 770 (A. D. 1392), whose son Omar was inspector of Mecca and Medina, and whose brother Sheraf-ed-din is buried in this Quarter. It is close to the preceding on the north, and adjoins the Quarter of Hayaderé. The Quarter Saltein adjoins that of Sheraf on the south-west; Haret-er-Rîsha, and the Jews' Quarter on the east. The Quarter of Sion is west of the Jews'. The Quarter Dhawi, north of that of Sion, and the Quarter of the Beni Hareth, without the City, near the Fortress.

§ xxix. *The Street of David.*—This is the great Street which commences at the Gate of the Chain (Salsala) of the Mesjid el-Aksa, and leads to the City-gate, once called of the Mihrab, now of Hebron (Kahlil). Its parts bear different names. Thus the part from the Gate of the Mesjid to the house of the Koran of Selami is called Suk-es-sagha (the Goldsmiths' Mart); from the gate of Selami to the gate of the Quarter of Sheraf, Suk-el-Kashash (faggots); from the Quarter of Sheraf to the Khan Fakhm, Suk-el-mobidhîn (the Whitesmiths' Mart); from the gate of the Khan to the arch (Kantara) Jobeili, Suk-Khan el-Fakhem (the Mart of the Charcoal Inn); from the arch Jobeili to the steps (duraj) Harafîsh, Suk-al-tabakkin (Tobacco Mart); from the steps Harafîsh to the gate of the Jew's Quarter, Khat-bab-el-wakali (the Line of the Gate of the Wakil's Office). It is a large Khan, (the revenues of which are assigned to the Mosk el-Aksa, and let for four hundred ducats a year), in which various sorts of goods are sold. From the Jews' Quarter to the Khan Essarf (Money-changers') is called Suk el-Hariri (the Silk Mart); and from the Khan es-Sarf to the City-gate, Khat-'arsat-el-ghalal (Line of the Place of Produce).

All these parts are comprised in the Street of David, so named from a subterranean gallery which David caused to be made from the Gate of the Chain to the Citadel called the Mihrab of David. It still exists, and parts of it are occasionally discovered. It is all solidly vaulted.

§ xxx. *The Street of the Merzeban (probably Landgrave).*—It is divided into different parts, like that of David. From the Gate El-Katanin to the end of the Akba it is called Akbat-el Katanin. From the head of the Akba to the Khan Jobeili is known as Hamman Ala-ed-din, which joins on the west the lane (shaari), known as the quarter of Sheikh Mahommed el-Karmi, and on the north, a lane (shaari), known as the quarter of the Hasryé (Mat Merchant), which is followed on the east by the quarter of Ibn-es-Shentîr, because he dwelt there; and the whole of this is comprehended under the Khat of the Merzeban. (I know not the reason of this name, but it is so written in the legal decisions.)

Near the Merzeban's quarter on the west is the Plan of the Square, and the Stuff Mart, followed by those of Herbs and Spicery: and close to it the street of the Derkah, where is the Hospital of Saleh-ed-din, and the Church of the Sepulchre. Near this the Christians' Quarter extends to the south-east from the Gate of Hallil to the Gate of Serb (Drinking). And within the Christian Quarter is the Quarter of the Rahbeh. The Quarter Jewalidi joins the Christian Quarter on the west, without the city.

§ xxxi. *The Lane (Shaari) of the Valley of the Mills.*—This is the greatest street, from the south towards Damascus, which extends from the steps of the fountain to the Gate of the Column (el 'Amûd)—one of the city gates, and includes many lanes (shaari). First, that of the Gate of the Cotton Mart, and this is the Gate of the Mesjid, so called because they sell cotton in the Bazaar near it. That of the Gate of the Inspector (en Nazir), opposite to which on the west, is Market Street (Akbat-es-Suk), now known as Lady's Street (Akbat-es-Sit), so called from a house built by Dame Tonshok, in 794 (A. D. 1416). Near it on the west is the Oil Mart, and by it is an Akbat on the east, known as Akbat Abû Shama (the Mole's Father—it is the title of an unpublished tale of the Thousand and One Nights). On the east side of the Mill Valley is the Quarter Ghuanimi, named from the Beni Ghanem, and opposite on the west is Akbat ez-Zahari, so called from an oratory of that name. On the south is Akbat es-Sudan, by which, on the north, is the Akbat known as the Arch (kantara) of Green. At the northern end of Akbat ez-Zahari is the Bazaar of Fakhr, so called from the founder of the school of that name. Here are the soap manufactories. On the north-west of this Bazaar is the Quarter of the Beni-Merri, joined on the west by the Quarter Zeraini, and that of Malath, without the city, joining the Christians' Quarter on the west. Lastly, the Quarter of the Column, where the Valley of the Mills and the City terminate on the north-west.

The Quarters of the Beni-Saad and Baila are on the east of the Mill Valley, joining on the north the Ottomans' Quarter, followed on the north by Akbat-es-Showekh, on the north of which again is the Quarter of the Beni Zied, and that of the Gate Ed-Dagu, at the northern extremity of the city. The Quarter Deraj-el-mola is near the Quarter Osaila on the east, joined on the south by the Quarter Sheriff-el-Umbia (Nobility of the Prophets), now called that of the Dewatar. It is near the Quarter Mehmazi, and leads to the Gate Zaharai. The Quarter of the Gate of Hitta on the north of the Mesjid el-Aksa, joined on the north by the Orientals', which joins the city walls. The Quarter Tori, from the Gate of the Tribes to the northern wall of the city, and to the Quarter called the Faster's.

There are besides a great number of Quarters, but we have only mentioned the more celebrated; of which the most remarkable is that of the Gate Hitta. All these Quarters are on the north and west sides of the Mesjid. On the south and east is the desert, as was before said.

§ xxxii. *The Castle.*—This is without [?] Jerusalem on the west side, formerly called the Mihrab of David, who dwelt there. It is said that the building joined the Convent of Sion. It has a great tower named of David, and built by Solomon. . . . . . The Franks and Greeks erected some buildings in the Castle, when they were masters of Jerusalem. There is in the Castle a Castellain different from the governor of the city, who has the privilege of a Mint, and a military band every afternoon, according to the usage of the Castellains of the castles in the great cities. This usage is now discontinued by reason of the general disorder. Formerly the Governor resided in the Castle.

The buildings of Jerusalem are all of great strength, built in stone with vaulted roofs, or terraced without timber. Travellers say that they know no city better built for appearance than Jerusalem, and none better in reality than Hebron. The architecture of Jerusalem resembles that of Nablûs. These three cities are all of stone, because they have the advantage of being situated near mountains where there is an abundant supply of this material. The *coup d'œil* of Jerusalem taken from a distance is very beautiful, above all on the east side, from the Mount of Olives, and also from the south. On the west and north only very little is seen from far. Behind are the mountains which surround Jerusalem and Hebron, and render the approach difficult. . . . . .

§ xxxiii. *The City Gates.*—The first, situated on the south, is that of the Moghrebins' Quarter, then that of Sion, now called the Jews'. On the west is a small secret gate adjoining the Armenian

Convent. The Gate of the Mihrab, now called that of Khalii. Moshrif in his Defence of the Traditions says, that, according to the words of the prophet, the Gate by which Jesus shall enter at the end of the world to oppose Antichrist, is not the Gate of the Church towards Ramla, but the western Gate of David near the Mihrab, called by the name of Lid, and another known as the Gate of Rahbi [*i. e.* wide place]. On the north are the Gates of Serb, el-'Amud ed-dazje, Ez-Zahari, and on the east that of the Tribes. In all, ten gates.

REMARKABLE PLACES IN THE ENVIRONS OF JERUSALEM.

§ xxxiv. *The Fountain of Siloam.*—This is without the city, on the south, in the valley adjoining the southern walls of the city.

[Then follow traditions, &c., showing how highly it is esteemed by the Moslems, who rank it with Zemzem,—the sacred Well of Mecca.]

§ xxxv. *The Fountain of Accused Women.*—Said, son of Abd-el-Aziz, says that there was in the time of the Israelites, near the Fountain Siloam, another fountain, to which women accused of adultery came, and drank the water—with impunity if they were innocent, but with fatal effect if they were guilty. When Miryam was found with child and accused to her husband, she called God to witness her innocence, and drank of this water only with benefit. She then prayed that this water might never do harm to any faithful woman, and from that day the fountain disappeared.

[This is doubtless the Fountain of the Virgin, of which a similar tradition is often recorded by Christian pilgrims of the middle ages.]

§ xxxvi. *The Well of Job.*—This is near the Fountain Siloam. The author of the Ins mentions that he has read the following in the writings of Ibn Omar, son of Mohammed el-Kasem. "I have read in history that in a drought of water this well was dug to the depth of eighty Ziraas, ten long, and four wide. This well is entirely cased with large stones, each of which is five Ziraas long and two high, more or less. I was astonished at the size of these stones, and at the difficulty of getting them down there. The water was fresh, and during the whole year at the depth of eighty Ziraas, except in the winter, when it overflows, inundates the valley, and turns a mill. I descended in the well with the laborers to dig there. I saw that the water there issued from a stone of nearly two Ziraas [in diameter?] There is a cave, the entrance to which may be three Ziraas in height by one and a half in width. A very cold wind came from this cave. I entered it with a lighted candle, and saw there a cave all in stone; I advanced, but the wind which issued thence extinguished the candle. This well is in the depth of the valley, and the cave in the middle of the well, which is surrounded by enormous rocks and high mountains, up which one climbs with difficulty. This is the well whereof God said to Job, "Place thy foot in this cold hole." The water which overflows in winter, for a month or more, forms a torrent which floods the valley.

There are at Jerusalem six pools constructed by Ezechiel (Hezekiah), one of the ancient kings of Israel. Three of these pools are in the city—Birket Israil, that of Solomon, and that of Ayad. The three others are without the city, Birket Mamillah and the two pools called El-Merje, which were constructed as reservoirs of water for the city. The first, which is very celebrated, is north of the Mesjid el-Aksa, near the wall, at the Gate of the Tribes (es-Sabat) and the Gate Hitta: it is of majestic appearance. As to the Pools of Solomon and Ayad, I know not where they are, unless, at least, they are the two pools, one of which is at the Street of the Merzeban, and serves as a reservoir for the bath of Ala-ed-din Bazir [Hammam es-Shefa], and the second in the Christian Quarter [Birket Hammam el-Batrack], which serves as a reservoir to the Patriarch's Bath, whose revenues belong to the Convent of Saleh-ed-din. These two pools I suppose to be those of Solomon and Ayad. That of Mamillah is universally known; the two pools named Merja are near the village Urtas, distant half a farasang, whence the water is conducted by pipes to Jerusalem.

In the vicinity of Jerusalem are everywhere seen vineyards and orchards. The most beautiful situation is that called El-Kaat [Bukà in MS.], without Jerusalem on the south-west, the revenues of which were granted by Saleh-ed-din to the Convent of the Sofis. These country houses are elegantly and solidly built, and their owners pass several months there in the summer.

There was formerly at Jerusalem only one palm, supposed to be that which the Koran says bowed to Miryam. According to El-Kortobi, it was planted more than a thousand years since.

There were at most three palms in the Mesjid el-Aksa, one near the oratory at the side of the royal path at the place of the Sakhrah. This withered about the year 802 (A. D. 1424). The two others still exist, one at the Gate of Mercy, the second at the south of the Sakhrah, known as the Palm of the Prophet. [Have long since disappeared.]

§ xxxvii. *The Convent of Abû Tor.*—On the side of this Bukà, on the north, is a small village in which is a convent, built by the Greeks, known in ancient times as the Convent of Mar Kaibûs. Its present name is derived from a pious Sheikh, to whose family this village was bequeathed by Saleh-ed-din, A. H. 594 (A. D. 1216). The Sheikh Abû Tor is buried there. His tomb is visited by many pilgrims. The village is near the gate of the city called the Gate of Hebron.

§ xxxviii. *The Mount of Olives.*—This is the mountain on the east which commands the Mesjid el-Aksa. [Moslem Traditions.] It is here that Jesus ascended to heaven. On the summit is a church built by Helena; in the middle is the Dome of the Assumption [*i. e.* the Ascension]. The church is in ruins, but the place is highly reverenced by the Christians. On the Mount of Olives is a karubeh [the Carob-tree], and near it a beautiful Mosk. Beneath the Mosk is a cave frequently visited by travellers. This tree is called the Karubeh of the Ten—I know not the reason of this name. This Mount of Olives is also called the Mountain of Khamer; it abounds in fruit and shade. When Saleh-ed-din conquered Jerusalem he gave this property to the Sheikh Weli-ed-din Abul Abbas Ahmed, &c., and to the Sheikh Abul Hassan Ali, &c., and their families. The deed of grant is dated the 17th of Zilhajeh, A. H. 584 (January, A. D. 1206).

§ xxxix. *The Tomb of Miryam.*—This is in the Church named Jesmanye [Gethsemane], at the foot of the Mount of Olives, outside the Gate of the Tribes. This place is frequently visited by pilgrims, Moslem and Christian. The Church was built by Helena, mother of Constantine. When Omar conquered Jerusalem, he passed by the Church of Mary situated in the valley, and offered there two prayers. He afterwards repented, remembering the word of the Prophet, who said that this valley is one of the Valleys of Jehennom. "What occasion," said Omar, "had I to pray in the Valley of Jehennom?" According to Kaab, he said "Go not to the Church of Mary which is at Jerusalem," that is the Church of Jesmanye. In the Church of the Mount are two columns of wonderful workmanship. Near the Tomb of Mary, in the Valley of Jehennom, is a Dome built by the Greeks, called by the people the Mound of Pharaoh, at which they throw stones. Near it, at the foot of the mountain, is another Dome of stone, named Kufyeh, after the wife of Pharaoh. It is said that the first of these is the Tomb of Zachariah, and the second that of John. I have read in some learned writings that Zachariah and John were buried on Mount Olivet, in the Tombs of the Prophets. Others say that their sepulchres are at Sabtye, near Neblûs, others at Damascus. God knows best how it is!

§ xl. *Ez-Zahara.*—This is the valley west of the Mount of Olives. Ibrahim, son of Abû Abbas, says that this valley is described in the Koran by the word Zahara. In the traditions of Ibn Omar it is related that the land of judgment is called Zahara, which is properly "a plain." Travellers quicken their pace to get out of it, and never sleep there. This Valley is without the city on the north. There are graves of Mohammedans.

§ xli. *The Cave Edhemieneh.*—It is beneath the Mount of Tombs in a wonderful rock. The Tombs of Zahara are above, so that, should the rock be bored, one would come from the tombs to the oratory Edhemiene (of the Fanatics); but the distance is great and the rock of enormous thickness, so that it may here be said that the dead are above the living, and I have seen it with my eyes. This oratory was formed by the Emir Menjek, prefect of Syria. There are tombs of many pious persons of distinction.

§ xlii. *The Cotton Grotto.*—Opposite the Zahara on the south, under the northern wall of the city, is a large oblong cave named the Cotton Grotto; which some say extends as far as beneath the Sakhrah.

§ xliii. *Graveyards without Jerusalem.*—The Tombs of the Gate of Mercy, near the eastern wall of the Mosk above the Valley Jehennom, preferred to all others as being the nearest to the Mosk. The Sepulchral Chapel on the north was built by the Emir Kansu El-Badawi, Governor of Syria, when he visited Jerusalem, which he quitted in the year 892 (A. D. 1514). He finished the building in 895 (A. D. 1517). The Tombs of Ez-Zahara, of which I have spoken above, on the north of the city. The Tombs of the Martyrs, near the preceding on the east [?]: few persons are buried there. The Tombs of Mamilla, without the city on the west: these are the largest of all. The name Mamilla seems to be corrupted from the words "Ma-min-ullah" (What is from God!), or as others think, from "Babullah," (the Gate of God). The Jews call it Beit-Mollo, the Christians, Babila; the common name is Mamilla.

The Kalenderien Tombs. In the middle is an oratory known as Kalenderieh, in which are great buildings, and this oratory was a Greek Church. It is known as the Red Convent, and the Christians believe in it. Sheikh Ibrahim Kalenderi there collected the poor Kalenders [a sect of fanatical Fakhirs], in the time of Dame Tonshok, daughter of Abd-ullah El-Mozaffer, who built the great institution known by the name of the House of the Dame Tonshok, and the Dar-el-akba near the Gate of the Inspector. By her liberality Sheikh Ibrahim built this Convent in 794 (A. D. 1416), but it is in ruins since it fell in 893 (A. D. 1515). There are seen the Tombs of the most illustrious personages of Jerusalem.

The Kebkebian Tombs, near the Turbet Mamilla. It is a building solidly constructed, raised by the Emir Ala-ed-din Aidi Ghadi, son of Abdullah el-Kebkebi, who is there buried. He died in 688 (A. D. 1310).

CHAPTER XIV.

JERUSALEM UNDER THE TURKS.

EXTRACTS FROM JOURNAL OF HENRY MAUNDREL.—1697.

BUT that which has always been the great prize contended for by the several sects, is the command and appropriation of the Holy Sepulchre, a privilege contested with so much unchristian fury and animosity, especially between the Greeks and Latins, that in disputing which party should go into it to celebrate their mass, they have sometimes proceeded to blows and wounds even at the very door of the Sepulchre, mingling their own blood with their sacrifices, an evidence of which fury the father guardian showed us in a great scar upon his arm, which he told us was the mark of a wound given him by a sturdy Greek priest in one of these unholy wars. Who can expect ever to see these holy places rescued from the hands of infidels? Or, if they should be recovered, what deplorable contests might be expected to follow about them, seeing, even in their present state of captivity, they are made the occasion of such unchristian rage and animosity?

For putting an end to these infamous quarrels, the French king interposed, by a letter to the Grand Vizier, about twelve years since, requesting him to order the Holy Sepulchre to be put into the hands of the Latins, according to the tenor of the capitulation made in the year 1673, the consequence of which letter, and of other instances made by the French king, was that the Holy Sepulchre was appropriated to the Latins. This was not accomplished till the year

JERUSALEM UNDER THE CRUSADERS.

WATERS.

A Lacus Germani—Lower Gihon.
B Lacus Patriarchæ—Upper Gihon.
C Lacus Patriarchæ interior—Hezekiah's Pool.
D Probatica Piscina—Bethesda.
E Piscina a Francis inventa, or Piscina Grandis Valde.
F Piscina ad latus Templi.
G Piscina ad latus Templi, exterior.
H Fons Siloe.
I Natatoria Siloe.
J Puteus Jacobi—detectus a Germano.
K Fons Draconis—Virgin's Fount.

CHURCHES AND APPENDAGES.

1 Monasterium Surianorium.
2 Monasterium et Ecclesia ascensionis.
3 Ecclesia St. Pelagii.
4 Ecclesia Pater Noster.
5 Ecclesia Dei Genetricis Mariæ.
6 Capella Gethsemane.
7 Monasterium de Valle Josephat.
8 Ecclesia Salvatoris (St. Saviour?)
9 Turris Josephat.
10 Capella St. Jacobi.
11 Uzziah's Sepulchre, near to which was also the Church De Leon.
12 Ecclesia Gallicantus.
13 Ecclesia Sionis.
14 Ecclesia St. Petri.
15 Church Holy Ghost—Cœnaculum, or House of Caiaphas.
16 Pretorium Pilati.
17 Ecclesia Martyris Procopii, or House of Annas.
18 Bridge and Tree of Judas.
19 Carnariarum Leonis—Mamilla or Babilla.
20 Ecclesia St. Stephani (?)
21 St. Stephen's Stables.
22 Templum Domini.
23 Capella in honorem St. Jacobi.
24 Templum Salomonis (domus regia Francorum).
25 Domus Templi seu officiane Fratrum Militæ Templi.
26 Ecclesia St. Mariæ.
27 Ecclesia Cunabuli Jesu. The Temple of St. Simeon was either identical with this or immediately contiguous.
28 Equitia Salomonis (below).
29 Porta Speciosa.
30 Portis Douleureuses.
31 Monstier le Repons.
32 Pretorium.
33 Ecclesia St. Sepulchri.
34 Ecclesia Mariæ Majoris. Adjoining this Church was the Hostel of Charlemagne, the Church of St. John the Apostle, the Church of the Holy Trinity, and the Baptistery
35 Ecclesia St. Johannis Baptisti.
36 Ecclesia Mariæ de Latina.
37 Ecclesia Mariæ Magdalene, seu Mariæ Parvæ.
38 Claustrum Dominorum St. Sepulchri.
39 Changes des Suriens.
Syrian Church of St. Mark.
40 Ecclesia St. Charitonis.
41 Dyeing Establishment.
42 Castle of the Pisans—Tower of Hippicus.
43 Cœnobium—St. Saba.
44 Church of St. Zion—St. Zion's Place.
45 Church of St. Simeon.
46 Ecclesia St. Jacobi Minoris.
47 Ecclesia St. Jacobi Majoris.
Church of St. Thomas midway between the two preceding.
48 Ecclesia St. Petri ad Vincula.
49 Monstier St. Martin.
50 Ecclesia St. Stephani (?)
51 Ecclesia St. Petri.
52 Ecclesia St. Johannis.
53 Ecclesia St. Mariæ Magdalene.
59 Ecclesia St. Annæ.
60 Dungeon of Jeremiah.
61 Zenodochium of Dame Tonshok, afterwards called Hospital of St. Helena.
62 Place of Stephen's Martyrdom.
63 Viri Galilæi.
The Church or Convent of the Cross is one mile west of the city.
The Church of St. Zebedee was also one mile distant—direction not stated.

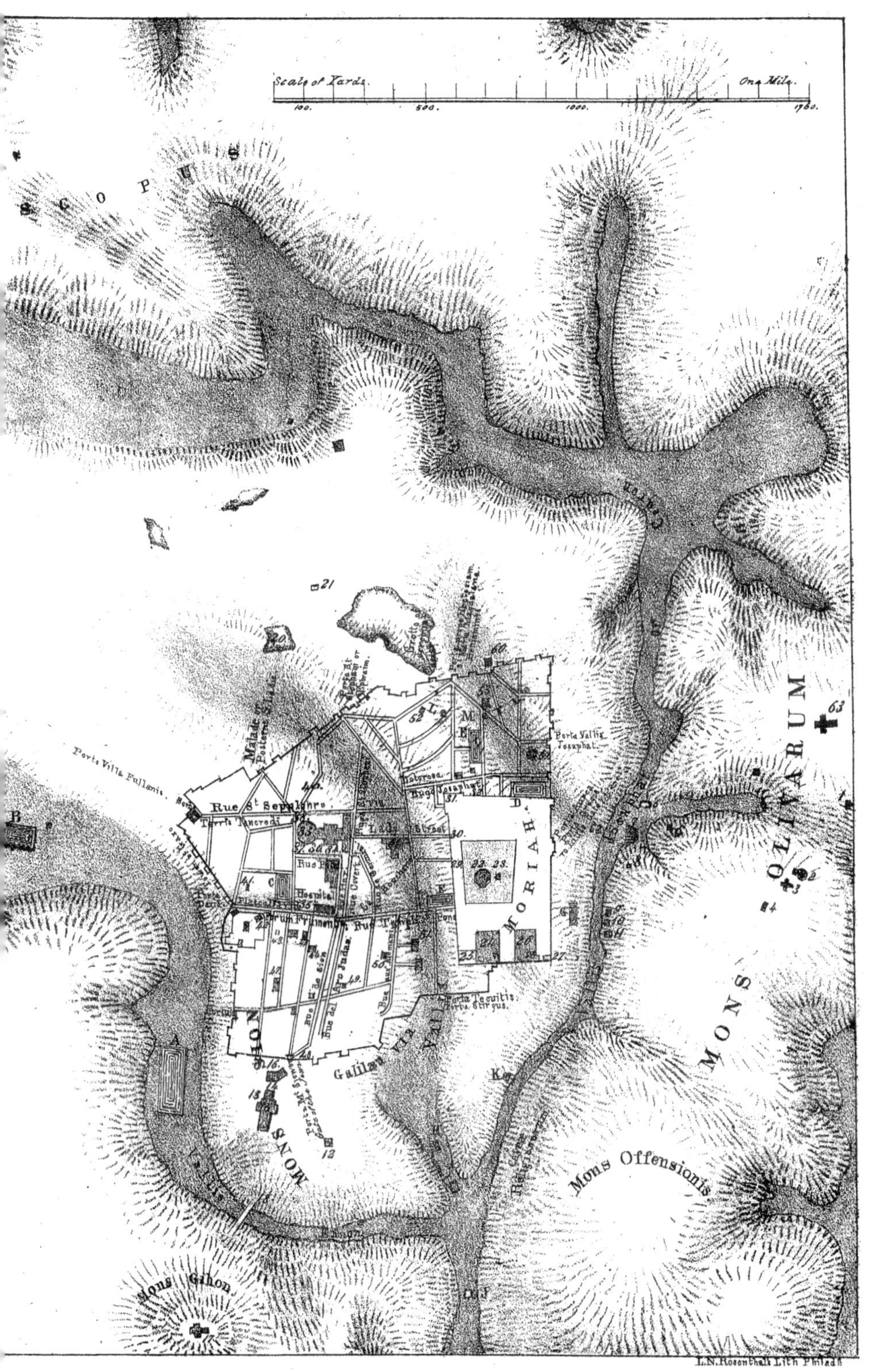

L.N. Rosenthal's Lith Philada

JERUSALEM.
Under the Crusaders.

1690, they alone having the privilege to say mass in it; and though it be permitted to Christians of all nations to go into it for their private devotions, yet none may solemnize any public office of religion there but the Latins.

The daily employment of these recluses is to trim the lamps, and to make devotional visits and processions to the several sanctuaries in the Church. Thus they spend their time, many of them for four or six years together; nay, so far are some transported with the pleasing contemplations in which they here entertain themselves, that they will never come out to their dying day, *burying themselves* (as it were) *alive in our Lord's grave.*

The Latins, of whom there are always about ten or twelve residing at the Church, with a president over them, make every day a solemn procession, with tapers and crucifixes and other processionary solemnities, to the several sanctuaries, singing at every one of them a Latin hymn relating to the subject of each place. The Latins being more polite and exact in their functions than the other monks here residing, and also our conversation being chiefly with them, I will only describe their ceremonies, without taking notice of what was done by others, which did not so much come under our observation.

Their ceremony begins on Good Friday night, which is called by them the *nox tenebrosa,* and is observed with such an extraordinary solemnity that I cannot omit to give a particular description of it.

As soon as it grew dusk, all the friars and pilgrims were convened in the chapel of the apparition (which is a small oratory on the north side of the holy grave adjoining to the apartments of the Latins), in order to go in a procession round the church; but, before they set out, one of the friars preached a sermon in Italian in that chapel. He began his discourse thus: "*In questa notte tenebrosa,*" &c., at which words all the candles were instantly put out, to yield to a livelier image of the occasion; and so we were held by the preacher for near half an hour, very much in the dark. Sermon being ended, every person present had a large lighted taper put into his hands, as if it were to make amends for the former darkness; and the crucifixes and other utensils were disposed in order for beginning the procession. Amongst the other crucifixes, there was one of a very large size, which bore upon it the image of our Lord as big as the life. The image was fastened to it with great nails, crowned with thorns, besmeared with blood; and so exquisitely was it formed, that it represented in a very lively manner the lamentable spectacle of our Lord's body as it hung upon the cross. This figure was carried all along in the head of the procession, after which the company followed to all the sanctuaries in the church, singing their appointed hymn at every one.

The first place they visited was that of the Pillar of Flagellation, a large piece of which is kept in a little cell just at the door of the Chapel of the Apparition. There they sung their proper hymn; and another friar entertained the company with a sermon in Spanish, touching the scourging of our Lord.

From hence they proceeded in solemn order to the prison of Christ, where they pretend he was secured whilst the soldiers made things ready for his crucifixion. Here, likewise, they sung their hymn, and a third friar preached in French. From the prison they went to the altar of the Division of Christ's Garments, where they only sung their hymn, without adding any sermon. Having done here, they advanced to the Chapel of the Derision, at which, after their hymn, they had a fourth sermon (as I remember) in French.

From this place they went up to Calvary, leaving their shoes at the bottom of the stairs. Here are two altars to be visited, one where our Lord is supposed to have been nailed to his cross, another where his cross was erected. At the former of these they laid down the great crucifix (which I but now described) upon the floor, and acted a kind of resemblance of Christ's being nailed to the cross; and after the hymn one of the friars preached another sermon in Spanish upon the crucifixion.

From hence they removed to the adjoining altar, where the cross is supposed to have been erected, bearing the image of our Lord's body. At this altar is a hole in the natural rock, said to be the very same individual one in which the foot of our Lord's cross stood. Here they set up their cross, with the bloody crucified image upon it; and, leaving it in that posture, they first sung their hymn, and then the father guardian, sitting in a chair before it, preached a passion sermon in Italian.

At about one yard and a half distance from the hole in which the foot of the cross was fixed, is seen that memorable cleft in the rock, said to have been made by the earthquake which happened at the suffering of the God of Nature, when (as St. Matthew witnesseth*) "The rocks rent, and the very graves were opened." This cleft, as to what now appears of it, is about a span wide at its upper part, and two deep, after which it closes; but it opens again below, as you may see in another chapel contiguous to the side of Calvary, and runs down to an unknown depth in the earth. That this rent was made by the earthquake that happened at our Lord's passion, there is only tradition to prove; but that it is a natural and genuine breach, and not counterfeited by any art, the sense and reason of every one that sees it may convince him; for the sides of it fit like two tallies to each other, and yet it runs in such intricate windings as cannot well be counterfeited by art, nor arrived at by any instruments.

The ceremony of the passion being over, and the guardian's sermon ended, two friars, personating the one Joseph of Arimathea, the other Nicodemus, approached the cross, and, with a most solemn and concerned air, both of respect and behavior, drew out the great nails, and took down the feigned body from the cross. It was an effigy so contrived that its limbs were soft and flexible, as if they had been real flesh; and nothing could be more surprising than to see the two pretended mourners bend down the arms, which were before extended, and dispose them upon the trunk in such a manner as is usual in corpses.

The body being taken down from the cross, was received in a fair

* Matt. xxvii. 51.

long winding-sheet, and carried down from Calvary, the whole com pany attending as before, to the Stone of Unction. This is taken for the very place where the precious body of our Lord was anointed and prepared for the burial. Here they laid down their imaginary corpse, and casting over it several sweet powders and spices, wrapped it up in the winding-sheet. Whilst this was doing they sung their proper hymn; and afterwards one of the friars preached, in Arabic, a funeral sermon.

These obsequies being finished, they carried off their fancied corpse, and laid it in the Sepulchre, shutting up the door till Easter morning; and now, after so many sermons and so long, not to say tedious, a ceremony, it may well be imagined that the weariness of the congregation, as well as the hour of the night, made it needful to go to rest.

Sunday, March 28.—On Easter morning the Sepulchre was again set open very early. The clouds of the former morning were cleared up, and the friars put on a face of joy and serenity, as if it had been the real juncture of our Lord's resurrection; nor, doubtless, was this joy feigned, whatever their mourning might be, this being the day in which their Lenten discipline expired, and they were come to a full belly again.

Coming to the Church of the Holy Sepulchre, we found it crowded with a numerous and distracted mob, making a hideous clamor, very unfit for that sacred place, and better becoming Bacchanals than Christians. Getting with some struggle through the crowd, we went up into the gallery on that side of the church next the Latin Convent, whence we could discern all that passed in this religious frenzy.

They began their disorders by running round the Holy Sepulchre with all their might and swiftness, crying out, as they went,* "Huia!" which signifies "This is he," or "This is it," an expression by which they assert the verity of the Christian

* The words they utter now are—God save the Sultan—this is the tomb of our Saviour.

religion. After they had, by these vertiginous circulations and clamors, turned their heads and inflamed their madness, they began to act the most antic tricks and postures, in a thousand shapes of distraction. Sometimes they dragged one another along the floor all around the Sepulchre; sometimes they set one man upright on another's shoulders, and in this posture marched around; sometimes they took men with their heels upward, and hurried them about in such an indecent manner as to expose their nudities; sometimes they tumbled around the Sepulchre after the manner of tumblers on the stage. In a word, nothing can be imagined more rude or extravagant than what was acted upon this occasion. In this tumultuous, frantic humor they continued from twelve till four o'clock: the reason of which delay was because of a suit that was then in debate before the Cadi, betwixt the Greeks and Armenians, the former endeavoring to exclude the latter from having any share in this miracle. Both parties having expended, as I was informed, five thousand dollars between them in this foolish controversy. The cadi at last gave sentence that they should enter the Holy Sepulchre together, as had been usual at former times. Sentence being thus given, at four o'clock both nations went on with their ceremony. The Greeks first set out in a procession around the Holy Sepulchre, and, immediately at their heels, followed the Armenians. In this order they compassed the Holy Sepulchre thrice, having produced all their gallantry of standards, streamers, crucifixes, and embroidered habits, upon this occasion.

Towards the end of this procession there was a pigeon came fluttering into the cupola over the Sepulchre, at sight of which there was a greater shout and clamor than before. This bird, the Latins told us, was purposely let fly by the Greeks, to deceive the people into an opinion that it was a visible descent of the Holy Ghost.

The procession being over, the suffragan of the Greek Patriarch (he being himself at Constantinople), and the principal Armenian bishop, approached to the door of the Sepulchre, and cutting the string with which it is fastened and sealed, entered in, shutting the door after them, all the candles and lamps within having been before extinguished, in the presence of the Turks and other witnesses. The exclamations were doubled as the miracle drew nearer to its accomplishment, and the people pressed with such vehemence towards the door of the Sepulchre, that it was not in the power of the Turks set to guard it, with the severest drubs, to keep them off. The cause of their pressing in this manner is the great desire they have to light their candles at the holy flame as soon as it is first brought out of the Sepulchre, it being esteemed the most sacred and pure, as coming immediately from heaven.

The two miracle-mongers had not been above a minute in the Holy Sepulchre, when the glimmering of the holy fire was seen, or imagined to appear, through some chinks of the door; and certainly Bedlam itself never saw such an unruly transport as was produced in the mob at this sight. Immediately after, out came the two priests, with blazing torches in their hands, which they held up at the door of the Sepulchre, while the people thronged about with inexpressible ardor, every one striving to obtain a part of the first and purest flame. The Turks, in the mean time, with huge clubs, laid on them without mercy; but all this could not repel them, the excess of their transport making them insensible to pain. Those that got the fire, applied it immediately to their beards, faces, and bosoms, pretending that it would not burn like an earthly flame. But I plainly saw that none of them could endure this experiment long enough to made good that pretension. So many hands being employed, you may be sure it could not be long before innumerable tapers were lighted. The whole Church, galleries, and every place seemed instantly to be in a flame, and with this illumination the ceremony ended.

It must be owned that those two within the sepulchre performed their part with great quickness and dexterity; but the behavior of the rabble without very much discredited the miracle. The Latins take a great deal of pains to expose this ceremony, as a most shameful imposture and a scandal to the Christian religion; perhaps out of envy that others should be masters of so gainful a business. But the Greeks and Armenians pin their faith upon it, and make their pilgrimage chiefly upon this motive. And it is the deplorable unhappiness of their priests, that having acted the cheat so long already, they are forced now to stand to it for fear of endangering the apostasy of their people.

Going out of the church after the riot was over, we saw several people gathered about the Stone of Unction, who, having got a good store of candles lighted with the holy fire, were employed in daubing pieces of linen with the wicks of them and the melting wax, which pieces of linen were designed for winding-sheets; and it is the opinion of these poor people, that if they can but have the happiness to be buried in a shroud smutted with this celestial fire, it will certainly secure them from the flames of hell.

Upon this finishing day, and the night following, the Turks allow free admittance for all people, without demanding any fee for entrance as at other times, calling it a day of charity. By this promiscuous license, they let in not only the poor, but, as I was told, the lewd and vicious also, who come hither to get convenient opportunity for prostitution, profaning the holy places in such manner (as it is said) that they were not worse defiled even when the heathens here celebrated their Aphrodisia.

CHAPTER XV.

CLIMATE AND PRODUCTIONS OF JERUSALEM AND VICINITY.

"A delightsome land, saith the Lord of Hosts."

PROPERLY speaking, there are but two seasons in Palestine at the present time—and indeed the Scriptures mention no others—"winter and summer, cold and heat, seed-time and harvest," or wet and dry. As soon as the winter rains set in, all nature becomes re-animated, and the parched surface of the earth is "decked in living green;" but it is not till after the vernal equinox that it becomes arrayed in its gaudiest floral mantle. Then "the winter is past, the rain is over and gone, the flowers appear on the earth, the time of the singing of birds is come; and the voice of the turtle is heard in the land." The splendor of a Syrian sky, and the gorgeous effulgence of the setting rays on its rainless summer clouds, have been greatly extolled by travellers; but if not excelled in brilliancy by the sky of the United States, it is certainly surpassed in variety and softness of hue. The transparency of its atmosphere, however, is justly proverbial; and the occasional influence of this characteristic property, in bringing up distant objects apparently to one's immediate vicinity, is quite bewildering, and occasions the traveller anxiously approaching a desired locality a disappointment similar to that resulting from the *mirage*—making the heart sick by hope deferred.

Yet there is occasionally a kind of dry mist or haziness, like smoke, that renders the vision of distant objects very indistinct and unsatisfactory—in appearance not unlike the "Indian Summer" of the United States.

The isothermal line is much higher in the old than in the new world: consequently this region, though lying in the same parallels of latitude as those embraced between Washington City and New Orleans, its climate is materially warmer, and in consequence of the diminished amount of rain, rivers once figuring very conspicuously upon its map, now no longer exist.

Elevation of temperature, diminution of humidity and verdure (and the consequent electrical changes), are all the necessary sequents of this partial suspension of the latter rains.

The fruitful seasons promised to the Israelites by Jehovah, were all suspended upon obedience to the terms of the covenant; for he expressly threatens to diminish, withhold, or "turn to dust and powder" these fructifying showers on disobedience, and it would seem that not only did this intimate connexion between temporal welfare and moral conduct exist under the Jewish dispensation, but is also to be the rule of the incoming millennial dispensation! (And it shall be that whoso will not come up of all the families of the earth unto Jerusalem, to worship the King, the Lord of Hosts, even upon them shall be no rain: Zech. xiv. 17.) And often has the threat been executed to a greater or less extent in times of defection: "He turneth rivers into a wilderness, and the water springs into dry ground: a fruitful land into barrenness for the wickedness of them that dwell therein." Therefore the showers have been withholden, and there hath been no latter rain," says Jeremiah (iii. 3). At one time they were entirely withheld in judgment for the space of three years and six months continuously: at other times only for a few months; and sometimes very partially, and specially, as recorded by the prophet Amos (iv. 7), "I have withholden the rain from you, says the Lord, when there were yet three months to the harvest; and I caused it to rain upon one city; and caused it not to rain upon another city; one piece was rained upon, and the piece whereupon it rained not withered; so two or three cities wandered to one city to drink water." Most of these instances of the cessation or paucity of the showers of heaven were manifestly the immediate result of Divine infliction. But although it may appear that the present deficiency of rain is ascribed to natural causes, yet these natural agencies being brought about by Divine causation, the results are no less referable to the same source. After the destruction of Jerusalem by Titus, and the dispersion of the few remaining Jews, the tenure of property in Palestine became so very insecure and uncertain that systematic agriculture was entirely neglected. The marauding incursions of the predatory bands of Saracens, Persians, Mamelukes, and Turks, with innumerable herds of camels, goats, horses, and cattle of every description, like so many swarms of destroying locusts soon denuded the country of verdure, and hence the failure of summer clouds—for there exists between the clouds of heaven and the verdure of earth a reciprocal reaction, founded upon the most intimate meteorological connexion—the production of clouds and rain being greatly promoted by trees and herbage. The continuous existence of the one necessarily implies the presence of the other: and the absence of the one necessitates the diminution of the other.

If then the present sterility of Palestine be chargeable to the absence of summer rains, or of more extensive and copious fall, winter, and spring rains, on account of its denuded condition, and it should again be clothed in verdure, by cultivating in the first place such trees, grains, and herbs as need but little moisture, and can be successfully cultivated in the present condition of the country; it requires no prophet to foretell that the genial influences of earlier and later, if not of summer rains, would soon be realized.

Absorption of the rain by the ground, would be greatly facilitated, were it once protected from the scorching rays of the sun, by such a mantle of foliage and herbage; and evaporation being also greatly checked, fountains would again spring forth in places where they have long since disappeared. Such a result too would be in exact accordance with the arrangements of the Divine economy—both natural and revealed—even though it be effectuated by chemical and electro-magnetic influences. Many model orchards, farms, and gardens have lately been established in Palestine—like so many little oases in the desert—and the result already justifies the conjecture that this is the Divinely appointed means of restoring to the Holy Land the fructifying influence of the long-suppressed rains, and exhausted fountains and depths,* at least so far as to justify a partial return of the Jews—the rightful proprietors of the land. But that we are to expect the direct *Divine* interposition, in behalf of the land, at a later period, is unquestionable.

It will be seen by reference to the appended pluviometrical table that the total annual average fall of rain at Jerusalem, is 56.5 inches; but if the last column be discarded from the calculation, the average would be 61.6, and if an average be formed from the first five columns only, it mounts up nearly to 70 inches. No appreciable portion of this rain falls in June, July, August, or September; and very little either in May or October—more than nine-tenths of it falling in December, January, February, and March, and more copiously in February than any other month. The greatest amount of rain tabled in any year during the period of observation is 85 inches, which fell in the season of 1850–51; the smallest, that of 1853–54, 26.9 inches; but this amount is so small compared with any other year, that there is good reason to question the accuracy of this column. The average annual fall of rain throughout the United States is about 45 inches; and perhaps in no one year has so great an amount of rain fallen as in Palestine during the winter of 1850. But in California the rain averages only about 20 inches per annum.

* Nothing is better established than the fact that the fountains and streams of all wooded countries diminish, and in many instances entirely disappear, on clearing the forests and cultivating the ground. It was observed, both by Humboldt and Baussingolt, that the waters of Lake Tacariga were considerably diminished by the denudation of the surrounding country; and that they were restored to their former level by the regrowth of forests. The Jordan was no doubt decreased somewhat by the denudation of the forests about its sources, to supply Egypt with timber and fuel.

It is thus perceived that the rains are about one-fourth more abundant in Palestine than in the Atlantic portion of the United States, and two and a half times more abundant than in California, even at the lowest estimate. The rain sometimes falls continuously for several days very gently, but generally more hastily, and at the rate of half a dozen or a dozen or two showers per day, and that too when but little is expected. But each spell of rain or succession of showers is sure to be succeeded by several days of fine, bright weather—"clear shining after rain." And although the rainy season is not marked by an entire cessation of rain at any time, producing as decided an interval as might be supposed from the works of occasional travellers; yet an interregnum of several weeks' dry weather generally occurs between the middle of December and the middle of February, somewhat distinguishing the "former rains" of the season from the latter.

The greatest range of the thermometer in any one year of the period through which the observations extended was 52°, and the widest during the whole period 54°. The highest elevation of the mercury 92°, and the lowest 38°, though 143° in the sun on one occasion; and, under favorable exposure, immediately before sunrise on one occasion, was only about 28°. Pellicles of ice, an eighth of an inch in thickness, remained in the shade the whole day. The mean annual average of temperature is 66.5°, while that of Boston is 49°, Philadelphia 52°, Washington 53°, New Orleans 62°, and San Francisco, California, 56°. July and August are the hottest months, but June and September are nearly as warm. January is decidedly the coldest month in the year. The climate is remarkably uniform—though an opposite opinion might very naturally be drawn, when the relative positions of the snow-capped Lebanon, and the burning desert of Arabia, are considered. The thermometric variation in the same latitude on the Atlantic coast of the United States is nearly twice as great. California and the peninsula of Florida are the only portions of the United States through which the isothermal line of Jerusalem passes. In point of temperature and periodic seasons of rain, there is the closest analogy between Palestine and California.

The sun-stroke would appear not to be as fatal as it once was, judging from the Scripture allusions to it; though I have known very injurious consequences to result from exposure to the full blaze of a mid-day sun, on the part of strangers. Sleeping beneath the rays of a full moon is also supposed to be very prejudicial to health.

CALENDAR OF THE VEGETABLE KINGDOM FOR JERUSALEM AND THE SURROUNDING COUNTRY.

In giving a brief synoptical view of the vegetable productions of Palestine, it will be most expedient, as it also is most natural, to exhibit the subject in the order of its development by nature—ploughing, sowing, and reaping—and open the calendar with the usual commencement of the rainy season, which happens also to begin with the Jewish civil year. The parching drought of summer having prevailed for more than half the year, the whole vegetable kingdom appears to be held in durance and abeyance, until the windows of heaven are once more opened, and the reviving showers begin to fall about the period of the autumnal equinox. The Feast of Tabernacles or ingathering of crops, at the end of the year (Ex. xxiii. 15, 16), was celebrated on the 15th Tizri (Sept.), at the end of the year.

The annual routine of vegetation being now completed, and the husbandman having reaped all that he has sown, or indeed can sow, without the mollifying influence of rain to restore the cracked and indurated earth, he anxiously awaits the first shower, that he may lay the foundation of another series of crops. Having gone to the banks of the river Jordan, and selected a bifurcated limb, with such crooks and proportions that one prong may serve as a beam, another as a handle, and the remainder as a stock for the attachment of a piece of iron, he hitches to this primitive plough a cow and a donkey, and stirs up the soil—if not as effectually, at least as rapidly as an "unclean" pig would do.

October.—Under favoring circumstances much wheat and barley are sown this month. All the ordinary garden esculents are also committed to the earth, as well as sesame, chickpea, and other lentiles.

The grape season is still well maintained, but pomegranates are becoming scarce. Olive-trees threshed for the last berries. Pistachio nuts make their appearance in the bazaars. If the rains have set in early, a few flowers begin to appear towards the close of the month: and radishes, lettuce, and other vegetables of rapid growth are already sufficiently matured for use. The seed that was sown in the spring may now be gathered. The cotton crop is now fully matured. The species of cotton heretofore cultivated in Palestine, has not commanded a good price abroad; but Mr. Smith, the able and enterprising American Consul at Beirût, having made a large experiment with American seed, near Jaffa and Tyre, succeeded in raising an article of excellent staple, which, though its production only cost 3½ pence per pound, readily brought one shilling in London. Fig leaves begin to blacken and fall.

November.—The principal sowing of wheat and barley is made in this month. Deciduous trees are now generally denuded. Such dates as have matured are now collected; but it is only on the plains that they attain to much perfection. A few olives still gleaned. The vintage terminates this month. The grapes not heretofore consumed as an article of diet, or converted into raisins, are trodden in the wine-press, and set fermenting in the vat for wine or vinegar. Some of the expressed juice, however, instead of being thus appropriated, is boiled down to the consistence of molasses, under the name of *dibs* or *dibes*, and is far superior to any kind of sugar-cane treacle. The raisins, as well as figs, are rather indifferently cured, and are mainly consigned to the still by the Jews and Christians, and converted into arrak, and alcohol of no mean *bead*—but great quantities of them are consumed as a cheap and wholesome article of diet. Although Ichabod is evidently written upon Eshcol, yet it still produces most delicious grapes, particularly a seedless species, very much sought after by housekeepers. The vines are generally permitted to lie upon the ground in a state of the utmost neglect, without the slightest bracing or training; but in some of the vineyards of Eshcol, a bracing is most effectually accomplished by tying together the tops of three or four neighboring vines.

December.—The earth fully clothed with rich verdure. Wheat and barley still sown, also various kinds of pulse. Sugar-cane in market. Cauliflowers, cabbages, radishes, lettuce, lentiles, &c.

Ploughing still continues at intervals.

January.—Last sowing of wheat and barley. Last roasting ears of American maize—being the third successive crop from the same piece of ground! A few trees in leaf. Beans in bloom. The almond-tree blossoms, and, in rapid succession, the apricot, peach, and plum.

Cauliflowers, cabbages, &c. Oranges, lemons, citrons, and limes. New leaves on the olive-tree. Doura planted. The mandrake in bloom—also the wormwood—absinthium, santoreium judaicum.

This is midwinter, and fire becomes indispensable to the comfort and health of the Frank population of the city; though the natives build no fires, for merely warming themselves (except, perhaps, a few exposed out-door shopkeepers), contenting themselves throughout the winter with additional clothing.* Charcoal is the principal fuel made use of for domestic culinary purposes. But many thousand bundles of sticks and brush are also consumed: both are brought from Hebron and the banks of the Jordan, eighteen or twenty miles

* There is not in all Jerusalem a single fire-place, and perhaps not half a dozen chimneys, even to the bakeries and soap manufactories. A few stoves, however, have been introduced amongst a few Frank families residing there as consuls, missionaries, &c. But the cooking and warming of the natives is almost exclusively done by means of a few pieces of charcoal burnt in a pile of ashes, in a little furnace made of clay and straw, about the capacity of two gallons.

distant. In the large baking establishments, the only fuel used is green thorns, brushwood, and thistles, in bunches the size of sage, brought from a considerable distance on donkeys, and great is "the crackling of thorns under the pots." Lime-kilns are built in the midst of fields that abound in thorns, thistles, and rank weeds and grasses; which are dug up, and thrown into the furnace, through a narrow aperture—and such is the disposition of much of "the grass which to-day is, and to-morrow is cast into the oven,"—for mountain-like piles of it are required for these various purposes. All the village bakeries are heated by the excrement of cows and camels. It is to be hoped that the late discovery of good coal in Mount Lebanon, will lead to great improvement in the social condition of all Syria.

February.—Barley may still be sown. Snap-beans begin to mature sufficiently for table use. Apple-trees in bloom.

Hyacinths, daffodils, tulips, ranunculuses, lilies, narcissus, geraniums, scarlet poppies, anemones, daisies, and many other familiar flowers in bloom, spreading themselves over the country in rich carpets; besides vast numbers of unknown herbs, springing everywhere in the fields. Cauliflowers, onions, carrots, beets, radishes, &c. Oranges, &c., &c.

March.—Beans and peas in market. Trees all in full leaf. Pear-trees in bloom—also the apple-tree, palm, and black-thorn.

Sage, thyme, and other aromatics. Various kinds of mint. Both fruit and flowers on orange and lemon-trees. The fig-tree blossoms. Date-palm in flower.

Cauliflowers now in their highest state of perfection, equal to the best English or American.

The pod of the carob-tree nearly ripe—very much like the honey-shuck.* The crop of celery sown in July now perfected. Rue, parsley, hyssop, leeks, onions, garlic, &c.

* This carob fruit is sometimes called the "food of John the Baptist;" and also supposed to have been the *husks* on which the Prodigal Son sustained himself in his direful extremity!!

The flowers of last month are still to be found either in the valleys or mountains.

April.—Wheat and barley harvest already commenced on the plains of the Jordan, if the rains have not been more than usually protracted. Sugar-cane set. Grass very rank, and all vegetation very luxuriant.

Horses are now universally tethered in the green barley fields, to enjoy uninterruptedly, for several weeks, the "spring grazing."

Beans, onions, peas, artichokes, lettuce, cucumbers, a species of onion much resembling a large turnip, very acrid and pungent when raw, but mild and edible when well boiled. The uncultivated and unimproved Arab potato is now seen in great abundance.

Lavender, rosemary, &c. White mulberry ripe. Cistus roseus in bloom—the supposed rose of Sharon. Oleander in bloom.

Great variety and numbers of plants—one of them entirely unknown, has several different kinds of flowers on it. The fields abound in the richest carpets of brilliant flowers—that luxuriate in the frequent alternations of sun and shower. Early roasting ears. First ripe apricots.

May.—Harvest in progress both on the mountains and in the valleys. Almonds ripening. Apples in market, but very inferior, as all kinds are throughout Syria. The "mandrakes" give forth a smell and ripen their fruit. Many vegetables still sown; and vegetate without rain—as pumpkins and various kinds of squashes. Many esculents are raised as well at the conclusion of the rainy season as at the commencement. Vegetation having attained its maximum, now begins rapidly to decline for want of rain.

Late in the month watermelons, muskmelons, cantelopes, &c., are in market; but generally only from the plains. The Sultan is supplied with those grown upon the shores of Lake Tiberias, pronounced the finest in the world. Cucumbers, onions, tomatoes, potatoes, maize. Oleanders still in bloom. Walnuts and blackberries ripe. First crop of sycamore figs—the jimaze or mulberry fig—for such is the import of its Greek name.

June.—Threshing still continues. Figs in market, cherries, plums, damascenes, now abundant. Cedar berries. Herbage becoming parched, the nomad Arabs begin to move northward with their flocks. The Fellahin, with a view of improving the quality, and hastening the process of maturation, are observed touching the fig with an oiled rag, affixed to the extremity of a long pole. Olives, almonds, figs, quinces, plantain fruit, and bananas: a few grapes ripe also. Licorice-plant and dandelion. Egg-plant in great perfection and abundance; will continue in market for months. Doum fruit from Jericho. Henna gathered to dye the hands, by way of checking perspiration, as well as beautifying them.

The season of making rose-water, by distilling the fragrant petals from "Wadi el Word" (Valley of Roses), and exposing the jars in the sun.

July.—Abundant supply of pears, nectarines, peaches, grapes, melons, potatoes, tomatoes, egg-plants, &c. The Indian fig, prickly pear, or cactus fruit, now ripe, and largely consumed. The trunk of the Jerusalem variety is about as thick as the human body, and usually but little longer, generally recumbent—its oval leaf is eight or ten inches long, five or six broad, and nearly one inch thick—well studded with prickles—each leaf (with few exceptions) grows from the end or side of another, and soon becomes converted into a limb. The gaudy yellow flowers that also put forth from the edges of its mammoth leaf, produce a delicious golden-colored cucumber-shaped fruit. These leaves, if placed a yard or two apart and covered ever so slightly with earth, even in midsummer, soon take root, and form one of the most impenetrable hedges imaginable.

If the cochineal insect really thrives as well upon it as is reported, the inexhaustible supply about Jerusalem opens a wide field for an industrial enterprise of a very laudable and remunerative character—the employment of the poor Jews in Palestine. The cocooneries are in full operation this month. Fine plums, damascenes, peaches, dates, cucumbers, pumpkins, and watermelons—the latter are sometimes preserved through winter. Their seeds are also salted and preserved for eating. Various kinds of gourds likewise.

Millet, doura, linseed, and tobacco. There are several species of tobacco cultivated in Palestine—being incessantly smoked by men, women, and children; but always being suffered to run to flower, it is milder than that raised in the United States. First grapes ripe.

August.—All the fruits and vegetables of this goodly land are now mature. Figs, grapes, citrons, and pomegranates still abound. Tomatoes, egg-plants, &c., &c. Turkish corn or doura, and millet ripening. That truly rich and valuable tree, whose beautiful silvery leaf has been so long the emblem of peace—the perennially green olive of the earliest species—has now fully matured its berries, which being gathered, first by shaking, and then by beating the trees, are taken to the mill, and being ground into pulp, the "sweet oil" is extracted by pressure.

September.—Grapes, olives, pomegranates, pears, plums, citrons, peaches, tomatoes, potatoes. Cotton rapidly maturing, and hemp in bloom. Millet, doura, maize (Egyptian). Most of the lentiles are gathered within four months after planting chick-peas, lupins, beans, fenugreek. The crop of sesame, sown immediately on the removal of the barley, is now somewhat matured, but not gathered, till next month: its expressed oil is called *serage*, and is used very extensively for culinary purposes, and of late for burning—since the price of olive oil has advanced so much. The castor oil plant (palma christi), which in the United States is generally an annual, or at most a biennial plant of six feet height, is here a perennial tree twenty feet in height. Wild fennel is now matured, several species of flowers spring up through the hard desiccated earth, without a particle of moisture—and yet are very esculent.*

* There are certain plants here that seem to have the remarkable faculty of attracting moisture from the atmosphere, even when it is exceedingly arid. This phenomenon may be observed in some of the sepulchres and caves, through whose fissures minute radicles have forced their way, and may be seen at all times bespangled with myriads of minute drops of water; while not a particle is visible or in any way appreciable, elsewhere.

The grape gathering season continues a month or two longer, but by the end of this month, the earth having made an abundant return of all her varied productions, refuses all assistance from man, and makes the rains a *sine qua non* to further effort.

The foregoing calendar is by no means complete. No mention whatever has been made of many evergreens and medical plants, to which much interest attaches; such as the juniper, cedars of Lebanon, cypress, pine, tamarisk, terebinth, mistletoe; wall plants—rhubarb, aloes, datura stramonium, colocynths, squill, henbane, cucumis prophetorum, &c., &c. Nor has a complete list of vegetables been given, for any one month whatever. Mention too is only made of such as are raised without the slightest forcing or artificial irrigation. It must also be borne in mind that nearly every article mentioned in the calendar, can be had from irrigated gardens for six, eight, or ten months of the year, and many, indeed, the entire year round. The sylva of Palestine is truly meagre at this time, compared with what it was in the days of its prosperity; but even amid all of its desolation, its flora is by no means contemptible, nor its list of fruits and esculent vegetables to be carped at. Nearly every species of vegetable in common use in the United States has been successfully cultivated in Jerusalem and its immediate vicinity. But amongst all those that I introduced in the spring of 1851, none has succeeded so well as the sweet potato. Oranges, limes, and lemons of various kinds are to be had in the greatest profusion and perfection almost the entire year round, and on terms surprisingly low.

May is the great harvesting month, and the vintage extends from July to October.

The American agricultural colonists have successfully cultivated nearly every variety of American vegetables, grain, and fruits, most of which they first introduced, not only upon the low plains of Sharon near Jaffa, but at the Valley of Artos (or Etham near Bethlehem), and on the heights about Jerusalem. It is matter, however, equally of surprise and regret that the apple seems to be almost insusceptible of acclimation to that region.

The foregoing notices are intended to apply mainly to Jerusalem. Very material alterations would be required for the region of the sea-coast, and all lower districts of country, and especially for the valley of the Dead Sea, and the lower portion of the Jordan, which is quite a tropical region.

It is said that between the top of Jebl-Sannin and the lower valley of the Jordan—a distance of sixty miles, there exists almost every climate between the torrid and the frigid zone. In relation to this famous spur of the Lebanon range, it may be truthfully said, after the manner of the Arabs, that his towering head is ever crowned with a resplendent turban of snow; spring smilingly sports upon his breast; exuberant autumn reposes in his lap; and at his feet—if they really extend so far as to be laved by the Jordan and Dead Sea—ever-enduring summer revels in luxuriance.

Meteorological Tables.—The register of the weather from which the following abstract is made, although possessing no special claims to rigid accuracy, is yet sufficiently reliable for all ordinary purposes. The thermometer used is one of McAllister's best instruments, though not self-registering. During the first year of observations it was well situated beneath an out-door shelter, entirely free from all disturbing causes; but was afterwards kept in a small isolated building, which, though sufficiently well ventilated during the day, was closed at night—owing to which the sunrise temperature is always marked too high in cold weather. The coldest period is about sunrise, the warmest about noon; and sunset very fairly represents the average temperature of the twenty-four hours. The barometer was by no means a first-rate instrument; but though it might not be reliable for ascertaining heights, yet its *relative* indications are perfectly reliable. Observations made at sunrise, noon, and sunset. The rain gauge made use of was quite an ordinary instrument; and not at all favorably situated for exact measurement: preference is therefore given to the more extensive registration made at the Anglican Hospital under the superintendence of Dr. McGowan, according to Newman's gauge. The last column, however, contains the indications of the common rain gauge; but are so far below the average of Newman's pluviometer that their accuracy is by no means unquestionable.

The period of time through which the meteorological observations extend is quite remarkable for variety of weather—the deepest snow, the heaviest rain—the severest drought, the lowest depression of the mercury, and perhaps its highest elevation. It therefore affords all the elements necessary to the formation of a correct idea of the climate of Jerusalem.

Table of Average Monthly Temperatures.

Years.	January.	February.	March.	April.	May.	June.	July.	August.	September.	October.	November.	December.
	°	°	°	°	°	°	°	°	°	°	°	°
1851	....	....	....	....	....	72.8	79.8	78.2	75.	72.3	67.	53.3
1852	49.6	52.1	56.	62.2	69 6	73.8	78.	78.	74.1	76.6	62.7	55.3
1853	51.4	60.4	60.2	64.	77.6	77.3	78.	80.	80.2	74.9	61.1	52.9
1854	49.6	50.8	51.	58.1	74.1	76.9	80.8	80.9	77.3	72.9	64.3	56.6
1855	47.1	....	....	....	....	....	....	....	....	....	....	....
Average . .	49.4	54.4	55.7	61.4	73.8	75.2	79.1	79.3	77.	74.2	63.8	54.5

Average annual temperature, 66.5°.

Register of the fall of Rain at Jerusalem from 1846 *to* 1854 (*in inches*).

Months.	1846-7.	1847-8.	1848-9.	1849-50.	1850-1.	1851-2.	1852-3.	1853-4.	Average.
October	4.	4.	0.	Not registered.	0.	0.	0.	.2	1.
November	6.4	0.	.2		6.4	0.	1.8	2.3	2.
December	0.	19.	16.		33.8	15.2	9.4	3.6	14.
January	9.8	24.6	19.4		14.6	13.6	4.2	4.4	13.
February	32.8	5.8	13.2		24.	25.	4.	5.8	16.
March	6.	0.	11.8		4.	8.8	21.4	6.5	8.
April	0.	.2	0.		2.2	0.	1.2	3.6	1.
May	0.	1.4	0.		0.	2.4	2.	.5	1.
Total per annum .	59.	55.	60.6		85.	65.	44.	26.9	56.5

It must be borne in mind that the foregoing observations are applicable only to Jerusalem and its immediate vicinity: for the temperature, atmospheric pressure, and amount of rain on the low plains (and especially in the depressed valley of the Jordan), are so much greater as to change the whole vegetable calendar.*

* Those wishing farther particulars on this subject may find them by consulting the Thesis of Dr. R. Gutzlaff Barclay, Physician to the Jerusalem Mission, by whom the foregoing observations were made. This Dissertation on "The State of Medical Science in Syria" is published in the September Number of the Medico-Chirurgical Journal.

REMAINS OF JEWISH TOWER NEAR THE SERAGLIO.

CHAPTER XVI.

WALLS, GATES, TOWERS, &c.

"Is this the city which men call the perfection of beauty—the joy of the whole earth?"

JERUSALEM at this time has no cross-walls in the interior, unless the northern and western sides of the Temple enclosure may be regarded as such. The present wall of the city is about two and a half miles in circumference, and very respectable in appearance—albeit somewhat patched and piebald. It will average about forty feet in height; but in a few places is about twice that height inclusive of its symmetrical embrasures. It would appear from inscriptions on the gates that it was erected about the year 1542; and, as

REFERENCES TO MAP OF MODERN JERUSALEM.

GATES.

A St. Stephen's Gate—Bab Sitte Myriam.

B Golden Gate—closed; immediately to the left of which there is a small gateway, also closed.
C Triple Gateway—to the right is a small Saracenic doorway, and at junction of wall the double gateway—the traditional Gate of Huldah.
D Mugrabin Gate—Bab el-Mugarebeh—generally closed.
E Zion Gate—Bab en-Neby Daûd.
F Jaffa—Bab el-Khalil.
G Damascus Gate—Bab es-Sham.
H Herod's Gate—Bab ez-Zahara—permanently closed.

POOLS, ETC.

a Birket Mamilla—Upper Pool of Gihon.
b Birket es-Sultan—Lower Pool.
c Pool of Siloam—Birket Silwan taht.
d Ain Sitte Myriam.
e Birket Hammam Sitte Myriam.
f Birket el-Hijjeh.
g Pool of Hezekiah—Amygdalon.
h Bathsheba's Pool.
i Royal Cistern beneath the Temple Area.
j Birket Israel—Bethesda.
k Tanks at En-rogel.

TURKISH QUARTER.

1 Mosk of Omar—Kubbet es-Sakhrah.
2 Mosk el-Aksa.
3 Mosk Abû Bûkr.
4 Mugrabin Mosk.
5 Mart of Science.
6 Sidna Iesa—Cradle of Jesus.
7 Serai or Seraglio—site of Tower of Antonia.
8 City Castle—Tower of Hippicus in the north-east corner.
9 Melaweh Church and Mosk—situated over Cotton Megara (Cave).
10 Mahmooneh Church and Pottery.
11 St. Anne's Church.
12 French Consulate.
13 Austrian Consulate.
14 Baldwin's Bath.
15 Church of Flagellation—immediately to the right of which is Dier el-Addas.
16 Turkish Bath.
17 Indian Moslem Khan.
18 Pasha's Residence.
19 Ain Hammam es-Shefa and Bath.
20 Residence of Baskatib and Cadi.
21 Mekhemeh—Council Chamber—Sanhedrim.
22 House of Town Clerk—Abû Seud.
23 Remains of Tyropœon Bridge.
24 Helena's Hospital.
25 Prussian Consulate.

CHRISTIAN QUARTER.

26 English House of Industry.
27 Greek Church and Nunnery.
28 Greek Convent, Archimandrite's Residence, &c.
29 Latin Convent, Nunnery, &c.
30 Casa Nuova.
31 Greek Convent of St. Theodore.
32 Greek Hospital.
33 Greek Convent of Constantine.
34 Coptic Convent.
35 Greek Church and School.
36 French Hospital.
37 Palace of Latin Patriarch.
38 Greek Church and Convent of the Forerunner.
39 Prussian Hospice.
40 Anglican Church.
41 Anglican Hospital.
42 St. Mark's, Syrian Church.
43 St. James's Church, Armenian.
44 Palace of Armenian Patriarch.
45 Armenian Hospital.
46 Dier ez-Zeitun.

JEWS' QUARTER.

47 Jews' Dispensary.
48 Great Synagogue.
49 Khulid Perusim.
50 American Christian Mission Premises.

IN THE ENVIRONS.

51 Tombs of Kings—Kûbr Molûk.
52, 52, 52 Tell el-Massabin—Ashmounds.
53 Rockmound.
54 Turbet Zahara—Mohammedan Cemetery.
55 Mohammedan Wely and Cemetery.
56 Greek Church—St. George—el-Khûdr.
57 English Cemetery.
58 American Cemetery.
59 Neby Daûd—Tomb of David.
60 Armenian Convent—House of Caiaphas.
61, 61, 61, 61, 61, 61 Aqueduct from Solomon's Pools.
62 Aceldama—Monument of Ananas.
63 House of Annas, Dier el-Khadis Modistus, Dier et-Tor.
64 Kefr Silwan—Village of Siloam.
65 Site of Bethphage.
66 Tomb of Zacharias.
67 Tomb of James.
68 Jehoshaphat and Absalom.
69 Garden of Gethsemane.
70 Church of Virgin Mary.
71 Tombs of the Prophets—Kûbr el-Umbia.
72 Village of Jebl Tûr—Church of Ascension.
73 Kûsr—Watch Tower.
74 Deep Tanks—Ruins—Viri Galilæi?

MODERN JERUSALEM

is generally admitted, by Suliman I., the second of the Ottoman Sultans that reigned over Jerusalem. It would appear that the present walls are nearly identical in position with those erected by Hadrian; though often partially destroyed and rebuilt. They were so much decayed in 1178—about the close of the Frank domination—that large sums were sent from Europe for their reparation. And they were again repaired and strengthened in 1192, by Saladin (Seleh-ed-Din), after the expulsion of the Franks. In 1219, however, they were all thrown down by order of Sultan Melek el-Miadh-Shem, except the Haram walls and El Khala, but were restored in some measure by the Christians, when delivered to them in 1243. The city soon afterwards fell into the hands of its present usurpers, by whom it was placed very much in the state we now find it, by order of Sultan Suliman. It must be admitted, however, that the lions carved in such bold relief on St. Stephen's Gate savor much more of the Crusaders than of the iconoclastic Moslems, and are probably referable to the age of the Crusades, as are also many other portions of the existing walls. It seems to have been well defended by a fosse on its most assailable points, but is now very shallow; and in many places quite effaced, by accumulation of rubbish. At a few points the native rock is merely faced with masonry; in others, built upon it—as on Mount Bezetha.

The city has four principal gates, facing the cardinal points of the compass—*the Jaffa* or *Bab el Khalîl* (*gate of a friend—i. e. Abraham*—the friend of God), on the west; *the Damascus* or *Bab es Sham* or *Bab el Amûd* (*gate of Syria or the column*) on the north; *the St. Stephen's* or *Bab Sittè Miriam* (*St. Mary's gate*) on the east; and *Zion* or *Bab en-Nebi Daûd* (gate of the prophet David) on the south. They are quite respectable in point of architecture; and are kept open from sunrise to sunset every day, except an hour on Friday—the Moslem Sabbath—noon, when they are closed with religious care while services are being held in the Haram. The *Mugrabin Gate, Bab el Mugharibeh*, situated in the Tyropœon, is never opened except during seasons of scarcity of water, when it is kept open several hours every day for the convenience of water carriers, who supply the city with water brought on donkeys from Bir Ayuab. There were formerly several other gates, but they are all now walled up with substantial masonry. One of these, called Herod's Gate, or *Bab ez Zahari* (*gate of Flowers*), is on the north side. On the east is situated a large and beautiful structure called the Golden Gate (Bab ed Dahariyeh, the Eternal Gate), nearly midway the Temple wall on the east; and fifty feet below it is a small gate or door, also walled up. On the south there is a small closed gate or door one hundred and five feet from south-east corner, and a hundred and sixty-three feet beyond this is the large triple gateway described in the section on the Temple. The city wall proper unites with the southern wall immediately east of the large double gateway known as Huldah's.

There are many structures in the wall that might be styled battlements and towers—though scarcely worthy of the name—but there are several mural structures in the *el Khalah*, besides the Hippic Tower or city castle, that may well be thus denominated. This fortification is entirely surrounded by a fosse, very deep generally, and a portion of it sloped off and substantially walled as a bulwark or buttress. When the Holy City fell into the hands of the Crusaders in 1099, this stronghold was the last to be captured. It was then known as the Tower or Citadel of David, but is also mentioned under the name of the "Castle of the Pisans." The large massive structure, situate in the north-eastern corner of the fortress, is undoubtedly of the highest antiquity, and is unquestionably the celebrated "Tower of Hippicus." It is still called the Tower of David, by those who suppose that the palace of that old warrior bard was on this part of Mount Zion: but this is an egregious misnomer. It is about seventy feet in length and fifty-six in breadth: the upper portion is of modern and inferior workmanship, but the original structure to the height of about forty or fifty feet still remains, the rocks apparently in situ as in the days of Herod, some of them ten or twelve feet in length and three or four in thickness.

It is probable, in the highest degree, that in the projection at the north-east corner of the Haram enclosure we have the remains of the Tower of Hannaneel. In the north-west corner of the city are seen the remains of a large piece of fortification called "Goliath's Castle" (Khalil Julil), better known as "Tancred's Tower"—and it was certainly in this immediate neighborhood that he was encamped.

It will be observed, on comparing the existing city wall with its original boundaries, that it only occupies about one-third the site of the ancient city, in its utmost extent; much of Mount Zion being excluded on the south, and nearly all of Cœnopolis on the north.

THE STREETS.

Alas! how different from the marble-paved streets of ancient Jerusalem! They cannot, with propriety, be said to be paved at all; yet they are covered with stones and rocks of all sizes and shapes imbedded in the earth; very narrow and filthy—many of them having a trench or ditch in the middle designed for horses and camels, between the elevated side-paths, which are used for foot-passengers. This ditch is frequently two feet in depth; and as only one beast can pass at a time, battles are constantly being fought for the right of way. Their average width is not more than ten feet; and many are not half that breadth. However indispensable to convenience the designation of streets by special names may be regarded amongst us, this is a convenience unknown in Jerusalem—there being only two or three streets known amongst the natives by any special name. The Franks, however, are endeavoring to supply this awkward inconvenience to some extent, by reviving a few of the names by which they were called by the Crusaders—as follows:—

Street of Mount Zion.—That part of the main street, if such we may call the rude passage-way, running between Zion and Damascus Gates, which divides the Jews' Quarter from the Armenian, is known by this name. The remainder of it, separating the Latin and Greek Quarters from the Turkish, is generally called St.

Stephen's Street (in virtue of a *former* tradition of the Latins, that assigned the martyrdom of the courageous deacon a site not far from Bab-es-Sham), but by many it is designated, and certainly more appropriately, *Damascus Street.*

Street of David, is the name by which they designate that portion of the great thoroughfare leading from Jaffa Gate to the Temple, dividing the Latin and Greek Quarters from the Armenian; and that portion of it running between the Turkish Quarter on the one side, and the Jews' and Mugrabin on the other, is called *the Street of the Temple.*

Mill Valley Street, is the designation by which the low lane running from Mugrabin Gate to its junction with Damascus Street, is appropriately styled.

The zigzagging street, lying between St. Stephen's Gate and the north-western corner of the city, is called *Via Dolorosa* from St. Stephen's Gate to Damascus Street, and from that point westward, *Street of the Holy Sepulchre.*

Street of the Patriarch, is the name of the short and straight street lying between Hezekiah's Pool on the one side, and the Greek Convent of the Forerunner on the other—running from David Street to the Street of St. Sepulchre.

Palmer Street runs directly in front of the Church of the Holy Sepulchre, from a point midway Patriarch Street, on to the Street of Damascus.

The short street, lying between Damascus and Valley Streets, immediately in front of Helena's Hospice, is sometimes called *Market Street;* but generally *Tarik es Sitte—Lady Street*, in honor, no doubt, of the lady by whose munificence that magnificent structure was erected—either the Empress Helena or Dame Tonshok.

BAZAARS—SUK.

The Jewish Bazaars are located mainly on the street immediately east of the Zion highway and the street leading thence by the great synagogue. *The Turkish Bazaars* occupy nearly the whole of David and Temple Streets, Damascus Street, and the network of alleys at its southern extremity. Patriarch Street is the principal seat of the *Christian Bazaars;* but the Court of the Church of the Holy Sepulchre is the great "house of merchandise" for "holy wares," "pious trinkets," and "sacred relics"—the Grand Spiritual Bazaar! *The Arab Bazaar* is situated on the lower portion of the Via Dolorosa and the street entering it nearest the Church of St. Anne. *The Corn Market* is a term applied to the vacant space around the el-Khalah. But besides these leading bazaars, each sect of Christians has its own special shops, generally near their convents, for the sale of particular articles.

The Cotton Bazaar—once a magnificent structure, and still in a tolerable state of preservation—is now entirely abandoned, and made the receptacle of all manner of filth; though even now susceptible of restoration at a comparatively trifling cost. The principal avenue to the Haram leads through this bazaar, immediately north of Hammam es-Shefa.

The domestic architecture of this once magnificent city of palaces, is of the simplest possible character. The houses are all constructed of the common limestone of the country, with the exception of a few public edifices. There being no timber in Palestine, this material is exceedingly high-priced here; and the doors and casements of the windows are the only portion of the houses made of wood—not a particle being used about the floors, roofs, or any other part whatever. The windows, which, by-the-by, are very few and small, are all grated with iron—if sufficiently large to admit a thief; and hence the the jail-like appearance of the houses. And it is only within the last few years that window-glass has been introduced into a few houses of the better classes. There being only one outer door to the largest establishments, no windows below, and those above generally concealed by lattice-work, the inmates enjoy as much seclusion as could well be desired. The entire absence of timber necessitates the most extensive use of crypts, arches, vaults, and domes, in the construction of buildings. This imparts a very pleasing appearance to the interior of the rooms; and the ceilings are generally very properly ornamented with mouldings in mortar. The stones of which private houses are constructed, are generally quite small and roughly squared: but those used in the construction of public edifices are very nicely and accurately squared into large blocks.

INTERIOR OF A JERUSALEM HOUSE.

All the rock anywhere to be found in the neighborhood of Jerusalem, with the exception of occasional deposits of flint (of which, that on Mount Olivet, and in the Valley of the Kedron, is very richly variegated), is *limestone.* But it varies greatly in quality, color, and consistency. There is a highly variegated reddish species, quite abundant about the city, so compact and fine-grained as to be quite well entitled to the appellation by which it is known—Jerusalem marble. The sparkling white variety, found at Anatta (or Anathoth), out of which the Anglican Church is built, is quite a handsome building material; but so rapidly disintegrates that not a few rocks in the lower tiers had so far exfoliated as to require removal and substitution before the entire completion of the building. In consistency and texture there is the greatest variety, some being so hard, fine-grained, and compact as to rank as good lithographic stone, and much of it as soft and friable as chalk. The facility with which much of it disintegrates will alone account for the disappearance of the immense piles of wrought stones which every traveller expects to find amongst the ruins of the Holy City—and the consequent deposit of a "*heap*" of rubbish, forty feet deep, on the site of the Holy City.

QUARTERS OF THE CITY.

Jerusalem is divided into three general sections, called Quarters—the Jewish, Christian, and Mohammedan—Haret Yehudy—Haret En Nassaraneh—and Haret el Mussulmin. The Christian Quarter comprises all that portion of the city lying west of the main thoroughfare that runs between the Zion and Damascus Gates, through the principal bazaars. The Jewish or Zion Quarter is bounded by the southern portion of the above street on the west, the central part of Temple Street on the north, the base of the hill (Zion within the wall) on the east, and a portion of the city wall on the south—being the more north-eastern corner of Mount Zion, comprising only about one-fifth its area. And all the remainder of the city is embraced under the Turkish Quarter, to which appertain also two reservations in the Christian Quarter—the large fortification and barracks at the Jaffa Gate, called El-Khalah, and the miserable string of huts at Zion Gate, belonging to the Lepers.

I. *The Jews' Quarter.*—Perched upon a bold, rocky promontory of Mount Zion, at an elevation of ninety-one feet above the present level of the Tyropœon, is a cluster of rudely-constructed houses, now occupied as the premises of the American Christian Mission. This spot is undoubtedly one of the most notable localities about the Holy City, though heretofore it has failed to

AMERICAN CHRISTIAN MISSION PREMISES, ON THE STRONGHOLD OF ZION.

attract the attention not only of tourists and pilgrims, but of professed antiquarians and topographers. It is the north-easternmost projection of "the Holy Hill Zion," and is distant only one hundred and eighteen yards from the western wall of the Haram es-Sheriff, which being identical in position with that of the western cloister of the Temple, defines the width of the Tyropœon Valley at that spot; between Mount Moriah and Mount Zion—the Mugrabin Quarter of the city.

This lofty cliff was the great bulwark of the ancient city of the Jebusites, and is first mentioned in 2 Samuel (v. 6–9), being unquestionably the "stronghold" of Zion, where King David was so derided by the king of Jebus in the taunting language of insult and defiance—"Except thou take away the blind and the lame, thou shalt not come in hither—thinking David cannot come in hither." And well might the insulting and overbearing Jebusites so think; for even Joshua himself, that pious and pre-eminently successful old generalissmo of the hosts of Israel, had not succeeded in reducing this "fort," though the "children of Judah" afterwards captured and burnt the lower city on Acra, which in all probability was Salem, the ancient city of "Melchisedec, the King of Righteousness." "Nevertheless, David took the stronghold of Zion—the same is the city of David;" and now the united cities of Jebus and Salem became Jebus-Salem, or, for euphony's sake, Jerusalem—the proud capital of the son of Jesse. How often have the halls with which he crowned this lofty summit resounded to the mellifluous strains of the harp of "the sweet Psalmist" and bard of Israel, as he sang the "sweet songs of Zion," which he indited as he was moved by the Holy Spirit. How beautiful, too, for situation, when the Holy Hill of Zion was "the joy of the whole earth!" But alas! how changed is the appearance of this world-famed hill, under its Turkish owners! The very first expression that now usually escapes the lips of the traveller (and has, perhaps, already been suggested to the reader by the truth-telling photograph print), queries whether this can possibly be "the city that men call beautiful, the joy of the whole earth," the place that the Great Ancient of days "hath chosen to dwell at for ever," and over which the great Melchisedec will yet reign gloriously before his ancients.

This commanding situation must ever have been a very important one, whether in the possession of heathen, Jew, or Christian; and accordingly we learn from Josephus that it was successively the site of the royal palaces of the Davidian, Asmonean, and Herodian dynasties of Israel. Herod the Great, however, required a larger area for the display of his magnificent designs; and hence he erected another, and perhaps still more sumptuous palace near the Tower of Hippicus (which he seems mainly to have occupied), on the site of the present splendid Anglican Church and Consulate—quite on the opposite side of the city. But not only did Herod Agrippa (called king) have his magnificent palace on this identical spot, but also built by its side another for his beautiful but meretricious sister, Berenice, so unsparingly satirized by Juvenal—before both of whom, as well as Festus, Felix, and Drusilla, Paul delivered his celebrated address at Cæsarea. Here also, was the famous hall "for feasting and compotations," to which the great Jewish historian and priest thus alludes: "King Agrippa built himself a very large dining-room in the royal palace in Jerusalem, near to the portico. Now this palace had been erected of old by the children of Asamoneus, and was situated upon an elevation and afforded a delightful prospect to those that had a mind to take a view of the city, which prospect was desired by the king, and there he could lie down and sit, and thence observe what was done in the temple, &c., &c." (Ant. book 20, chap. ix. sec. 10.) And truly it was a most delightful prospect. The beautiful, purplish, chatoyant mountains of Moab and Ammon, bounding a part of the horizon at the distance of twenty-five or thirty miles; the hallowed ridge of Olivet forming the remainder at the distance of a mile. Then, only one hundred and fifty yards distant was the gorgeous Temple, "exceeding magnifical, and of fame and glory throughout all countries," crowning Mount Moriah. The deep gorge of the Tyropœon, at that time, perhaps, about two hundred feet below the palace, adorned by the magnificent Xystus Porticos which lay below—the towering Castle of Antonia loomed aloft on the north, and on the right were Ophel, Kedron, Siloam, En-rogel, &c. Immediately adjacent on the north was unquestionably situated the "Armory of Solomon," or "the House of the Forest of Lebanon," and just in its rear, in the direction of the Tower of Hippicus, was the "House of the High Priest." The east end of the palace was connected with the Temple by that cyclopean bridge so often mentioned by Josephus, spanning the Tyropœon, and forming a noble highway between Moriah, the colossal remains of which are still to be seen at its abutment against the Temple wall—the highway or "ascent" of Solomon, so much admired by the Queen of Sheba.

This spot was subsequently occupied by the Crusaders, who (if we may form a judgment from present indications) crowned it with a magnificent church, in one sense, at least, resembling a city set on a hill, that cannot be hid. The tent, pitched on the top of one of the houses, now jumbled on its ruins, covers one of the circular skylights of the ancient church ; and the little court beneath this tented skylight is the humble tabernacular chapel of the Mission.

Immediately at the base of this perpendicular cliff, more than a hundred feet below the ancient palace, was situated the Xystus, so often mentioned by Josephus. By this term, we are not only to understand the long gallery beneath the palace, running parallel to the western cloister of the Temple, at a distance of about three hundred feet to the west, but also the intervening Tyropœon, or Cheesemongers' Valley of Josephus, called here, both by Josephus and the sacred writers, the suburbs (and truly the situation is literally *sub urbe*)—Mount Zion overhanging it on one side, to the height of one or two hundred feet, and Mount Moriah nearly as much on the other. It seems originally to have been mainly appropriated to gymnastic purposes, but in process of time evidently became the theater of the grand Jewish convocations, for the discussion of great national concerns. Hence it was probably the place where Herod the Great convened the Jews to consider his proposition for the reëdification of the Temple. And here it certainly was that King Agrippa assembled the Hosts of Israel, to address them on the occasion of their rebellion against their oppressive Roman masters, the circumstances of which Josephus details, as well as the king's speech, in the 16th chapter of the Second Book of the Wars of the Jews.

It was across this portion of the Tyropœon occupied by the Xystus that Titus caused Josephus to remonstrate with the infatuated Jews, after he had dispossessed them of the Temple; and across it also that Marc Antony held his celebrated parley with that stubborn people after he had captured Mount Zion—the bridge, in each instance, having been broken down.

Many other circumstances concur to invest this place with peculiar interest in the eyes of the Jews. But the bare probability that it was just at this spot that the great "promise" was made unto us (Gentiles) and our children, and to all that are afar off, is calculated to invest it with a thousand-fold more interest in the eye of every

Christian. And that it really was just to this place of assembly that the "multitude came together," attracted by the "sound from Heaven, as of a rushing mighty wind," and were there addressed by the Apostle Peter, on the ever memorable day of Pentecost, is in the highest degree probable. Indeed, with Josephus in one hand, and the Bible in the other, I am utterly unable to arrive at any other conclusion than that the devout representatives of the Jews in every nation under heaven amongst which they were scattered, were here gathered together when the terms of the new Dispensation were announced by the Apostle Peter. Indeed, so far as we can learn, there was no other place of convocation in all the city, where such a vast multitude could be accommodated, except the Temple; and most obvious is it that the circumstances narrated could not have transpired there. The "Law of the Lord," embodying the new institution, was ordained to go forth, according both to Isaiah and Micah, not only from Jerusalem, but "out of" that part of the city called Mount Zion. And where else could the adorable Redeemer have been more appropriately justified of the Spirit than just at this point, directly opposite the Temple—to the utter confusion of the stiff-necked hierarchs of disannulled Judaism, and "the betrayers and murderers of the Prince of Life!" The "*upper room*" to which the Apostles "went up," after they had witnessed the Ascension, was probably the "*one place*" in which they were assembled when the day of Pentecost was fully come, and may have been situated on this very brow of Zion; and had they but stepped forth upon Solomon's Bridge, what a noble pulpit would that elegant structure of "the King that was Preacher in Jerusalem," have been for the delivery of the great message of salvation with which these heaven-coronated ambassadors were charged!

The reader is candidly informed that the foregoing locations of sites and events are entirely different from those of all former Biblical antiquaries and topographers; but it must also be remarked that the investigations resulting in these conclusions have been conducted in the enjoyment of advantages and facilities never heretofore possessed by any explorer of the "Sacred Localities." The photograph—of which the wood cut is an exact transcript—was taken from the embankment of the "causeway" upon which the lower part of Temple street is situated. Immediately in the foreground is the top of a Mugrabin house, upon which a few pieces of clothing are suspended for drying. The pointed dome-building, farther on in the foreground, is a *weli* or mausoleum of a Moslem *santon.* In the elevated garden in the middle-ground, a man is seen looking through a hole in a large rock, that serves the double purpose of window and chimney to the bakeries and mills—several of which there are beneath this garden—and are entered by doors in the wall along the street, where an Arab is seen riding a camel. The pottery aqueduct, that brings water from Solomon's Pools to the great mosk, enters the city beneath the wall beyond the farthest copse of cactus, and passing along just at the foot of the old palm, penetrates by a channel cut through the solid rock on which the Mission premises are situated; and issuing through the lowest door seen in one of the corners of the house, passes along the base of Mount Zion into the Haram, via the causeway. The two elevated windows in the most projecting part of the Mission premises (above which there is also a smaller one), give light to the *hackhmeh*, or dispensary of the Mission. The distant hill seen over the city wall, by the Mugrabin Gate, is the top of one of "the mountains round about Jerusalem," on the south.

The locations of the leading synagogues, lection and transcription rooms, are indicated on the large map of the city: two or three of them are quite large, but very plain and indifferent buildings.

The open space called "Deir" marks the site of an old convent, some portions of which, on the east, are still standing, though miserably patched; and at a short distance, in the rear, is an old ecclesiastical building—a dilapidated portion of which is observed on looking at the view of the American Christian Mission premises. It is indicated by the two farthest windows. It would seem to be one of the St. Peter's Churches built by the Franks. The remains of another of these old Crusaders' churches may be found near the Jewish Bazaar, contiguous to the minaret and mosque on the south.

The public school of the Jews is kept in a building occupying the south-west corner of the city.*

The Jewish dispensary, under the able management of a liberal-minded German Hebrew physician, Dr. Frankel, situated in the north-west portion of the Jewish Quarter, is the only other public building in this quarter worthy of mention.

Few travellers possess sufficient nerve to pass, or even approach the vicinity of the shambles, but the little pottery, midway between this disgusting place and the lepers' huts—though altogether uninviting and insignificant in appearance—will scarcely fail to recall the 18th chapter of Jeremiah's prophecy, and excite in the reflective mind of the Scripture reader profitable reminiscences and reflections.

This quarter of the city, though assigned to one-half of the entire population, is by far the smallest, being about one-third the size of the Christian, and one-fifth that of the Mohammedan. It is by far the filthiest and most unhealthy—the very home of squalid poverty and wretchedness. A few families, however, of the better class dwell by sufferance in other parts of the city; and these are sufficiently numerous in the immediately adjacent portion of the Armenian Quarter, to have a reading-room.

Amongst the accumulated heaps of filth and rubbish along the city wall, east of Zion Gate, the traveller will observe with mingled emotions of pity and disgust the tabooed row of huts appropriated to the lepers.

II. *Christian Quarter.*—This division of the city may be farther subdivided into the Armenian, Latin, and Greek sections—the Armenian occupying all below the Jaffa or David street, the Greek the north-eastern portion, and the Latin mainly the western and

* The credit of the large hospital now being erected on the hill west of the "Lower Pool of Gihon," is due in great measure to the munificent donation of a wealthy Jew of New Orleans—Mr. Touro.

PALACE OF ARMENIAN PATRIARCH—AND CONVENT OF ST. JAMES.

central parts. All the public buildings and places of interest are indicated on the large map.

ARMENIAN.—*The Armenian Convent* is one of the largest establishments in the city. It occupies several square acres in the centre of the quarter; and is capable of entertaining about eight thousand pilgrims.

The Armenian Church of St. James (brother of John). This convent is a fine building and gorgeously decorated within; but most of the pictures and ornaments are tawdry and puerile in the extreme; and some of them are absolutely idolatrous and blasphemous.

The Patriarchal Palace, a short distance south of the Church, is a new and quite elegant building.

The Armenian Hospital is another new and fine building, situated near Zion Gate.

The Church of St. Thomas is situated on the street immediately north of the convent, but is disused at present.

The Church of Yacobeiah (St. James the Less) in the rear of the

English Church, is also claimed by the Armenians. The Armenians are also the proprietors of the large irregular conventual building, just outside Zion Gate, called the *Palace of Caiaphas* the High Priest, once known as the Church of St. Salvator. "Here under the altar," says Maundrel, "(and they repeat the same story to this day), is deposited the very stone which was laid to secure the door of our Saviour's sepulchre.* * * It is two yards and a quarter long, high one yard, and broad as much. It is plastered all over, except in five or six little places, where it is left bare to receive the immediate kisses and other devotions of pilgrims. Here, likewise, is shown a little cell, said to have been our Lord's prison, till the morning, when he was carried from hence before Pilate, and also the place where Peter was frightened into a denial of his Master. The 'Cœnaculum' may also be conveniently mentioned here. This '*upper room*' where tradition says the last passover was kept, and the Lord's Supper instituted, is to be seen, in virtue of a good buckshish, in the second story of one of the rooms of the jumble of buildings called Neby Daûd, a short distance from the House of Caiaphas."

Tradition also locates the *Tomb of David here*, immediately beneath the Cœnaculum, and hence it is that none but the *élite* of Islam are permitted to reside in this revered hamlet.

The Greek Convent of St. George (*the Hebrew*), and Dier el Zeitûn (Convent of the Olives), are in the south-eastern part of this quarter; as well as the *Syrian Convent and Church of St. Mark.*

Just above the Church of St. George, is a *Church of the Crusaders* (that of *Mount Zion*), in a tolerable state of preservation; and some distance farther north the *Reading-Room* of the Polish Jews. The extensive gardens attached to the convent, form a very pleasant place of retreat, where some of the clergy while away a portion of their time very pleasantly. The upper portion of this quarter is mostly appropriated by the English and Prussians.

"*Christ's Church,*" as the *Anglican Cathedral* is called, is situated very conspicuously in the north-western corner of the Armenian Quarter, on the grounds (in part) of the great Herodian Palace, and inclusive of the English Consulate—to which it is architecturally as well as civico-ecclesiastically united—is decidedly one of the most costly and magnificent edifices of modern erection in the city.

Quite a large parcel of land is attached to the church, upon which there are various offices, gardens, &c., all the property of the *London Jews' Society.*

The *English Hospital*, a large, well appointed, ably managed, and liberally endowed establishment, under the faithful and long-continued superintendance of Dr. McGowan, is situated in the north-east corner of this quarter.

The Prussian Hospice occupies a very eligible position on the northern border of the Armenian Quarter, and is under very excellent management, chiefly in charge of female medical nurses.

The Greeks are much wealthier in ecclesiastical property than the Latins, as may be seen by comparing the following schedule—independently of their interest in the pile aggregated around the Church of the Holy Sepulchre, which, however, is by no means inconsiderable:—

The Church and Convent of Gethsemane, immediately in front of the Church of the Holy Sepulchre:

The Church and Convent of St. John the Forerunner, occupying the southern end of the large square lately presented to the French Emperor by the Sultan:

The Convent of Constantine, separated from the Holy Sepulchre Square, only by Patriarch Street:

Greek Church between the Latin Convent and that of Constantine:

Greek Convent on opposite side of the street:

Archimandrites' Residence adjoining:

Adjacent Greek Nunnery:

Nunnery and Almshouse of St. Basil:

Convent of St. Theodore, adjoining the Casa Nuova Buildings:

Church of Schismatics:

School Buildings near Jaffa Gate:

The Consulate of Russia, on the opposite side of the street from the Church of Constantine.

But besides these properties in that quarter, the Greek Church also owns the *Church of St. George* in the Armenian portion of the Christian Quarter; and a church of the same name on the hill about three hundred yards east of el-Khalah; also at the Convent of the *Cross*, and Mar Elias, &c.

The COPTS have a *small convent* adjoining their fine, large *Caravanserai*, on the north of the Pool of Hezekiah, and a chapel immediately in the rear of the reputed rock Calvary, as well as a claim upon some valuable property adjoining the Church of the Holy Sepulchre on the east, called *Dier es-Sultan.*

The London Jews' Society own some very valuable property not far from Damascus Gate, called the *House of Industry*, where its neophytes are well maintained and taught some handicraft occupation. The *Anglican Bishop* resides in this quarter, until his palace can be erected. His residence is hard by that of His Grace the *Latin Patriarch.*

There are two *minarets and mosks* in this quarter—the one situated immediately in the rear, and the other just in front of the Church of the Holy Sepulchre—very much to the annoyance of the Christian pilgrims, as well as the native Christians. The one on the south is the celebrated *Khankey Minaret.*

The Hammam el-Batrarch, or *Pool of Hezekiah*, is situated between a row of houses on the west side of Patriarch street, and the residences of their Graces of England and Rome; and though not accessible by any street, may be readily seen by entering the large new hotel, or any one of the shops on its eastern side, or still better from the top of the Coptic Convent.

A *Bathing Establishment* on the east of Patriarch street is supplied with water drawn from this pool in leathern buckets, and conducted across the street in an arch-shaped aqueduct.

LATIN.—*The Church of the Holy Sepulchre* and adjacent buildings, occupy a large part of the great square contained between a portion of the Via Dolorosa, Patriarch street, Palmer street, and the street leading south from Damascus Gate—somewhat between the Latin and Greek districts of the Christian Quarter. It is unquestionably an object of more general interest than any other in all that quarter, or any in the whole city, with the single exception of the Mosk of Omar; but a minute description of this colossal mausoleum will be found in the chapter on sepulchral monuments.

Besides the interest which the Latins have in the massive pile of building, known under the general appellation of the Church of the Holy Sepulchre, which is almost paramount at this time, they possess the following edifices :—

The extensive and well furnished "*Convent of St. John the Divine*," in the north-west corner, conspicuously erected on the highest ground in the city. *The Latin Nunnery* in the same neighborhood: *the Casa Nuova* or Hostelry of the Convent, separated from it only by a street: a kind of hotel, designed not only for sheltering Latin pilgrims, but for the entertainment of all kinds of travellers.

The well-conducted French Hospital, near the Coptic Convent, enjoying the able services of the talented Dr. Mendelsohn. The *Palatial Residence* of the Patriarch, near Jaffa Gate. The ruins of the *Palace of the Hospitallers*, east of the Church of the Sepulchre, which, together with the large square in which it is situated, have been lately presented to Louis Napoleon, the avowed patron of the Romish Church in the East. The traveller will linger a long while admiring the ornate and elaborately carved gate of this renowned establishment, despite the yelping of dogs and the abominable stench issuing from the tannery on the opposite side of the street, and the accumulations of filth within.

The *Church of St. Anne*, near St. Stephen's Gate, also lately presented to the French Emperor. The Latins also own the *Church of the Flagellation*, adjoining which is *Dier el Addas*.

There is a *Weli* in the north-west corner of the city, where the body of a Moslem saint reposes; and near it is "*Goliath Tower*," or the Castle of Tancred, as it is sometimes called.

The *Sardinian Consulate* is just above the Latin Convent. The large court and appendages east of the Church St. Sepulchre, called *Dier es-Sultan*, are occupied by the Copts and Syrians; but regarded as the property of the Sultan. Beneath is the large pool, called the "*Treasury of Helena.*"

III. *Muhammedan Quarter.*—This quarter may be very conveniently subdivided into four or five parts—the *Turkish*, situated on Bezetha Hill and the lower part of Akra; the *Arab*, in the north-eastern corner of the city, and the *Mograbin* in that part of the Tyropœon lying between the Haram and Mount Zion; to which may be also added the Turkish fort and barracks called *el Khalah*, and the *Haram ash-Sheriff.*

The Mekhemeh or *City Hall*, located probably on the site of the ancient council chamber, is situated on the causeway in the extreme south-east corner of the Turkish division, and adjoins the Haram.

On the opposite side of the street is the *the residence of the Cadi or Chief Judge*, and also that of

The Bashkatib or Secretary of the City. There is also a clerk's office in the establishment of Abu Seud, opposite the American Mission premises. But the portion of that pile of buildings located within the Haram wall is, at least, the representative of the *Convent of Fakhr*—founded by a Coptic convert.

The Pasha's Establishment is on the western side of the Haram, near the north-west corner; and here the *Divan Effendi* also has his office in the same cluster of buildings; in which also is the *city prison.*

The Kaim Makam, Bim Pasha or Military Governor, resides in the Seraglio or *Serai*, near the corner of the Haram, on the north side—the site of the celebrated fortress of Antonia.

Besides *the three mosks* connected with the Haram, there are two others in this quarter, both on Bezetha Hill. The mosk

THE SERAI (SERAGLIO) THE RESIDENCE OF THE MILITARY GOVERNOR—ON THE SITE OF FORT ANTONIA.

attached to the upper one—that of Melawieh, which is very large and conspicuously situated, is an old church, the paintings on whose walls are occasionally exposed by the peeling off of the plaster with which they were concealed in transforming the church into a mosk. There are eleven mosks in Jerusalem and its immediate environs.

The Turkish Hospital is situated a short distance from the Pasha's residence on the street leading to Damascus Gate.

The Custom House is immediately north of the Jaffa Gate.

Quarantine, until quite recently, was performed at Jeremiah's Cave; but at this time respectable travellers are permitted to undergo quarantine in their own tents at any point they may select a short distance from the city, while Arabs and Turks of the lower order are cast into the deep fosse of Hippicus to serve out their sanatory term as best they can—entirely unsheltered.

El Tekiyeh (*Helena's Hospital* or rather *Hospice*), a very fine and extensive building (though now somewhat ruinous), is used as a soup establishment for the poor, and is situated upon the slope of Akra on Sitte street, a short distance west of the Pasha's residence. Opposite to the northern entrance of the Pasha's premises is a large *Khan* or convent for Moslem pilgrims from India and Tartary.

A short distance south of the Pasha's residence, on the street leading from el-Tekiyeh to the Haram, is the "*College for blind Derwishes.*"

There are several large *Bathing Establishments* in this quarter of the city—one at St. Stephen's Gate, supplied by a trench leading from a pool just without the wall—another at the east end of the Cotton Bazaar, supplied from the Bîr esh-Shefa or Well of Healing, and another at the western extremity, the water for which is mainly brought from the Pool of Siloam. The largest and finest by far, was that of King Baldwin at the junction of the streets leading from Damascus and St. Stephen's Gates, but it is now in a somewhat dilapidated condition. The stable supplies the fuel with which the water of all these baths is heated.

There are several very beautiful *Saracenic Fountains* in the lower part of this quarter—one at St. Stephen's Gate, another opposite the door of the Mekhemeh, and two others at intermediate points along the street running parallel to the western side of the Haram. The accompanying view of that at the Mekhemeh will convey a correct idea of these fontal structures.

Near the lower corner of the Serai, close by *a square tower* of Jewish architecture, is a Mohammedan *wely* much revered; there is also another very jealously watched, near a large house of curious architecture, on the cross street south-west of Helena's Hospital, as well as several others along the western wall of the Haram. They not only contain the remains of some celebrated Moslem saints, but are also used for devotional purposes.

SARACENIC FOUNTAIN.

Opposite the Serai is the *Church of Flagellation*, the property of the Latins; and just to the east, *Dier el Addas*, which seems to be yet in the hands of the Mohammedans. There is a large church in ruins on the side of Bezetha Hill in the north-eastern portion of this quarter, called Mahmooneh—used in part as a pottery, where a much revered imprint of a foot is found on a rock. It was doubtless one of the "*Mary churches*," and gave name at one time to all that part of the city—"Merie." Considerable remains of a church are found between Baldwin's Bath and the Serai. The Church of St. Anne, now said to be the property of Louis Napoleon, is in a tolerable state of repair, but has become decidedly hermaphroditish in undergoing so many transitions between Romanism and Islamism.

There are three *Consulates* situated in this quarter:—that of *Prussia*, on Sitte street, about midway between Helena's Hospital and the Church of the Holy Sepulchre; the *French*, near the

Damascus Gate; and the *Austrian*, a short distance south-east of the French, in the house first occupied by the American Christian Mission; where, in recently making excavations, several rooms and a grotto once apparently occupied as a church, were discovered at a distance of fifteen feet below the surface of the ground.

The principal khan or caravanserai in the city, is found in this quarter, near the large bazaars, and was once a magnificent establishment.

The legendary Pool of Bethesda forms the boundary line of the Haram for more than one-third of its extent on the north; and was, doubtless, designed as the most effectual defence that could be constructed at that very assailable point of the ancient Temple area. The eye of the tourist will be at once arrested by the traditionary arch, *Ecce Homo*, spanning the street near the north-west corner of the Serai; and farther up the "Via Dolorosa," between Baldwin's Bath and "the *house of Dives*," situated at the acute angle of the street, near the Turkish Hospital, "the *Bowl of Lazarus*" will be noticed.

The north-eastern part of the Mohammedan Quarter, like the southern, is almost houseless; and is either appropriated to horticultural purposes, or abandoned to chapparals of cactus.

Haret el-Mugareby is mainly peopled with negroes from the west of Africa—extremely black. *The "Wailing Place,"* and other places of interest connected with the Temple wall being described in connexion with the Haram, there remains nothing worthy of special note in this quarter, not already noticed.

The Leper huts, built along the city wall, east of Zion Gate, though so widely differing in locality, must be regarded as appertaining to the Mohammedan Quarter, and should have been located in the outskirts of this retired spot, inhabited in part by the swarthy eunuchs, the conservators of the Haram enclosure.

The villages of Silwan and Jebl Tûr, being immediate dependencies of Jerusalem, may be appropriately mentioned in this connexion.

Kefr Silwan, or the village of Siloam, is suspended in the cliff, at the north-western portion of that spur of Olivet called the Mount of Corruption, Offence, or Scandal: and surely a more corrupt, offensive, and scandalous set of scamps is nowhere to be found! They are, with few exceptions, real troglodytes—dwelling not only in natural caves, but in the tenements of the dead, with which that cliff abounds—the best of their residences being mainly the hewn sepulchres merely faced with an ante-room of masonry. Its population does not probably exceed two hundred.

The village of Jebel Tûr, or Mount Olivet, is far more respectable than that of Siloam, both in point of architecture and inhabitants. It is situated on that elevation of the Mount of Olives nearest Jerusalem, but not on its highest point, which is two or three hundred yards farther back. Near the centre of this little village, contiguous to the minaret and mosk, is the legendary Church of the Ascension—or at least all that remains of the magnificent structure erected by the Empress Helena. It is now the property of the Turks; but is accessible to Christians, at all times, on payment of a small fee. All that now remains is a large octangular court, surrounded by a high wall and the sides of adjoining houses, along which are arranged altars belonging to various Christian sects, and a kebli for the Moslems. Upon the living rock, in a small circular chapel, situated in the centre of this court, is the imprint of a foot, universally revered by pilgrims as the real impress of the Saviour's foot, made in springing upward to heaven—confirmation of which is found, by the credulous pilgrim, in the puncture made by the co-operating staff!

Proceeding along the western side of the village to the south-west corner, the traveller, by warily watching his opportunity, may succeed in effecting a furtive peep into the cave of Pelagius—a spot, which however highly revered both by Jews and Christian, is most jealously guarded against their unhallowed intrusion by the watchful eye of the jealous Turk, who claims it also as the resting place of one of his honored santons. It is here—as tradition alleges with every probability of truth—that the notorious courtesan Margarita of

Antioch, in the guise of a monk, spent her life in doing penance after her conversion, under the assumed name of Pelagius; and here too the poor Magdalen finally found her resting-place. The sepulchre, however, in which it is alleged by the Christians that she was buried, is claimed by the Jews to have been that of Huldah the prophetess. It is a large, plain sarcophagus of coarse marble, six feet eight inches in length, three feet nine inches in breadth, and three feet four inches in height—outside dimensions.

The following old Greek inscription is copied from a rock in the cave of Pelagius: (I affix the English orthography of the words, that the reader not acquainted with the ancient Greek alphabet, may the better note the anagram contained in the second line, on comparing the inscription with the accompanying extract.)

"Put thy faith in God, Domitela: no human creature is immortal."

There is a very valuable stone here like that at Neby Kamah—placed like that too, as a lintel over the door. Who knows but that it once figured amongst the precious stones of the Temple! Its shape and material may well justify the conjecture that it once formed part of the low wall separating the Court of the Priests from that of Israel, or the Court of the Gentiles from the inner portions of the Temple.

NETHER JERUSALEM.

Subterranean Passages, Excavations, Caves, &c.—The citizens of Jerusalem tell marvelous tales about its subterranean passages, galleries, and halls: and that there are many passages perforating the city in various directions, is expressly stated by Josephus. The Talmud also mentions that "there were not a few caves in the city hollowed out of the rock; but this subject having but slightly engaged the attention of explorers, we have as yet but little reliable information on this point; and they probably lie at such a depth that they will not be brought to light for many years. Of the various subterraneous passages mentioned by Josephus or incidentally alluded to in the Bible, some were designed for the conveyance of water, whilst others were clearly intended for use in time of war. The aqueduct conveying water into the Pool of Siloam has long been known; and has been fully explored and described by Drs. Robinson and Smith. Professor Johns has also partially explored a similar conduit passing from the neighborhood of Hippicus down towards the Temple. But the rock-hewn conduit of Hezekiah, by which he brought the waters of Gihon into the city, has never as yet been exposed to view at any point, unless the channel entering that between the Virgin's Fount and Siloam be a portion of it. (See *Virgin's Fount.*)

There is quite an extensive conduit running from Damascus Gate down the Valley street through the city at the depth of fifteen or twenty feet below the surface; but it is evidently a mere sewer for draining all that part of the city. This drain discharges its contents at present a short distance below the Mugrabin Gate; but originally must have made its exit below the southernmost portion of the city. It was through this passage that the Fellahin effected an entrance into the city during the war of Ibraham Pasha and captured it—emerging from it at a point not far from the Cotton Bazaar. I have penetrated about one-half its length; and can truly testify, that though the poor creatures may have regarded it as a mere pleasure trip, yet I certainly had rather an ugly time of it.

I made an effort to explore a subterranean passage commencing in the premises of a Rabbi on Mount Zion, formerly a church of the Crusaders (Zion Church, I think), which he assured me led into the country almost *two hours.* But I found it so much obstructed by rocks and debris, that I was compelled to abandon it after going a short distance. My success in exploring the subterranean passage that issues from the ground underneath the upper Kedron Bridge, (by St. Mary's Church)—said to lead to the northern side of the city, was no better—for I was glad enough to abandon it after crawling on hands and knees fifty or a hundred yards, where I found daylight gleaming in through some of the loosened rocks above. An account will be found, in connexion with the exploration of the Virgin's Fount, of a channel which I explored from that place to a point within a short distance of the Mugrabin Gate, where it turned abruptly to the west, and became too much choked with rubbish and earth to allow farther penetration. The use to which this passage was originally appropriated yet remains a mystery: it would rather appear, however, that its design was to discharge surplus water into the Ophel channel, in order that it might be reservoired in the Pool of Siloam, instead of flowing directly out of the city and thus being lost: and may possibly be the continuation of Hezekiah's channel.

Having often heard it positively asserted, that persons had actually entered a cave near Beit Hanina about four or five miles from the city, and traversed it to its termination in Jerusalem, I determined to venture on the subterranean excursion; but soon became so bewildered in its damp labyrinths, that I was glad to effect a safe retreat, and abandon the hope of successfully exploring it.

But, though foiled in many attempts to ferret out the regions of the nether city, my efforts were quite successful in effecting an entrance into a very large excavation beneath Mount Bezetha. And inasmuch as there have been rather discrepant accounts of this discovery, I will insert an account of its exploration, written for a Philadelphia journal,* by a member of our Mission:—†

"The Nazir Effendi (a State-Church dignitary, only a few grades below the Pasha), while admiring the fine view from the terrace of

* The Ladies' Christian Annual, edited by James Challen, the gifted author of the "Cave of Machpelah," &c., &c.

† Dr. R. G. Barclay.

CITY WALL ON BEZETHA HILL, OVER "COTTON MEGARA," THE GREAT CAVERN QUARRY.

our house, remarked that ancient Jerusalem was several strata below the superficies of the present city; and that it would be interesting to explore the magnificent subterranean remains of the gorgeous palaces of King David, Solomon, and various other monarchs of former times,—could an entrance but be effected. Having received some intimation of the existence of an entrance to a very extensive cave near the Damascus Gate (entirely unknown to Franks), we resolved upon its exploration, on the strength of the Nazir's permission. Accordingly, a few days afterwards, father, brother, and myself repaired thither; and after several hours of vain labor, finding it utterly impossible to effect an entrance unperceived in the open light of day, we concluded to return in the shades of the evening—resolving to pass the night *under* Jerusalem in making a thorough exploration.

"Having provided ourselves with all the requisites for such a furtive adventure—matches, candles, compass, tape-line, paper, and pencils—a little previous to the time of closing the gates of the city, we sallied out at different points, the better to avoid exciting suspicion, and rendezvoused at Jeremiah's Pool, near to which we secreted ourselves within a white enclosure surrounding the tomb of a departed Arab Sheik, until the shades of darkness enabled us to approach unperceived,—when we issued from our hiding-place, amid the screeching of owls, screaming of hawks, howling of jackals, and the chirping of nocturnal insects. The mouth of the cavern being immediately below the city wall and the houses on Bezetha, we proceeded cautiously in the work of removing the dirt, mortar, and stones; and, after undermining and picking awhile, a hole (commenced a day or two previous by our dog) was made, though scarcely large enough for us to worm our way serpentinely through the ten-foot wall.

"On scrambling through and descending the inner side of the wall, we found our way apparently obstructed by an immense mound of soft dirt, which had been thrown in, the more effectually to close up the entrance; but, after examining awhile, discovered that it had settled down in some places sufficiently to allow us to crawl over it on hand and knee; which having accomplished, we found ourselves enveloped in thick darkness, that might be felt, but not penetrated by all our lights, so vast is the hall.

"For some time we were almost overcome with feelings of awe and admiration (and I must say apprehension, too, from the immense impending vaulted roof), and felt quite at a loss to decide in which direction to wend our way. There is a constant and in many places very rapid descent from the entrance to the termination, the distance between which two points, in a nearly direct line, is seven hundred and fifty feet; and the cave is upwards of three thousand feet in circumference, supported by great numbers of rude natural pillars. At the southern extremity there is a very deep and precipitous pit, in which we received a very salutary warning of caution from the dead—a human skeleton! supposed to be that of a person who, not being sufficiently supplied with lights, was precipitated headlong and broke his neck, or rather his skull, I should judge, from the fracture I noticed on picking it up! There is also near this pit a basin excavated in the solid rock, about five feet in diameter and two and a half feet deep, into which the percolating water trickles; but it was in vain we tried to quench our thirst with water of such bitter, disagreeable taste. A little, however, was bottled for analysis. Water was everywhere dropping from the lofty ceiling, which had formed numerous small stalactites and stalagmites—some of them very resplendent and beautiful, but too fragile to be collected and preserved.

"We noticed bats clinging to the ceiling in several places, in patches varying from fifty to a hundred and fifty, hanging together, which flew away at our too near approach, and for some time continued to flit and scream round and about our heads in rather disagreeable propinquity. Numerous crosses marked on the wall indicated that, though unknown to Christendom of the present day, the devout Pilgrim or Crusader had been there; and a few Arabic and Hebrew inscriptions (though too much effaced to be deciphered) proved that the place was not unknown to the Jew and Arab. Indeed, the manner in which the beautiful white solid limestone rock was everywhere carved by the mason's rough chisel into regular pillars, proved that this extensive cavern, though in part natural, was formerly used as the grand quarry of Jerusalem.

"Also, from the close correspondence in the strata of rock in this cave and the opposite hill, we came to the conclusion that this cavern and the Grotto of Jeremiah, two or three hundred yards distant (the intermediate hill having been carried away for the construction of the city wall, Temple, &c.), constituted one immense cave. There are many intricate meandering passages leading to immense halls, as white as the driven snow, and supported by colossal pillars of irregular shape—some of them placed there by the hand of nature, to support the roof of the various grottos, others evidently left by the stone quarrier in quarrying the rock to prevent the intumbling of the city. Such reverberations I never heard before!

"Though disappointed in our fond expectations of working our way to the Sanctum Sanctorum, Hippicus, or Antonia, as we had vaguely conjectured we might be enabled to do, we were nevertheless highly delighted with our little jaunt in nether Jerusalem.

"From the former entrance of the cave down to the Temple area is a gentle inclined plane—a fact that suggests a satisfactory solution of what has heretofore been regarded as a very puzzling question—the difficulty of placing such immense masses of rock *in situ*, as those found at the south-east and south-west corners of the Temple wall.

"We entered the cave at 7 P. M., with the intention of passing the night in its dark recesses; but after making a plan, were so fatigued that we concluded, that were we to yield ourselves to the influence of Somnus, the rising sun would probably reveal to the jealous Mussulmans the opened entrance to the scene of our nocturnal adventure. Therefore, at 2 A. M., we repaired to an old vacated oil-mill adjacent, and having kindled a brush and grass fire, passed the remainder of the night in a state of no little discomfiture—longing for the light of morning.

"The numerous burrows, into which we so often sank knee-deep, served to confirm the construction we had put upon the report made to us by our faithful dog in this arduous reconnoissance—and proved that here 'the foxes had holes,' as well as 'the birds of the air their nests'—for the bones that lay strewn about proved that the voracious jackal was now the 'lord of this manor,' whose interminable halls had for centuries resounded to the busy din of the hammer and chisel. What untold toil was represented by the vast piles of blocks and chippings, over which we had to clamber in making our exploration! A melancholy grandeur—at once exciting and depressing—pervaded these vast saloons. This, without doubt, is the very magazine from which much of the Temple rock was hewn—

the pit from which was taken the material for the silent growth of the Temple. How often, too, had it probably been the last place of retreat to the wretched inhabitants of this guilty city in the agonizing extremities of her various overthrows! It will probably yet form the grave of many that are living over it! for the work of disintegration and undermining is going on surely, though slowly. We can now account for a terrible fright we all felt one Sunday evening, which caused our little Bible class to break up and retreat to the court in great alarm. We had always been under the impression that it was the shock of a distant earthquake—though we could but think it strange that it was felt more severely on Bezetha Hill than elsewhere: but the immense masses of rock which had evidently fallen quite recently from the ceiling of one of the unsustained halls, plainly declared that *they* had made the earth to quake—at some period, if not at the time alluded to—and the Mission premises being situated only a few yards from the southern extremity of the cave, had of course felt the concussion very sensibly."

In the following humorous and graphic account, taken from the Boston Traveller, will be found some additional particulars and reflections of interest:—

"It has long been more than suspected that a gallery of this quarry extended under the wall of the city itself, but nothing was positively known regarding it, as it has been kept carefully closed by the sucessive governors of Jerusalem. The mouth of the cavern was probably walled up at least as early as the times of the crusades, to prevent its falling into the hands of a besieging army; earth was then thrown up against this wall, so as effectually to conceal it from view, and it is only upon the closest scrutiny that the present entrance can be perceived.

"Drs. Smith and Robinson, during their tour through Palestine, made an effort to effect an entrance, but in vain, and so far as I know, all other attempts have been equally unsuccessful, until about a year ago, when the dog of an American gentleman, a resident of Jerusalem, attracted by the smell of some animal, scratched a hole just at the surface of the ground and suddenly disappeared; he soon came back, and his master attempted an exploration, but owing to the want of candles he was obliged to give up the attempt. He returned, however, with his sons and a servant just about sunset, and, allowing themselves to be locked out of the city, they succeeded without attracting observation, in descending and making a survey of the whole extent. The report of this was soon bruited abroad, and before the authorities took any action in the matter it was visited by several parties, and by ours among the number.

"The afternoon on which we proposed to explore the quarry, I returned to my hotel from a walk, and changing my clothes, was soon equipped and ready for the rest of the party, when a waiter informed me that they had been gone some minutes. Fearful of missing the only opportunity I should have, I ran down into the street and hastened along in the direction of the gate, in perfect ignorance of the proper way, when fortunately I met the servant of the American Vice Consul, who had already served me as guide and showman, but always through the medium of an interpreter. Summoning to my aid almost the only Arabic words I knew, I shouted 'Bab el Shem,' or 'The Damascus Gate.' He understood me, and turning set off as fast as his dignity, his large trowsers, and his crooked sword would permit him. As we turned out of the gate I saw the rest of the party standing at a little distance, preparing for the descent, and immediately joined them.

"There was a good deal of dispute among us, as to which of the Franks should have the honor of leading the party, but as we found all were anxious to see Dr. M., a tall and very pompous man, humble himself, the question was soon decided. An Arab servant was the pioneer, and you can hardly imagine our astonishment when we saw him lie flat on his face, and *worm* himself feet foremost into a hole, into which a man with his arms by his sides could not possibly have inserted his shoulders. Next came the doctor, who was dressed in a drab overcoat, cut in the height of the present fashion; turning the long skirts up over his back, he prostrated himself amid the shouts and laughter of the lookers-on. First there was a digging of the toes into the ground and a pulling, then a pushing with the elbows. Slowly and with difficulty was the feat performed, and the agonized look of the poor man, as he took the last look of earth, was indescribably ludicrous.

"My turn soon came, and it was certainly the most awkward position in which I ever found myself: but after a few minutes' struggling and kicking, I was seized by the ankle, and my foot guided downward to a crevice in the wall, along the top of which I had been crawling. The passage was some ten feet in length, and from the top of the wall to the loam upon which we stood, was some six feet. At first all was utter darkness, but my eyes soon became accustomed to the obscurity; and lighting my candle, I was ready for a start by the time the last of the party joined us.

"For a few rods the descent was very rapid down a slope of rich loam, but soon we began to ascend over immense heaps of rubble and the chippings of hewn stone. The turnings were frequent, but not abrupt, the main direction being south-east. We took the precaution to fasten a clue at the entrance, which an Arab unwound as we advanced; and at every turn we stopped to examine the bearings of our compasses, so that our progress was slow. We labored on, however, now running against some of the huge pillars left for the support of the roof, and again stumbling over some massive block, which we could not see in the obscurity. We followed up the different galleries, and examined them all thoroughly, in hope of finding some other outlet, but were stopped in every direction by the solid rock.

"Suddenly there was a cry of 'take care, here's a precipice!' We all pressed forward to the spot to examine it, and found ourselves on the edge of a pit some ten or fifteen feet deep, and about a hundred feet across. The floor was of rock, smooth, but extremely uneven, the inequalities being caused by breaking off the blocks at the bottom, instead of cutting them away; the roof, too, presented a similar appearance. Near this, at the end of a long gallery, was a fountain, supplied by water dropping from the roof. It was delightfully cool, but unpleasant to the taste, being strongly impregnated with lime.

"Our advance was, in one or two places, obstructed by the heaps of broken stone, which reached so near the roof, that we were obliged to creep on our hands and knees. I could understand well what a grievous penance it must be, to walk with one's shoes full of peas, for crawling on cobble stones is near akin to it. At the end of the chambers was a crevice in the rock, through which one or two of us squeezed, and, looking up, we thought we had discovered an old shaft, but, on climbing thirty feet or more, we found that it was a natural fissure, and had no outlet above, as we hoped. Our disappointment was lessened, however, upon discovering that the sides of the fissure were covered with stalactites of a rose color, and we immediately availed ourselves of a hammer, produced by one of the party, to break off specimens, with which we filled our pockets.

"But the most interesting portion was the extreme end of the last chamber. Here were blocks of stone but half quarried, and still attached by one side to the rock. The work of quarrying was apparently effected by an instrument resembling a pickaxe, with a broad chisel-shaped end, as the spaces between the blocks were not more than four inches wide, in which it would be impossible for a man to work with chisel and mallet. The spaces were many of them four feet deep, and ten feet in height, and the distance between them was about four feet. After being cut away at each side, and at the bottom, a lever was probably inserted, and the combined force of three or four men could easily pry the block away from the rock behind; the stone was extremely soft and pliable, nearly white, and very easily worked, but, like the stone of Malta and Paris, hardening by exposure. The marks of the cutting instrument were as plain and well defined as if the workman had but just ceased from his labor.

"Having thoroughly examined every nook and corner, we turned back toward the entrance, examining the ground as we went. Near a pillar in about the centre we found a quantity of bones, brought in by the jackals, the smell of which had first attracted the dog. We then looked along the surface of the wall which closed the entrance, but, though the light streamed in at one or two cracks, there was no other hole large enough to admit even a dog; and, satisfied that we had come in at the only possible entrance, we one after another climbed up, and worked our way out.

"The sun was just setting, and, blazing full in our faces, nearly blinded us; as soon as we could see there was an universal shout at the forlorn appearance each and all of us presented. It was impossible to tell the original color of hat, cap, clothes, or hair, for we were covered from head to foot with lime dust, and looked like a company of millers. We dusted and brushed each other, but to no purpose; we were marked men, and our merry party was greeted with many a stare by the staid old Turks, as we marched through the streets and bazaars.

"Upon comparing a subsequent measurement of our guiding line, and the time spent in returning from the extreme end, we judged the length of the quarry to be rather more than a quarter of a mile, and its greatest breadth less than half that distance.

"There had been some doubt expressed by one or two of the party, who had made a previous visit, as to its being a quarry; but we all agreed that though it might originally have been a grotto, it had been worked, and then the question arose 'By whom?' The answer was, 'King Solomon,' and for this opinion there seemed to be many reasons. The stone is the same as that of the portions of the Temple wall still remaining, and referred by Dr. Robinson to the period of the first building. The mouth of the quarry is but little below the level of the platform on which the Temple stood, making the transportation of the immense blocks of stone a comparatively easy task.*

* Tyro is evidently in error on this point. The mouth of the quarry is many feet higher than any portion of the Temple area.

"The heaps of chippings which lie about show that the stone was dressed *on the spot*, which accords with the account of the building of the Temple: 'And the house, when it was in building, was built of stone, made ready before it was brought thither; so that there was neither hammer, nor axe, nor any tool of iron heard in the house while it was building.' The extent of the quarry, the amount of stone which must have been worked out there, and the size of some of the blocks themselves. The extreme age of the part which has been exposed to the action of the elements, and which dates back in legends and traditions to the time of Jeremiah. The fact that there are no other quarries of any great size near the city, and especially the fact that in the reign of Solomon this quarry, in its whole extent, was *without the limits of the city*.

"Whether the hole through which we effected an entrance will be closed again, it is hard to say; but it seems probable that it will, as the quarry lies directly under the Mohammedan Quarter of the city, and, in case of an insurrection of the Jews, it would be almost impregnable if taken possession of by insurgents, and at the same time they would have it in their power to blow up all that quarter of the city. I hope, however, that it may be thoroughly explored before the close of this season, and a better account given of it by some more able pen than that of a TYRO."

I must add, that though I had never heard of the slightest traditional hint relative to this cave until I undertook its exploration, yet I have since found an *allusion* to it in the "Description of Jerusalem" by Kadi Mejr-ed-din, under the name of "Cotton Grotto."

A dotted plan of this cave, as well as its exact location, may be seen on inspecting the large Map of Jerusalem.

The Cave Edhemieneh or *Grotto of Jeremiah* is quite a large cavernous expansion beneath the opposite hill of Zahara or Mount of Tombs, and was, no doubt, continuous with the Bezetha Cave before the removal of the intervening portion of the mountain. Its roof is supported by two large pillars; and being not more than fifty yards in depth, the whole cave is so well lighted from its large mouth that no artificial illumination is necessary for its exploration. A beautiful miniature lake covers its floor during a large portion of the year. There is a capacious court in front of it, enclosed by a substantial wall, and several well constructed houses, besides the few recessed domicils within the cave. It has served for many years as a quarantine station; and a more isolated and pleasant place (bating the vicinage of the city of the dead) could not well have been selected. The usual order of nature is here reversed; and the rare spectacle of the dead above the living may be noticed at any time. There seems formerly to have been a communication between the cave and the surface of the hill, which may once have been one of the strongholds of Jerusalem. It was used by the Mohammedans at one time as an oratory. The polite Derwish who resides here is very particular in exhibiting to his visiters the exact spot where the prophet usually reclined, as indicated by the impression which, like that of Elijah at Mar Elias and the many foot-prints and hand impressions about the Holy City, remains to this day! How much more impressible were the rocks in days of yore, than the *people* of this generation! There are vast numbers of caves all around the city in a natural state, besides the multitudes that have been remodelled by the hand of art and converted into sepulchres. But of all the subterranean excavations and passages about the city, no greater interest attaches to any than to the two rock-hewn passages leading from the Temple, the one from the altar to the Kedron, by which the sacrificial blood was conducted away, and the other from a Temple Gate to the Tower of Antonia by which troops could at any time be sent into the Temple; for the discovery of either of these passages would indicate the position of the sacred fane—the latter only approximatively, but the former exactly. All my efforts to explore them, however, have hitherto proved fruitless.

CHAPTER XVII.

NOBLE SANCTUARY.

EL-HARAM ES-SHERIF—MESJID EL-AKSA—TEMPLE MOUNT.

THERE is no place on earth concerning which there has existed a curiosity half so intense and prurient as that in relation to the sacred enclosure of the Temple, the Haram es-Sherif, which can only perish with the faith it typifies. But so great is the fear inspired by the clubs and cimetars of those blood-thirsty savages, the Mauritanian Africans, to whose jealous custody the entire Haram is committed, that few indeed have been found of sufficient temerity to hazard even the most furtive and cursory reconnoissance of this tabooed spot. It is an ascertained fact that every religious community in the Holy City has a firman from the Sublime Porte, empowering them to kill the members of any other communities intruding on their premises; and that the Moslems, at least, delight to execute the decree upon any *infidel*, whether Jew or Christian, that may be caught intruding upon this sacred spot, is well known. So wild and ungovernable is their fanaticism that the protection of the Effendis is entirely unavailing. On making an attempt on a certain occasion to measure the length of the street entering the Enclosure, near the supposed site of the Sanhedrim, these bigoted fanatics deliberately drew a line across the street ten or fifteen yards from the gate of the Haram, and with most defiant looks and threatening gesticulations, declared that if I dared to set foot over the mark there drawn, they would put me to death instantly—notwithstanding the presence of two influential Effendis, under whose protection I had placed myself, and who vainly sought to negotiate terms of accommodation. I scarcely need add that no portion of the lofty Haram wall was a more effectual barrier against my entrance than was that emphatic thus-far-shalt-thou-go-and-no-farther mark to my progress towards the gate. I knew an American gentleman so seriously injured by a stone-pelting that he received on unintentionally stepping into one of the Haram gates, notwithstanding his immediate precipitate retreat, that he was confined to his room for many days. A well-known resident physician, who, though attending one of the Haram officers professionally, under special protection, was so severely beaten for merely passing along the cloisters, that he was confined to his bed for many weeks in a critical condition. It is understood, however, since the Turko-Russian war, that permission will now be granted by the Pasha to travellers, on payment of a liberal buckshish, to walk through the enclosure under escort of soldiers. And for many years past all travellers who were willing to incur the expense and trouble of procuring an order, have been permitted to enjoy the privilege of viewing the enclosure from the top of the Serai or Governor's house. Until lately, however, no Christian or Jew, with a few exceptions, under peculiar circumstances, has been permitted to set foot within its walls, for six long centuries.

In 1818 Dr. Richardson was officially permitted to make a hasty reconnoissance of it in return for medical services rendered some of the dignitaries of the Haram. And in 1833, Mr. Catherwood and his companions, by practising a bold and hazardous ruse, obtained entrance to nearly every part of the Haram, often enough to execute many valuable drawings and make quite a minute survey; but unfortunately he does not seem to have made the subject a matter of critical study beforehand, and hence his attention was not directed to many matters that possess the deepest interest. I have known several persons well disguised to spend a few minutes, or even several hours, there at night, on payment of thirty or forty pounds in money, and a still heavier expense in conscience; being compelled to go through the Mussulman form of prayer, bow the knee to Mecca, &c.: but it was found utterly impossible to accomplish anything, under such circumstances.

My excellent friend, the late Mr. Bartlett, gives the following amusing account of his abortive effort to make a nocturnal visit to this all-attractive spot.

"I will now add an account of one attempted by myself," he remarks, "which, though it proved abortive, may amuse the reader, as showing, that in spite of the bigotry of the Mussulmans in general, individuals are always to be found, and often of high standing, who are willing, for the sake of a bribe, not only to smuggle the infidel into the holy places, but also, rather than fail, to violate the established proprieties and rooted prejudices of their countrymen.

"The agent in this instance was a character common enough in comedies, viz. an intriguing servant, belonging to a friend, whose profession as *hakim* brought him into contact with many of the better class of Moslems. By his contrivance a meeting was brought about, at a house on the brow of Mount Zion, looking out on the ruined bridge, with an old Turk, who, having been previously sounded, had expressed his willingness to undertake the job. On repairing to the spot, I found one of the finest-looking old men I ever saw, with an open, benevolent countenance and a long silvery beard, dressed in a turban and white robes, and looking the very impersonation of one of the patriarchs. After mutual salutations, the business was opened by my interpreter, and the best means of effecting it were canvassed with great earnestness. As I wore neither beard nor moustache, and besides, had not been long enough in the country to get thoroughly bronzed, the old man at first proposed that I should be dressed as a Turkish woman, and walk behind him about the mosk. This plan, however, had its objections, and, on further reflection, he was struck with a most original idea, and certainly the last of which I should ever have thought. I was to come to his house after dark, apparently as a hakim sent for to prescribe for his family, with the intriguing servant carrying a box of medicines before me, in order to lull suspicion. On arriving at his domicile, he would have a woman's costume all ready, in which I was to dress myself—a disguise, in which no doubt many more nefarious pranks have been played than I was about to commit. Having put on this feminine attire, I was then to accompany his wives to the mosk, which would at that time be brilliantly illuminated, this being the season of Ramadan. The only difficulty, he said, would be to talk over his women; but to persuade them into the scheme, he trusted to the efficacy of a certain five hundred piasters, which I promised to pay down as soon as we came back to his house, after the successful conclusion of the adventure.

"I now returned home, and from the terrace of the hotel watched the red light fade off Mount Olivet, and heard the gun fired to give notice to all good Moslems that they might now lawfully eat their dinners. Darkness soon invested the city, relieved only by the brilliant stars and the red glimmer of the lamps suspended on the tops of the minarets. As the time drew near when the servant was to come and fetch me, it now suddenly struck me that I had embarked in a rather hazardous affiair, without anything to justify it, but the mere desire of an adventure; since it would be impossible, muffled up in female attire, to examine the architectural peculiarities of the mosk, even if the act of staring about would not of itself be enough to betray my disguise. In the event of discovery, there hardly could be a doubt that death by stoning, or some more horrible fate, would be the penalty inflicted upon me by the frantic mob, doubly enraged by the violation of the sanctity of the place, and at the indecent manner in which it had been effected.

"It was, then, with no little nervousness that I listened for the tap at the door which was to announce the messenger. About nine he made his appearance, informing me that the old man had succeeded in talking over his womankind, and that everything was in readiness. We then stole forth, the servant gravely preceding me, and carrying before him a travelling box of medicines. This precaution was all but useless, for the streets were so dark that it was with difficulty we could grope our way; but here and there we came upon a group of Turks sitting out of doors and smoking by the light of paper lanterns. The last of these was in the Via Dolorosa, near St. Ann's Church; and I thought I recognised among them the ugly visage of a lad who had thrown stones at me in the morning for approaching too near the mosk, and who regarded me with a look of suspicion.

"At length we reached the house of the old Turk. On stepping in, I was conducted, with an air of mystery, into an upper chamber, when the old Turk came forth and welcomed me. I could not but remark that, notwithstanding the confidence he had previously expressed, his countenance betrayed no little agitation. He uttered, from time to time, a deep sigh, stroked his long beard, and, looking up to heaven, muttered what I understood was a prayer for the happy success of the enterprise. In fact, he must have been conscious that, should a discovery take place, he would be certain to forfeit all consideration and character, even if subjected to no farther punishment, which, however, would most probably be the case.

"The articles of female dress intended for my disguise were now produced, and I was invited to put them on. The first difficulty occurred with the boots of yellow leather, in which the Turkish women waddle, rather than walk, about the streets. These were so small that it was impossible to get them on, and I had therefore to content myself with slipping my stockings into a pair of red shoes, which only half covered them. My feet seemed alarmingly large and clumsy, and very likely to betray my real sex; but the Turk and servant said these would do. The next affair was to draw over my pantaloons a pair of female inexpressibles, which, though of very spacious width, turned out, like the boots, to be too small, scarcely reaching down to the ankles, which stood out in strong development. Their sole fastening was a pair of strings, intended to be drawn around the slender waist, and to rest upon the swelling hips of the fair owner; but from the want of any such support in my case, they threatened to slip bodily down upon the slightest movement. A dark veil was now put over my head, so as to entirely conceal the features, but through which I was enabled to see with tolerable clearness; and, finally, a large white wrapper, but also too short, was thrown over me, completely enveloping all but the face. Although I fancied this disguise far from complete, the old man and the servant, after studying it attentively, and asking me to walk up and down, dropping my head a little, and affecting something of a female waddle, looked at one another with approving glances, and authoritatively pronounced it to be 'taib.'

"The servant now explained to me the manner of proceeding. When the women were dressed, which would be in a few minutes, we were all to sally forth together, and enter the enclosure by the neighboring gate. I was instructed to keep in the middle of the party, to do precisely as they did, and to be careful not to stare too much about me. We were to go first into the Mosk of Omar, which at that moment would be brilliantly lighted up, and from thence to that of El Aksa; returning, after a short stay, to the house, where I was then to count down the five hundred piasters which I had stipulated to give.

"All was now ready, and I awaited the arrival of my female conductors with intense anxiety, not altogether unmingled with apprehension. To say truth, besides doubts as to my own successful deportment, I was not without misgivings as to the discretion of my companions, in a case where the slightest misconduct would involve the most serious consequences; and feared no less, that in case of alarm they would suddenly scatter about the enclosure, and leave me to get out of it as I could. My distrust was greatly increased when I heard much chattering without, and when the head of the chief lady was projected into the apartment, beckoning forth her husband, who followed her into an adjoining room. He returned in a moment, evidently much disconcerted, declaring that his wives would only consent to accompany me on previously receiving payment. Stroking his beard, he declared that he himself had no misgivings whatever, and trusted entirely to my honor, but that his wives were rebellious, and would listen to no reason. I was doubly annoyed at this—not only because it involved a personal affront, and displayed the avaricious eagerness of the women in a disgusting light, but also because it confirmed me in my distrust of their conduct. To pay them beforehand what was so evidently their only inducement to go with me, would deprive me of the sole check I might have upon their behavior, and I firmly resolved not to surrender it. Producing the money, which I had brought with me, I declared that it should be paid down the very moment we returned, but that, after the formal agreement which had been entered into, it was doubting my honor to insist upon receiving it beforehand. A spirited discussion now ensued, the women thrusting their heads into the room and taking part in it. I found they were divided in opinion, and that it was the obstinacy of the chief lady which prevented the conclusion of the bargain. The poor old Turk seemed passive in their hands, and altogether it afforded a curious insight into the manifold tribulations besetting the possessor of many wives, proving that polygamy is to be regarded, as Byron says—

"'Not only as a sin, but as a bore.'

"As the women still persisted in their demands, I at length got wearied, and throwing off the feminine garb in which I was half-suffocated, broke off all further negotiation.

"The servant resumed his lantern and medicine-chest, the old Turk preceded me into the street, and took leave with every demonstration of courtesy, and regret that the matter had come to so untoward an issue. The harem was, no doubt, in a pretty state of combustion after our departure."

Glad indeed were we the next morning to find that the misadventure had eventuated no worse; for, having been made acquainted with his intention, we spent a night of no little anxiety.

But I was myself doomed to experience a somewhat similar disappointment soon afterwards. One of the highest officials of the Haram, whom I had laid under considerable obligations by medical services, voluntarily proposed to incur the responsibility of permitting me to spend several nights securely guarded, in the various parts of the enclosure, on payment of a few pounds to his sub-officers. I readily acceded to the terms, and in order to avail myself of the opportunity to the greatest advantage, I waited for a full moon, which would enable me the better to make some measurements of the area. Accordingly, being habited *à la Turc*, as an Effendi myself, one of my sons as an Arab, and the other as pipe-bearer, we made our entree about 10 o'clock: but scarcely had we satisfied our longing eyes with the enchanting moonlight view of the Mosk of Omar, before some of the Haram officers, not in the secret, were seen approaching. We were immediately ensconced in the Mugrabin Mosk, and our faithless guide (for so it afterward appeared that he was) reported to us, that we were detected, and unless we would agree to give an additional buckshish to stop the mouths of the guard, we might be murdered outright. But being near the Mugrabin Gate, we concluded to abandon the enterprise and effect our escape, which we accordingly did, but not quite as leisurely as we had entered; and who would not fly from a choice between the Koran and the cimetar—the alternative presented to any individual caught within this sacred enclosure? Quite an army of dogs being aroused and effectually cutting off our homeward retreat, we were compelled to flee with all dispatch, around through the Jews' Quarter, and here we were challenged by the night watch, and for sometime threatened with a night's lodging in the common prison; but making a virtue of silence, and frowning indignation in true Effendi style, I outbraved them, and they were content to let us go our way without farther molestation.

A most fortunate circumstance, however, soon made ample amends for this sad disappointment. The Sultan's architect, having petitioned the *Mejlis* of Jerusalem for permission to associate me with him in designing the proposed improvements about the Haram, procured my official and unrestricted admittance to every part of the sacred enclosure, both above and below ground, without fee or reward.

I was not even required to undergo the important ecclesiastical lustration by water on the occasion. In order, however, to avoid the appearance of anything that would savor of the observance of a Mohammedan rite, I took care to go voluntarily and submit to the rubbing, scrubbing, bumping, thumping, racking, cracking operation of the Turkish bath, so as to forestall all difficulties on the score of uncleanness.

Whoever has once enjoyed the luxury of a Turkish bath will almost realize the operation a second time on reading the following account from the graphic pen of Curtis :—

"The lofty hall which we enter is lighted through a dome, and is paved with varied marbles. Three deep alcoves are raised above the court, in the sides of the wall, and in the centre of the pavement is a fountain, upon whose margin stand clusters of nargilehs, wreathed with their serpentine tubes. A mat is spread for us in the most spacious alcove. A boy holds a fine linen veil before us while we disrobe, and instantly an attendant girds us with linen over the shoulders and around the loins, and a flat turban of the same is pressed upon our heads. Then carefully treading in clumsy wooden pattens, which slide upon the polished floor, we enter a small room.

"It is misty with steam, and warm, entirely bare, and of smooth marble walls and floor. We pass into another of the same kind, hotter and more misty, and a group of parboiled spectres regard us languidly as we advance.

"Then we emerge in a long oblong hall, reeking with moist heat, in which we gasp and stare at the figures—some steeped to the neck in a cauldron of steaming water, their shaven heads floating, like livid pipkins, upon the surface—some lying at full naked length upon the floor, in a torpor of sensual satisfaction—some sitting meekly upright upon little stools, and streaming with soapsuds, while nude officials, with a linen fig-leaf, rush rapidly about with a black horsehair mitten upon the right hand, making occasional sallies upon the spectres, and apparently flaying them with the rough hand of hair.

"These spectres are all shaven and profoundly solemn. They undergo parboiling, boiling, soaping, and flaying, with a melancholy seriousness of western gentlemen dancing at a ball, heroically resigned to happiness.

"But we may not pause. Persuasive hands are urging us toward the cauldron. We are suddenly denuded, and hover affrighted on the very verge of the steaming abyss. But we will not be pipkins. We will not join that host of shaven Saracens, who look at us from the cauldron as lifelessly—for *les extrèmes se touchent*—as the victims in the ice glared upon Dante and his guide. We remember Hylas with an exquisite shudder. We gasp '*la, la,*' (no, no,) with an emphasis that makes us the focus of all the languid glances in the misty limbo.

"Then the persuasive hands urge us toward a door opening into a small marble chamber. A fountain gushes hot water at the side, a linen is suspended over the door, and we are removed from the view of the pipkins. The thick hot air is absorbed at every pore, and the senses are soothed as with opium fumes. We pant, resistless, sitting upon the floor, streaming with perspiration. Beyond, struggling, we see a hairy-handed spectre enter under the linen of the doorway. He rubs his fingers upon our naked bodies, as a barber rubs the chin he is about shaving. The hairy-handed says, 'Täib, täib,' (good, good,) and lays the Howadji flat upon his back.

"Sitting by his side, he dips the hair glove into the running water, and rubs with a smooth, steady firmness the inside of the infidel arm. Not a spot escapes. You muse of almonds in the process of blanching, and are thus admitted to mysterious sympathies. You are no longer panting and oppressed. You respire heat and mist at every pore, and perceive yourself of the consistency of honey. The hairy-handed whispers coaxingly, as you sink more deeply in the sense of liquefaction 'Khawadji, bucksheesh.' You look at him with the languid solemnity of the pipkins in the cauldron, but are sure that you would only bubble and gurgle, should you attempt to speak.

"The hairy-handed turns you like a log, and like the statue of great Ramses at Memphis, lying with its face in the mud, so lies the happy Howadji with his nose upon the wet marble floor, torpid with satisfaction, while his back is peeled in the same skilful manner.

"The ceremony of the glove is finished, and you lie a moment as if the vague warm mist had penetrated your mind. A stream of clear hot water is poured over you, and pleasure trickles through your very soul.

"Then lo! the hairy-handed, smiling upon you as you lie, and whispering, 'Bucksheesh, Howadji,' steps with his naked feet upon your spine, and stands on your body between your shoulders. But he has scarcely touched the back than he slides off down the ribs, his large moist feet clinging to your back. So, sliding and slipping, and kneading your body, he advances toward the feet, accumulating in your misty mind new ideas of luxury, and revealing to your apprehension the significance of the Arabic word 'kief,' which implies a surfeit of sensual delight. He steps off and leaves you lying, and there you would willingly lie for ever, but that he returns with a pan of soap and a mass of fibres of the palm-tree—the Oriental sponge.

"The next moment you are smeared in suds, from the neck to the heels, and it is rubbed in with a vigor that makes you no longer Ramses in the mud of Memphis, but a Grecian wrestler, anointed and oiled with suppleness. He rolls you over, and your corporeal unctuation is completed.

"Then hairy-hand sits you upright upon the floor, like the mild-eyed lotus-eaters, who sit sudded upon stools in the vicinity of the pipkins; and suddenly the soap is planted in your hair, and you are strangling in the suds that stream over your face. You cannot speak or gasp; for the hairy-hand mercilessly rubs along your face up and down, as if you were merely Marsyas; and as you sit half terrified, and with a ghostly revery of anger at your heart—for positive emotions are long since melted—you perceive a burning stream of water flowing over you and washing soap and rage away. Hairy-hand deluges you with the hot water, which he bails out of the fountain with the pan that held the soap, then folds his hands meekly to signify that you are done, and whispers gently, 'Buckshish, Howadji.'

"You rise and enter the Sudarium beyond. No unbelieving Verde Giovane is there to scoff; but another spectre approaches with razor and scissors. You tremble lest you be too much done to resist the shaving process, lest you re-enter the world utterly bald as a Saracen. But a glance at the pipkins nerves your heart. Feebly this time, and truly with liquid accents, you murmur, 'la, la,' and the spectre with razors vanishes into the mist with a scornful smile. You pass into the next chamber and clean linens are thrown around you as when you entered, and you stumble along upon the clumsy pattens out into the large hall.

"You reel into the alcove and stretch yourself at length upon the mattress covered with gold-fringed linen. A boy lays other linen over you, skilfully flapping a heavenly coolness as he lets it fall. Your eyes close in dreamy languor. Something smooth touches your lips; it is the amber mouth of a nargileh tube, upon whose vase, filled with tobacco from Shiraz, a bit of aloes is burning. It is the same boy who kneels and hands it to your lips, and offers in the other hand a cup of orange sherbet.

"You sip and inhale, and a few moments, restful as a year to the sleeping princess, pass. Then you are gently raised, all your drapery is changed, and fresh, fair linen is spread over you again, with the same exquisite coolness in falling.

"Your eyes wander in revery around the hall. In one alcove, lie a pair of Sybarites like yourself, also dreamily regarding you, and your glances meet and mingle, like light vapors in the air. Another is praying—bending and kissing and muttering—others are robing and disrobing, entering or going out. The officials move as quietly as shadows, and perfect silence reigns under the dome, broken only and deepened by the plash of the fountains; clouds of azure smoke wreathe away, and the faint bubbling of the water in the nargileh hums soothing through the space. By reason of the windows in the dome, the bath is lighter than the bazaar, and you watch through grated windows opening upon the bazaar, the passers in that dim region, the camels, the horses gayly caparisoned, the Bedowins and Sakkas, and *bright-robed merchants*, who all go by like phantoms.

"But the boy kneels again and with firm fingers squeezes your arm slowly from the shoulders to the finger tips. Then he proceeds along your legs—firmly, but gentle at first, then more strongly kneading, and passes off at your fingers, cracking every joint, nor unmindful of the toes. He retires and leaves you to another interval of dreams, smoke, and sherbet. The draperies are changed, again with sweet coolness in the changing. Finally a strong man, Uncle Kühleborn himself, kneels behind you seriously, and lifts you up. He thrusts his arms under yours, and bends you ruthlessly backward and forward, straining and squeezing in every direction, forcing your body into postures which it can never know again, actually cracking your backbone, until seizing you quite off the mattress, old Kühleborn twists you upon his knee into an inextricable knot, then suffers you to fail exhausted upon the couch.

"It is the last stroke, the crown of delight. You exist in exquisite sensation, but are no longer conscious of a body. You comprehend an 'unbodied joy whose race is just began.' The cool, fragrant dimness penetrates your frame. You fall softly into sleep, as into an abyss of clouds."

But, however anxious to explore the mysteries of that sacred spot, I was fully resolved to submit to none of the degrading ceremonies to which Christian and Jewish mechanics had been required heretofore to do on entering the Haram for the purpose of making repairs. It is well known that every kind of handicraft avocation is regarded as degrading by all classes of Moslems; and hence when the clock of the Mosk needs repairing, they are compelled, however reluctantly, to employ a Frank. But in order to have a clean conscience in the commission of such an *abominable piece of sacrilege* as the admission of an *infidel* upon the sacred premises, they adopt the following expedient. The mechanic selected being thoroughly purged from his uncleanness by ablution *à la Turc*, a certain formula of prayer and incantation is sung over him at the gate. This being satisfactorily concluded, he is considered as exorcised, not only of Christianity (or Judaism, as the case may be), but of humanity also; and is declared to be no longer a man but a donkey. He is then mounted upon the shoulders of the *faithful*, lest, notwithstanding his depuration, the ground should be polluted by his footsteps; and being carried to the spot where his labors are required, he is set down upon matting within certain prescribed limits; and the operation being performed, he is carried back to the gate, and there, by certain other ceremonies, he is duly *undonkeyfied* and transmuted into a man again! But the poor brutalized mechanic may at least "lay the flattering unction" to his wounded pride, that if he has been made to play the part of a *donkey* for a while, his juggling employers are *asses* evermore.

In conferring this signal favor upon me, the Effendi was influenced mainly by gratitude for medical services, but in no small degree also by a desire to become familiar with the use of several philosophical instruments I had, and most willingly did I undertake the instruction of himself and brother. The opportunities thus extended for some weeks, were much greater than have ever been heretofore enjoyed by any Frank since the possession of this place by the Turks, and the expulsion of the Franks from the Holy Land. Still I have to regret that owing to the importunate application, on the part of an Englishman and a Frenchman, the range of my observations was somewhat controlled after a short time. A remark made by the Effendi in his speech before the Mejlis on the occasion, is characteristically Oriental. The claims of these gentlemen were urged before the Mejlis by one of the chief dignitaries of El-Khuds, in very eloquent terms (for a good fat buckshish can even make the stolid Turk speak eloquently), being based principally upon alleged principles of honor, and the duty of reciprocity devolved upon the subjects of the Sultan, in consequence of the assistance of England and France, rendered against the Russians, while America afforded them no aid. "It is true," said the Effendi, "that England and France are our allies, and that America is not: but the truth is, my lords, that the Haram is sick and needs medicine (not gunpowder), and the *Hakim American* has the right kind of medicine, and knows how to administer it." The result of the discussion was that I was retained and they were denied admittance.

*The Enclosure of the Haram es-Sherif,** or the Noble Sanctuary, as the area of the Temple is now called, contains about thirty-six acres. The east side of this large quadrilateral enclosure runs due north and south, but no other side is either perpendicular or parallel to it, nor any two sides the same length. The course of the south side is south 86½° west; the west side north 5° west; and the north side south 89° east. The diversity of result exhibited by the following tabular view of its admeasurement by different persons must be regarded as evincing the great difficulty of making correct measurements about Jerusalem at present, rather than the incompetency or carelessness of the observers.

* Sometimes also called "Mesjid el-Aksa," the most distant sanctuary, because more distant from Mecca than Medina is. Mesjid differs from Jamey as a churchyard differs from the church—a distinction which it is important to bear in mind.

Dimensions of the Haram—discrepant accounts.

Observers.	Sides of the Enclosure.			
	E.	N.	W.	S.
Catherwood	1520	1020	1617	932
English engineers	1520	1188	1520	877
Robinson	1528	1060		955
Smith	1528	1060		906½
Tipping and Walcot	1533			915
Richardson	1489	995		
Schwarz	1498			995
Maundrel	1539			
Assaad Effendi	1521	1047	1617	945
Medjr-Eddin	1471	893		
Ali Bey	1369			845
Omar Effendi	1489	995		
Another Mussulman account	1563	938		
My own measurements	1523½	1038	1600	916

These discrepancies are much to be regretted, but by no means to be censured, for such is the nature of the ground, and such the difficulties arising from impenetrable copses of cactus, interposing buildings, and accumulations of rubbish, that error is unavoidable; and no measurement that it is practicable to make, on any side, at present, except the eastern, can be regarded as absolutely reliable. Another measurement of the south end, made with the utmost care, upon trigonometrical principles, varied but slightly from this number; but a very careful measurement, made directly along the wall, from each corner to the pile of buildings around the double gateway—added to the best estimate that could be made of the breadth of the walls and rooms, makes the length of this end as much as 936 feet: but it is probable that what was supposed to be a single wall, was in reality a small room. Though I found no difficulty in measuring and drawing anything out of sight of the Mugrabin guard, entirely at my leisure, yet I had no sooner commenced measuring the area of the Haram, than the Effendi took alarm at the fanatical demonstration of the guard, and we deemed it prudent to desist for awhile, in the hope that they would become better reconciled.

The surface of this enclosure is by no means a uniform plane, there being a general declination towards the south and east. The ground immediately south of the Golden Gate is quite low, that around Solomon's Throne is elevated, and the rock surface in the north-west corner is considerably higher than any other part of the area—the platform of course excepted.

These walls are about eight or nine feet in thickness at the foundation, though the parapets are not more than three feet thick, and average about fifty in height on the exterior, and at the south-east corner are seventy-seven feet high. On the interior only twelve or fifteen feet are visible above the surface of the flat area of the enclosure; and upon the north and west and a portion of the south, ranges of cloisters form the internal boundary; but about the north-west corner, the native rock, on which the Tower of Antonia was built, forms the enclosing wall for the height of twenty or thirty feet in some places.

Three gates give entrance to the Haram-yard on the north:—Bab es-Sitte Myriam, or es-Sabat, in the north-east corner; next Bab es-Sawatta or Dewatar; and the Bab el-Hitta or Ettim. On the west, there are eight gates or doors, as follows:—commencing near the north-west corner and proceeding south, Bab el-Guauney or Guanimi, Bab es-Seraiyah, Bab en-Nazir or el-Bassery or el-Alsdeen, Bab el-Hadid, Bab el-Muthara, Bab el Katanin, Bab el-Makhemy or es-Sekine or Salsala, and Bab el-Mugaribeh.

On the east there were formerly a small portal and a magnificent gate, though both are now closed. The former, which appears to be unnamed at present, is the "Little Gate" of the Franks, sometimes called "Porta Jehosaphat sive Gregis;" and the latter is called, in Arabic, Bab ed-Dahareyeh, and is the celebrated Golden Gate—the Porta Aurea of the Crusaders.

The course of the eastern wall several times varies from a straight line—there being numerous projections and recessions—as observed on the plan. There are a great many pillars built transversely into this wall, generally said to be porphyry and verde antique (but erroneously, inasmuch as they effervesce with acids). One of these pillars, projecting a few feet from near the top of the wall, about a hundred yards from the south-east corner, is a spot very much revered by Mussulmans; being no less in their estimation, than the very judgment seat upon which Mahommed will sit in the last day, and judge the world, assembled in the valley below. They even contend that a very fine wire extends horizontally over to Olivet, at this time, upon which the souls of the faithful pass safely over to Paradise—while that of no Jew, Christian, or other *infidel*, can possibly pass over that Islamic-wire-suspension-Paradisaic bridge.

The Golden Gate is situated 456¼ feet from the north-east corner of the Haram. It is fifty-five feet in width, and projects about six. It was through this gate, tradition says, the Son of David made his triumphant entry into the city, and through it the Emperor Heraclius also entered triumphantly, bearing the Cross, which he had recovered from the Persians.

Whether it was blocked up by Christians or Moslems, is uncertain; but evident it is, that the latter are well content to let it remain closed, having the fear of the Bedawin as well as the Christian before their eyes.

All the gates of the city are scrupulously kept closed for an hour or two on every Friday (the Mohammedan Sabbath), because of a universal belief that an attempt will, sooner or later, be made by Christians to take the city at Friday noon. Nothing is positively known of the history of the small closed door, 50½ feet south of the Golden Gate, near which is an empty stone basin, formerly supplied with water from within, which has so much puzzled travellers. It is probable, however, that it was merely intended to substitute the Golden Gate, after its closure, and is the "Little Gate" that led down to the valley by many steps—mentioned by chroniclers of the crusading times. Nor is anything certainly known concerning the closed doorway, with pointed arch, on the south, 105 feet from the south-east corner. It is possible that horses may once have been stabled amongst the splendid colonnades within, according both to

Moslem and Christian tradition: and if so, this was the "Stable Door."

On the south side is the Triple Gate, 277 feet from the south-east corner (51 feet in width and 25 feet in height, now built up also), which may either have led through the substructions below to a Christian church or heathen temple; or, more probably, was originally the gate through which the bovine victims were led to the altar above.

HULDAH'S GATE.

The double doorway, partly concealed by the offices in the rear of Aksa, built up at the junction of the city and Haram walls, 334½ feet from the south-west corner of the Haram, is supposed to be the Huldah Gate of the Talmud by many, and is undoubtedly alluded to by Josephus (Ant. xv. xi: 5). It has all the characteristics of Jewish architecture, but the exterior entablature is unquestionably a Roman addition. The doors were originally 18 feet wide and 20 feet high. A double, vaulted archway of pure Jewish architecture, 258 feet long, leads to the area above.

I discovered an ancient doorway, quite similar to this, on the west side, about 270 yards from the south-west corner, which is also walled up.

The subjoined sketch shows a portion of the lintel of this doorway, beneath the lowermost iron-grated windows in the Haram wall—part of it being within the room underneath the vault that sustains the street leading up to the Haram. This gate is without doubt one of the two mentioned by Josephus as leading into Parbar; and is an important element in the restoration of the Temple. It also affords another proof of the reliability of the Hebrew historian.

LINTEL OF ANCIENT GATEWAY OF TEMPLE.

It is immediately beneath the present Mugaribeh Gate, and much of it entirely occluded by the house of Abu Seud Effendi, one of the city secretaries. Twenty feet two inches of the lintel now appear, which is six feet nine inches in breadth. This is probably only about one-half its width. The lintel is only four feet above the surface of the ground at present, just above the level of the basement of the Mekhemeh building; and is about twenty feet below the surface of the Haram area.

This gateway is about seventeen feet lower than Huldah's. Originally it doubtless gave admission to the area above by a flight of steps in a way similar to the passage from Huldah's Gate; and without doubt is one of the gates mentioned by Josephus as leading to the suburbs. During the period of my admission into the Haram enclosure I discovered in this immediate vicinity, on the interior, a portion of a closed gateway, about fourteen or fifteen feet wide; but whether it is connected with that on the exterior, I was not enabled to determine—for the guards became so much exasperated by my *infidel* desecration of the sacred room, el-Borak, where the great prophet tied his mule on that memorable night of the Hegira, that it was deemed the part of prudence to tarry there but a short time, and never to visit it again. But the accompanying illustration, though rather hastily taken, will convey a better impression of this place than the most prolix description.

Only the upper portion of the gateway can be seen—the lower part being excluded from view by a room, the roof or top of which is formed by the floor of this small apartment.

OLD PORTAL IN WESTERN WALL OF TEMPLE ENCLOSURE.

At the northern extremity of the eastern wall of the Haram may be noticed its projection eastward, about five feet six inches for the distance of eighty-three and a quarter feet. It is a very massive structure, and is no doubt on the site of one of the towers of the Antonia precincts, mentioned by Josephus; and while much of its upper portion is of inferior materials and workmanship, being evidently modern reparation, cyclopean stones extend to the very top at its northern termination, and apparently *in situ*—but they were no doubt thrown down by Titus, and replaced by Hadrian or some subsequent rebuilder of the city. Many of the stones are from fifteen to twenty or twenty-five feet in length, and vary in depth and width from three to eight or nine feet. These large Jewish stones are found in every part of the wall, sometimes however, only in one, two, or three courses, and frequently, indeed, only a few scattering ones, whose intervals are filled up by small ill-shaped stones, broken columns, capitals, pedestals, entablatures, &c.; but it is at the corner that they are seen in most colossal proportions, as chief "corner stones." At the south-east corner the stones, though cyclopean, are not quite as large as they are at the other corner, where the wall was more easily assailed. The wall here is seventy-seven feet in height, and is truly imposing. From some of these rocks may be observed cubical projections of more than half a foot extent; and a cavity of similar shape and dimensions in others, as if the prominences of the one were made to fit into the depressions of the other. The same fact is observed in the wall at the Wailing Place, and also on the Tower of Hippicus; and has caused a great deal of controversy, some supposing that they were originally so arranged as to form a stairway, others that they were designed to facilitate their handling. My own opinion is, that they were merely intended to secure the junction of an abutting wall, built subsequently to that against which it abuts.

Pursuing our survey around the patched wall of the Temple, on the south, we observe amongst its cyclopean masonry, immediately west of the Triple Gate, a stone, four feet wide and five and three-quarters long, standing on end—being built perpendicularly into the wall. It has a beautiful moulding on one edge, and probably once formed part of the decoration around the top of the old Temple wall, which Josephus says "was of excellent workmanship upwards and around the top of it." (Ant. xv. xi: 3.) The observant traveller will not fail to scan it with a critical eye. Just above the right hand upper corner of the subterranean gateway lintel, at the junction of the city and Temple walls, we find another proof of the hasty and imperfect manner in which this wall has been rebuilt, in the inverted inscription of one of its stones. Some of the letters are nearly effaced by the erosive influence of time and the elements; but the inscription may be satisfactorily made out as follows, by the aid of glasses:—

Titoailhadriano TITOAILHADRIANO

Antoninoavpio ANTONINOAVGPIO

pppontifaugvr PPPONTIFAVGVR

DD

From this inscription it may safely be inferred that the wall was rebuilt at a period certainly somewhat posterior to Antoninus Pius. At the south-west corner these colossal blocks of stone are found still larger than those at the other corners, as might be reasonably inferred from the vicinity of the immense bridge, *probably* just as they were placed by the architect of Solomon or his immediate successor. They vary in size from five to six and a quarter feet in thickness, and from twenty to thirty feet in length. Nearly all of the upper part of the wall, however, is rather indifferently constructed of small stones.

At a distance of thirty-nine feet from this corner, we reach the abutment of the celebrated Templo-Zion or Tyropœon Bridge, first identified by Dr. Robinson. It was fifty-one and a half feet in width, and extended at least three hundred and fifty feet in length, from abutment to abutment, across the Tyropœon. The radius of the arch, as correctly ascertained by repeated experiments on the spot, is twenty feet six inches. The span of the arch was therefore forty-one feet. The pier upon which this arch rests, projects eighteen inches from the wall; but not more than two feet of its height is now visible above ground—indeed none on its northern side, where trash is every day thrown from above.

From the top of the pier, where the arch springs, to corresponding level on the opposite side of the Tyropœon, is but little more than three hundred feet, though it is about three hundred and sixty from the level of the Haram-yard above to the corresponding level on the opposite cliff of Zion. Allowing a sufficient thickness of piers for such a massive structure, there were, probably, five or six arches across the Tyropœon. One of the blocks in the remaining portion of the bridge measures twenty-one feet, and another twenty-five, in length, by five and three-quarters in breadth.

WAILING PLACE OF THE JEWS.

At the "Wailing Place," which occupies a space of forty yards from a point about one hundred yards north of the corner, these large rocks are again visible, and in the pool beneath the causeway, they are in fine preservation; but the rest of the wall is concealed by houses as far as the Moat of Antonia, beyond which the wall is constructed of much smaller stones until it unites with the tower at the north-east corner.

Although many of these stones have been quarried and dressed nearly three thousand years, yet the *rebatement* or *rabbeting* on most of them is perfectly distinct and well defined. This supposed characteristic of Jewish architecture is generally designated by the term "bevelling," which term, however, signifying, as it does, an oblique rebatement, is incorrect: the sides of the channel being perpendicular, though very shallow (generally less than half an inch in depth), and one or two in width, and extend all around the exposed face of each rock.

A few of these lower tiers of stones have lain many centuries inhumed. And there is no *proof* that some of them have ever been removed from the position in which they were first placed: but this cannot justly be construed into a non-fulfilment of our Saviour's prophecy, recorded by Luke (xix. 44), in relation to the stones of the city. That relating to the Temple itself (Matt. xxiv. 2) has been so completely and literally fulfilled, that, so far as is known, not a single stone of that "magnifical" building is *left* in situ. That in Luke has been fulfilled in *spirit*, just as completely—the enemy *did* lay the devoted city even with the ground, and her children within her—in the sense intended; and in the same sense, "not one stone was left upon another," and yet no doubt there were millions of stones, actually lying one upon another in every part of the city!

Josephus informs us that, in building the outer wall of the Temple, it was necessary to commence the foundations in some of the ravines of Moriah, very far beneath the general surface of the earth. (Ant. viii. iii: 1, & W. v. v: 1.) Now the Saviour certainly did not intend us to understand that the Romans, in overthrowing the city, would dig down into the bowels of the earth, and draw up these immense stones, there "bound together by lead and iron!" Nor was it to be expected that, when the Roman soldiers had thrown down the upper tiers of stones, and their accumulation at the base of the wall had so far obstructed the work of subversion, as to render it impracticable, without carrying these stones away into the country, to get at the foundation stones, they would thus remove these immense masses, in order to remove the *foundation* of the wall! Josephus uses language still more explicit and sweeping than this; and declares (W. vii. i: 1) that after the subversion of the city by Titus, "There was left nothing to make those that came thither believe it ever had been inhabited!" And yet who that understands the nature of language, would think of charging that historian (as sceptics have so foolishly charged this prophecy) with falsification!

BUILDINGS WITHIN THE ENCLOSURE.

Kubbet es-Sakhrah—Dome of the Rock—Mosk of Omar—Temple.—A marble-paved platform, very similar in outline to the enclosing bounds of the Haram es-Sherif, but only one-sixth its area, is situated within it, and near its middle, but rather closer to its western and northern than its southern and eastern boundaries. The surface of the Haram area being not perfectly plane, but more elevated on the north-western quarter, where it is entirely composed of rock, than elsewhere, the platform is not equally elevated above the ground on all sides; but its average height is at least ten feet, though the central portion of the north side is not half that height. It is ascended through eight portals of Saracenic style, some of which are truly elegant.

The superb edifice called by Moslems Kubbet es-Sakhrah (Dome of the Rock), and by Franks, the Mosk of Omar, is situated rather below the middle of the platform—being nearest to the western side, and farthest from the northern. It is about one hundred and seventy feet in diameter and the same in height. The lower story, or main body of the building, is a true octagon, of sixty-seven feet on a side; but the central and elevated portion is circular. A more graceful and symmetrical dome than that which crowns the building, is perhaps nowhere to be found; and the lofty bronze crescent that surmounts the whole gives a pleasing architectural finish, despite its soul-sickening associations. The dome appears to be covered with copper, also the roof to the investing building; but laterally it is everywhere covered with porcelain tiles of richest color, except the lower half of the octagonal sides, which are encased with rich marble of various colors and devices. And a *very dim*, religious light is shed through sixteen windows of the richest stained glass, with which the circular body of the building is pierced. The lower story is forty-six feet high, and has seven windows of stained glass on each side—fifty-six in all.* Just above the windows, numerous extracts from the Koran, in very large Turkish letters, run all around the building. There are four doors, and as many porches, each facing a cardinal point, the southern one affording the main entrance.

The dome and its circular shaft are supported by four very massive piers, and twelve arches resting on pillars, within which, enclosed by a gilt iron railing, and overhung by the richest crimson silk canopy, is the celebrated rock (Sakhrah) which gives name and interest to the building. Around this inner building there is an octagonal aisle thirty feet wide, and around this, separated only by eight piers and sixteen pillars, is another, the outer one, thirteen feet in width. The columns are mostly composed of a purplish breccia kind of marble or porphyry, with gilded Corinthian capitals. The ceiling of the octagonal portion is studded with large gilded rosettes; but there was not sufficient light beneath the interior dome to enable me to make out the intricate gilt patterns above.

Immediately beneath the centre of the dome, is the venerated rock about which so much has been written. In the estimation of the Jew, this is by far the most hallowed spot on earth: for, according to the Rabbins, this is the identical rock upon which Jacob pillowed his head "and set it up for a pillar and poured oil upon the

* The arches of these windows are, on the outside, slightly pointed, Tudor fashion; but this applies only to the outer tile-work—the stonework being semicircular. The windows in the interior, however, are slightly pointed.

top of it; and he called the name of that place Bethel"—House of God. (Gen. xxviii. 17, 22). It is the general belief also, that it is the threshing-floor of Araunah the Jebusite—the spot where the faith of Abraham was so sorely tried in his determined obedience to God to offer up Isaac; and the site of the Holy of Holies of the Temple—which glowed beneath the Divine manifestation of Deity in the Shekinah. The Mahommedans affirm, with assured confidence, that it was from this very rock also, that their ubiquitous time-and-space-annihilating prophet bounded upwards though seven heavens; and in attestation of the fact—to the confusion of all gainsaying blasphemers and opposers—they show the imprint of his foot in the solid rock, the impress of the angels' fingers in withholding the rock that it might not accompany the prophet in his celestial flight (as it *actually* commenced doing, and hence its inclined position they say), and the veritable ring still suspended from a staple in a neighboring wall. When brought to light by Omar, it was inhumed beneath an immense mound of rubbish and filth. But it had previously been crowned by Hadrian's splendid Temple of Jupiter Capitolinus. The present noble structure over and around it, is undoubtedly the work of the munificent Khaliff Abd-el Melek, though often supposed to be a Christian edifice.

The shape of the Sakhrah is irregular, though approximating somewhat that of the platform on which it is situated, but in reverse position. It is about sixty feet in length from north to south, and fifty-five in breadth. It rises about five feet above the marble floor of the Mosk, and would consequently be about fifteen feet above the central portion of the ground, but, inasmuch as it is situated immediately on the ridge, it is probably not elevated more than eight or ten feet above the contiguous ground.

In the south-east portion of this rock is a small room, irregularly square and roughly finished, about eight feet in height, and fifteen on each side—"The Noble Cave." Its ceiling is about four or five feet below the upper surface of the rock, from four to six feet thick, and pierced with an oval-shaped hole about three feet in diameter: the sides are plastered in order to produce the *impression* that this immense rock is *now* supported by a wall of masonry. They allege that it is *really* sustained by *nothing*, and this *wall* was merely placed here to deceive the pilgrims, on account of fatal accidents to persons who had gone below and found themselves beneath such an immense *unsustained* rock! An empty, hollow sound being emitted on striking the northern side, shows undoubtedly that vacant space is beyond. On stamping upon a circular stellar-constructed piece of variegated marble about the centre of the floor, sonorous reverberations are emitted, clearly evincing the existence of a large excavation below this stellated slab, which they say closes the door to Hades. This is the Bîr Arruah, or "Well of Souls," which was formerly kept open for the convenience of holding intercourse with departed spirits; but on account of urgent prudential considerations, deeply affecting the honor of certain hareems of the city, it was deemed best to close it. Is this the "*Lapis pertussus*" of the pilgrim fathers, that the Jews so much venerated? Access is had to this room by a pair of steps cut in the native rock, just above which, on entering the door of the room, is a tongue very highly revered by good Moslems. This whole rock is fine limestone, or coarse marble somewhat mottled, and the tongue is nothing more than a small portion of it, developed in making the entrance, that being somewhat like the tougue in shape and color, received that designation: but *truly*, if we may credit their legends, this "unruly member" has uttered some things hard to be understood! There are various recesses cut in the rock both above and below, indicating the spots where Abraham, Elijah, David, Solomon, and other renowned Hebrews were in the habit of praying; and a prayer offered there even by us *infidels*, as all Christians are termed, they say, must be effectual. But, besides these operations of the chisel, large portions of the rock have also been cut away for no obvious reason, particularly on the west where it has been nicely squared off and lowered; on the north also it has been chiselled away to the thickness of only a foot or two. It is supposed, how-er, to have been done by the Crusaders, when they covered it with iite marble, and reared an altar upon it, calling the building the Temple of the Lord," under the impression that this is the rock on which David sacrificed in order to stay the progress of the ague.

The Moslem tradition concerning the Sakhrah is that it fell from aven about the time that the spirit of prophecy was imparted. iis holy stone, they say, wished to accompany the prophet in s nocturnal flight to heaven; and actually started; but in response the "great prophet's" prayers, the angel Gabriel was dispatched stay its flight: and so firm was the grasp by which it was retained, at the impression of the angels' hands are to be seen there to is day.

They allege also that the Mosk contains the scales for weighing e souls of men, the shield of Mohammed, the birds of Solomon, e pomegranates of David, the saddle of el-Borak, and an original py of the Koran the parchment leaves of which are four feet ng. A well of soul-refreshing water is also alleged to exist there. green slab of marble is also shown, formerly nailed down by ghteen silver nails, three of which still remain. This, it seems, is a ind of chronological table: a nail having been withdrawn for each rand epoch in their history, and when the last nail takes its flight, e consummation of all things will occur. So rapid, they say, was e prophet's flight through the heavens, that although he had various onversations with Moses and others whom he saw in heaven, he eturned in time to prevent the falling of a silver urn, which abriel's wing happened to strike as they mounted on high! Such re a few of their absurd legends concerning this marvelous rock. hey serve at least to exhibit the puerility of Moslem ideas and the rength of their credulity.

This edifice was no doubt built by Abd-el-Melek Ibn Marwan, hough some attribute it to Khalif Omar. But no one should ccuse such a creature as this filthy Arab of building such an edi ce: and moreover, we learn that the Mosk built by him was a very inferior structure except in size: and besides all this, there is a Mosk specially known by his name under the roof of Aksa.

Mosk el-Aksa—Palatium—Porticus seu Templum Solomonis—Church of the Presentation.—The large barn-like structure built against the southern wall of the Haram, on the interior, rather nearer its western than its eastern side, is called by the Moslem, Jamey el-Aksa—Mosk of Aksa. Apart from its modern additions on the east, which are mere workshops and magazines, it is a regular parallelogram in shape—two hundred and eighty feet in length, and a hundred and eighty-three in breadth. The central portions, on the east and the west, only rise thirty or forty feet; the central body of the building is about twice that height; and the dome at its southern extremity is nearly as lofty as that of Kubbet es-Sakhrah, though considerably smaller.

There seems to be no particular style of architecture predominant; but rather a jumble of various orders, composite *ad infinitum.* It looks as if it may have been built in cruciform shape originally, and been brought into quadrangular form by lateral additions to the breadth of the transepts. Its portico, which is on the north, directly facing the Dome of the Rock, extends the entire breadth of the present building, and is not specially imposing. There are seven front doors, corresponding to the number of arches in the porch, the easternmost of which gives entrance into the isolated apartment, where alone the women are permitted to worship.* Scarcely a doubt can be entertained that this is one of the *Mary-churches* built by the Emperor Justinian, and described by Procopius, the thaumaturgic historian of his architectural works. The Saracens seem to have converted it into a mosk, and metamorphosed it as much as possible. Its portico is said, by Arabian historians, to have been as completely covered with gold plate, by one of their

* The arches throughout this church are erroneously represented as pointed, in Mr. Catherwood's beautiful drawings—a circumstance upon which a false theory has been reared by several writers.

halifs, as ever any portion of the Temple of Solomon was; but, at his time, has neither gold nor anything else valuable about it.

The Crusaders, on becoming possessed of it, greatly enlarged it y additions on the east—a dormitory, refectory, infirmary, and ther offices, as well as a church. I observed, in walking over the south-eastern part of the Haram area, large patches of tesselated pavement, closely resembling that of the present Mosk el-Aksa; which, in all probability, indicate the locality of the church there erected by the Franks. "The poor fellow-soldiers of Jesus Christ," as they quaintly enough styled themselves, had quarters assigned o them here by Baldwin II., A. D. 1119; and hence the name *Templars*, by which they became known. According to Hovenden, he murderers of Thomas à Becket lie interred in front of this building—"*Hic jacent miseri qui martyrizaverunt beatum Thomam Archiepiscopum Cantuariensum.*"

Mosk of Abû Bekr.—This building is situated between el-Aksa Mosk and the western wall, being about two hundred and forty feet in length, and seventy in breadth—used for educational as well as devotional purposes—a very plain hall with the exception of a fine pulpit or two.

The Mugrabin Mosk.—At a distance of about thirty feet from the western wall this Mosk of the Western African negroes runs off at nearly right angles to the Mosk Abû Bekr, and parallel to the western Haram wall. It consists of a single hall one hundred and seventy-three feet long and twenty-five wide, having a portico in front. The space between this Mosk and the wall is a large public court, in front of the premises occupied by Abû Seud Effendi, one of the Town Clerks, the southern end of which is covered by four pretty little domes. And on the wall is quite a picturesque kiosk or summer-house belonging to this functionary.

The Colonnade running around the remainder of the northern and western sides of the Haram, includes within it various cells, cloisters, &c., for religious and educational purposes, as well as dormitories for the Mauritanian Eunuchs, and Dervish snake charmers. In a room beneath one of these cells, the entrance to which is just above the Mogrebin Gate, is an iron ring, very much venerated by the *faithful*, as being the identical martial ring, *they say*, where the Great Prophet tied the celestial mule the night of his never-to-be-forgotten-or-questioned ascent to heaven! It happens, however, to be quite a new piece of pious manufacture.

Sidna Issa is the name of a small domed building in the south-east corner of the Haram, called "of our Lord Jesus," in the lower room of which is an irregularly shaped trough, made of Jerusalem marble, usually called a sarcophagus, but is more probably a baptistery—at least it resembles such as I have seen in the Greek Churches for the baptism of children. There is a genuine sarcophagus, however, in the Mekhemeh, in which the drinking-water of the city council is kept—a royal one too—being brought, as they affirm, from the Tombs of the Kings.

The Mart of Science, strangely enough so called, is another small domed building immediately adjacent on the west.

The Altar of David, now in ruins, is situated midway between the Mart of Science and the Mosk el-Aksa. *The buildings around the platform* are principally used for offices, though some of them are occasionally occupied by pilgrims.

Coursi Sûliman, where the faithful profess to exhibit the Royal Throne of the Son of David, is a much venerated and very sacred locality, adjoining the east wall, about half-way between the Golden Gateway and the north-east corner.

The Dome of the Chain, or *Judgment Seat of David*, is a beautiful little fane, situated twenty feet east of the Dome of the Rock. It is said to have been built as a model for the Kubbet es-Sakhrah; but if so, it has been but poorly imitated. The idea that it was a treasure house is equally absurd. It was no doubt designed merely as a praying-place. There are many little oratories scattered about the sacred precinct, as may be seen by reference to the plan, and innumerable niches for private devotions, accommodating but one person. *The pulpit*, situated a few feet north-west of the gateway, immediately between el-Aksa and Kubbet es-Sakhrah, is a perfect gem of art. It is from this "*Sacred Stand*," that prayers are regularly offered up for the Sultan.

The Minarets of the Haram, to which there are no less than four attached, contribute not a little to its architectural beauty. The dark green cypresses that so gracefully wave their tall heads over the sacred enclosure once adorned by the most splendid marbles and precious stones contrasting so richly with the silvery olive and stunted acacias, cannot fail to remind the observer of the fulfilment of the prophecy denounced by Micah the Morasthite (iii. 12); and this interest is keenly enhanced on learning that some of these trees, as if in derision to Zion, were specially imported from Stamboul, the very head quarters of the "worst of the heathen!"

Substructions of South-east Corner—Solomon's Stables.—The substructions under the south-east corner of the Haram are doubtless alluded to by Josephus in describing the construction of the Temple wall. The declination of the hill being greater here than elsewhere, it was found more advantageous to bring it to a general level, by erecting vaults upon lofty columns, than by filling up either with solid masonry, or by earth as in the case of the narrow ravines.

The length of the rock galleries or substructures from east to west is three hundred and nineteen feet; from north to south the length of the avenues varies considerably, being two hundred and forty-seven and a quarter feet at the triple gateway; they are quite short on the east, with the exception of the colonnade leading from this gateway, but become one hundred and eighty-six feet six inches in length as they approach the eastern wall. (See plan on large Map.) The keenest controversies have been waged about these substructions, which are undoubtedly of the highest antiquity, and pre-eminently possess the peculiar features of Jewish architecture: and as they are more or less involved in all the various schemes for the restoration of the Temple, it will be well to give the details of my measurements*—a bird's-eye view of which is seen, *in situ*, at the south-east corner of the Haram enclosure—which will enable the reader the better to appreciate the accompanying perspective view of these remarkable substructures.

SUBSTRUCTIONS SUSTAINING THE SOUTH-EAST CORNER OF THE HARAM ES-SHERIF YARD.

Measurement of Substructions.—Proceeding westward from the eastern wall along the second row from the southern wall, the following is a correct statement of the sizes of the pillars or piers, and walls, with the distance between each in feet and inches.

* It is to be regretted that there is not a closer coincidence between my measurements and those of that able architect and engineer, the late Mr. Catherwood, who also had an opportunity of making a plan of these substructions.

Measurement of ground plan.

Spaces from interior of wall to pier . .	10 ft.	1 in.	Thickness of pier . .	3 ft.	5 in.
Next space " " . .	10	1	" " . .	3	5
" " " . .	12	10	" " . .	3	5
" " " . .	13	8	" " . .	3	3
" " " . .	23		Thickness of wall . .	4	10
" " " . .	23	4	" " . .	3	3
" " " . .	17	10	" " .	3	6
" " " . .	17	7	" " . .	3	6
" " " . .	14	9	" " . .	3	6
" " " . .	17	3	" " . .	3	6
" " " . .	17	6	" " . .	3	6
" " " . .	17	4	" " . .	3	6
" " " . .	18	3	" " . .	8	3*
" " " . .	15	10	Thickness of pier . .	4	
" " " . .	5	3	" " . .	4	
" " " . .	14	1	Projection of pier . .	1	8
	258	7		60	6
	60	6			
	319	1			

The three last spaces comprise the interior of the Triple Gate, embracing a distance of fifty-three feet two inches: but deducting from it the projections from the two walls, one foot eight inches from the western, and six inches from the eastern, it corresponds exactly with the width on the outside—fifty-one feet.

Measured from south to north along the third row from the eastern wall, their length is one hundred and eighty-six feet seven inches, divided as follows:—

Space from interior of wall to pier . .	11 ft.	8 in.	Thickness of pier . .	3 ft.	8 in.
" " " . .	11		" " . .	3	5
" " " . .	11	5	" " . .	3	6
" " " . .	11	4	" " . .	3	6
" " " . .	12	10	" " . .	3	5
" " " . .	12	9	" " . .	3	7
" " " . .	12	10	" " . .	3	8
" " " . .	12	2	" " . .	3	6
" " " . .	11	10	" " . .	3	5

* Projection.

South-east corner of Haram.					Position and size of its sustaining pillars.			
"	"	"	12 ft.	2 in.	"	"	3 ft.	5 in.
"	"	"	12	2	"	"	3	5
"	"	"	12		"	"	3	11
			144	2			42	5
			42	5				
			186	7				

There are seven rows of this length, but the next two are only about half as long; and the remaining three are still shorter, embracing the width of only three ranges. Then comes the Triple Gate passage, the westernmost arcade of which extends two hundred and forty-seven feet, but the middle and easternmost are both shorter. Measured on the westernmost wall, the recesses and pilasters alternate as follows:—

Jam projection					3 ft.	6 in.
Projection of wall, or broad pilaster					8	3
Recess of wall	10 ft.	7 in.	Pilaster or projection of wall		4	
" "	10	7	" " "		4	1
" "	10	7	" " "		4	
" "	10	8	" " "		4	
" "	10	7	Wall		167	
	53	00			194	10
					53	
					247	10

At the commencement of the *wall* the solid rock forty-two feet long projects about a yard from the ground, the upper end of which is arched for about fifteen feet. In front of the western door of Triple Gate is an oval-shaped well five or ten yards in diameter. In the third recess is a doorway, now blocked up, but formerly, perhaps, communicating with the Mosk el-Aksa.

The following arrangement obtains in the two rows of piers in the triple gateway passage:—

Position and size of pillars of substruction.

Internal projection of triple gate pier				10 ft.	8 in.
Space to next pier	11 ft.	7 in.	Thickness of pier	5	
" "	9	8	" "	5	
" "	9	8	" "	4	11
" "	9	7	" "	4	10
" "	7	8	" "	3	8
" "	7	8	" "	5	
" "	9	6	" "	5	
" "	9	6	" "	5	
" "	9	6	" "	5	
" "	9	6	" "	4	11
" "	9	6	" "	4	11
" "	9	6	Length of wall	74	
	112	10		137	11
	137	10			
	250	08			

Two octagonal columns, $2\frac{1}{3}$ feet in diameter, support the arches on each side of the gateway, that rest upon the gate piers, and the next two succeeding piers, as represented in the accompanying woodcut.

TRIPLE GATE UNDER MESJID EL-AKSA.

Between the sixth and seventh piers are large masses of live rock, and a descent into the earth; but entirely choked with rubbish—as is also a large archway. There is a gradual ascent from the Triple Gate to the termination of the passage, which nearly comes in contact with the vaults. May not the bullocks and other large victims have been introduced into the Temple by this gentle ascent?

Measurement across the northern end of Substructions, going westward.

	ft.	in.		ft.	in.
Interval from east wall to first pier .	12 ft.	0 in.	Thickness of pier . .	3 ft.	5 in.
Pier to pier	13	11	" " . .	3	5
"	14	4	" " . .	3	5
"	13	9	" " . .	3	9
"	23	6	" " . .	4	10
"	22	10	" " . .	3	2
"	19	6	" " . .	3	5
	119	10		25	5
	25	5			
	145	3			

It is thus perceived that these arcades, instead of running parallel with the eastern wall, and with each other, are divergent—having gained nine feet four inches in the space of seven ranges; by which arrangement the remainder are made perpendicular to the south wall.

The piers near the south wall are composed of five of these quadrilateral stones, whose breadth and thickness are always less than their height, which is about five feet. The vaults are here about thirty feet high; though the lower portions of the piers are so much concealed by rubbish, that not more than twenty-five feet appears. The Saracenic door is entirely concealed by a large heap of dirt and rubbish. The windows on the exterior are about one foot below the vaulted ceiling. The thickness of the vaults, inclusive of the earth upon them, is about five feet. The large stones in the south-east corner, serving as a foundation for Sidna Issa, are very irregularly piled together—indicating great carelessness in its construction. The lower courses of stones in the eastern wall of the Temple project very irregularly, and have never been squared off.

About midway the easternmost range of arcades, we were shown the rock in which Solomon tortured the demon. The guides informed us very gravely that some of the faithful, conceiving the idea that there was treasure concealed in it, attempted to get at the contents by means of a pickaxe; but the first blow caused the devil to cry out, "Let me alone." And, sure enough, they did; nor has any one been since found with courage requisite to the task of repeating the experiment! Its height is six feet, its length four and a third, and its breadth three and three-fourths; and is precisely like those now serving as pedestals to the Triple Gate piers. Hundreds of small pyramidal piles of stones are seen all about the floor—the Ebenezer memorials of devout Moslem devotees from the ends of the earth. Large roots of olive-trees have found their way through the northern portion of some of the vaults, where they are but a short distance above the floor; and slender radical filaments several yards in length are gracefully pendent from many parts of the vaulted ceiling. This is also a favorite haunt for owls, hawks, and ravens.

Judging from appearances, these piers may all be ascribed to Solomon or his immediate successors, though the vaults are apparently more modern. At the Triple Gate, the floor within coincides with the surface of the ground without; but at the south-east angle it is about twenty-two feet higher.

Substructures of el-Aksa.—Having described the substructions in the south-east corner, we pass on to those beneath the Mosk el-Aksa. Immediately within the double gateway, usually called "Huldah's Gate," is a vestibule or entrance-hall fifty feet long, and forty-two wide, which is the width of the passage throughout. In the centre of this hall, is a monolithic column of the ordinary limestone of the country, six and a quarter feet in diameter, and twenty-one feet high, with foliated capital of no special order, but yet tasteful, from the top of which spring the arches that

SUBSTRUCTIONS OF EL-AKSA.

support the four domes, composing the ceiling. There are four white Corinthian columns attached to the doorway—one to each side of each door; but they are by no means well paired. From between the two middle Corinthian pillars, a pier projects inward about twelve feet, whose termination is pillar-shaped. At the middle of the northern end of this hall, is an oval pillar, whose diameters are six feet eight inches by four feet six inches, in the midst of a flight of steps once extending the whole breadth of the room; but now only to be seen on its western half, those on the eastern side being concealed by some large blocks of Jewish stones; and a modern Turkish wall. These nine steps at the commencement of this upper passage, occupy a space of about nineteen feet in length, and eight and three-quarters elevation. The floor of this passage is horizontal for a distance of one hundred and twenty-four feet; there is then a gentle inclined plane for the space of twenty-five and a half feet, after which it is again level for the space of thirty-eight feet, to its termination at the north foundation wall of el-Aksa, where entrance is had to the area above by a flight of steps, being two hundred and fifty-nine feet long. This passage is divided throughout its entire length by either piers, pillars, or a wall. Several short walls also run across to its eastern side, either from piers or the longitudinal wall. The eastern half of the passage is either really or thus apparently made shorter than the other. Two low segmental vaults overspan this double passage its entire length. This passage is not situated medially beneath el-Aksa Mosk, but somewhat east of its central line. The entire workmanship of the vaulted passages is characteristically Jewish, with the exception of some trifling Turkish additions and alterations. But the lower room or vestibule to the passage has been considerably Romanized; and the entablature on the exterior must also be referred to Roman architects. The idea is entertained by some, that much of the furniture and treasures of the ancient Temple lie concealed on one side or the other of this passage, and a closed door on the eastern side of the vestibule seems to indicate that there is vacant space between this passage and that of the Triple Gateway. But none of the keepers of the Haram are of that opinion; nor had they even heard that there is any void space westward of the passage.

An attempt to penetrate the wall on the west of the vestibulum has been made, and half a dozen large stones removed from the interior face; but whether the remaining thickness of the wall was found too firmly fixed to be removed, or has been partially removed and (no vacuity being found) was replaced, I could not learn—the attempt not having been made in modern times. The suggestion that hidden treasure might be concealed in that unknown place, so excited the good Effendi's *curiosity*, that he expressed his intention to explore it, should it not prove utterly impenetrable. But it is highly probable, that even if there were no projecting native rock there originally, that the position of such an immense bridge as that abutting against the neighboring wall, would require that this place should be filled with solid masonry. The subterranean pools discovered during these explorations are noticed under the water resources of Jerusalem.

CHAPTER XVIII.

WATER RESOURCES OF JERUSALEM.

ACCORDING to Mejr ed-Din, "the Mohammedans believe that all the water on earth comes from under the Sakhrah, which is a marvel, because being without support on any side, it is supported only by Him who supported the heavens, which can only fall on the earth by His permission;" and yet, at this time, there is not a single perennial stream of water in the whole city of Jerusalem; and only one is to be found throughout all its immediate environs. There is a small stream which for a few weeks in the winter flows down a short bifurcation of the Kedron Valley, half a mile above Jerusalem; and a mile below the city another ephemeral fountain (ain ed-Durrage) gushes forth violently a few weeks in the winter, whenever the well En-rogel overflows—running a few hundred yards in conjunction with the En-rogel stream, and then sinking into the earth like the one above. But Siloam is the only perennial stream about Jerusalem—if indeed that can be called a *perennial stream* which only flows a few hours daily, and runs only a few hundred yards before it is all absorbed by the earth—the Siloam gardens. Nor is this deficiency of running water compensated by numerous wells of living water: for there is but one such well within the limits of the city, and one without. Some writers mention another, situated between Absalom's Pillar and the Kedron Bridge; but the Fellah whom I lowered down to explore it, reports that it is supplied entirely (as it evidently is in part) by the rains, and is more than one hundred feet in circumference. Some writers enumerate the Well of Flagellation and the two large tanks at Damascus Gate amongst the living waters of Jerusalem; but improperly so. For the two latter (the northernmost one of which is sometimes called the "Pool of the Cotton Grotto") are entirely dry the latter part of summer, and evidently supplied by rain-water conducted into them by drains on the side of the road. The Well of Flagellation was dug in Ibrahim Pasha's reign, and seems at no time to have less than a depth of three or four feet of water; but it has no perceptible inlet or outlet—the water apparently oozing into it from the surrounding rubbish, and finding no way of escape, overflows in the winter. It is not specially palatable, and abounds in animalculæ: but "good padre Charley" serves it to his visiters with such special good grace, that the traveller likes to sip a little of it that he may with better grace *buckshish* the good-natured friar with a few piasters.

Such is the scanty supply of water at present: but if the site of Jerusalem was not originally well supplied with water, why was not Etham, Betir, Mispah, or other places in its neighborhood, abounding with water, and equally defensible, selected as the capital of Israel? The inference is, that it was at least sufficiently well supplied. Referring the reader, however, to Chapter IX. for an account of the supply of water with which the city was furnished at former periods; the object of the present chapter will be simply to speak of the now existing water resources of the Holy City.

Bîr Eyûb—Bîr Yûab—Well of Job or Joab—Well of Nehemiah —Well of Fire—Lucilliana—En-rogel.—Just below the junction of the Hinnom and Kedron Valleys, at the head of *Wady en-Nair*, or Valley of Fire, is a deep well of living waters, called by the present Christian population of Jerusalem, the Well of Nehemiah; but known amongst the Turks and Arabs under the appellation of Bîr Eyûb, or Yûab—Well of Job or Joab. It is called Nehemiah's

Well because "tradition saith"* that here the zealous old reformer recovered the holy fire of the altar from a cave communicating with the bottom of this well, where it had been concealed ever since the destruction of the Temple by Nebuchadnezzar. In consequence of this legend it was for many ages called "*Puteus ignis*"—hence, also, the name of this valley—Valley of Fire—Wady en-Nair. No plausible reason is assigned why it should be named after the pious old patriarch of Uz; but the Arabs allege that this is the well whereof God said to Job, "Put thy foot in this cold hole." Nor is the secondary part played by Joab in the rebellion of Adonijah here concocted, a very plausible reason for naming it after that reckless chieftain. This well† occupying precisely the spot where we should expect to find the En-rogel of Joshua, it is doubtless that famous landmark between Benjamin and Judah; but as nothing is heard of it for many long ages, it was probably sealed by some of the various possessors of Jerusalem, in order to deprive their enemies of its use, and left in that condition for centuries. That this was temporarily the case in the days of the Crusaders, we may be assured; for we are told by various chroniclers of the Crusades, that all the fountains about the city were thus stopped. Nor can it be doubted that it was one of the fountains stopped by Hezekiah. (2 Chr. xxxii. 4.)

It has probably been frequently deepened and enlarged in the lapse of ages. Mejr ed-Din reports from other authors that "it is constructed of large stones, each ten cubits long and four wide, and it is marvellous how they can have been let down such a depth. It was dug to the depth of eighty cubits in a time of drought; the water is fresh, and at that depth, except in the winter, when it overflows, inundates the valley, and turns a mill.‡ I descended into the well with the laborers, to dig there." Its present depth is one

* For full account see 2 Mac. i. 18-36.

† Josephus calls it a *fountain*—in the Latin version *fons*—in the Greek πηγή.

‡ A large millstone still to be seen in the valley below gives some slight confirmation to this assertion.

hundred and twenty-four feet: but the height at which the water stands is exceedingly fluctuating—and sometimes actually overflows—not generally at its mouth, but finds exit under an arch about ten feet below, on its south side—rising out of the ground behind a stone fence, forty yards lower down the valley.

The following extract from my note-book will give a sufficient idea of the height of water at various seasons, and the quantity vented when it overflows.

Oct. 26th, 1852.—Depth of water in Bîr Yûab (before the fall of rain), 42½ feet. Hundreds of donkey loads of water daily carried to the city—perhaps a thousand.

Sept. 12th, 1853.—Two thousand donkey loads daily carried to the city = 4000 skins or 25,000 gallons.

Oct. 7th.—Only 6½ feet depth of water.

Nov. 18th.—21 feet deep. This increase of depth is not due to the few showers that have fallen; but because much less is now required for city consumption—since a little rain has found its way into the tanks.

March 2d, 1854.—The well has been overflowing vigorously for some days—also the fount ed-Durrage—the former venting at least two or three hundred gallons per minute, and the latter perhaps forty or fifty. Well continued overflowing till the last of March—twenty-four or twenty-five days in all.

April 6th.—Well has been again overflowing two or three days; though not venting more than twenty gallons per minute—and this stream is absorbed into the earth before it reaches Ain ed-Durrage, four hundred yards below.

Adjacent to the well, on the north, is a small stone building, within and around which are five or six stone-plastered troughs, about ten feet long and four or five wide and deep. Anxiously did I await such a period of exhaustion of its waters that I might be enabled to explore it; but during the whole period of my sojourn at the Holy City, never did it subside sufficiently. But the Arabs who had descended the well assured me that there was quite a lake connected with it; but so low was the passage connecting it with the well, that it could only be entered when the water was nearly exhausted. Ten or fifteen yards south-west of the well is a small wely called Lewan, and a tank in front of it, about forty feet square, now usually filled by the winter rains.

Ain ed-Durrage.—This ephemeral fountain, situated four hundred yards below this well, undoubtedly derives its water either directly from Bîr Eyûb, or from a source common to them both:—for it never flows till the former is actually overflowing, or nearly full enough to vent itself through the underground passage outwards. A tradition, current amongst the Moslems, and challenged by none, declares that there is a flight of steps reaching from the bottom of the Well of Joab to this fountain, by which access was once had to these nether aquatic regions!

VIRGIN'S FOUNT—DRAGON'S FOUNT.—*Fount of Siloam—Fount of the Sun—Bath of Samuel—Bethesda—Ain Silwan Fowk—Ain Sitte Myriam—Ain Om ed-Durrage.*—This celebrated fountain is nowhere mentioned in the Scriptures or the writings of Josephus, though known at various times by the name of almost every piece of water about the Holy City. It makes its appearance in the pierced side of Ophel, on the west of the Valley of Kedron, about 365 yards from the south-west projection of that ridge, and is well worthy of minute examination: but the accompanying diagram and illustration enable us to dispense with much verbal description. The usual depth of water in this receptacle is only about three feet at present, on account of loose stones and rubbish within it. Its main stream issues from beneath the north end of the lowest step, but it also rises about midway the pool on the south side, boiling up with considerable force. A dropping and trickling may also be heard, showing that it descends considerably. This stream ebbs and flows quite irregularly; but generally three or four times per day in autumn, and oftener in spring—running from two to four hours in the twenty-four, and appearing perfectly quiescent during the remainder of the day; although a little water

VIRGIN'S FOUNT.

always runs. In general, its flow is not perceptible thirty minutes after the first gush, and sometimes not even fifteen: but this depends entirely upon the amount of rain that has fallen the previous season. Its temperature is very uniformly about 65° Fahrenheit, throughout the year. The tortuous channel that conveys this stream to the Pool of Siloam has been thoroughly examined by Drs. Robinson and Smith, as well as by some few other adventurous explorers; but I was not so successful myself—having reached a point (after crawling several hundred feet) where, owing to an accumulation of rubbish, there was barely room to keep my mouth out of the water, even when my head was pressed against the upper surface of the channel, I was compelled to abandon the enterprise, and *crawfish* it, as best I could. But though thus thwarted in my effort, this was quite a fortunate issue of the adventure compared with that of the Abbe Des' Massures, in 1819, who was compelled to remain twenty-four hours in the canal through fear of the Arabs. The length of this passage is stated at 1750 feet by Dr. Robinson, and no doubt correctly—though, in a direct line, the two extremities cannot be much more than 1000 feet apart. These gentlemen, however, are evidently mistaken in their conclusion that there is no "lateral passage by which water might come in from another quarter." On closely examining a passage turning north, at a distance of forty-nine feet from the upper extremity, it was found to be the termination of the channel leading across Ophel from Mount Zion, and explored as far as a point near the present Mugrabin Gate.

This receptacle was evidently more capacious at one time—at least in its southern and eastern dimensions. The present masonry has probably not been there much more than three centuries; for Felix Fabri mentions that the fountain was descended "*sine gradibus in arena*," and originally it must, in the nature of things, have run down the Valley of the Kedron. There was formerly an inscription above the entrance, but it is now no longer decipherable. There are two Mihrabs (or praying-places), one within on the middle platform, and the other without, on a paved platform; but the Mosk that once adorned its entrance has long since disappeared. That this place was once sealed and used as a well is rendered highly probable by an opening in the solid rock over the lower flight of steps, now partially stopped. This, of course, was one of the fountains sealed by Hezekiah; and perhaps that great aqueductor also perforated Ophel with its present channel. But if Hezekiah is not the actual author of this work, it was at least dictated by similar policy. The conclusion that this fountain, pool, or well (for it either is or has been entitled to each designation) originally flowed down the Kedron, is irresistible, unless resort be had to the far-fetched theory that it is brought, not by a natural, but artificial channel, and diverted from some other quarter—a surmise which, though adopted by high authority, is not only entirely untenable, but too unreasonable to need serious refutation. It was, no doubt, always outside the walls; but by means of this canal was effectually diverted from the use of the enemy, and *sent* where it would either be consumed for domestic purposes or turned into the "Lower Pool" for defence. The top-most step is five feet above the channel of the Kedron at this point, and twenty-nine higher than the surface of the water: the difference of level therefore between the Kedron Valley and the surface of the pool within is twenty-four feet. But the Kedron soon sinks far below the level of this water.

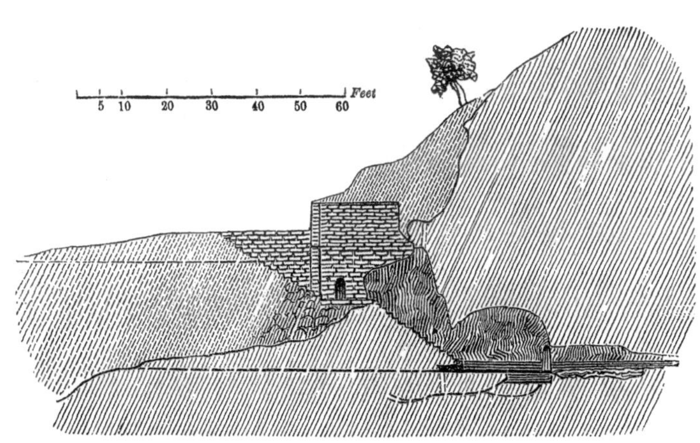

PLAN OF VIRGIN'S FOUNT (PERPENDICULAR SECTION).

*In beautiful contrast with the general nudity and arid sterility of the soil around Jerusalem, during the larger portion of the year, is "her garden and her pleasant green;" that "sparkling gem" occupying the ancient site of the "King's Gardens and wine presses," in the "King's Dale," hard by Tophet—a paradise by Gehenna! The luxuriant vegetation that characterizes this charming spot is due to the fertilizing influence of the waters of a pool, elevated a few yards above it, in the mouth of the Tyropœon, not far from

* This sheet of water having become the subject of much discussion, I append an extract from an article I published on a former occasion.

Isaiah's Tree—the world-renowned "Pool of Siloam." These are the "waters of Shiloah, that go softly"—*softly* at least—thus far, as saith Esaias; yet on reaching the brink above this lovely spot they tumble, dash, splash, and rush from a hundred little cascades, and are distributed in a thousand murmuring rills for the irrigation of this paradisaical spot. This famous pool, however, is only the temporary receptacle of the water, and by no means its source, as was formerly supposed. Descending into the earth by a rude flight of steps just above its upper extremity, you perceive the terminus of a low, narrow channel, cut through the solid rock of Mount Ophel, barely large enough in some places to admit your prostrate body; and if you have the curiosity and perseverance of a Pater Julius, a Robinson, a Smith, a Tobler, or a Paul Pry, and can so far humble yourself as to creep *à la serpent* seventeen hundred and fifty feet, you find yourself at last in a waist-deep little pool, three or four yards wide and six or eight long, where you can once more stand up and breathe freely; though you are still far below the surface of the earth and twenty yards from daylight, which you reach on ascending two long flights of steps.

The accompanying pictorial illustration represents a partial glimpse of the recesses of this celebrated fountain as seen from above. Dr. Williams, in his "Holy City," pronounces this "one of the most picturesque '*pieces*' about Jerusalem;" and my highly gifted friend, the late Mr. Bartlett, whom I once accompanied there, was lavish in praise of its picturesque beauty. This little subterranean pool is no other than the far-famed "Fount of the Virgin," so called because ecclesiastic tradition saith, that it was "here the mother of Jesus was accustomed to wash her linen." Its waters, though perennial, do not flow regularly, but intermit with considerable irregularity, rushing furiously like a mountain torrent for twenty or thirty minutes, then intermitting for one or two hours, or in dry seasons, even a day or two. This phenomenon, though doubtless due to the natural action of a syphon-shaped reservoir in the heart of the mountain, is *religiously* supposed by the Turks and

Arabs to be caused by a huge amphibious animal inhabiting the cavernous mountain, and hence the name by which they designate this mystic water—the Dragon's Fount. They sagely conclude that when the monster reposes, the water being thus effectually dammed, ceases to flow; and can only run during his perambulations! and by this simple article of faith, most philosophically and satisfactorily account for this hydrodynamical phenomenon. A learned contributor to the Bibliotheca Sacra, partly on account of its supposed propinquity to the "sheep" [market], but mainly on account of this phenomenon, supposes it to be the Bethesda of the Scriptures, where "Jesus said unto a certain man which had an infirmity thirty-and-eight years, 'Rise, take up thy bed and walk,' and immediately the man was made whole." But, for reasons elsewhere assigned, I can by no means concur in this opinion, not only because of the somewhat neological squinting of the reasoning by which this conclusion is argued—(the idea being that the "troubling of the waters by the angel" was nothing more nor less than this irregular rushing of the stream)—but for many other reasons, and especially because the assumed premises are most probably untrue. For there is no proof whatever of the intermittent character of this fountain, until a period long subsequent to the subversion of Jerusalem by the Romans, when the curse of God rested so signally upon the land, as entirely to dry up the sources of the Kedron and many other streams throughout this whole country once so abundant in brooks of water, of fountains and depths that spring out of valleys and hills." Had it been intermittent in the days of the Saviour and the apostles, Josephus, who so frequently speaks of the waters of Jerusalem in general, and so specifically describes the Pool of Siloam, would not have failed to inform his heathen readers of a phenomenon so curious and to them so inexplicable. And besides this significant silence of the great Jewish historian, Tacitus, Aristeas, and Strabo, who all make special mention of the singular distribution of water about Jerusalem, are equally silent. But not only is Josephus profoundly silent on the subject, but he makes special mention of a fact which is entirely inconsistent with such intermission of its current, *i. e.* that "it had *sweet water* in it, and this in *great plenty* also." For it is perfectly obvious that a *great plenty* of water would entirely arrest this intermission. This sweet taste is also a proof of its abundance: and were it to flow copiously again it would doubtless lose its present taste. Apropos, of its taste—Josephus pronounces it *sweet;* the author of "The Acts of God by the Franks," calls it *tasteless;* another Crusader says *bitter;* one modern tourist *brackish;* and another *milk-and-waterish!* Sweet, bitter, tasteless, brackish, milk-and-waterish! truly "*de gustibus* * * * *disputandum est!*" What a salmagundi potation! Few, however, could be induced to decide upon its taste at Siloam, after having witnessed the foul ablutions practised by the Arabs and Turks in the waters of the upper fount. It is a very popular collyrium for ophthalmic offections; and is believed by all classes of Moslems to be largely endowed with healing qualities: hence the numerous ablutions performed in it by men, women, and children, at all hours, from the first call of the muezzim at daylight to the last cry at bedtime.

This is the mysterious *Zemzam*, or fountain of living waters, for which Jerusalem, like Mecca, is celebrated by some. Mohammed declared that this stream flowed from Paradise, and in our own lyrics it is much celebrated as

> "The brook that flows
> Fast by the oracle of God."

Williams, Ferguson, and other eminent Biblical topographers, contend that it comes directly from the site of the threshold of the ancient Temple; while others affirm that it is the very stream brought down subterraneously by Hezekiah when, seeing "that Sennacherib was come, and that he was purposed to fight against Jerusalem, he took counsel with his princes and his mighty men to stop the fountains which were without the city, and the brook that ran through the midst of the land, saying, Why should the kings of

Assyria come and find much water?" But endless are the theories and surmises concerning this interesting stream.

The thought occurred to me one very warm day, whilst residing on Mount Olivet, that an attempt to ascertain the true origin of this mysterious streamlet might neither be an unprofitable nor unpleasant way of spending an hour or two. I accordingly commenced my subter-aquatic explorations as stealthily as possible, for fear of raising a mob, crawling about with only a single candle in hand. Having loitered in the pool till the coming down of the waters, I soon found several widely separated places where it gained admittance, besides the opening under the steps, where alone it had formerly been supposed to enter. I then observed a large opening entering the rock-hewn channel, just below the pool, which, though once supplying a tributary quite copious—if we may judge from its size—is now dry. Being found too much choked with tessara and rubbish to be penetrated far, I carefully noted its position and bearing, and, on searching for it above, soon identified it on the exterior, where it assumed an upward direction toward the Temple, and entering it through a breach, traversed it for nearly a thousand feet; sometimes walking erect, at other times bending low, now on hand and knee, and not unfrequently inching my way snake-fashion, until at last I reached a point near the wall, where I heard the donkeys nimbly tripping along over my head; and then the pioneer of our party getting lodged, we were compelled to back out and retrace our way. I was perfectly satisfied, however, on subsequently locating our course above ground with the theodolite, that this subterraneous canal derived its former supply of water, not from Moriah, but from Zion. Being foiled in my effort to ferret out the true source of the fountain in this direction, I then sought the Sheikh of the overhanging village of Silwan, who claims lordship of the fount, and deemed myself very fortunate in bargaining with him for permission to remove a few of the lower steps, beneath which the main stream entered the pool, for the moderate sum of only one hundred piasters, or one pound sterling, for the light of his countenance thus graciously vouchsafed! I accordingly repaired there about ten o'clock at night, with all the secrecy practicable, in such a region of dogs and Arabs, and soon found him faithful to his appointment: not so, however, to his bargain; for he immediately took me aside, and with palavering flattery, such as an Arab's tongue alone can ply, assured me that he was merely jesting about the paltry sum of a hundred piasters; that the "Angleseys" (the English) had repeatedly offered him five hundred piasters, which he had indignantly refused, but that as I was "Hakim American" and his special friend, he would only charge me four hundred! My curiosity immediately sank to zero, however anxious I had been to make exploration in this direction, and I at once abandoned the adventure.

Pool of Siloam—*Sent—Ain Silwan taht.*—The present Pool of Siloam (which occupies undoubtedly the site of the ancient fountain or pool of that name) is situated in the Valley of the Tyropœon on the Ophel side, about one hundred yards from its termination. It is fifty feet long, fourteen and a half at the lower end, and seventeen at the upper—its western side being somewhat bent. It is eighteen and a half feet in depth, but never filled—the water either passing directly through, or being maintained at a depth of three or four feet. This is effected by leaving open or closing (with a few handfuls of weeds at the present day, but formerly by a flood gate) an aperture at the bottom. At a height of three or four feet from the bottom its dimensions become enlarged a few feet, and the water attaining this level falls through an aperture at its lower end into an educt; subterranean at first, but soon appearing in a deep ditch under the perpendicular cliff of Ophel, and is received into a few small reservoirs and troughs. A rude pair of steps, in the south-west corner, leads down to the water; and a still ruder flight, just above its upper extremity, gives admission to the enlarged extremity of the aqueduct that brings the water from the Fountain of the Virgin, and vents the water beneath these steps. Six pillars of Jerusalem marble are half embedded in its

POOL OF SILOAM—

Seen from above; and exhibiting the site of the "Lower Pool," now cultivated as a garden—the "Tree of Isaiah" on its dam, and (beyond the "King's Gardens,") the site of En-rogel at the two houses in Wady en-Nair.

eastern wall in most ruinous condition, said to be the remains of a Basilica over the pool. It receives its supply of water entirely from the Virgin's Fount by the tunnel chiselled through Ophel—hence its name Siloam—Sent.

WATERS OF THE HARAM.—*Great Reservoir of the Temple—"Royal Cistern"—Subterranean "Sea" of the Temple.*—During our exploration of the Haram enclosure, we observed on removing a half-buried marble capital on one occasion, a rude subterranean passage, leading to a long flight of steps. The Effendi immediately dispatched some of the workmen for flambeaux, and prepared for a thorough exploration. Descending a broad flight of forty-four

THE ROYAL CISTERN OF THE TEMPLE.

wide steps cut in the native rock—but so worn in some places as to have required partial re-cutting, only a few centuries ago to all appearance—we reached a beautiful sheet of water. The Effendi mounted the shoulders of a Fellah and seemed to navigate the waters very pleasantly; while my sons and self spent our time certainly as pleasantly, in wading through its rude but venerable halls; and making an accurate ground plan of it—finding the water nowhere much more than knee-deep. We afterwards spent a good portion of another day in its dark nether regions, completing and verifying the plat, taking other measurements, and making an accurate sketch—that here figured—a few minutes' inspection of which will convey a better idea of this long-lost place than many pages of written explanation.

This sheet of water is, without doubt, the "Sea," of which the Son of Sirach and the Commissioner of King Ptolemy speak in such rapturous terms. It is now however quite a rude piece of work—the massive metal-covered pillars having given place to ill-shaped piers, apparently of unhewn rocks, badly plastered; the rapacity of some of the various spoilers of the devoted city—Syrian, Roman, Persian, Saracenic, Turkish, or Frank—having left it minus the lead or brass with which it was formerly encased. It is seven hundred and thirty-six feet in circuit and forty-two in depth: and according to the best estimate I could make, its capacity falls but little short of two millions of gallons! The rain from el-Aksa is conducted into it by a small trench, and much also finds its way through small superficial channels leading from various parts of the Temple area into the same opening near El-Aksa Porch. We discovered no fountain in connexion with it, nor did we find the entrance of the aqueduct from Solomon's Pools, which, we were told by one of the old keepers who had formerly visited this subterranean lake, enters it on the west, yet we cannot positively affirm that there is none; nor did we discover any exit from it into the neighboring pool under el-Aksa; yet, as that pool, which is said to be very capacious, has no visible source of supply, there is probably a communication between them. It formerly had eight apertures above, through which the water was drawn up; but only one remains open at this time.

I am not able to say how many wells there are in the Haram enclosure—the larger ones having several mouths each; but there are no less than thirty-two well-mouths; though some of these reservoirs are now disused and nearly filled with rubbish. The dimensions of only the few marked on the map could be ascertained. That under el-Aksa is forty-seven feet deep, that at Mugaribeh Gate twenty-seven and a half, and that on the right hand of the Cotton Bazaar, near Hammam es-Shefa, is only thirty-three feet in depth—a conclusive proof that it can receive no water by lateral connexion with the latter, as some have contended—being less than half its depth. According to Mejr ed-Din there were thirty-four of these wells or reservoirs in the Haram yard about three and a half centuries ago, and seven more beneath the great central platform. The most remarkable amongst these wells was that near the entrance to the Cotton Bazaar, thirty-three feet deep, entitled "Well of the Leaf." (See his account, section 3 of his Treatise.)

AIN HAMMAM ES-SHEFA—*Well of Healing.*—The entrance to this mysterious well is situated ten feet south of the Cotton Bazaar, one hundred and twenty-five and a half feet from the Haram wall, and one hundred and seventy-six from the Valley Street. Its apparent depth is nearly eighty-five feet; but subtracting eighteen and a half of this for the height of the house, upon the top of which its mouth opens, its real depth beneath the surface of the ground is only sixty-six and a half feet. Its mouth being ten feet higher than the general level of the Haram area, its bottom is, therefore, seventy-five feet below the level of the Haram.

The following extract, from the pen of the accomplished Williams (Holy City, ii. 457), will serve to evince the interest felt in this mysterious *Zemzam*, and entertain the reader by recounting an amusing adventure:—

"The next fountain which I shall mention is one within the city, near the area of the great mosk, known only by report until very lately, when an enterprising traveller undertook to explore it; and the company to whom he related his adventure in the small shed built over the mouth of the well by which he effected his perilous descent, will not easily forget the thrilling sensations which his narration produced. This fountain now supplies the Bath of Healing (Hammam es-Shefa), which is entered from the ruined Cotton Mart. The present mouth of the well is on the roof of the buildings attached to the bath, and is found to be about twenty feet above the level of the street. Dr. Robinson had in vain sought permission to explore this well, but the reports which he had heard of it excited the curiosity of a countryman of his who was at Jerusalem in the winter of 1841–2, and he resolved, at all events, to descend. Having endeavored, without success, to induce the keeper of the bath to aid him in the undertaking, he prevailed on two peasants of a neighboring village to assist him. This was in the month of January. At the dead of night, attended only by a servant lad, and furnished with candles and matches, measuring-rule moreover, and a compass, forth he sallied, equipped as for an aquatic excursion.

"Arrived at the well's mouth, he tied a cord around his body, and was lowered through the aperture by these *fellahs*, who had kept their appointment, but would, without doubt, have let the rope slip, and left their employer to his fate, on the slightest alarm. However, he survived to tell the tale; an outline of which shall here be given.

"The entrance to the well is not quite two feet square, but a few feet lower down it expands and becomes about twelve feet square, and is apparently hewn in the rock. His first adventure in this aerial journey was meeting the leathern bucket which had been tied at the other end of the rope as a counterpoise. It was 'streaming at a dozen apertures, and for the rest of the way he was under a cold shower-bath, and could with difficulty keep his light without the circle of it.' The well was eighty-two and a half feet deep, and the water about four and a half. On arriving at the bottom, the vibrations of the rope, before he could get a footing, extinguished his light, and he was left in total darkness. He had observed, in his descent, four arched recesses in the rock, facing one another, and lower down, six feet above the water, a door-way leading into an arched chamber, which he contrived to reach, and here he refitted for his further voyage. The matches were dry, and other candles soon illuminated the darkness. The excavated chamber in which he found himself was only three or four feet in height, fifteen long by ten broad, and did not seem to be constructed with any reference to the water. Opposite to this chamber he discovered a passage which formed the water-channel. He had taken the precaution of bringing with him an India rubber life-preserver, which he found useful in his further explorations. He now descended into the water; and, entering the passage, soon passed another excavation in the rock, of which he could make nothing. The passage beyond this was two or three feet wide, and about five feet high, covered with stones laid transversely, but very irregularly; in some places were fragments of polished marble shafts, and in one place the end of a granite column had sunk obliquely into the passage. The bottom of the channel was not flat, but grooved; the passage not straight, though its general course was direct; and 'the cutting so uneven as to suggest the thought that advantage might have been taken of a natural seam or fissure in the rock.'

"Having followed this passage eighty feet, he was stopped by a basin or well of unknown depth, on the opposite side of which the wall shut down to the water, and presented another obstacle, even could the water have been passed. Unhappily he was obliged to return without any more satisfactory result. His exit is amusingly characteristic of cool intrepidity. He had barely breathing room or space for his candle between the surface of the water and the roof of the passage; and one would think must have felt rather uncomfortable in such a position; but he first measured the passage with his rule, then illuminated it with his spare candles, and having taken a last fond look, left them burning there, and returned to the well to prepare for his ascent. The rope was still there, and the natives above. The signal was given, and he again found himself swinging in mid-air, and in darkness; the candle which he had reserved having been extinguished as before. His descent had been uniform, but he was necessarily drawn up at intervals, which caused a greater vibration. He spun around the dark vault, striking against one side and another, and was not sorry to find himself again beneath the open heaven. It is deeply to be regretted that this daring exploit was not attended with better success. Its results are very unsatisfactory to Mr. Walcott himself. He does not imagine that this excavation was originally a well: the artificial recesses and chambers in the rock he thinks are against it. It more nearly resembles some of the sepulchral excavations without the city. The direction of the passage he cannot positively determine, as he had injured his compass in the descent. He thinks it runs eastward in the direction of the Haram; but if so, it stops short of the enclosure forty-four feet. The passage may extend further, the water descending into a lower gallery; if so, it could only be explored when the water is very low. Two English travellers were anxious to attempt this at the end of a dry summer, but no one could be prevailed on to aid the undertaking, and it was abandoned. At that time it was necessary for a man to descend to the well in order to bring the water from a distance to supply the bath, as the floor of the chamber was dry. A close cross-examination of this man elicited that the water proceeded from an immense reservoir beneath the Haram, but it did not appear that he had penetrated so far. It must be remarked that the water is identical in taste with that of Siloam."

Marvellous tales being still reported by the wonder-exciting Mohammedans concerning the wondrous subterraneous apartments yet unexplored, and startling theories based upon them, I felt no little desire to examine for myself and complete Mr. Walcott's exploration. Accordingly—having obtained consent of its proprietor—and that too without buckshish and without stipulation—(a fact so unprecedented in the ways and doings of the Turks, that it could but be interpreted most favorably)—I hired and spliced together two rope ladders, bought a new cord, and made all suitable arrangements for a descent; and, accompanied by our Dragoman and one of my sons, with a Silwan fellah, well acquainted with the place, as cicerone, I accomplished the descent of this wonder-exciting well on the 19th of November, 1853—being fully equipped with lights, measuring-line, compass, &c., and spent an hour or two in the exploration of its mysterious waters.

Descending ten feet through the small four-sided funnel, not quite two feet square at top, and becoming still smaller at its lower end, the shaft was found gradually expanding in size and soon becoming cilindric. At a depth of twenty-eight feet are four small doorways, facing the cardinal points of the compass, and apparently shallow recesses behind them. The shaft enlarges to the size of ten or twelve feet about midway, and again becomes square: but a few yards before reaching the bottom it diminishes again and terminates in a basin eight feet square, covered with loose stones and gravel. At eleven feet from the bottom, in the north side of the well, is a doorway four feet thick, leading to a vaulted room eighteen feet long and fourteen wide. A passage rather circumscribed, varying in width from one and a half to several feet, leads from the south side of the well, which is mostly an artificial wall nine feet high—the passage being about ten or twelve feet wider here than elsewhere; and for fifteen or twenty feet arched over with rocks apparently two feet by one and of very good workmanship. Only half of the vault is seen (in its longitudinal extent), the remainder being apparently concealed by later additions of masonry—though as these half-arches are very common in the east, the other half may probably never have been constructed. At the end of this archway, about twenty-four feet from the well, the passage is reduced in height to about six feet, and for eight or ten feet is overlaid by coarse slabs of marble a foot wide and half a foot in thickness at a point thirty-nine feet from the commencement—the course which the passage thus far has run—south 5° east, turns south 20° west, for eight feet, and is ceiled with eleven small white marble pillars, and one large one of coarser material, one end of which is partly fallen through—the last-mentioned twenty inches, and the former only seven in diameter. The passage now leads with slight variations of width, height, and direction due south thirty-five feet, where the flow of the water is interrupted by a rock, equal in length to the width of the passage, and about a foot in height, or rather in thickness, cemented across it transversely, serving as an occasional dam. Thus far the passage gradually ascends (perhaps only half a foot in all), but now it suddenly deepens three feet, and continues that depth with an increased width as far as it could be measured, which however was only fourteen and a half feet. The ceiling of the passage which, as far as this reservoir, is nowhere less than four or five feet, here gradually declines till it comes in contact with the water, thus effectually arresting all further progress—greatly to our disappointment.

The bottom of the passage from this reservoir to the well whence the water is drawn up, is not flat but concave, and has a small channel a few inches deep, cut perhaps—not by the hard chisel but by the soft waters—for, in the lapse of ages, "waters wear the stones."

About twenty feet south of the well is a rough, irregular cave a few yards in extent on the east side, the mouth of which is about six or eight feet above the channel. There is also a square opening in the ceiling of the passage, a few yards farther south, leading to a small cave above. Various other small openings are also observable both in the lining wall and the native rock communicating with fissures and small caves. The total length of the channel of water as far as measured is one hundred and four and a half feet; but the guide, who has often been down when the water was at a low stage (to empty it from the southern reservoir into the channel conveying it to the well), assured me that it extends at least a hundred feet farther in the same direction: but the low narrow passage can only be traversed when it is nearly exhausted of water. Although the native rock is visible at many places, for many yards in extent, yet most of the passage and the shaft is cased with masonry—of very inferior kind—though the room north of the well is hewn out of solid rock, which continues visible several yards above it. It was found impracticable to effect a landing in the small recesses indicated by the doors observed fifty or sixty feet above the water, though they appeared to be merely ornamental, and may have been in full view at the former level of the city. Touching the "large arched room supported by fourteen marble columns with capitals," the report of which is even credited by the tradition-hating authors of the Biblical Researches,* I have to report that it was not only "*non-come-at-able*," but "*non inventus erat*."

The conclusions to which I had been necessarily brought by investigation elsewhere, in relation to the most interesting matter

* Bib. Res. i. 508.

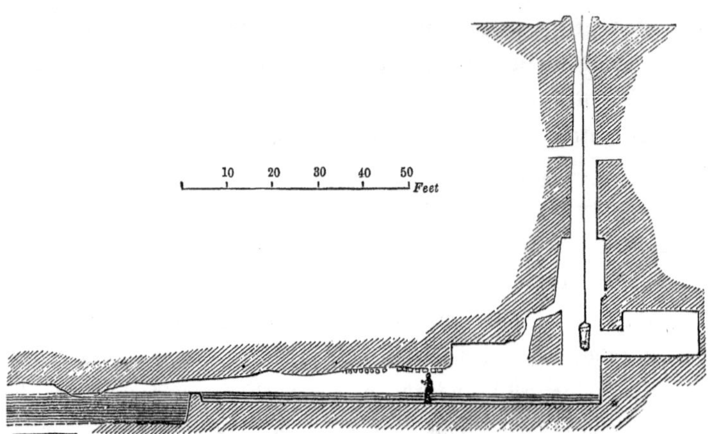

PLAN OF HAMMAM ES-SHEFA—(PERPENDICULAR SECTION).

connected with the subject, were fully confirmed by this exploration, though materially different from any heretofore expressed, and are certainly justified by the facts of the case. Even had I not proved by previous analysis the fallacy of the assertion that this water is identical with that of the Virgin's Fount, Flagellation Well, Cotton Grotto, reservoir, &c., this examination would have induced a contrary conviction—for instead of coming from the north, as such an opinion necessarily implies, the source of this fountain is directly from the south, and therefore cannot be derived from either of the above-mentioned places. And having witnessed an unusually copious outflow of the Virgin's Fount of thirty-seven minutes' continuance on the preceding Friday, about mid-day, after seven or eight hundred skins (four or five thousand gallons) had been drawn up for the bath and its supply well nigh exhausted, I was convinced that the outflow could not be owing, as is generally supposed, to the discharge of this alleged over-filled reservoir, by a rude kind of natural syphon. That it is not derived from a large fountain within the precincts of the Haram es-Sherif, as others contend, is also fairly inferable from the fact that the channel along which it flows, instead of coming from the east, in the direction of the Haram, approaches the well from the south as far as is ascertained either by report or actual examination; so that when protracted it falls considerably short of even touching the most westerly corner of the Haram enclosure.

But that its source is entirely independent of and totally disconnected with any of the waters alluded to, or indeed any others whatever, is obvious from the fact (at least when considered in connexion with their small supply), that no such source is discoverable, and that water trickles into it from nearly every portion of the interior; and though only *guttatim*, yet, considering the large surface from which it exudes, is fully adequate to the daily demand, which is only about three or four hundred skinsful—except on Friday. Upon this Sabbatical day of the Moslem, about eight hundred skins are demanded for expurgatorial ablution. My own impression is, that a well (probably from former indications of moisture in the neighborhood) was originally sunk to the depth of the room, now ten feet above the bottom; which, being plastered and shaped as cisterns generally are, was probably the original cistern, and long used as the receptacle. But the supply proving inadequate to the demands of later times, after the cessation of the latter rains, it was deepened and enlarged; in process of which—following no doubt the leaky veins of porous chalky formation—a cave of crumbling material was reached, which required to be walled in and supported by masonry. Does not the profuse use of broken marble pillars for such common purposes indicate that this enlargement was subsequent to one of Jerusalem's sad overthrows—perhaps after the return from Babylon? The smaller ones perhaps may once have adorned a little Temple over the well! Although there was not as much to be seen in these nether regions as was reported, yet, inasmuch as I was enabled to clear up some difficulties connected with an interesting subject—at least to my own satisfaction—I was highly gratified with this Plutonic excursion: but right glad was I to regain the surface of the earth once more in safety—for I could but be most feelingly impressed by the perilous position in which I found myself on the sudden snapping of one of the slender ropes of the ladder, when, even despite the cord fortunately tied around my body by way of security, the brittle thread of life had well nigh been severed.

The fond tenacity with which many persons cling to the idea that this well is in connexion with an inexhaustible fountain under the threshold of the ancient Temple, is truly astonishing. In a late and interesting, but highly speculative work on the Holy Land, by Captain Allen, of the Royal Navy, he remarks in relation to the account of my exploration given by Mr. Bartlett ("Jerusalem Revisited"*), "Dr. Barclay succeeded in examining this (Hammam es-Shefa), and says 'the theory which ascribes its supply of water (to reservoirs under the Haram) is entirely disproved by the exploration.' I am not disposed fully to agree with this, although the hypothesis of the long passage being intended for the purpose of increasing the 'guttation,' is very plausible; yet he did not, as it appears, reach the end of the passage, where alone the mystery is to be solved."

Most evident is it, however, from what has been already stated, that this well does not communicate with any source of living water of the Haram, and more especially with one immediately under the threshold of the Holy Oracle. Nor can it be in connexion with any of the Haram reservoirs—for it is thirty-three feet lower than the large reservoir between Kubbet es-Sakhrah and el-Aksa, forty-two lower than that between the well and the supposed site of the Temple, and twenty-eight below that in el-Aksa—the most southern and the deepest reservoir in the Haram enclosure.

Hezekiah's Pool—*Amygdalon—Birket Hammam el-Batrak—Pool of Patriarch's Bath.*—This pool is situated between Patriarch street and the Latin Patriarch's residence, and though entirely surrounded by houses, can at all times be seen by ascending to the top of the Coptic Convent, or any of the shops bordering upon it. Its

* Page 87 of this very interesting and admirably illustrated work—the last production of this gifted author and arti t.

POOL OF HEZEKIAH.

average breadth is about one hundred and twenty-six feet, and its present length two hundred and fifty-two feet; but was formerly longer. Its depth below the average surface of the earth may be eight or ten feet—perhaps more; but it is considerably deeper at the southern than at the northern extremity. It derives its supply entirely from the Mamilla Pool; and usually has from two to six feet of water; though it sometimes becomes entirely exhausted late in autumn. The water is drawn up to a considerable height at great expense of labor by two stout Fellahin, and sent across the street over a large stone arch to supply a bathing establishment—which being lower than the pool, might easily be supplied by a small leaden pipe acting as a syphon. But such a device as this, emanating from Christians, the Simon-pure Moslem spurns.

Birket Israel—*Pool of Israel—Moat or Trench of Antonia—Bethesda!*—This capacious pool is three hundred and sixty-five feet in length and one hundred and thiry-one in breadth; and at its south-western corner is a continuation of it westwardly, nearly one hundred and forty-two feet in length and forty-five in breadth. This breadth, however, is divided most of the way by a wall into two nearly equal parts, and vaulted over as a foundation for houses. The wall now terminating this extension being quite modern, it is probable that it once extended farther west. Both the main pool and the extension were once more than fifty feet in depth; but are now in some places nearly filled. The cement has generally fallen off above, and no doubt below also—hence, though much water runs into this pool during the winter, and continues to drain into it a long while after the rain has ceased, still no water is ever observed in it. That this trench cannot be Bethesda is abundantly shown elsewhere.

MEKHEMEH POOL.—Temple street passes over quite a large pool adjoining the wall between the Mehkemeh and the residences of the Cadi and Bashkatib, which I discovered in searching for remains of the Temple gates. Eighty-four feet of the Temple wall forms its eastern side; its northern side is forty-two feet in length, and starts from the wall at the foundation of the minaret pertaining to Kubbet es-Sakhrah; its southern extremity was also at one time forty-two feet in length, and its western side the same length of the eastern; but the foundation of a house seems to have been built up in its south-western corner which diminishes its northern end to twenty-five feet and makes an angle in its western side. It probably extended much farther west originally. It is coated with cement, and is in a very good state of preservation, though much filled with rubbish. Its widely expanded vault is well executed; and all the workmanship is of quite superior style of execution. There is a fine arch and keystone over a new closed door ten or twelve feet from the bottom, in its northern extremity. It is not improbable that it was once much larger on the north as well as the west. It is only accessible at this time by passing through several dark cellars and passages from the Mekhemeh Garden, by way of the gate at the Wailing Place. There is also quite a large pool of water kept well filled, between this and Hammam es-Shefa—quite near the latter.

HIPPIC CISTERN.—There is a large cistern in el-Khala, near the Tower of Hippicus, said to be one hundred feet in length; but we were not permitted to make any explorations there, on the only occasion upon which I ever visited the castle.

BATH OF BATHSHEBA.—Monro describes this pool in his "Summer Rambles," as a mere "oblong pit, twenty feet deep, lined coarsely with small stones," thus intimating its modern origin. But Schubert says, "the architecture and the size of the stones seem to belong to the works of the ancient Jerusalem." The situation it occupied was immediately to the left on entering Jaffa Gate; but it has been so completely filled up in the course of the last eight or ten years that no trace of it is now visible. Tradition has not yet decided whether this is the veritable pool at which Uriah's wife laved herself, or whether the honor should be accorded to Birket es-Sultan, which also lays claim to this mark of distinction. But here again tradition is most egregiously at fault. For it could be at neither of these pools that Bathsheba was bathing when David saw her, as neither of them could, by any possibility, have been seen from "the roof of the king's house, where David was walking in an evening-tide, when he saw the woman washing herself." (2 Sam. xi. 2.) The legend is evidently based upon the erroneous impression that the Tower of Hippicus, built by Herod the Great, was the Palace of David: and is entirely unworthy of credit.

HELENA'S CISTERN—*Treasury of Helena.*—This reservoir is situated near the reputed rock of Golgotha, in the Coptic Convent: it is about sixty feet long and thirty wide, and has a constant supply of cool sweet water, said to be inexhaustible—"*nullus fons vel puteus.*" Quaressimus says it was not far from "the 'Baptisterium,' which was square without—within, rose-shaped."

LOWER POOL OF GIHON—*Birket es-Sultan—Sultan's Pool—"Great Pool"—Lacus Germanicus.*—This immense pool, averaging six hundred feet in length by two hundred and sixty in breadth, is situated in the Valley of Ben Hinnom, about a quarter of a mile below Jaffa Gate; but at present retains water only a short time. It is by far the largest piece of water in all the environs—containing a sheet of more than three and a half acres, when full.

"UPPER POOL OF GIHON"—*Birket el-Mamilla—Serpent's Pool.*—The traditional reservoir thus called, is situated at the head of the Valley of Hinnom, nearly half a mile north-west of Jaffa Gate, and is at present supplied entirely by the rains that drain in it from the surrounding basin. It is three hundred and fifteen feet in length, and about two hundred and eight in breadth, with a depth of fifteen or twenty feet. The water is conducted to Birket el-Hammam by a very inferior kind of aqueduct—a mere ditch, running on the surface of the ground most of the way, but dipping quite deeply in passing beneath the city wall. Being surrounded with Moslem tombs, it is a place much resorted to by the women; it is much used also as a swim-pool by men and boys, in the early part of the season, when so full that they can run and tumble into it without danger of striking the bottom; but it is generally exhausted before the winter rains set in. It is now entered by only one pair of steps—that in the south-west corner; and has a contrivance in a small subterranean room beneath its lower side, or dam for regulating its outflow of water.

BIRKET COTTON MEGARA.—This cavity is situated on the exterior of the northern wall, about seventy yards north of Damascus Gate. It does not appear to have been originally designed for a pool, but has been made simply by closing the entrance to the great cave beneath Bezetha Hill, and running a wall across the deep cut through which the quarried rocks were once brought out of the cave. It derives its present supply of water almost entirely from the hill in the interior of the city, through a small hole cut in the wall; but it was formerly brought, by a subterranean aqueduct, the remains of which are still visible, from a beautiful sheet of water that every rainy season collects in the Cave of Jeremiah.

BIRKET EL-HIJJEH—*Jeremiah's Pool or Dungeon.*—The double tank of water, situated immediately outside of the northern wall, in the valley that separates the main hill of Bezetha from the low hill east of it, is thus designated in the traditionary vocabulary of Jerusalem. They have every appearance of ordinary tanks beneath houses of the better class; but as they are favorably situated for receiving water, they have been rendered accessible in modern times by a flight of steps at the south-east corner. Water is generally to be found in the one that is still vaulted over, until midsummer; but seems to be derived entirely from the winter rains. There are many such, but generally in a state of disrepair, scattered around Jerusalem; particularly north of the city. This name, el-Hijjeh, is also applied to the pool at Stephen's Gate by some authors. It is evident, from the account given by Jeremiah himself (Jer. xxxvii. 21, 38), that his dungeon could not have been situated anywhere in this quarter of the city, inasmuch as it was within the precincts of the King's House.

Birket Hammam Sitte Miryam.—This pool can lay claim to no higher antiquity than the adjoining city wall, as it is evidently made to receive the rains that flow into the fosse formerly existing all the way up the city wall on the east; but is now so completely filled with rocks and rubbish as scarcely to be distinguishable; though still permitting the rain-water to percolate below. It is situated a short distance north of St. Stephen's Gate, and its only design, apparently, was originally to supply the Turkish bath immediately within—which it generally does throughout the year: a flight of steps, however, in its corner towards Gethsemane seems to indicate that its water is sometimes used for other purposes.

Hammam Tabareyeh—*Bath of Tiberias.*—The Baths of Tiberias are assigned a place on the south-west quarter of Zion, not far from the English Cemetery, by Mr. Williams.

Lower Pool—*Natatoria.*—The depressed spot of ground between the points or promontories of Ophel and Zion, is the site of the "Shorn Skin Pool" of the Talmud, and the Natatoria of the Crusaders. But although the lower wall is in a good state of preservation, it holds no water—the cement having long since fallen off.

There are several large reservoirs and tanks within a mile of the city, several of them very large and uncovered, being merely walled in, mainly with unwrought stones; but others were originally natural caves, merely enlarged and plastered, and having the superincumbent rock supported, in some instances, by large rough columns, all filled with rain-water, conducted into them by natural valleys or artificial trenches. Two or three of these are in the upper part of the Kedron Valley—on the plain of Rephaim, in the direction of Bethany—and one or two in Wady en-Nair. Vestiges of a dam may still be observed, lying across the valley north-west of Damascus Gate; and about two hundred yards north-east of Stephen's Gate, the traveller may see a specimen of many other rock-hewn reservoirs in the neighborhood.

Baths.—There are five or six fine bathing establishments in the city, and most of the better kinds of residences have private baths also.

But, besides these public reservoirs and tanks, *every private house has beneath it one or more cisterns*, into which the water from the court and top of the house is conveyed through pipes, or vacuities in the walls, in sufficient quantity to serve all the purposes of the family—and, though teeming with animalculæ, becomes very cool and pleasant on reaction and clarification.

Specific Gravity of the Waters of Jerusalem and Environs, the Jordan and Dead Sea—distilled water being 1000.

Cistern-water from the Mission premises	1002½
From inner well of Flagellation Church	1002
From Ain Hammam esh-Shefa	1004½
From Virgin's Fount	1003½
From En-rogel	1002½
From Jordan	1001
From the Dead Sea	1128

Residuum yielded by Evaporation from Ebullition.

128 oz.	of water	from	Ain Hammam esh-Shefa	185 grains.
128	"	"	Virgin's Fount	93 "
128	"	"	Flagellation Well	32 "
128	"	"	Mission cistern	16 "

It would appear, from the foregoing experiments, that according to the table of densities, the purity of the waters of Jerusalem ranks in the following order:—1st. Well of Flagellation Church; 2d. En-rogel; 3d. Cistern; 4th. Virgin's Fount; 5th. Ain Hammam esh-Shefa.

But, according to the trial by ebullition, the order is somewhat different, as follows:—1st. Cistern Water; 2d. Flagellation Well; 3d. Virgin's Fount; 4th. Ain Hammam esh-Shefa. (En-rogel not tested.)

The existence of carbonic acid gas, or other volatile matter, may account for the discrepancy of result as to the amount of impurity; but the experiments having been only once performed, it is quite probable that they are not free from error. It is evident, however, from the taste, as well as the density, and amount of deposit by ebullition, that of all the Jerusalem waters that of Ain Hammam esh-Shefa is the most impure.

AIN LIFTA—NEPHTOAH.

CHAPTER XIX.

WATERS BEYOND THE IMMEDIATE ENVIRONS—BUT WITHIN SEVEN MILES OF THE CITY.

AIN LIFTA.—Ain Yalo is generally supposed to be that celebrated "fountain of waters" on the boundary between Judah and Benjamin called Nephtoah; but it is very evident from Joshua's indication of the dividing line between the lots of these two tribes, that the present *Ain Lifta* is identical with the Nephtoah of the Scriptures. In describing the boundary of Judah, he tells us (xv. 9) that "the border went up by the Valley of the Son of Hinnom unto the south side of the Jebusite (the same is Jerusalem) and the border went up to the top of the mountain that lieth before the Valley of Hinnom westward, which is at the *head* of the Valley of the Giants northward; and the border was drawn from the top of the hill unto the fountain of the waters of Nephtoah, and went out to the cities of

Mount Ephron; and the border was drawn to Baalah, which is Kirjath-jearim"—the present village of Abû Ghosh.

In describing the boundary line of Benjamin, where it co-extends with that of Judah, he reverses the direction and informs us (xviii. 15) that "the south quarter was from the end of Kirjath-jearim, and the border went out on the west, and went out to (at) the well of waters of Nephtoah; and the border came down to the end of the mountain that lieth before the Valley of the Son of Hinnom, and which is in the Valley of the Giants on the north, and descended to the Valley of Hinnom to the side of Jebusi on the south, and descended to En-rogel." Now it will readily be perceived on tracing this dividing line upon a correct map, that while a line passing from the head of the Valley of Ben Hinnom or Rephaim, to Baalah by Ain Yalo, would form a right angle, and that too without following any natural landmarks, and without any apparent reason, a line passing through Lifta would not only be very nearly straight, but would pursue a course indicated by nature. An argument in favor of this conclusion is also drawn from the name of this fountain—for while Yalo has no analogy whatever to Nephtoah, the transition from Nephtoah to Lifta is very easy and natural in the mouth of an Arab—*l* being frequently substituted for *n*, and the difference in termination being perfectly admissible—and especially if considered as a contraction. Such instances are of constant occurrence throughout Palestine.

This bold fountain is beautifully situated a short distance above the village of Lifta, not far from the head of the valley that runs into Wady beit-Hanina, and about two and a half miles north-west of Jerusalem. It pours forth from a spout into a stone trough at the upper end of a large sunken court, just below which there are two or three small receptacles for the water, and further down one or two more, used now, as of old, to irrigate the rich gardens below. What a delightful "gathering-place" this famous landmark must have been for the children of Judah and Benjamin to enjoy themselves beneath the cool shade of those delightful groves of orange, lemon, apricot, pear, and pomegranate trees! This enchanting spot is now within the limits of the *sheikhdom* of Abû Ghosh the renowned freebooter, so much dreaded by travellers: and it was just here we once found ourselves in rather an unpleasant predicament. Some of the mission family had ridden out to this place one afternoon, for the first time after a long attack of Syrian fever: and just as we were taking a sketch of the fountain, and a picturesque group of women with their water jars and goat-skin bottles, a number of well mounted and fully armed Fellahin were seen to descend the sides of the valley in rapid succession, and secure their horses to a limb, a craggy rock, or the ground by a spear or iron spike which they always carry. The number soon increased to many scores, and the cry was "still they come," horse, foot, dragoon, donkeys, camels, and all, until they amounted to hundreds. It immediately became painfully evident that we were regarded as intruders if not spies, and were not only closely watched but somewhat "held in durance vile," notwithstanding they knew that I was a *hakeem*—for the person of a physician is regarded as sacred amongst Arabs. Soon, however, a dignitary of stern mien approached the fountain, and took his seat beneath an old olive-tree on a raised platform of masonry a few yards distant; and forthwith order and decorum prevailed—all marching up in the most respectful manner to kiss his hand and bow at his feet. All of our inquiries as to the object of this gathering being evasively answered, we could obtain no clue to this strange procedure until a handsomely equipped deputation of Damascenes made their appearance, and a regular Arab council commenced its palaver. We had heard that the Pasha of Damascus was about to send an embassage to Leham and Abû Ghosh, two rival chiefs who had been at war with each other for some months; and though we did not dream that we were in the presence of such a terrible Arab chieftain as Abû Ghosh, yet on seeing such an imposing military display down in this wild glen, we could but come to the conclusion that it was about time to be off: and accordingly we hastened our departure—leaving the sketch, like the tale of "Hudibras, the bear and fiddle—commenced—but broke off in the middle." One of the soldiers called at our premises in the city early next day to admonish us of our danger, and beg us, for "Ullah's" sake, not to venture beyond the walls any more during the continuance of the war—a piece of advice which, however well meant and well received, was entirely unnecessary, as it had now become known that the forces of Abû Ghosh had rendezvoused at Lifta, for the purpose of having a pitched battle with those of Leham the next day on the old battle-ground of the Philistines—the plain of Rephaim: and for several months the most daring robberies and atrocious murders were committed with entire impunity, until at last the Pasha of Jerusalem, taking the field in person, and bringing his cannon to bear effectually on some of their villages, and actually pulling down one or two of them, succeeded in bringing the belligerents to terms.

AIN YALO is situated about four miles south-west of Jerusalem in Wady el-Werd, or Valley of Roses—several plantations of which are there cultivated, for the purpose of making rose-water. On the summit of a hill in the rear of the spring, the traveller from the "Old Dominion," in the New World, may meet with some old acquaintances, much in request at Jerusalem during the solemnities of the Feast of Tabernacles and Palm Sunday—veritable *Virginia old field pines!* This fountain is rather weak; though irrigating several gardens, and supplying the city with fifty or one hundred donkey loads of water daily, throughout the summer. A pool twenty feet square, entered by a pair of steps at one corner, receives the surplus water, which serves both for bathing and irrigation. It is situated a short way up the declivity, on the south-east or left hand side descending the valley.

AIN ALEEK is situated in a valley that enters this (Wady el-Werd) nearly a mile below, from the north; and just below the entrance of this valley into el-Werd, is another copious spring, called AIN HANNIYEH (ST. PHILIP'S FOUNTAIN). It gushes profusely from a beautiful piece of fountain architecture, on the declivity of the hill, a dozen or two yards to the left of the luxuriant gardens in the rich flats of the valley below. It is first received into a small semicircular basin, six or eight feet in diameter, and, after flowing about twenty yards, falls into a rectangular basin, twenty-five feet in breadth and forty-one and a half in length, executed almost entirely in the living rock, and supplied, as usual, with a broad flight of steps at one corner. Some of our party were anxious to refresh themselves with a bath in this reservoir; but the "faithful" were so much scandalized at such an outrageous desecration of the place by the "*infidels*," that it became necessary to forego that pleasure, tantalizing as it was. Just in front of the fountain stands a section of a coarse marble pillar, about three feet in diameter; and higher up the hill are to be seen some smaller columns entire—indicating that there was once here either a church or a village of some importance.

Unlike the fountain works at Jerusalem, which are purely Saracenic, this is evidently Corinthian—the two piers terminating the semicircle being crowned with beautiful Corinthian capitals: and while, from general similarity of style, compared with the Golden Gate and other supposed Hadrianic structures, we might well refer it to the age of Hadrian, they probably date back no farther than the visit of the Empress Helena, to whom I am inclined to ascribe this structure, on account of the tradition that signalizes this water. For the Latins will have it that this is the "certain water" at which Philip baptized Queen Candace's treasurer. But it must be confessed that Wady el-Werd is at present, and always must have been rather "a hard road to travel" in a "chariot." Indeed the road to Jordan, proverbially difficult as it is regarded, is yet a graduated highway, compared with the neck-breaking pathway along the sides and bottom of this narrow defile. Nor can this course be said, with any propriety, to be "toward the south"—"the way that goeth down to Gaza, which is desert;" for it is decidedly the most northern route to Gaza, if indeed there ever was any kind of road leading this way to that city. Certain it is that there are two roads south of it leading to Gaza, through a much more accessible tract country—that passing through Eleutheropolis being much more irect and superior in every respect.

Rather more than a mile lower down this valley, and on the same de of it, is AIN BETIR, bearing also north-west from the city. It an exceedingly bold fountain, and bursts out from the rock near e top of a high ridge, supposed, by Mr. Williams, with high pro-ability, to be one of the mountains of Bethir, of which he considers e present name to be an Arabic corruption. The water is con-ucted a considerable distance in stone troughs, and then falls into a ne large pool, whence it is distributed in hundreds of rills through-ut extensive falling gardens; a large surplus portion also rushing npetuously down the horse pathway. To the wearied traveller this truly an enchanting spot—a garden of delights! But the inhabit-nts of the village are reputed the most villanous set of Arabs in all Iussulmandom: and so I esteemed them on first entering the town. ut, after I had prescribed for a few patients, I was treated with arked consideration; and when I subsequently visited the place, company with Drs. Robinson and Smith, although they had rought themselves to the conclusion that we were making a survey the country, preparatory to its re-occupation by the Franks, yet ey offered no insult or molestation whatever. This picturesque ot is regarded by many traditionists as the scene of the Ethiopian randee's baptism: but the considerations that deprive Hanniyeh that distinction, apply here with still greater force.

The "GREAT WATERS OF GIBEON," referred to by the prophet Jer. xli. 12), are no more to be seen: the curse under which "whole alestina groaneth and travaileth in pain together until now," hav-g long since dried them up. But near the eastern base of the hill ere is quite a capacious cavern, in which are both a fountain and eservoir of water that formerly supplied a pool, in a field about fifty ards below it, thirty-three feet wide and fifty-one long. This being upplied with living water was, perhaps, always a place of resort; nd may well have been the pool Helkath-hazzurim, where "Joab, he son of Zeruiah, and the servants of David, went out and met together: and they sat down, the one on the one side of the pool and the other on the other side of the pool; and Abner said unto Joab, Let the young men now arise and play before us. And Joab said, Let them arise. Then there arose and went over by number twelve of Benjamin which pertained to Ish-bosheth the son of Saul, and twelve of the servants of David, and they caught every one his fellow by the head, and thrust his sword in his fellow's side; so they fell down together, wherefore that place was called Helkath-hazzurim—the field of strong men." (2 Sam. ii. 13.) Considerably farther south, there is another pool, of much smaller dimensions, however; and the dribbling spring that supplies it is barely perennial. Dr. Robinson mentions a pool one hundred and twenty feet long and one hundred wide; but this, no doubt, derived its supply of water only from the rains.

At Neby Samwil, the Mispeh of the Scriptures, there are more than half a dozen small fountains and receptacles of water: the lowest of these is fifty-seven feet in length and thirty in breadth, massively constructed on one side with rebated stones—the upper side being the native rock, merely scarped down.

They are to be found on both sides of the mountain; and are turned to very good account by irrigating some very productive gardens. A few of them are situated quite near the top of the mountain; and tradition states that their waters were once conducted to Jerusalem. I have not succeeded, however, in finding such an aqueduct; and the boldest spring is certainly too low for that purpose. But all these waters may easily have been *reservoired* quite *near* the city.

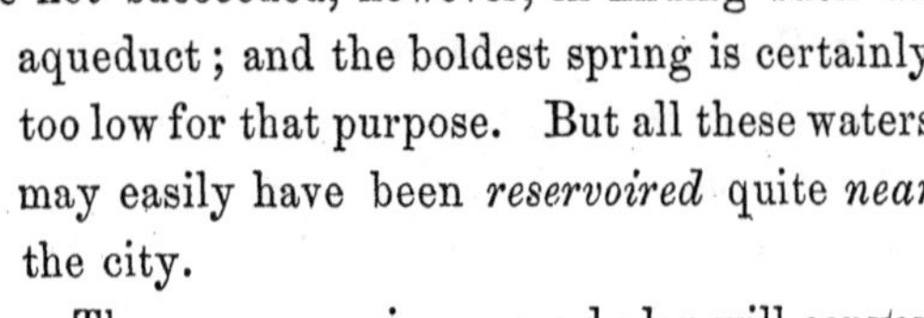

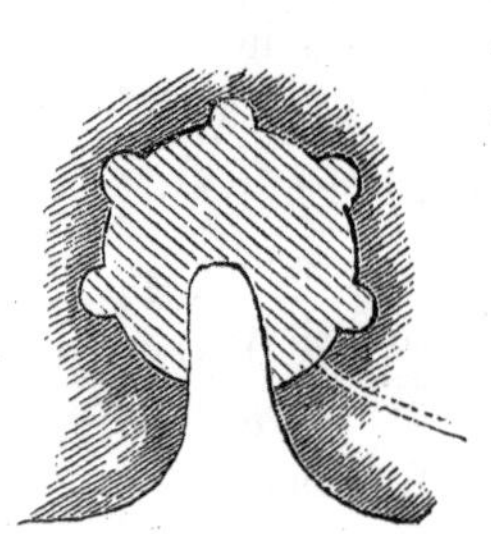

SUBTERRANEAN FOUNTAIN AND POOL AT NEBY SAMWIL.

The accompanying ground plan will convey a correct idea of a small basin of water, situated beneath and within a large projecting rock, near the top of the mount, east of the present mosk, which appears to be a metamorphosed convent of the Crusaders. The old chroniclers speak of a "Fountain of St. Samuel." They locate it, however, in another quarter; and it is probably that situated near the mosk just beyond the ridge. Can this excavation have been a Jewish bath? Or was it designed as a baptistery by the Empress Helena, either for a church once erected over it, or for the one now in ruins, considerably south of it?*

A mile or two south-west of Neby Samwil, and four or five north-west of Jerusalem, is Ain Kirbet Losa. And a mile farther south, at the junction of the Valley of Kirbet Losa with Wady Beit Hanina, are several fountains and pools, near the foundations of an old city, called Beit Tulmeh. Half a mile farther down Wadi Beit-Hanina is quite a bold fountain near some old Jewish ruins, and an Arab village called Kulonieh—a little above the point at which the road from Jerusalem to Jaffa crosses the valley over a stone bridge. A few hundred yards up the road to Kastul the traveller may slake his thirst at a very weak fountain on the wayside, called Ain Arsafear; not far from which, over on the north, is another, called Ain Adjous. In this neighborhood are also Ain Ras Kabàlli, on the west, and on the south, Ain Sataf, Ain Habis, Ain Kaudak, Ain Arawas, and Ain Karim. The last of which is rather more than four miles due west from Jerusalem, and, according to the tradition of the Greeks, who here have a fine church and convent, is the birthplace of the great forerunner, John the Baptist.

"The Fountain Sealed."—A few hundred yards up the shallow valley, above the old Saracenic castle at the head of Solomon's

* This singular structure may well remind us of the elegant octagonal baptistery in the Basilica of St. John Lateran, at Rome, built by Constantine for his own baptism; and in which proselyted Jews and Infidels are to this day ceremoniously baptized the Saturday before every Easter. At all events, it is very natural to suppose that the Empress would model all the ecclesiastical structures she built in Palestine very much after the fashion prevailing in Italy; and especially after the style of that great model church at Rome so highly honoured and regarded by her imperial son—"Omnium urbis et orbis Ecclesiarum Mater et Caput," as it was designated. Webster remarks that, "primitively, baptisteries were in buildings separate from the church; but in the sixth century they were taken into the church-porch, and afterward into the church itself."

Pools, the traveller may discover, amongst the luxuriant growth of weeds and grass, a large round rock, which he will find, on inspection, to close the mouth of a shaft of masonry, leading to a subterranean, rock-hewn room, containing a fountain. This, tradition confidently asserts, is the celebrated fountain to which the Wise Man compares his spouse—"A spring shut up, a fountain sealed." (Cant. iv. 12.) Nor can the tradition be disproved. The united strength of many men is required to unseal the entrance. The accompanying engraving gives a correct view of this interesting font-room, which, in all probability, was constructed by Solomon—being the main source from which the pools derive their supply. (See next article.)

"THE FOUNTAIN SEALED."

Besides the Fountain Sealed, and the other fountains at el-Burak, whose waters flow to Jerusalem through the present Pottery Aqueduct, there are several others in that vicinity. AIN DIER EL-BENAT, AIN HAUD KYBRIAN (Trough of Cyprian), AIN AHMED, several small unnamed springs, and the bold fountain of Wady ARTAS or Ortos, the waters of which, issuing from its strong reservoir into an aqueduct, were formerly conducted into a large pool called BIRKET ES-SULTAN (or Royal Reservoir), and a smaller one, EL-MARMOODIEH, the bath-house or baptistery at the base of Herodium or Frank Mountain—the Beth-haccerem of Scripture, called by the Arabs Jebl Fureidis or Mount Paradise, on account of the splendid gardens once irrigated from these pools. The monks strenuously contend that "Artas" or "Ortos" is a corruption of the Latin "*Hortus*," and that this valley is no other than the "Hortus clausus" or "Garden enclosed" of Canticles. (iv. 12.)

If the water for which David so ardently longed, saying, "Oh that one would give me drink of the water of the well of Bethlehem that is at the gate!" was living water, as it most assuredly must have been, it has long since disappeared, as so many others have done elsewhere—there being no fresh water there now, except the current passing through the aqueduct from Solomon's Pools to Jerusalem. But between Bethlehem and Jerusalem there are several fountains; only one of which, however, is perennial—that near Surbahet village—AIN SURBAHET.

About two and a half miles south-east of Jerusalem, on the road to Jericho, is AIN EL-HOARTH, OR THE FOUNTAIN OF THE APOSTLES, which, tradition says, they never passed without tarrying.* A thin stream issues from a rather inferior piece of fountain architecture, near an old, dilapidated khan: and, after passing through a large stone trough into a pool five or six yards square, all not thus retained is immediately absorbed by the thirsty earth. There are several other places in this vicinity where the water merely oozes out in small quantities—both above and below the "Apostle's Fount." This is probably en-Shems or es-Shemish, mentioned Josh. xviii. 17.

No remains of the pools mentioned by the rabbis are now to be

* "And indeed it is a thing very probable, and no more I believe than is done by all that travel this way, the fountain being close by the roadside, and very inviting to the thirsty passenger"—says Maundrel.

found immediately at Bethany; but there are several very large ones a few hundred yards east of the isthmus by which Bethany Mount is connected with the main ridge of Olivet.

EL-BURAK—SOLOMON'S POOLS.

Solomon's Pools and Aqueduct—*El-Burak.*—The only living water with which the Haram es-Sheriff seems now to be supplied, is derived from three pools thus denominated by the Franks, but by the Arabs called merely "El-Burak"—The Pools. They are distant from Jerusalem about eight miles by the usual road, and are situated near the head of a long valley, called Wady Urtas, supposed to be the site of ancient Etham. This is rather far for Etham, according to the usual estimate of the furlong or stadium; for Josephus states it to be sixty furlongs from the city, but if he alluded to that portion of the valley near Bethlehem, where its largest expansion occurs, and where it is most probable that the royal pleasure gardens, orchards, and parks would be located for the benefit of irrigation, the confines of it might there be reached within the specified distance—seven and a half miles. The upper pool, which is quite near a large quadrangular Saracenic fortress in a tolerable state of preservation, derives its supply of water solely from a fountain about two hundred yards above it. This fountain is about thirty feet below the surface of the ground, accessible only through a rude, roughly walled declivitous passage. But the illustration given under the last article imparts to the reader a better idea of this renowned fountain-head of Jerusalem waters than the most minute written description. In order to keep it permanently sealed, the pastoral Arabs that graze their flocks hereabouts in great numbers, close its conical mouth so effectually with a large round stone that it requires powerful mechanical force to remove it. Hence it was effectually sealed during the whole period of my sojourn in Palestine, until a short time before my return, when I had the good fortune to gain admittance and make a full exploration of it. The water, being collected into a central receptacle from various surrounding fissures, is conducted far beneath the surface of the ground to the upper pool, just before entering which it is again accessible by descending a rude stairway of rocks. I can but concur in opinion with the monks that this is the very fountain that the "king that was preacher in Jerusalem" had in mind when he compares his spouse to "a spring shut up, a fountain sealed," in his beautiful Song. (Cant. iv. 12.) One hundred and sixty feet below this pool—the shortest distance, allowing the bottom of the upper pool to be rather higher than the top of the next—we find the second or middle pool: and similarly situated in respect to this is another, the third and lower one, at a distance of two hundred and forty-eight feet. They are not very symmetrically situated or regularly made—adaptation to the local features of the valley at the highest available level being evidently the governing feature in their construction. Their respective dimensions are as follows:—

Upper Pool—length 380 feet; breadth at the upper end 229 feet, at the lower 236; greatest depth 25 feet.

Middle Pool—length 423 feet; breadth at upper end 160 feet, at lower 250; greatest depth 39 feet.

Lower Pool—length 582 feet; breadth at upper end 148 feet, at lower 207; greatest depth 50 feet.

The walls are built of large hewed stones, well lined with cement, as is also the bottom, which is very narrow in the middle, but becomes wider and wider—the different strata of rock forming successive terraces—not horizontal, but slightly inclined longitudinally, so that the water on each plateau differs materially in depth. More delightful swim-pools than these, heart could not desire: and that they were formerly much used as such, is rendered highly probable by the well-arranged flights of steps descending into them. The lower one, however, at the present day, is never entirely filled, even at the close of the rainy season; and the middle one frequently becomes nearly exhausted before the expiration of the dry season; but the upper one is generally well filled. The water brought from the "fountain sealed" may either be turned into the pools or conducted by the rapidly descending aqueduct alongside of it. There must of necessity be an educt as well as an induct connected with each pool for regulating its supply of water, though the exact *modus operandi* is not observable. The lower pool receives an additional supply, at least in winter, from two superficial channels running around the hill on the south; and the main aqueduct having passed a short distance below the pools, receives a considerable accession from another conduit coming from the south; and having crossed the valley just below the lowermost pool, enters the aqueduct some yards farther down, having itself received two small tributaries, the one from *beneath* the pool, and the other from a point certainly lower than the top of the pool, and probably lower than its bottom, which unite in a room under the lower wall and dam of the pool.

The style of architecture in this room very closely resembles that of the "fountain sealed." The disproportionate length of the rocks in the vaults is a peculiarity that I have observed only in these two rooms. The atmosphere being subject to but little variation in humidity or temperature in these deep subterranean partially closed recesses, the vaults as well as the arches (with their keystones too) are found in admirable state of preservation:—a very significant fact in deciding the much mooted question as to the antiquity of the arch—for no one questions the high antiquity of these great water-works. The aqueduct is made almost exclusively of suitably shaped cylinders of red pottery, twelve or fifteen inches long and eight or ten in diameter, cemented into each other and buried usually a foot or two in the ground; but having occasional watering-places of stone with open mouths through which the water can be easily obtained. About one mile below the pools the aqueduct passes just above the ruins of the town of Artas, where a few enterprising Americans settled, and for a time succeeded in the culture of the most valuable American esculents—vegetables, fruits, grains, &c; but were soon compelled to desist on account of the most virulent opposition on the part of those who should have been their most cordial co-operators. A powerful fountain bursts forth from the side of the hill just below the ruined village, and being received into a reservoir, is now appropriated to the irrigation of the highly cultivated gardens in that lovely vale; but was formerly carried to Herodium or Frank Mountain for the purpose of adorning and watering the *Paradise* of Herod the Great, hence called by the Arabs to this day Jebl *Furidis*—an Arabic corruption of that term, as Artas is also of the name assigned it by the monks, and not altogether unwarrantably "*Hortus clausus*"—from the simile used by the Wise Man, "*a garden enclosed* is my sister, my spouse: a spring shut up, a fountain sealed." The aqueduct passes on hence to Jerusalem, reposing on the slopes of the hills, slightly descending, and pursuing the tortuous course laid down on the "Vicinity Map" twelve and a quarter miles; but not as sinuous as represented by travellers—for instead of passing around Bethlehem, as is generally maintained, it goes directly through the centre of the town after reaching "the well;" and also tunnels another hill about a mile and a half from the city. Having reached the Valley of Hinnom, it passes around the lower pool of that valley, about seventy-five yards above it, on nine or ten arches, now nearly concealed by accumulated earth; but before doing so sends off a short branch to the troughs of a monumental fountain situated midway the lower side of the "Great Pool." According to the deciphering and translation of the late lamented Dr. Schultz, so long the able representative of the Prussian government at the Holy City, the inscription on this fountain reads as follows: "In the name of the most merciful God,—our lord the Sultan El-Melik en-Nassir the Lord of the Faith and of the faithful, Mohammed son of the Sultan el-Melik el-Mansur Kelaun, ordered this blessed aqueduct to be built." (A. D. 1294—1340.) After coursing around Mount Zion at the highest attainable level, it passes through the city wall at the spot indicated on the map, and having penetrated by a short tunnel the solid rock on which the premises of the American Christian Mission are built, it reaches Temple street, down which it turns at right angles and enters the Haram esh-Sherif.

This is perhaps the "canal which rushed forth in a copious stream introduced from a distance," of which Felix Fabri speaks in 1480. Or was the aqueduct of Pontius Pilate then remaining? Scarcely.

The water-works of el-Burak are doubtless the pools to which the "Preacher" alludes in the 2d Chapter of his Ecclesiastes: "I made me pools of water, to water therewith the wood that bringeth forth the trees,"—probably not only at Etham, but all the way along thence to his magnificent capital.

ENON—ÆNON—Αινων—Αινον εγγυς του Σαλειμ—*Salim—Foxes or Paths—Aiyûn* or *Ainyûn—Wady Farah—Fountains of the Valley of Delight.*—Of all the fountains in the neighborhood of Jerusalem, the most copious and interesting by far are those that burst forth within a short distance of each other in Wady Farah, about six miles north-east of the city. The following extracts from "The History of the Jerusalem Mission," though somewhat extended, will not be found too detailed, it is hoped, for a spot to which so much interest attaches:—

WADY FARAH—ÆNON ?

* * * "Finding it impossible to procure, in the immediate environs of the city, a suitable place for the proposed asylum, on account of the high price demanded for land, I have extended my researches a little farther than heretofore, and have at last found a very eligible place about six miles from the city, which is 'merie'—a term used to designate the public domain or property of the Sultan; and I have accordingly written to our highly esteemed minister at Constantinople, to ascertain upon what terms it can be obtained. I have every reason to believe that the sum demanded will not exceed that to which I am limited by the Board; and as it is a very interesting spot, entirely unknown to Christendom, and is surrounded by places of stirring interest, I will give you a brief account of my visit there. Crossing Mount Olivet near the Church of Ascension, and taking the road down Wady Ruwaby, fifty minutes' walk brought us to the ruins of Al Kuby Sufre; and turning abruptly to the left, after crossing a few inconsiderable hills, we found ourselves opposite the venerated Irkhan Ibrahim (Cave of Abraham), on the top of a commanding hill, where, according to Arab tradition, the old patriarch watched his flocks as they grazed in the neighboring valleys and plains, more than three thousand seven hundred years ago—just as many groups of them were doing as we passed along; and in half an hour more we were on the verge of a great valley within a few hundred yards of Wady Farah, the object of our visit. But having heard of a wonderful monster fountain a mile or two below, near the

junction of this wady with Wady Fuwah, we determined to visit this mysterious Zemzam before descending the valley of Farah. Our Moslem guide informed us, that though it burst forth from the earth as copious as a river, yet he could stop at command the rushing flood, merely by chanting a certain formula of prayer, the chorus and burden of which was—'the colored man whipped the white man;' and, what to our occidental ears was equally marvelous, could call the 'spirits from the vasty deep,' and again cause the pent-up torrent to rush off down the valley, by reversing his declaration, and making 'the white man whip the colored man.' Arrived at the spot, we found that, though *not exactly* realizing the American idea of a river, it was certainly a most copious 'fountain and depth springing out of the valley,' capable of driving several mills as it gushes forth from the earth; and although we were not at all anxious to see such a noble spring suppressed, yet he proceeded at once to redeem his promise, as if unwilling that his professed character as a thaumaturgist should be doubted a moment longer. Imagine, if you can, what astonishment filled our minds, when, despite our disbelief in the miraculous pretensions of this follower of the 'great prophet' and apostle of Islam, the water actually began to disappear; and in a few minutes not a single drop escaped from the yawning fissure. It had entirely subsided and retired within the earth. In order apparently that we might be the more fully convinced of his miraculous powers, he inquired, after a minute or two, if we did not wish to see him cause the water to flow again? to which, of course, we responded in the affirmative; and forthwith this rival of Canute, Xerxes, and Moses commenced his lugubrious incantation, and soon, exultingly calling attention to the gurgling sound below, had the satisfaction of seeing the water burst forth furiously from its apparent imprisonment. In order to remove from our minds the least shadow of doubt, he again subjected the obedient waters to his magic influence. And as we still lingered at the fountain, he was about to renew his conjurations; but I thought it was now time to show this tricking son of Ishmael that 'Saul was also among the prophets;' and, by way of making my 'rod swallow up the rod of this modern magician,' told him I would neither sing nor pray about the white and colored men fighting, nor wave a hand or wand over the water as he did, but would even walk out of sight, and yet make it appear and disappear at my bidding; for I noticed that it flowed about six minutes, ebbed six, and was quiescent about three; and the idea occurred to me at once, that the water from the fountains above, which he had told me disappeared after flowing about a mile, was received into a subterranean reservoir, which emptied itself every twelve or fifteen minutes by a kind of natural syphon. Anxious still to maintain his pretensions to familiar intercourse with infernal aquatic spirits, he defied me to do so at first; but, seeing me pull out my watch and mark the moment of the water's subsidence, he discovered he could gull us no longer, and reluctantly confessed the trick he had been attempting to palm on us.

"Returning by a circuitous route to the place whence we had started, from the brow at Wady Farah, we descended with some difficulty into that 'Valley of Delight'—for such is the literal signification of its name—and truly I have seen nothing so delightful in the way of natural scenery, nor inviting in point of resources, &c., in all Palestine. Ascending its bold stream from this point, we passed some half-dozen expansions of the stream, constituting the most beautiful natural natatoria I have ever seen; the water, rivalling the atmosphere itself in transparency, of depths varying from a few inches to a fathom and more, shaded on one or both sides by umbrageous fig-trees, and sometimes contained in naturally-excavated basins of red mottled marble—an occasional variegation of the common limestone of the country. These pools are supplied by some half-dozen springs of the purest and coldest water, bursting from rocky crevices at various intervals. Verily, thought I, we have stumbled upon Enon!* 'Many fountains,' I believe, is what Professor Robinson, the great Biblical geographer and lexicographer, prefers rendering the 'polla hudata' of Enon; and here are not only many fountains, but literally 'much water'—thus accommodating each translation. Portions of aqueducts, both of pottery and stone, and in a tolerable state of preservation, too, in many places, are still found remaining on each side of the valley, indicating the extent to which the valley was at one time irrigated; and richer land I have never seen than is much of this charming valley; capable, too, of being made yet richer by the guano of goats, many large mounds of which—the accumulation of long ages—are here found. Several herds of cattle were voraciously feeding on the rich herbage near the stream; and thousands of sheep and goats were seen approaching the stream, or 'resting at noonday' in the shadow of the great rock composing the overhanging cliff here and there. The cooing dove and the 'kharking'† raven are here seen in strange affinity. And many birds of many kinds—from the chirping little sparrow to the immense condor-looking vulture—were sweetly carolling, or swiftly flitting across the valley, or securely reposing upon its lofty cliffs; and the most delicious perfume pervaded many spots in this beautiful little Eden. Rank grasses, luxuriant reeds, tall weeds, and shrubbery and trees of various kinds, entirely conceal the stream from view in many places; forming around its pebbly little pools just such shady and picturesque alcoves and bowers as classic poets picture out for the haunts of their naiads, sylphs, and fairies. But instead of nymphs and sylphs, a very wizard-like old Arab was wading about, gathering crabs—and snails also, which here grow on weeds and shrubs as thick as blackberries—for the dignitaries of the Greek convent at Jerusalem. Half a dozen young Arab women from a neighboring encampment were also wading about in one of the expansions of water, filling their goat-skin bottles less gracefully than disgracefully; their solitary garment—if garment it could be called—being well tucked up by the girdle! One of our party, on coming up from one of these secluded bathing-places, found himself minus every particle of his clothing—a *liberal-minded* son of the desert having arrayed himself in them, apparently in sport: and, professing to humor the joke as best we could, succeeded after a while—and a long while, too, it seemed—in getting him disrobed, or rather *disrobbed* of them. By-the-bye, whence came the fishes that were sporting about in these pellucid little ponds elevated at least two thousand feet above the Jordan? A *per saltum* ascent is entirely out of the question. Have they made their escape from the muddy waters of the Jordan, and wended the uneven tenor of their way through subterranean channels to this great height? or are they the remains of an old piscatory colony planted here by the old Canaanitish, Jewish, Roman, Persian, or crusading residents of this valley? Certainly not by rude improvident Turks or Arabs. This being the only *accessible* water for many miles, herds of gazelles that graze on the neighboring hillsides resort here in great numbers; and the dense forests of cane-brakes are the favorite resort of wild boars, which abound below—hog-hating Islamism to the contrary notwithstanding!

---

* See page 564.

† This bird is very fond of calling its own name in Arabic—for ever crying, as it flies "khark! khark! khark!"

"Higher up, the valley becomes very narrow, and the rocky precipices tower to a sublime height, and at one point seem to have been connected by an airy bridge. In the perpendicular faces of these towering walls are found many caves of great extent; and what we at first took for sepulchral excavations, were found, on further examination, to have served as habitations for the living, furnished with receptacles for water, and other conveniences; but especially well devised for defence. But though the eremite tenants of these rock-tenements have long since been swept off by the bloodthirsty sons of Ishmael, whose hands are against every man, and every man's hand against them, yet some kind of 'folks' still dwell high up in the rocky cliffs. Now 'the conies are but a feeble folk, yet make they their houses in the rocks,' and maintain possession there in great force. A short distance below the upper fountain were very evident remains of a sugar or oil mill; and scattered about were also tessara, fragments of pillars, and other indications of ancient buildings. We also found several Roman coins. But what impressed me more than anything else that I saw, was a large, somewhat regular, though altogether natural hemispherical—or rather amphitheatrical—excavation in the cliff, with its overhanging dome of dizzy height—a kind of natural clerestory or void—like that over the Oracle of the Temple, unfathomable by the sight. Oh, what a devotion-inspiring cathedral for the worship of that exalted Being that 'dwelleth not in temples made with hands,' and who has made this gigantic temple himself, with the exception of the semicircular ranges of seats that have probably been chiselled out by the hands of the Crusaders!

"Ascending a neighboring hill, we had a most commanding view of Mount Olivet, the hill country and wilderness of Judea, the land of Moab, the Dead Sea, the Arabah or Jordan region, Michmash, Rimmon, Geba, Ramah, Gibeah, and other interesting localities; and then, after having spent a most delightful day, we reluctantly left this sweet retreat, and reached our quarters in an hour and a half, passing through Anathoth, near to which lay the field of Jeremiah; where we entered upon the devastating track of the haughty Assyrian monarch advancing to the investment of the Holy City. And crossing Mount Olivet near Nob, where there is a commanding stand-point in full view of all the stations mentioned in the glowing description of the prophet (Isaiah x. 28–32), could but greatly enjoy it.

"'He is come to Aiath, he is passed to Migron
At Michmash he hath laid up his carriages:
They are gone over the passage:
They have taken up their lodging at Geba;
Ramah is afraid;
Gibeah of Saul is fled.
Lift up thy voice, O daughter of Gallim!
Cause it to be heard unto Laish,
O poor Anathoth!
Madmenah is removed;
The inhabitants of Gebim gather themselves to flee.
As yet shall he remain at Nob that day:
He shall shake his hand against the mount of the daughter of Zion,
The hill of Jerusalem."

The valley upon which we entered on crossing Mount Olivet (Wady Ruwaby), I afterwards identified as a locality of some interest. It runs a nearly straight course from Mount Olivet for three miles, directly towards Jordan, and offers the nearest, though not the best route to it. The pathway is on the right hand (descending), on which side the slope is quite gentle, but on the opposite side is very precipitous, and much of it entirely inaccessible. Wady Khark enters it from the north near its head, not far from a small wely of an Arab Santon, just below which are a few broken columns and vestiges of a former city; and at its lower end it unites with another valley (from the west) called Wady Seleim, where there are also ruins of a city called Kirbet al-Kubr Suffre; and just above, on the northern side of Wady Seleim, are the remains of Deir es-Sid, surrounded also by the ruins of an old city. All the circumstances attending David's flight from Absalom, lead to the conclusion that this wady, the upper part of which is called Emkaitham and the lower portion Ruwaby, is the identical valley along the side of which the weeping king of Israel fled; and the ruins indicate the site of Bahurim, out of which "came forth Shimei, and cursed still as he came, and he cast stones at David, and at all the servants of King David * * * Then said Abishai the son of Zeruiah unto the king, Why should this dead dog curse my lord the king? let me go over, I pray thee, and take off his head * * * * And David said, Let him alone, and let him curse * * * And as David and his men went by the way, Shimei went on the hill's side over against him, and cursed as he went; and threw stones at him and cast dust." (2 Sam. xvi.) It was in this place, too, that "Jonathan and Ahimaaz came to a man's house who had a well in his court, whither they went down, and the woman took and spread a covering over the well's mouth, and spread ground corn thereon, and the thing was not known; and when Absalom's servants came to the woman to the house, they said, Where are Ahimaaz and Jonathan? And the woman said unto them, They be gone over the brook of water. And when they had sought, and could not find them, they returned to Jerusalem." (2 Sam. xvii. 18–20.)

The Chaldee renders Bahurim Almath; and it was probably identical with Almon or Alemeth (Josh. xxi. 18, and 1 Chr. vi. 60), where it is associated with Anata, in the canton of Benjamin. It was a city of refuge. There is now no stream in the wady, except occasionally through the winter months; nor is there any proof that there was a permanent stream at the period of time referred to: so that the present failure of water is by no means fatal to the recognition suggested, for great numbers of streams known to have existed at one time have long since disappeared. But the subterranean stream not far from this spot—though separated by a hill—may possibly be the representative of a former stream, that ran beneath the hill and burst forth in this valley—certainly not an impossible fact, nor even an unfrequent case in Palestine.

*Although this *conjecture*—that Ain Farah was Ænon—must be set down to the account of a mere random suggestion of the moment, yet a more intimate acquaintance with the geography of the neighborhood has brought me to an assured conviction that this place is indeed no other than the "Enon, near to Salim, where John was baptizing, because there was much water there." But it may be well to assign the principal reasons by which I have been led to form a conclusion so different from the generally received opinion in relation to Enon and Salim. Biblical geographers have generally concurred in opinion with Eusebius and his commentator Jerome, in supposing that Enon was near a town in Galilee called in their day "Alim, Vicus Salumias, Salem or Salim, about eight miles from Scythopolis or Bethshean" (the Beisan of the present day), first brought to notice by those fathers in the 4th century. And this venerated patristic tradition has perhaps never been called in question, but is uniformly received in trust down to the present day, and that too not on account of a definite locality characterized by "many waters or much water," but simply because there happens to be

* "Enon, juxta Salim, ubi baptizabat Joannes, sicut in Evangelio κατα Ιοάννην—scriptum est; et ostenditur usque nunc locus in octavo lapide Scythopolios ad meridiem juxta Salim et Jordanem."

water of some sort somewhere in the neighborhood of a village called Alim, Shalim, Salem, Shulumias, Salumias—the ancient "Shalem, a city of Shechem," before which Jacob pitched his tent. But surely, never was tradition so poorly sustained—indeed it is self-refuted. Enon, they allege, was not only near to Salim, but also near the Jordan. Now, Salem is at least twenty-five miles from Scythopolis, and twenty from the nearest point on the Jordan. Enon being only eight miles from Scythopolis, with what propriety can it be called "near to Salem," when it is necessarily more than sixteen miles distant! and that too in a country teeming with towns and cities. And if near to Salem, how could it be near also to the Jordan—being necessarily at least ten miles from each, even if situated midway. Nor does even tradition speak of any place "near to Salem," answering John's description of Enon.

Perceiving therefore the incongruities of the traditional allocation of these places, and finding that Ain Farah answers so admirably to Enon in every respect except the vicinity of Salim, I could but institute an investigation of the matter. And being unable to hear of any ruins called Salim thereabouts, I secured the services of an Arab of that neighborhood, and commenced a regular "furrage," (as the Arabs term an exploration;) and on inquiring, when within a mile and a half of the fountains, "*Shu ismo hatha wady?*"—"What is the name of this wady?" had the satisfaction of hearing him pronounce the identical word; and soon was conducted to the site of an ancient city. It is true that, on further inquiry of others, it was pronounced somewhat differently—Sillim, Silim, Sulim, Saleim, Sallem, Selam, &c., quite as near an approximation, however, to the present Hebrew orthography as could be expected from the slippery tongue of Arabs. For they use the vowels very arbitrarily; and indeed nothing is more common than the same exchange of consonants, apparently without rhyme, rhythm, or reason. This will abundantly appear from the following specimens of Arabic pronunciation of Hebrew names.

Salim.

Hebrew.	*Arabic.*
Anathoth	Annatta
Bethel	Beitin
Jezreel	Zerim
Emmaus	Amwas
Joppa	Yaffa
Siloam	Silwan
Babilla	Mamilla
Kerith	Kelt
Jericho	Riha
En Gannim	Jennin

This valley (Wady Selim) commences on the eastern slope of Mount Olivet, rather more than a mile above the city; and passing between a small village called Isawiyeh and Annata (the ancient Anathoth), runs almost due east about three miles, when it unites with Wady Ruwaby at Kirbet el Kubr Sufre. There is also a valley commencing at Tell el Fûl, called usually Wady Sunam, but sometimes also Suleim or Senam or Selam, which, after running about two miles somewhat parallel to the above, unites with Wady Zreek, and is then known under the name of Wady Farah, the valley in which the fountains gush forth, rather more than a mile before their junction. The position of Salim would seem to have been well known: and if situated either at the ruins on the ridge around Deir es Sid, near some wine and oil presses, or at Kubr Sufre, it would have been quite a conspicuous object from Mount Olivet. It would thus be well known not only to all the "dwellers at Jerusalem," but all Israel being compelled to attend the feasts "from Dan even unto Beersheba," its location would be familiar to all: and hence the position of Enon would be well understood by the Apostle's reference to this "city set on a hill." We have no account that John exercised his ministry anywhere else than at Enon, in the wilderness, and at the Jordan; nor is it at all probable that he ever preached elsewhere (unless it was when he reproved Herod) during the brief period of his ministerial career: if, therefore, Enon and Wady Farah be identical, it is probable in the highest degree that Enon is the place alluded to in the passage where the Saviour inquires of the people "what went ye out into the wilderness for to see? a reed shaken with the wind?"—for it abounds in reeds, and is now, as it probably always has been, the dividing line between the wilderness and the cultivated country, or rather an oasis a short distance in the wilderness of Judea where the Saviour was tempted of the Devil. The first entrance into the desert was three miles from Jerusalem, and that place was called Bath Chadudo, one of the scapegoat stations, according to the Talmud.

On consulting the work of the very learned Dr. Lightfoot I find in sections 1, 2, 3, 4, of his "Chorographic Inquiry into some places mentioned by the Evangelist St. John," the following unexpected confirmation of this view of Enon. In speaking of the generally received opinion that Salim is indicated in the 18th verse of the 33d chapter of Genesis, where Moses is made by our translators to say that "Jacob came to Shalem (or Salem), a city of Sichem," he remarks that

"Neither the Jews nor Samaritans acknowledge any such thing. For the Jews render it, and that not without reason, 'Jacob came *safe* into the city of Sichem.' The Samaritan text hath 'he came *in peace*.' And certainly there is no part of mankind could be more likely to judge than the Samaritans whether Shalem or Salem in that place were the name of any city, yea or no. * * * * If now the reader can pitch upon any places he may have met with in his reading, as that which our Evangelist here meaneth, let him consider whether the article tou may properly be prefixed to it, whereas the names of all cities and towns are of the feminine gender generally, and yet St. John hath it tou Saleim, which gives some ground of conjecture, that the passage is to be understood not of any town or city but of some other matter: which by way of exercitation it may not be amiss a little to enlarge upon. Every one that hath but dipt into the Chaldee Paraphrasts must know that the Kenites are called by them Salmeans of *Salameans*. . . . . But the Kenite is not termed a Salamean from any place or country where he dwelt; for the Kenites in the southern parts of Judea are called Salameans; so, also, Heber the Kenite in Galilee, the Kenites amongst the Amalakites, and the Kenites beyond Jordan. Whence so called is not to our purpose; it sufficeth that they were vulgarly known by the name of Salame, which how near akin to Saleim (Salim) let the unbiassed reader judge. Who knoweth, therefore, but the Evangelist should mean thus—John was baptizing in Enon near the *Salamean* or Kenite—giving that name to that people which at that time they were commonly called by? But supposing this should be granted us, what Kenite should we understand here, either those that were in the wilderness of Judah, or those on the other side the salt sea? If the Essene might be called Salamean as well as Kenite (and certainly he seems to have as much claim to it if the word denote perfection or austerity of life), then I could more confidently place our Salim in the wilderness of Judah, because there I find Enon mentioned in the Greek version. (Josh. xv. 61, 62.) Where the Hebrew hath it thus: 'In the wilderness Betharabah, Middin, and Secacah, &c.;' but the Greek (instead of Middin) a i n o n (Ænon) where it is plain that a i n o n (Enon) is put for Middin; but why it should be so is more difficult to tell. This only we may remark that the word Middin occurs Jud. v. 10, which if I should render 'ye that dwell by Middin,' I should have Kimche to warrant me, who, in his notes upon this place, tells us that Middin is the name of a place mentioned in Joshua. But now when a i n o n (Enon) signifies a place of springs or waters, see what follows—'from the noise of archers among the places of drawing waters.' . . . . So that if you ask the Greek interpreter why he should render Middin by a i n o n (Enon), a place of springs, he will tell you that it was a place of those that draw waters. The Essens succeeded the Kenites in their dwelling* in the wilderness of Judah (Pliny, lib. 4, cap. 17), and not only so, but in strictness and austerity of life as Josephus and others assure us. Now if we will but allow the Essenes to be called *Salamean,* as the Kenites were, then the words of the Evangelist might bear such sense as this—'John was baptizing in Enon near the Essenes.' And it may be supposed that as the Baptist had already conversed with two of the Jewish sects, the Pharisees and Sadducees, and had baptized some of each, he would also now apply himself to a third sect, viz. the Essenes, and baptize some of them too. But herein, I will not be positive."

"While we are treating upon the word A i n o n (Ænon), I cannot but observe that the word is *divided* both in the Syriac and Arabic version—S y r. a i n - j o n (or I o n or Y o n) = A i n - y o n : Arab, A i n - n u n†—'In the Fountain Jon, Ion, or Yon, and in the Fountains Nun.' The words of the Evangelist seem to discover the signification of the name—'oti hudata polla een ekei,' because there was much water there, for we could not have rendered the word more significantly than '*a place of springs,* or a watery place.' So Nonnus,

Hudati baptizon bathuh—monos eggathi Saleem.
Baptizing near the waters of deep-waved Salem.

Why, therefore, did these interpreters take the word in two, when it was plain and etymological enough of itself? . . . . . Whilst we are in this watery country [he is here speaking of the 'many springs' in the region of the Castle Macharus, in which John the Baptist was incarcerated by Herod], are we not got amongst the rivers of Arnon? The learned Beza commenting upon those words of St. John—'for there was much water there'—affirms it, commenting thus: namely, 'many rivers of which, also in that tract about Aroer, there is mention in the Books of Moses. . . . . But here we find no place that is either called Ænon or Salim.' True, indeed, but the place, for the very wateriness of it, deserves to be called Ænon, that is a place of springs; and if Salem may be the same with Salamean, here we

* It is certainly within the range of reasonable probability that the cells which I have conjecturally ascribed to the eremite monks of the era of Frank domination in Palestine, may have been the habitations of the Essenes here alluded to.

† "Aiyûn" is the plural of ain, as at present pronounced by the Arabs about Jerusalem; but it is doubtless a contraction for Ainyûn—quite a near approach to a i n o o n or Enon.

have also the Salamean or Kenite. (Gen. xv. and Num. xxiv.) However, in a thing so very obscure, it is safest not to be positive; and the reader's candor is begged in this modest way of conjecturing. The way we tread is unbeaten, and deserves a guide, which as yet we have not obtained." (Vol. ii. 498, 499.)

Thus writes the great Oriental Scholar: but the obscurity that then beclouded the matter has been dissipated by the discovery of Wady Selim, which affords the clue to the identification of this interesting locality.

The etymology of the term affords another argument in favor of this identification. Its Hebrew name is a i n o o n and not Enon; and this is almost exactly the Chaldaic Hebrew for fountains. The perfectly limpid water of the upper fountain being received into a somewhat hemispherical or bowl-shaped excavation in reddish and greenish mottled marble eight or ten feet diameter and about half as deep, is not inaptly compared to a bird's eye, when reflecting the hues of the sky. And it is to this fact, according to many excellent scholars, that the etymology of the term points. But there is yet another matter of interest connected with these waters. On inquiring of the *natives*—if such we may term the nomadic bipeds that roam through these wilds—where these waters emptied into the Jordan, I learned that on sinking into the earth and again emerging just below the junction of wadys Fuwar and Farah, the stream is called Kelt; and after flowing or rather tumbling eastward about ten miles, passing directly by the Castle of Jericho, empties into the Jordan a mile or two below. Now the recognition of the Hebrew word Cherith in the Arabic garb Kelt may seem rather far-fetched to a person unacquainted with such latitudinous transitions of names in Palestine: but it is nevertheless true that Kelt is an Arabic corruption of Kerith—and accordingly we find this same stream at Jericho styled "Flumen Krith," by some old authors. But in corroboration of this assertion I quote the following passages in relation to the stream at Jericho from the Biblical Researches (Vol. ii. 288.) "So far as it depends upon the name, this Wady Kelt may have been the brook Cherith where the prophet Elijah hid himself and was fed by ravens. The Arabic form Kelt and the Hebrew Cherith are indeed not exactly the same, though the change from *Resh* to *Lam* and that of *Kaph* into *Koph* are sometimes found." And in relation to the position of Cherith, Dr. Robinson farther remarks very appropriately that "there is also an apparent difficulty in the circumstance that the brook Cherith is said to be *before* Jordan; which is usually understood as meaning *east* of Jordan. But the difficulty vanishes if we translate it *towards* Jordan; and that this may be done is shown by Gen. xviii. 16 and xix. 28, where the angels and Abraham, in the vicinity of Hebron, are said to have looked '*towards* Sodom'—the expression in Hebrew being the very same as here. So too Judges xvi. 3."

It is a matter of pleasing surprise that amongst the many parallels that might be drawn between Elijah the Tishbite and John the forerunner (the "Elias that was for to come") is evidently the fact that they both spent a portion of their time, in this delightful, grand, and fearful wady—for doubtless it was to the ravines of this very valley that the prophet fled when the Lord said unto him (1 Kings xvii. 3, 6) "Get thee hence and turn thee eastward, and hide thyself by the brook Cherith that is before Jordan. And it shall be that thou shalt drink of the brook; and I have commanded the ravens to feed thee there. So he went and did according unto the word of the Lord: for he went and dwelt by the brook Cherith which is before Jordan. And the ravens brought him bread and flesh in the morning, and bread and flesh in the evening, and he drank of the brook." And surely a more admirable place of seclusion could nowhere be found. Some of its yawning chasms are absolutely frightful to behold. The ruins of an old convent are to be seen toward the lower end of the valley where possibly tradition once located the retreat of the hermit-prophet *pro tem.*, so situated that nothing short of the ravens and other privileged orders of the feathered tribe could ever reach it, unless the most desperate efforts of the Arab species of bi-manu-ped Homo might succeed in scaling it. And it is still a mootable point whether Elijah was fed y the ravens or by the Arabs. The word rendered raven, being ointed by the Masoretic Doctors so as to read Orebim, is properly ranslated ravens by King James's translators, but might also have een pointed so as to mean Arabs! The distinction being made lone by the Masoretic points; for the original consonants without he affixed points were convertible either into a proper name Orebim r susceptible of being rendered ravens, Arabs, or strangers. Nor eed any one be apprehensive lest such a version should detract rom the value of the miracle: for when we consider the innate ntipathy and hatred borne towards the Jews, by those "whose hand is against every man" in general and the Jew in particular, it would be almost as miraculous for a poor despised Jew to be thus fed by an Arab as by a raven. It is a little remarkable, however, that these wild fastnesses should still be the favorite abode of ravens nd other rapacious birds that now dispute with the Arabs the nastery of this valley.

Extracts from a letter transmitting a Journal of an excursion to Gaza, &c.

.... I scarcely know whether such a mere itinerary as the accompanying journal is embraced in the request contained in your last kind communication, and I therefore feel some reluctance in sending it: but, inasmuch as it contains certain matters of interest, interspersed here and there, which I think you would like to present to the public, I conclude to send it just as it is—devolving upon you the onerous task of separating the few grains of wheat from the mass of enveloping chaff—provided you have patience to turn your quill into a winnowing shovel, and toss it up a few times on the threshing floor of your table editorial.

Several considerations that I could not well resist induced me to undertake this trip. I had concluded, after much deliberation, to spend the summer at Jaffa, or somewhere else on the seacoast; and it therefore became necessary to make a preliminary visit of reconnoissance. The delicate state of my own health, as well as that of my sons, rendered it highly advisable to take a few days' recreation beyond the influence of Jerusalem's mephitic vapors: and, while so doing, we concluded to take Gaza and "a *certain* water" in our route, with the view of determining a point about which there has long existed the greatest diversity of opinion.

May 14*th*, 1853. Accompanied by Mr. L., of Scotland, and Messrs. C. and A., of the United States, we made our exit from Zion Gate, Ethiopia-ward, soon after sunrise, nine souls, all told, including muleteer and guide. Descending the western steep of Zion, we crossed the Valley of Hinnom on the southern wall or dam of the "Lower Pool of Gihon," once a beautiful sheet of water, covering about four acres, and entered upon the beautiful Plain of Rephaim, just at the foot of the Hill of Evil Council.

Forcibly reminded of David "fetching a compass behind the Philistines" at this spot, when he heard a "going in the tops of the mulberry-trees," by the extensive orchard of these trees planted just here to supply the large cocoonery and silk-house lately erected by the Philistinian Greeks, out of the fine limestone of the adjacent tombs. Expecting soon to have their religion firmly planted here as the established religion of Judea, they are making rapid strides in the acquisition and improvement of property. But it is probable that the detection of their late gunpowder-smuggle plot has so aroused the jealousy of the Turks, as effectually to arrest their farther aggrandizement for the present. Leaving to the left the Hill of Evil Council and the curious-looking tree whereon *Judas hung himself*, we soon reached the Well of the Magi, where, "they say," the star reappeared to the wise men of the east. A few hundred yards farther we passed the Greek Convent of Elijah on the left, and on the opposite side, in the hard limestone, the impression of the prophet, where, hardly bestead and hungry, the poor fugitive seer lay down to repose. For a wonder, no Mussulman was praying on the top of the little building here erected, strangely enough for the double purpose of a Mohammedan oratory and general watering-place. Thus far and for half a mile farther, the small pottery conduit bringing water from Solomon's Pool to the city is on the left at various distances, according to its horizontal meanderings; and to the right I have traced for several miles a much more substantial and capacious one of stone, evidently very ancient, and having a handsome little marble reservoir near el-Khamis, on the water-shed between the Mediterranean and Dead Seas. Pursuing the same general track no doubt once traversed by Jacob, as he journeyed from Bethel to the tower of Edar, we soon came to a small domed building, whence "there was but a little way to Ephrah, which is Bethlehem," which it is highly probable that tradition is not much at fault in handing down to us as the place where the pious old patriarch buried his beautiful and well-favored Rachel. Instead of the commemorative pillar mentioned by Moses as existing in his day, there is now within the wely a mere rude oblong tumulus which, however, is a favorite place of pilgrimage for the daughters and sons of Israel. What "lamentations and weeping and great mourning" did I witness here a short time ago—Rachel's daughters weeping, not for their children but for themselves! The men also moaned and groaned most piteously; but principally manifested their emotions by reeling to and fro, and by violent contortions of countenance. In less than half an hour we reached Bethlehem, where we were joyfully received by some of the inhabitants; and whilst most of the party went into the convent to examine its rare aggroupment of "sacred localities," I took my stand at the main door, and seeing some of our old patients and friends, I told them I not only had along with me medicine for the body, but for the soul—at the same time displaying a bundle of tracts I had lately printed for the special benefit of the Bethlemites. Had I offered them an equal weight of gold, there could scarcely have been a greater rush. In less than one minute the whole bundle was exhausted, and many applicants went away unsupplied. But though they scrambled for the tract as though it were "sweet as honey," it will doubtless prove a bitter pill on deglutition, at least to the vitiated taste of the priests, like "the little book" of the Apocalypse. . . . .

Leaving this heaven-honored "House of Bread" (Beth-lehem), still called by the natives Beit-leham (House of Flesh), out of which came forth He "whose goings forth have been from of old, from everlasting," we returned to the main Hebron road, and in less than an hour reached those wonderful pools of water, made by the wise preacher who was king in Jerusalem, "to water therewith the wood that bringeth forth trees." These immense pools

› only supplied in part by a fountain, and hence, owing to the unusually light rains dur- g the past rainy season, are only partially filled—indeed, the lower one was nearly dry. ıitedly, they expose a surface of water, when only half filled, equal to an area of ten or elve acres; and owing to the slightly declining ledges or steppes on their sides, possess depths at all seasons or stages of water from their greatest depth of forty or fifty feet the centre to the superficies on the upper shelving rocks.

Leaving the pools after a short delay, and pursuing a southerly course through the battle- ld of Ibrahim Pasha and the Fellahin, down Wady el-Beer—well so named from the ımber of wells or tanks it contains, we reached Beer Hadji Ramadan at 12 o'clock, having ssed Subbeek and several other ruins. Having watered the horses, I descended into the nk by its short flight of stone steps, but though the water was quite cool, it was rather un- latable. It seems to be a very weak fountain, or shallow well, and perhaps never overflows cept during very rainy seasons. It was only a few inches in depth where the steps entered ; but seemed to be four or five feet deep at the farther end of the vault. At 12½ o'clock ached Kirbet Opheen, where there are some ruined buildings, a mosk, and many large ones lying about in wild confusion, and some of them beveled after the Jewish style. . . . . little farther on we discovered, on rummaging amongst the ruins, a natural cavernous reser- ir of water, and on descending it by means of a limb with projecting knots, found quite a etty little sheet of water, shallow in front, but apparently quite deep in the rear. The iling of the cave is supported by a rude artificial pillar. . . .

. . . . At the end of the next hour we had passed Neby Yunas or Halhul, and ed-Dirweh. nere appear to be two distinct places of this name near each other; this was Essor ed- irweh, supposed by Dr. Robinson, with every reasonable probability of truth, to be Bethzur Judah. If so, the water, which in the days of Eusebius was absorbed in the sand, is now ceived into a well-cemented reservoir. Many cattle, horses, and persons, besides our own mpany, enjoyed the refreshing beverage as it poured into the trough and flowed off into e pool—the latter three or four yards square, and the former about fifteen feet long and early three in breadth. One of the Arabs pertinaciously held on to my bridle, demanding buckshish. Another took a more quiet way of taxing us for drinking on the Sultan's ighway, by abstracting a handkerchief from Mr. J.'s pocket; but returned it evidently with ss grace than regret, when detected. As we passed through the plains, half an hour's ride nis side Hebron, we turned aside from the main road to visit the far-famed tree under which they say" Abraham dwelt. This is the land of the Anakim, and truly it is an Anak of a ee, measuring about twenty feet in circumference, and its shadow at noon covering several housand square feet. . . . . That this is not the tree which it is piously affirmed to be, is vident, not only from the express declaration of Jerome that it had disappeared in the ourth century, but from the fact that the Father of the Faithful dwelt under a terebinth or utm tree, while this is an oak ! ! ! There are very fine and extensive vineyards in this part f Arba, producing a seedless grape. . . . . Several small aqueducts observed just before eaching town; and also several wells and fountains, with their attendant pools.

We reached Hebron at half past four, and pitched our tents on a gently declining plain ear the Lazaretto, commanding a fine view of this venerable old city—"built seven years efore Zoan in Egypt," now called Khaleel or Friend by the natives. Having secured our orses and set our tabernacle in order, we sallied forth, stirred by the recollections of so nany memorable events in the history of the "Friend of God"—of the faithful spy who "followed the Lord wholly,"—and "of the man after God's own heart." Our first effort was, if possible, to get a peep into the high enclosure containing the "Cave of Machpelah before Mamre, the same is Hebron, in the land of Canaan, which Abraham bought for a possession of a burying-place." But the jealous soldier on guard frowned indignation and seemed to say to us, "*Procul, O procul esti profani!*" and lest we should not understand the logic of surly looks, pointed his musket directly at us. We found it convenient forthwith to veer to the left, and interpose a wall between us; being content now to climb a hill and view this "tabooed" spot at a more respectful distance. Perceiving a glass foundry in full blast, we called in to see the Arabic operation of blowing glass; and found this Ishmaelitish branch of Abraham's family quite expert in making vials, lamps, tubes, &c. A short distance farther we found them making bottles, such as are mentioned in Scripture, still in universal use throughout all this country. These are made not from mineral, but from animal matter—not by fire, but by water. A goat is carefully drawn out of his skin, with as small an opening as possible at the neck; and very slightly tanned with the hair on. It is then filled with chips, and water being introduced, the wood, by swelling, expands the bottle considerably, and it is now ready for use. Visited the two pools—over the lower, larger, and better one of which, called "the Pool of Hebron," it was that David hung up the heads of the murderers of Ish-bosheth. In wandering about the estates of Abraham and his confederates, Eschol and Aner, we stumbled upon several beautiful fountains and shallow wells, arched over, but accessible by steps—some of them perhaps "the upper springs," and some the "nether springs." . . . . We didn't visit the reputed tomb of Abner, nor the place where Cain killed Abel, nor did we bring away any of the red earth out of which, "they say," Adam was made! What incredulous pilgrims! We were repeatedly hooted at, cursed, and stoned by the Moslem children—worthy successors of the Anakim in brutality and iniquity. . . . .

After reading many incidents in the life of the "Father of the Faithful"—doubly interesting under existing circumstances, we commended ourselves to the God of Abraham, Isaac, and Israel, and sought for our wearied limbs the refreshment of balmy nature's sweet restorer.

May 15*th*. In such exercises as reading the word of the Lord, meditating upon his ways and works, social and secret devotions, the Lord's day passed sweetly, swiftly, and I trust, not unprofitably away.

Owing to the delay caused by refurnishing our larder, "the sun had risen upon the earth" at Hebron as well as at Sodom, before we had resumed our journey on Monday morning. . . . . Going northward for one hour. . . . . At seven, tarry awhile at Ain el-Oaf, where there are several fountains issuing from the crevices in the rocks, some poorly tilled gardens, and a pool, nine by fifteen feet. Great resort for birds. . . . . Two large millstones here lying half buried, seem to indicate that the fountains above were once much more copious, and after being used for irrigating the gardens, their united streams were brought to this spot for the purpose of driving a flour-mill. . . . . At ten o'clock reached Beit Jebrin. This is the ancient Beto Gabra, or Eleutheropolis, an important episcopal city of the early Christian ages, discovered in 1844 by the laborious researches of Drs. Robinson and Smith, after lying many centuries unknown. . . . . We here first noticed the rude machinery by which water is drawn from the deep wells by camels, somewhat as the gardens at Jaffa are watered. There were several of these wells with their capacious pools and troughs continually kept in requisition for watering the immense herds around us, and we also noticed the remains of a small aqueduct. Learning that several tribes of Arabs on the "desert" road to Gaza, contrary to what we had learned in Jerusalem, were at war with each other, and apprehending from the suspicious movements of the crowds around us, that foul play might be brewing, we concluded to cut short our visit, and strike for some of the villages a few miles higher up where we might lodge in safety, instead of pitching our tents in the Hassy country amongst the belligerents, as we had designed doing. We therefore left Beit Jebrin without staying to explore those wonderful excavations in the adjacent hills, or even visiting the Church of St. Hannah or Ain Judeia, the reputed fountain of Samson. . . . . Leaving Beit Jebrin at 11¼ o'clock and threading our way amidst a fleet of "ships of the desert," heavily laden with barley, at 12½ we reached Zeita, a picturesque Arab village, situated on a conical hill, and inquiring for water, are directed to a well at the foot of the hill: arriving there, we found several persons drawing water for themselves, donkeys, horses, and cattle. And notwithstanding the water was rather warm and considerably muddied by a Fellah who was wading about in the deep fountain, or more correctly speaking, shallow well, yet so thirsty were we that we drank it with decided gusto. It was eight or ten feet deep, and four or five yards in diameter, with the usual supply of stone troughs for watering animals. . . . . Such a vast expanse of grain we had never seen before. And constant were the exclamations of surprise elicited by such a cheering sight—Where can the people come from to consume all this ocean of breadstuff? What a silly notion— that of Volney and others—that Palestine was not adequate to the sustentation of the population anciently assigned to it! The immense fields of doura (a species of millet, the small grains of which somewhat resemble Indian corn), occasionally alternating with the wheat and barley, concealing only partially the fertile red earth, were peculiarly rich. . . . .

Reach Burrier (called generally by the natives Elbrier), at 4.20, and pitch our tents a short distance from the mud huts, between the great threshing floors and the public well. This Sakieh or well, supplied with machinery for raising water, is plied day and night by camels. A beautiful marble Corinthian capital supports the shaft of the main wheel. There are eighty-five stone jars, each containing two or three gallons, fastened at intervals of four feet on the two endless grass ropes going over the large rough pulley wrapped with grass cords. The water, which is incessantly poured out of these jars, is received into a channel cut into a marble pillar laid horizontally, and thus delivered into a reservoir twenty-four feet square, and thence let off into a trough of masonry thirty-six feet long and two and a half broad, the outer border of which is made of marble pillars worked in horizontally, as in other instances. But copious and unremitting as is this supply of water, it would seem totally inadequate to the demand. Herd after herd, and flock after flock, came crowding in about sunset, and the cry was, "still they come," until it was too dark to count them. . . . . How often have we been reminded of Ruth and Boaz, since leaving Bethlehem, where women were to be seen gleaning, and men, women, and children busily engaged on the threshing floors! . . . . Many were washing in the pool and praying on its wall, and some of them quite patriarchal in appearance; but though there were many things calculated to call up the scenes recorded in the lives of Abraham and Job, yet no suitable representatives of these old patriarchs could be found amongst all the worthies of Burrier. . . . . In the assured hope that the God of Israel would soon grant the church the victory over all her enemies, with emotions unfelt before, did I sing aloud the triumphant song of Israel—

"Strike the cymbal,
Roll the tymbal,"

slightly paraphrasing some of the stanzas impromptu—for we had been passing near the supposed site of Gath, and not very far from Elah. . . . .

Soldiers from Gaza, and Sheikhs from several neighboring villages, had assembled for the purpose of attending a parley between the delegates of the contending parties of whom we had heard at Beit Jebrin—the death of four hundred in a late battle having disposed them for peace—but news came just before sunset that the conference would be held at a neighboring village. We now supposed it would be safe and practicable to return to the main route and visit El-Hassy at a point on the direct route from Jerusalem or at least from Beit Jebrin to Gaza, where Dr. Robinson locates the scene of the eunuch's baptism. And accordingly we first engaged one man, and then another and another, to accompany us there in the morning: but on a little reflection or remonstrance from their friends, they all declined, notwithstanding liberal offers of buckshish—through fear of falling into the hands of one or the other enraged belligerent parties. We were the more anxious to visit El-Hassy on account of information received recently from a Sheikh of Felluge and abundantly confirmed at Burrier, that in Wady-el-Hassy about two or three hours distant, at Ras Kussahbeh and at Moyat es-Sid, in the same wady, the stream of water is as broad as our tent (twelve feet), and varies in depth from a span to six or seven feet—occasionally sinking and reappearing. This was doubtless (Moyat es-Sid) the certain water of which we were in quest; but we were constrained, however reluctantly, to abandon the idea of seeing it.

Leaving Burat at 5 A. M., pass near some broken columns and a pool an hour afterwards. . . . . At seven pass a reservoir or pond fifty yards square, lately supplied with water but now almost dry near Beit Hannun. . . . . Arrive in Gaza 8.20—having travelled since leaving the immediate vicinity of Hebron, over one of the very best roads (with slight exceptions), and one of the most fertile countries, that I ever beheld. . . . . Vegetation peculiarly rank—so much for water, for the sandy soil seems to be peculiarly barren. The palms are peculiarly majestic, though they have so long ceased to be emblematic of Hebrew grandeur. . . . . On further inquiry about a "certain water," learn in addition to what I had heard above, that there is abundant water four or five hours from Gaza called Sheriah—the name by which the Bedawin designate the waters of the Jordan. The two or three pools about the city seem now merely to be receptacles for rain-water, though they may once have been supplied from fountains. The present Guzzeh (as the Arabs call it) is but a poor representative of the ancient Gaza "the strong," the key of Egypt and Palestine, and one of the capitals of the lords of the Philistines, which had so often and successfully resisted the armies of Israel, a Pharaoh and an Alexander, and alternately the Saracens and Crusaders. It occupies but in part, if at all, the site of the old heaven-accursed city, and has been rebuilt in a very shabby manner out of the wreck of old materials, with the largest addition of mud. Most completely has the prophecy been fulfilled—that "Gaza shall be forsaken"—indeed it was probably deserted as early as the days of Luke. And as we gazed upon the naked white sand-hills upon which the ancient city seems to have been mainly situated, I thought in a moment of the prophetic declaration—"baldness has come upon Gaza." Of all her splendid palaces once decorating the surrounding hills, we saw no remains whatever larger than a man's hand—merely a few fragments of various-colored marbles—though it is said that, buried far below the surface of the long-accumulating sand of the desert, large cks and pillars are to be found on laborious excavation. To gaze on Gaza, is well calcu-ed to excite stirring emotions, and convey a profitable lesson on the vanity of all human eatness. . . . .

Leaving Gaza at 9¾, and passing the extensive pottery works in the suburbs, we proceed a northwest direction to the quarantine station on the beach, which we reached at 10.25, d were quite cheered by the rather unusual sight of a large foreign merchant vessel, just out to bear away the productions of Palestine to the lands of the Gentiles. . . . . Passed me wells on the beach, where we are informed that good water is obtained by digging only few feet. . . . . At 12.40 stopped to water at a sweet little stream issuing from a beautiful eet of water just on the coast, called Herbea, around whose banks many cattle, birds and ild fowls were feeding and sporting. Pursuing our lonely way along the beach, we arrived Askalon, about half past two, and took lunch under some magnificent trees near a lovely ttle mosk embowered in vines, shrubbery, and trees; amongst these trees is a very large g sycamore (Ficus Sycamorus), called by the natives Jimaze—a basket full of the fruit of hich (more than a peck) an Arab furnished us for 10 paras (about one cent), and delightful uit it is too. Sycamore fig trees attain an immense size; but bifurcating as they almost always o at a height of only two or three feet, and mainly extending horizontally, they are very asily climbed, which at once suggested the probability that this was really the kind of tree at the reformed publican of Jericho ascended in order to see his Lord. . . . . What appeared a distance to be rocks on a sand-hill proved on examination to be a strong wall built on semicircular rock-ridge—almost entire in many places. Immense columns of granite, arble, and limestone were scattered about in wild confusion. The several hills embraced ithin the semilunar wall are terraced on a magnificent scale, and as well as the valley, richly ored with fruit trees and vegetables, looked like a little paradise in a desert. . . . . There e many wells of water on the hills, as well as in the valleys: and we noticed the entrance numerous subterraneous passages. Though offering so many inducements for residence its ruins, yet there is not a single dweller within its walls—the gardens altogether culti-ated by the Fellahin of Jura, an adjacent mud village. That its present wall has been uilt out of the fragments of a former and magnificent city, is evident from the great num-er of splendid marble and granite pillars built into it transversely to bind it together. . . . . Why a place possessing such great and rare advantages should be thus neglected, seemed uite a mystery, until we remembered that thus it is written, and therefore thus it must be—"Askelon shall be a desolation"—"Askelon shall not be inhabited"—"woe to the inhabitants f the seacoast, O land of the Philistines, I will even destroy thee, that there be no inhabit-ants; and the seashore shall be dwellings and cottages for shepherds and folds for flocks." And surely never was there a more literal fulfilment of the sure words of prophecy! There s not a single inhabitant of this once mighty city; and the few Arab villages constructed ere and there by these pastoral Ishmaelites, are designed almost entirely as folds for the ccommodation of flocks. . . . . We left this very interesting spot at 4¼ o'clock, and in twenty inutes reached Ibrahim Pasha's barracks, wells, &c., a detour half a mile to the right, to ee a ruin called Mished. . . . . A few minutes more brought us to a beautiful grove and arden, with its well, cistern, &c., called a Biera, whose refreshing water we much en-joyed. . . . .

At half past five we found our tent pitched in Mijdil (the ancient Migdal?) . . . . It seems to derive an abundant supply of water from large wells; and the towering palms, interspersed here and there, and the numerous fruit trees, by which it is surrounded, impart to it a peculiar rural and oriental aspect. . . . . As soon as they learn that we have medicines to distribute, patients are forthcoming in large numbers. Greatly enjoyed a fine large watermelon as dessert after our fishfry. . . . . Received the same accounts of the water in the Hassy country that I had so frequently received elsewhere. Reminded of Boaz and Ruth by observing the guards rise with early dawn from the heaps of barley on the threshing floor, where they had slept all night.

. . . . At Ashdod we learned from some intelligent Turks that Jaffa, instead of being taken by the Russians, as we had heard reported, had simply been saluted with twenty-four guns from an American man-of-war. . . . . At the base of the hill is a beautiful and highly sculptured piece of marble composing the front of a trough attached to the pool at the well, and here, as well as at all these pools, bees are found in great numbers. Being now "found at Azotus," what pleasure it would have afforded me to preach the gospel that Philip preached, to these bigoted idolatrous creatures, bowing down as they do to Dagon Mohammed, but under existing circumstances it appeared worse than casting pearls before swine to do so. . . . . Forcing our way through the thousands of goats, sheep, camels, and donkeys that crowded around the pool and troughs, we slaked our thirst with the cool water drawn up so copiously by the patient blind-folded camel; and much enjoyed our lunch under an umbrageous olive. . . . . At 11.25, took leave of Yebna, and at the same time Philistia, with its cattle upon a thousand hills, and a thousand cattle upon a hill. At 12, opposite Hubaby, and at 12½, cross the fertile Wady Haneen, and refresh ourselves at the waterworks in the Beira of Khawager Markus, the American consular agent for Ramley, where we find ripe Indian corn! (May 17th.) . . . .

At 4 o'clock reached the renowned city of the Son of Noah, beautifully situated upon a hill on the sea shore—having the sea on the west, and beautiful gardens on the east. Pleased to find seven quite large merchant vessels in the harbor, besides a great many smaller smacks for the coasting trade; and what was far more beautiful, to behold the stars and stripes of America waving over the waters of Palestine! "Ho! to the land shadowing with wings!" The town has certainly improved since I visited it about two years ago. At the house of our highly esteemed Consul, Yacob Murad, we met with the Hon. Caleb Lyon, and Capt. Ingraham and officers of the corvette St. Louis, which had figured so largely down the coast, and whose visit to these shores is worth not a little to us, and to American interests in general in these ends—or rather the beginnings—of earth. The gardens of Jaffa are estimated at one hundred and fifty, one hundred of which have quite large pools, constantly supplied from shallow wells—wherewith all the trees as well as vegetables are daily watered. Whilst the citron, orange, lemon, banana, and palm strongly impress upon these gardens the peculiar features of tropical scenery, the appearance of the apple, pear, quince, Indian corn, and sweet potatoes seemed almost to carry me "back to old Virginny." Such luxuriant vegetation I never saw anywhere else except on the plains of the Jordan. . . . .

Left Jaffa at 3½ o'clock, and passing by Yasur, Beit Dejan (where there are some broken columns and pleasant Beiras), and Surafend where there is a small disused aqueduct, we arrived in Ramleh at 5¼, and pitched our tents by the side of a very substantial and apparently ancient pool a hundred and sixteen feet square, in which some Arabs were bathing, preparatory to praying. Arab women at the same time were bearing away large jars of water on their heads or in bottle skins on their backs. The pool is entered by two pairs of steps, and affords a supply of water throughout the year. . . . .

Colonia.

Leaving Ramley at 4½ o'clock on 19th, at 5 we were opposite Berea (not the Scripture-searching place), half a mile to the right, at 5½. . . . . At 7.25, stop to water at Ayouab, a deep fountain or shallow well, about five feet in diameter and six feet in depth, containing three or four feet of water. . . . . At 10½ midway between Kirjath-jearim and Kastue, are the fountain and ruins of El Dib, and a little further on to the left is Beit Nacouba. . . . . Still pursuing the track which, I doubt not, from the physical nature of the country, David pursued in bringing the ark from Kirjath-jearim to Jerusalem, we soon commence the descent of the worst hill on the road; and here it was, in all probability, that Uzza was smitten for "his error." And close at hand, no doubt, were also the sites of the threshing floor of Nachon, and the house of Obededom. The good Lord grant that we may profit by the events thus "written aforetime, 'concerning Perez—Uzza,' for our learning," and may we be kept from error of heart, head, and hand. . . . . At 11½ drank at the fount of Arsafear, and at 11¾ stop a few minutes at Kuloney (Colonia) to examine the stone bridge, large ruins, fine pools, and copious fountains there.

After ascending several large and steep hills, reach the table land; immediately to our left, but more than one hundred yards, is Ain Lifta—a bold fountain—the water of which, being collected in pools, is used for irrigating the fine gardens of the village below.

We arrived in Jerusalem safely at 1 o'clock—the Lord being merciful unto us. This was the Mohammedan Sabbath, and the gates, which are always closed from twelve to one on this day (Friday), were just being opened as we reached the city. But owing to a great fanatical demonstration, consequent upon the administration of the seal of the Abrahamic covenant to a young sprig of Turkish nobility, our way was completely blockaded, as it had been during the night preceding our departure, by an overwhelming torchlight marriage procession—and we were compelled to beat a retreat precipitately, and take shelter a length of time in a mill, before the uproarious crowd attending his gilded little Effendiship would allow us to proceed homewards.

CHAPTER XX.

MISSIONARY OPERATIONS.

To be "followers of the Apostles even as they followed Christ," is at once the duty, the honor, the interest, and the distinctive characteristic of all whose earnest object it is to restore primeval Christianity to the world. Hence the American Christian Missionary Society (under whose auspices the mission to Jerusalem is conducted), in entering upon the prosecution of the missionary enterprise, resolved—as wisely as unanimously—in imitation of apostolic example, to make the first offer of salvation to Israel, that noble race from whom it came—"for salvation is of the Jews."

"I am not sent," said the Messiah in addressing a Syro-Phœnician heathen, "but unto the lost sheep of the house of Israel."—"O Jerusalem! Jerusalem!" he exclaims, while gazing on the devoted city, "how often would I have gathered thy children together, as a hen doth gather her brood!" And the twelve Apostles he also instructed to "go—not into the way of the Gentiles—but rather to the lost sheep of the house of Israel," during his continuance upon earth. And when finally commissioning these missionaries, just before his ascension, to go into all the world and preach the gospel to every creature, he specially charges them to witness for him first in Judea, "beginning at Jerusalem." And that they thus manifested a decided preference for the Jews in announcing the word of life, is most evi dent from such of the acts of the Apostles as the Holy Spirit has recorded. The Apostle Paul declares also, in the tenth chapter of his letter to the Romans, "my heart's desire and prayer to God for Israel is, that they may be saved:" and in the ninth chapter he expresses his concern for them in still stronger terms—"I have great heaviness and continual sorrow in my heart, for I could wish that myself were accursed from Christ for my brethren, my kinsmen according to the flesh—who are Israelites—to whom pertain the adoption, and the glory, and the covenants, and the giving of the law, and the service of God, and the promises—whose are the Father's, and of whom, as concerning the flesh, Christ came, who is over all, God blessed for ever more." In the eleventh chapter, he assigns still more important reasons for preaching the word "to the Jews *first*"—declaring that they are not hopelessly cast away by an obdurate fate or irreversible decree of Heaven (as some affirmed even at that early day), but that they were only blinded *in part* UNTIL the fulness of the Gentiles should come in, and so *all* Israel should be saved: alleging that it is even easier to graft a Jew (who is of the native branch) upon the olive-tree of the kingdom, than the Gentile (who is wild by nature); and contending that if the casting away of them were the reconciling of the world, the recovery of them would be like recovering the world to life from the dead: for if the fall of them was indeed the riches of the world, and the diminishing of them the riches of the Gentiles, much more would their fulness be the riches of the world. No wonder, then, that we find him so pertinaciously adhering to this course (*the Divine rule*); not only in Judea, but in every part of the world wherever a son of Abraham was to be found—never turning to the Gentiles till the Jews judged themselves unworthy of everlasting life. Nor should gratitude on our part the less strongly concur with the honor and interests of Christianity to commend to us the same line of policy at this remote day—for upon the conversion and resumption of Israel is unquestionably suspended the destruction of Antichrist and the salvation of the world.

That the Hebrew race is the noblest that has ever adorned the annals of humanity, will not be questioned even by the proud Anglo-Saxons themselves: nor can it be doubted that if converted—speaking, as they do, all the languages of earth, habituated to all customs, and acclimated to every region—they would make the best missionaries on the face of the globe.

It is a fact as significant as it is singular, that notwithstanding the degradation, persecution, and robbery to which the Jews have for so many long ages been subjected by every nation on the earth (ourselves alone excepted), there is not a single department of life in which you may not find a son of Abraham preëminent. There is, perhaps, not a wealthier family amongst all the nations of the earth than the Rothschilds. Where is a more astute or enlightened politician than D'Israeli? Where a purer patriot and philanthropist than Sir Moses Montefiore? A brighter ornament to the church than Neander, or to literature than Messelshon? In music they boast of (A) Braham. Nor does the world at present possess a more gifted dramatist than Mad. Rachel. But time would fail, were an attempt made even to mention the names of the many gifted Hebrews that adorn humanity in every sphere of life.

Influenced by such considerations as these, the American Christian Missionary Society determined to plant its first mission in Jerusalem, mainly in reference to the Jews—not unmindful, however, that Jerusalem possesses various other claims upon our consideration as a field of missionary operations. The Holy City is essentially a *religious* city. No stronger emotions are experienced anywhere upon earth than at the "City of Solemnities," in some form or other—a consideration, certainly of no small moment in the selection of a field for missionary operations. Thither go up in pilgrimage, not only the tribes of Israel, and all the sects of Christianity (that of Protestantism only excepted), but the various factions of Islamism also. "Thus saith the Lord God," by the pen of Ezekiel. (v. 5, 6), and it is certainly as true now as it was then, "this is Jerusalem: I have set thee in the midst of the nations and countries that are round about her: and she hath changed my judgments into wickedness more than the nations, and my statutes more than the countries that are round about her, for they have refused my judgments, and my statutes they have not walked in them." Although it may savor somewhat of contradiction to assert that this same *religious* city (distinctively styled "*Holy*," even in the Bible itself, and which is yet destined preëminently to be "a city of truth" and holiness), is more remarkable for error and iniquity than any city on earth; yet, perhaps nothing is hazarded in asserting that it is at this time the favorite "camping ground" of the prince of the power of the air—"the father of lies and author of evil!" And in view of the fact that accountability is directly proportioned to available light, this awful and disgraceful state of matters constitutes a special claim upon the consideration of those who have the truth, and profess to know how to wield it as an antidote to all error and evil.

In no other city, perhaps, on earth, are there so many and such distinct races of men and grades of religion as are to be found in Jerusalem—the sensual, fair-skinned Turk—the swarthy, turbulent Arab—the barbarous, ebony-skinned African—the superstitious, circumventing Christian of every hue and dye, and the down-trodden, Banquo-like Israelite, the wanderer of every clime—a stranger everywhere—at home nowhere—not even on his own heaven-given soil!

From Jerusalem as a central point 75,000 of the Arab family can also be reached in every direction. Situated on the medimarinean isthmus, between the continents of Asia and Africa on the one hand, and the Mediterranean or Western Sea and the Indian or Eastern Ocean on the other, leading to the abode of Japhet in Europe, and the Isles of the Gentiles in all Oceanica:—it is thus accessible to all nations, tribes, kindreds, and tongues. Nor is there another spot on the face of the earth so well situated as Palestine for the erection of a mighty Pharos, for the diffusion of moral light amongst those that are sitting in the region and shadow of death. Hence the importance of creating an immense Bible Magazine in Jerusalem. Equally obvious too is the importance of the Holy City as the most suitable place on all the earth for a "school of the prophets"—a great mission establishment for preparing missionaries for the whitening fields of the East—that "the law may go forth of Zion, and the word of the Lord from Jerusalem." What a noble and inviting enterprise!

And what an inexhaustible fund of encouragement is found in the "sure word of prophecy—(*whereunto we do well to take heed*")—assuring us that whatever may betide other nations, the time is coming when every Jew upon earth shall be ransomed—"so *all* Israel shall be saved!" "This people have I formed for myself, saith Jehovah: they shall show forth my praise. Israel shall be saved in the Lord with an everlasting salvation, ye shall not be ashamed nor confounded, world without end: in the Lord shall all the seed of Israel be justified and shall glory; and I will place salvation in Zion for Israel my glory!"

And that the universal conversion of the Jewish nation shall occur prior to that of the Gentiles, is most manifest. Does not policy, then, concur with every other consideration in specially commending them to the first and best efforts of the Church? Nor let scepticism supinely start the inquiry, "*can* these dry bones live?" or venture to intimate that "the time is not come—the time that the Lord's house shall be built:—the year of recompenses for the controversy of Zion"—for "the time to favor Zion, yea, the *set* time is come; *for her people take pleasure in her stones, and favor the dust thereof!*"

The American Christian Mission was planted in Jerusalem about six years ago—the mission family having reached that city on the 8th day of February, 1851. After a sojourn of about three years and a half in the Holy City, it was deemed expedient to suspend operations for a time: but the causes that operated its suspension no longer existing, it will be immediately resumed—Providence permitting—and established upon a much more extended scale and permanent basis than formerly. The history of this mission having been given to the public in a volume published by the late Corresponding Secretary of the Society, D. S. Burnet, the mere summary of its operations, contained in the following extract from the last Annual Report of the Mission (February 9th, 1854), must here suffice :—

. . . . In entering upon the fourth year of our missionary effort at the Holy City, under circumstances of such distinguishing mercy, we cannot but call upon our souls and all that is within us, to praise and bless the name of the Lord, that we have been so long permitted to enjoy the privilege of witnessing for the truth of the Gospel, in a place invested with so much interest and importance. And although the sanguine expectations that some have indulged rather overweeningly, in relation to the success of "the ancient Gospel" amongst "God's ancient people," may not have been realized, yet surely, if the Bible estimate of the worth of a soul be not exaggeration, we have abundant reason to "thank God and take courage," that, during the three years' existence of the Mission, more than a score of poor, blinded Jews and benighted Gentiles have been brought (savingly, as we trust) to a knowledge and reception of the truth as it is in Jesus. Of these, eleven have been added during the past year, making in all twenty-eight.* Had it been my object merely to establish a congregation of immersed professors of the Protestant religion, this number might easily have been increased many fold; but designing, if possible, to have none on the list but such as should evince and maintain pure motives and principles, in the love of the truth, I have been constrained amidst the most perplexing doubts and difficulties to exercise such a prudential discrimination, as compelled me, in the fear of God, to reject many applicants, who appeared to be influenced by sinister motives. . . . . . Consular and ecclesiastical power, threats and entreaties, love and money, the grossest misrepresentations, and appeals at once the basest and most alluring, have all been perseveringly plied, in order to seduce some of our converts into some one or other of the various religious communities here—all of which, odious as most of them are, enjoy a higher degree of popularity than is accorded to the religion planted here by the meek and lowly "Just One" and his Galilean followers.

I am thus tediously minute upon this disagreeable topic, in order that you may be the better enabled to appreciate the difficulties of our position, and aid us by your counsels, prayers, and co-operation. But whilst your sympathies will be painfully excited by the recital of these discouragements, you will rejoice with me, I am sure, when you learn that I have never anywhere seen greater devotion to the Gospel than that manifested by some of those whom I have had the privilege of introducing into the kingdom.

Failing to get the font of Hebrew type of which we were in expectation, we have been unable to issue the few sheets we contemplated for the benefit of the Jews. But we have struck off a few small tracts for the benefit of Italian pilgrims and residents, directed against the machinations of the "Scarlet Lady," which, brief and imperfect as they are, have been decidedly productive of good; though "at the same time there arose no small stir about that way!"

* The number was subsequently increased to thirty-one.

The necessity of spending a large portion of the year beyond the reach of the unhealthy exhalations of the city, renders it impossible for us to accomplish much in the way of school-teaching. But this is matter of less regret, inasmuch as there are no children of our converts requiring instruction. We have, therefore, made no special effort for a regular school; and, indeed, have refused many applications in behalf of children already attending school —being content merely to instruct such adults as voluntarily apply for instruction—deeming it best, under existing circumstances, to leave mere literary instruction to the well sustained English and German institutions here.

Setting as high an estimate as ever upon the importance of pioneering the Gospel by "healing all manner of sickness, and all manner of disease among the people," I have to regret that neither the number of patients treated at the dispensary, nor those visited at their houses, has been as great as formerly, owing not only to our absence from the city the greater portion of the year, but to the recent establishment of other gratuitous curative institutions; the French having lately established a very fine hospital, the Prussians quite an extensive hospice, and the English another dispensary—all eleemosynary: so that whatever else they may need, there is now no lack of gratuitous relief to the indigent sick of Jerusalem. And for the accommodation of such Jews as are unwilling to receive relief as beneficiaries, two educated Jewish physicians have also settled here. Still we have a goodly number in attendance at our dispensary on three days of the week: and I cannot but regard the medical department of the Mission as highly important, and, under existing circumstances, almost indispensable—furnishing the most favorable access to all classes.

My eldest son has been greatly importuned to return to Bethlehem, where, until the violent measures of the Latin Patriarch, he had from fifty to a hundred patients daily: but the prospect of benefiting them spiritually, since their purchased reconciliation to the authorities of the Convent, is not sufficiently encouraging to justify such a measure. It is a lamentable fact, that of the hundreds that promised so fairly a year ago, there is only one who appears to be seriously interested at this time; and there is too much reason to suspect, from his long procrastination, that the loaves and fishes of the Convent stand greatly in the way of his obedience. Poor creatures! Forming a judgment from their zeal in observing the feasts, fasts, and ceremonies of their church, one might suppose them very religious; and so they are, truly, in their own way: but like the Samaritans of old, who "feared the Lord greatly, but served other gods," this mongrel cross of wild Arabs with eremite ascetics and knight-errant Crusaders "fear the Lord and serve their graven images—as did their fathers, so do they unto this day."

Although the possession of a place of temporary shelter for indigent and persecuted converts is so very desirable, yet I have not deemed it expedient to attempt the purchase of such a place during the troubled state of the country that has prevailed almost ever since our dispossession of Wady Farah. . . . .

Very little has been done in Bible distribution during the past year; and I have been pained to see importunate applicants for the Word of Life go away empty-handed! . . . .

You will be pleased to learn that the Mohammedans are much more accessible than they formerly were, and occasionally listen, not only with patience and forbearance, but with evident interest. . . . . We lately held a long and interesting discussion with the Chief Mufti (the spiritual head of the church); and although he manifested much warmth of feeling in defending his views and practices, he was much moved by the sublime morality of the

"Sermon on the Mount," which was read to him for the purpose of contrasting Christianity with Islamism: and I am certain, from subsequent circumstances, that he went away favorably impressed. This is something new under the sun! A Fellah of very good character, who, as well as his wife, is altogether disposed to embrace Christianity, is now here—though he has been absent for some time; and his case has caused me no little moral perplexity: but not being satisfied that, under existing circumstances, it is the part either of duty or propriety to urge immediate obedience, I am acting rather passively; for there is every reason to believe that his open profession at this critical juncture would not only cost him his property, but his life—the Toleration Firman to the contrary notwithstanding.

The kindness and consideration with which we are treated by Mohammedans of all grades, and especially by those of the highest circle, is matter of great astonishment, and augurs well for the future.

Deeming it important that you should be correctly informed of the ecclesiastical statistics of the field in which your Mission is established, I submit the following statement, which has been collected with much care from the most reliable sources, that you may be the better enabled to form a proper estimate of the fruit to be expected from the labor bestowed upon its culture. . . . .

The Jews are composed of two principal classes—the Sephardim and Askenazim. Of the Sephardim, the Spanish Jews number about nine thousand, and the Mugrabin only about fifty. Of the Askenazim class, the Perushim (or Pharisees) number about one thousand two hundred; the Khassydim (Pious), about eight hundred; the Khabaad (or Hebronites), one hundred; and the Kairaites (distinguished for discarding the Talmud), only forty. The remaining subdivision of the Askenazim—the German Jews—number about one hundred. About two hundred and forty-six Rabbis (so called) preside over these various classes of Jews, as lords temporal as well as spiritual; and a more grinding despotism is not, perhaps, exercised upon the whole face of the earth. About fourteen houses, dignified by the name of "Synagogues," are used for the purpose of worship, though only three or four are worthy of this appellation; and for special indoctrination in Talmudic philosophy, they have various other more retired places of study. The very partial literary instruction received by the children is imparted in the most disorderly and imperfect manner, either in private families or a public school--there being only one such for all the fraternity of Israel.

The annual foreign contribution by which the Jews are almost exclusively maintained, is exceedingly precarious, both in collection and disbursement. This fund is said to yield to a large number of the Jews only about ten paras (one cent) per day, after passing through the hands of the messengers and rabbis, the latter of whom especially, it is said greatly to enrich, *in transitu*, and afford the means of completely lording it over the conduct and consciences of their poor, abject, dependent lay brethren. Half a piastre (or rather more than two cents) would be a liberal average for the general daily allowance to each Jew! And how they can eke out the scantiest livelihood, with the little employment they can get, is one of the wonders of Jerusalem. Many of them, however, are vicarious residents, and this class are said to be quite well sustained by the special contributions of those whom they thus substitute—a kind of residence by proxy thought to be almost as meritorious as an actual abode in *propria persona*.

The Mohammedans of Jerusalem are all Turks, with the exception of a few proselytes from the Jews and Greeks, one or two hundred Arabs, and three or four hundred negroes from the west of Africa. . . . .

Missionary Report, &c.

Church and State affairs are so intimately blended, that it is difficult to say what special functionaries are peculiar to each; but it would seem that their ecclesiastical affairs, in this city, are under the jurisdiction of a Cadi Moolah, two or three Muftis, three or four Imaums or preachers proper, one Nakeeb, half a dozen Chief Dervishes, and about one hundred of subordinate character, one hundred Sheikhs, two dozen Muezzim, and a great number of still inferior officers and servants. . . . .

The following brief statement will convey a correct idea of the variety, numerical strength official staff, and resources of the different Christian sects now in Jerusalem:

THE GREEK CHURCH has 1 Patriarch, 1 Archimandrite, 6 Bishops, 150 Priests, 90 Nuns, 100 Boys in training for the priesthood, 1 Theological and 3 Common Schools, 12 Convents, with 12 Churches attached, 1 Dispensary, with Physician and assistants—Total Membership . . . 2250

THE LATINS.—1 Patriarch, 100 Priests, 10 Nuns, 2 Churches, 2 Convents, 2 Hospitals, with Male and Female Physicians, 1 Almshouse, 1 House of Hospitality, 1 Printing Establishment, 1 Theological Seminary, 2 Common Schools, Superiors, Vicars, Procurators, Reverendissimos, &c. Members (50 of whom are Franks) 1350

ARMENIANS.—1 Patriarch, 2 Bishops, 32 Priests, 10 Deacons, 51 Subdeacons, 25 Nuns, 1 Printing Establishment, 2 Schools, 3 Convents and Churches 464

COPTS.—3 Priests, 1 Convent and Church 100

ABYSSINIANS.—1 Bishop, 15 Priests, 1 Convent and Church 80

GREEK CATHOLICS.—1 Bishop, 2 Priests, 1 Candle Officer, 1 Church 20

SYRIAN JACOBITES.—1 Bishop, 2 Priests, 1 Nun, 1 Convent and Church—total 4

PROTESTANTS.—1 Bishop, 2 Priests, 5 Missionaries, &c.—Aggregate Membership 250

Total number of Christians 4518

In addition to the above enumerated places of worship, all these sects have also chapels in the "Church of the Holy Sepulchre," as also have the Nestorians, the Maronites, and other denominations whose shrines are only occasionally used. The Latins and Greeks have also several thousand members in their various convents near the city, principally Arabs.

Officers, Agents, Agencies, Statistics, &c., of the English Episcopal Society for Promoting Christianity amongst the Jews; the Mission of the "Prussian Evangelical Church;" and the Church Missionary Society; all co-operating in Jerusalem.

FIRST.—THE EPISCOPAL SOCIETY FOR JEWS, &c.

1 Lord Bishop (Sam'l Ang. Hierosol.), salary £1455

1 Chaplain, 300*l.*; Sexton, 40*l.*; Sundries for Church, 28*l.* 368

4 Missionaries, Assistants, Scripture Reader, &c., 702*l.*; Schools for Jewish Children, 178*l.*; salary and expense of Architect, 281*l.*; purchase, rent, and repairs of mission premises . . . 1391

1 Bible and Tract Depository, 80*l.* (amount distributed unknown) 80

Superintendent of House of Industry, 100*l.*; annual expense of sustaining the institution, inclusive of boarding, clothing, and three to eight piasters weekly pocket money to each inmate, 345*l.* 445

Industrial Institute for Females.—3 Teachers, 50 Jewesses (only partially reported) . . . 129

Hospital.—Salaries and allowance of Physician, Surgeon, Dispenser, &c., 421*l.*; rents and purchases of leases, 202*l.*; Wages of Dragoman and servants, 104*l.*; Housekeeping, furniture, and clothing, 431*l.*; Drugs and dispensary expenses, 70*l.* 1230

Secretary and Treasurer 250

Total £5328

Hebrew College, now transferred to London, 700*l.* per annum; Consulate, 600*l.* 1300

Auxiliary Mission Branches at Nablous, Nazareth, Jaffa, and Safet, 130*l.* each; House-rent at Hebron, 9*l.* 529

Annual Expenditure of the Special Funds.—Jewish Converts' Relief Fund, 140; Fund for Relief

Missionary Report, &c.

of Inquiring Jews (not reported); Fund for assisting to establish in business Inmates leaving the House of Industry (not reported); Fund for Widows and disabled Missionaries (not reported) . . . .

Outfit for a Missionary, 100*l.*; allowance for voyage to or from London, 40*l.* to each member of the family.

Property owned by the Mission.—Church and adjoining premises, with Consulate and other offices for Museum, Library, &c., 70,000*l.*; Cemetery, with School buildings and other houses attached, 450*l.*; Industrial buildings, 1000*l.*; Botanic Garden, Machinery, Printing Establishment, &c. ? 71,450

In Contemplation.—A Farming Establishment, Episcopal Palace, Female Seminary, &c., &c.

Property Rented.—Hospital and Dispensary Buildings, 150*l.*; Bishop's Residence, 75*l.*; four or five houses, at 35*l.* to 40*l.* per annum, 170*l.*; several others for Depositories, &c., 50*l.* . . 445

The Lyceum in connexion with the Anglican Consulate and Mission already contains the nucleus of a valuable Museum and Library; and, if conducted on less exclusive principles, might be productive of much good.

SECOND.—CHURCH MISSIONARY SOCIETY.

1 Missionary, Assistant, Dragoman, Schools, &c.—17 members; total expense £700

THIRD.—LUTHERAN EVANGELICAL DEPARTMENT.

1 Minister, 5 Deaconesses, 1 School, 25 German and 5 Arab Members, 600*l.*; 1 large Hospice, 100*l.* per annum £700

The Basle Missionary Society has also an establishment here, in which there are four or five lay missionaries, but its efforts are mainly of a secular character, and only as yet of indirect proselyting tendency.

In the English Diocesan boarding school, which is under the management of five teachers, assisted by a steward and stewardess, there are sixty-two boys and girls, three or four of whom are Jews. The "Jewish Intelligencer" asserts, that "the community (worshipping in the English Hebrew Church on Mount Zion) consists of some two hundred members: some are Arabs, and others members of the Mission; but there is also a goodly number of Hebrew Christian converts, and native Christians." The "Hebrew Christian converts" amount to fifty-two; of whom twenty-five are adults and twenty-seven children. The proselytes, from the native Arab Christians (under the care of the Church Missionary Society), number about seventeen; and the remainder consist of the missionaries, their families, auxiliaries, and English and German servants, &c., together with the Lutherans. The total number of Jewish converts, from the beginning to the present time, amounts to ninety-nine. "Sixty-seven adult Jews (says the last Annual Report of the London Jews' Society, page 85), and thirty-two children, are, or have been, members of the congregation on Mount Zion. This number, however, includes some that have been baptized elsewhere, but subsequently settled here, and others that have been imported from other parts of the world to be educated and baptized here: and also those that have relapsed again into Judaism—of whom there have been some sad cases. These ninety-nine Jewish converts (the only legitimate object of the Mission's effort) have been made at the cost of several thousand pounds per annum. The expenditure for Jerusalem during the past year was about forty thousand dollars—rating interest at only three per cent. on its property; by the London Society alone, independently of the Church Missionary and Lutheran Societies, the cost of the consulate established for its protection, and exclusive also of various heavy items unreported—some idea of which may be had by reference to page 122, of last annual report—bearing in mind at the same time, that beside Miss Cook's legacy of sixty thousand pounds (much of which is devoted to this favorite mission), the regular annual contributions to this mammoth London Society range from twenty to thirty thousand pounds.

Missionary Report.

Chronological Chart of the Operations of the London Jews' Society.

YEAR ending Mar. 31.	PROMINENT FEATURES IN THE HISTORY OF THE SOCIETY.	MISSION COMMENCED.	JERUSALEM MISSION.	COMMENCEMENT OF COTEMPORANEOUS LABOR IN THE CAUSE OF ISRAEL.
1728	. . . .	. . . . . .	. . . .	Callenberg Institution at Halle (closed 1792)
1738	. . . .	. . . . . .	. . . .	Missionaries of the Church of the United Brethren (until 1764)
1809	The London Society founded			
1810	The "Jews' Chapel," Spitalfields, opened for Lectures to the Jews A Printing-office established for Converts			
1811	Ann. Sermon preached by Rev. C. Simeon			
1813	April 7.—First stone laid of the Episcopal Jews' Chapel and Hebrew Schools, Palestine Place, by H. R. H. the Duke of Kent			
1814	July 16.—Episcopal Jews' Chapel opened			
1815	March 14.—The Society becomes a Church of England Society Sir Thos. Baring, Bt., becomes President Rev. Lewis Way's donation of £10,000 First issue of a Hebrew translation of the New Testament			
1816	Bps. Ryder and Burgess become Patrons	. . . . . .	. . . .	American Society for Evangelizing the Jews (afterwards "for Ameliorating the condition of the Jews")
1817	Journey of the Rev. L. Way to prepare the way for Missions abroad			
1819	First Missionary sent abroad Temporal Relief discontinued as an object of the Society "Jews' Chapel," Spitalfields, disposed of Hebr. Boys' School, Palestine Place, opened	. . . . . .	. . . .	Edinburgh Society for promoting Christianity among the Jews The American Board of Missions send Missionaries to the Jews in Palestine
1820	. . . .	Holland Frankfurt-on-the Maine	First Mission of Inquiry to Palestine	Society of Friends of Israel at Basle Ditto, Frankfurt-on-the-Maine Ditto, Brussels
1821	Hebrew Girls' School and Seminary opened	Poland	Messrs. Fisk and Parsons visit Jerusalem on behalf of the American Board of Commissioners for Foreign Missions	
1822	. . . .	. . . . . .	. . . .	Berlin Society Elberfeld ditto
1823	. . . .	. . . . . .	Visit of the Rev. Lewis Way	Dresden ditto
1824	. . . .	Jerusalem	Dr. Dalton sent out to Jerusalem as Medical Missionary	
1825	. . . .	Posen Rhine District	Rev. J. Nicolayson arrives, Dec. 31	
1826	First complete edition of the Hebr. Bible published	Strasburg and France	Dr. Dalton dies, Jan. 26	
1827	. . . .	Konigsberg Danzig	Political events compel Mr. Nicolayson to leave	
1829	. . . .	Smyrna North Africa		
1831	. . . .	London	. . . .	Toulouse Society
1832	Seminary discontinued Conferences with Jews in Aldermanbury	Berlin		
1833	. . . .	Cracow	Rev. J. Nicolayson returns	
1834	. . . .	. . . .	. . . .	Neuchatel Society
1835	. . . .	Constantinople	Appeals issued for a Hebrew Church	Strasburg ditto
1836	Hebrew Translation of the Liturgy published Death of Bps. Burgess and Ryder; and of the Rev. C. Simeon			
1837	The Bishop of Ripon becomes Patron The "Old Paths" published Divine Service in the Hebrew language commenced in the Episcopal Jews' Chapel, on February 5			

Missionary Report.

Chronological Chart—continued.

YEAR ending Mar. 31.	PROMINENT FEATURES IN THE HISTORY OF THE SOCIETY.	MISSION COMMENCED.	JERUSALEM MISSION.	COMMENCEMENT OF COTEMPORANEOUS LABOR IN THE CAUSE OF ISRAEL.
1838	Revised edition of the Hebrew New Testament published	. . . . . .	Purchase of Mission premises effected, and first Medical Missionary sent out	
1839	. . . .	. . . . . .	. . . .	The General Assembly of the Church of Scotland send a Deputation to inquire into the state of the Jews; and establish Missions in consequence
1840	Hebrew College established Death of the Rev. L. Way	. . . . . .	First Stone laid of Christ Church	
1841	Archbishop of Canterbury becomes sole Patron Jerusalem Bishopric established Nov. 7.—Consecration of Bishop Alexander	. . . . . .	. . . .	Bremerlehe Society
1842	. . . .	. . . . . .	Jan. 21.—Arrival of the first Protest'nt Bishop	British Society for the Propagation of the Gospel among the Jews
1843	. . . .	Safet Beyrout Sweden	College established (closed 1847)	Free Church of Scotland Missions Presbyterian Church of Ireland ditto Rhenish Westphalian Society
1844	Special Temporal Relief Fund established	Bagdad	Hospital opened Dec. 12	Netherlands Society (Amsterdam) [Church of England Young Men's Society] Society at Frankfort-on-the-Oder, for Proselytes
1845	. . . .	. . . . . .	Death of Bp. Alexander, Nov. 23	The Glasgow Christian Society on behalf of the Jews (afterwards "Scottish Society for the Conversion of Israel")
1846	. . . .	Bucharest	Arrival of Bish'p Gobat, Dec. 23	Stavanger (Norway) Society
1847	. . . .	Salonica	Turkish subjects declared free to change their religion	
1848	Death of Sir Thomas Baring, Bart. Lord Ashley (Earl of Shaftesbury) becomes President	. . . . . .	House of Industry opened, Dec. 21	
1849	. . . .	. . . . . .	Consecration of Christ Church, Jan. 21	
1850	. . . .	Breslau		
1851	Death of Miss Jane Cook, whose donations to the Society (including her last bequest) amounted to £60,000.	Jassy Adrianople	First Annual Conference of the Palestine Mission, Dec. 1851	Mission of Am. Chn. Missionary Society established at Jerusalem

The accompanying synoptical view of missionary effort in behalf of the Jews in general, and of those at Jerusalem in particular, will sufficiently evince the interest now felt on this subject by various Christian communities. It is extracted from the "Report" of the "London Jews' Society."

How handsomely the Jerusalem station of this colossal missionary corporation is endowed with available funds, as well as with other ways and means, will also abundantly appear from the appended statement, taken also from the report above.

By	Fund towards Stipend of Minister of Christ Ch., Jerusalem, Stock £8500	£8289	6	3
"	Fund towards repairs of Church at Jerusalem, Stock £1000	975	4	5
"	Fund for Circulation of Scriptures in Palestine, Stock £2000	1950	8	11

Missionary Report.

	£	s.	d.
By Fund for House of Industry at Jerusalem, Stock £2 000	£9752	4	4
" Fund for assisting to establish in business Inmates leaving the House of Industry at Jerusalem, Stock £200	195	1	1
" Fund towards salary of the Apothecary to the Hospital, Jerusalem, Stock £2000	1950	8	11
" Fund for the relief of Inquiring Jews, or Infirm or Aged Converts at Jerusalem, Stock £4000	3900	17	9
" Fund for Widows and disabled Missionaries, Stock £15000	14628	5	11
" General Fund, as per account	5904	4	2
" Fund for Relief of Jewish Converts, at Jerusalem	169	10	0
" Fund for Relief of Inquiring Jews, &c., do.	300	0	0
" Fund for assisting to establish in business Inmates leaving the House of Industry at Jerusalem	9	0	0
" Reserve Fund	100	0	0
" Suspense account for sundry drafts of Committee charged to account of 1851–52, but not paid	3411	16	5
" Bills payable under acceptance	1711	19	5

In real estate possessions it is still more richly beneficed. Its splendid church edifice, the Anglican Cathedral—called at first "Church of St. James," but now known as "Christ Church," is said to have cost—inclusive of the Consular Residence attached—several hundred thousand dollars, though only containing sittings for two hundred persons. It must be remembered, however, that it was built in "troublous times," and under most disadvantageous circumstances.

The general principles upon which the Mission was designed to be conducted, will sufficiently appear from the following manifesto of the Archbishop of Canterbury to his brethren—"their Holinesses" of the Oriental *Apostolic Churches!*

To the Most Reverend our Brothers in Christ, the Prelates and Bishops of the Ancient and Apostolic Churches in Syria and the Countries Adjacent, Greeting in the Lord.

We William by Divine Providence Archbishop of Canterbury, Primate of all England and Metropolitan, most earnestly commend to your brotherly love the Right Reverend Michael Soloman Alexander, whom we, being well assured of his learning and piety, have consecrated to the office of a Bishop of the United Church of England and Ireland according to the ordinances of our Holy and Apostolic Church, and having obtained the consent of our Sovereign Lady the Queen, have sent out to Jerusalem with Authority to exercise spiritual jurisdiction over the Clergy and Congregations of our Church, which are now, or which hereafter may be, established in the countries above mentioned. And in order to prevent any misunderstanding in regard to this our purpose, we think it right to make known to you that we have charged the said Bishop our Brother, not to intermeddle in any way with the jurisdiction of the Prelates or other ecclesiastical dignitaries bearing rule in the Churches of the East, but to show them due reverence and honor, and to be ready on all occasions, and by all the means in his power, to promote a mutual interchange of respect, courtesy, and kindness. We have good reason to believe that our Brother is willing, and will feel himself in conscience bound, to follow these our instructions; and we beseech you in the name of our Lord Jesus Christ to receive him as a Brother, and to assist him, as opportunity may offer, with your good offices.

We trust that Your Holinesses will accept this communication as a testimony of our respect and affection, and of our hearty desire to secure that amicable intercourse with the ancient Churches of the East, which has been suspended for ages, and which, if restored, may have the effect, with the blessing of God, of putting an end to the divisions which have brought the most grievous calamities on the Church of Christ.

In this hope and with sentiments of the highest respect for your Holinesses, we have affixed our Archiepiscopal seal to this letter, written with our own hand at our palace of Lambeth, on the twenty-third day of November, in the year of our Lord one thousand eight hundred and forty-one.

W. CANTUAR. [L. S.]

Signed and sealed in the presence of
CHRIS: HODGSON,
Secretary to the Archbishop.

The Lutheran Church sought an alliance with the English in conducting missionary operations in Jerusalem, at an early period of its history; and still maintains a cold and formal co-operation—in a kind of politico-ecclesiastical relationship. This singular copartnery was secured through the zealous efforts of the great Chevalier Bunsen, special envoy of the king of Prussia to the court of St. James; who was instructed by his majesty to ascertain "In how far the English National Church, already in possession of a parsonage on the Mount Zion, and having commenced there the building of a church, would be inclined to accord to the Evangelical National Church of Prussia a sisterly position in the Holy Land." His royal overtures of "aid and comfort" were received—as may readily be supposed—as graciously as offered. Amongst many other marks of the special favor by which Frederic William manifested his interest in behalf of the Mission, was the donation of $75,000 in aid of the Jerusalem bishopric. And all the consideration for which he stipulated in return for his munificent contributions, was the occasional use of the

38

Cathedral when not occupied by the English; together with the right to alternate with Queen Victoria in the appointment of the incumbent of the See; who, by-the-bye, must always be an Englishman, by hook or by crook, before he can wear the mitre of Zion, and claim spiritual jurisdiction over Palestine, Syria, Chaldea, Egypt, and Abyssinia—his diocesan province!

The branch of the Church Missionary Society at Jerusalem, it is understood, is designed to supply a very serious deficiency in the *modus operandi* of the London Jews' Society—its efforts being directed exclusively to the Gentile population of the city; and is entirely under the control of the Anglican Bishop.

The Presbyterian Mission, faithfully conducted for some years at Jerusalem under the auspices of the American Board of Commissioners for Foreign Missions, by an able band of devoted missionaries, was discontinued in 1844, and transferred to Beirût.

The Sabbatarian Baptists have also made some proselyting efforts at the Holy City; but with what success is not known.

The present condition of the Jews of Jerusalem is precisely what it is represented to have been by Hanani, when Nehemiah attempted its restoration—"The remnant that are left of the captivity, there in the province, are in great affliction and reproach;" and their case is well calculated to produce upon us the same effect it did upon the pious old Reformer, when he "sat down and mourned and wept certain days, and fasted and prayed before the God of heaven." But alas! how few there are that "sigh and cry for all the abominations that be done in the midst thereof! Who shall have pity upon thee, O Jerusalem? Or who shall bemoan thee; or who shall go aside to ask how doest thou?"

The Jews of Palestine are all under the spiritual domination of a Chief Rabbi, called *Chackam Bashi*, "the first in Zion," who is assisted by a special council of seven leading Rabbis, and a large number of Sub-Rabbis. They exercise also a domineering temporal authority; and a more despotic government, in certain respects, scarcely exists this side the regions of Dahomey.

It is no wonder that these down-trodden outcasts of Israel are poor, illiterate, and bigoted, for they are almost entirely disfranchised and constantly maltreated, not only by their Turkish masters, but by those styling themselves Christians and philanthropists. Even in this year of grace 1857, it would cost any Jew in Jerusalem his life to venture into the so-called Church of the Holy Sepulchre, or within even the Outer Court of his beloved Temple. They are principally maintained here by the contributions of their brethren abroad—and whether lazy or not (as charged upon them), are certainly very idle. But even though the Jews were ever so industrious, and could obtain constant employment, they could barely procure a livelihood—so many are the sacred rabbinical days, upon which they are compelled to abstain from labor; and in this matter both Mussulmans and Christians seem to emulate them. The gate or door of every Jew, whatever else he may lack, is always supplied with the phylactery, enclosed in a tin case, as an amulet and antidote to all ill. Poor Israel is truly in an evil case; but distressing as their physical condition is, their spiritual and mental state is far worse. It were enough to swell the bosom of a brazen statue with indignation, and draw the tear of pity from the eye of the cold marble, to witness the grinding oppression under which they groan, body, soul, and spirit.

The portion of the Temple wall approached by a narrow lane through the Mogrebin Quarter, is esteemed the most sacred of all places to which they have access, on account of its vicinity to the site of the Holy of Holies, and there they repair every Friday—indeed in greater or less numbers every day—and weep and pray for the advent of the Messiah. And yet, to get so drunk at the feast of Purim, as to be unable to distinguish between "blessing Mordecai and cursing Haman," is an injunction of the Talmud which, though so much "more honored in the breach than the observance thereof," is very generally observed by men, women, and children! While their services at the Wailing Place are affecting, even unto tears, and are evidently from the heart, those of the Synagogue are mere empty, formal lip-service. Poor Judah! not only the sceptre, but the Urim and Thummim have long since departed from thee, and Ichabod is everywhere emblazoned on thy once fair escutcheon!

With the exception of some of the Mosks around the Haram es-Sherif, the Moslem houses of worship are very plain, unless of Christian origin, and even then the painting and sculpture are generally concealed by plaster or whitewash. But whatever else they may lack, they are always supplied with abundance of matting, a large movable kind of platform, for the reading of prayers, and the indispensable Kebla, or niche in the south wall, as a spiritual magnet to pioneer the orisons of the *Faithful* to the Paradisaical Mecca. As Mussulmans never pray "except they wash," a supply of water is indispensably requisite, and a praying-place of some sort is an almost universal accompaniment of every fountain and pool—There is no Mosk without its minaret from whose lofty spire the humdrum, drawling Muezzim five times a day calls the faithful devotees of Islamism to prayer.

Allah hoo achkbar—Allah hoo achkbah,
OO Ishad la illa il Allah, oo ishad la illa il Allah
OO inno Mohomed el-Resûl Allah.
God is greater—God is greater;
And bear testimony to one God—and bear testimony to one God;
And testify that Mohammed is the Prophet of God.

Five times a day is this summons repeated—at mid-day, in the afternoon, at sunset, after dark, and, with this addition, at daybreak—

Es Salat ophdel min en-nôm
Es Sullah koom wa Khedden es-Salat.
Prayer is better than sleep—rise up and offer prayers.

In common with all religionists of the East, the Mohammedans observe a great number of feasts, fasts, and other *solemn* rites During the month of Rhamadan they fast so rigidly that no good

Mussulman suffers any food or drink to enter his mouth from daybreak till after sunset, during each day of the whole moon. And yet it is notoriously and emphatically a month of feasting and revelry—sleeping all day and frolicking all night! But, not satisfied with this, at the end of the sacred month they observe a special feast of three days, called "Beiram," in which each tries to excel the other in gluttony. Sickness, as may well be imagined, is more rife at this time than during any other period of the year, whether Rhamadan occur in summer or in winter. Amongst many other foolish acts of fanatical superstition performed on such occasions, scores of the most pious and zealous Moslems prostrate themselves in the street, *supine*, for the purpose of being ridden over by some dignitary of the "Faithful"—and unfortunate indeed is he on whom the horse treads not. No one, they affirm, has ever been known to die, or even suffer any serious inconvenience, from submitting to this Juggernautic ceremony. The church and state are so intimately combined that it is quite difficult to distinguish the Mohammedan ecclesiastic from the civil and military officer; but it would appear that the Sheikhs or Imaums, and Dervishes comprise the two main orders of the clergy.

So much do good Mussulmans dread anything unclean, that they are as much afraid of coming in contact with a dog as with a "Muscoob" (Russian)! They are so conscientiously scrupulous, that they never drop the least crumb of bread without asking God to forgive them. And the application of a crumb of bread to the erasure of pencil-marks from paper, they regard with a kind of holy horror. On gaping or sneezing, they invariably thank the Lord that Shatan (Satan) didn't jump down their throats! To kill a chicken without devoutly exclaiming "Allah acbar" (God is great)! were an iniquity to be punished by the judges. And the same pious ejaculation escapes upon the occurrence of the most trivial circumstance. Indeed, they rarely ever leave the room without thus "taking the name of the Lord in vain." The same may be said of the Jews, with slight variation. Of all the exhibitions of wild religious fanaticism that I have ever witnessed, the services set forth occasionally at night on the minarets by the dervishes, are the most extravagant. One is forcibly reminded of the Tishbite's in-season-and-out-of-season, timous and ill-timed jestings with Jezebel's ecumenical council of her state church—so vociferous and frantic do they appear—and can scarce refrain from inquiring, if Mohammed is "asleep or gone a hunting!" To curse a Jew or Christian seems to be regarded rather as an act of devotion than as a sin, or even impropriety. And the vindictiveness and comprehensiveness of their maledictions—extending, as they do, not only to all the members of your person, but to your progenitors and descendants—however astonishing, is easily understood when it is remembered that this pious kind of malediction is systematically taught the children from early infancy by every *religious* family!

The most revolting of the abominations and iniquities enumerated in the 1st chapter of Romans, are committed unblushingly; and, with the exception of murder, almost with impunity.

"Judgment is turned away backward, and justice standeth afar off; for truth is fallen in the streets, and equity cannot enter. Yea, truth faileth; and he that departeth from evil maketh himself a prey." * * * "Run ye to and fro through the streets of Jerusalem, and see now and know, and seek in the broad places thereof, if ye can find a man, if there be any that executeth judgment, that seeketh the truth, and I will pardon it." * * * "Woe unto thee, O Jerusalem! Wilt thou not be made clean? When shall it once be!"

This being a true picture of the present moral condition of Jerusalem, it is not very surprising—however much to be deplored—that the result of Protestant missionary effort has not been more cheering. But Moslem opposition, it is confidently believed, is now at an end—indeed, the impression is almost universal among themselves that the days of Islamism are numbered—at least for the present. Some there are, however, and they are much to be dreaded for their ungovernable fanaticism, that still seem to think "the Faithful"

W. H. Bartlett. A. L. Dick

are invincible. But when we remember the imbecile state of the Ottoman Empire, we can but be reminded of the declaration of the Latins—"*Quem Deus vult perdere prius dementat.*" Mussulman views of destiny can but prove as certainly paralyzing under the waning moon, as they were irresistibly stimulating under its crescent phases. It is now far too late in the day for Moslem prestige to avail, as in days of yore!

Jerusalem was under the Pashalic of Damascus until quite recently, when all at once Palestine was promoted to the dignity of a separate Pashalic. The Pasha of Jerusalem (or *Basha** as he is universally called in Syria) is sent directly from Constantinople, and is permitted to remain in office until—at the usual rate of extortion—he is supposed to have had opportunity of sufficiently indemnifying himself for his outlay in farming it of the Sultan. And this he soon accomplishes.

The Basha is assisted in the administration of justice by the Divan Effendi, Cadi, &c. The Mejlis or Congress of the Holy City can scarcely be called a legislative body, though its functions are altogether of that character as far as they go. One delegate is now permitted to represent the interests of Christianity! and the Jews are assigned another!! But it would appear that the Arab population are entirely unrepresented except so far as they can operate through buckshishes—which, however, are omnipotent, should they have enough of the *wherewithal.*

Justice, if to be had at all, is administered in a very primitive and summary manner; and the government is excessively despotic.

The military establishment is under the control of the Kaim Makam or Beem Basha, the military governor—an object of no little dread at all times; but particularly during periods of conscription. The most heart-rending scene I ever witnessed was the parting of these poor conscripts from their parents, wives, and

* We borrow our orthography of the word from the Persians: for in Syria this functionary is never called *Pasha*—there being no such letter as P in the Arabic alphabet.

children—to be sent they know not where—and to return they know not *when*—if ever. Revolting as is the thought of parental affection maiming its own offspring, it is yet not much to be wondered at that the mother so often puts out the eye of her own darling son, or chops off a finger from his right hand, in order to exempt him from the horrors of the conscription! This humane policy is not, however, as prevalent as it was before the Viceroy of Egypt discovered that a soldier minus his right eye and index finger, can still be made available in destroying his fellow-creatures!

Although there have been for many years various vice-consular agencies in Jerusalem, conducted mainly by natives, yet it was not until 1843 that Jerusalem had so far recovered from her insignificance in the eyes of the nations, that regular Consulates were established and supported. In that year France, Prussia, and Sardinia deputed regular salaried Consuls to take up their permanent abode in the Holy City.

The Austrian Consulate was established five or six years afterwards. Great Britain had then only a Vice-Consul; but has ever since that time been fully represented by a well-sustained Consulate.

The Spanish Consul was appointed in 1853. But the United States of America was not represented by any regular Consul until 1856—consular functions having been regularly and nobly discharged by the excellent Murad family for more than thirty years—whose faithful services—be it confessed with shame—have never yet received any remuneration whatever from government.

The Consuls at Jerusalem are not only much respected, but greatly feared; and, indeed, may be said to exercise an all-controlling influence, when they can be brought to co-operate; but, owing probably to the peculiarity of their situation, they are too often in a state of hostility to each other, for any union of action whatever.

As far as his own subjects are concerned, a Consul is, virtually, "King in Jeshurun," and plays the despot with perfect impunity;

hence the importance of exercising great care and circumspection in consular appointments. It is by no means an uncommon occurrence for a Consul to deprive a subject of his passport (which, in that country, is not only to disfranchise him, but to expose him to every species of insult and injury, without the possibility of redress), simply because he has changed his religion.

I have seen a Protestant Consul hand over a respectable subject to the tender mercies of his janissaries for imprisonment, simply because he had agreed to assist in teaching a Protestant school. And to arrest a subject and send him out of the country for the most trivial offence, is a high-handed measure, not unfrequently adopted. But that such abuse of consular power will be effectually rebuked when made known to the various powers thus misrepresented, there cannot be a shadow of doubt.

But as far as *Moslem rule* is concerned in its exercise toward Christians, Jerusalem is no longer trodden down of the Gentiles. Nor can the least doubt be entertained as to the early enfranchisement and complete enlargement of the Jews. A better day has already dawned upon Zion.

Dr. Durbin, in speaking of the English Mission and Consulate at Jerusalem, makes the following very just remarks:—

"But the prospective *political* bearing of this Hebrew diocese is perhaps a matter of much greater interest than its immediate religious results. It is doubtless intimately connected with the restoration of the Jewish commonwealth in Palestine, chiefly under the auspices of England and Prussia. It is not to be affirmed that these governments instituted this measure with the sole, or even chief intent to accomplish this great prophetic event; yet without doubt they looked to the state of the Jewish and Christian mind, which these prophecies have produced with regard to the restoration, as a material, perhaps an essential element in their success. That the measure is considered by the five great powers as having an important political bearing, is evident from the fact that, since the organization of the diocese, France, Russia, and Austria have sent their consuls to Jerusalem, where there is neither trade nor commerce to be encouraged or protected. At this hour, the consular representatives of the five great guardians of Europe and the East are established in the Holy City, without any employment or object apparent to the public.

"The man may now be living who will see Jerusalem divide with Constantinople the discussions of the representatives of the nations for the settlement of the *Eastern Question*.

Its solution involves the fall of Turkey, the extinction of Mohammedanism, the restoration of the Jewish commonwealth, and the triumph of Christianity.

"In farther support of the opinion that the Hebrew diocese of St. James, at Jerusalem, has a deep hidden political bearing, I will assume the generally conceded fact, that the Turkish Empire is approaching its fall. It lies between Europe and the vast population and wealth beyond the Euphrates. The possession of its territories by any of the five great powers will destroy the political balance in Europe, and draw after it the control of India, China—indeed the whole Eastern world. The momentous question is, when the decayed fabric of the Moslem Empire shall fall to pieces, who shall possess its various parts? They must be occupied by new Christian states, or divided and appropriated by the five great powers. Their disposition is *the* great Eastern Question—perhaps the greatest political question of modern times—and its solution will quickly devolve on the Christian powers. For this they are preparing. They have long been gathered together at Constantinople, and have recently assembled at Jerusalem, as eagles gather where the carcass is. Each is augmenting its interest on the soil where the great question is to be solved. Austria, by means of the proximity of her territory, has influence in European Turkey, and access to its provinces. Russia has obtained a similar and even greater influence by like causes, and by her connexion with the large, influential, and wealthy population of the Greek Church, which is under her protection and in her interest throughout the empire. In *Syria alone* this population amounts to 350,000. France bears the same relation to the Roman Catholic population throughout the empire, which, with the Maronites of Mount Lebanon, amounts, in *Syria alone*, to 260,000. To these two communions add the thousands of Armenian Christians found in the principal towns, and it will appear that *one-third of the population in Syria is Christian*, and this, too, by far the most intelligent, wealthy, and active, and is increasing yearly. Prussia is too far distant, and being Protestant, has no interest on the soil in Syria; she therefore combines with England, whose influence lies in the weight of her name, and in the presence of her navy in the Levant. She has no population on the soil in her interest. The object of England and Prussia combined is to create such a population in their interest as a counterbalance to the great and growing Christian populations in the interests of Russia and France. England wants this population in Syria, which comprehends Palestine, because the possession or control of Syria will give her great commercial advantages and uninterrupted access to Persia, India, and the East. Considering the numbers and wealth of the despised Jews; the prophetic assurances of their return; their universal disposition to return at almost any hazard or sacrifice; and the influence of these facts on the common Christian mind, it was as natural as it was wise and good in England to seek to avail herself of all these influences to assemble a population in Palestine in her own interest, and take the great event so intimately connected with the regeneration of the world, under her immediate patronage and protection. When the time has come for the swoop of the eagles on the carcass, the predominant effect of a large Jewish population in Palestine in the interest of England will not be problematical with respect to the destination of Syria. The Jewish commonwealth will appear again under the protection of England, for which advantage compensation may be given to Austria in Bosnia and Servia, to Russia in Moldavia and Wallachia, perhaps at Constantinople, and to France in Egypt, to consolidate her African possessions."

Extract from Dr. Tyng.

The Rev. Dr. Tyng thus concludes one of his late letters from the Holy City :—

"The past of Jerusalem is overflowing with thought. But the future is equally impressive. These ruins are not always to remain. The future Temple, and the restored Israel, when 'Jerusalem shall be the throne of the Lord to all nations,' claim the most earnest thought. The day when 'the feet' of the Lord 'shall stand on the Mount of Olives, which is over against Jerusalem towards the east,' is full of importance; and whether we look back or forward, we have to speak of Zion as 'the joy of the whole earth,' for 'salvation is of the Jews.' The present missionary work in Jerusalem is deeply interesting. Now, what an accumulation of thought do all these facts and scenes prepare! I shall not attempt to enter into every particular scene; you must imagine for yourself. But surely there is no spot on earth like Jerusalem."

VALLEY OF JEHOSHAPHAT.

CHAPTER XXI.

JERUSALEM—AS IT IS TO BE.

"Glorious things are spoken of thee, O City of God!"

MILLENNIAL JERUSALEM.

Mene, mene, tekel upharsin, was the terrific verdict denounced alike against the empire of the Chaldees, its haughty monarch, and its mighty capital, "the beauty of the Chaldees' excellency;" and upon many a splendid city of antiquity has "Ichabod" been written: but of *Jerusalem*, Jehovah says, "I have graven thee upon the palms of my hands: thy walls are continually before me: I will make thee an eternal excellency." We accordingly find that however often doomed to utter destruction by her merciless spoilers and subverters, phœnix-like, she has always risen from her ashes in due time. For the same Almighty Being that not only suffered these chastisements to be inflicted upon the Holy City, but declares in judgment for her sins—"I will make Jerusalem heaps and a den of dragons—Zion shall be ploughed like a field, and Jerusalem shall become heaps, and the mountain of the House like the high places of the forest," also declares in fulfilment of his inscrutable decrees, "because they call thee an outcast—saying, This is Zion, whom no man seeketh after, behold, I will bring again the captivity of

Jacob's tents, and have mercy on his dwelling-places, and the city shall be builded upon her own heap, and the palace shall remain after the manner thereof"—"it shall not be plucked up nor thrown down *for ever.*"

It is strongly intimated in this comprehensive promise, that the city would not only be fully restored, but be built up according to her ancient land-marks. And that such a reëdification was literally accomplished under those great reformers and restorers, Ezra, Zerubbabel, and Nehemiah, we have abundant evidence in the memoirs of the admirable Tirshatha, and the zealous Scribe. But the same Divine Being who so graciously promised its restoration, is pledged also for its enlargement beyond its ancient boundaries. And to any one at all acquainted with the history of Jerusalem and the topography of the city and its environs, the truth of this declaration will abundantly appear from the following explanatory paraphrase of the prophetic text recorded Jer. xxxi. 38–40:—

38. Behold, the days come, saith the Lord, that the city shall be builded to the Lord from the Tower of Hannaneel to the gate of the corner.	38. Behold, the days come, saith the Lord, *after the expiration of the seventy years' captivity,* that the city shall be built to the Lord, *not only on its most impregnable foundations (in the southern quarter), but also the less defensible wall on the north*—from the Tower of Hannaneel even to the gate of the corner—*that portion of it most completely in ruins—from the most eastern point even to the westernmost—whence southward the fortifications are strong—so as to occupy all the site heretofore enclosed.*
39. And the measuring line shall yet go forth over against it, upon the Hill Gareb, and shall compass about to Goath.	39. *And not only so, but* the measuring line shall go forth yet *further* over against it (*the former northern boundary*), upon the Hill Gareb, and shall compass about *on that ridge and the rising ground that separates the Kedron Valley from the land around the north-east part of the city, commencing at the north-west corner of Zion and encircling a large district, even around to Goath, or Golgotha (a place of a skull)—that head of land that juts out into the Valley of Kedron, near Gethsemane, like a cape into the sea.*
40. And the whole valley of the dead bodies and of the ashes, and all the fields unto the Brook of Kedron, unto the corner of the Horse Gate, to-	40. *And this extended wall shall embrace in its north-east portion* the whole valley of ashes and dead bodies, as well as on the included portions of the sepulchral declivities o' Kedron; and all the fields or vineyards even unto the corner of the Horse Gate toward the east, shall be holy unto the

ward the east, shall be holy unto the Lord; it shall not be plucked up nor thrown down any more for ever.	Lord; and it (the city—at least under its original dimensions) shall not be plucked up nor thrown down any more for ever, during the present age (though it may be repaired and beautified), but shall remain throughout the whole millennial age, in one position or another.

And to this permanence and prosperity of the Holy City throughout the Millennium, Zechariah also abundantly testifies in the last chapter of his prophecy—10th verse. "And it shall be lifted up and inhabited in her place, from Benjamin's Gate unto the place of the First Gate, unto the Corner Gate; and from the Tower of Hannaneel unto the King's Wine Press." The land-marks here indicated seem expressly designed to mark out the ancient capital of the Jewish kings, and purposely to exclude much of Cœnopolis—the large addition made by the apostate Jews under Agrippa:—and not without special reason, for Jerusalem is yet to be surrounded by another enclosure, whose prescribed limits, of course, the city bounds must not transcend—a fact most significantly indicative of long-premeditated design and superintending providence. This wall of the sanctuary—seen in vision by Ezekiel—is a square of five hundred reeds, or rather more than a mile on each side, around which extends a narrow suburban strip thirty yards in width. If the southern boundary of this square be located so as to coincide with the southern limits of the ancient city, and the western line adapted to the western limits as closely as it can well be, there will be a considerable vacant surplus on the east and north of the city; and the Temple area will fall about the centre of the enclosure—in accordance with the intimation conveyed by the prophet in his description of the Holy City and vicinity. (Ezek. 45th chapter.) This extension of the bounds of the city will render its area rather greater than any phasis under which it has heretofore existed: and with this enlargement on the north and east, still more completely will "the whole valley of the dead bodies and of the ashes, and all the fields unto the Brook Kedron, unto the corner of the Horse Gate toward the east, be holy unto the Lord."

Whilst the Temple seen in vision by Ezekiel—so far at least as its details are given—bears a general resemblance to that of Solomon and the later structure erected by Zerubbabel and repaired by Herod, according to the accounts of Josephus and of the Talmud, it is yet not designed after either. In order to locate this Temple and the surrounding "sanctuary" within the compass of Moriah's surface, it has been seriously proposed to change the text and substitute *cubits* for reeds in some passages, after the example of the Seventy, who took the liberty of making such an alteration, no doubt under the impression—however ill-founded—that the prophet was describing the fashion of the Temple to be erected on the restoration of the Jews after the seventy years' captivity. But, as Dr. Scott well observes, "if men allow themselves to substitute one word for another in the sacred text, because the alteration would render that consistent with their systems which otherwise would be incompatible with them, there is no knowing to what lengths they may proceed. Surely it is better to acknowledge our ignorance on such abstruse subjects, than to support a favorite scheme of interpretation by giving countenance to so dangerous a measure."—A sentiment surely worthy of all acceptation; and especially in reference to the portion of Scripture now under consideration, which has always been esteemed by the Rabbins so abstruse and difficult of exposition in some respects: yet, the adaptation of the Temple and courts described by Ezekiel to the Temple Mount at least, is attended with no special difficulty—and certainly requires no such reduction as that proposed. The area of Mount Moriah is abundantly adequate to the accommodation of the projected Temple and all its courts. And there is certainly no kind of objection to the enclosure of the whole city within the five hundred reeds quadrilateral, constituting the boundary between the sanctuary and the profane place—provided, at least, that it be remodelled and inhabited only by the Prince, the Priests, Levites, &c., in attendance on the Temple service.

But while the exterior enclosure of the sanctuary described by

Ezekiel is so much more extended than those of the former Temples, the sacred fane itself, as well as the other corresponding structures, is but slightly larger. Their respective dimensions indeed are generally identical as far as recorded; but it must be remembered that the cubit used by "the man" in measuring Ezekiel's Temple is the "greater cubit"—being 21.648 inches in length, while the measurements of the other Temples were given in the "common cubit" of eighteen inches—shorter than the former by a hand-breadth, which is rated at nearly four inches. (Ezek. xl. 5, and xliii. 13.) And besides this discrepancy in size, there is also a considerable dissimilarity in the internal arrangements. In the former Temple there were four courts—that of the Priests, that of Israel, that of the Women, and that of the Gentiles: whereas in the Ezekiel Temple there are only two mentioned—the Inner and the Outer or "Utter court." But there are many points of difference between the Ezekiel or Millennial Temple, and the old Jewish Temple in any of its former phases—all going to show a modified ritual adapted to the Millennial age.

That this Temple is not to be erected before the final advent of the Messiah is obvious from the declaration of the Lord by Zechariah (vi. 12), "Behold the Man whose name is the BRANCH; and he shall grow up out of his place, and *He* shall build the Temple of the Lord."

The Temple and courts are described by the prophet as being in the midst of a square plat called the "*Sanctuary;*" surrounded by a wall five hundred cubits long on each side, situated in the midst of the "Holy Oblation," a special reservation of territory about fifty-one miles in length and twenty and a half in breadth, which is assigned to the priests as their place of residence. Contiguous to this "possession of the priests," is that of the Levites, of the same dimensions—lying immediately on the north; and to the south lies the "possession of the city," the same in length, but only half the breadth of the two other portions, called also the "profane place, for the city for dwelling and for suburbs for them that serve the

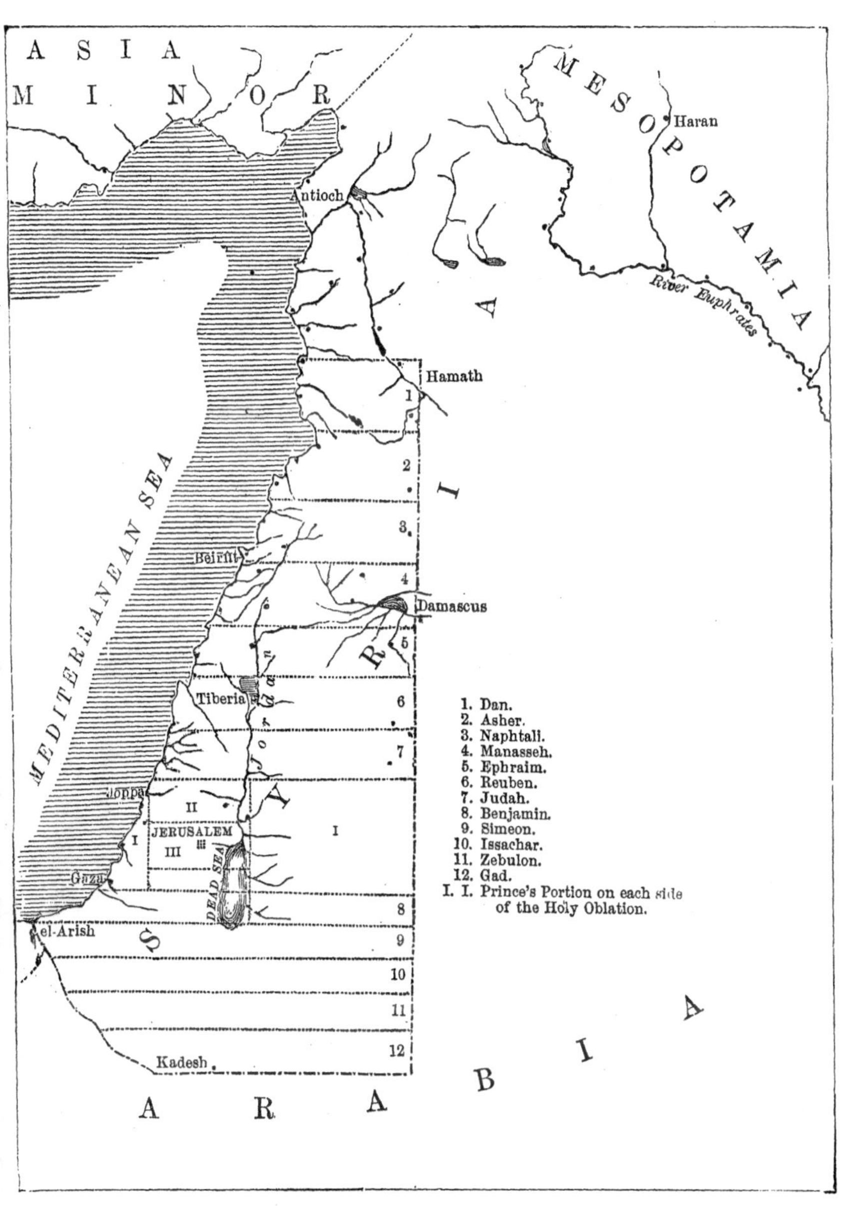

MILLENNIAL DIVISION OF THE HOLY LAND.

Locality of the Holy Oblation.

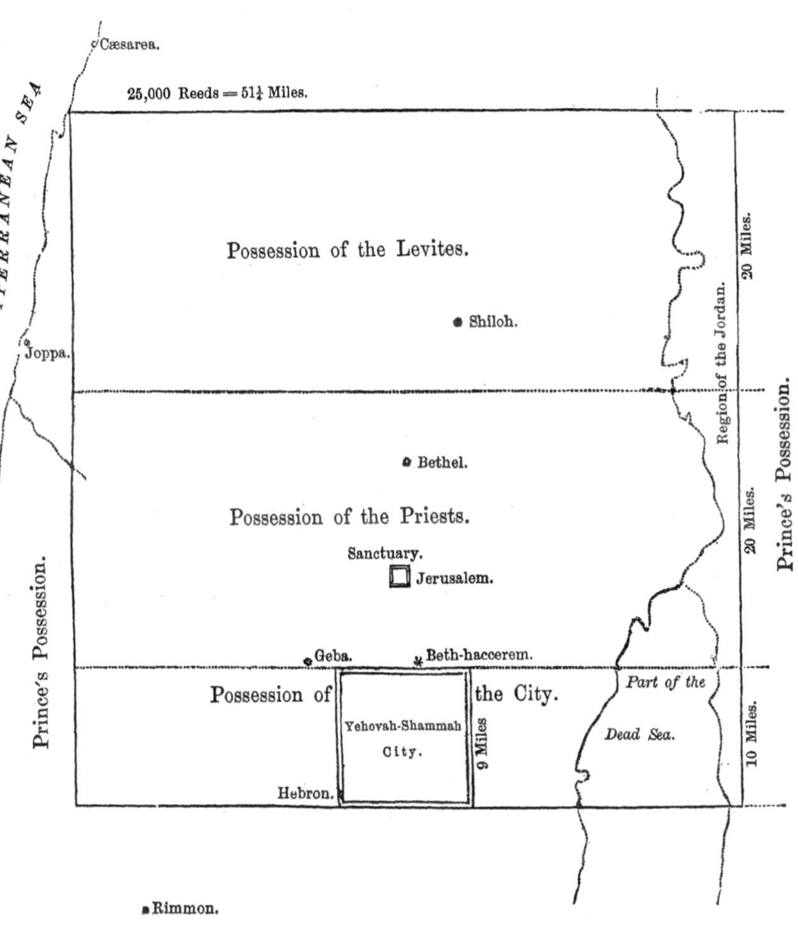

THE HOLY OBLATION. (See Ezekiel, xl.—xlviii.)

city." This great city—Yehovah Shammah—is a square of ten and a fourth miles on each side, inclusive of its suburbs half a mile wide, and occupies the exact middle of this last portion.

It is thus seen that these three portions united form a rectangular quadrangle of fifty-one miles on each side, quadrating with the cardinal points of the compass, which being protracted upon the map of Palestine, will be found to occupy nearly all the region of country lying between the Mediterranean and Perea. On the eastern and western faces of this immense square the prince is assigned his "portion"—the exact quantity not specified—but doubtless including all that triangular tract between the Holy Oblation and the Mediterranean, on the west; and the immense parallelogram extending from the eastern side of the oblation, between the new divisions of Judah and Benjamin, entirely to the border of Perea. It will be seen on inspecting the accompanying map, that the lots respectively assigned to the different tribes of Israel, differ very materially in position from the former partition under Joshua—being arranged nearly in a reversed order. And although this great Oblation is situated much nearer the southern than the northern border of the newly apportioned Holy Land, yet there being only five divisions below and seven above—and the land also being much wider below than above—the divisions are nearly equal in capacity, though so widely differing in length and breadth. And this remark will apply with equal truth to the entire country in its utmost boundaries, from the Euphrates to the Mediterranean in one direction, and from Mount Amanus to the Red Sea and Persian Gulf in the other—as it does to the restricted limits described by Ezekiel.

The *exact* location of the Holy Oblation within this district of country, though so minutely described, is not very clearly delineated, and hence cannot be determined with absolute precision. But upon the supposition that the Temple is to occupy its former site, and the "very high mountain" to the south of which the Great City is to be located is Jebl Fureidis or Frank Mountain (Beth-haccerem), its northern boundary will run due east from a point on the Mediterranean coast about twenty miles above Jaffa, to the western declivity of the Mountains of Ammon and Moab; its eastern side will lie a few miles east of Jordan on this declivity; and corner with the south line near the mouth of the river Arnon, thence crossing the Dead Sea, and passing a short distance south of Jebl Fureidis, and the ancient Jeba will unite with the western border eight or ten miles north of Beersheba. If "the living waters that go out from Jerusalem," as recorded in the fourteenth chapter of the prophecy of Zechariah, be identical with the waters described by Ezekiel in the twelve first verses of the 48th chapter of his prophecy, as issuing from the Temple (and they undoubtedly are), then must the Temple be built upon its ancient foundations in the Holy City. And that the city is to be rebuilt upon its ancient site (and if not under the very metes and bounds that circumscribed it at the period of its subversion by Nebuchadnezzar, at least as extensively), is also evident. (Jer. xxxi. 38–40, and Zech. xiv. 10.) That the "very high mountain," on the south of which the prophet saw the future city in vision, can be no other than Jebl Fureidis (that celebrated signal station in days of yore), is sufficiently obvious from a consideration of the fact that there is no other mountain in all southern Palestine to which this expression could apply with the least propriety. A circumstance strongly corroborative of this conclusion, too, is found in the fact that this mountain is situated just on the northern border of the belt of country that is be levelled "as a plain—from Geba to Rimmon, south of Jerusalem." And for what purpose is this rugged region to be reduced to an even surface, but as a site for the vast millennial city—Jehovah Shammah!

This city of cities will cover an area of more than a hundred square miles; and will number its inhabitants by millions. It can be rendered very accessible by a short railway from Al Arish, Askalon, or perhaps still better—Gaza—reputed the very best seaport on all the coast of Syria; and the construction of a railroad to Ezion Geber, Solomon's celebrated seaport at the head of the Elanetic branch of the Red Sea, is also entirely practicable at a small cost. The commerce of the East once flowed mainly through a channel almost identical in position with the route here indicated, between the Mediterranean and Indian Ocean; and it is doubtless destined again to become the great highway of trade and travel between the East and the West. Such a city, in such a climate, in a position so advantageous in a civil, commercial, and geographical point of view, might well claim to be the mistress of the world, when Judea shall have again become inhabited by its rightful owners. But still it is to its neighbor, a few miles to the north—the City of the Great King—the joy of the whole earth—that this supremacy is assigned in the coming age by Him who is Governor among the nations—the King of kings and Lord of lords.

We learn from the prophecy of Zechariah (xiv. 8), that at the coming of the Lord two most copious perennial streams of water shall burst forth from Jerusalem—one going forth towards the Mediterranean or "hinder sea," and the other towards the "former" or Dead Sea—developed apparently by the great earthquake.* And as this earthquake that shall rend Mount Olivet asunder and produce a "very great valley" running eastward, apparently for the purpose of conveying one of the life-giving streams to the parched desert below, will probably effect other physical changes in the immediate neighborhood of Jerusalem, as well as in the depression of the land from Geba to Rimmon, it will be useless to speculate as to the course the western stream will pursue—though it would seem from the 3d chapter of Joel, 8th verse, in connexion with the declarations of Ezekiel (xlvii. 1–12), that the course of the eastern river is very definitely marked out, though there is no valley in the neighborhood of Jerusalem known at the present day by the name there designated—Shittim. Wady anak-Nazal, however, would seem to be indicated as the most natural channel, and may originally have been called Shittim.

We are not informed *where* the healing stream bifurcates—if indeed there be only *one* source of the waters—or in what part of the Temple enclosure, or of the city, the second fountain arises—if there be *two* distinct sources. Ezekiel only measures and de-

* Quite a large river burst forth from a mountain in Armenia a few years ago: and a large stream of water is also said to have made its appearance in South America a few months since, during an earthquake.

scribes one; but Zechariah clearly indicates the existence of two, and inasmuch as that which flows eastward arises on the east of the Holy House, that which flows westwardly probably rises west of that building. If so, it must necessarily fall into the Tyropœon, and if left to itself, would naturally be carried down Wady en-Nair into the Dead Sea, unless it be conducted out of it westwardly by an aqueduct, or else the earthquake divert it in the same direction either by opening a new channel or by blocking up, or elevating some portion of the present Wady en-Nair. It would be perfectly practicable, with very little labor, to conduct a stream issuing from the Temple area to the region of the future Jehovah Shammah by a short serpentine canal conformed to the requirements of the ground about the upper portions of the Tyropœon, Mount Zion, Hinnom, &c.—situated as the ground now is. This western stream may thus readily be conducted to the great city, and thence, after irrigating a large portion of the arid region of southern Judea, enter the Mediterranean at el-Arish, or by any of the numerous valleys that empty into the Mediterranean. We have no positive information as to the size of *this* river; but, if it be as large as that emptying into the Dead Sea, it may be rendered very serviceable not only for the irrigation of a large district of country, but for internal boat navigation. If it be true that the desert of Arabia was once an inland sea or lake, and is still depressed below the level of the sea, may it not be re-filled either from the sea or by this river? It will be recollected that while Jerusalem is 3927 feet above the Dead Sea, its elevation above the Mediterranean is only 2610 feet; and that Jehovah Shammah will be much more depressed.

The waters that issue out eastward seem to undergo no increase in passing from the altar through the surrounding buildings, nor perhaps for a farther distance of six hundred yards; but at this point, at the least, the fountain becomes a stream ankle-deep; twelve hundred yards from the sanctuary it becomes knee-deep, at a distance of eighteen hundred yards it is found to be loin-deep; and when it is last measured, at a distance of two thousand four hundred yards (more than one and a third miles) from the wall of the sanctuary (by which time it has passed through the cleft in Mount Olivet), it has become more than chin-deep—"risen waters to swim in, a river that could not be passed over." Whether the river becomes still deeper, and what is its width, we are not informed; but it is probable that it receives no further increment. Its gradual augmentation thus far, at regular intervals of one-third of a mile, seems to be due to subterranean accessions received from the rent bowels of Mount Olivet.*

Should this river rush immediately down this valley into the Dead Sea, it would produce a succession of rapids, cascades, and cataracts unequalled in all the world; for the distance being only about fifteen or twenty miles, and the difference of altitude nearly four thousand feet, the rate of descent could not be less than an average of two hundred feet per mile, or one foot in twenty-six—a fall of four thousand feet in twenty miles! while the entire fall in the Mississippi, throughout its whole course of two thousand miles, is only fifteen hundred and seventy-five feet! What inconceivable power for the propulsion of machinery! What teeming luxuriance must crown the banks of this fertilizing and vivifying stream, and especially if the waters be made to meander along the declivities of the once frightful barren and desolate desert! How surpassingly beautiful the evergreen landscape in which this life-giving river sweetly meanders—where "grow all trees for meat whose leaf

* It is not a little singular that on descending a few yards below the surface of the earth, amongst some riven rocks, in a valley called Wady Anak Nazal, leading up to Mount Olivet, opposite Jerusalem, one may hear the faint ripple of a subterranean stream. By-the-bye, may not this *Nazal* have some connexion with the "Azal" to which the "valley of the mountains" is to extend? (See Zech. xiv. 5.) The transition from Azal to Nazal is by no means too violent for a Hebrew name to undergo in the mouth of an Arab. And besides—as the valley takes its name from an *ain* or fountain on its border, the *n* may properly belong to the *ain*, and the difficulty in distinctly separating the *n* from the *a* in pronunciation, may have led to its permanent connexion; but be this as it may, it is situated due east of Jerusalem in the precise direction indicated by the prophet. The traveller going down to Jericho will pass this valley about two miles below Ain el Horth (the Apostles' Fount), where it enters into Wady el Horth—written el Haud on some maps.

fadeth not, neither shall the fruit thereof be consumed—bringing forth new fruit according to his months—the fruit thereof for meat and the leaf thereof for medicine!" (xlvi. 12.) Then indeed will "the wilderness and the solitary place be glad, and the desert rejoice and blossom as the rose!" These are the gladdening waters of which the exulting Psalmist spoke in vision—"There is a river the streams whereof shall make glad the city of God, the Holy Place of the tabernacles of the Most High." (Ps. xlvi. 4.)

We are not positively told that the waters issuing to the west will possess those wondrous properties that characterize the eastern river; but it is altogether a legitimate inference, that they will be similarly endowed. And if on the banks of this refreshing and fructifying stream, adorned with those health-imparting and life-giving trees, the Highway of Holiness shall lead from Yehovah Shammah to the Holy City and Temple, through the desert of Tekoah, thus really become "an house of prayer for all nations," what a paradisaical avenue would conduct the millenarian pilgrim up to the House of the Lord! Thus shall "the ransomed of the Lord return, and come to Zion with songs and everlasting joy upon their heads!" "And it shall come to pass . . . . in the last days, that the Mountain of the Lord's House shall be established on the top of the mountains and shall be exalted above the hills, and all nations shall flow unto it. And many people shall go and say, 'Come ye, and let us go up to the mountain of the Lord, to the house of the God of Jacob, and he will teach us of his ways, and we will walk in his paths; for out of Zion shall go forth the law, and the word of the law from Jerusalem.'" (Is. ii. 2, 3.)

"See the streams of living waters,
Springing from eternal love,
Well supply thy sons and daughters,
And all fear of drought remove:
Who can faint while such a river
Ever flows their thirst t' assuage!
Grace, which, like the Lord the giver,
Never fails from age to age"

Great as are the temporal blessings of the Millennial age, greater by far are its spiritual blessings. Satan being then bound, and the evidences of the Lord's presence ever before their eyes, who can form even the faintest conception of the blessedness and splendor of the glorious era when the whole earth shall be filled with the knowledge of "the glory of the Lord, as the waters cover the sea!" For "wisdom and knowledge shall be stability of thy times and the strength of salvation."

The waters of the Dead Sea would not only be "healed," but doubtless much increased in depth and extended in length: for the latter rain being also fully restored would form in concurrence with these copious waters, far more than a counterbalance to the evaporation by which this mysterious sheet of water is now restricted to its narrow limits; and being walled in by perpendicular cliffs towering to the height of one or two thousand feet on each side, while its breadth would not be much increased, its length must necessarily be greatly extended—particularly towards the south. It would seem even from existing indications, that its length was formerly much greater than at present. And such a copious accession would doubtless cause its permanent outflow into the Red Sea—thus effectually sweeping away its bitter waters.

Very considerable geological changes will doubtless be produced by the great convulsions that accompany the subsidence and levelling of the tract of country lying between the Mediterranean and the Dead Sea, under the parallels of latitude separating Jeba and Rimmon. And one highly beneficial result, amongst many remarkable consequences of the earthquake, will, no doubt, be a literal verification of a prophecy of Isaiah (xxxv. 6, 7), that has heretofore been regarded as exclusively figurative—"in the wilderness shall waters break out, and streams in the desert. And the parched ground become a pool, and the thirsty land springs." How glowingly is the prosperity of the land and nation of Israel set forth by the prophets, when Judah and Israel shall have been restored and rought in complete subjection to their prince, David—the Beloved—. *e.* the Prince Messiah. (Is. lx. &c.)

But the most interesting and perhaps the most marvellous circumtance attending the Millennial condition of Jerusalem, remains yet o be mentioned. We are informed by Isaiah in the 4th chapter f his prophecy, that "when the Lord shall have washed away the lth of the daughter of Zion, and shall have purged the blood of Jerusalem from the midst thereof by the spirit of judgment and by he spirit of burning . . . . he will create upon every dwelling-place of Mount Zion, and upon her assemblies, a cloud and smoke by lay, and the shining of a flame of fire by night: for upon all the glory shall be a covering. And there shall be a tabernacle for a shadow in the day-time from the heat, and for a place of refuge, nd for a covert from storm and from rain" (3, 6) . . . . "the Lord hall arise upon thee, and his glory shall be seen upon thee; and he Gentiles shall come to thy light, and kings to the brightness of hy rising." (lx. 1, 3.) "The sun shall be no more thy light by lay: neither for brightness shall the moon give light unto thee; but the Lord shall be unto thee an everlasting light, and thy God hy glory: thy sun shall no more go down, neither shall thy moon withdraw itself, for the Lord shall be thine everlasting light, and he days of thy mourning shall be ended: thy people also shall be ll righteous, and they shall inherit the land for ever—the branch of my planting, the work of my hands that I may be glorified: a little one shall become a thousand, and a small one a strong nation: I the Lord will hasten it in his time." (lx. 19, 22.) "Moreover, the light of the moon shall be as the light of the sun, and the light of the sun shall be seven-fold in the day that the Lord bindeth up the breach of his people, and healeth the stroke of their wound." (xxx. 26.) "Then the moon shall be confounded and the sun ashamed, when the Lord of Hosts shall reign in Mount Zion, and in Jerusalem, and before his ancients gloriously." (xxiv. 23.) From these passages it would appear, that when the Lord shall again record his name on "his dwelling-place in Zion"—(for "this is the hill which God desireth to dwell in—yea, the Lord will dwell in it for ever"*)—there will be a revival, on a magnificent scale, of the "Glory of the Lord" as it anciently rested over the Tabernacle in the wilderness—"a pillar of cloud by day and of fire by night"—such a manifestation of Deity, perhaps, as was once seen in Eden! May it not be to this Shechinah, thus overshadowing the Holy City as a glorious luminary canopy, that the astonishing change of climate is to be ascribed? And need any more direct divine interposition be invoked in explanation of the wonderful effects wrought on the whole vegetable and animal kingdom in relation to the fertility of the soil, the domestication of destructive monsters of the forest, the transmutation of poisonous reptiles into innocent creatures, and the prosperity, happiness, and longevity of its inhabitants. Should any other influence be deemed necessary, we have it, without inconsiderately ascribing these wonderful changes to such an alteration of the axis of the earth, as would make the ecliptic and equator coincide (as some Millenarian writers rather fancifully conjecture).

Has not the Lord promised, in speaking of this very matter as portrayed in the 11th chapter of Isaiah, that he will make a covenant with the beasts of the field, and the fowls of heaven, and the creeping things of the ground? (Hos. ii. 18.) There is no calculating the wonderful consequences that would inevitably result from the alteration of electrical, thermal, and magnetic agencies, to say

* "Thus saith the Lord, heaven is my throne, and the earth is my footstool;" we are not, therefore, to infer from these and similar passages, that Jehovah will dwell at Jerusalem in any other manner than by delegation and the symbols of his presence. Nor do the Scriptures, rightly construed, intimate that the Saviour will actually *dwell* upon the earth in *propria persona*—as contended by many—or that he will ever be seen upon earth except at Jerusalem, which, however, there is every reason to believe he will occasionally and perhaps statedly visit in personal manifestations to receive the homage and adoration of his earthly subjects. The Throne of God and the Lamb—where of course is the real seat of the Divine Government—is the Heavenly Jerusalem above—the abode of the redeemed, whence, as kings and priests, and the partners of his throne, they will reign with Christ *over* the earth for ever and ever.

nothing of those of celestial light from the overhanging Golden City in a meteorological and climatic point of view! And who can divine the wonderful change that will be wrought not only on man, but in the brute creation also, and indeed even in the vegetable kingdom, by the life-giving stream that flows from the oracle of God! Would it be any marvel that the carnivorous beasts should not only become herbivorous by feeding upon the vegetation growing on the banks of this marvellous water, but have their entire natures changed into something like what it probably was when Adam gave them names in the garden of Eden? If the juice of the grape when fermented is capable of producing an effect so astonishing upon man—mentally, physically, and morally—is there anything unreasonable in the supposition that the water of this river and the vegetable productions on its banks—which are not only healing but life-giving—should effect such a change even in ravenous beasts and venomous reptiles? Certainly not: "*because their waters they issue out of the sanctuary*"—a fact to which the prophet directly ascribes their wonderful properties. If the properties of the nitrous oxide (or exhilarating gas) are so different from those of the atmosphere (though formed of the same elements, and differing only in their relative proportions), why should not a slight change in the waters of the sanctuary be adequate to the production of all the effects ascribed to this Millennial "*aqua vitæ?*"

There is no aspect in which the Millennial age can be regarded, that is not richly suggestive of the most pleasing and profitable themes of contemplation. Satan being bound, and man brought into complete subjection to Jesus Emmanuel, the whole creation, which had hitherto groaned in travail on account of man's sin, is vocal with praise—"the times of the restitution of all things" having now arrived! Who, that has a heart to feel, can refrain from praying and laboring for "a consummation so devoutly to be wished!"

INDEX.

THE END.

THE CITY OF THE GREAT KING.

Extracts from Lengthy Notices in Standard Papers.

Dr. Barclay's volume comes to us fragrant with memories of scenes and localities in the Holy City which his familiarity as a resident, and his perseverance and enthusiasm as an explorer, enabled the writer of this notice to visit to the best advantage. Dr. Barclay's skill as a physician, and his general repute as a man of science, gave him extraordinary facilities for exploring the ruins and the sacred places and localities of the city. He disarmed the prejudices of the Moslems, and received some marked acts of favoritism. He made good use of his privileges; and being a careful and persevering explorer, and an accurate observer, he has contributed much that is valuable to the topography of Jerusalem. In the main, Dr. B. sides with Dr. Robinson upon controverted points. His *facts* of personal observation will be invaluable in the future discussion of the topography of the city, if indeed they do not settle many points beyond dispute. The volume treats of Jerusalem in its Ancient, Medieval, and Modern periods, and is a good thesaurus of facts and authorities. Dr. Barclay does not pretend to literary accomplishments or to profound scholarship; but he has produced a work which will interest a variety of readers, and which, in connexion with his valuable map of Jerusalem, will furnish a complete guide to the Holy City. * * *

One of the most elegant books ever issued from the American press, as regards the various points of mechanical execution, is the "*City of the Great King*," which is noticed under the Editors' Table in this number. Though not specially intended for a holiday book, there are many students of the Bible and of history who would greatly prize a copy on account of its substantial worth, while the beauty of its typography and illustrations renders it a fair competitor for holiday favors.—*New York Independent.*

In its getting up, the book is a credit to our city: in its information, it is wonderfully condensed and full; and in even the plainest of its illustrations we have assurance of a perfect truthfulness, in the fact of their being from photographs taken on the spot. The chromographic illustrations of the Tomb of David, of the Temple and Mount Zion, and of the interior of the Mosque of Omar, are a novelty in such a work, and give it great additional attraction.—*Episcopal Recorder, Philadelphia.*

It is, beyond dispute, a work of the highest merit. In addition to its vast and peculiar interest as an authentic record of the latest discoveries in Jerusalem—many of which have been made by the author himself, and are now for the first time presented to the Christian public—the volume is highly embellished with chromographic illuminations, steel engravings by the best artists, a periscopic panorama of the entire circuit of the city and environs, explanatory maps and diagrams, and the finest of wood engravings. Nothing that could shed the faintest light upon the rare and priceless text has been omitted. It is equally exact and luminous. It is destined to produce a *profound impression* on the religious world.—*Louisville Journal.*

The publishers have done ample justice to the work. The splendid chromographs (printed in ten rich colors), fine steel and wood engravings, diagrams, maps, and panoramic views, impart to it an interest and value which no other work on the subject can claim.—*Philadelphia Ledger.*

We have space this week for only a brief notice of this valuable work. It is the fruit of the author's researches during a three and a half years' residence in the Holy City, and of such facilities for investigation as no Christian has enjoyed for many ages. His successful medical treatment of a case of disease in one of the Turkish dignitaries, procured for him access to "every part of the ancient Temple area, and 'holy places,' that have been seen by no Christian since the chivalric but unenlightened era of Frank domination." The work embodies much information from sources ancient and modern, on the local questions growing out of the facts and histories of the Bible. Its interest is greatly increased, also, by numerous engravings representing to the eye the objects, buildings, and scenes in and around Jerusalem with a clearness that no word-painting could give them. The general execution of the work is in the highest style of art, and is as creditable to our country in this respect as its contents are new and interesting to the world of letters. We bespeak for it a sale equal to its merits and the costliness of its execution.—*New York Chronicle.*

This is a very valuable contribution to Biblical literature. As to the topography of the Holy City, it has no rival. The author's residence there for nearly four years, his deep interest in the antiquities and whatever else is illustrative of the sacred records, his passion for exploration, and the extraordinary facilities afforded him, have imparted to his pages a great and permanent value. As to the Tyropœon and other points in the topography, Dr. Barclay differs from Dr. Robinson and others who have preceded him; but we are informed, on high authority, that Bishop Gobat and the Frank residents of Jerusalem generally concur with Dr. Barclay, and have great confidence in the accuracy of his conclusions and the general reliability of his researches. His map of Jerusalem is the best which has appeared, and his discoveries within the Temple enclosure—the arches of massive masonry beneath the Temple, the quarries and other matters connected with the sacred localities, are of great interest. The work is profusely illustrated with engravings in the first style of art, executed from photographs and drawings made by the author. We have been permitted to examine a portion of these photographs in connexion with the engravings, and can bear our testimony to the truthfulness and fidelity of the latter. The publishers deserve great credit for the liberality, taste, and enterprise displayed in getting up the work. The wood-cuts and steel engravings are of the best quality, the views printed in colors are gorgeous and elegant, and the paper and letter-press all that the most fastidious could desire. The millenarian and literalist views of the author in that portion of the book devoted to "Jerusalem as it is to be," are not in accordance with our opinions; but even these speculations will be read with interest. We cheerfully commend the work as one which will be a valuable addition to the library of the minister and the intelligent layman.—*Philadelphia Presbyterian.*

This is a large royal octavo volume, and is believed to contain more curious original and startling matter than any book that has ever been written on the Holy Land.—*Banner of the Cross, Philadelphia.*

I take pleasure in calling attention to the announcement of a new book on Jerusalem. It is by Dr. Barclay, a man of erudition and great religious zeal and devotion to whatever belongs to the Holy Land. I saw Dr. B. in Jerusalem, and had many proofs of his skill and energy in exploring the Great City, and in discovering whatever is most interesting in its topography. His advantages were greater than any writer who has attempted a description of that city and its environs.—*Christian Ambassador.*

hailed rather than rebuked. Its claim is supported on philological grounds, as well as on the general ground of local adaptation. * * * * *

The "Red Heifer Bridge," a lofty structure spanning the Kidron, opposite the eastern gate of the temple, is mentioned and described for the first time in English in this work on the Holy City. * * * * *

Another discovery, of which Dr. Barclay is entitled to the credit, is that of the great cave under Mount Bezetha, from which the stone was quarried for the walls and palaces of the city. The narrative of our author's nocturnal adventure is very entertaining. It was attended, not only with ludicrous inconvenience, but with serious danger, such as can be appreciated only by those who have crawled through the cavities, and threaded the mazes, and glided by dim candlelight along the edge of pitfalls in the Egyptian catacombs. The skull of some former adventurer, which one of the party picked up, was a caution against such hazardous attempts. The Turkish authorities are very jealous of these subterranean investigations, and during the day, a fanatical Moslem watches this quarter from the opposite grotto of Jeremiah. Dr. Barclay is convinced that the ravine between this grotto and Mount Bezetha is an artificial trench, made by the removal of the rock which once extended in a long ledge northward from the city. * * * * *

Another piece of good fortune which attended one of the expeditions of Dr. Barclay in the neighborhood of the Holy City was the discovery of that "Ænon near Salim," the place where John baptized, which Dr. Robinson, in his last visit, fruitlessly sought. Robinson, following Jerome and the tradition, looked for it in *Galilee*, in the neighborhood of Beisan. But the account of Jerome contradicts itself, and is of no real authority. * * * * *

The account of Jerusalem "*as it was*," is contained in fourteen chapters filling about two-thirds of the volume. These chapters treat, in succession, of the name of the city; its local features, hills, valleys, ravines, bridges, and surrounding villages;—its various quarters and their successive developments; the walls and trenches of the city from Melchisedec to Zedekiah, with an estimate of the population at the time of its destruction by the Romans, justifying the large numbers given by Josephus;—the Towers and Gates, a concise yet a full and valuable chapter,—the Castles and Palaces, with the names of the ancient streets, markets, and monumental pillars within the city;—the Tombs and Sepulchral monuments, including an elaborate discussion and description of the Holy Sepulchre, special notices of the numerous caves in the valleys of Jehosaphat and Hinnom, in which doubt is expressed as to the genuineness of the supposed pit of Aceldama, and a very interesting narrative is given of a visit which the author's daughter was enabled to make to the Tomb of David on Mount Zion, a Moslem shrine most jealously guarded, and described by no modern writer;—the Temple, a long and careful topographical study, reducing its dimensions, its arrangement, and its splendor to a picture before the eye as distinct if not as brilliant as the chromograph of the Mosque of Omar;—the Water Supply of the city, a chapter exhaustive in its fulness;—and finally, historical notices of the history of the city from its subversion by Titus to the present century, in which, in addition to the well-known stories of mediæval travellers and pilgrims, from Willibald to Maundrell, we have a long extract from the Moslem history of the Cadi Meji-ed-din, and an excellent summary of the chronology of the Crusades. This first portion of the work, though scientifically the most important, will have less interest for the general reader than the six chapters which treat of Jerusalem "*as it is*," in which are related the personal experiences and adventures of the author, and facts take the place of argument and conjecture. These chapters treat of the climate and productions, the walls, towers, and streets, the "Noble Sanctuary," the water resources within and around the city, and the missionary operations. They afford ample material for a comprehensive sketch of the Holy City. * * * * *

Dr. Barclay's family were able to enjoy the full hospitality of Turkish houses, and to the courtesy of a Moslem lady was due that visit to the reputed tomb of David, of which the gorgeous chromotype given in this volume is averred to be an accurate copy. The more important gratitude of a high official enabled Dr. Barclay to gain free access to the "Noble Sanctuary," and to bring away exact sketches of its parts and dimensions. * * * * *

Dr. Barclay's description of the Mohammedan sanctuary, its walls, its edifices, and its principal objects, is exceedingly interesting. His measurements of the outer walls differ materially from those of previous examiners, and his account of the *gates*, as they appear on close inspection, is very full. Several of these gates are now for the first time brought into notice, and they help to mark the true place of some of the ancient gates of the Temple. Dr. Barclay is able to correct the notion that columns of porphyry and verd-antique are built in the wall, having proved with acids that the grain of the stone is marble. He copies, from a block near the south-west corner, a Roman inscription, partly inverted, which only great patience and good glasses could fairly make out. Of the "Sakhrah" rock we have an elaborate picture, to which the chromotype only lends more vividness of coloring. He is able to bring facts in refutation of the Moslem pretence that this rock rests on nothing, and swings in mid air, supported by angels. * * * * *

But the most important revelations of the sacred enclosure which this volume gives us, are the minute descriptions of those parts which are ordinarily invisible, of the vast arches by which Solomon lifted the slope of the hill to a level with its summit. Bewildering measurements of these great artificial caverns leave us in equal admiration of the patience which has traced their dimensions, and the daring which raised their fabric. This underground architecture is indeed Cyclopean. Three hundred and nineteen feet in length, two hundred and forty-seven in breadth, with piers of three, four, and five feet in thickness, dating from the age of the magnificent Hebrew king. It is strange to find in these dark vaults the monumental cairns of hundreds of the pilgrims of Islam, and to see the radicles of olive-trees which have penetrated the crevices, hanging like stalactites from the roofs of the arches. Dr. Barclay has no hesitation in assigning the *piers* to the age of Solomon, although he thinks that the *arches* may belong to a later age. * * * * *

Dr. Barclay, whose love for tabular statements and skill in preparing them is remarkably evinced throughout this volume, has arranged in a schedule the churches, convents, hospitals, schools, patriarchs, bishops, priests, deacons, nuns, clergy, and laity, of the various sects of Christians, Protestants included, that inhabit all the westurn side of the city. The aggregate is somewhat larger than the usual estimates. * * * * *

We have no space to follow Dr. Barclay in his excursions around the city, his visit to the springs of water, to the great Pools of Solomon,—to the Jebl Fureideis, or Mount of Paradise, a curiosity for the archæologist as for the naturalist,—to Gaza on the south, where are the pillars of Samson, and the Mispah on the north, where is the monument of Samuel,—down the Valley of Kidron and up the Valley of Farah,—over the hills to Bethany, and over the plain to the convents of Elias and St. John,—or in his description of "Silwan," where Arab peasants burrow like marmots in the caves of the hill-side, and of "Jebl Tur," where accommodating Turks exhibit for a piastre the last footprint of the ascended Saviour,—or in his catalogue of fruits and flowers, so extensive as to clothe the hills of Jerusalem almost with the beauty of Damascus, and his observations of heat and cold which would bring its climate to be mild as the breeze of Madeira. For all these details, and much more, we refer our readers to the book itself. Its profuse engravings on wood, stone, and steel leave nothing to be desired in the matter of pictorial embellishment. The mechanical execution of the work corresponds to the importance of the theme, and to the scientific thoroughness with which the author has fulfilled his task.

Dr. Barclay, with the enthusiasm of the Christian, unites the taste of the antiquary and the thirst of the scholar; and with such advantages of observation, comparison, and exploration as no traveller could possess, he has pursued his labors with zeal, perseverance, and success. In this handsome octavo volume he has presented to the world the fruits of three years of careful research and reflection. The drawings with which the letter-press is illustrated, are profuse and elegant. Maps and sketches of the ancient and the modern city, serve to make the region and the specific localities more intelligible to the reader, while the colored plates of several of the most interesting and illustrious objects in Jerusalem will be contemplated with special interest. For some of these we are doubtless indebted to the accomplished daughter of the author, who we are told, was the first Christian female ever permitted to set her feet within the holy precincts of the Mosque of Omar. And this was effected by her assuming a disguise, and she happily escaped detection. Dr. Barclay differs on many important points from the conclusions which other writers have reached, respecting some of the most interesting localities in and around Jerusalem. His conclusions, however, are not stated with the air of a controversionalist, but with the spirit of a sincere searcher after the truth, and one anxious to throw all the light at his command upon the most interesting departments of study that can occupy the attention of the Christian mind. It cannot, therefore, fail to contain a vast amount of information, of which clergymen and other intelligent scholars will be glad to avail themselves.—*New York Observer.*

One of the most eminent reviewers in the Union thus notices this work:—

"The forthcoming reviews will doubtless give this magnificent contribution to Biblical Science an elaborate notice and an appropriate welcome. It is a royal octavo, of 600 pages, full of engravings, most of which are new and accurately copied from photographs, some of them, moreover, splendidly colored —and the whole mechanical execution of the work is in the highest style of art. The author's facilities for observation and inquiry have been unprecedented. His work has been prepared with great pains and care, and nothing which could illustrate the subject has been omitted. It is incomparably the fullest and most reliable treatise on 'Jerusalem' which has appeared in our language. Families, Sunday Schools, Parish Libraries, all will want it. Let those who would get a standard and remarkable book at a reasonable price, inquire for 'The City of the Great King,' by Dr. J. T. Barclay."

This is a magnificent volume, printed on fine paper in very superior style, and superbly illustrated with five admirable steel engravings, three richly illuminated plates, and with more than fifty engravings, illustrative of memorable places and scenes in the Holy City. The contents of this work are designed to elucidate the history of Jerusalem, the theatre of the most stupendous events recorded in the annals of the world. What hallowed associations, what sacred reminiscences cluster around Jerusalem—"the joy of the whole earth!"—where the King of Peace and Righteousness held communion with Abraham, "the friend of God;" where the Royal Psalmist tuned his soul-stirring harp, and composed his immortal songs; where Jesus Christ taught, suffered, died, and rose from the dead—whence He ascended to His throne in the heavens;—a city repeatedly visited with desolating judgments, yet still remembered in mercy for the Fathers' sake.——*Philadelphia Christian Observer.*

We commend this elegant volume to the notice of our readers, as a valuable work, worth possessing.—*True Union.*

THE CITY OF THE GREAT KING.

From the North American Review.

The author is a man whose views and opinions, even when they do not command acquiescence, are entitled to respect. At once a physician and a preacher, a practised chemist and a skilful draughtsman, he carried to his labors in Jerusalem more than the heart and faith of a missionary. The intervals of professional toil were filled by researches not less congenial; and extending, as they did, over so considerable a period, three years and a half, these researches have led to some novel conclusions. As a critic of facts in Jerusalem, Dr. Barclay had great advantages. His residence in several quarters of the city,—first in the Moslem neighborhood on Mount Bezetha, afterward between the Jewish houses on Mount Zion and the Mogrebin huts around the Mosque, and in the summer on the Mount of Olives,—the intimate association of his family with the various races, Jew, Armenian, Turk, Syrian, and Bedouin,—the assistance which he was able to secure in his explorations,—his signal good fortune in gaining free and frequent admission to the forbidden precincts of the "Haram es Sherif," mosques, chambers, vaults, and all, even to the extent of taking sketches and measuring dimensions,—his patient study, on the spot, of the various conflicting hypotheses, historical and topographical, would lead us to expect from him a very valuable treatise. He had the opportunity of seeing Jerusalem under all its aspects, in winter and in summer, in the dry season and in the rainy season, in its Easter crowds and its Hebrew festivals, by night as well as by day. Most of those who have written in English about the Holy City have stayed there only a few days or a few weeks, and have been obliged to borrow their facts from other authorities. Dr. Barclay was able to do for himself the work of examination. He had time and opportunity to go over all the ground. He had the photographic art as an efficient auxiliary. And his demonstrations of antiquities and proportions are verified by the stamp of the unerring solar ray. * * * * *

Professing the highest regard for the judgment and the conclusions of Dr. Robinson, in several important particulars Dr. Barclay ventures to disagree with that eminent writer. As to the direction of the Tyropœon he fully coincides with Dr. Robinson; but he pronounces very confidently that the ravine west of the city is *not the Valley of Gihon*, but is part of Hinnom, as it was formerly believed to be. * * * * * Unlike Robinson, he is not content with proving a negative, but never rests satisfied until he has found a place for every site or object mentioned in the Scriptures or the Rabbinical stories. Such a catalogue of fountains, aqueducts, pools, wells, cisterns, and the like, has nowhere else been brought together. * * * * *

Two important discoveries, on the hills around Jerusalem, are here confidently brought forward. The first is the site of Bethphage, "the house of figs," which Robinson settled by the concise remark that "no trace exists of it." The trace has since been found, and not only the place where it ought to be, according to the Evangelist's narrative, but the place where its ruins actually remain, has been ascertained. On this point Dr. Barclay's reasonings win our full assent, and it is only singular that a site so obviously appropriate should have so long escaped the scrutiny of investigators. * * * * *

The other discovery, which will not be so easily accepted, is the discovery of the true place of the Crucifixion, of Calvary, and of Golgotha. We shall not review the arguments which condemn the traditional site, or criticise those offered for the new site. In the absence of any other reasonable supposition, the new location of Calvary has a certain prerogative right, and should be

MAP OF JERUSALEM AND ENVIRONS,

BY J. T. BARCLAY AND SONS.

From actual and minute survey, made on the spot, and shaded from a verified model.

This map has been carefully examined by many persons who have visited Jerusalem. Prof. Robinson, of the Union Theological Seminary, Dr. Durbin, Rev. G. W. Samson, and others, highly commend its accuracy. We extract the following notice from the New York Independent, the largest circulating religious weekly in the Union.

"We are glad to be able to announce the appearance of Dr. J. T. Barclay's Map of Jerusalem and its environs. Having visited this brother, and seen his model of the city, at his house on Mount Zion, and out to Bethany, and thus learned something of his familiarity with the topography of the city and its environs, we have waited with much interest for the publication of his map. It strikes us as the most detailed and accurate map of *modern* Jerusalem we have yet seen. A residence of several years made Dr. Barclay familiar with every nook of the city; and having gained favor in high quarters as a physician, he enjoyed some special facilities for research. He has improved his advantages well."

Prof. E. Robinson, of the Union Theological Seminary, thus notices it:—

"The plan is undoubtedly the best that exists, so far as the physical features of the ground and the modern city are concerned."

The following is from Rev. J. P. Durbin:—

"I have received great satisfaction in carefully inspecting your new map of Jerusalem, just published; and take great pleasure, from personal knowledge of the 'Holy City' and vicinity, in testifying to its accuracy. I heartily commend it to the Christian public.

Very respectfully,

J. P. DURBIN."

Prices—plain, 50 cents; colored, 75 cents; pocket-book form, colored, $1, *postpaid;* mounted, colored and varnished, $1.75.

JAS. CHALLEN & SONS, PUBLISHERS,
PHILADELPHIA, PA.

www.ingramcontent.com/pod-product-compliance
Lightning Source LLC
LaVergne TN
LVHW021056110826
845150LV00001B/88

* 9 7 8 1 4 2 5 5 6 6 7 2 2 *